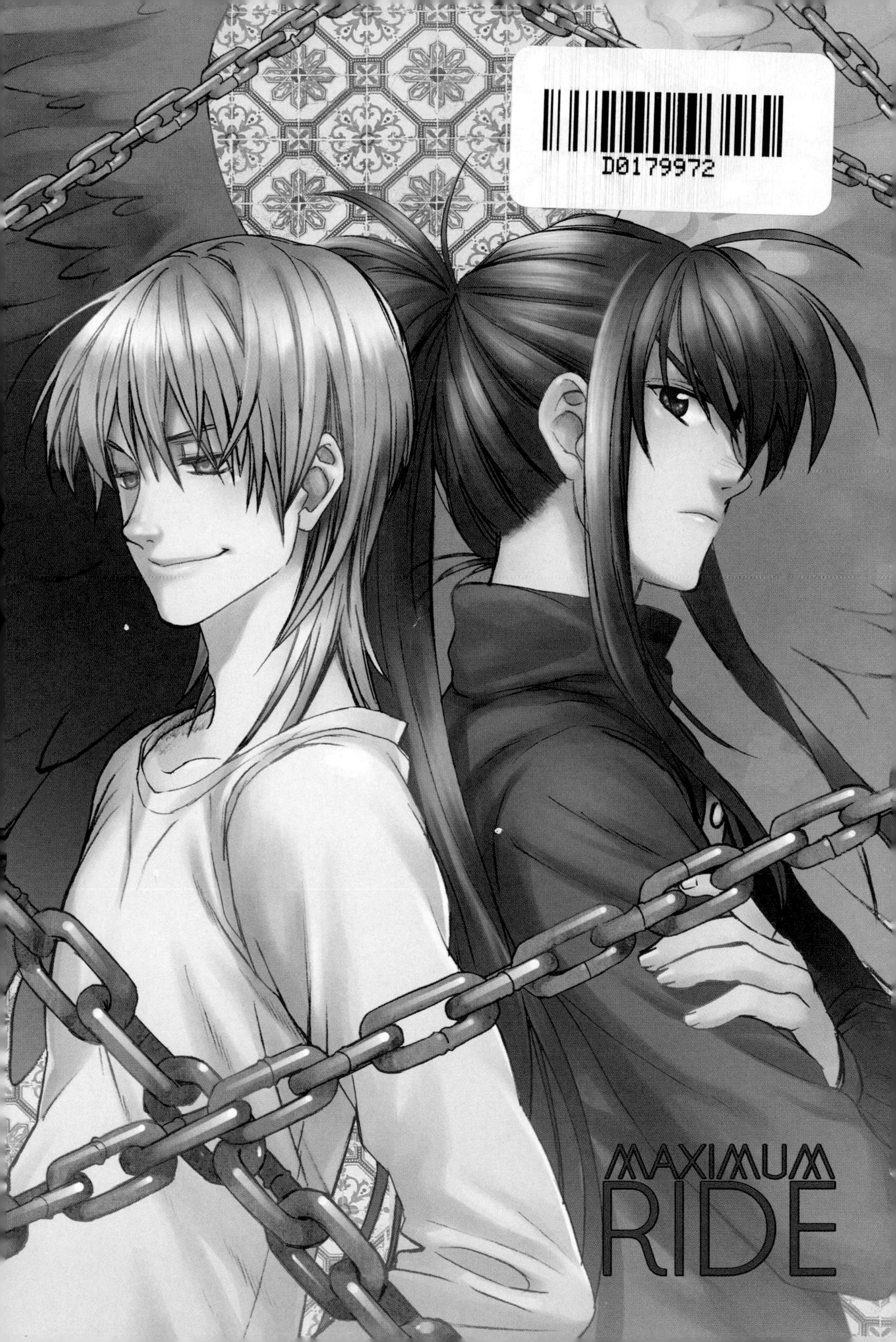
MAXIMUM
RIDE

MAXIMUM RIDE

CHAPTER 8 3

CHAPTER 9 35

CHAPTER 10 65

CHAPTER 11 95

CHAPTER 12 127

CHAPTER 13 159

CHAPTER 14 191

CHAPTER 15 223

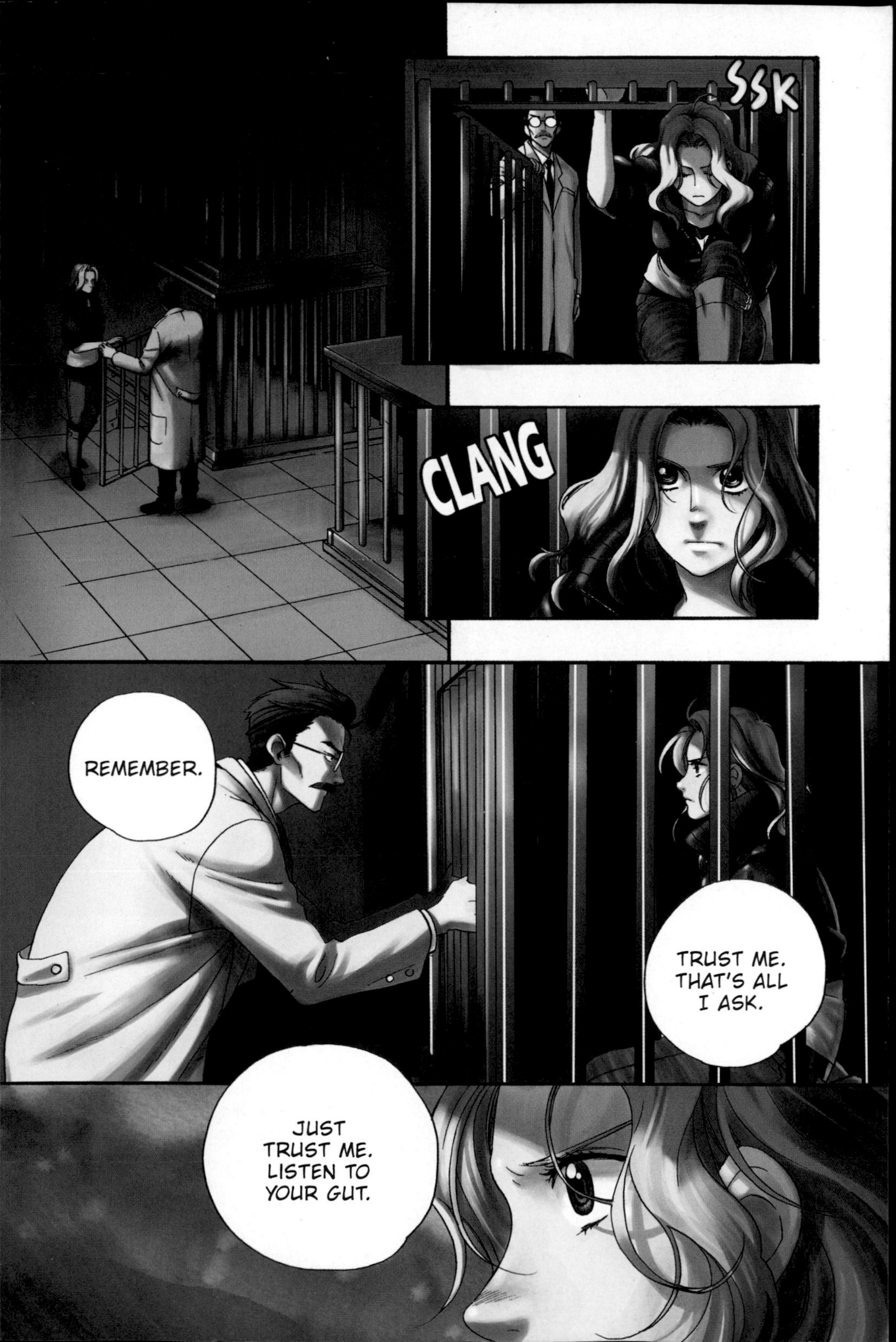
SSK
CLANG
REMEMBER.
TRUST ME. THAT'S ALL I ASK.
JUST TRUST ME. LISTEN TO YOUR GUT.

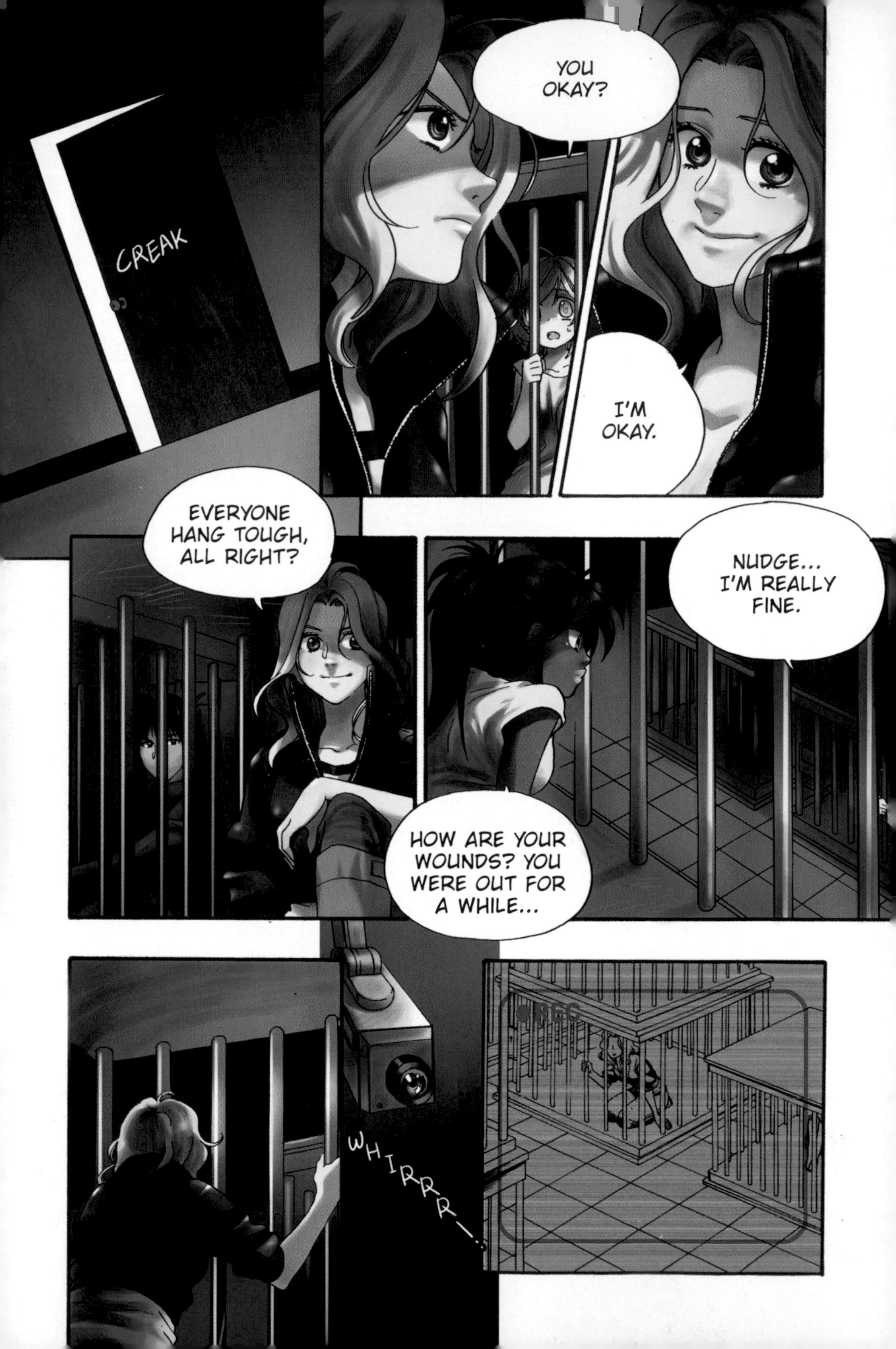
CREAK
YOU OKAY?
I'M OKAY.
EVERYONE HANG TOUGH, ALL RIGHT?
NUDGE... I'M REALLY FINE.
HOW ARE YOUR WOUNDS? YOU WERE OUT FOR A WHILE...
WHIRRR—
REC

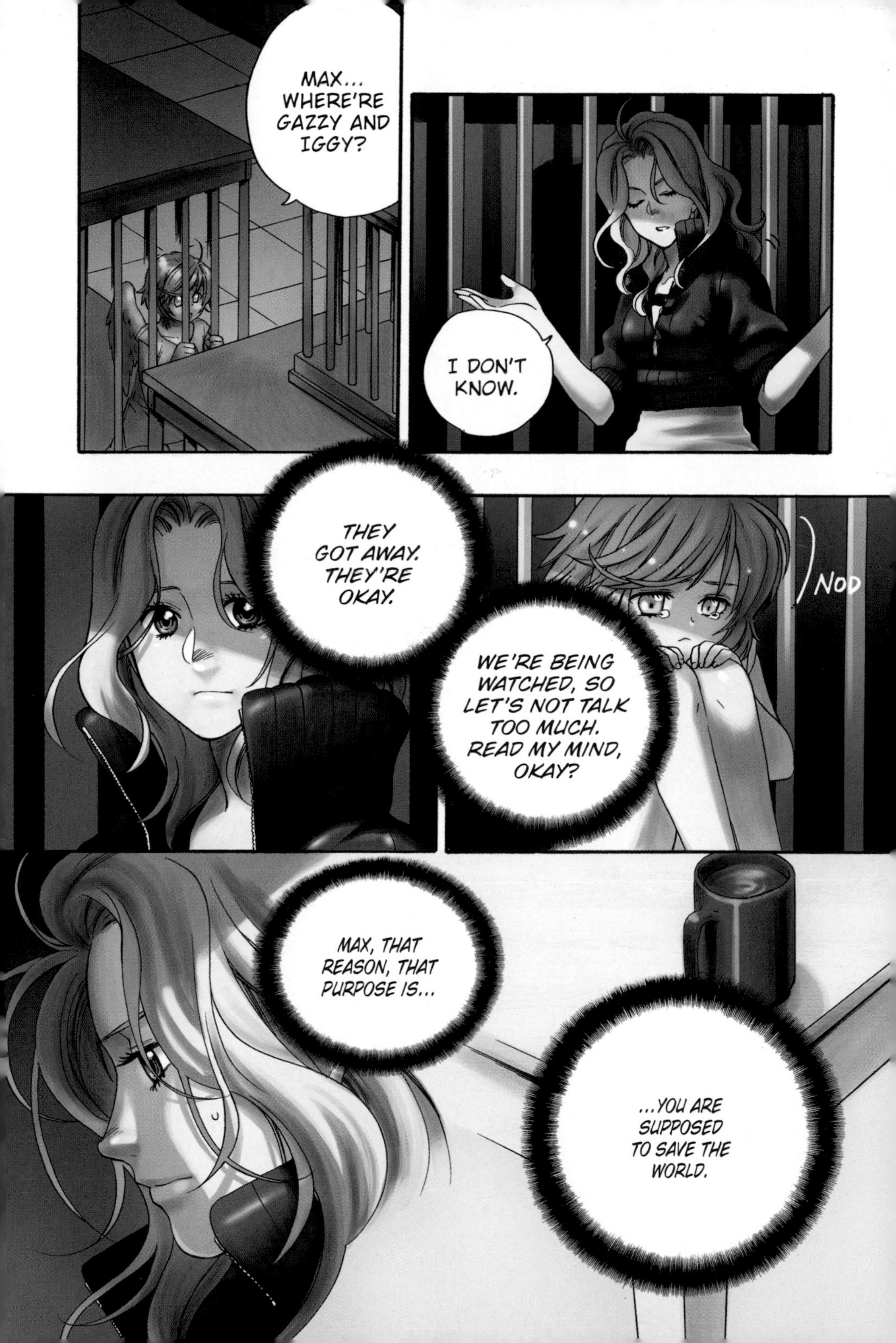
MAX... WHERE'RE GAZZY AND IGGY?
I DON'T KNOW.
THEY GOT AWAY. THEY'RE OKAY.
WE'RE BEING WATCHED, SO LET'S NOT TALK TOO MUCH. READ MY MIND, OKAY?
NOD
MAX, THAT REASON, THAT PURPOSE IS...
...YOU ARE SUPPOSED TO SAVE THE WORLD.

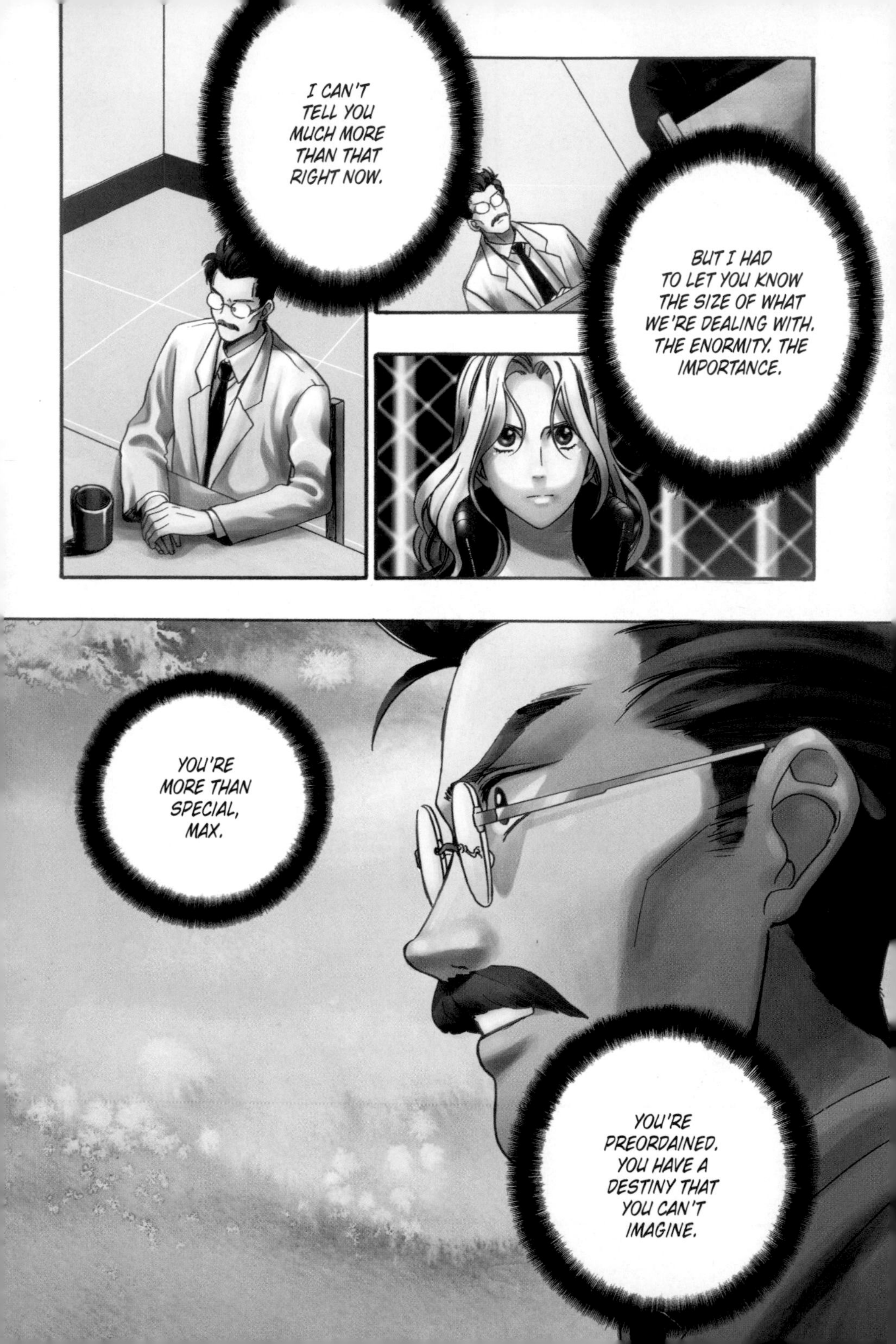
I CAN'T TELL YOU MUCH MORE THAN THAT RIGHT NOW.
BUT I HAD TO LET YOU KNOW THE SIZE OF WHAT WE'RE DEALING WITH. THE ENORMITY. THE IMPORTANCE.
YOU'RE MORE THAN SPECIAL, MAX.
YOU'RE PREORDAINED. YOU HAVE A DESTINY THAT YOU CAN'T IMAGINE.

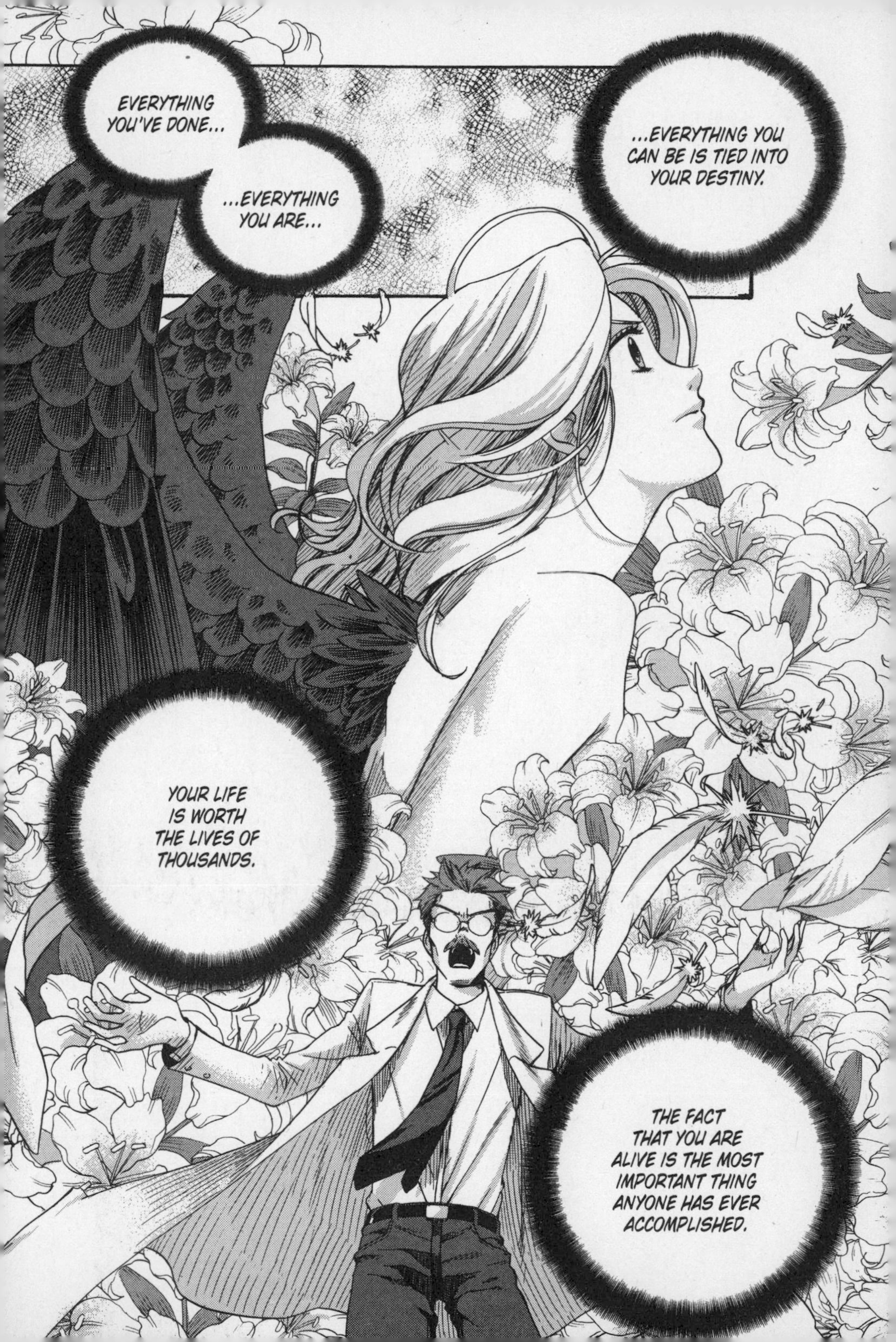
EVERYTHING YOU'VE DONE...
...EVERYTHING YOU ARE...
...EVERYTHING YOU CAN BE IS TIED INTO YOUR DESTINY.
YOUR LIFE IS WORTH THE LIVES OF THOUSANDS.
THE FACT THAT YOU ARE ALIVE IS THE MOST IMPORTANT THING ANYONE HAS EVER ACCOMPLISHED.

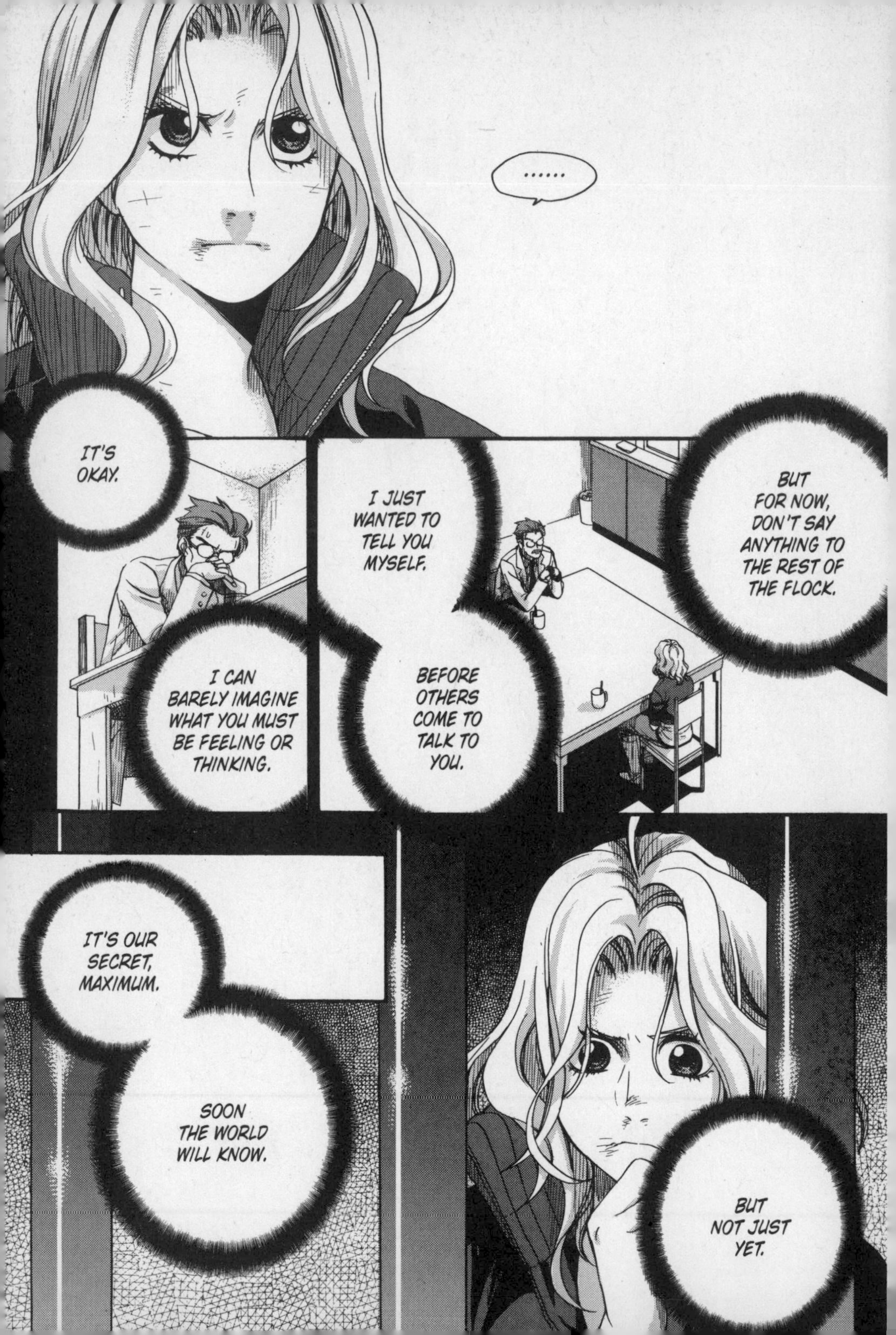

....
IT'S OKAY.
I JUST WANTED TO TELL YOU MYSELF.
BUT FOR NOW, DON'T SAY ANYTHING TO THE REST OF THE FLOCK.
I CAN BARELY IMAGINE WHAT YOU MUST BE FEELING OR THINKING.
BEFORE OTHERS COME TO TALK TO YOU.
IT'S OUR SECRET, MAXIMUM.
SOON THE WORLD WILL KNOW.
BUT NOT JUST YET.

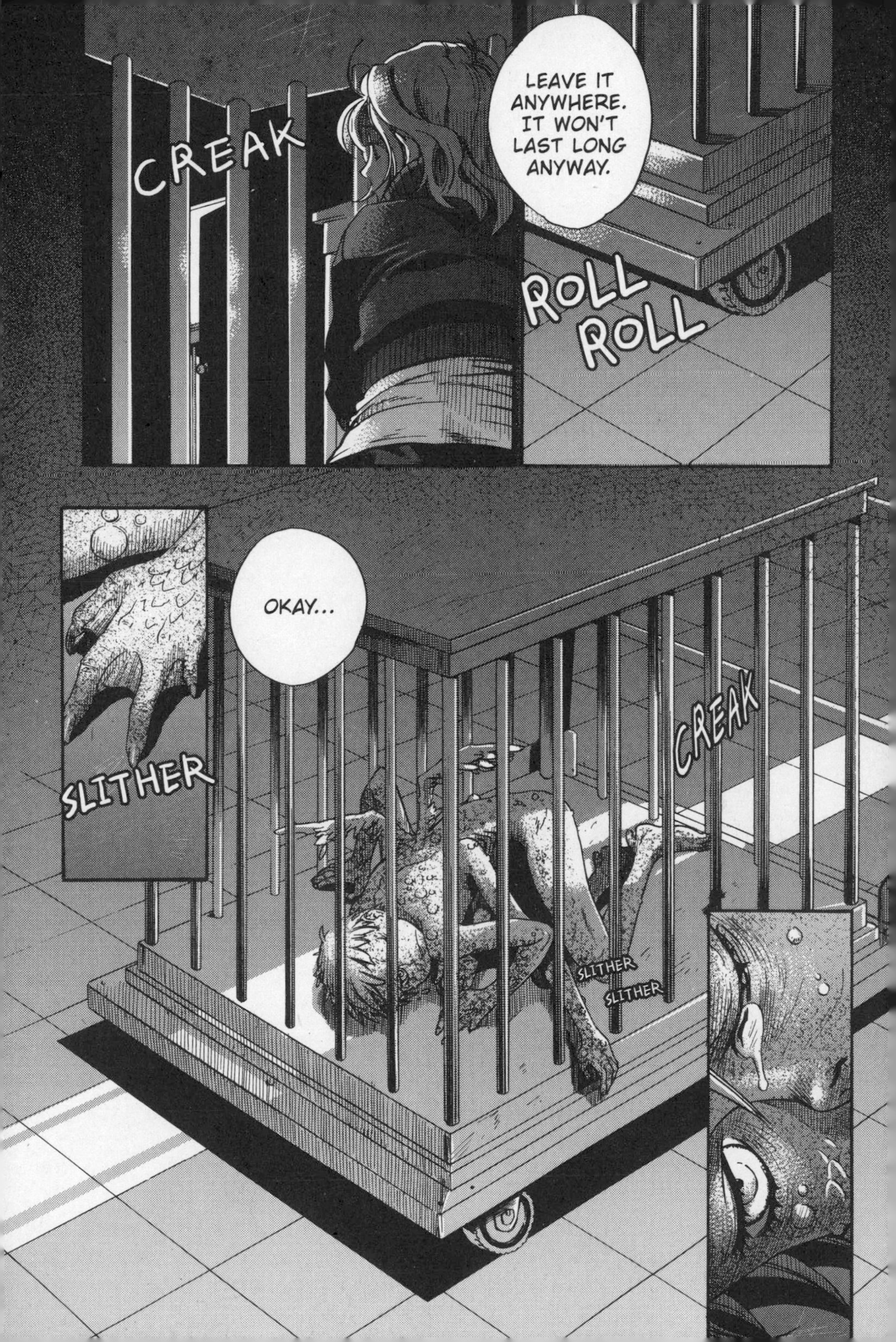
CREAK
LEAVE IT ANYWHERE. IT WON'T LAST LONG ANYWAY.
ROLL ROLL
SLITHER
OKAY...
CREAK
SLITHER
SLITHER

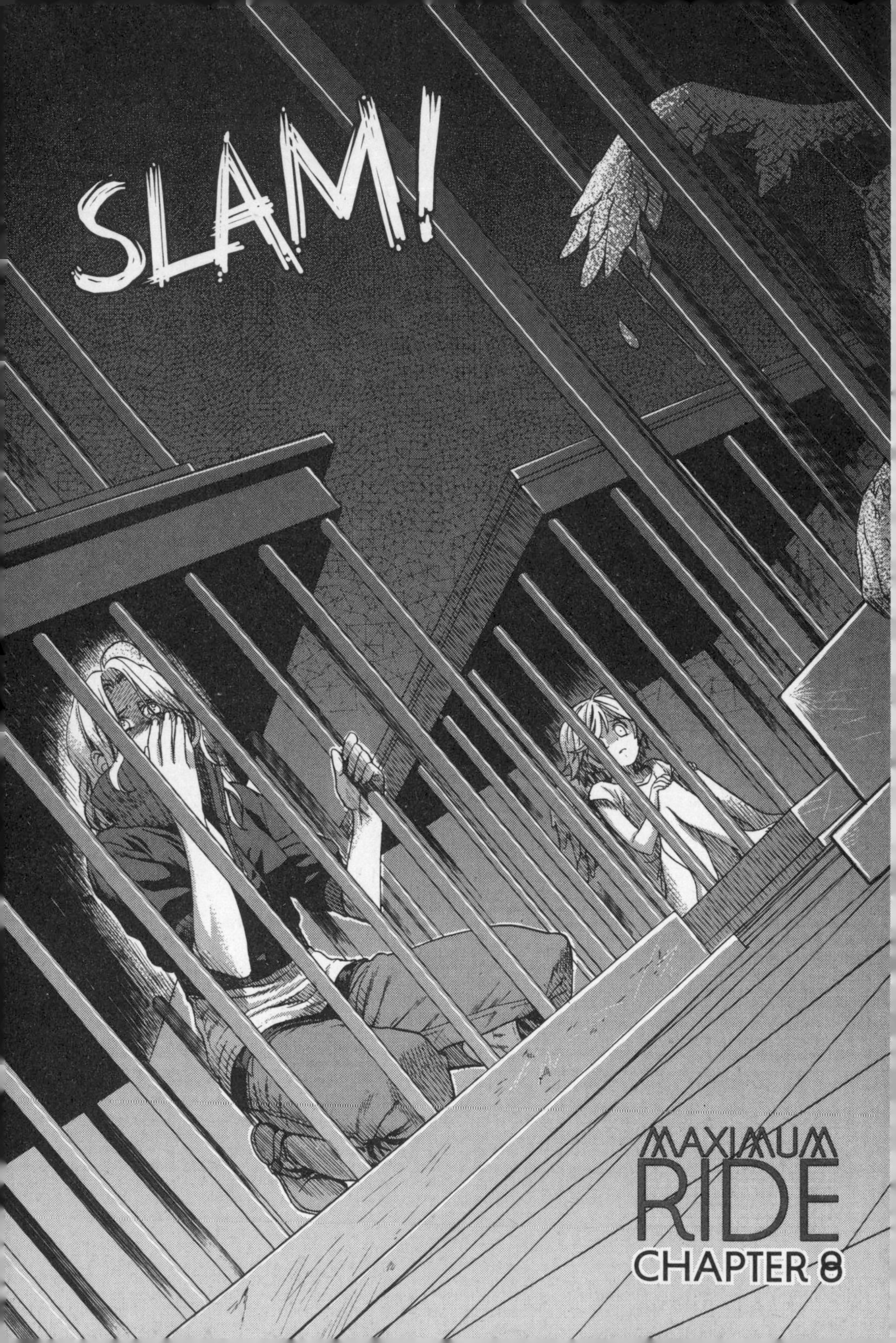
SLAM!
MAXIMUM RIDE
CHAPTER 8

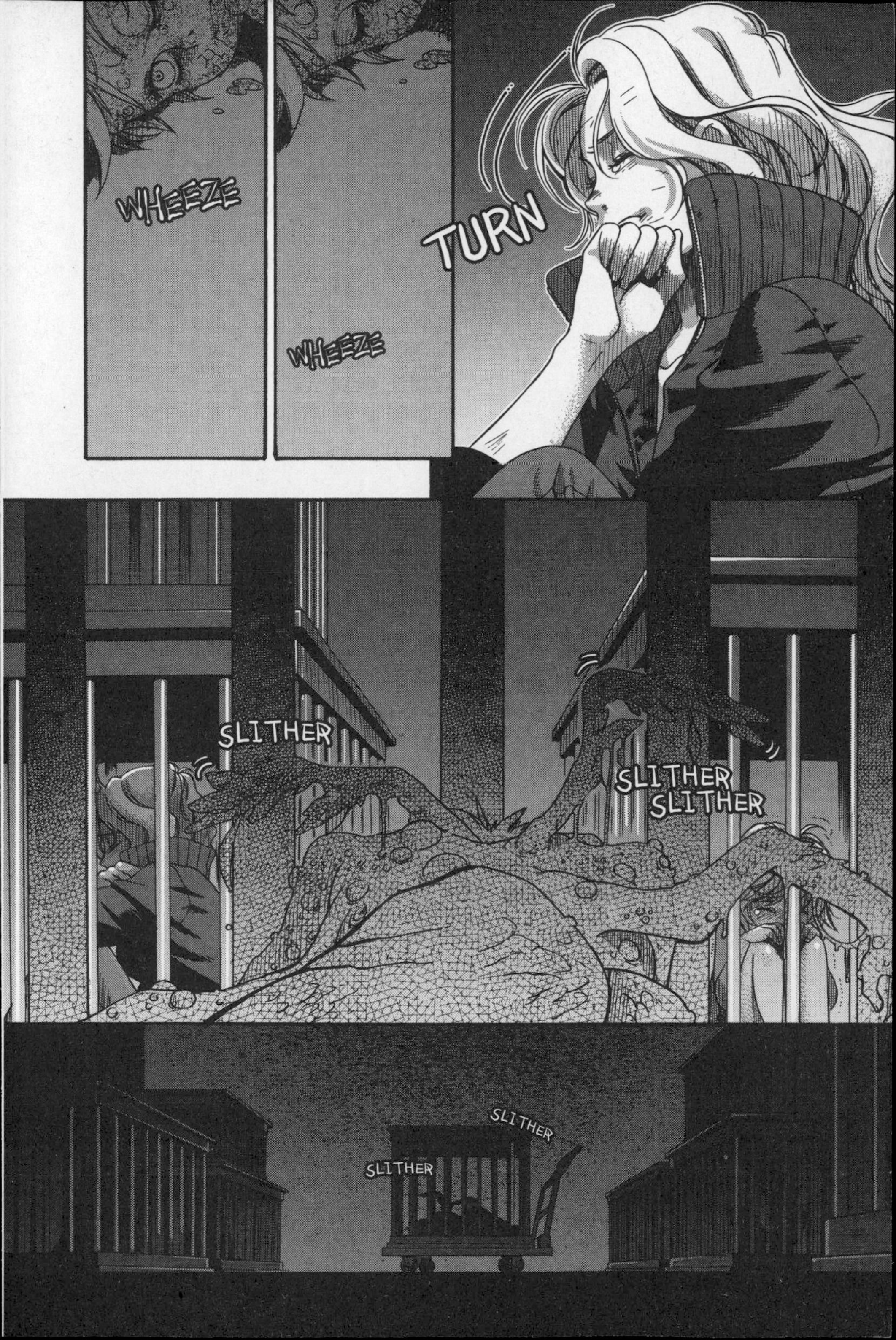
WHEEZE
WHEEZE
TURN
SLITHER
SLITHER
SLITHER
SLITHER
SLITHER

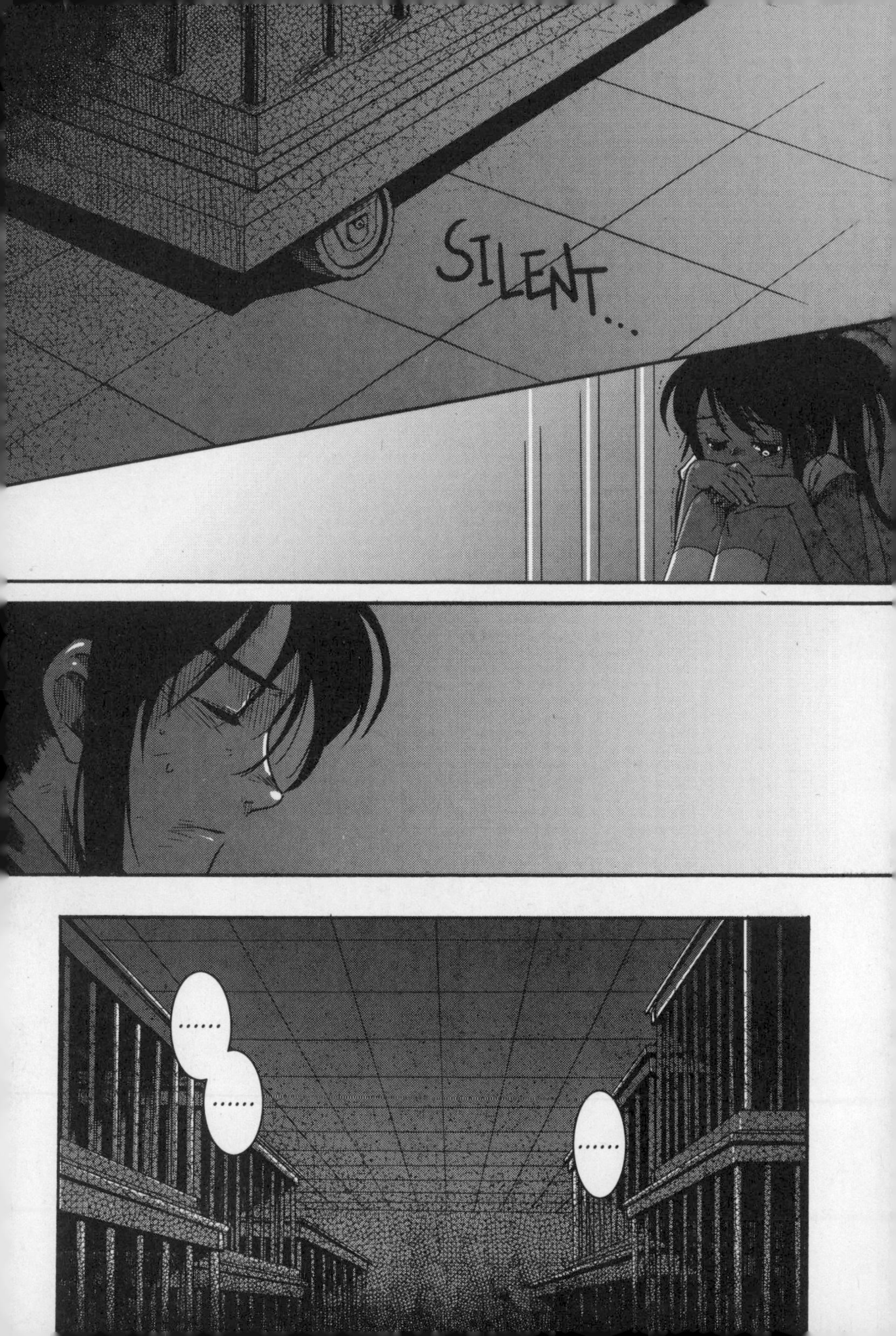
SILENT...
......
......
......

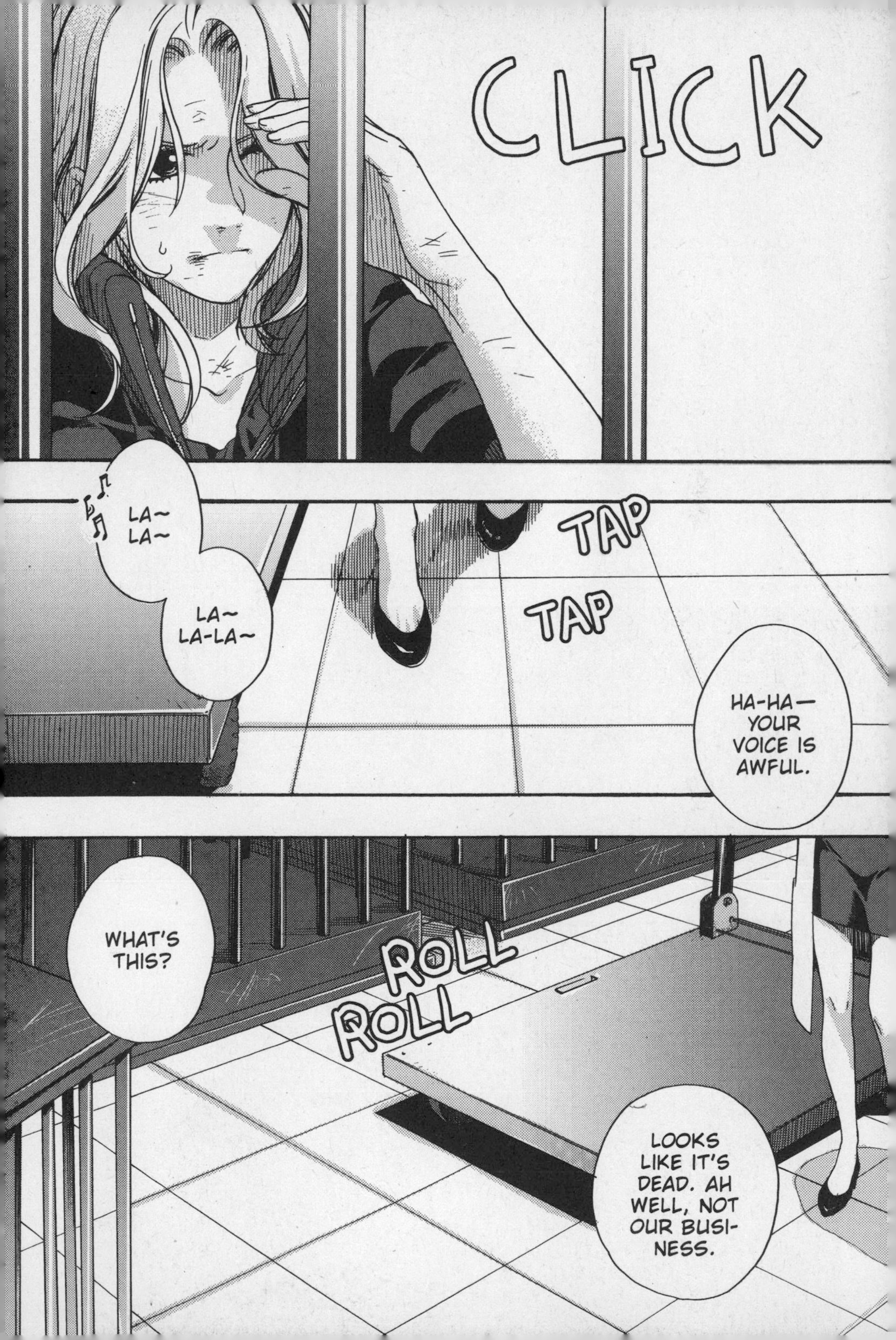
CLICK
LA~ LA~
LA~ LA-LA~
TAP
TAP
HA-HA— YOUR VOICE IS AWFUL.
WHAT'S THIS?
ROLL
ROLL
LOOKS LIKE IT'S DEAD. AH WELL, NOT OUR BUSI-NESS.

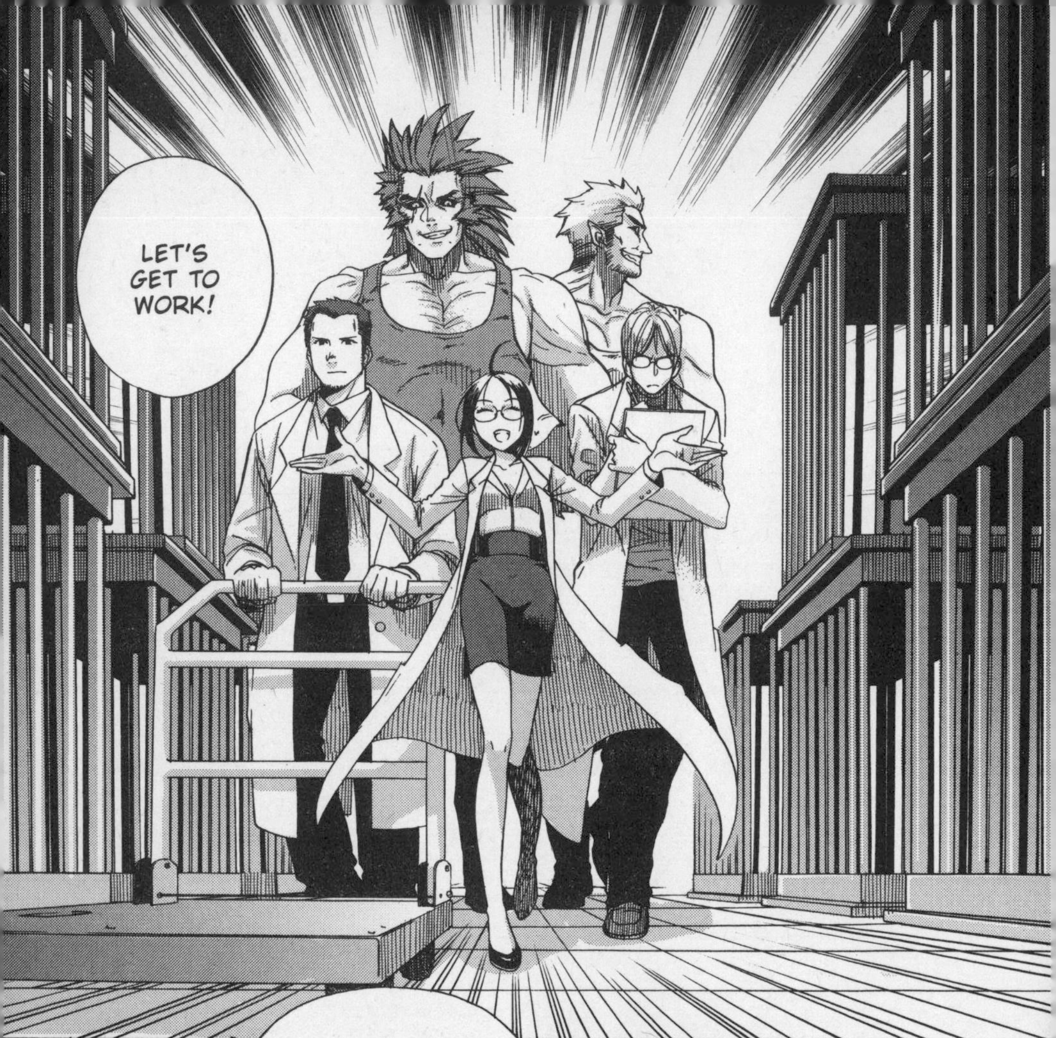
LET'S GET TO WORK!

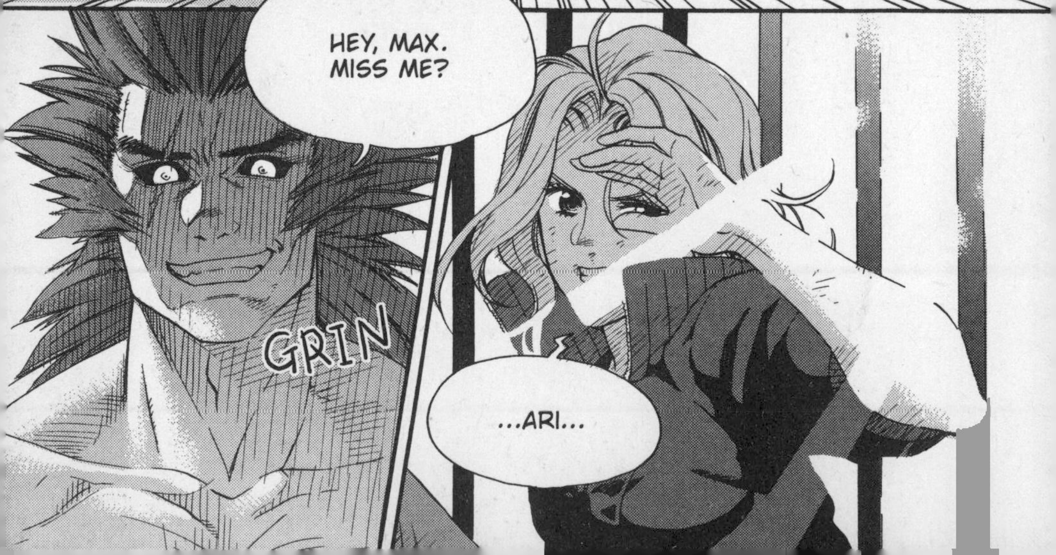
HEY, MAX. MISS ME?
GRIN
...ARI...

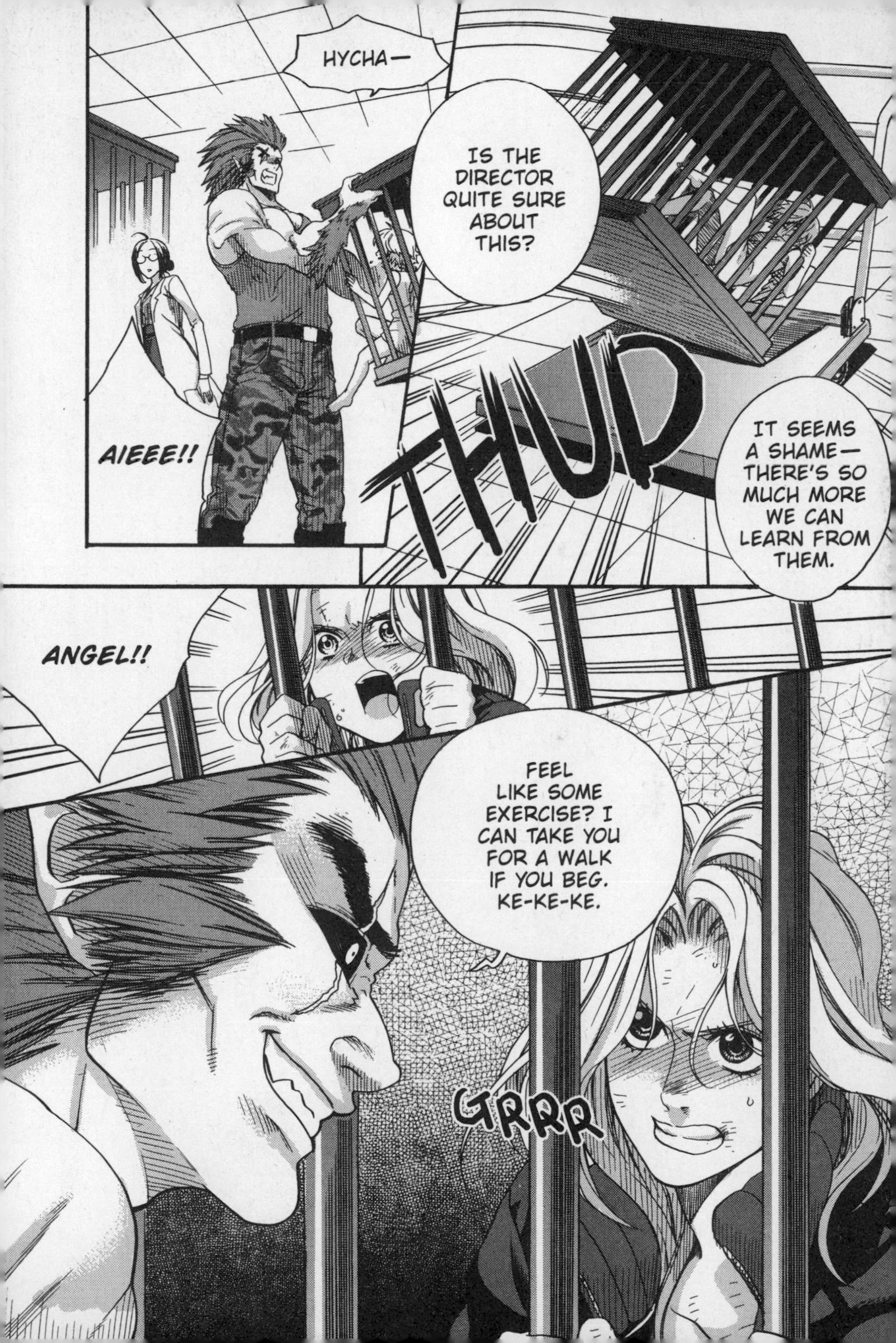
HYCHA—
AIEEE!!
IS THE DIRECTOR QUITE SURE ABOUT THIS?
THUD
IT SEEMS A SHAME— THERE'S SO MUCH MORE WE CAN LEARN FROM THEM.
ANGEL!!
FEEL LIKE SOME EXERCISE? I CAN TAKE YOU FOR A WALK IF YOU BEG. KE-KE-KE.
GRRR

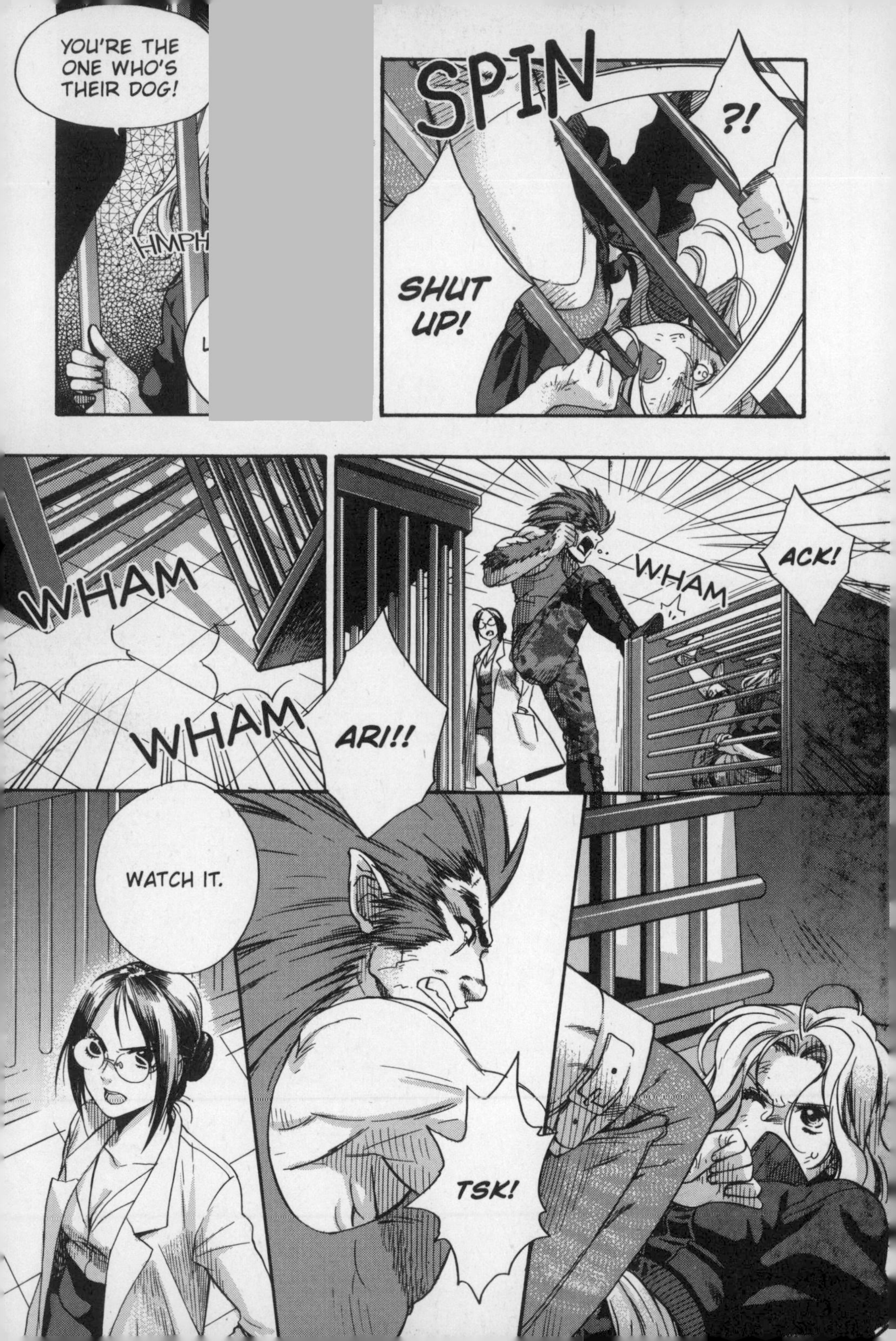
YOU'RE THE ONE WHO'S THEIR DOG!
SPIN
?!
SHUT UP!
WHAM
WHAM
ARI!!
WHAM
ACK!
WATCH IT.
TSK!

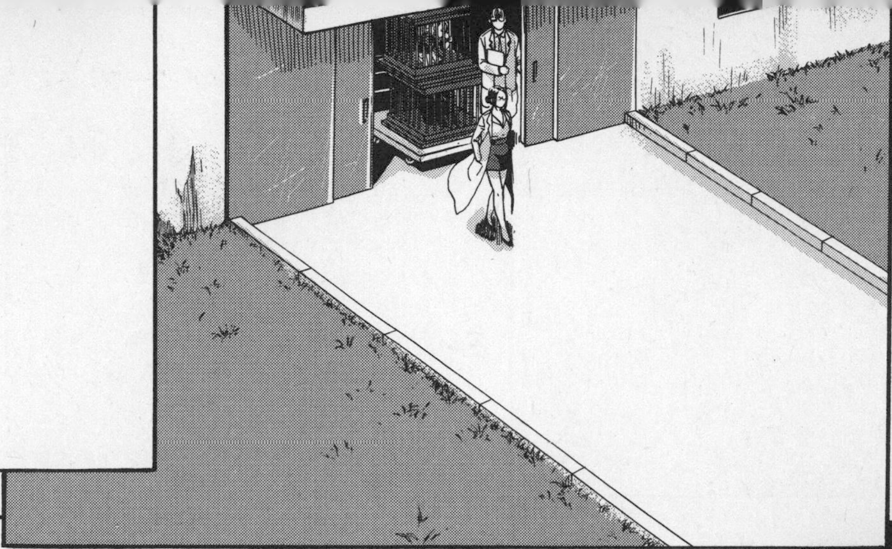
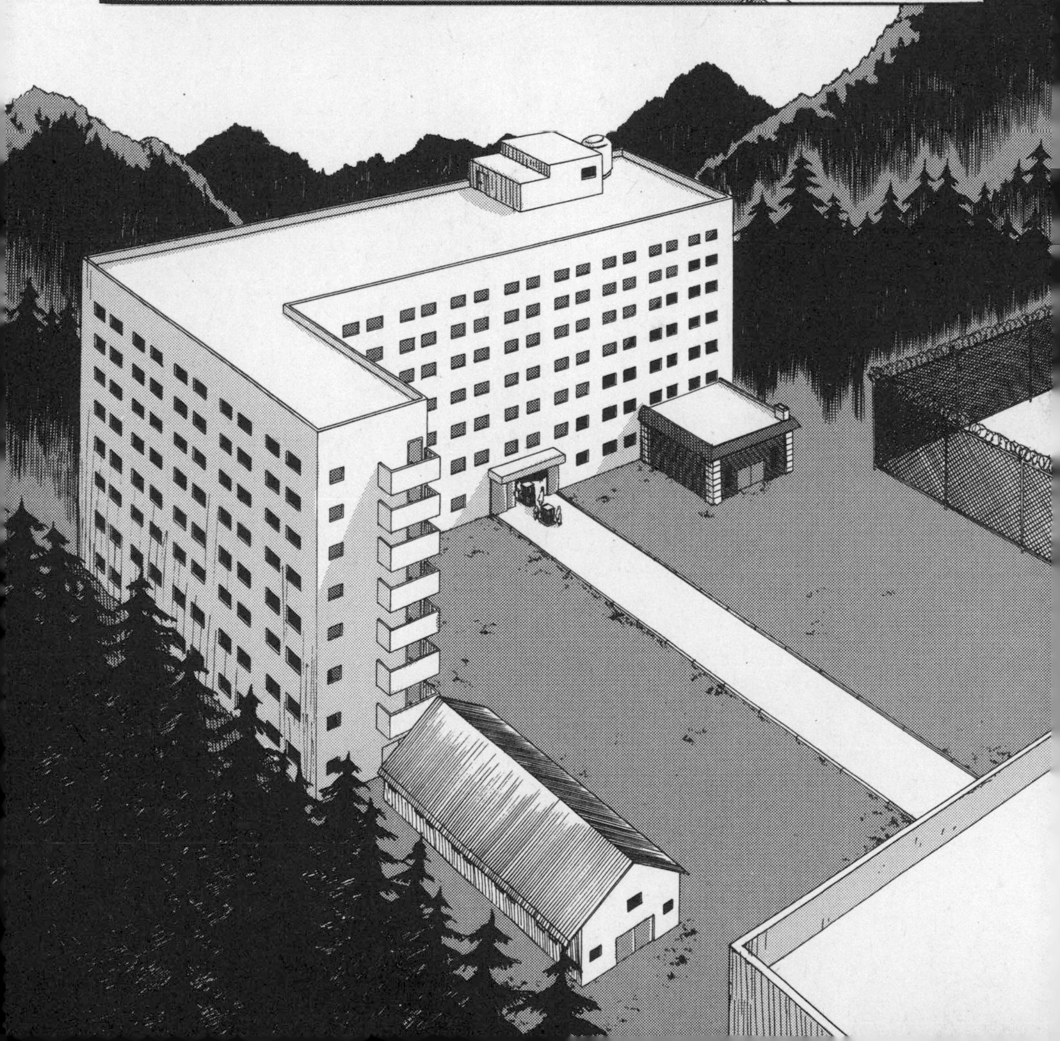

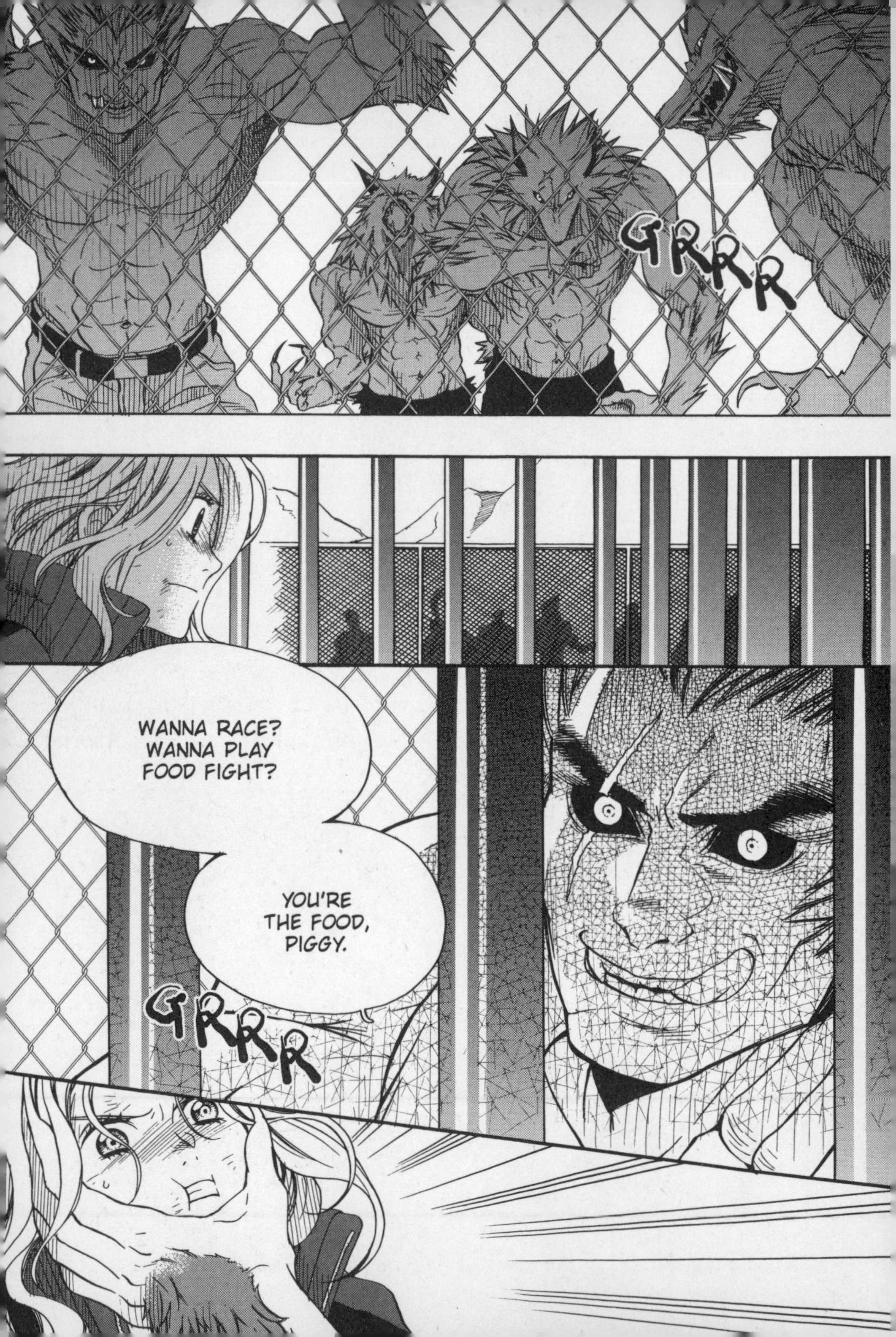
GRRRR
WANNA RACE? WANNA PLAY FOOD FIGHT?
YOU'RE THE FOOD, PIGGY.
GRRRR

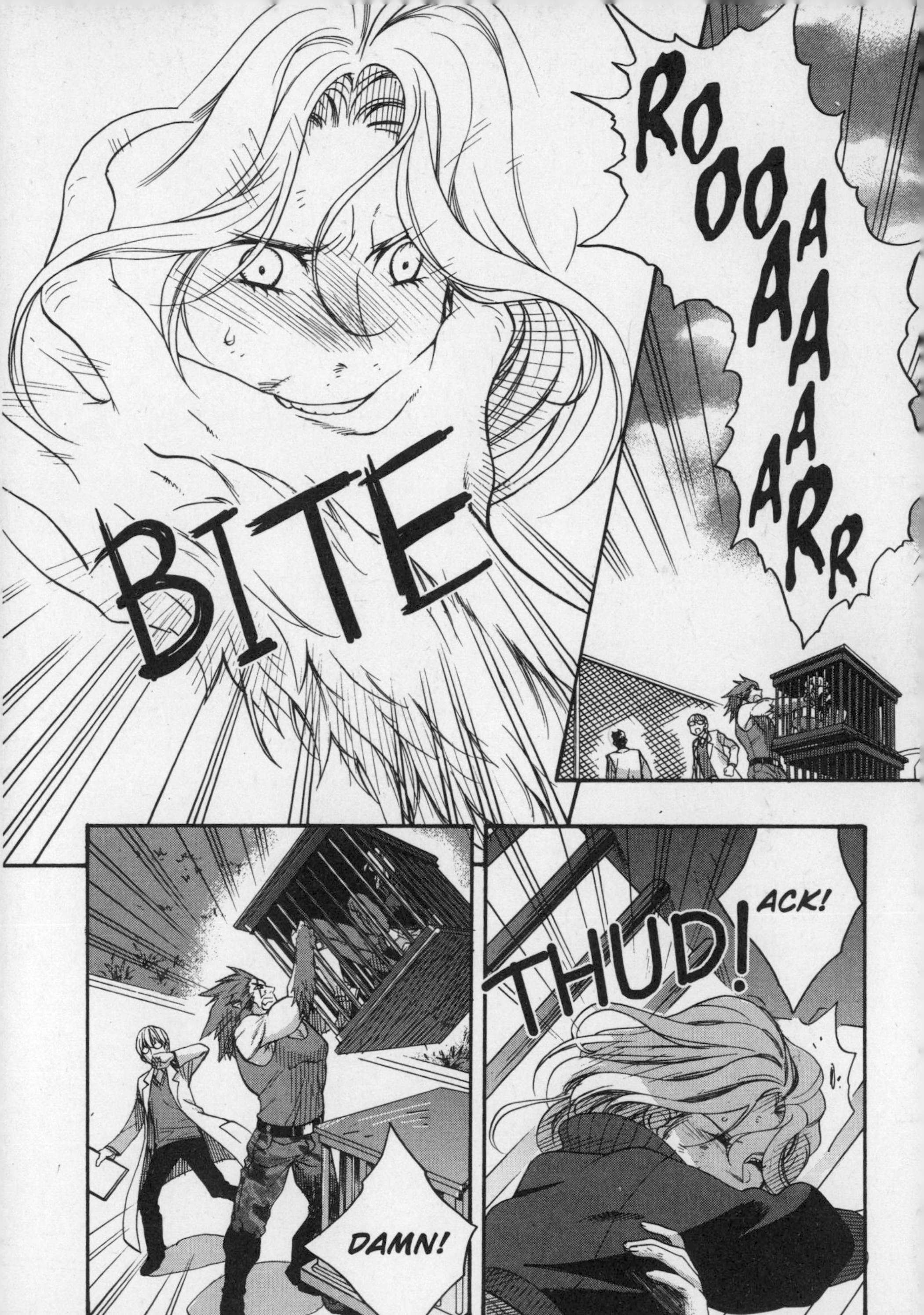
BITE
ROOOAAAAARR
DAMN!
THUD!
ACK!

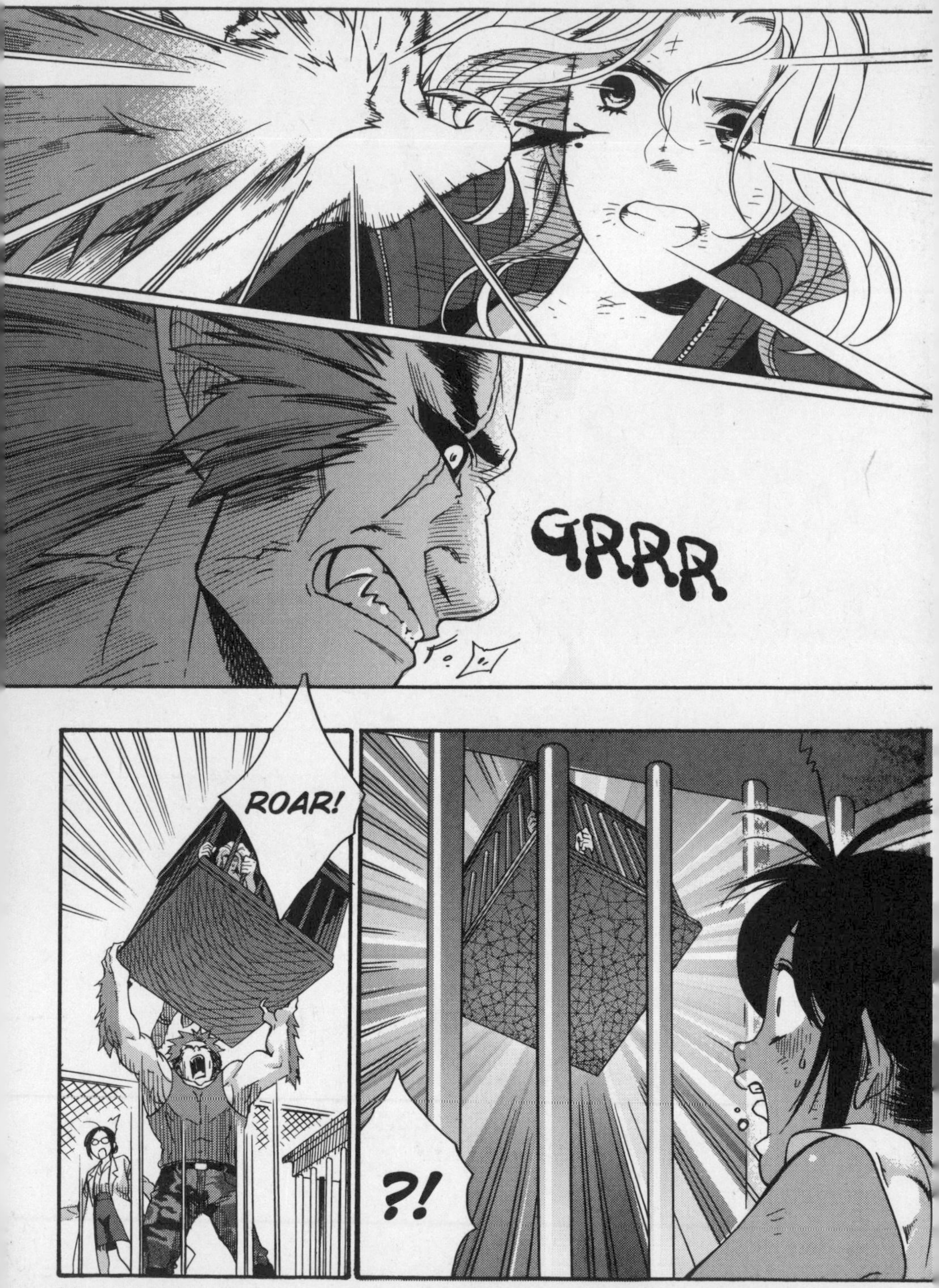
GRRR
ROAR!
?!

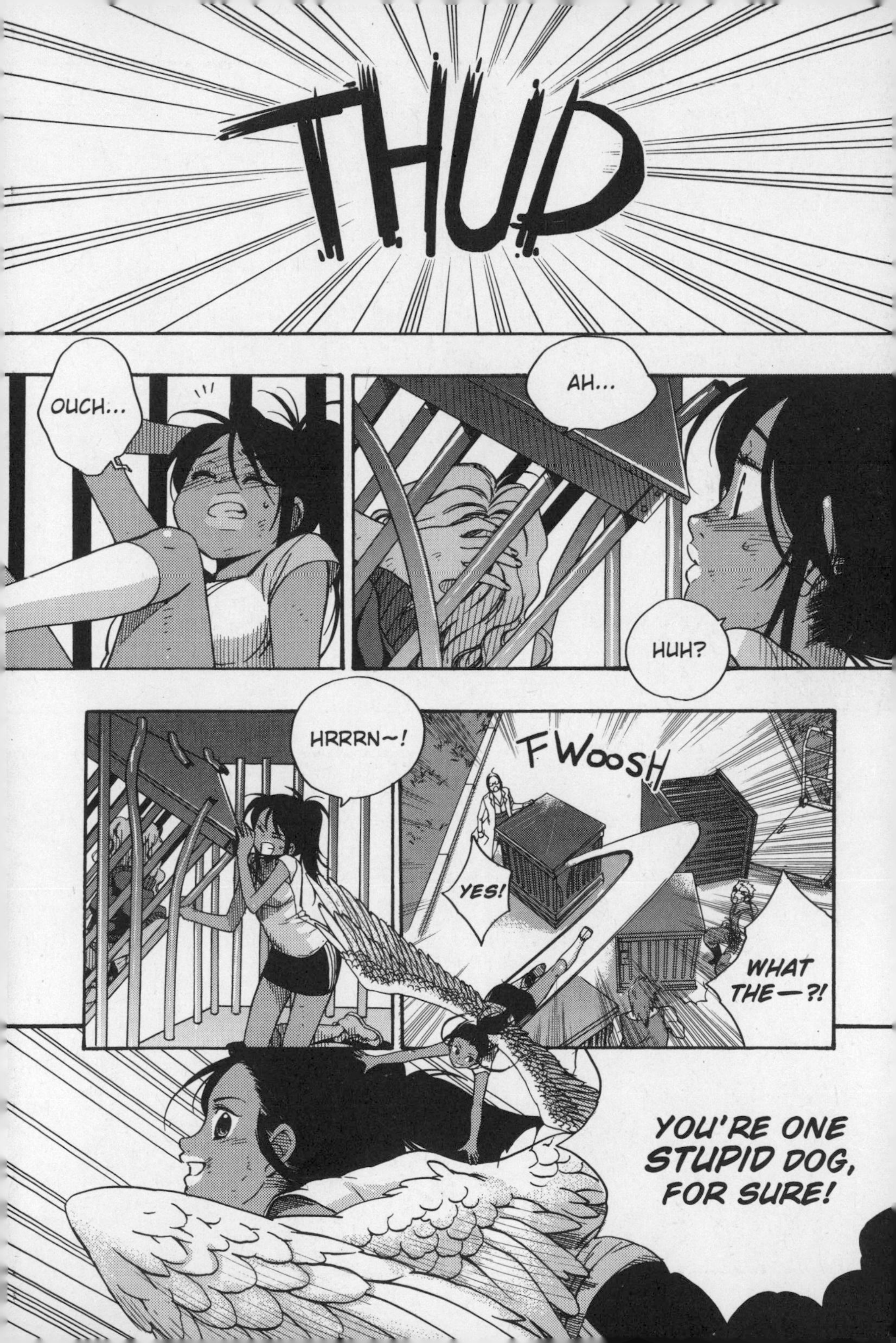
THUD
OUCH...
AH...
HUH?
HRRRN~!
FWOOSH
YES!
WHAT THE—?!
YOU'RE ONE STUPID DOG, FOR SURE!

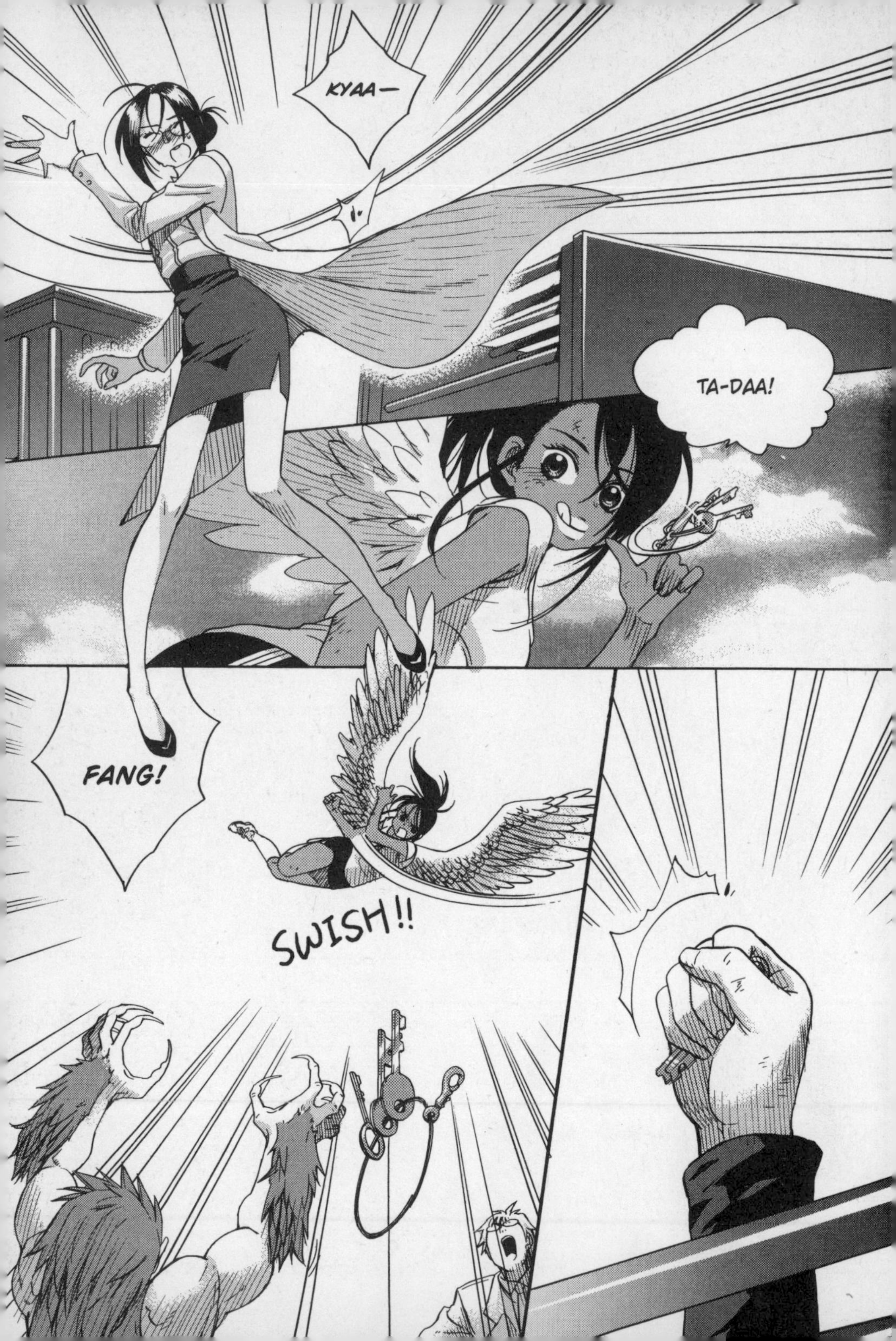
KYAA—
TA-DAA!
FANG!
SWISH!!

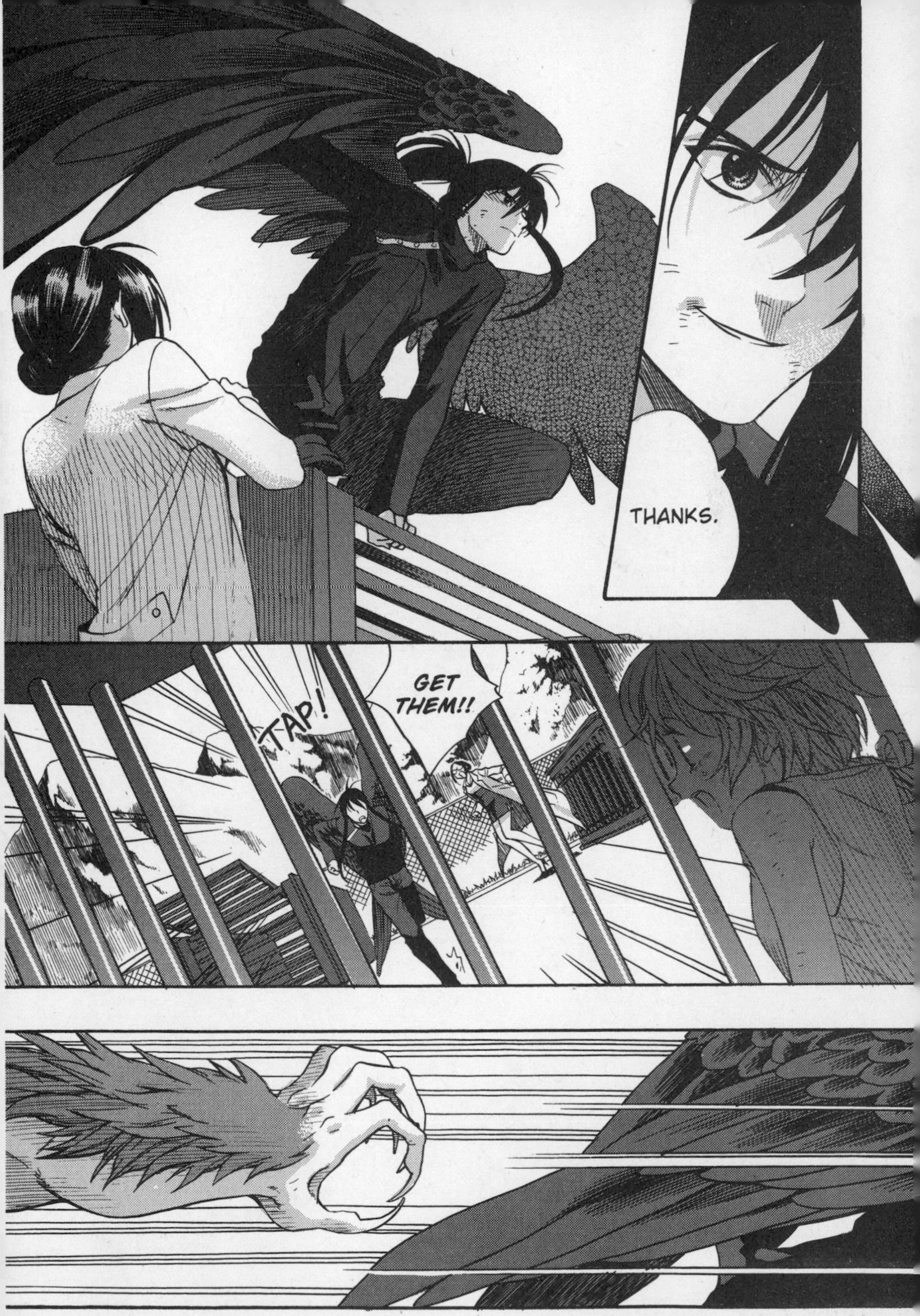
THANKS.
TAP!
GET THEM!!

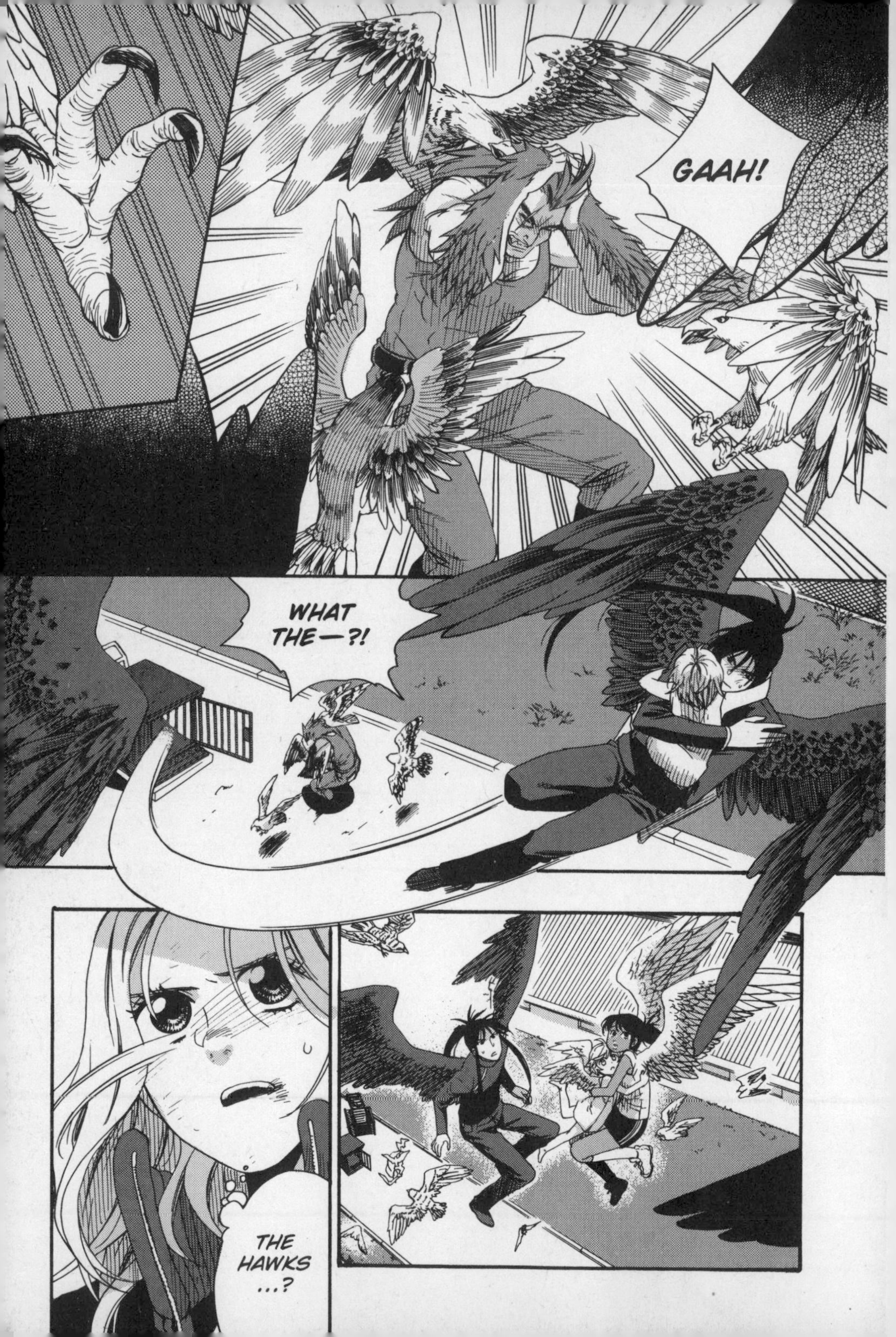
GAAH!
WHAT THE—?!
THE HAWKS ...?

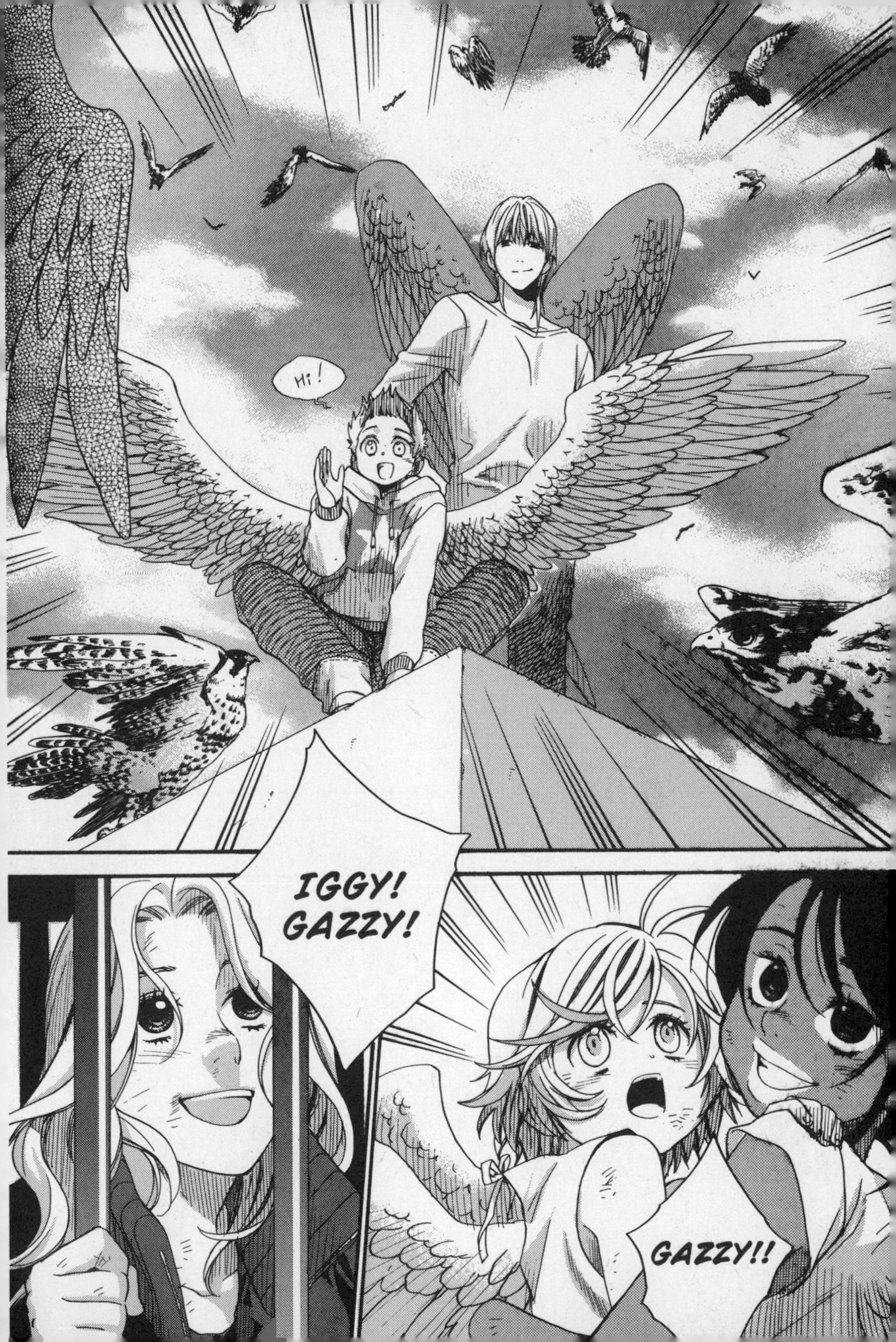
Hi!
IGGY! GAZZY!
GAZZY!!

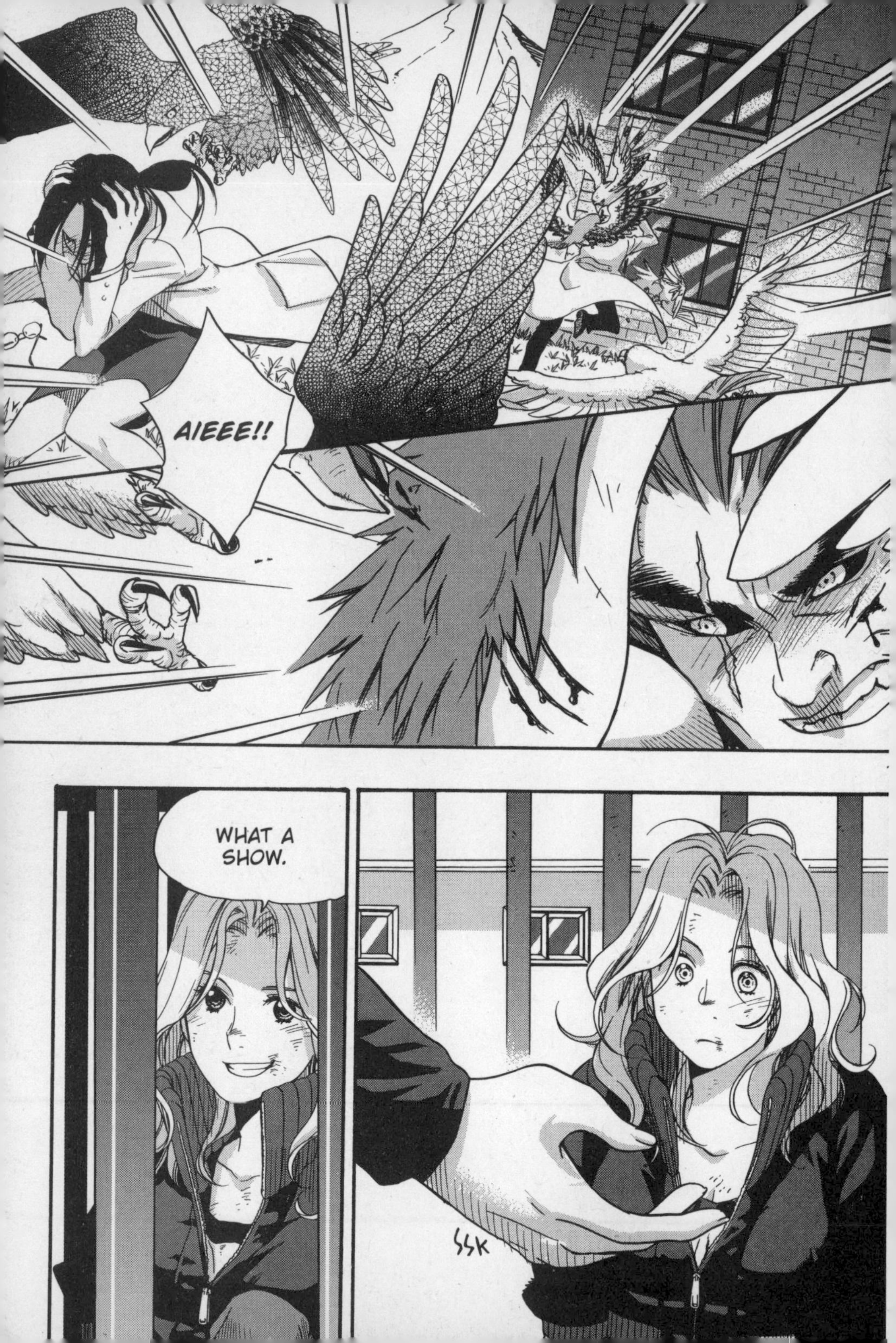
AIEEE!!
WHAT A SHOW.
SSK

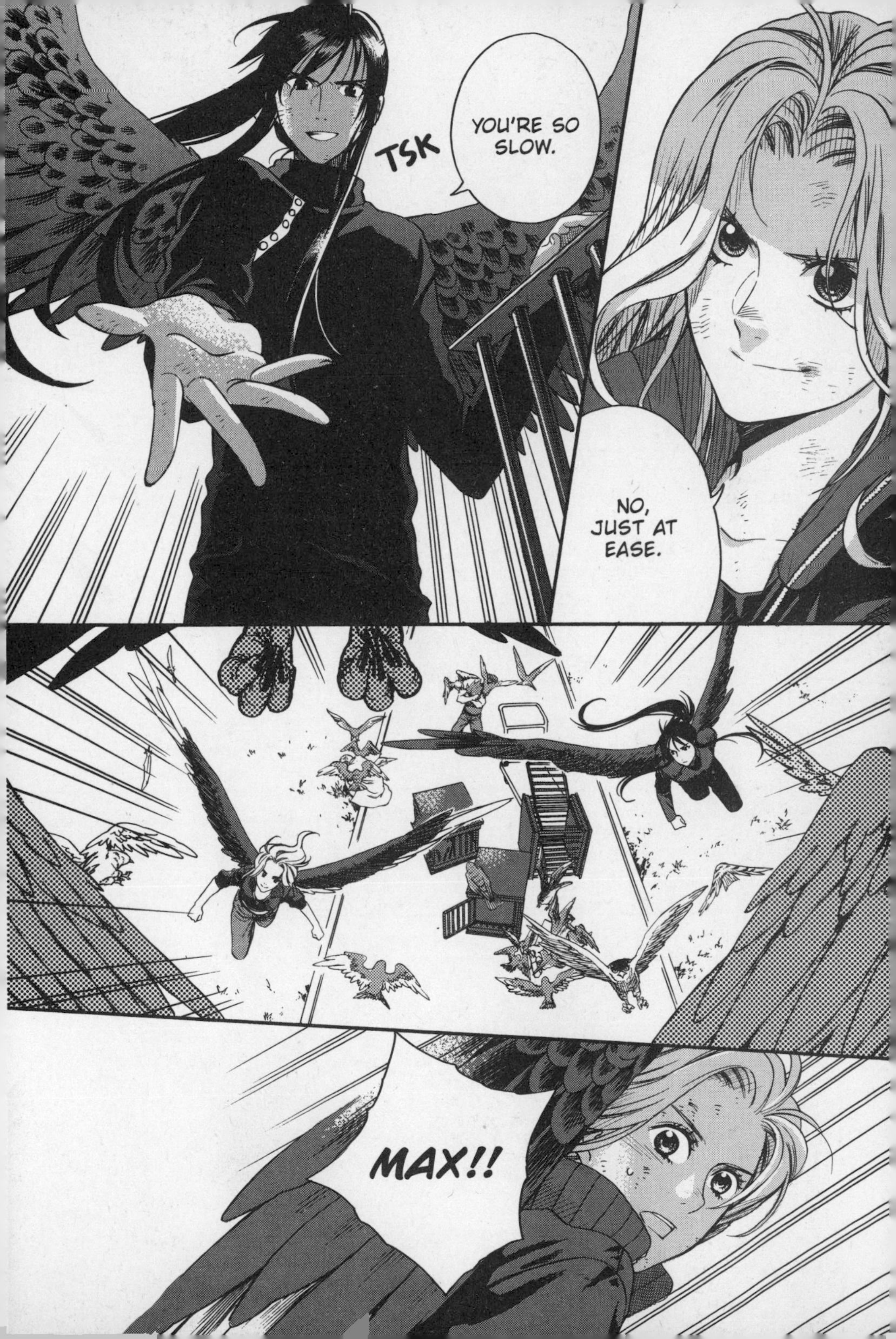
TSK
YOU'RE SO SLOW.
NO, JUST AT EASE.
MAX!!

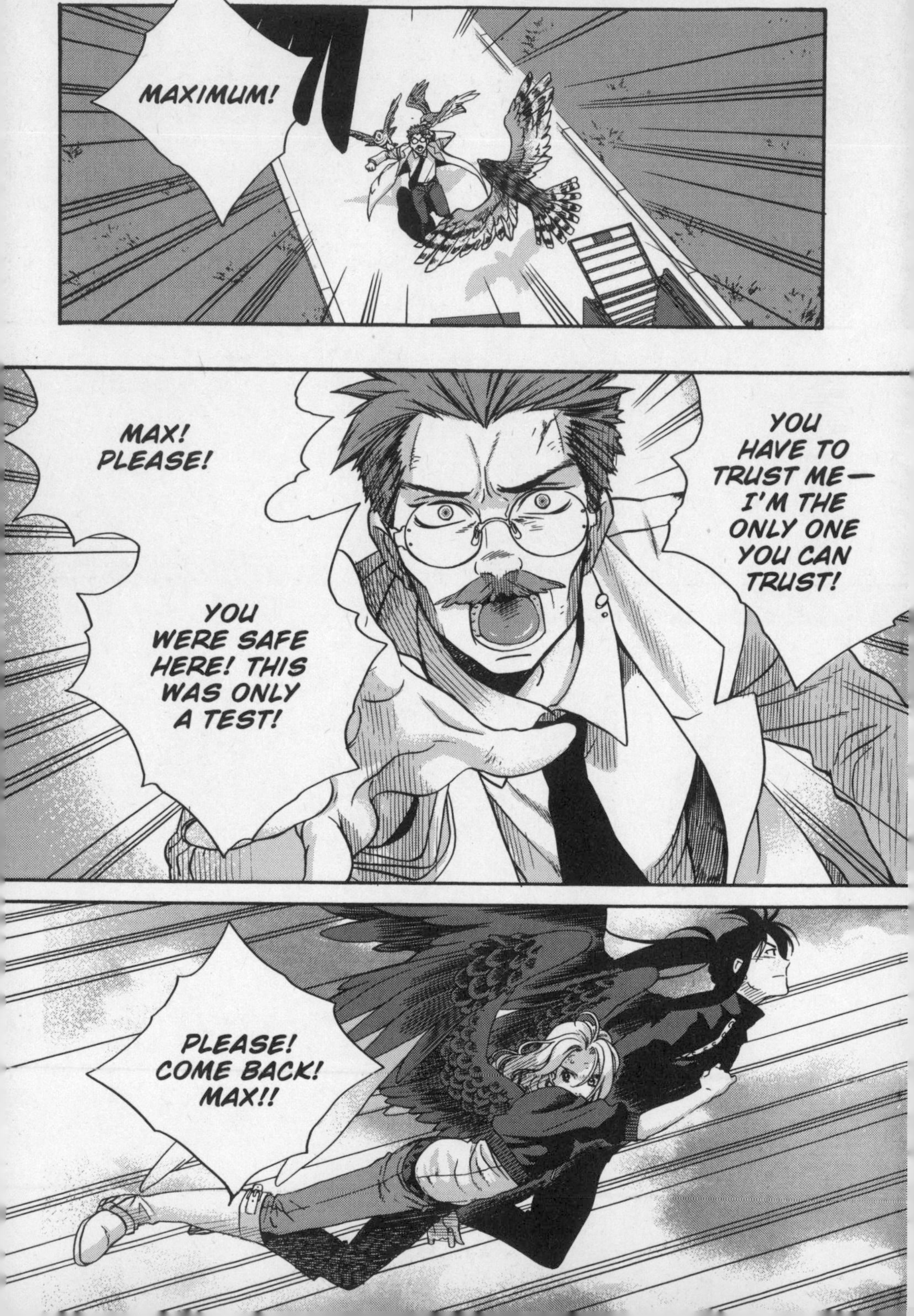
MAXIMUM!
MAX! PLEASE!
YOU WERE SAFE HERE! THIS WAS ONLY A TEST!
YOU HAVE TO TRUST ME— I'M THE ONLY ONE YOU CAN TRUST!
PLEASE! COME BACK! MAX!!

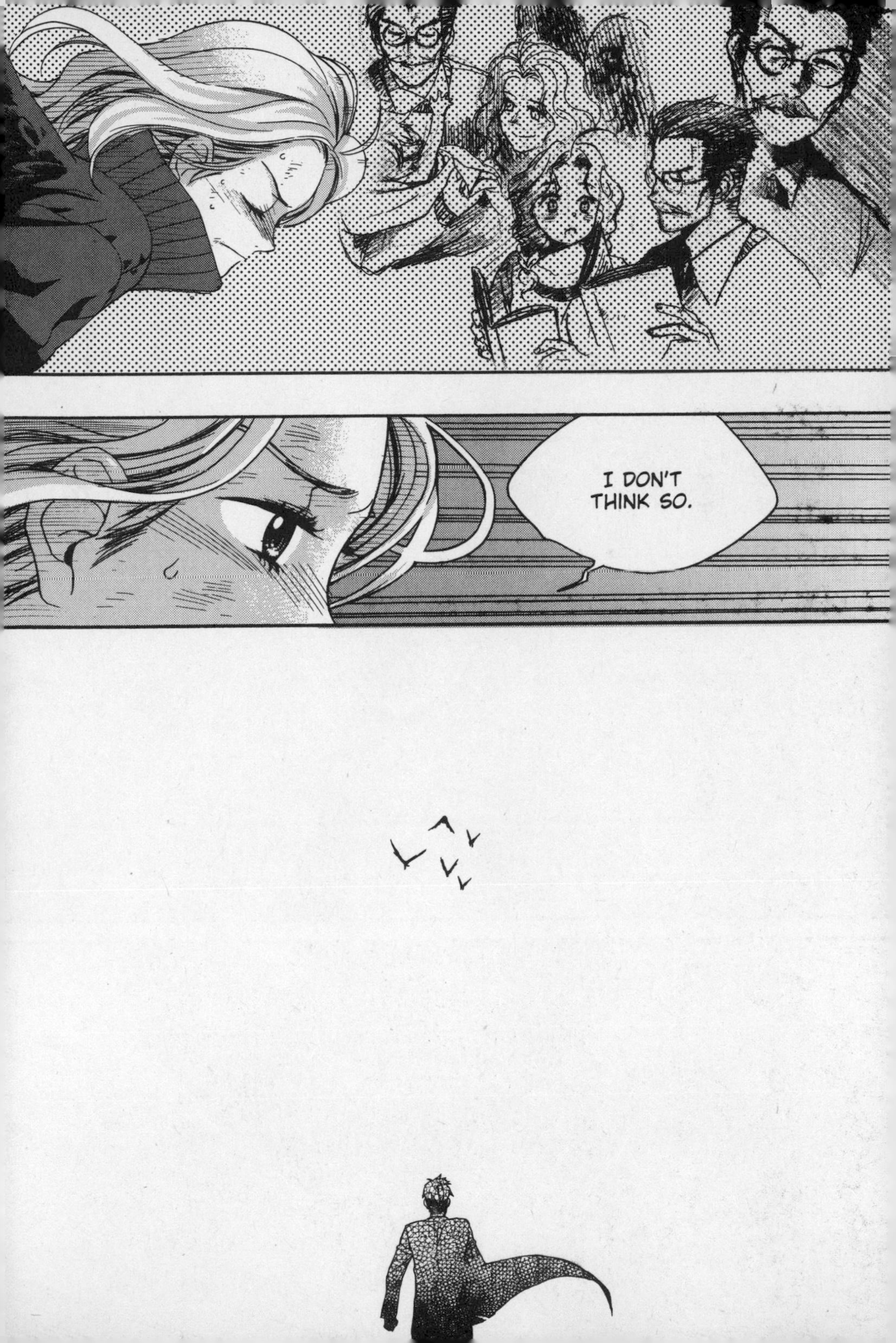
I DON'T THINK SO.

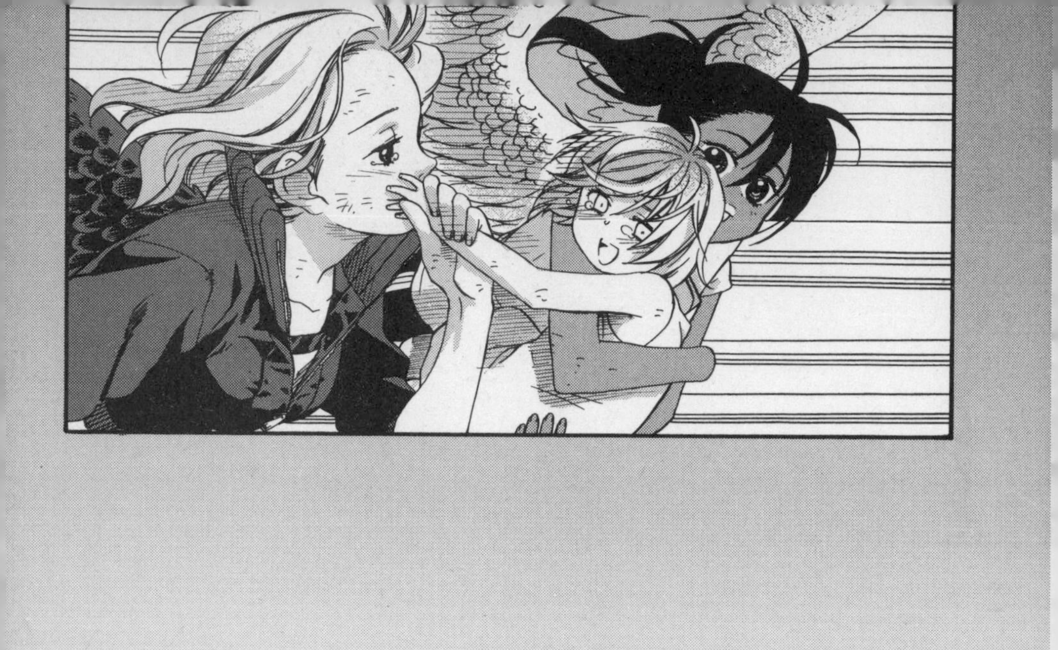
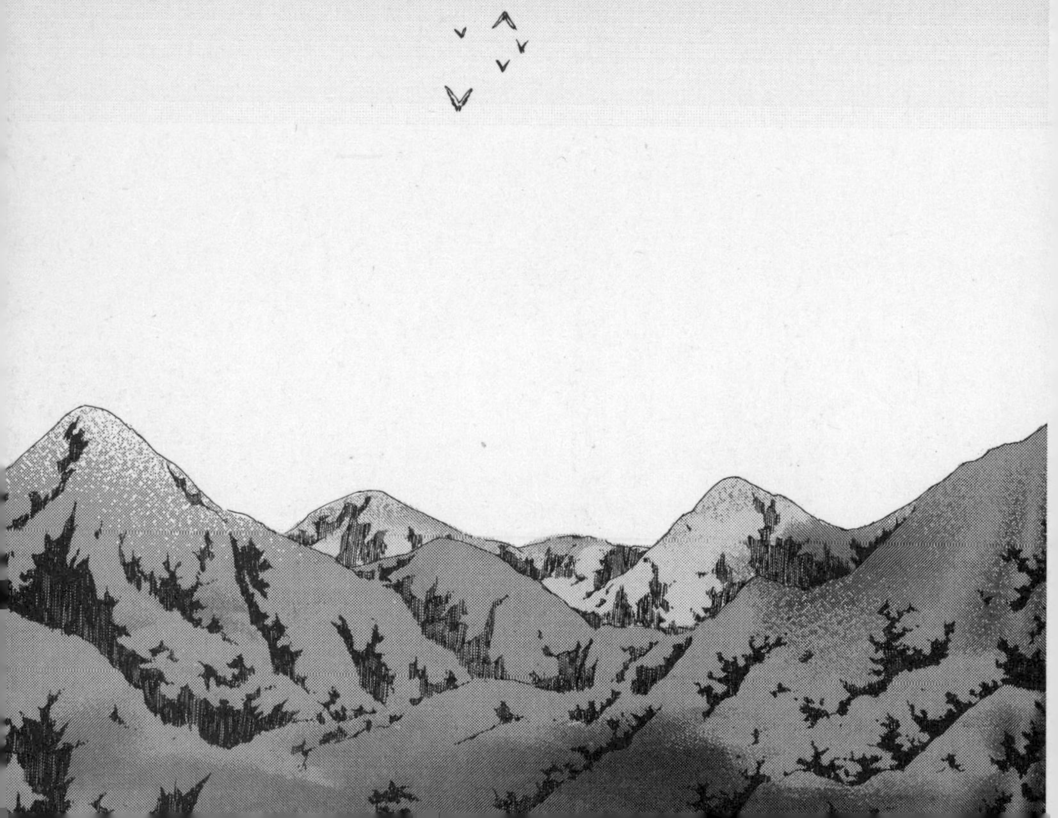

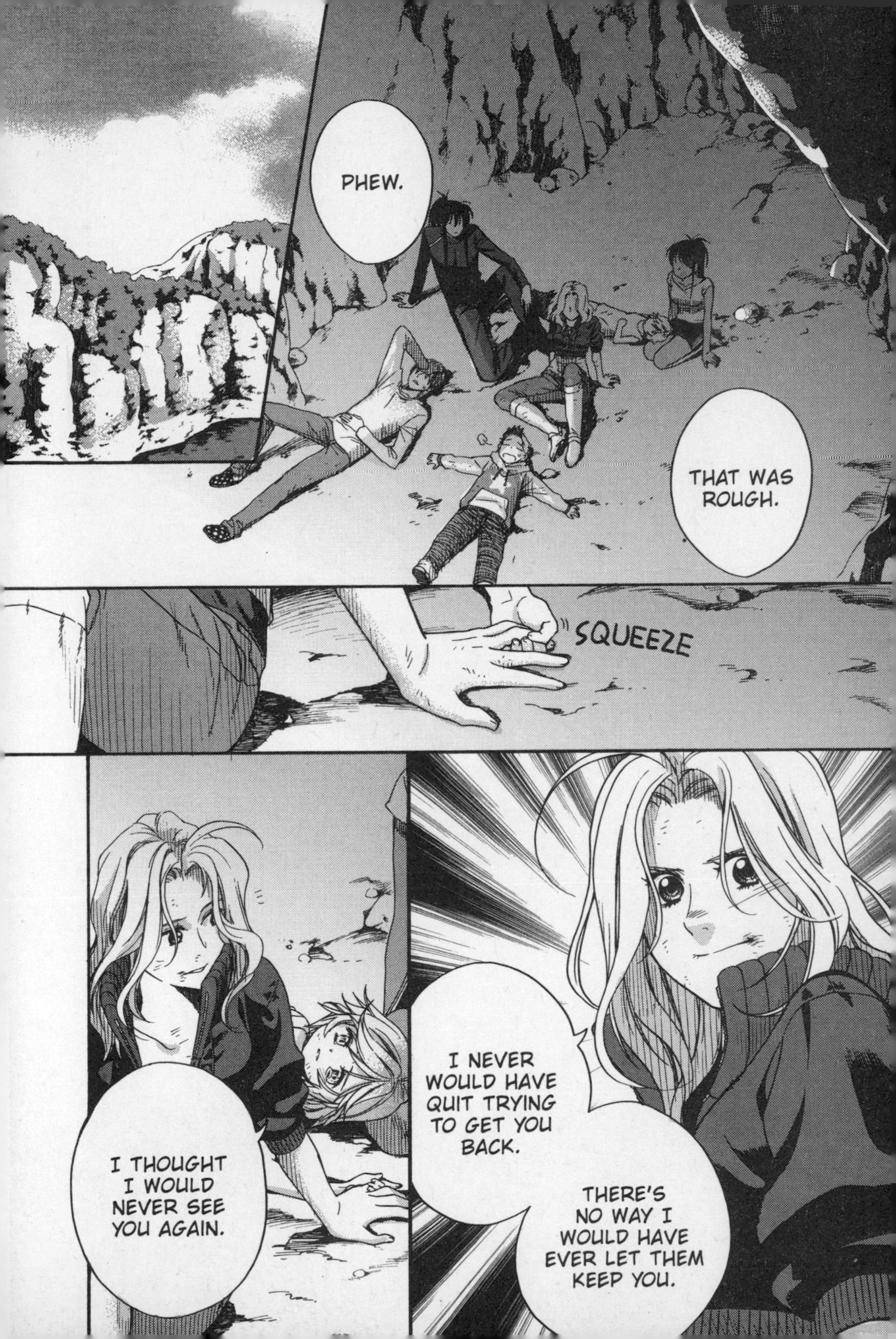
PHEW.
THAT WAS ROUGH.
SQUEEZE
I THOUGHT I WOULD NEVER SEE YOU AGAIN.
I NEVER WOULD HAVE QUIT TRYING TO GET YOU BACK.
THERE'S NO WAY I WOULD HAVE EVER LET THEM KEEP YOU.

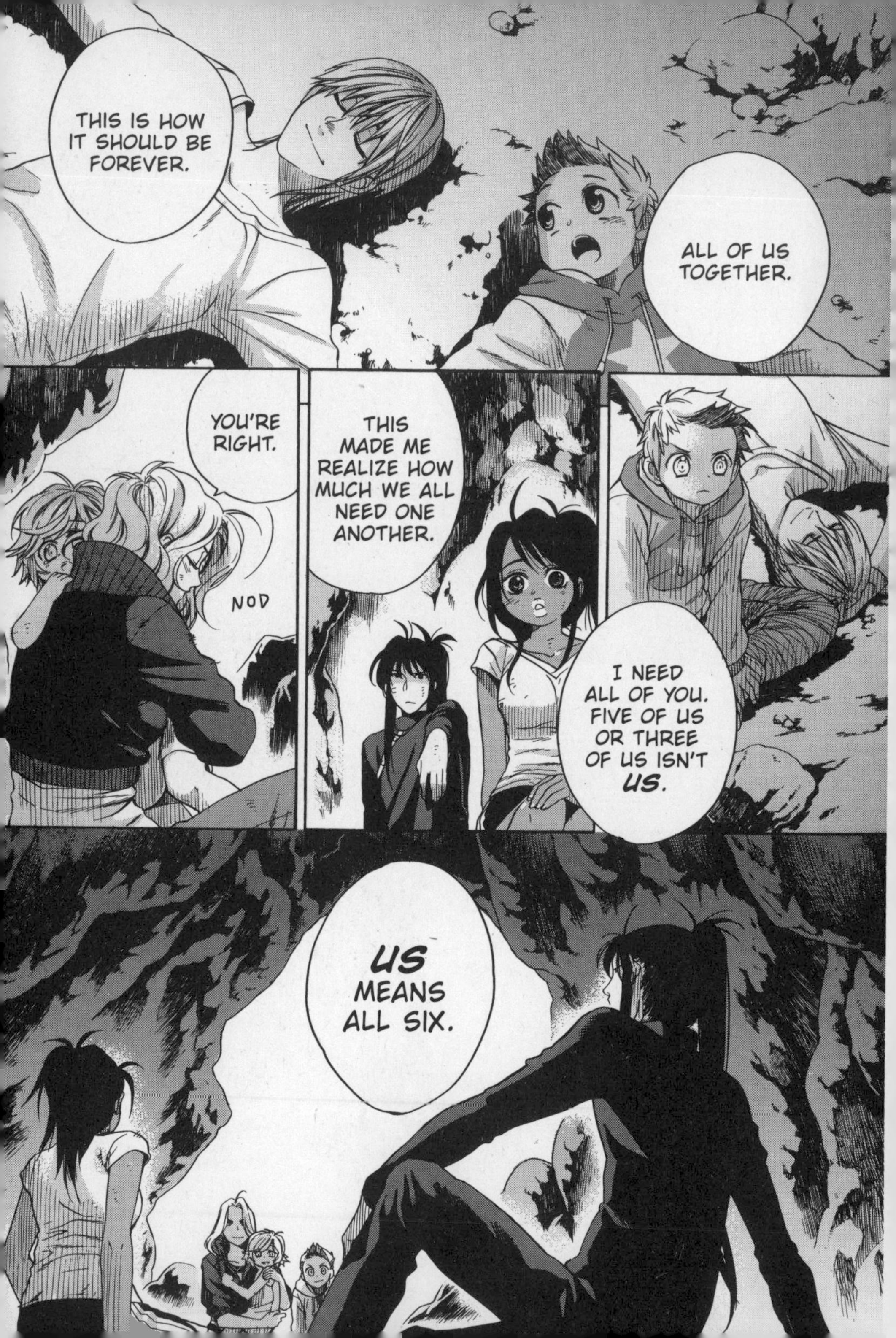
THIS IS HOW IT SHOULD BE FOREVER.
ALL OF US TOGETHER.
YOU'RE RIGHT.
NOD
THIS MADE ME REALIZE HOW MUCH WE ALL NEED ONE ANOTHER.
I NEED ALL OF YOU. FIVE OF US OR THREE OF US ISN'T *US*.
US MEANS ALL SIX.

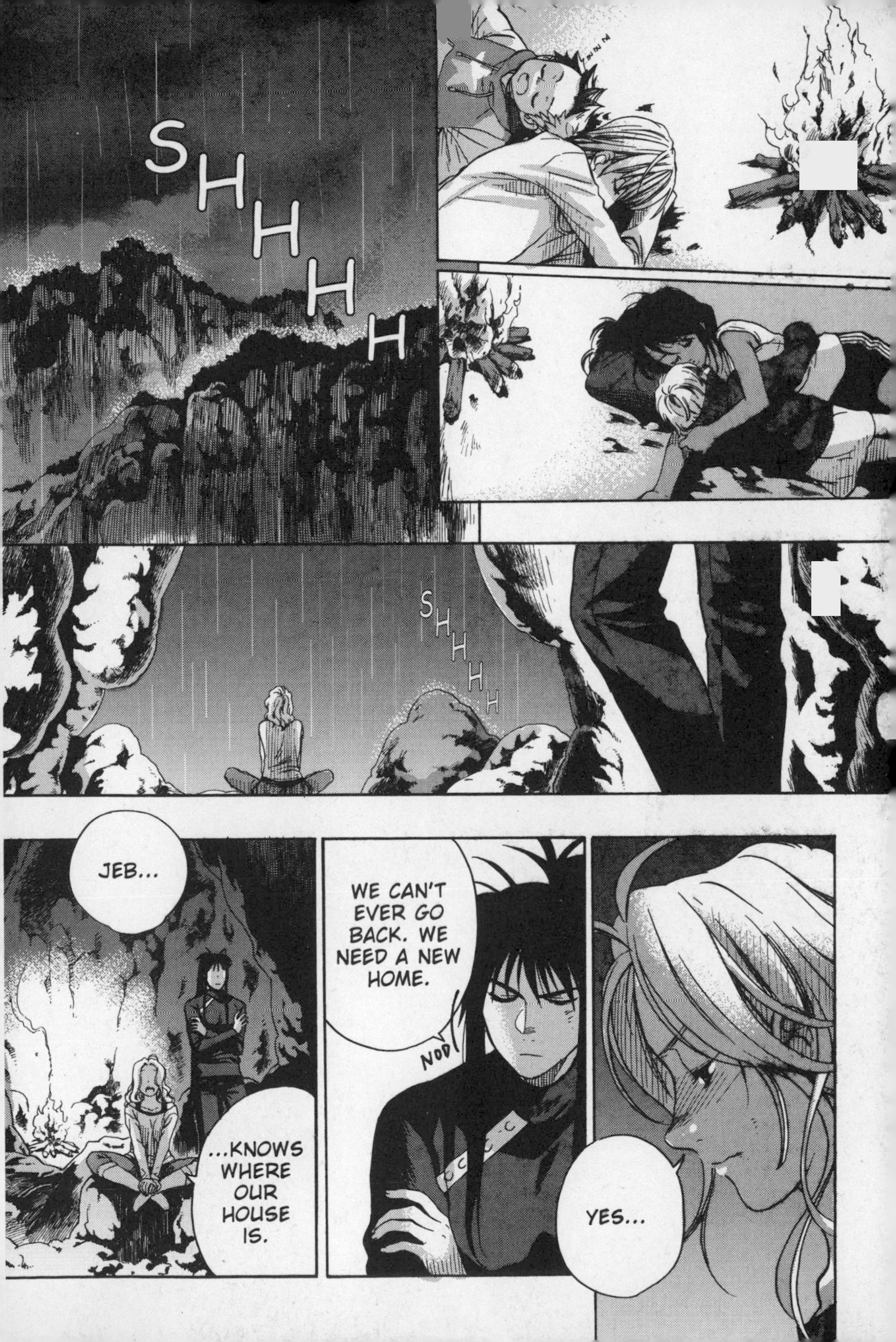
SHHHH
SHHHHH
JEB...
...KNOWS WHERE OUR HOUSE IS.
WE CAN'T EVER GO BACK. WE NEED A NEW HOME.
NOD
YES...

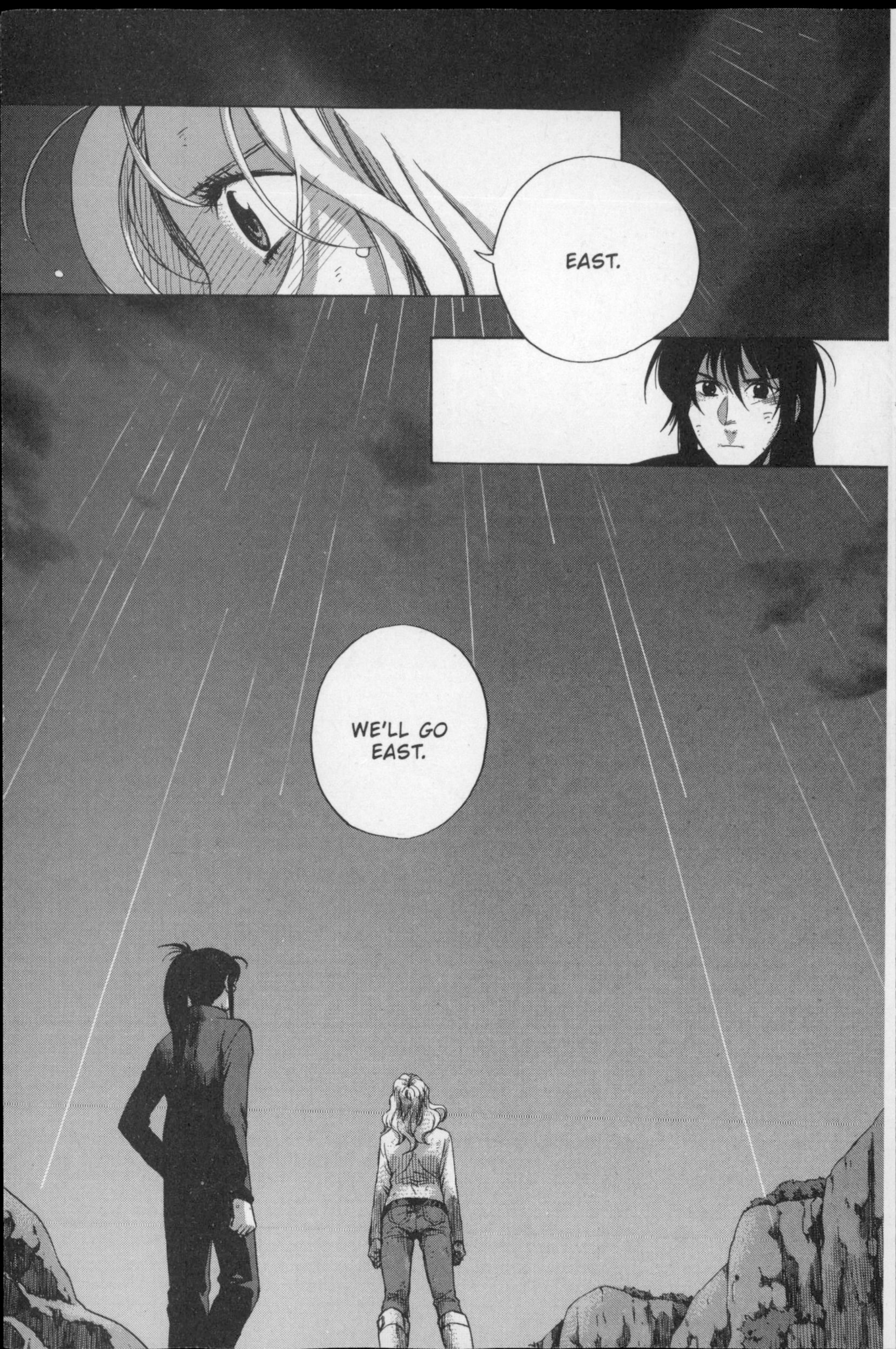
EAST.
WE'LL GO EAST.

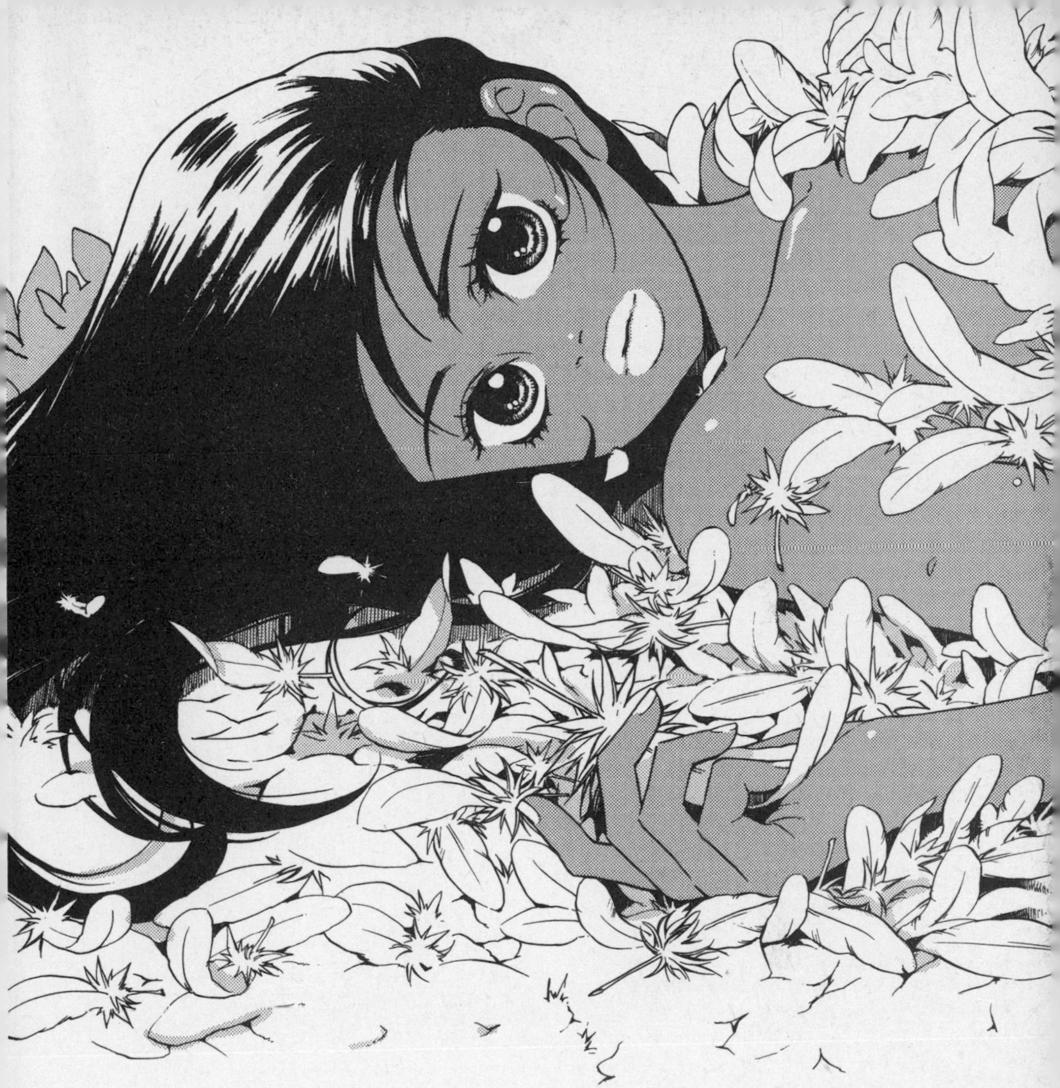

MAXIMUM RIDE
CHAPTER 9

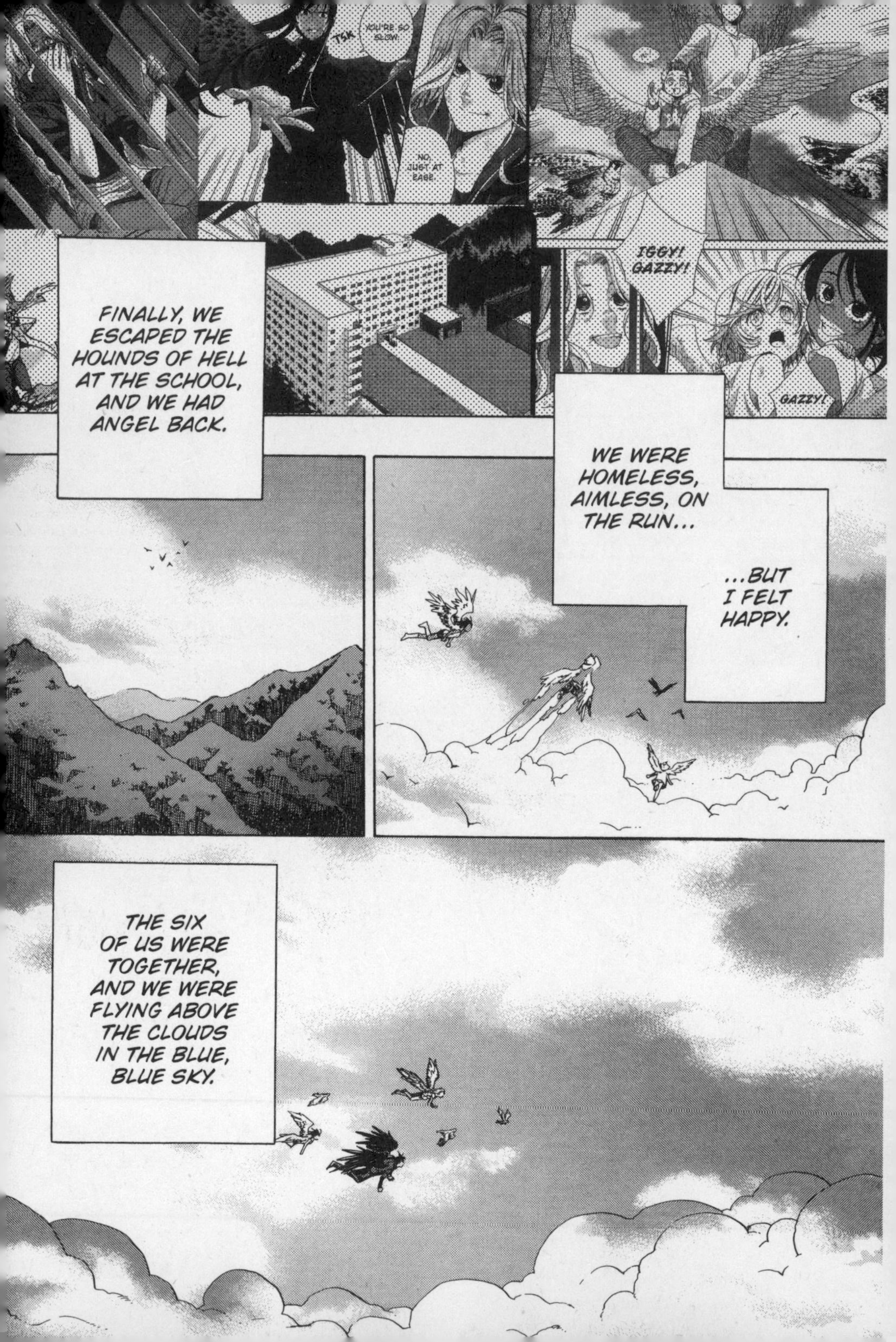

TSK
YOU'RE SO SLOW.
NO, JUST AT EASE.
FINALLY, WE ESCAPED THE HOUNDS OF HELL AT THE SCHOOL, AND WE HAD ANGEL BACK.
IGGY! GAZZY!
GAZZY!
WE WERE HOMELESS, AIMLESS, ON THE RUN...
...BUT I FELT HAPPY.
THE SIX OF US WERE TOGETHER, AND WE WERE FLYING ABOVE THE CLOUDS IN THE BLUE, BLUE SKY.

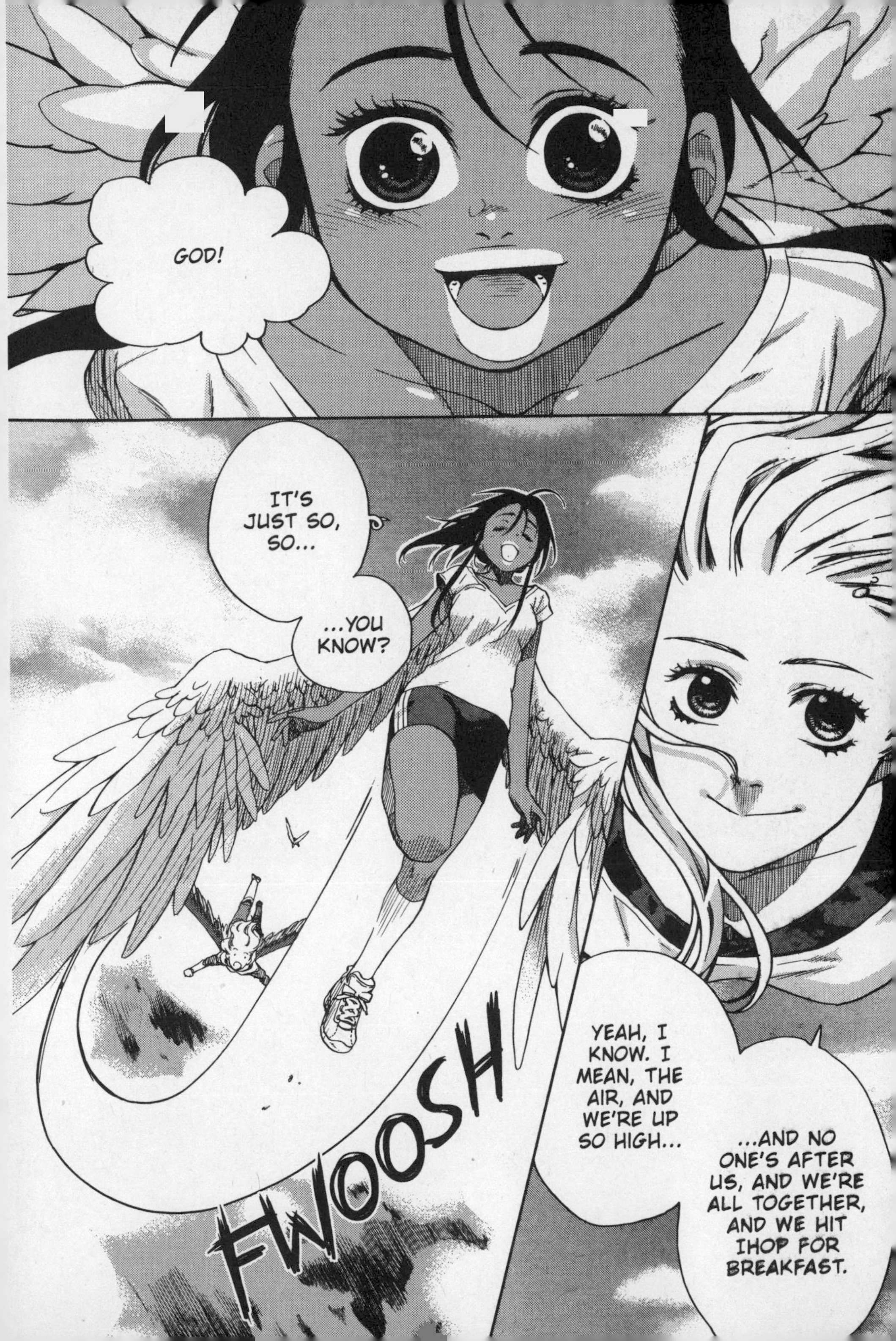
GOD!
IT'S JUST SO, SO...
...YOU KNOW?
FWOOSH
YEAH, I KNOW. I MEAN, THE AIR, AND WE'RE UP SO HIGH...
...AND NO ONE'S AFTER US, AND WE'RE ALL TOGETHER, AND WE HIT IHOP FOR BREAKFAST.

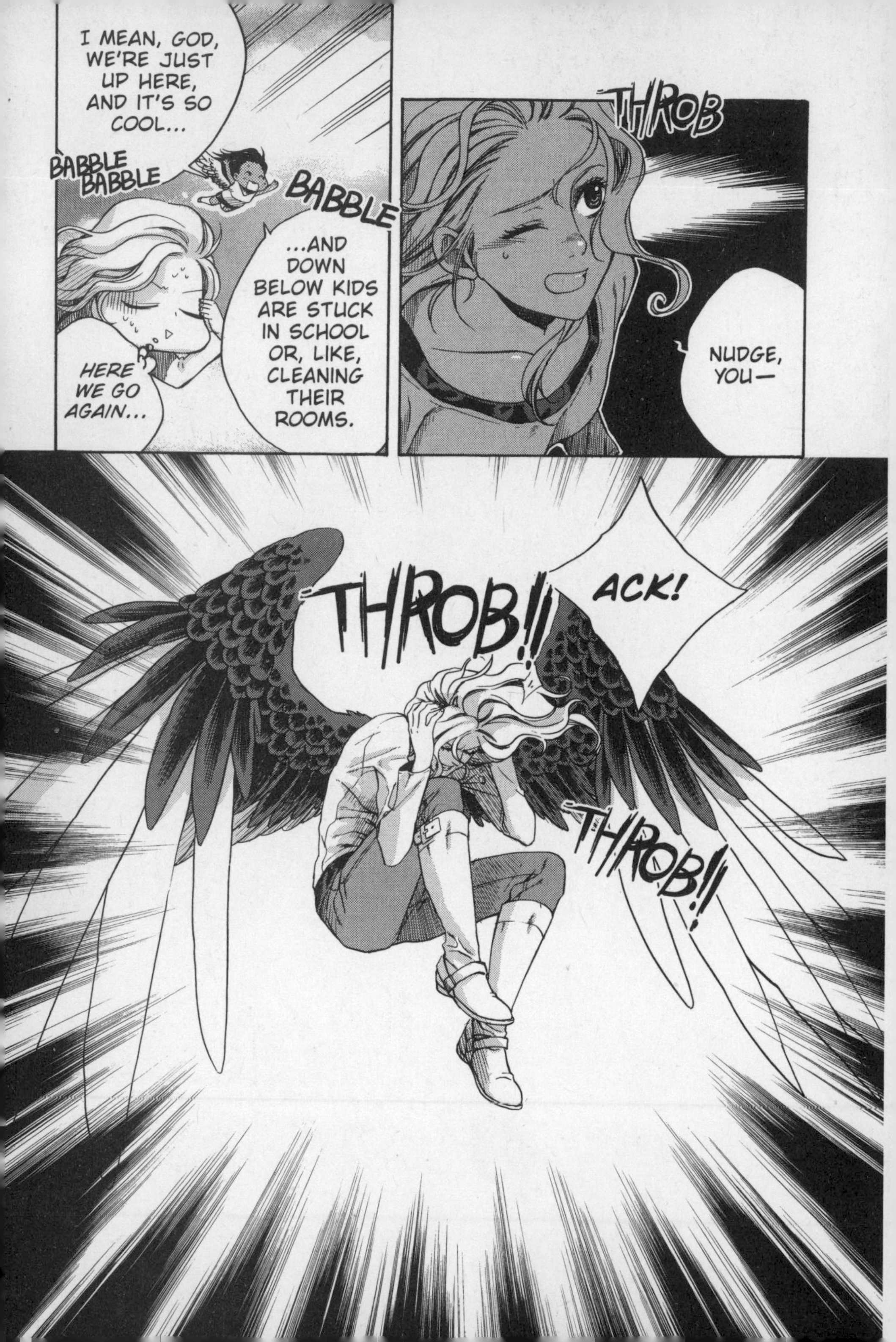
I MEAN, GOD, WE'RE JUST UP HERE, AND IT'S SO COOL...
BABBLE BABBLE
BABBLE
HERE WE GO AGAIN...
...AND DOWN BELOW KIDS ARE STUCK IN SCHOOL OR, LIKE, CLEANING THEIR ROOMS.
THROB
NUDGE, YOU—
THROB!!
ACK!
THROB!!

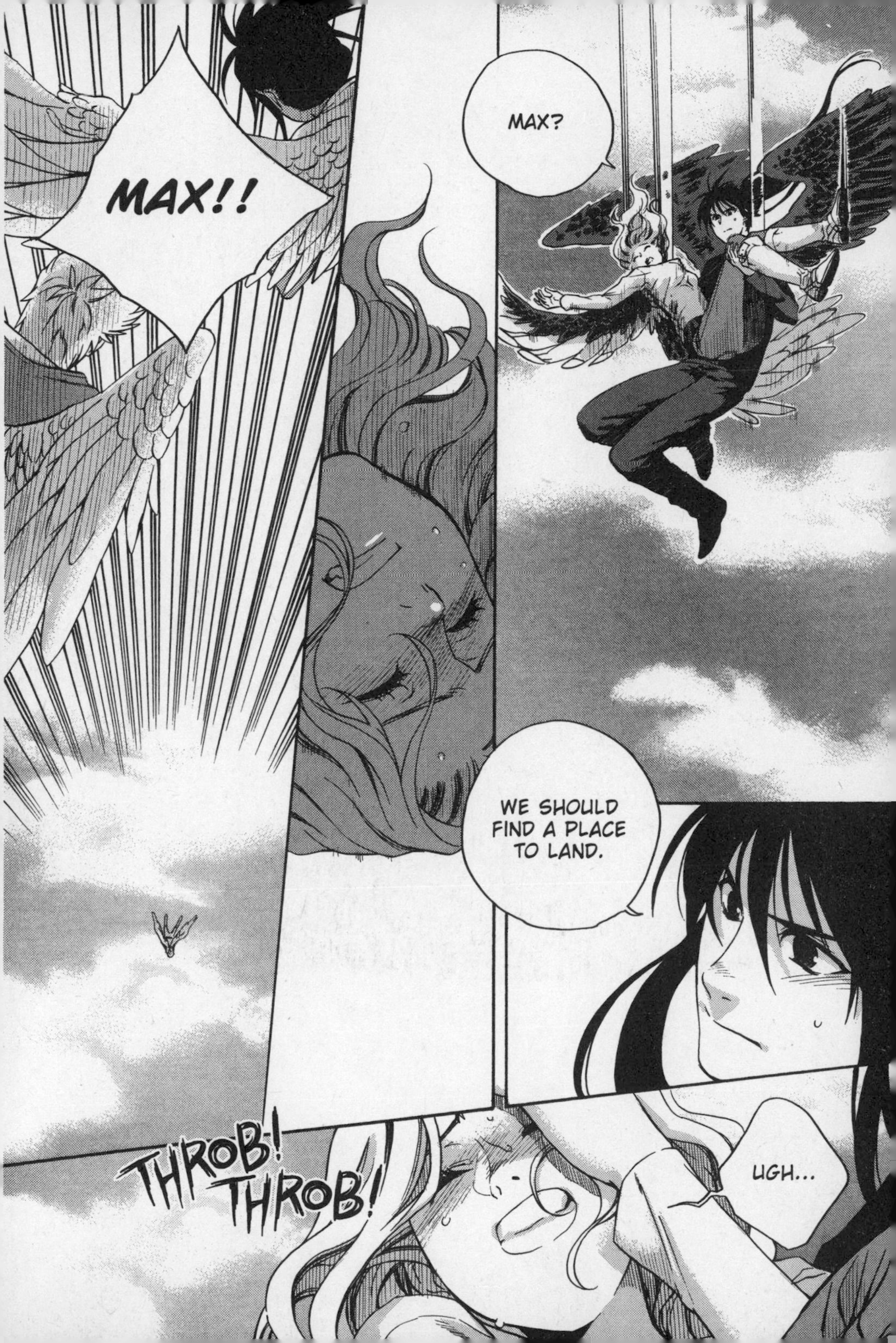
MAX!!
MAX?
WE SHOULD FIND A PLACE TO LAND.
THROB! THROB!
UGH...

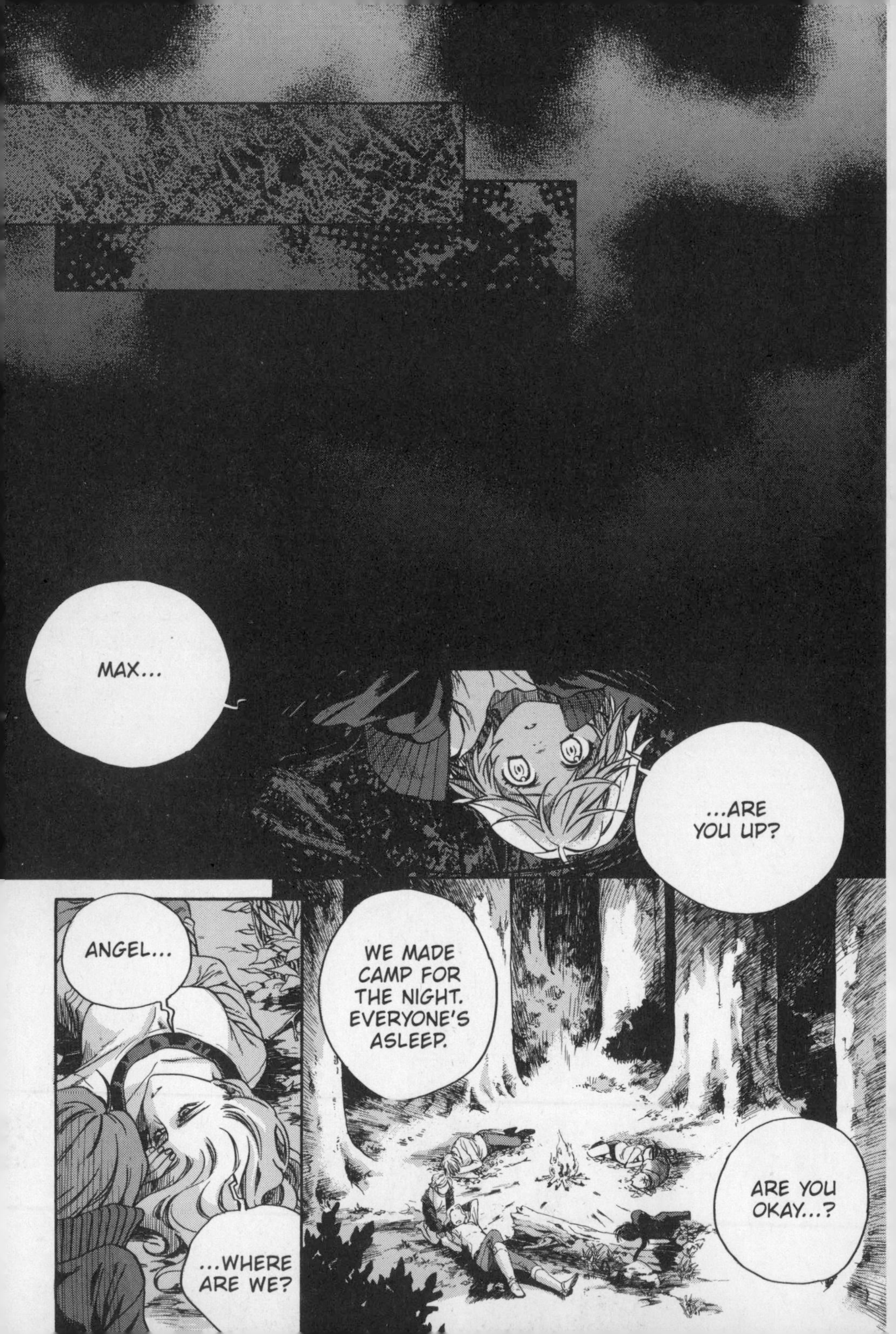
MAX...
...ARE YOU UP?
ANGEL...
...WHERE ARE WE?
WE MADE CAMP FOR THE NIGHT. EVERYONE'S ASLEEP.
ARE YOU OKAY...?

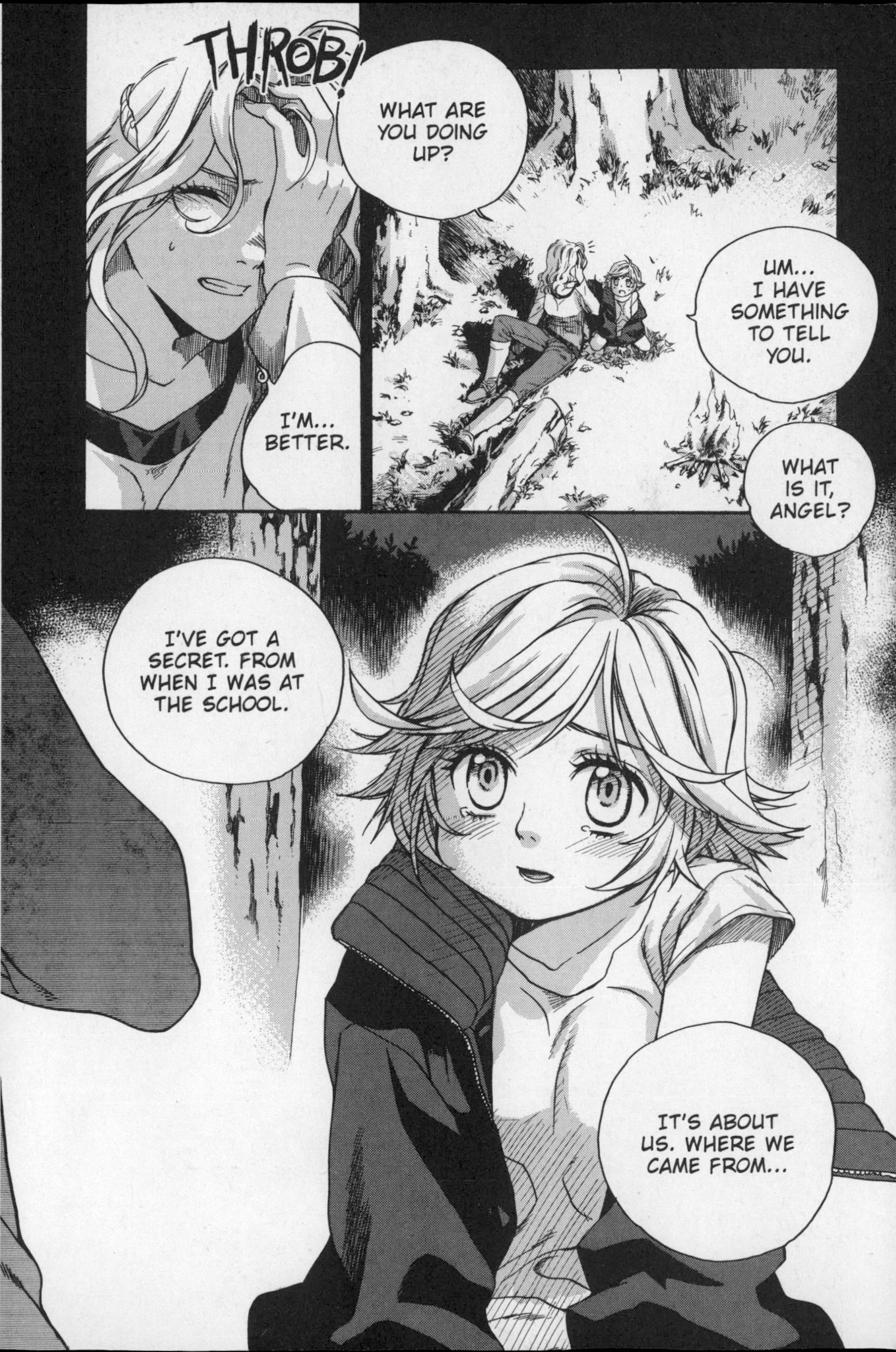
THROB!
WHAT ARE YOU DOING UP?
I'M... BETTER.
UM... I HAVE SOMETHING TO TELL YOU.
WHAT IS IT, ANGEL?
I'VE GOT A SECRET. FROM WHEN I WAS AT THE SCHOOL.
IT'S ABOUT US. WHERE WE CAME FROM...

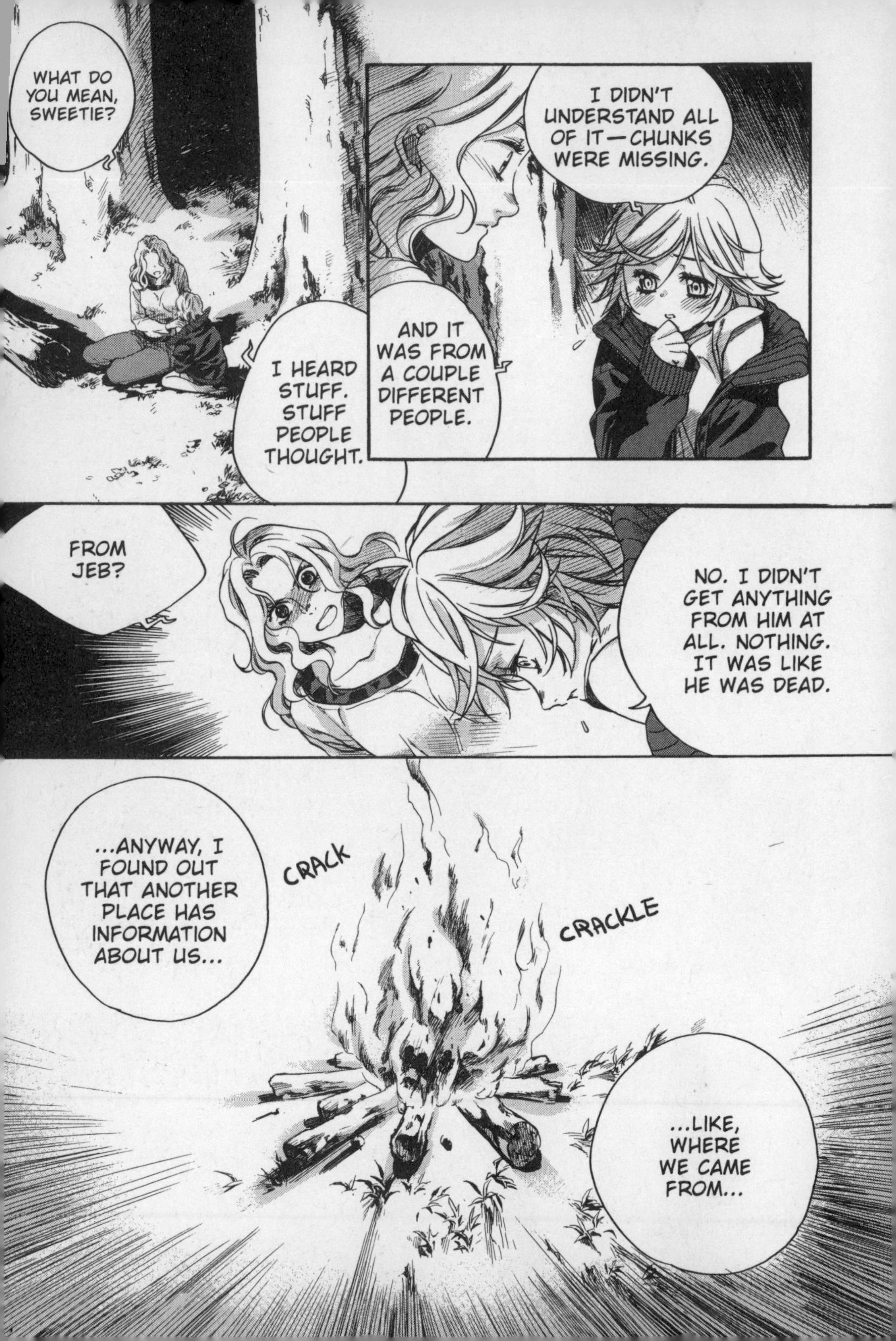
WHAT DO YOU MEAN, SWEETIE?
I DIDN'T UNDERSTAND ALL OF IT—CHUNKS WERE MISSING.
I HEARD STUFF. STUFF PEOPLE THOUGHT.
AND IT WAS FROM A COUPLE DIFFERENT PEOPLE.
FROM JEB?
NO. I DIDN'T GET ANYTHING FROM HIM AT ALL. NOTHING. IT WAS LIKE HE WAS DEAD.
...ANYWAY, I FOUND OUT THAT ANOTHER PLACE HAS INFORMATION ABOUT US...
CRACK
CRACKLE
...LIKE, WHERE WE CAME FROM...

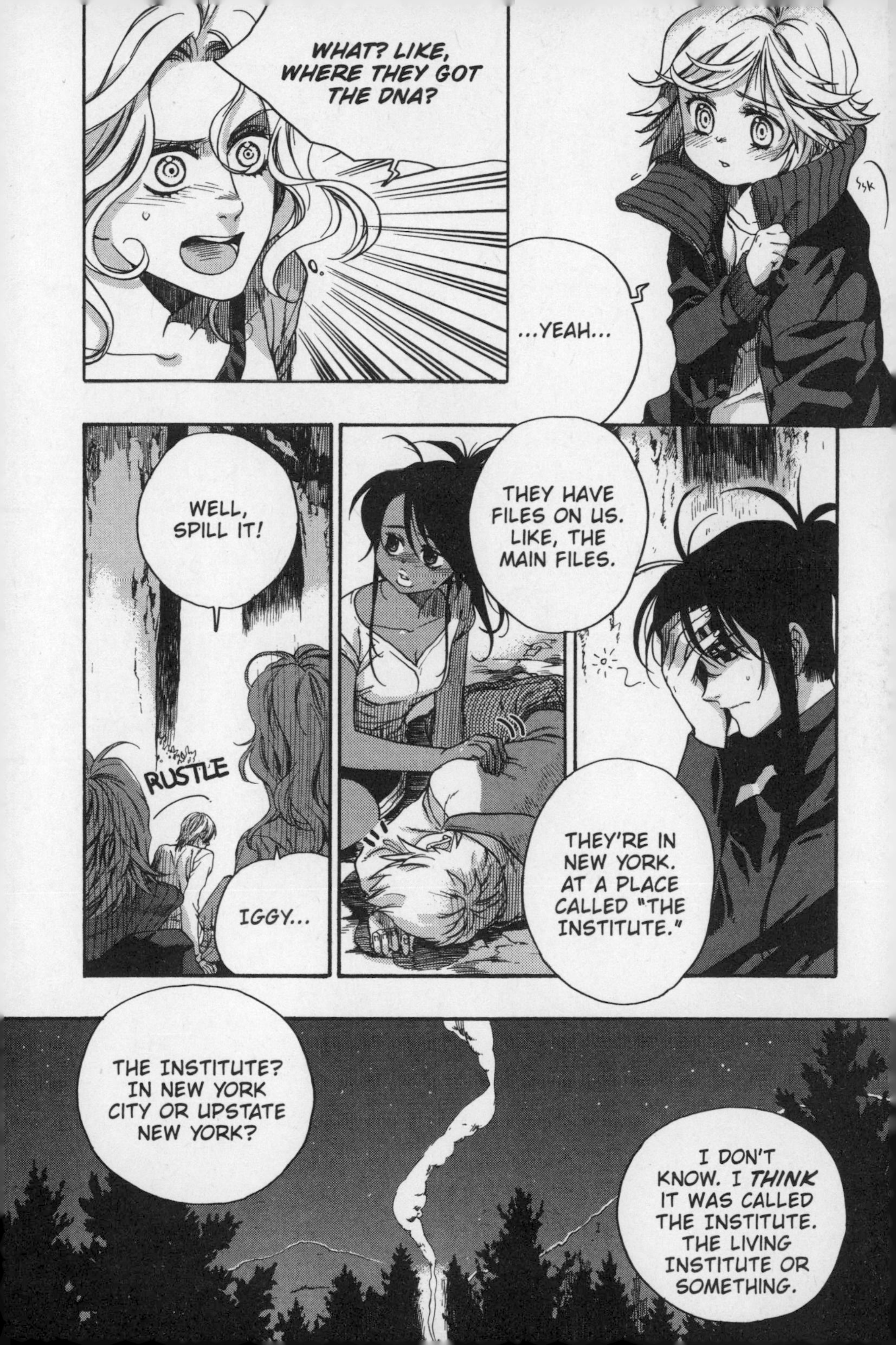
WHAT? LIKE, WHERE THEY GOT THE DNA?
SSK
...YEAH...
WELL, SPILL IT!
RUSTLE
IGGY...
THEY HAVE FILES ON US. LIKE, THE MAIN FILES.
THEY'RE IN NEW YORK. AT A PLACE CALLED "THE INSTITUTE."
THE INSTITUTE? IN NEW YORK CITY OR UPSTATE NEW YORK?
I DON'T KNOW. I *THINK* IT WAS CALLED THE INSTITUTE. THE LIVING INSTITUTE OR SOMETHING.

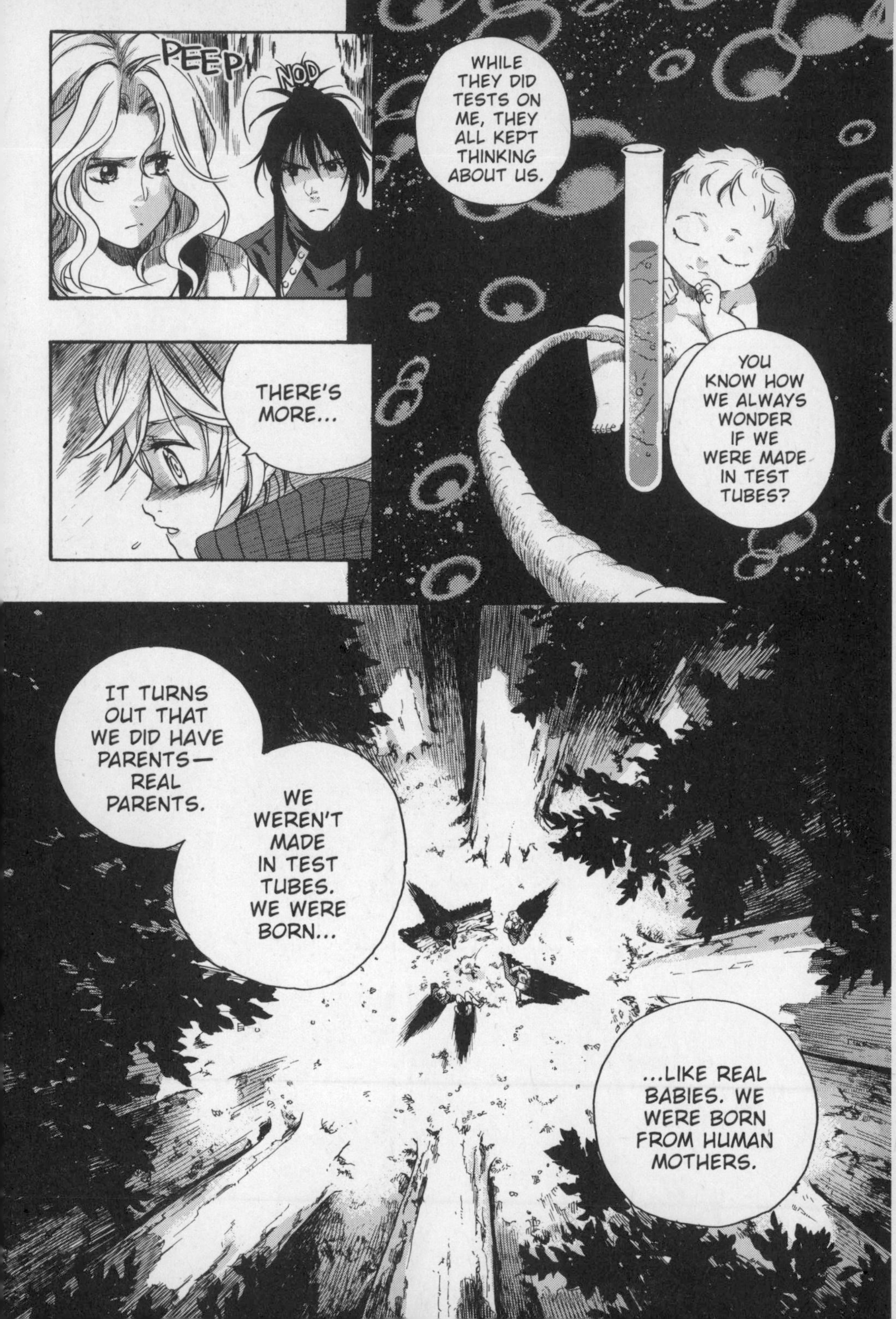
PEEP
NOD
THERE'S MORE...
WHILE THEY DID TESTS ON ME, THEY ALL KEPT THINKING ABOUT US.
YOU KNOW HOW WE ALWAYS WONDER IF WE WERE MADE IN TEST TUBES?
IT TURNS OUT THAT WE DID HAVE PARENTS—REAL PARENTS.
WE WEREN'T MADE IN TEST TUBES. WE WERE BORN...
...LIKE REAL BABIES. WE WERE BORN FROM HUMAN MOTHERS.

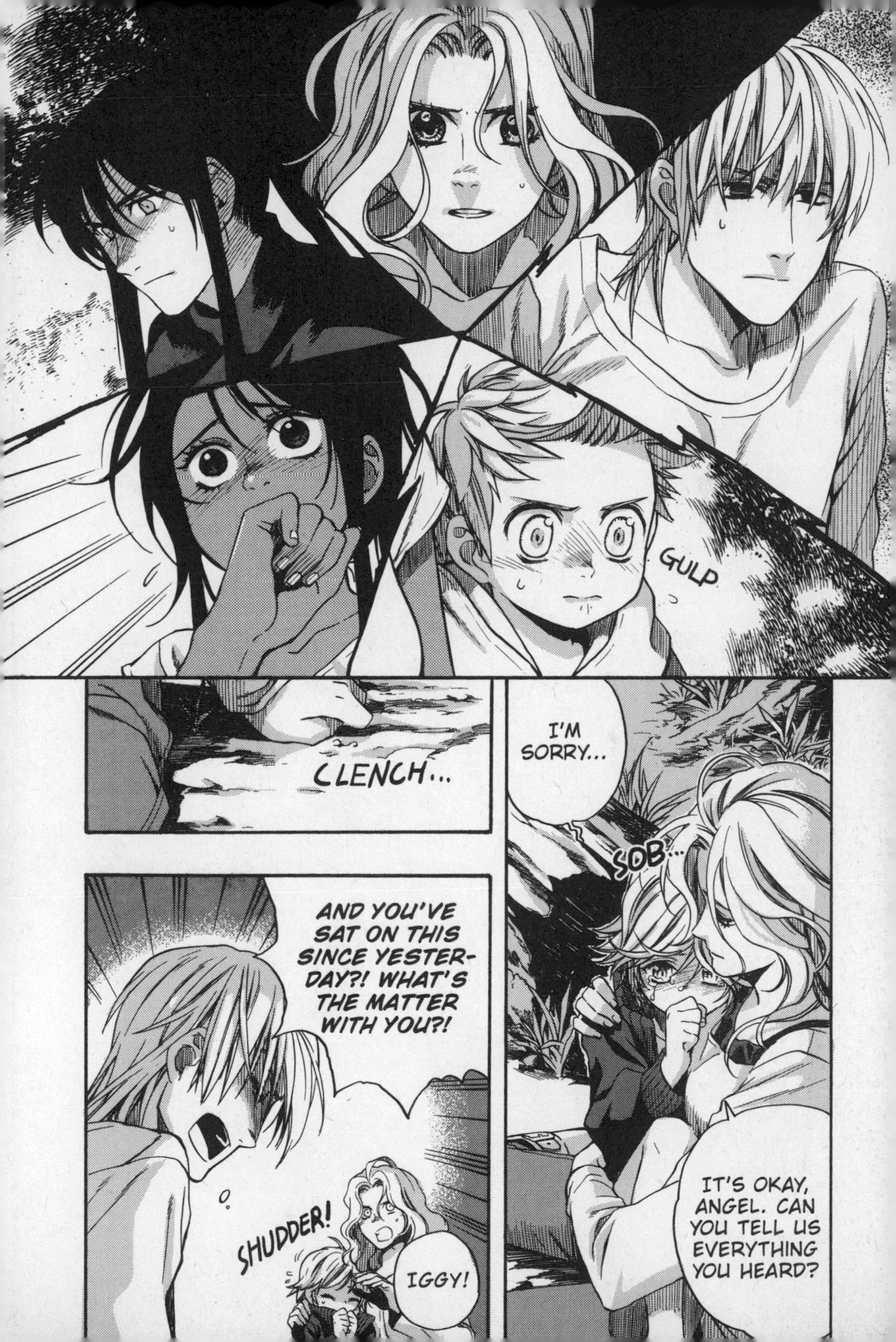
GULP
CLENCH...
AND YOU'VE SAT ON THIS SINCE YESTER-DAY?! WHAT'S THE MATTER WITH YOU?!
SHUDDER!
IGGY!
I'M SORRY...
SOB...
IT'S OKAY, ANGEL. CAN YOU TELL US EVERYTHING YOU HEARD?

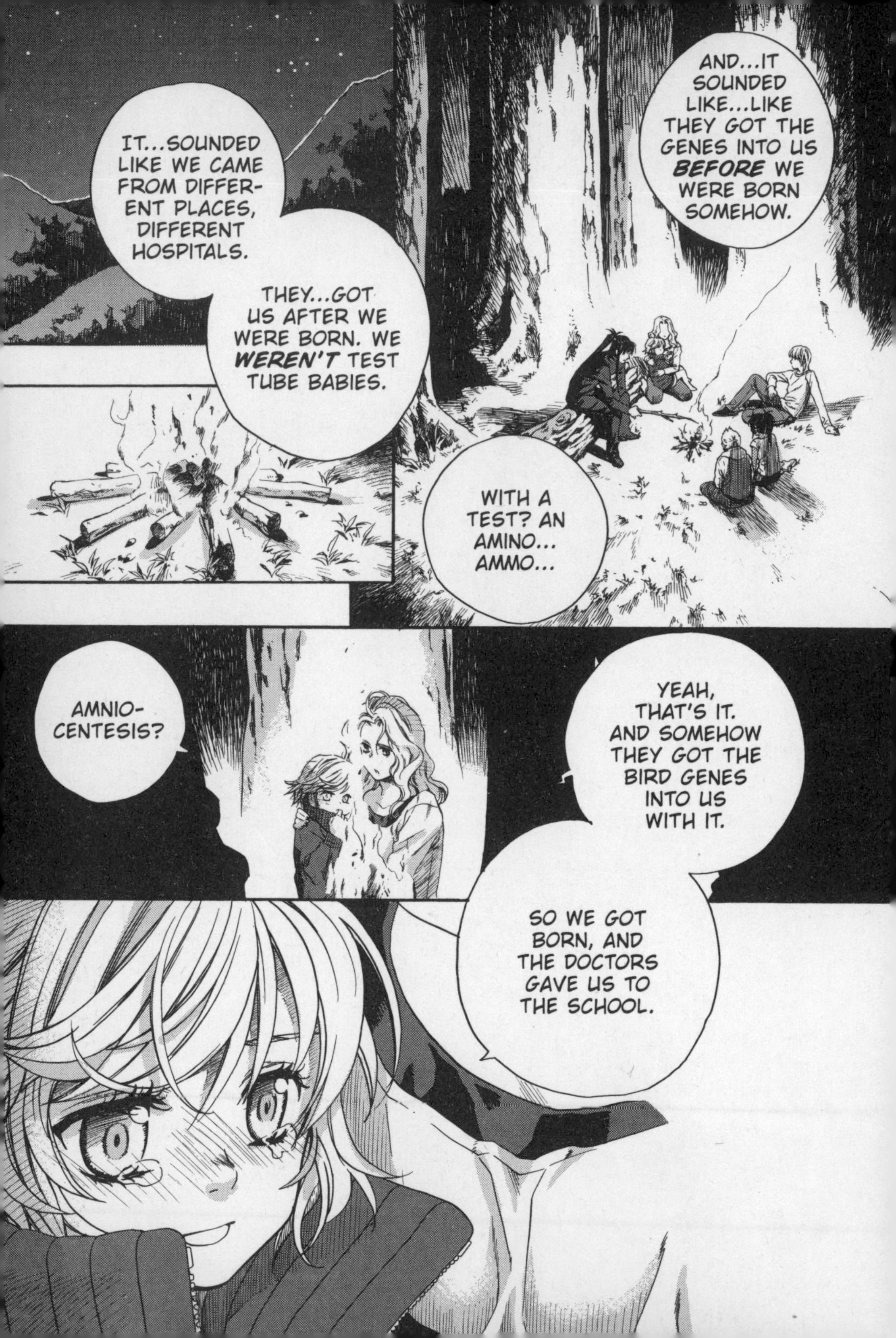

IT...SOUNDED LIKE WE CAME FROM DIFFERENT PLACES, DIFFERENT HOSPITALS.
THEY...GOT US AFTER WE WERE BORN. WE *WEREN'T* TEST TUBE BABIES.
AND...IT SOUNDED LIKE...LIKE THEY GOT THE GENES INTO US *BEFORE* WE WERE BORN SOMEHOW.
WITH A TEST? AN AMINO... AMMO...
AMNIO-CENTESIS?
YEAH, THAT'S IT. AND SOMEHOW THEY GOT THE BIRD GENES INTO US WITH IT.
SO WE GOT BORN, AND THE DOCTORS GAVE US TO THE SCHOOL.

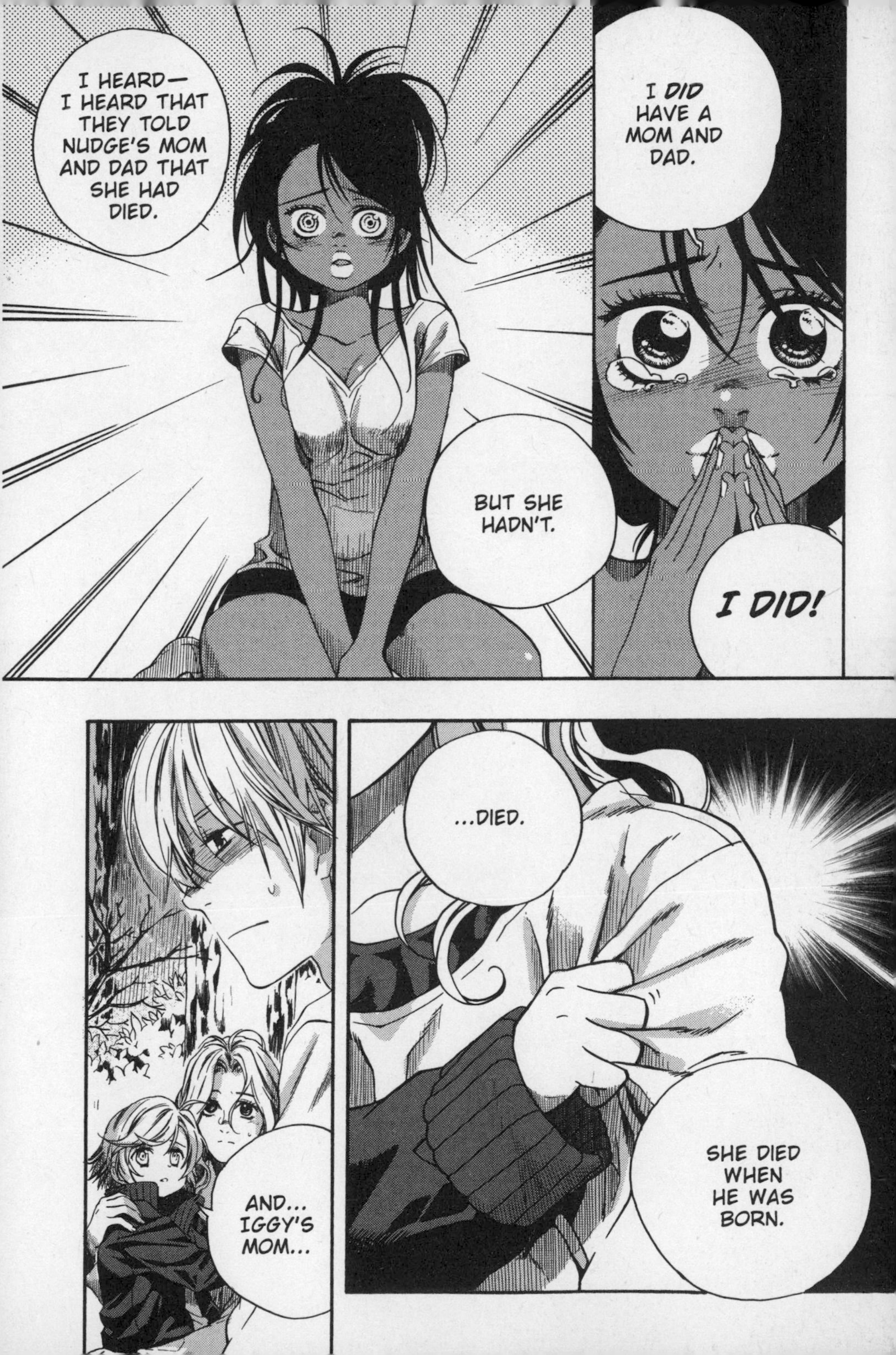
I HEARD— I HEARD THAT THEY TOLD NUDGE'S MOM AND DAD THAT SHE HAD DIED.
BUT SHE HADN'T.
I *DID* HAVE A MOM AND DAD.
I DID!
AND... IGGY'S MOM...
...DIED.
SHE DIED WHEN HE WAS BORN.

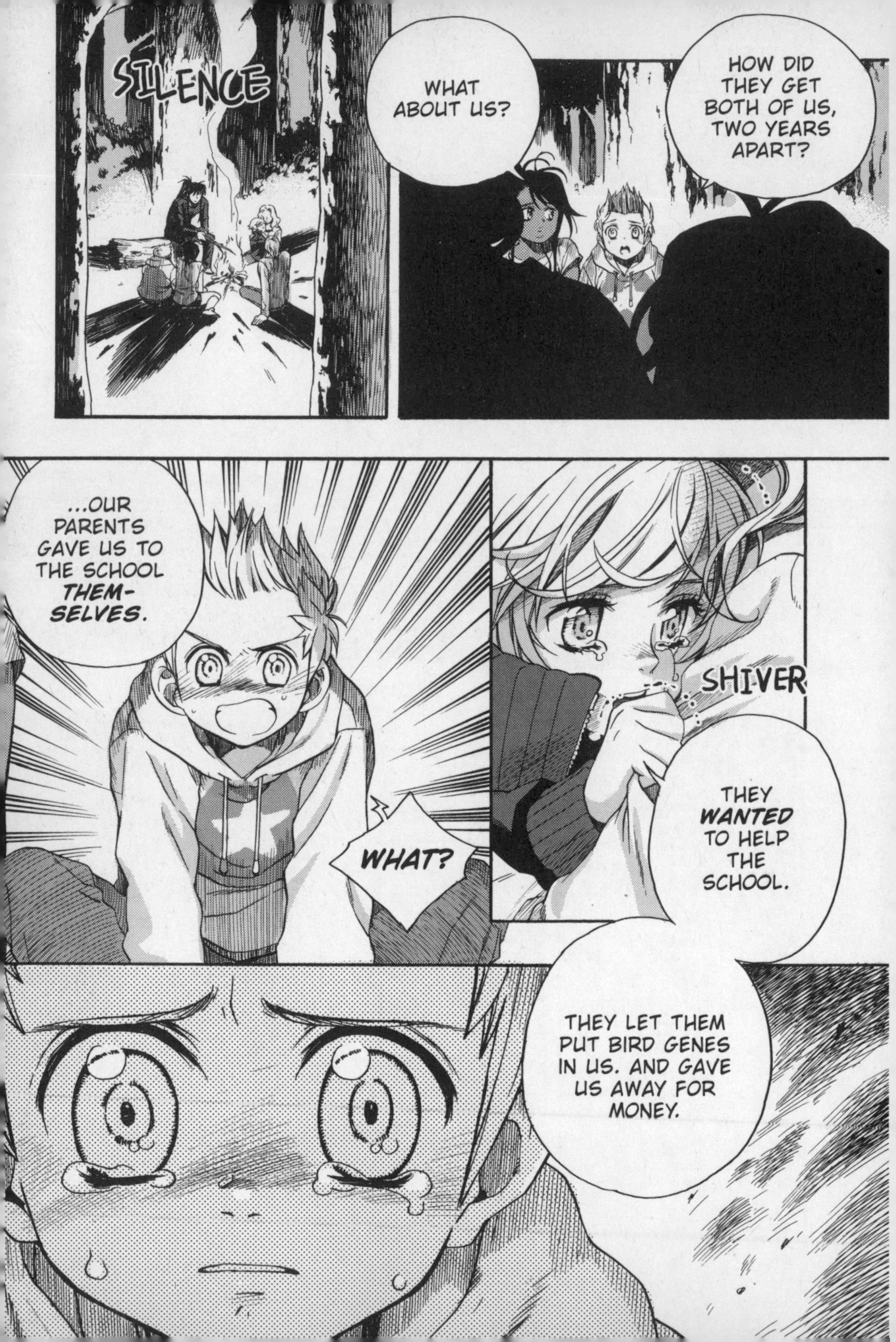
SILENCE
WHAT ABOUT US?
HOW DID THEY GET BOTH OF US, TWO YEARS APART?
...OUR PARENTS GAVE US TO THE SCHOOL *THEM-SELVES*.
WHAT?
SHIVER
THEY *WANTED* TO HELP THE SCHOOL.
THEY LET THEM PUT BIRD GENES IN US. AND GAVE US AWAY FOR MONEY.

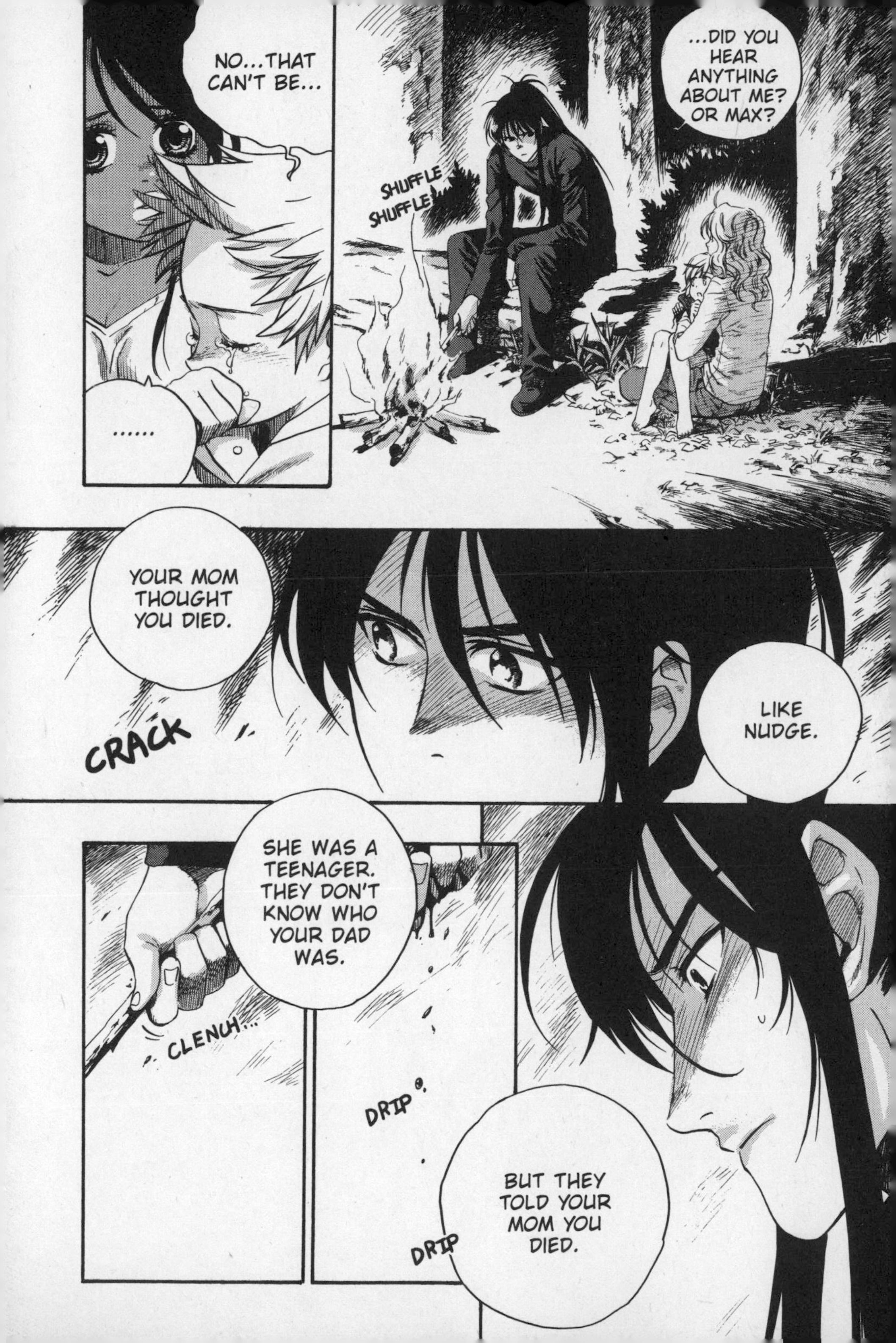
NO...THAT CAN'T BE...
......
...DID YOU HEAR ANYTHING ABOUT ME? OR MAX?
SHUFFLE SHUFFLE
YOUR MOM THOUGHT YOU DIED.
CRACK
LIKE NUDGE.
SHE WAS A TEENAGER. THEY DON'T KNOW WHO YOUR DAD WAS.
CLENCH...
DRIP
DRIP
BUT THEY TOLD YOUR MOM YOU DIED.

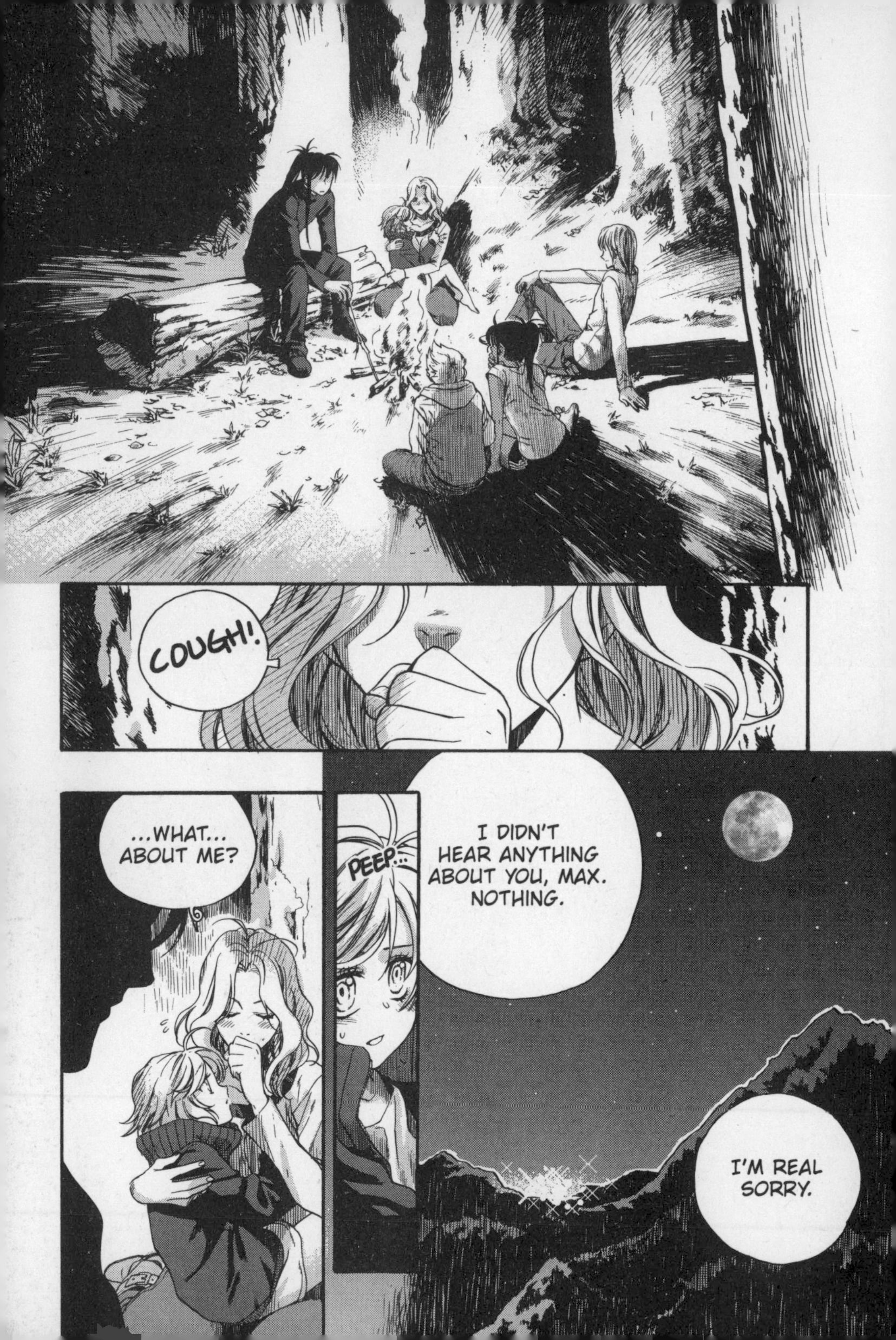
COUGH!
...WHAT... ABOUT ME?
PEEP...
I DIDN'T HEAR ANYTHING ABOUT YOU, MAX. NOTHING.
I'M REAL SORRY.

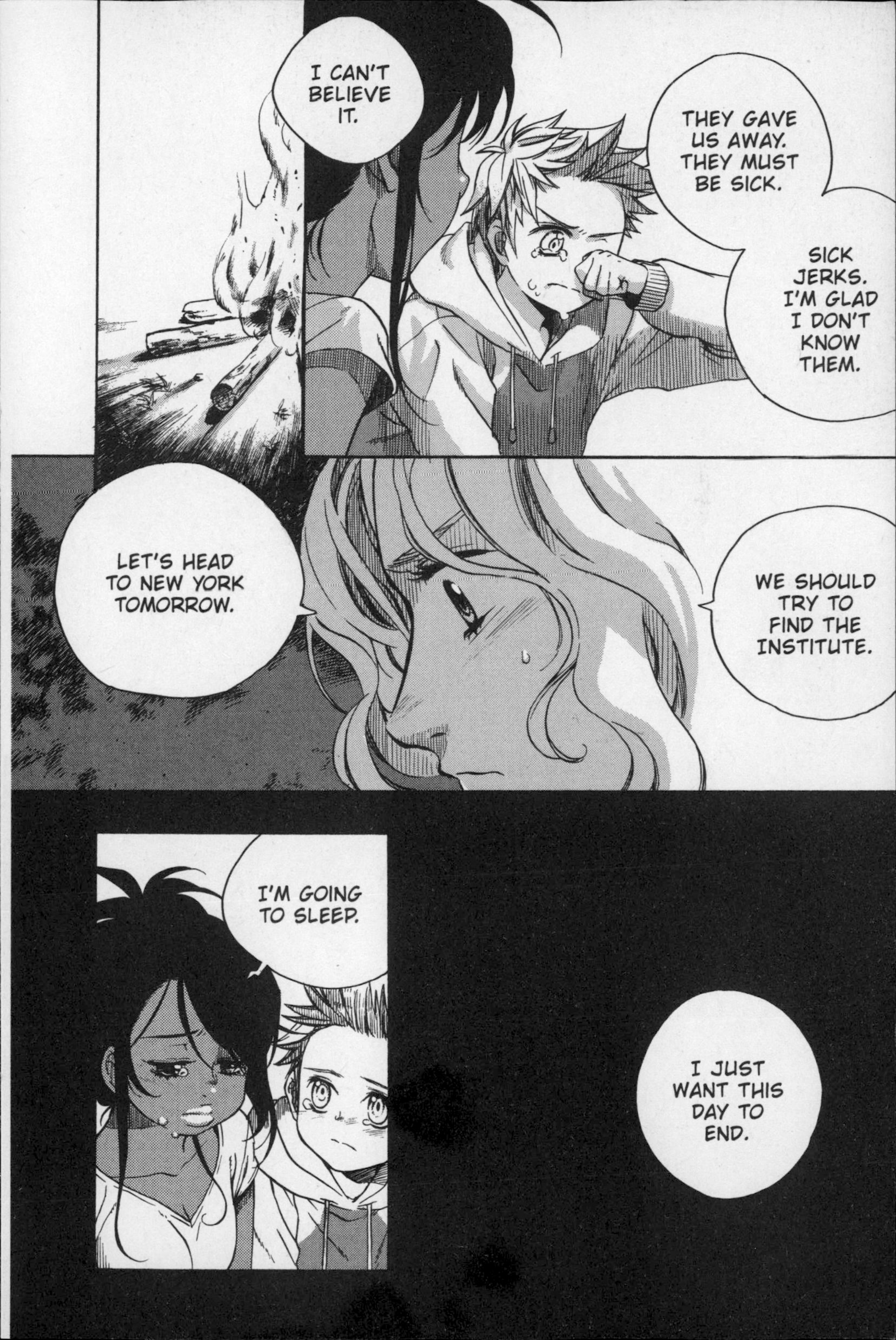
I CAN'T BELIEVE IT.
THEY GAVE US AWAY. THEY MUST BE SICK.
SICK JERKS. I'M GLAD I DON'T KNOW THEM.
LET'S HEAD TO NEW YORK TOMORROW.
WE SHOULD TRY TO FIND THE INSTITUTE.
I'M GOING TO SLEEP.
I JUST WANT THIS DAY TO END.

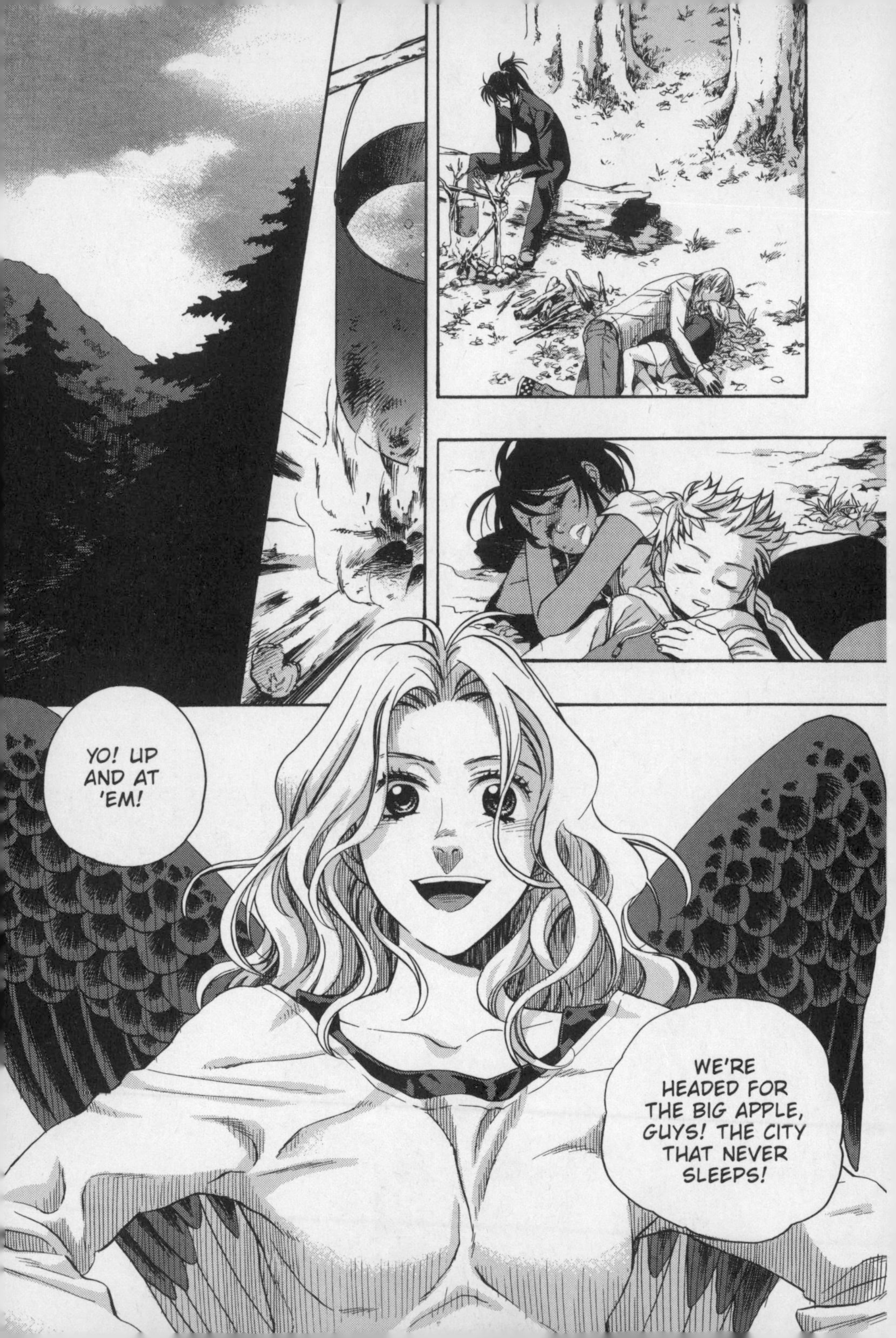
YO! UP AND AT 'EM!
WE'RE HEADED FOR THE BIG APPLE, GUYS! THE CITY THAT NEVER SLEEPS!

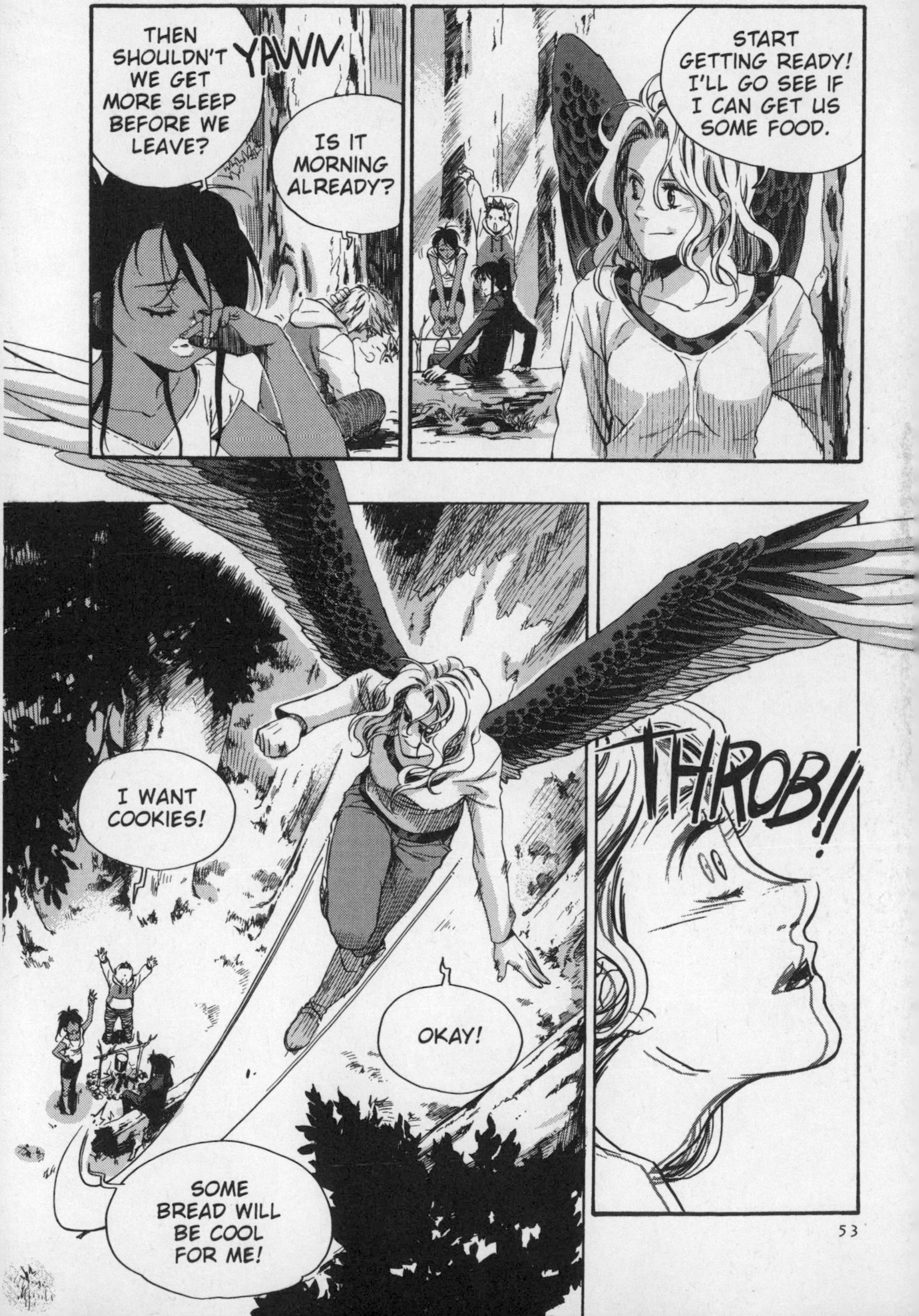
THEN SHOULDN'T WE GET MORE SLEEP BEFORE WE LEAVE?
YAWN
IS IT MORNING ALREADY?
START GETTING READY! I'LL GO SEE IF I CAN GET US SOME FOOD.
I WANT COOKIES!
OKAY!
SOME BREAD WILL BE COOL FOR ME!
THROB!!

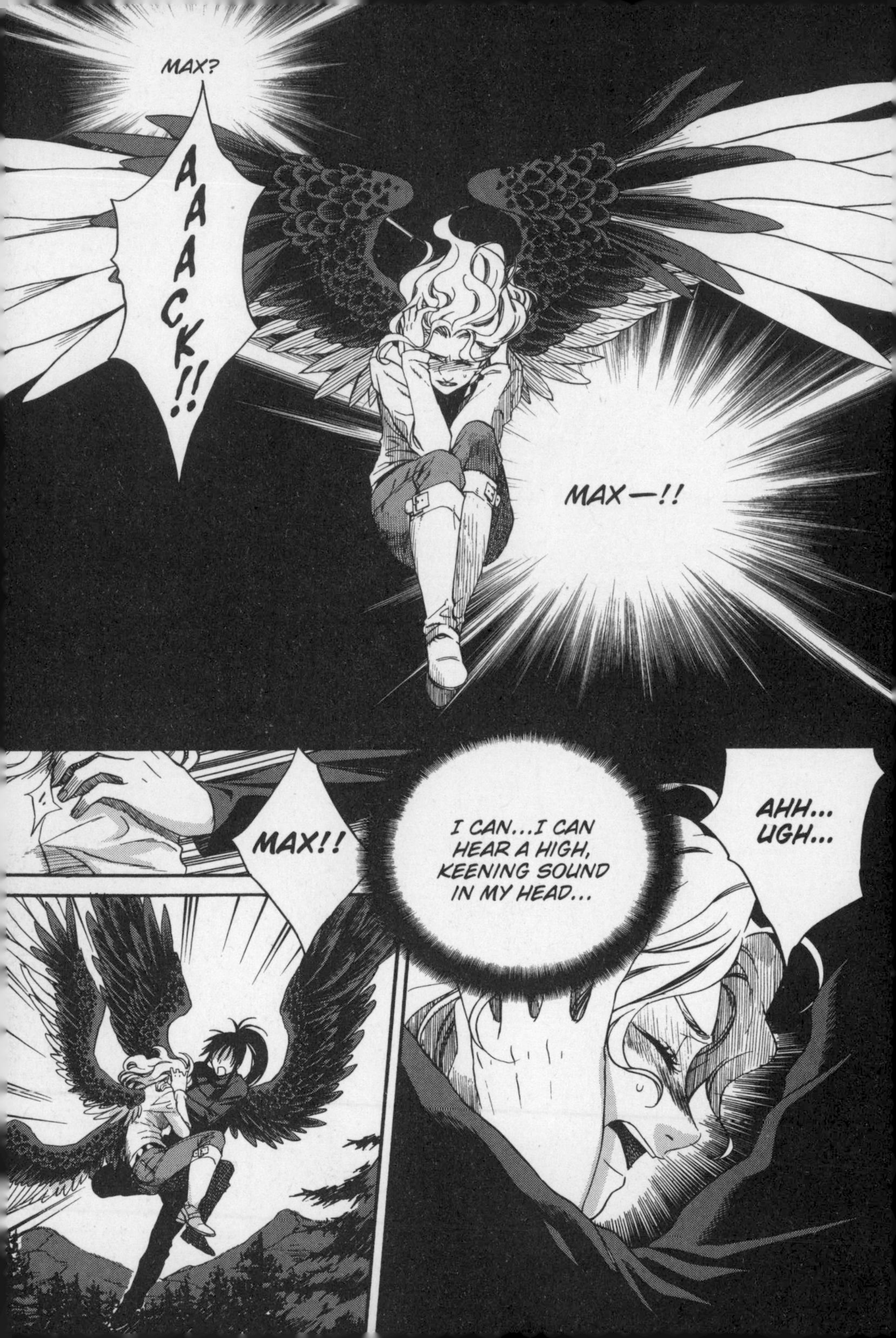
MAX?
AAAACK!!
MAX—!!
MAX!!
I CAN...I CAN HEAR A HIGH, KEENING SOUND IN MY HEAD...
AHH... UGH...

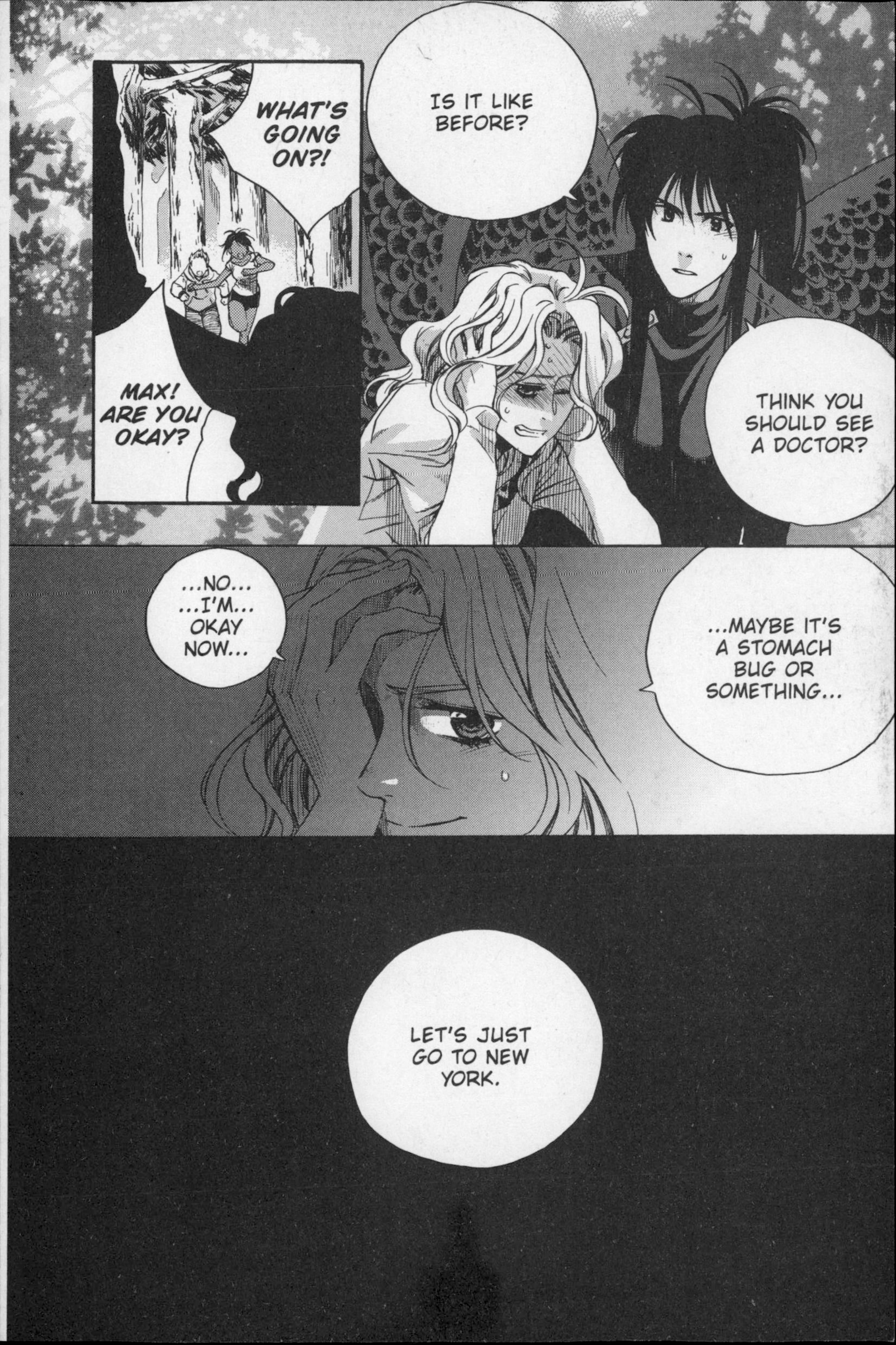
WHAT'S GOING ON?!
MAX! ARE YOU OKAY?
IS IT LIKE BEFORE?
THINK YOU SHOULD SEE A DOCTOR?
...NO... ...I'M... OKAY NOW...
...MAYBE IT'S A STOMACH BUG OR SOMETHING...
LET'S JUST GO TO NEW YORK.

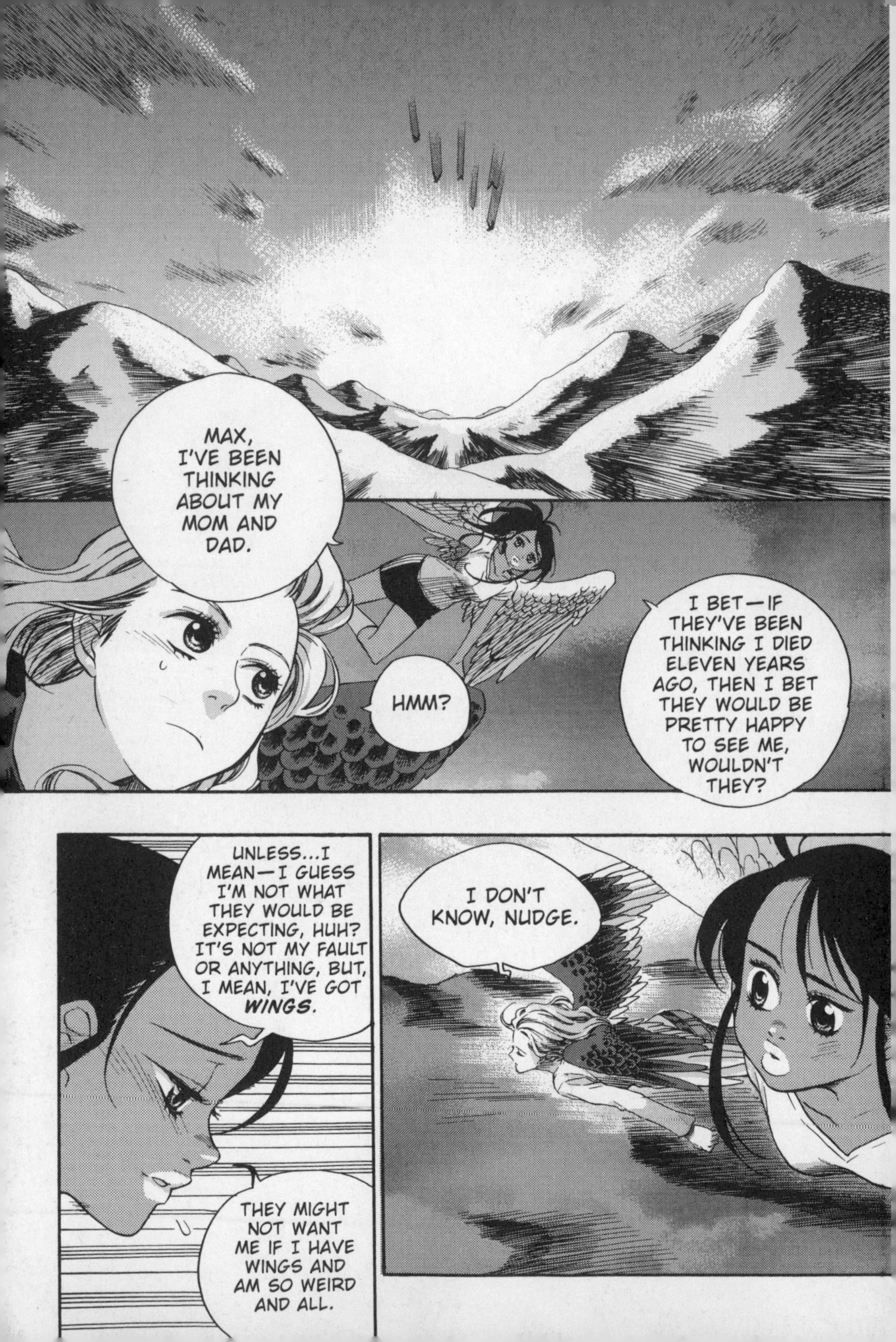
MAX, I'VE BEEN THINKING ABOUT MY MOM AND DAD.
HMM?
I BET—IF THEY'VE BEEN THINKING I DIED ELEVEN YEARS AGO, THEN I BET THEY WOULD BE PRETTY HAPPY TO SEE ME, WOULDN'T THEY?
UNLESS...I MEAN—I GUESS I'M NOT WHAT THEY WOULD BE EXPECTING, HUH? IT'S NOT MY FAULT OR ANYTHING, BUT, I MEAN, I'VE GOT ***WINGS***.
THEY MIGHT NOT WANT ME IF I HAVE WINGS AND AM SO WEIRD AND ALL.
I DON'T KNOW, NUDGE.

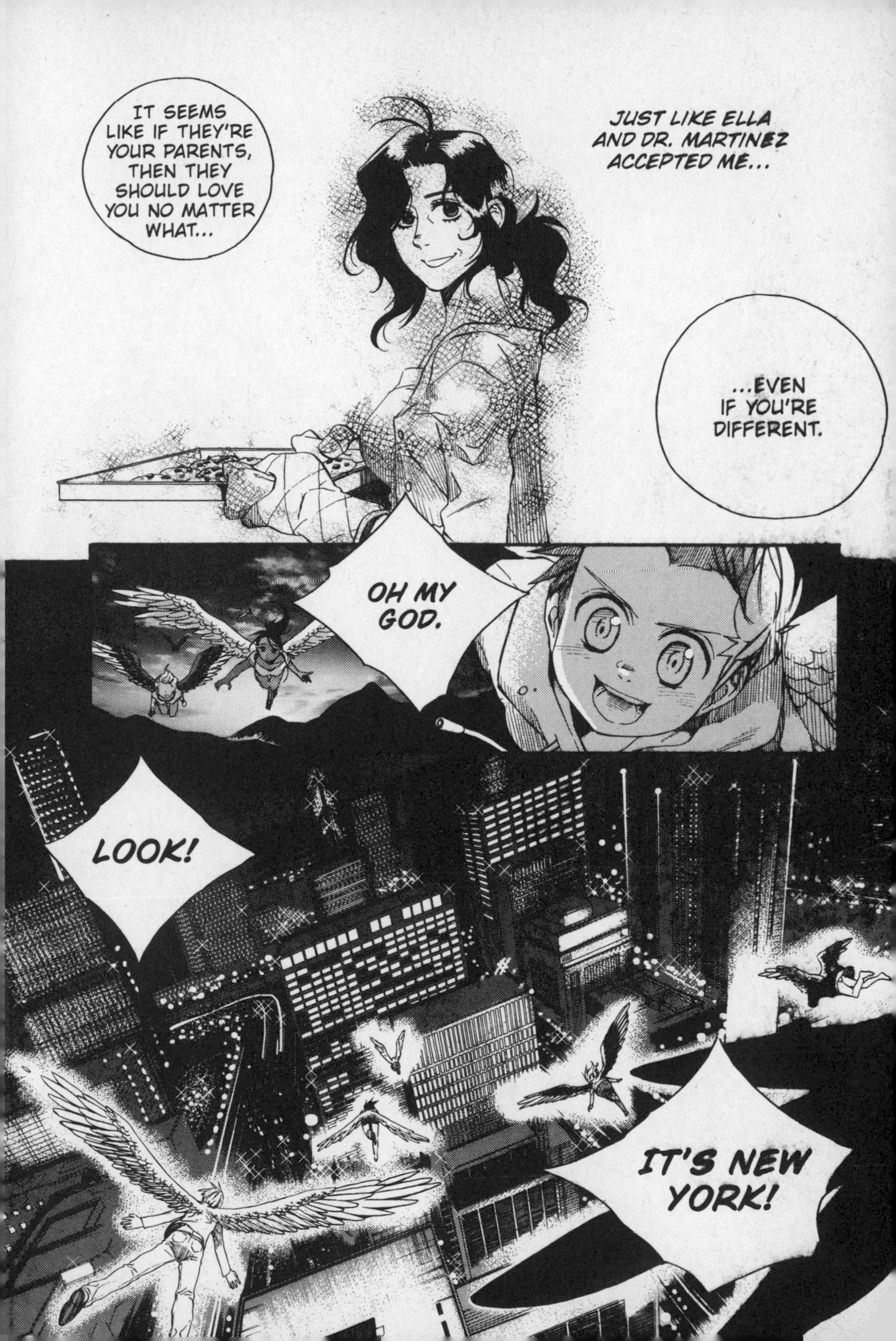
IT SEEMS LIKE IF THEY'RE YOUR PARENTS, THEN THEY SHOULD LOVE YOU NO MATTER WHAT...
JUST LIKE ELLA AND DR. MARTINEZ ACCEPTED ME...
...EVEN IF YOU'RE DIFFERENT.
OH MY GOD.
LOOK!
IT'S NEW YORK!

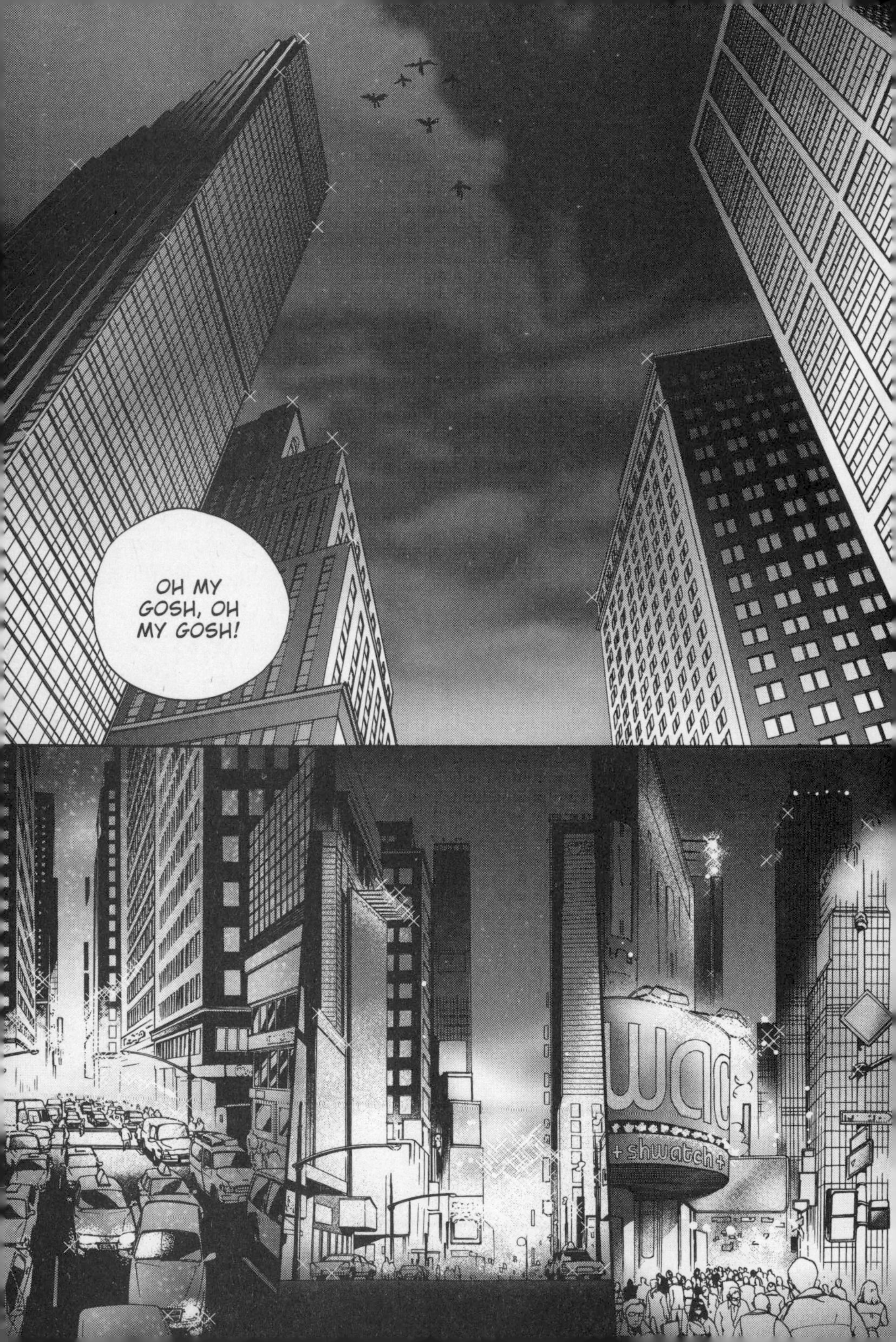
OH MY GOSH, OH MY GOSH!
shwatch

WHAT'S THIS SOUND? IS IT MUSIC? IS THERE MUSIC BELOW US?

I know this song!

I THINK IT MUST BE A CONCERT.

CAN WE GO? MAX, LET'S GO!

GRAB!

NO.

LET'S FIND A PLACE FOR THE NIGHT FIRST.

WE NEED TO REST AND FIGURE OUT HOW TO FIND THE INSTITUTE.

OKAY...

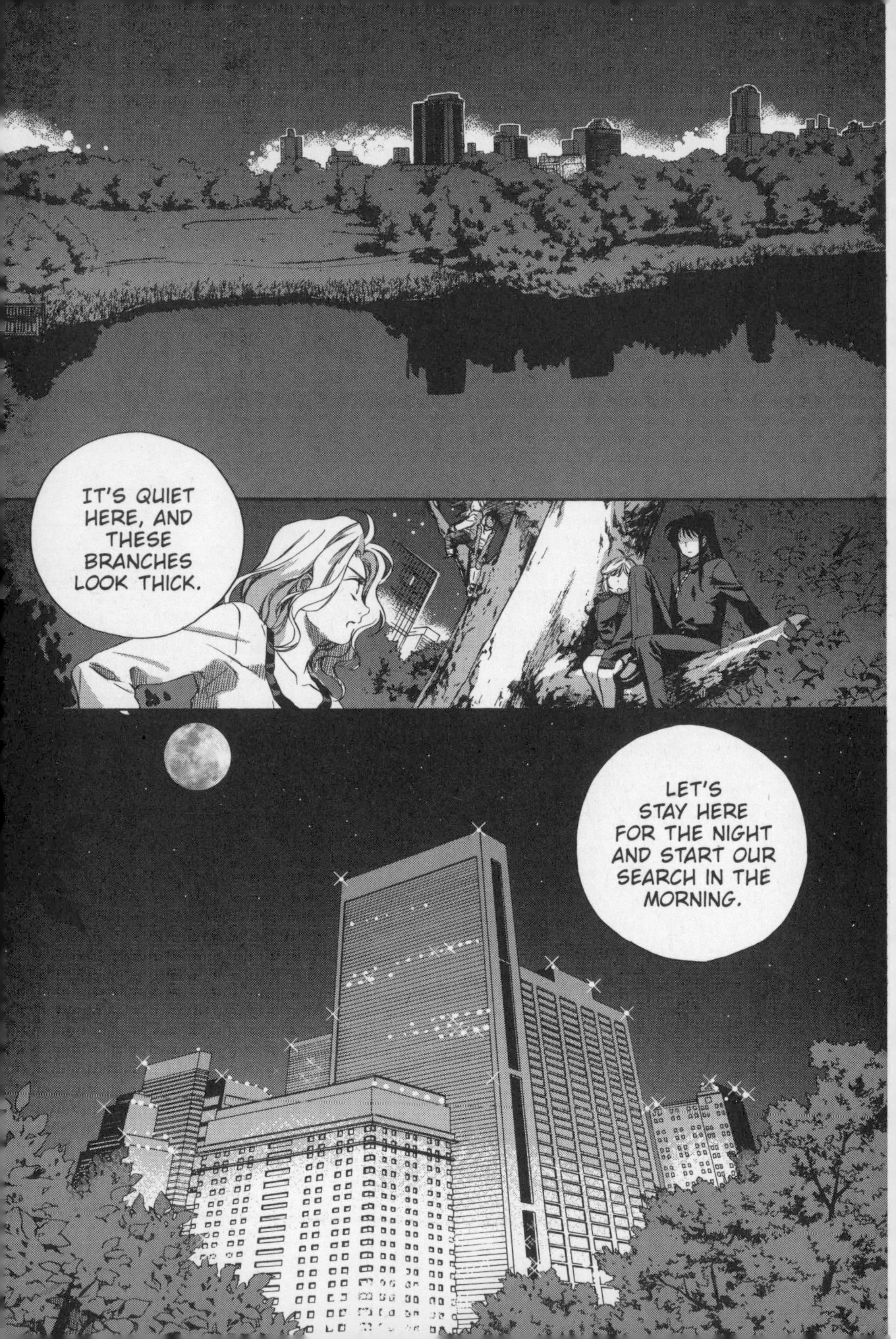
IT'S QUIET HERE, AND THESE BRANCHES LOOK THICK.
LET'S STAY HERE FOR THE NIGHT AND START OUR SEARCH IN THE MORNING.

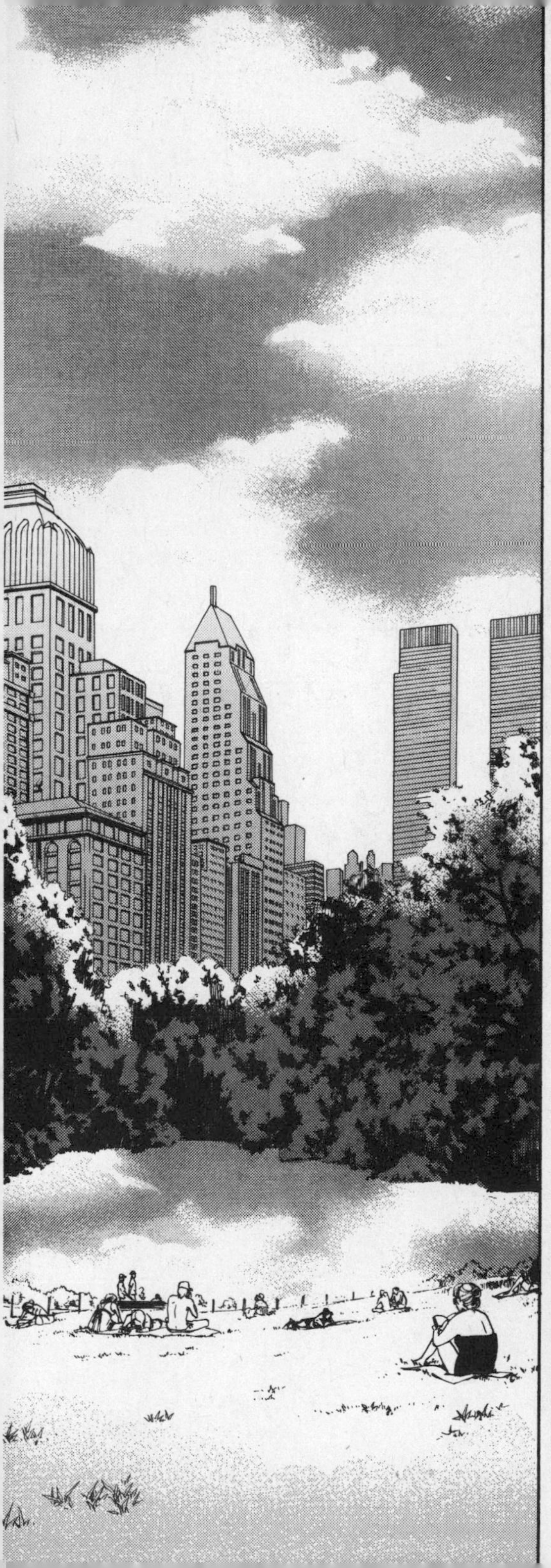

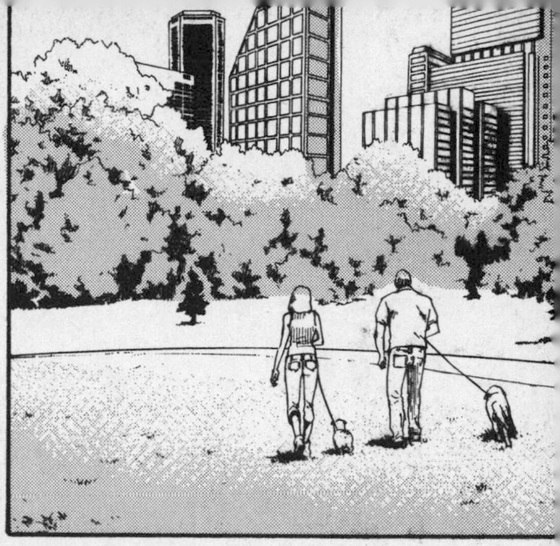

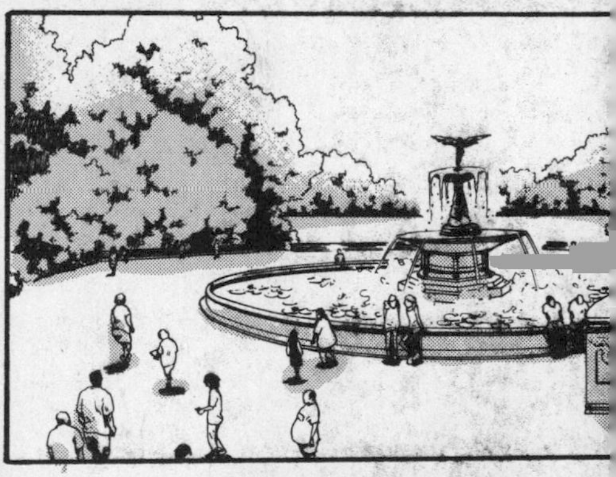

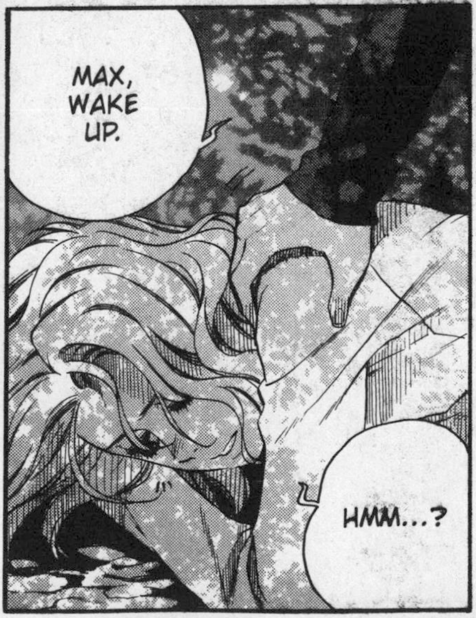
MAX, WAKE UP.
HMM...?

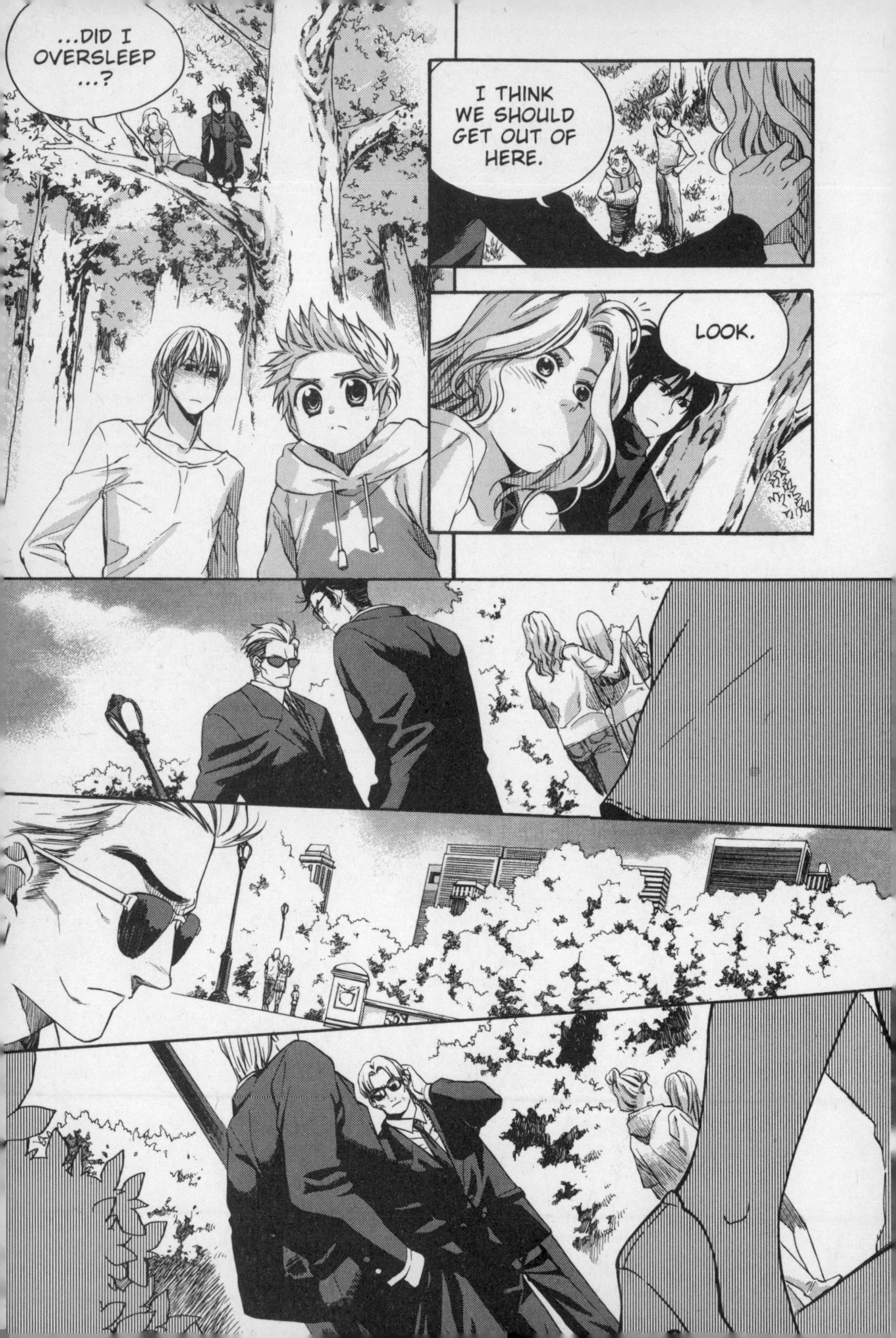
...DID I OVERSLEEP ...?
I THINK WE SHOULD GET OUT OF HERE.
LOOK.

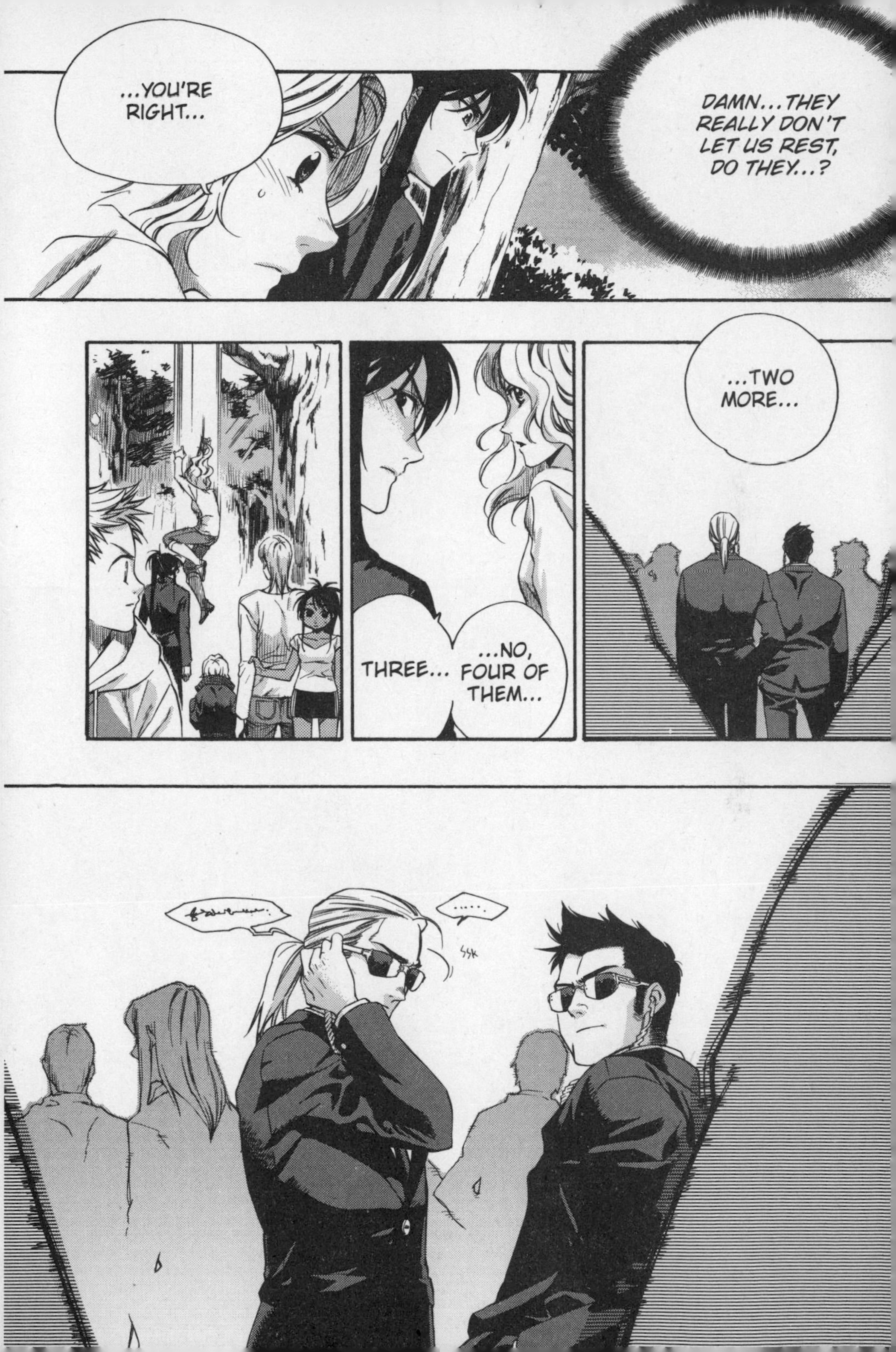
...YOU'RE RIGHT...
DAMN...THEY REALLY DON'T LET US REST, DO THEY...?
THREE...
...NO, FOUR OF THEM...
...TWO MORE...
......
SSK

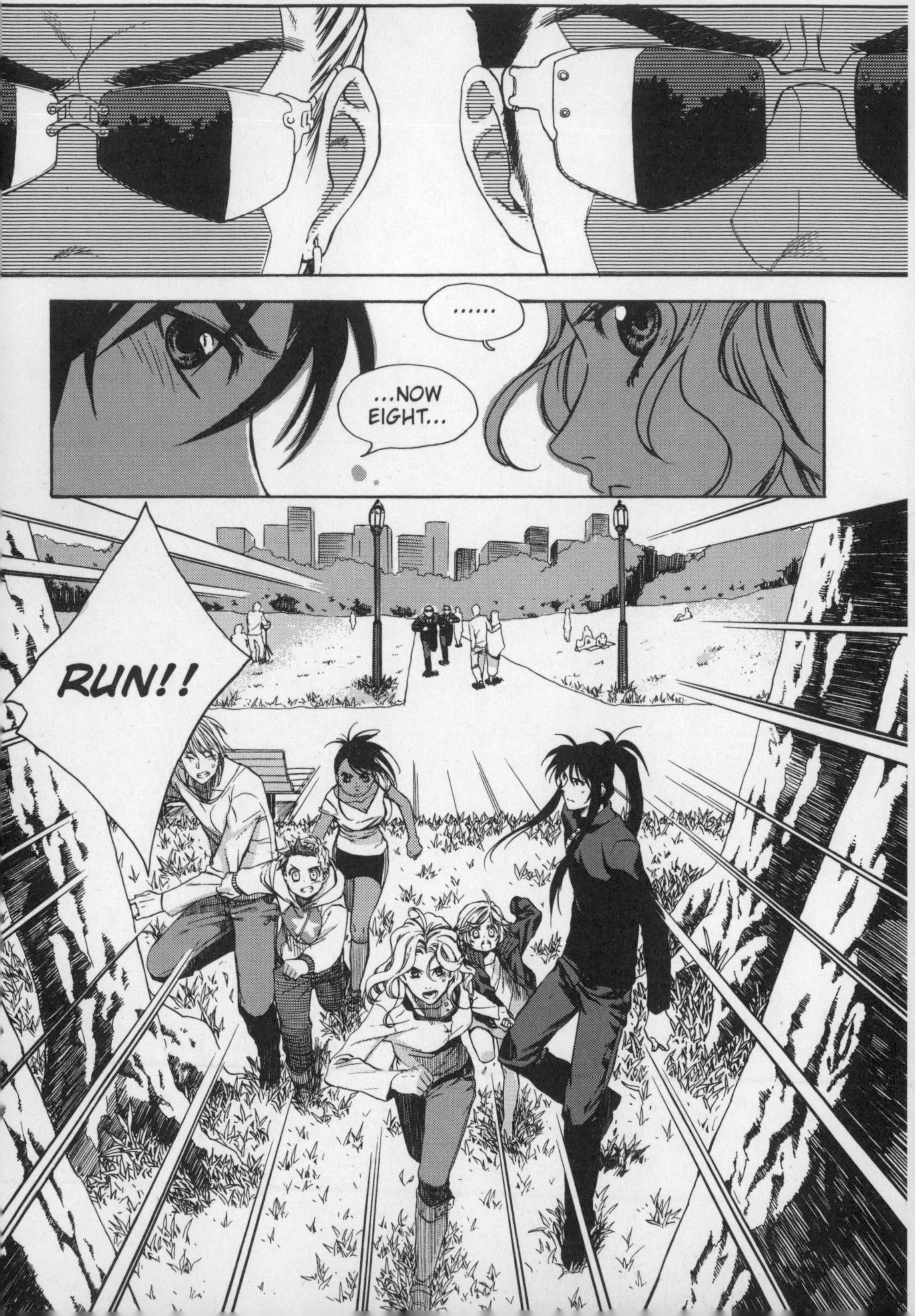
......
...NOW EIGHT...
RUN!!

MAXIMUM RIDE
CHAPTER 10

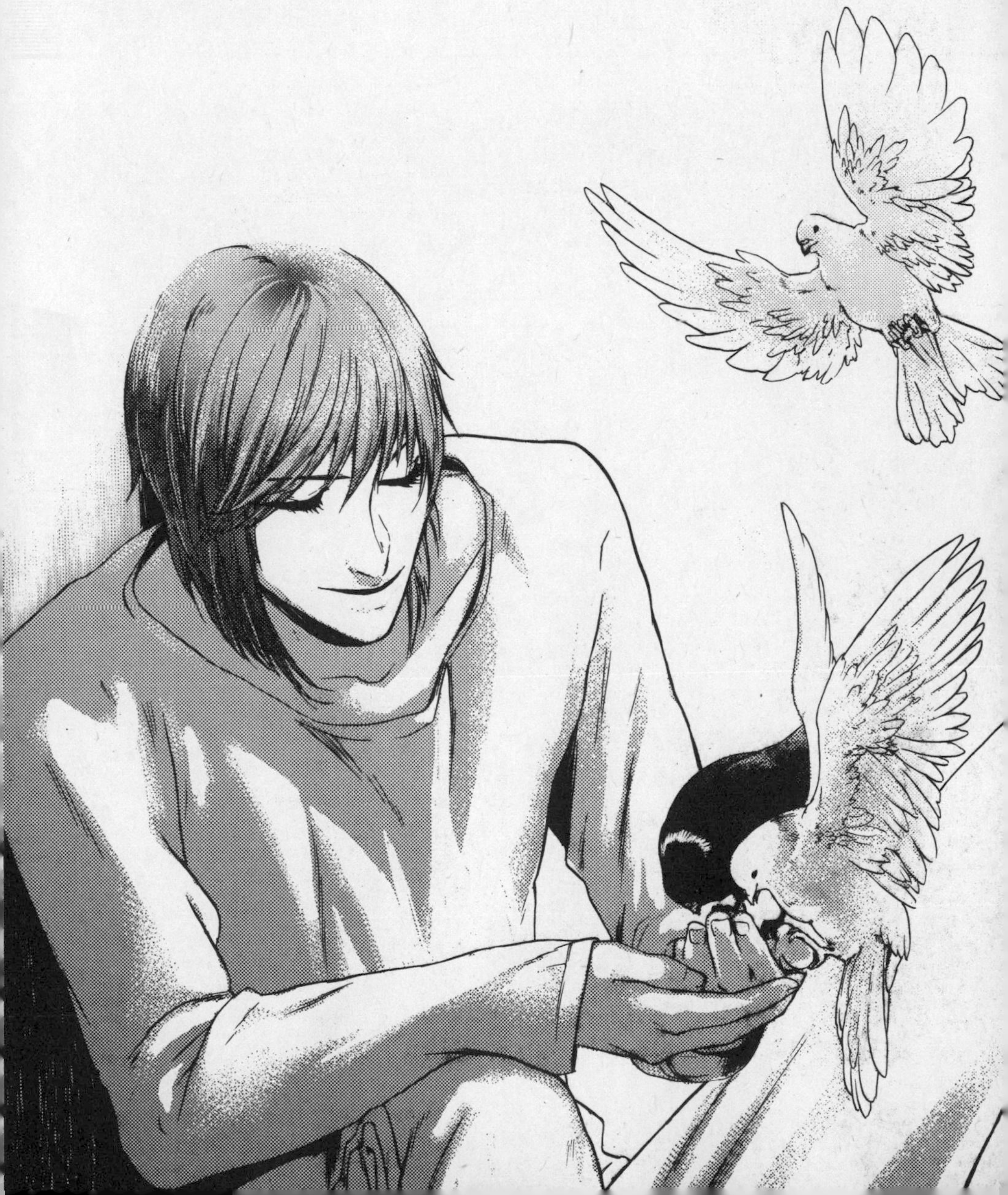

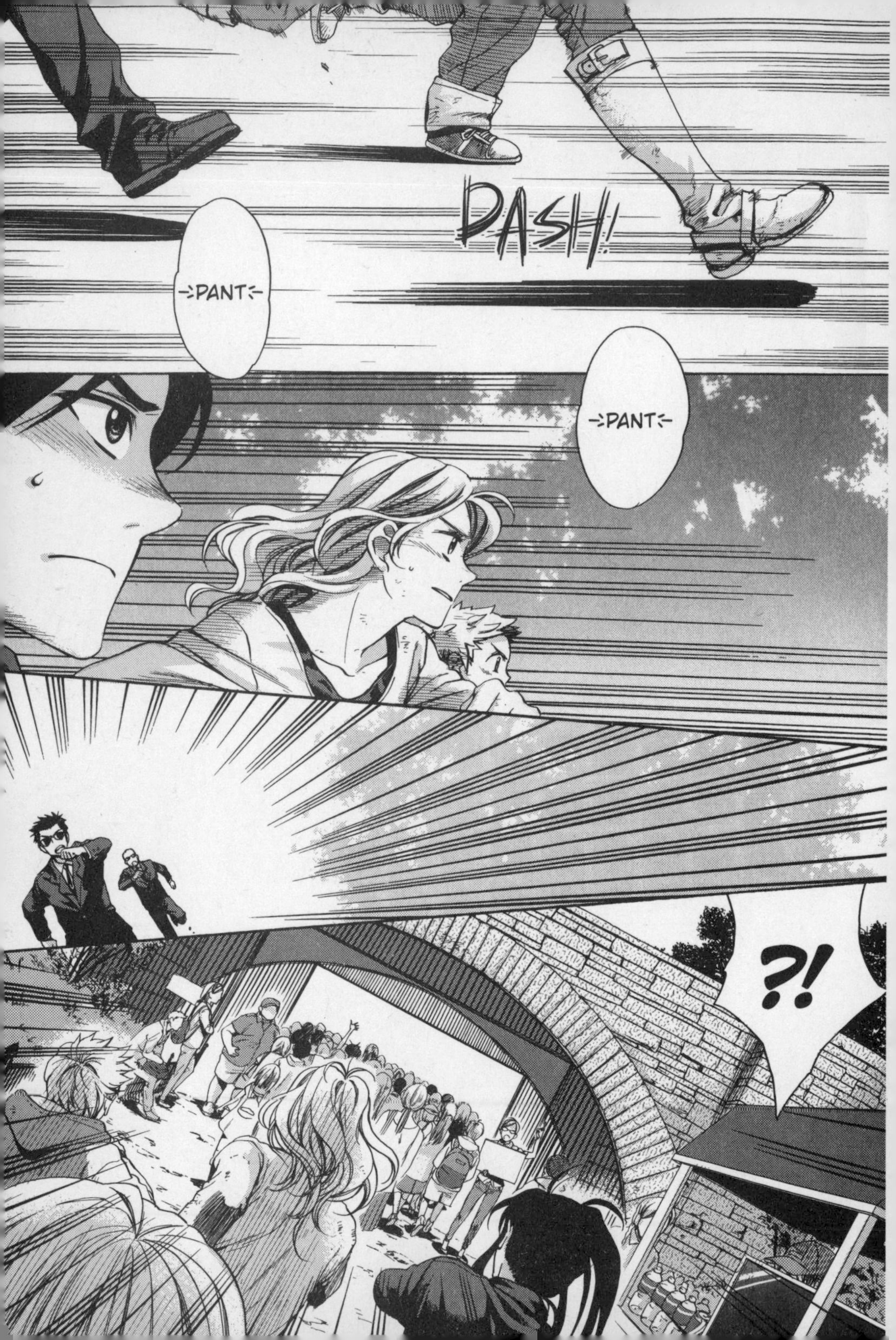
DASH!
-PANT-
-PANT-
?!

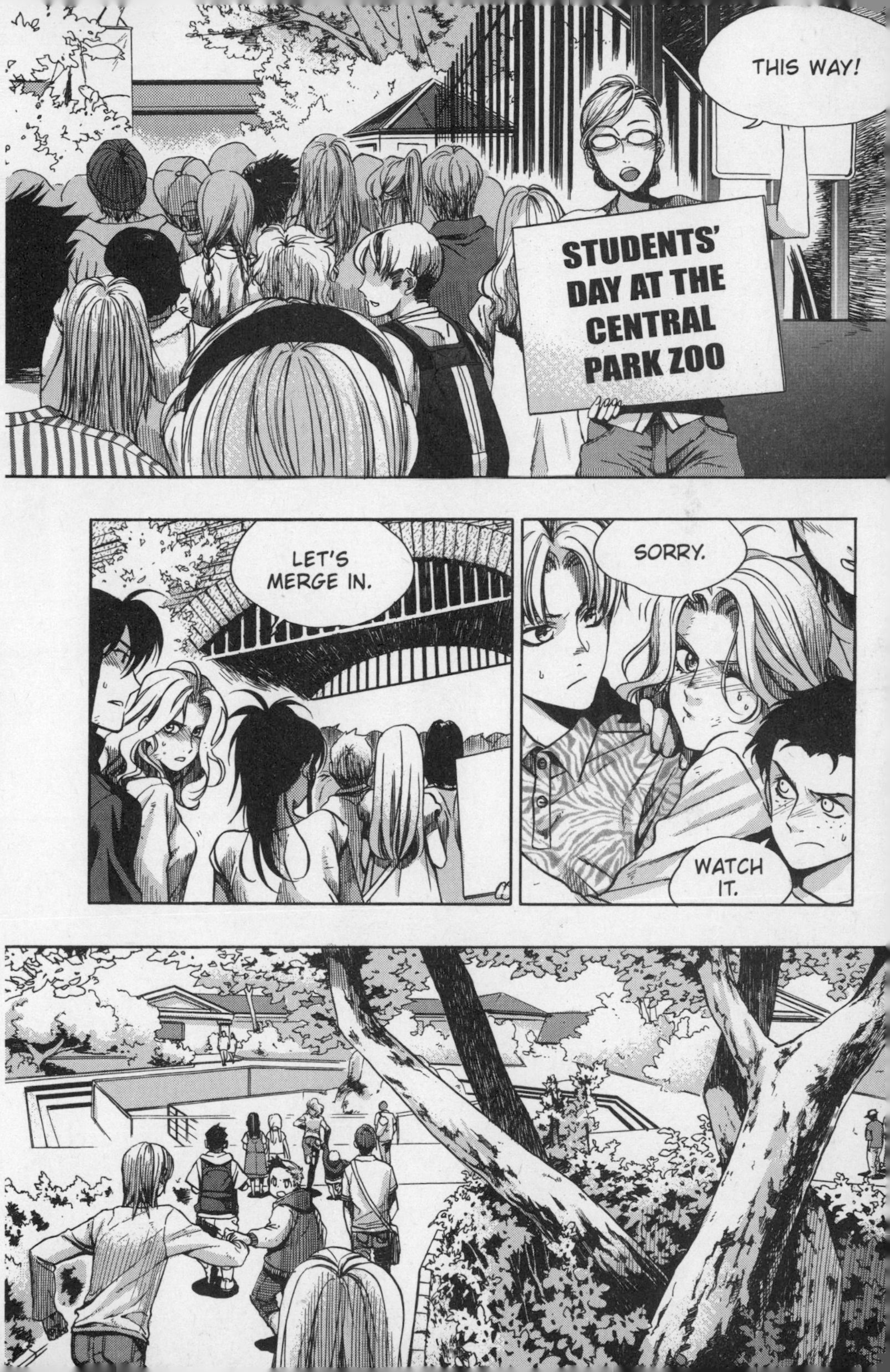
THIS WAY!
STUDENTS' DAY AT THE CENTRAL PARK ZOO
LET'S MERGE IN.
SORRY.
WATCH IT.

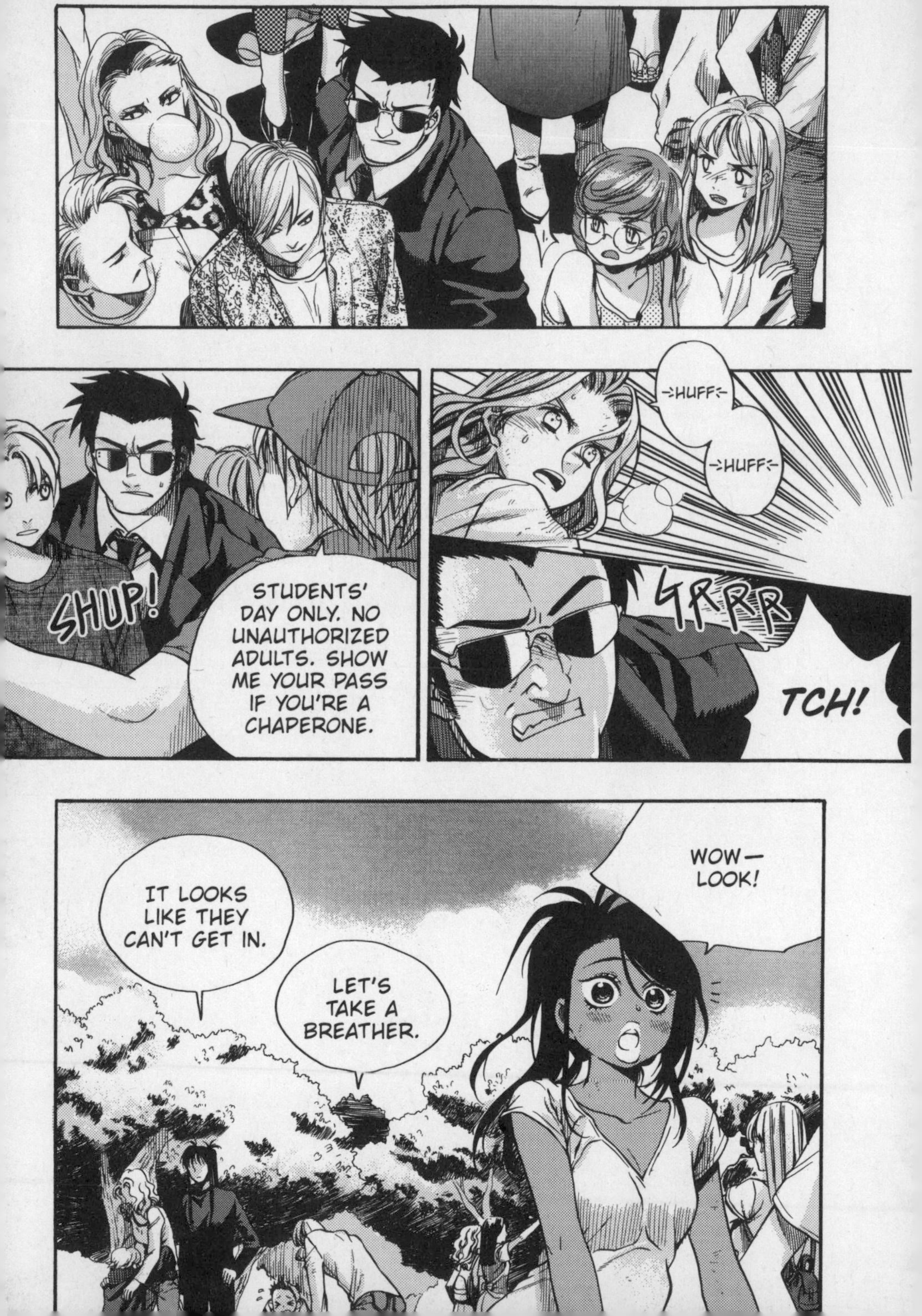
SHUP!
STUDENTS' DAY ONLY. NO UNAUTHORIZED ADULTS. SHOW ME YOUR PASS IF YOU'RE A CHAPERONE.
-HUFF-
-HUFF-
GRRR
TCH!
IT LOOKS LIKE THEY CAN'T GET IN.
LET'S TAKE A BREATHER.
WOW— LOOK!

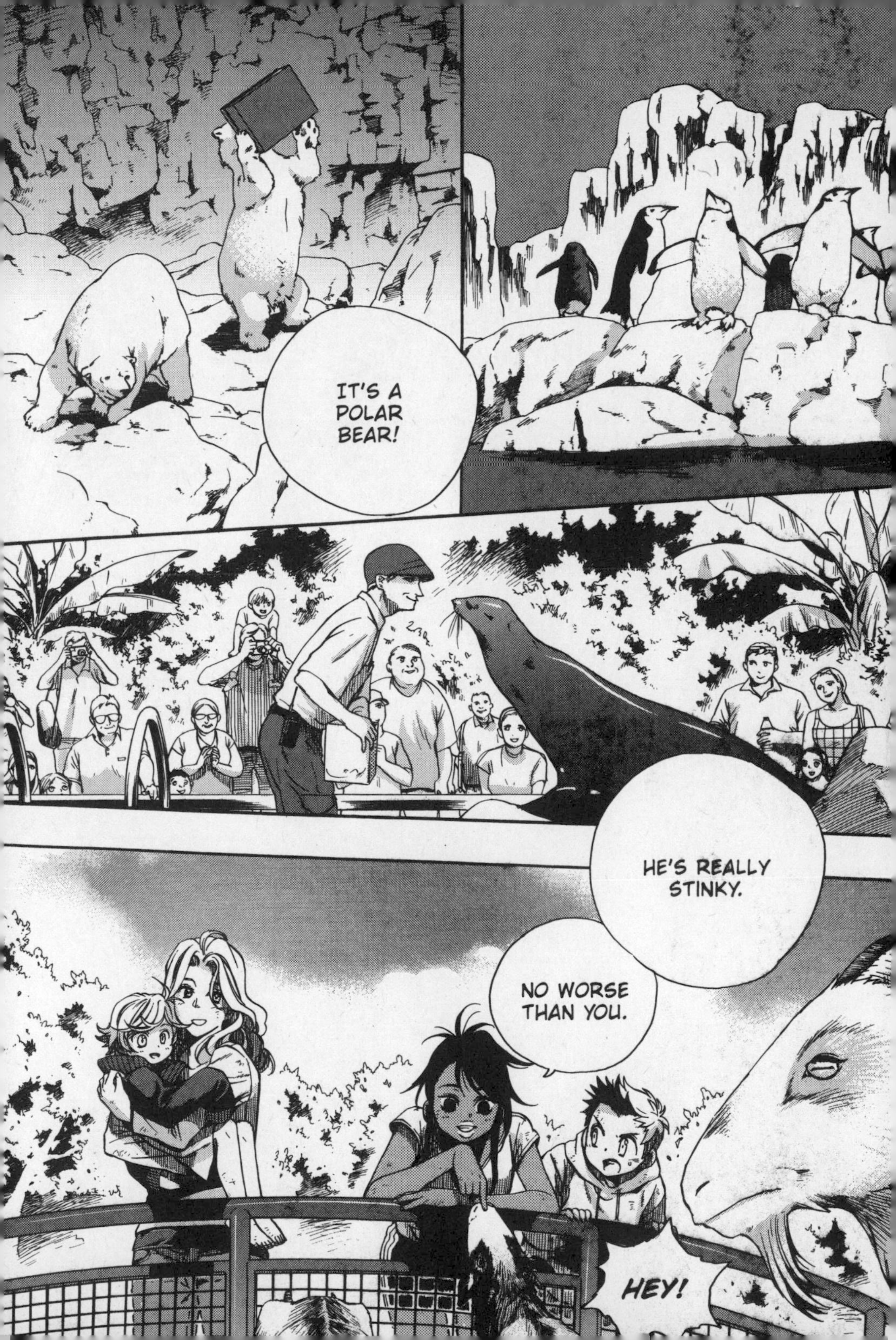
IT'S A POLAR BEAR!
HE'S REALLY STINKY.
NO WORSE THAN YOU.
HEY!

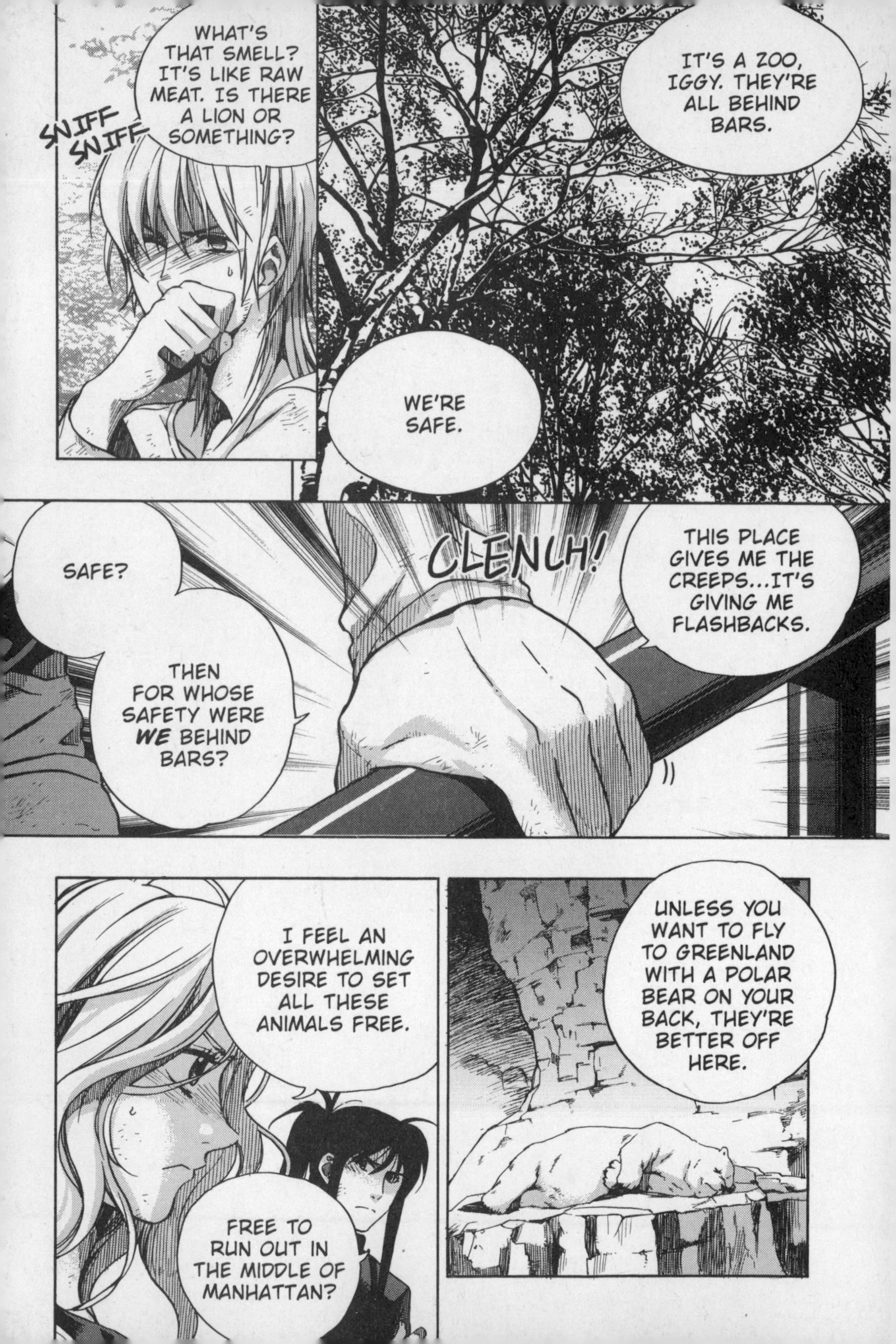
WHAT'S THAT SMELL? IT'S LIKE RAW MEAT. IS THERE A LION OR SOMETHING?
SNIFF SNIFF
IT'S A ZOO, IGGY. THEY'RE ALL BEHIND BARS.
WE'RE SAFE.
SAFE?
THEN FOR WHOSE SAFETY WERE *WE* BEHIND BARS?
CLENCH!
THIS PLACE GIVES ME THE CREEPS...IT'S GIVING ME FLASHBACKS.
I FEEL AN OVERWHELMING DESIRE TO SET ALL THESE ANIMALS FREE.
FREE TO RUN OUT IN THE MIDDLE OF MANHATTAN?
UNLESS YOU WANT TO FLY TO GREENLAND WITH A POLAR BEAR ON YOUR BACK, THEY'RE BETTER OFF HERE.

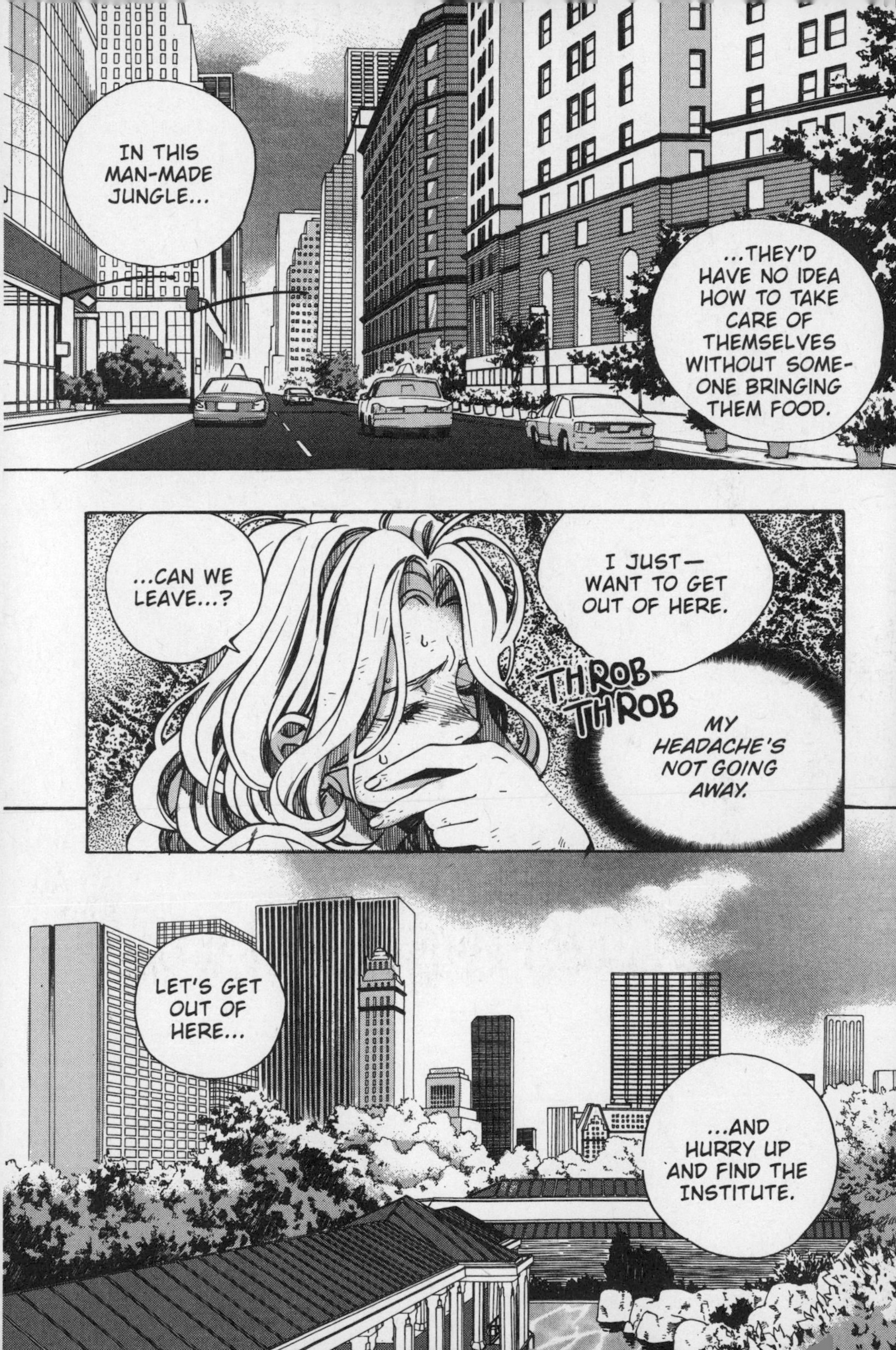
IN THIS MAN-MADE JUNGLE...
...THEY'D HAVE NO IDEA HOW TO TAKE CARE OF THEMSELVES WITHOUT SOME-ONE BRINGING THEM FOOD.
...CAN WE LEAVE...?
I JUST— WANT TO GET OUT OF HERE.
THROB THROB
MY HEADACHE'S NOT GOING AWAY.
LET'S GET OUT OF HERE...
...AND HURRY UP AND FIND THE INSTITUTE.

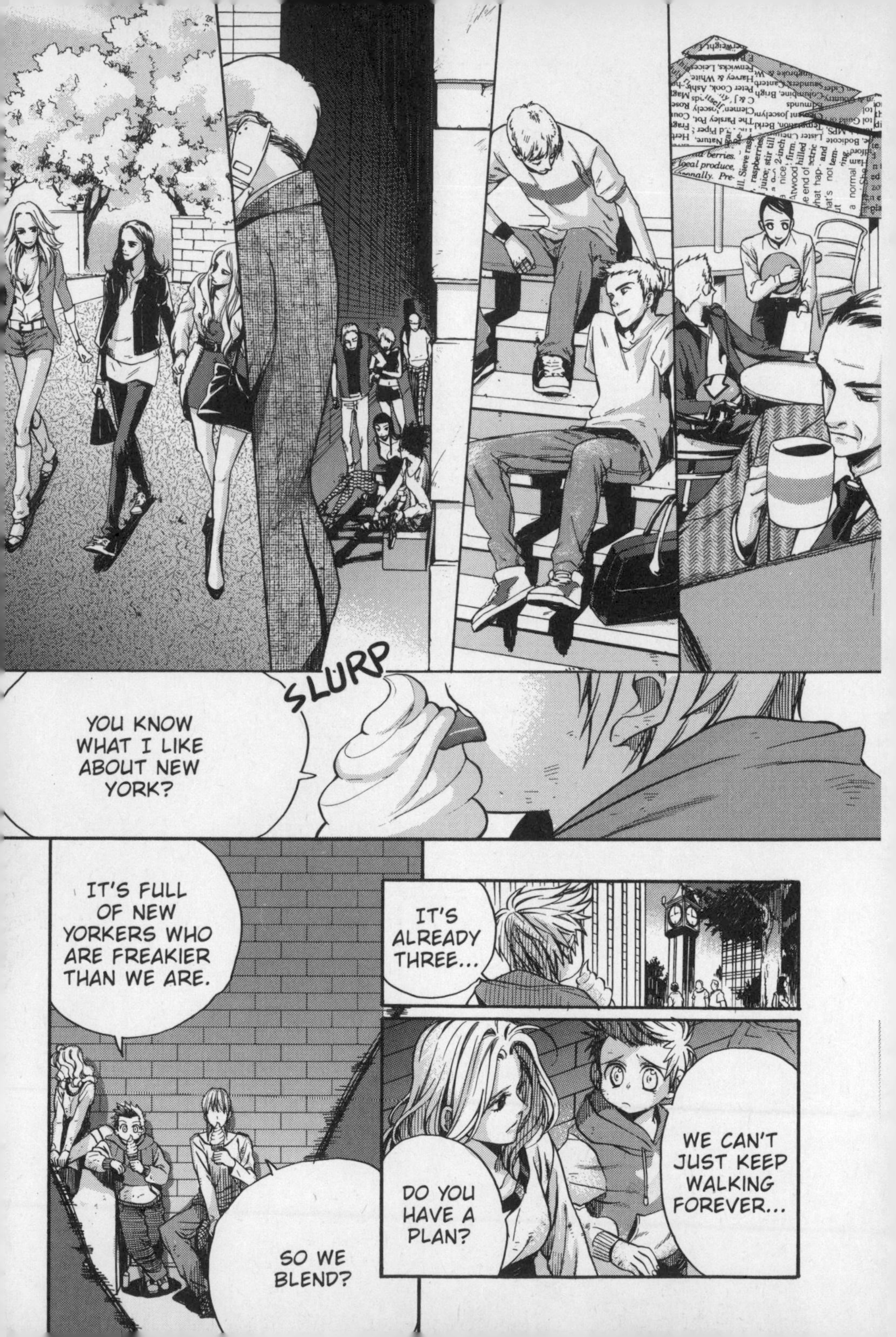
YOU KNOW WHAT I LIKE ABOUT NEW YORK?
SLURP
IT'S FULL OF NEW YORKERS WHO ARE FREAKIER THAN WE ARE.
SO WE BLEND?
IT'S ALREADY THREE...
WE CAN'T JUST KEEP WALKING FOREVER...
DO YOU HAVE A PLAN?

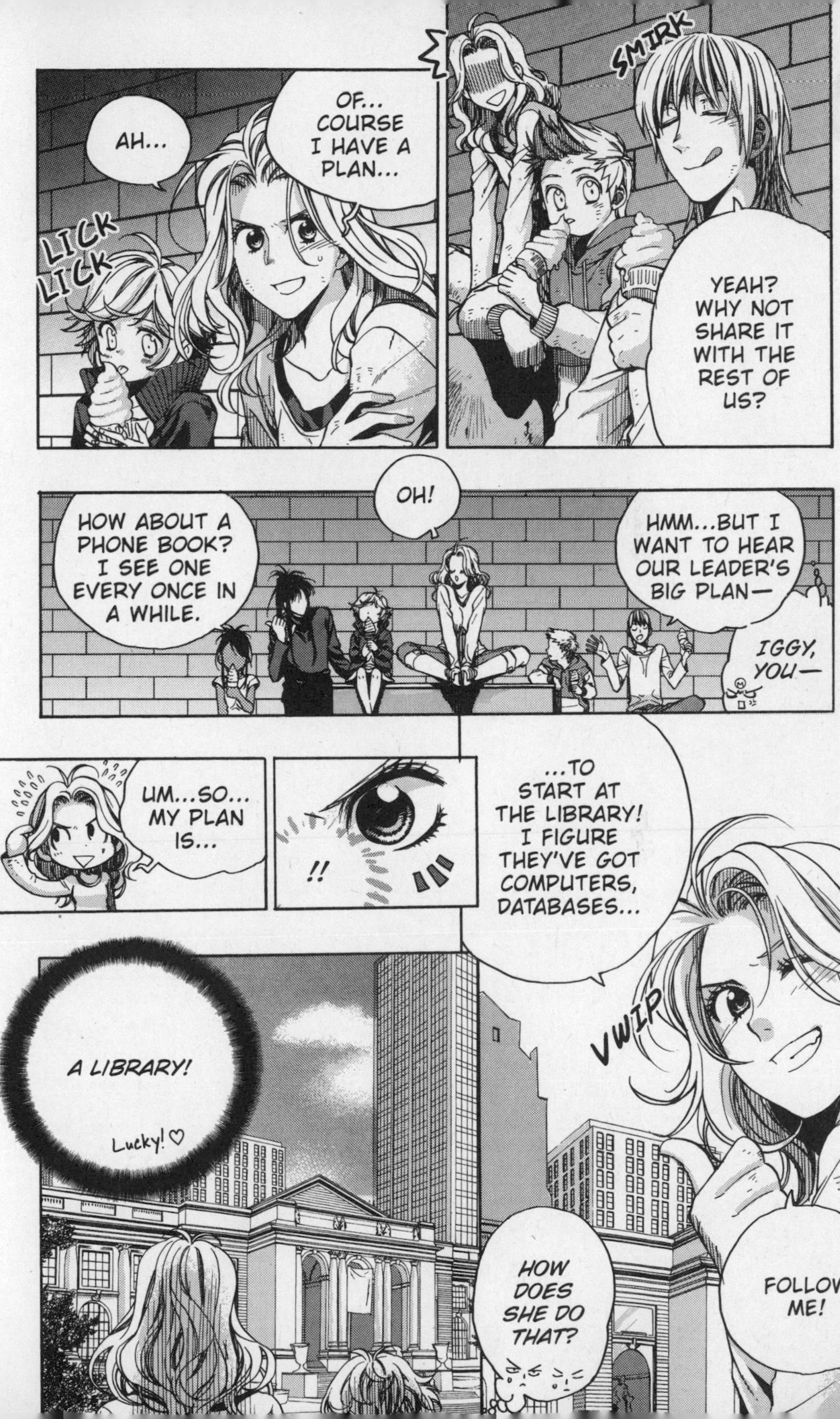
AH...
OF... COURSE I HAVE A PLAN...
LICK LICK
SMIRK
YEAH? WHY NOT SHARE IT WITH THE REST OF US?
HOW ABOUT A PHONE BOOK? I SEE ONE EVERY ONCE IN A WHILE.
OH!
HMM...BUT I WANT TO HEAR OUR LEADER'S BIG PLAN—
IGGY, YOU—
UM...SO... MY PLAN IS...
!!
...TO START AT THE LIBRARY! I FIGURE THEY'VE GOT COMPUTERS, DATABASES...
A LIBRARY!
Lucky! ♡
VWIP
HOW DOES SHE DO THAT?
FOLLOW ME!

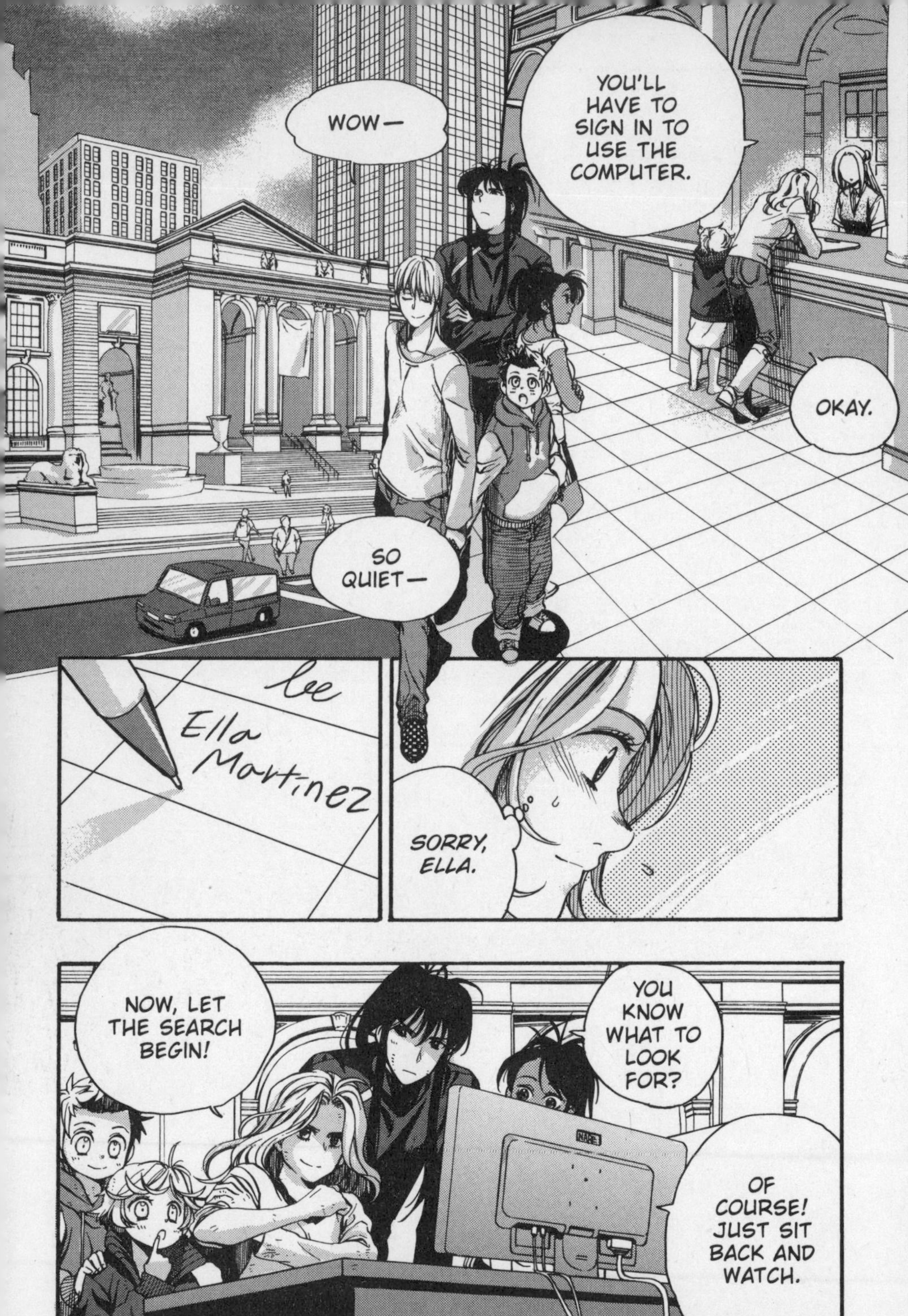
WOW—
YOU'LL HAVE TO SIGN IN TO USE THE COMPUTER.
OKAY.
SO QUIET—
lee
Ella Martinez
SORRY, ELLA.
NOW, LET THE SEARCH BEGIN!
YOU KNOW WHAT TO LOOK FOR?
OF COURSE! JUST SIT BACK AND WATCH.

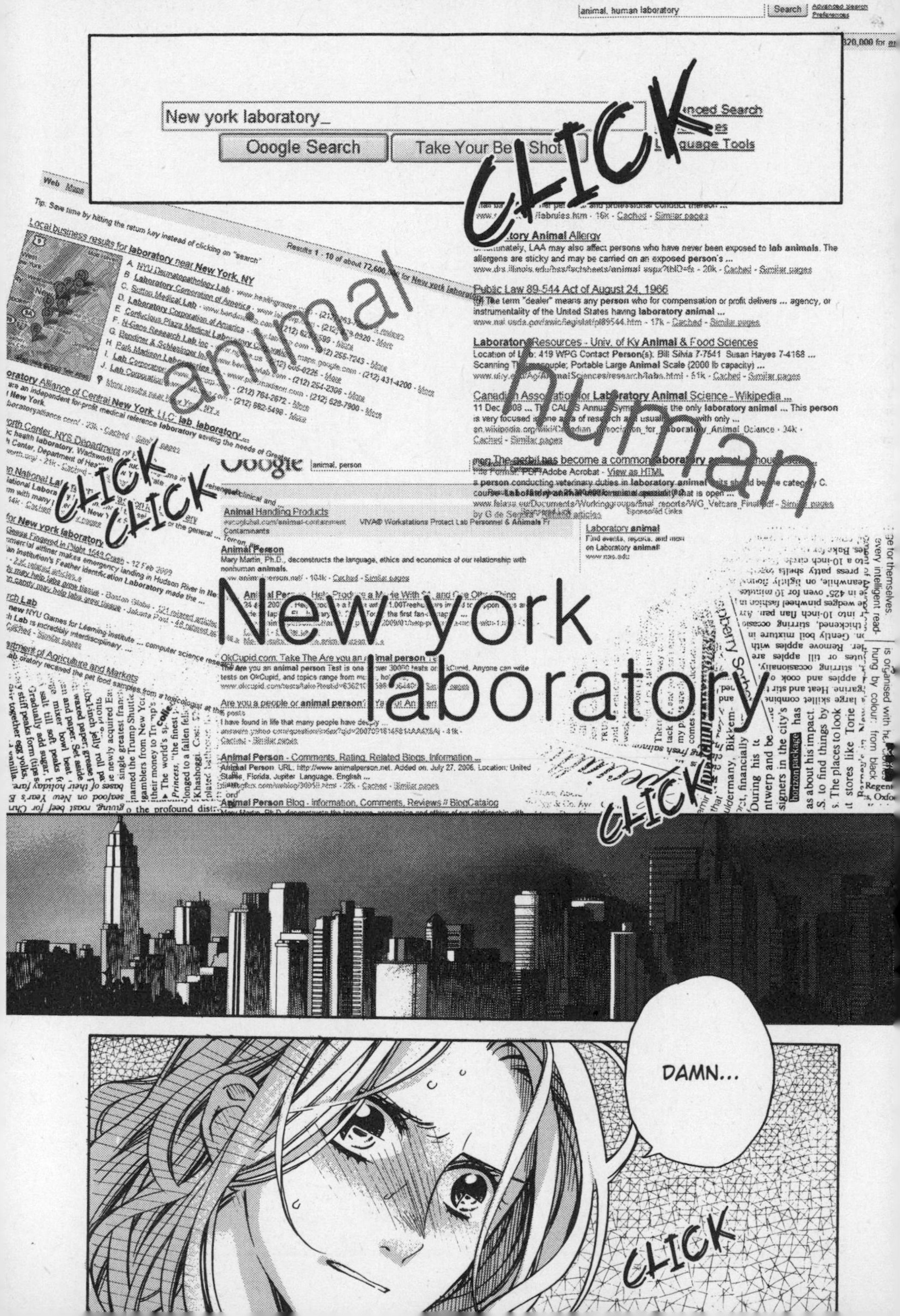
New york laboratory_
Ooogle Search
CLICK
animal
human
CLICK CLICK
New york laboratory
CLICK
DAMN...
CLICK

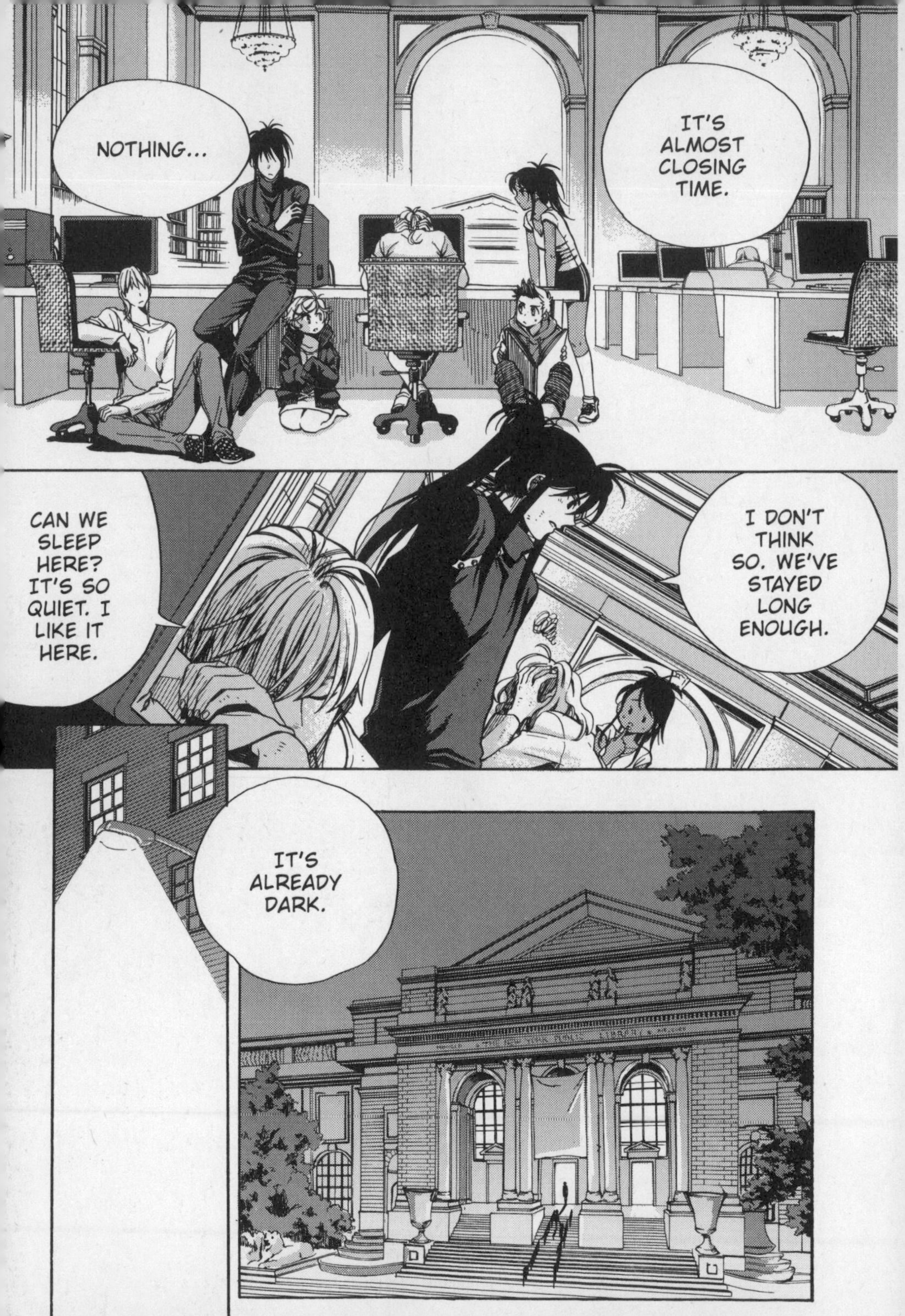
NOTHING...
IT'S ALMOST CLOSING TIME.
CAN WE SLEEP HERE? IT'S SO QUIET. I LIKE IT HERE.
I DON'T THINK SO. WE'VE STAYED LONG ENOUGH.
IT'S ALREADY DARK.

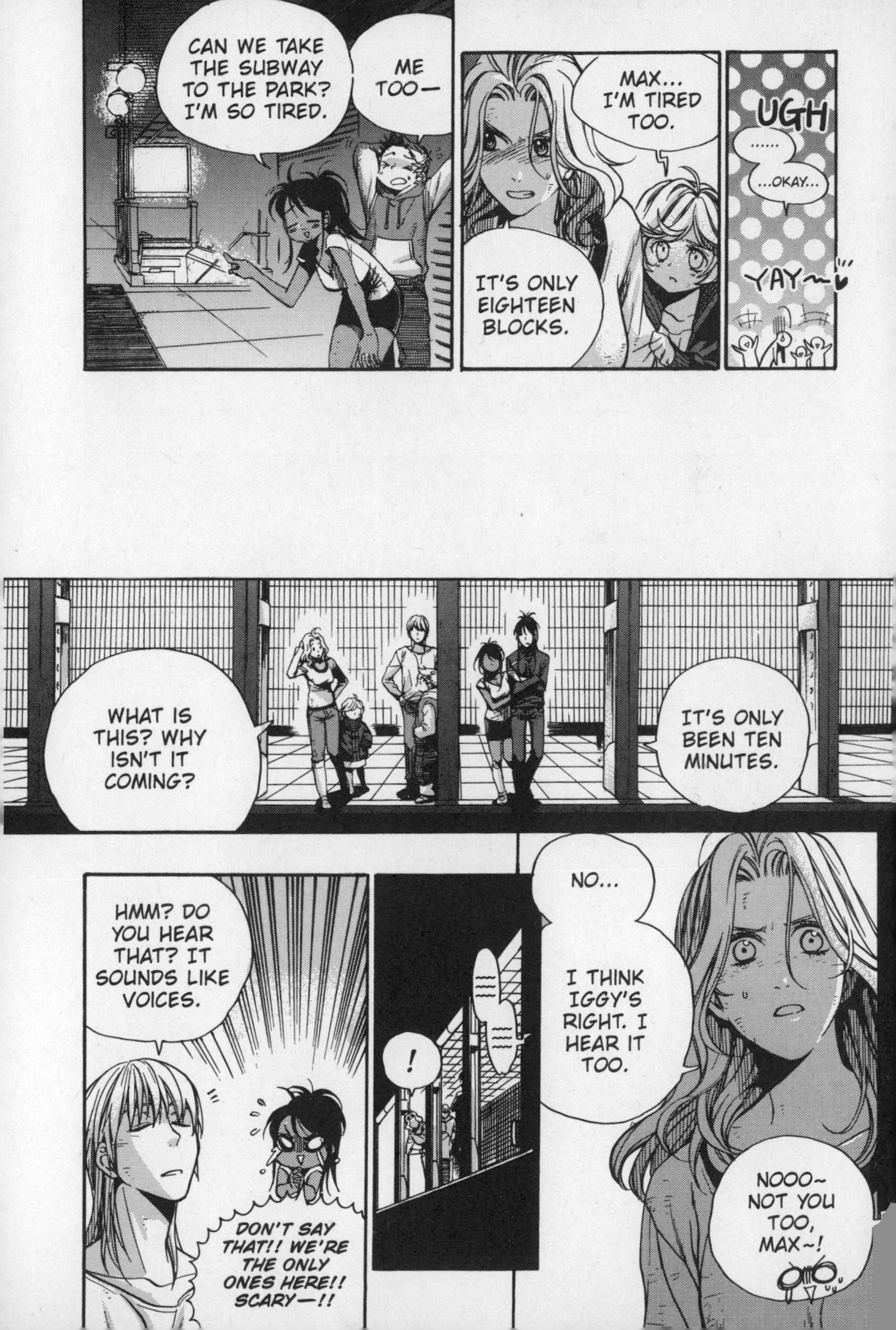

CAN WE TAKE THE SUBWAY TO THE PARK? I'M SO TIRED.
ME TOO—
MAX... I'M TIRED TOO.
IT'S ONLY EIGHTEEN BLOCKS.
UGH
......
...OKAY...
YAY~
WHAT IS THIS? WHY ISN'T IT COMING?
IT'S ONLY BEEN TEN MINUTES.
HMM? DO YOU HEAR THAT? IT SOUNDS LIKE VOICES.
DON'T SAY THAT!! WE'RE THE ONLY ONES HERE!! SCARY—!!
!
NO...
I THINK IGGY'S RIGHT. I HEAR IT TOO.
NOOO~ NOT YOU TOO, MAX~!

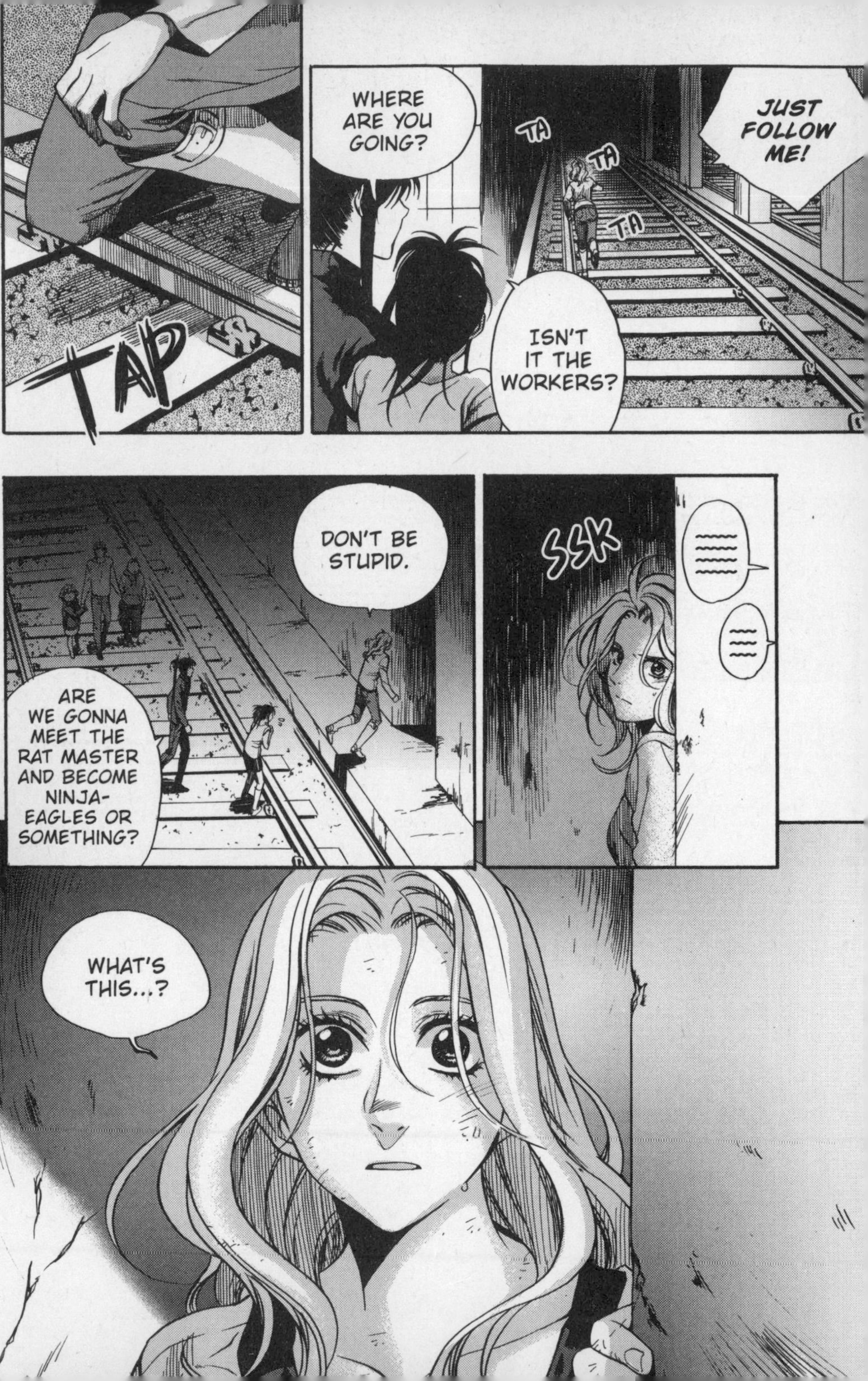
TAP
WHERE ARE YOU GOING?
TA
TA
TA
JUST FOLLOW ME!
ISN'T IT THE WORKERS?
DON'T BE STUPID.
ARE WE GONNA MEET THE RAT MASTER AND BECOME NINJA-EAGLES OR SOMETHING?
SSK
WHAT'S THIS...?

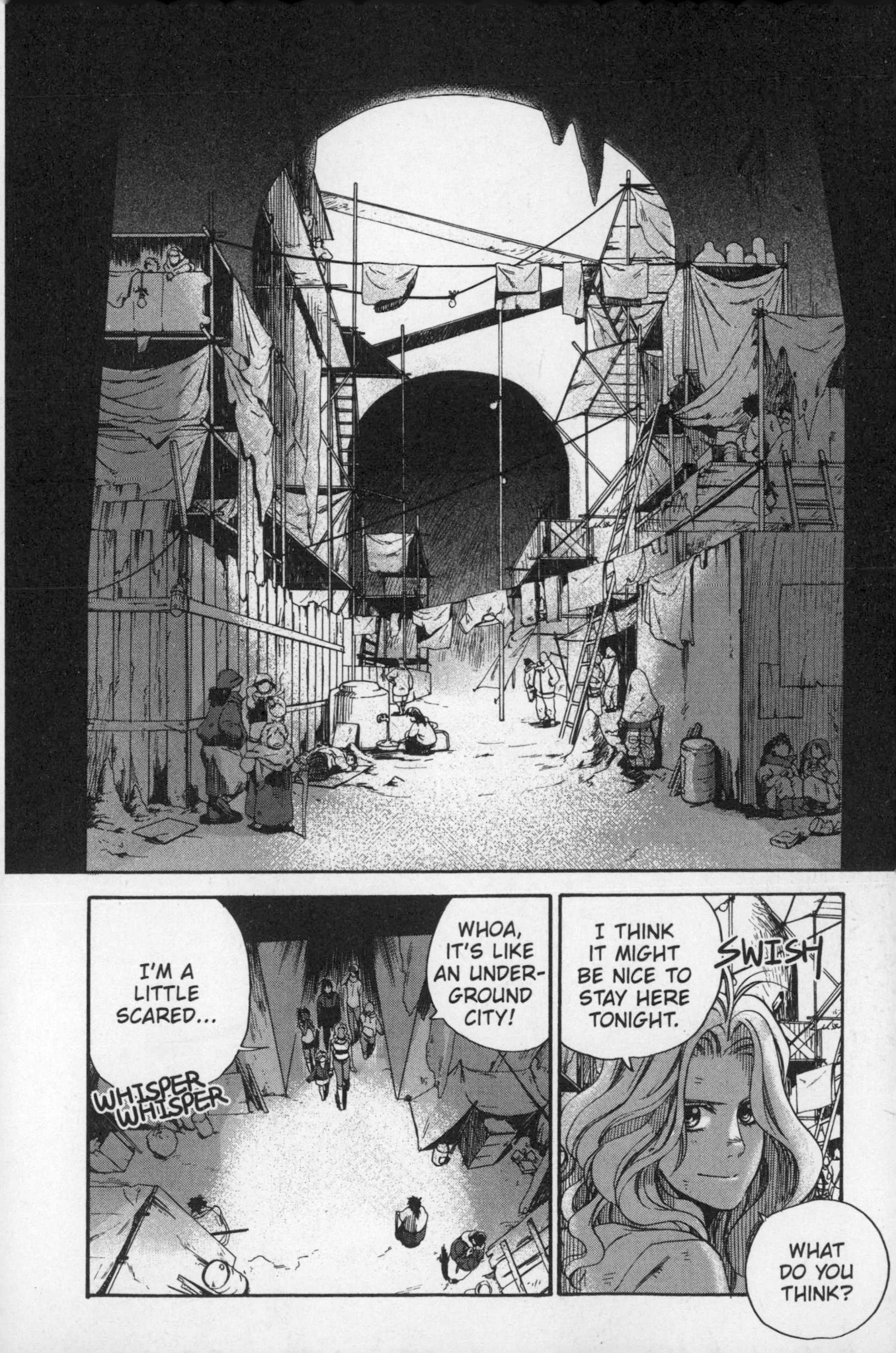
I'M A LITTLE SCARED...
WHISPER WHISPER
WHOA, IT'S LIKE AN UNDER-GROUND CITY!
I THINK IT MIGHT BE NICE TO STAY HERE TONIGHT.
SWISH
WHAT DO YOU THINK?

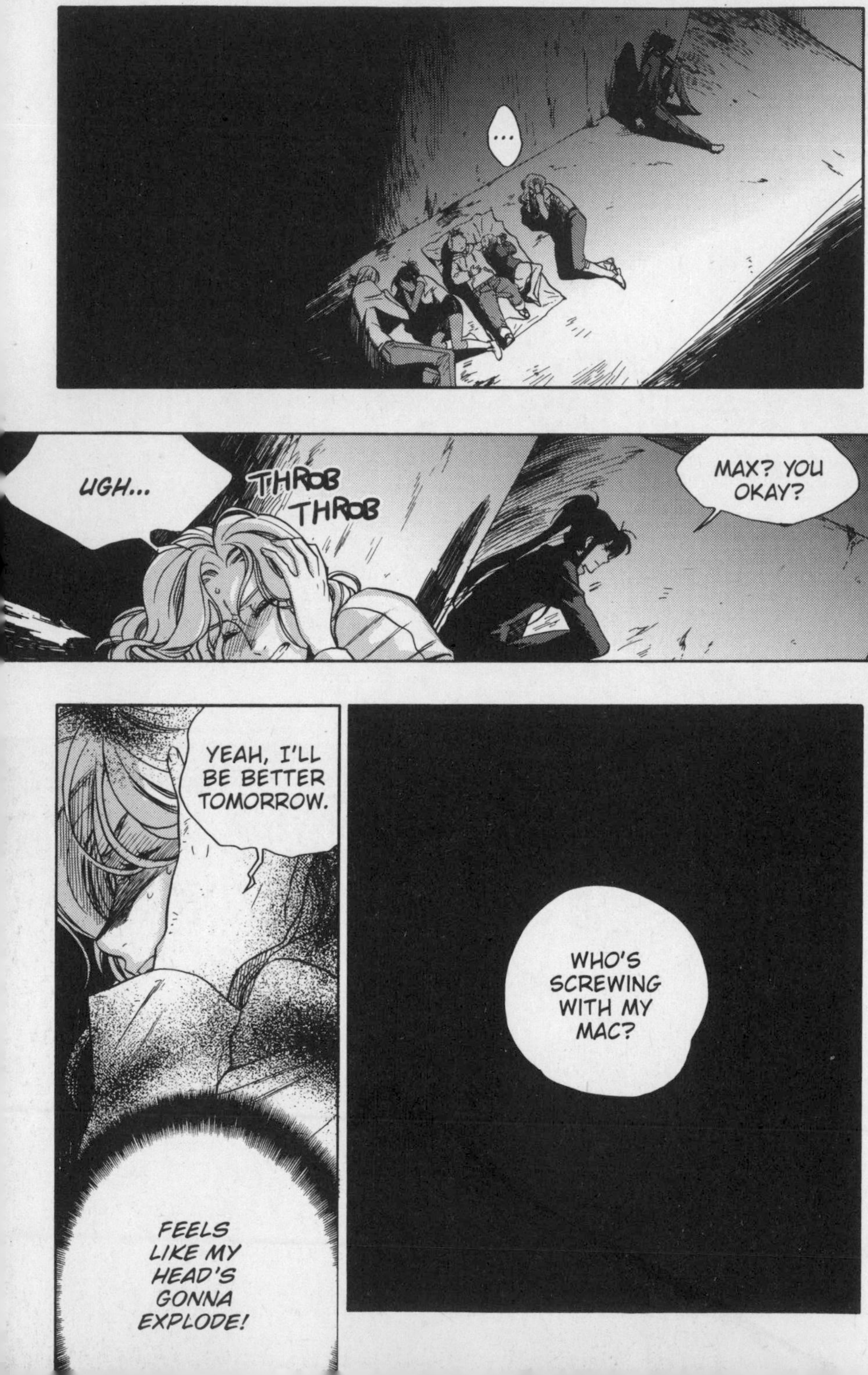
...
UGH...
THROB THROB
MAX? YOU OKAY?
YEAH, I'LL BE BETTER TOMORROW.
FEELS LIKE MY HEAD'S GONNA EXPLODE!
WHO'S SCREWING WITH MY MAC?

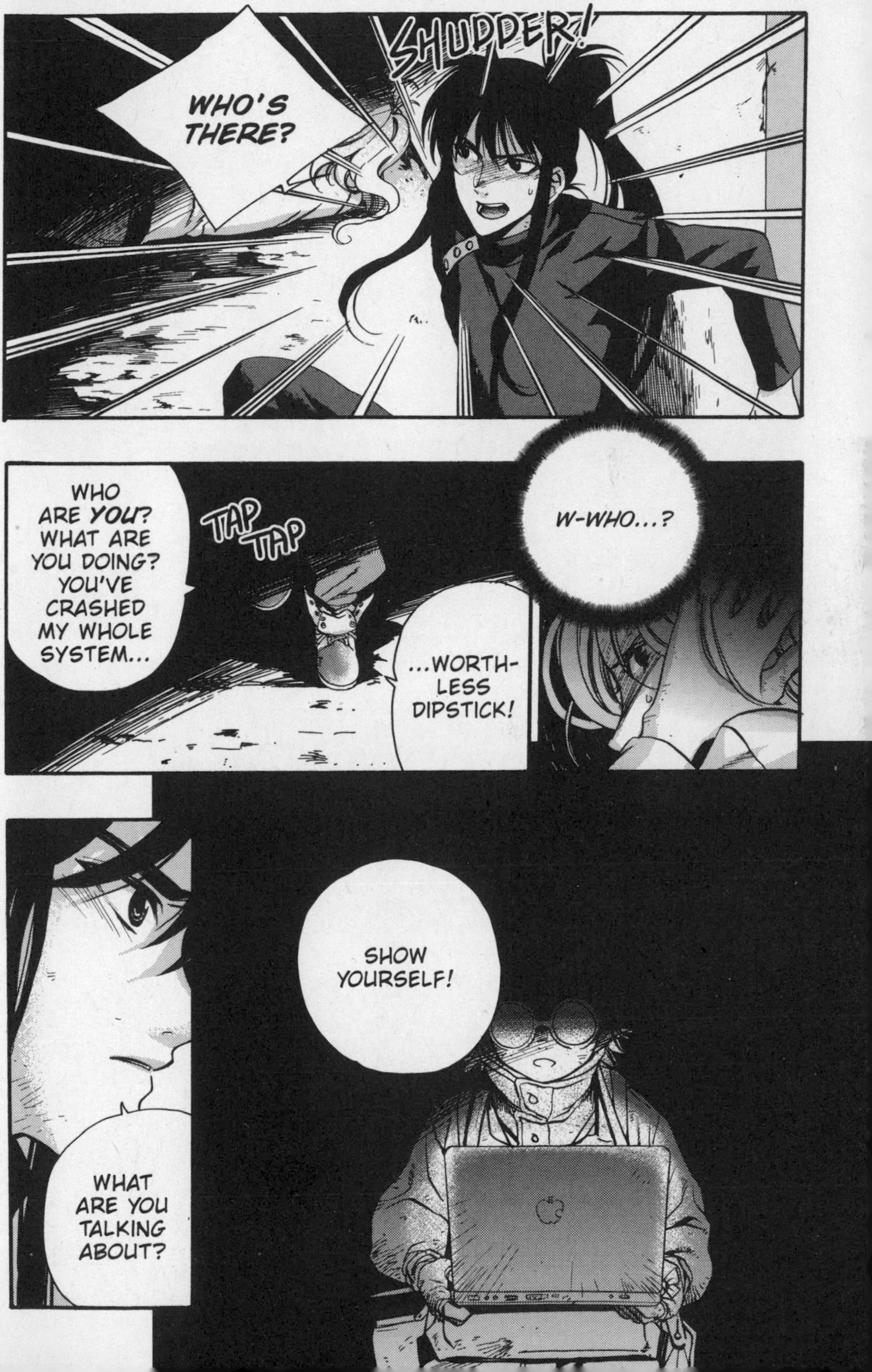
SHUDDER!
WHO'S THERE?
WHO ARE YOU? WHAT ARE YOU DOING? YOU'VE CRASHED MY WHOLE SYSTEM...
TAP TAP
...WORTH-LESS DIPSTICK!
W-WHO...?
SHOW YOURSELF!
WHAT ARE YOU TALKING ABOUT?

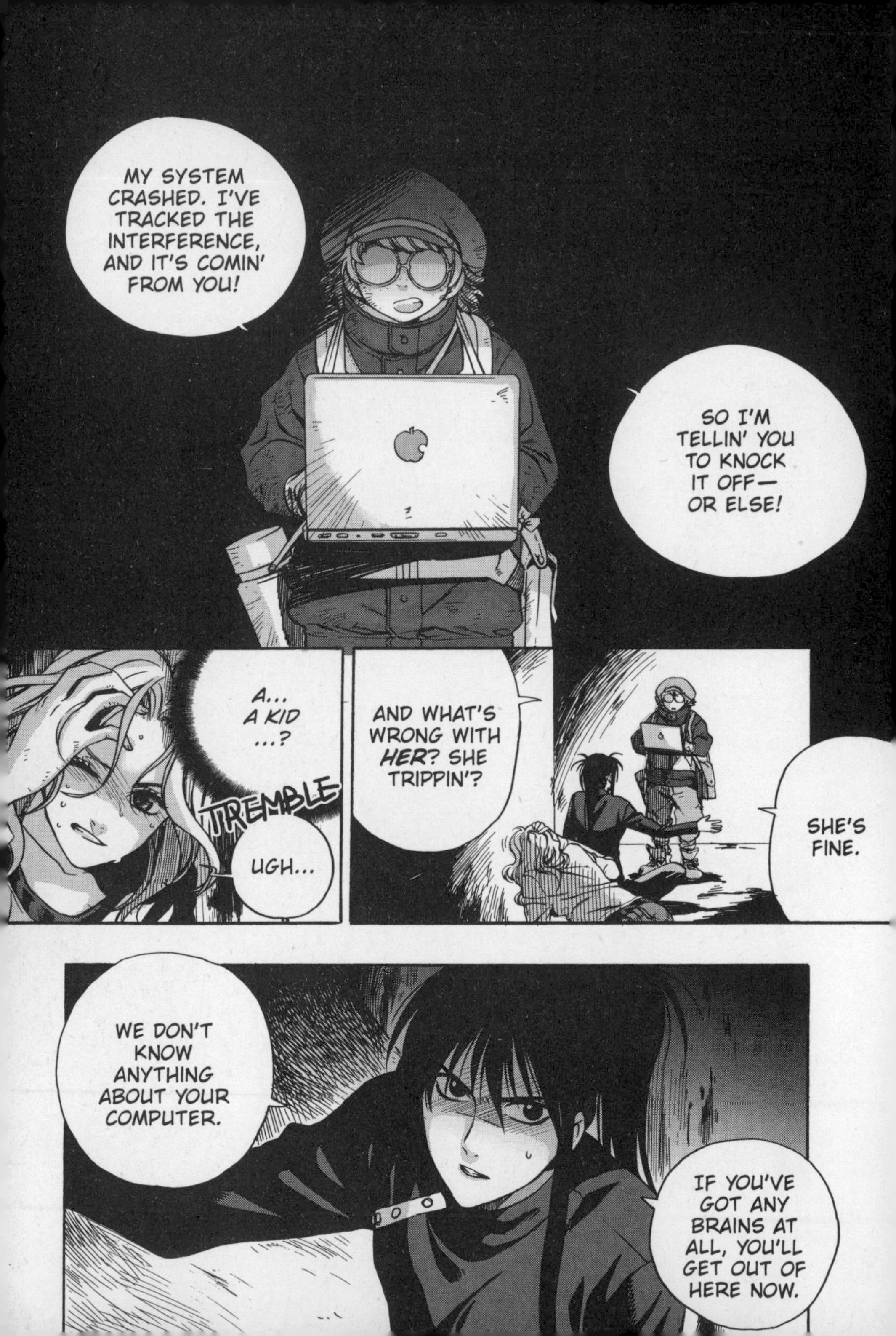
MY SYSTEM CRASHED. I'VE TRACKED THE INTERFERENCE, AND IT'S COMIN' FROM YOU!
SO I'M TELLIN' YOU TO KNOCK IT OFF— OR ELSE!
A... A KID ...?
TREMBLE
UGH...
AND WHAT'S WRONG WITH *HER*? SHE TRIPPIN'?
SHE'S FINE.
WE DON'T KNOW ANYTHING ABOUT YOUR COMPUTER.
IF YOU'VE GOT ANY BRAINS AT ALL, YOU'LL GET OUT OF HERE NOW.

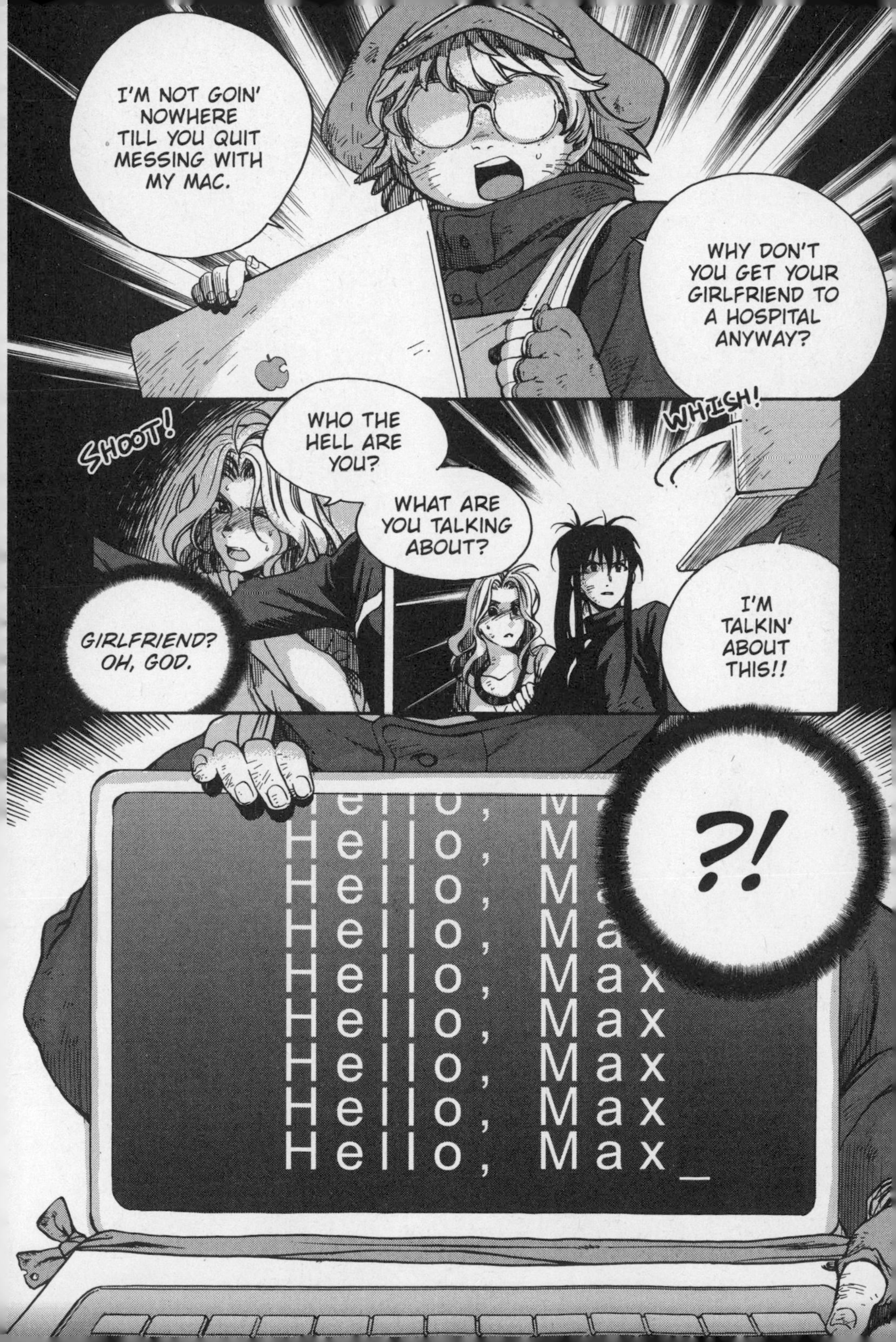
I'M NOT GOIN' NOWHERE TILL YOU QUIT MESSING WITH MY MAC.
WHY DON'T YOU GET YOUR GIRLFRIEND TO A HOSPITAL ANYWAY?
SHOOT!
WHO THE HELL ARE YOU?
WHAT ARE YOU TALKING ABOUT?
GIRLFRIEND? OH, GOD.
WHISH!
I'M TALKIN' ABOUT THIS!!
Hello, Max
Hello, Max
Hello, Max
Hello, Max
Hello, Max
Hello, Max
Hello, Max_
?!

Hello, Max

Welcome to New York_

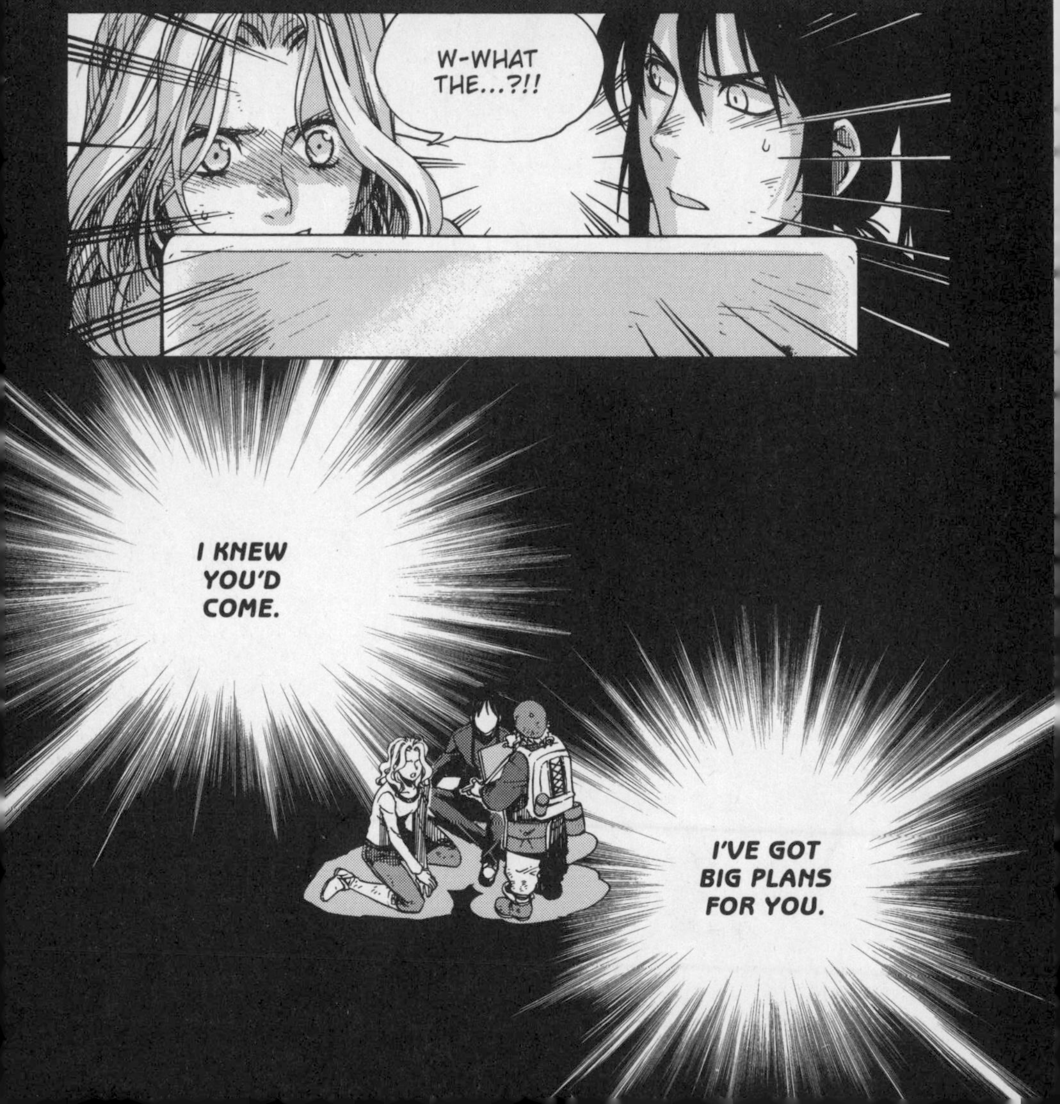
W-WHAT THE...?!!
I KNEW YOU'D COME.
I'VE GOT BIG PLANS FOR YOU.

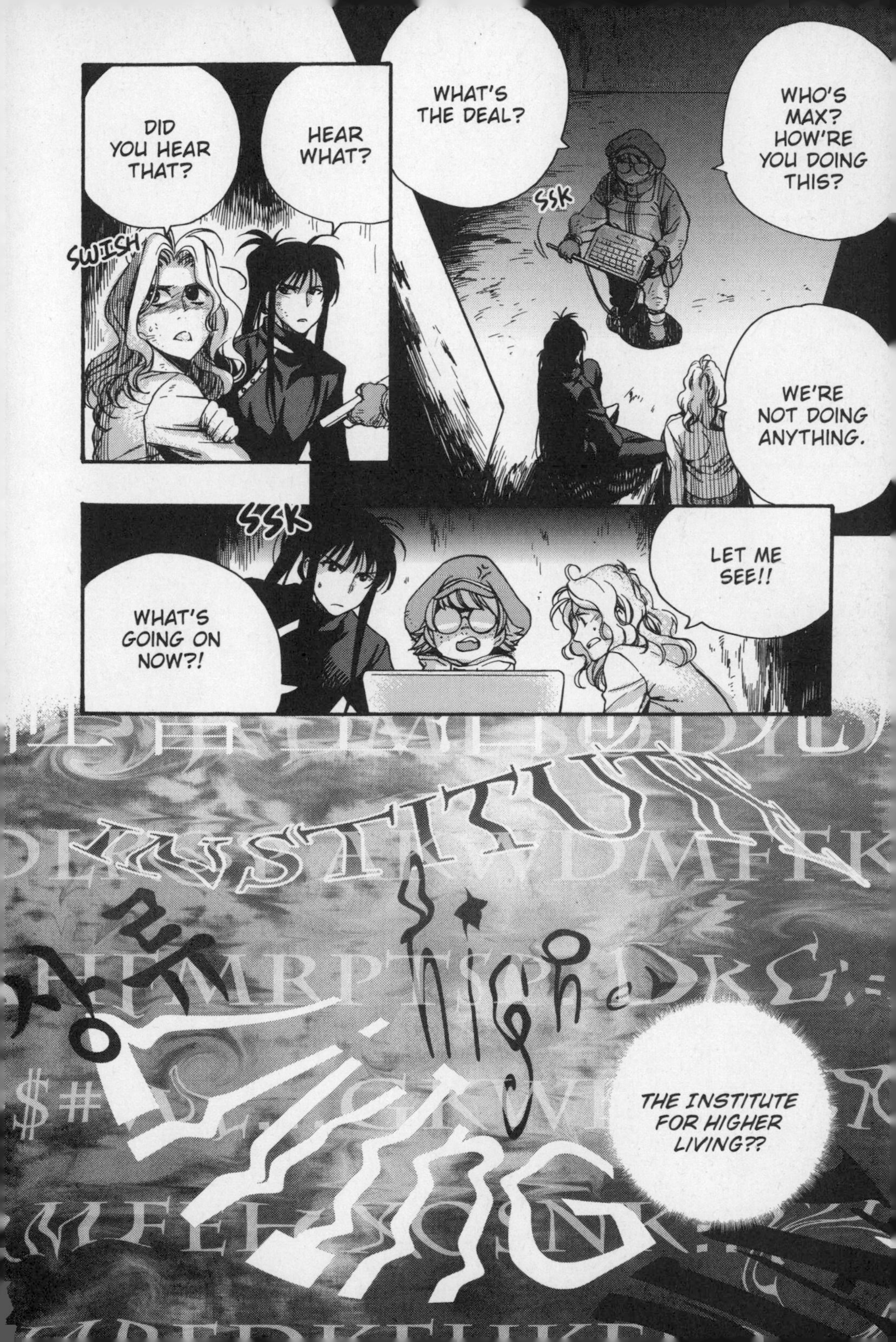
DID YOU HEAR THAT?
SWISH
HEAR WHAT?
WHAT'S THE DEAL?
SSK
WHO'S MAX? HOW'RE YOU DOING THIS?
WE'RE NOT DOING ANYTHING.
SSK
WHAT'S GOING ON NOW?!
LET ME SEE!!
THE INSTITUTE FOR HIGHER LIVING??

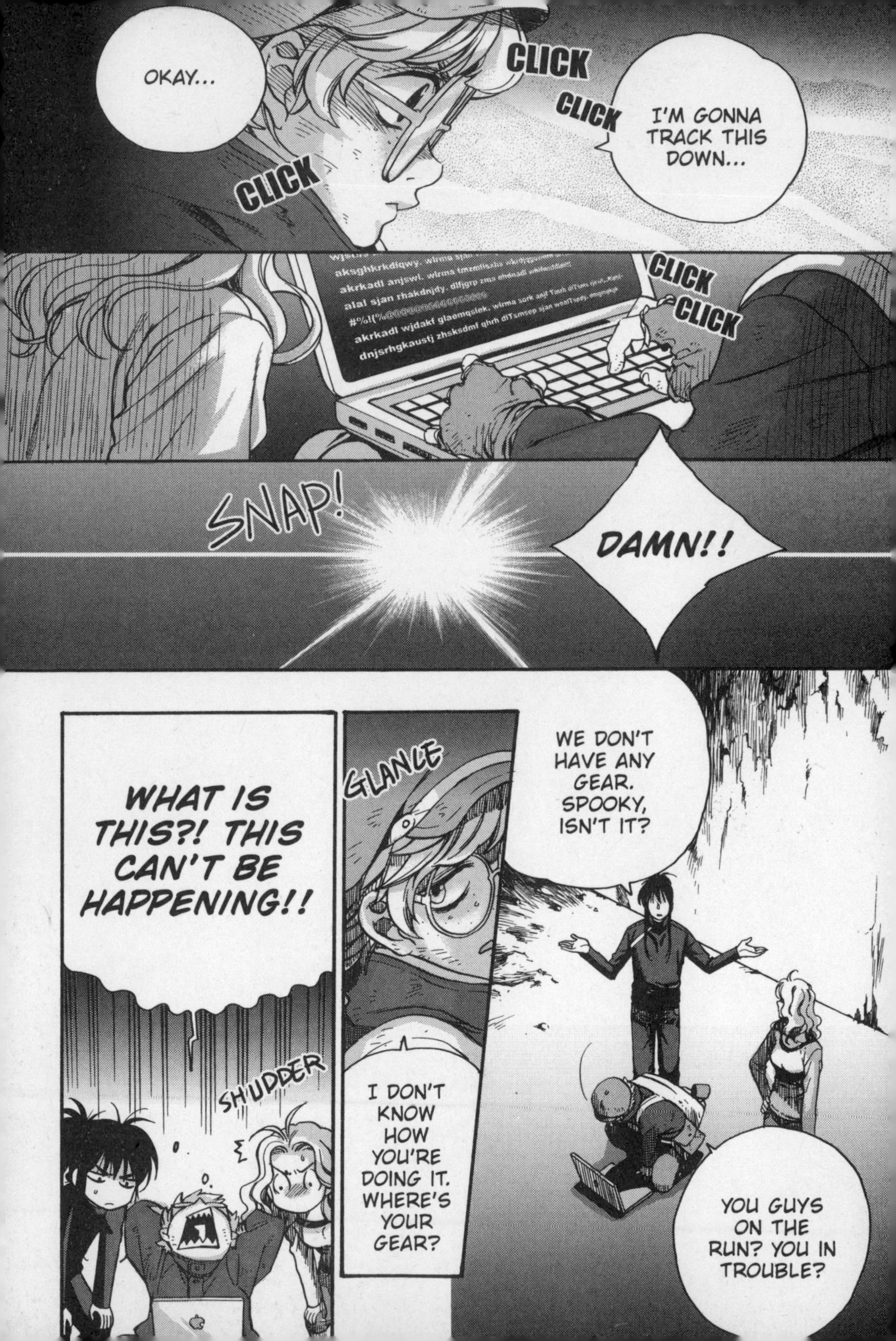
OKAY...
CLICK
CLICK
CLICK
I'M GONNA TRACK THIS DOWN...
CLICK
CLICK
SNAP!
DAMN!!
WHAT IS THIS?! THIS CAN'T BE HAPPENING!!
SHUDDER
GLANCE
I DON'T KNOW HOW YOU'RE DOING IT. WHERE'S YOUR GEAR?
WE DON'T HAVE ANY GEAR. SPOOKY, ISN'T IT?
YOU GUYS ON THE RUN? YOU IN TROUBLE?

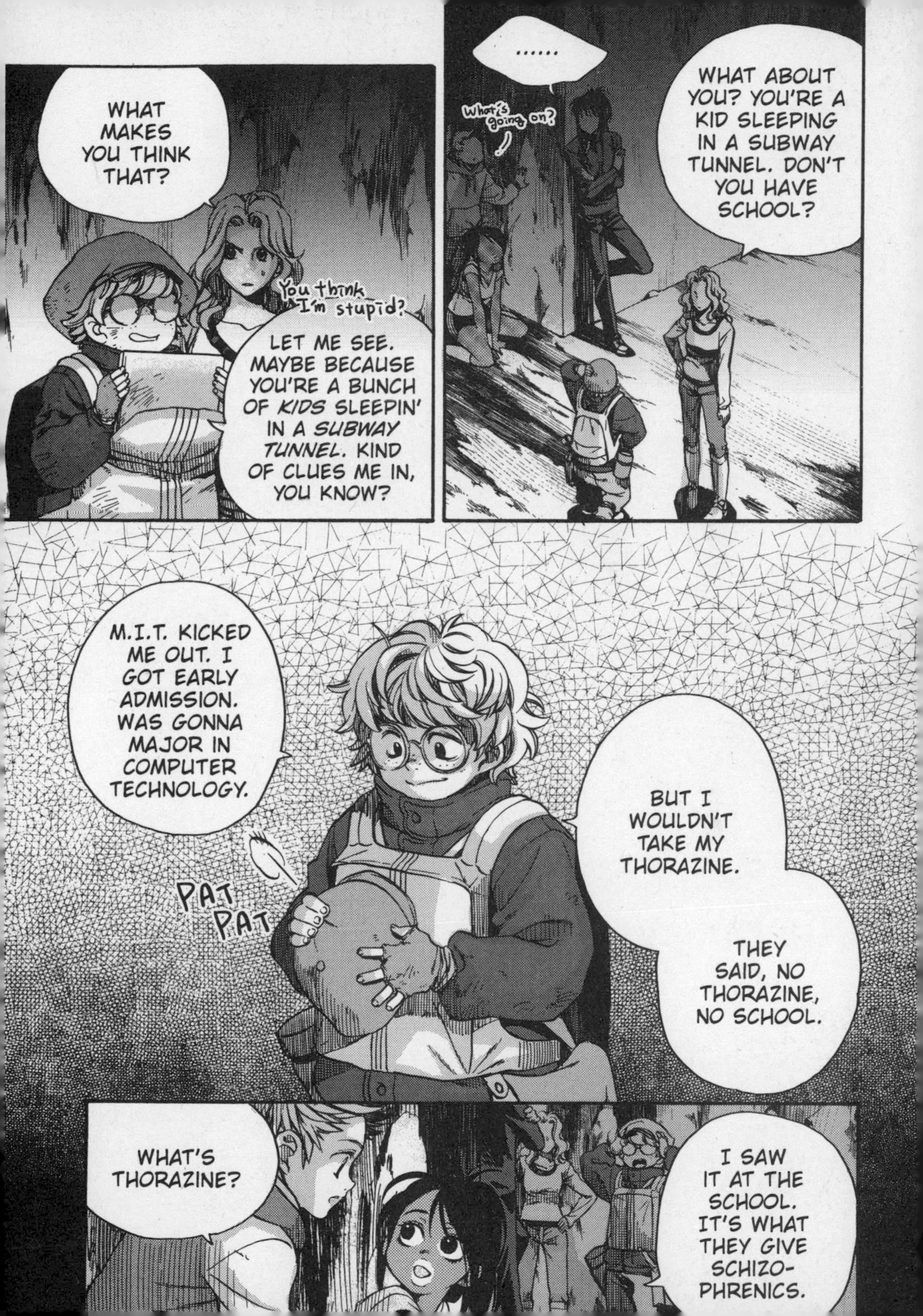
WHAT MAKES YOU THINK THAT?
You think I'm stupid?
LET ME SEE. MAYBE BECAUSE YOU'RE A BUNCH OF KIDS SLEEPIN' IN A SUBWAY TUNNEL. KIND OF CLUES ME IN, YOU KNOW?
......
What's going on?
WHAT ABOUT YOU? YOU'RE A KID SLEEPING IN A SUBWAY TUNNEL. DON'T YOU HAVE SCHOOL?
M.I.T. KICKED ME OUT. I GOT EARLY ADMISSION. WAS GONNA MAJOR IN COMPUTER TECHNOLOGY.
PAT PAT
BUT I WOULDN'T TAKE MY THORAZINE.
THEY SAID, NO THORAZINE, NO SCHOOL.
WHAT'S THORAZINE?
I SAW IT AT THE SCHOOL. IT'S WHAT THEY GIVE SCHIZO-PHRENICS.

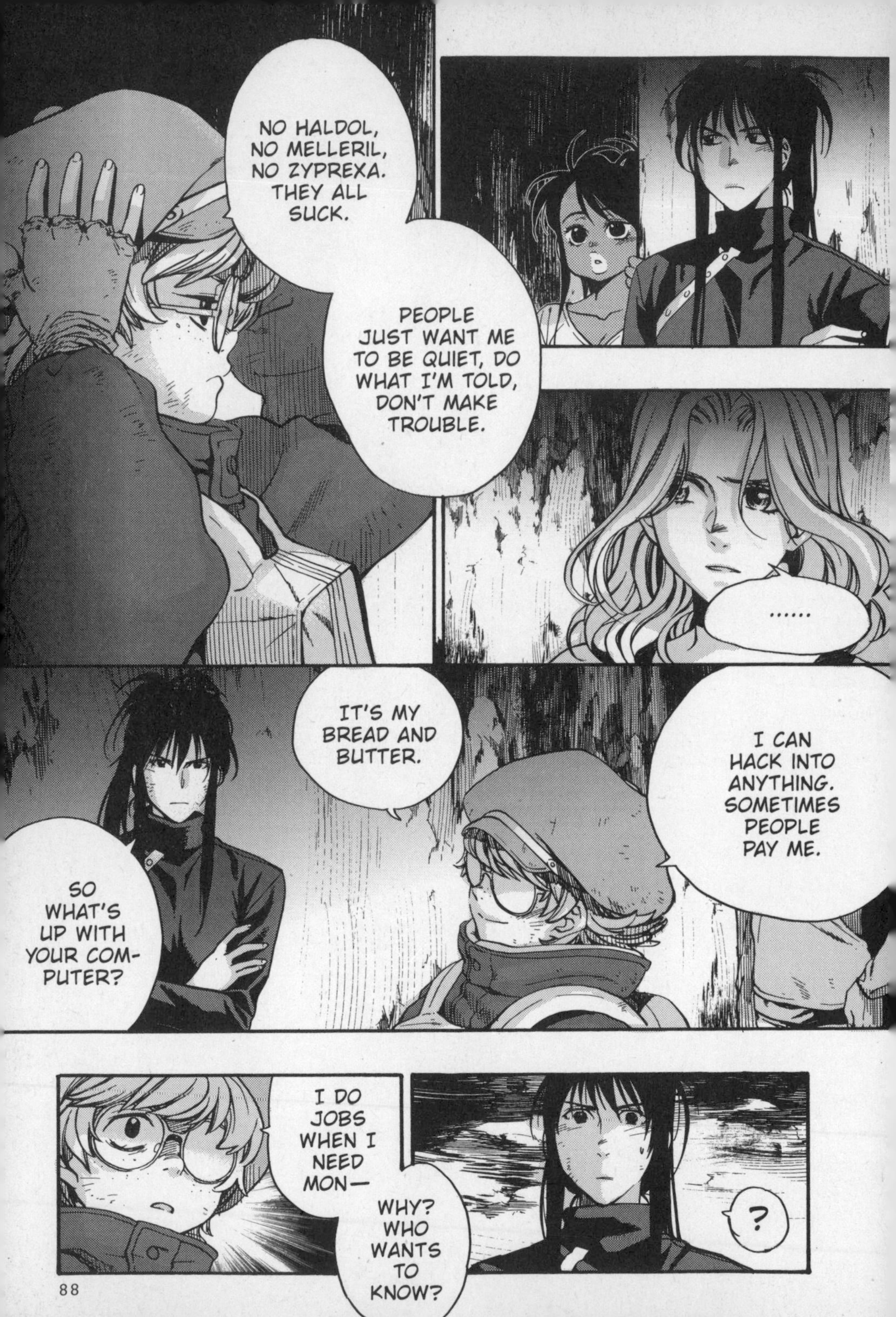
NO HALDOL, NO MELLERIL, NO ZYPREXA. THEY ALL SUCK.
PEOPLE JUST WANT ME TO BE QUIET, DO WHAT I'M TOLD, DON'T MAKE TROUBLE.
......
SO WHAT'S UP WITH YOUR COM-PUTER?
IT'S MY BREAD AND BUTTER.
I CAN HACK INTO ANYTHING. SOMETIMES PEOPLE PAY ME.
I DO JOBS WHEN I NEED MON—
WHY? WHO WANTS TO KNOW?
?

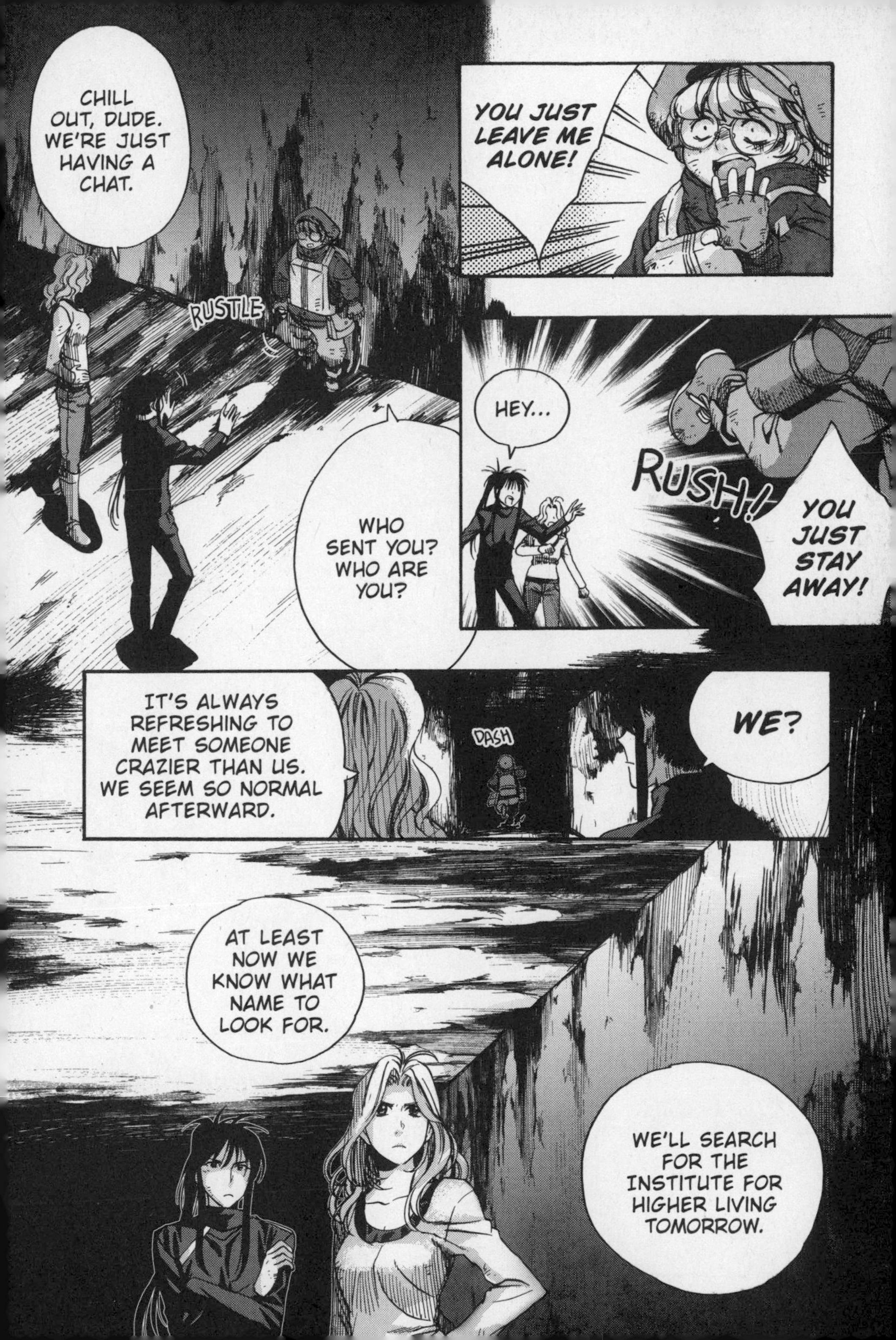
CHILL OUT, DUDE. WE'RE JUST HAVING A CHAT.
RUSTLE
WHO SENT YOU? WHO ARE YOU?
YOU JUST LEAVE ME ALONE!
HEY...
RUSH!
YOU JUST STAY AWAY!
IT'S ALWAYS REFRESHING TO MEET SOMEONE CRAZIER THAN US. WE SEEM SO NORMAL AFTERWARD.
DASH
WE?
AT LEAST NOW WE KNOW WHAT NAME TO LOOK FOR.
WE'LL SEARCH FOR THE INSTITUTE FOR HIGHER LIVING TOMORROW.

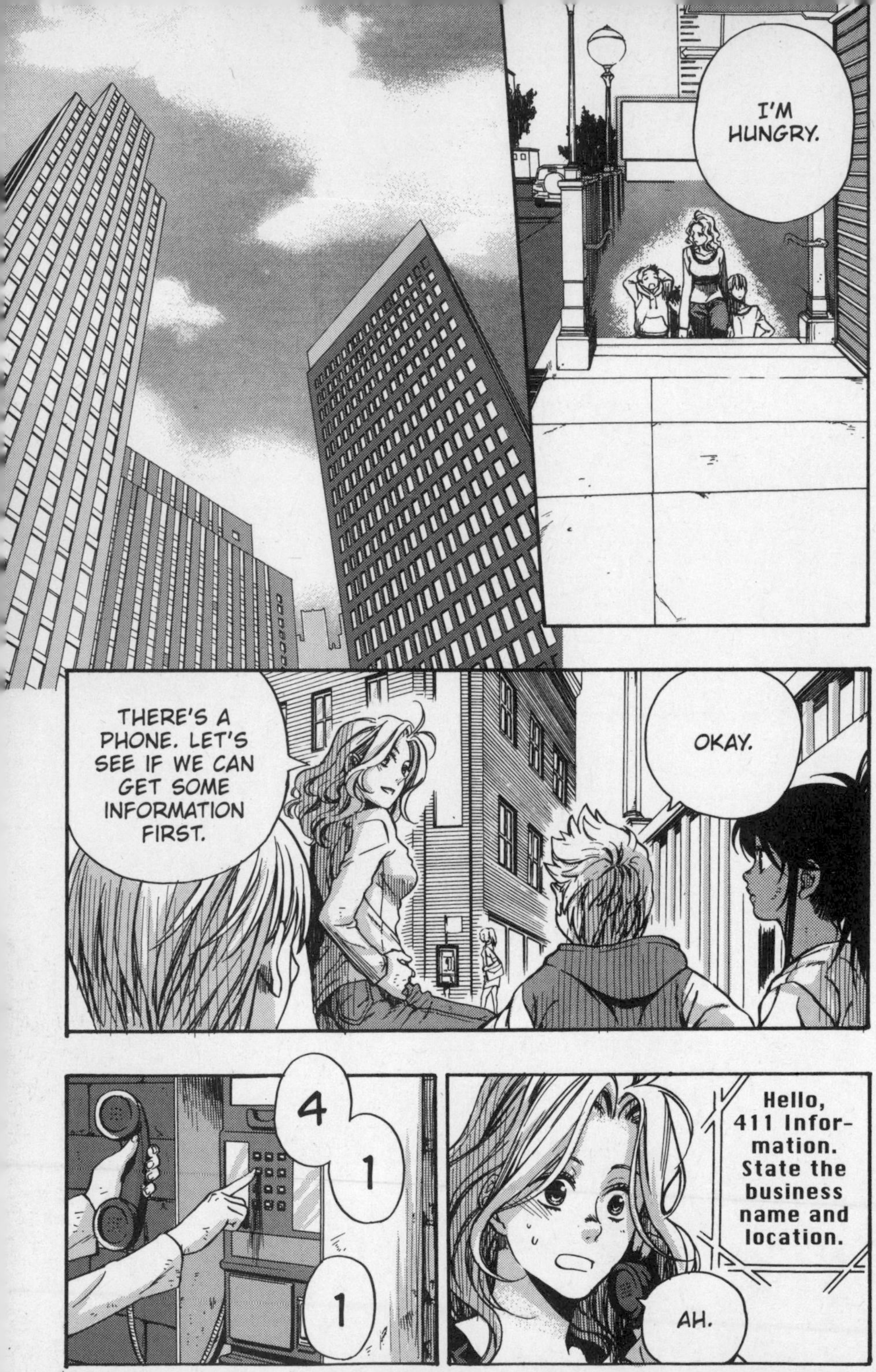
I'M HUNGRY.
THERE'S A PHONE. LET'S SEE IF WE CAN GET SOME INFORMATION FIRST.
OKAY.
4
1
1
Hello, 411 Information. State the business name and location.
AH.

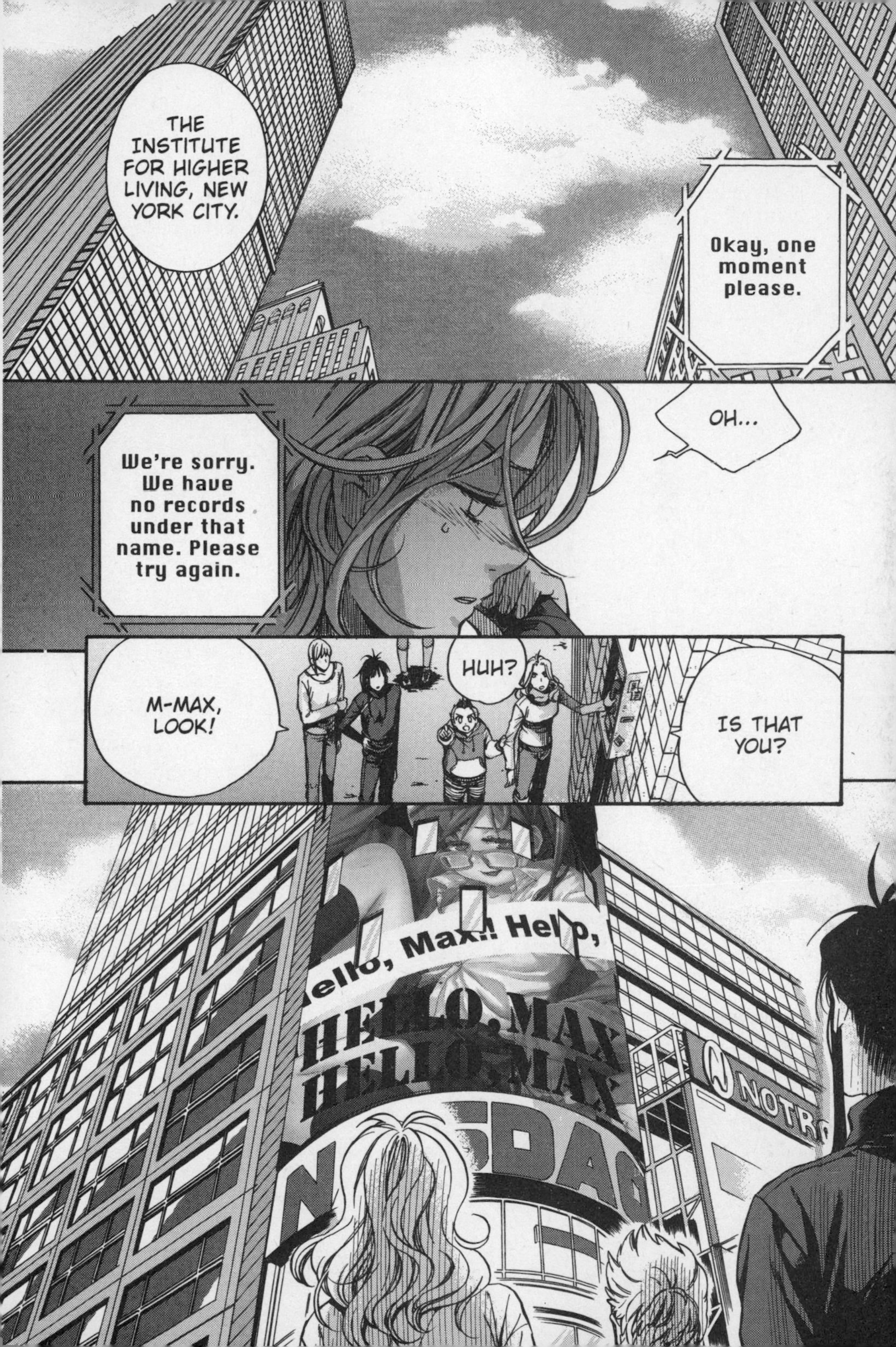
THE INSTITUTE FOR HIGHER LIVING, NEW YORK CITY.
Okay, one moment please.
We're sorry. We have no records under that name. Please try again.
OH...
M-MAX, LOOK!
HUH?
IS THAT YOU?
Hello, Max!! Hello,
HELLO, MAX
HELLO, MAX
NOTRO

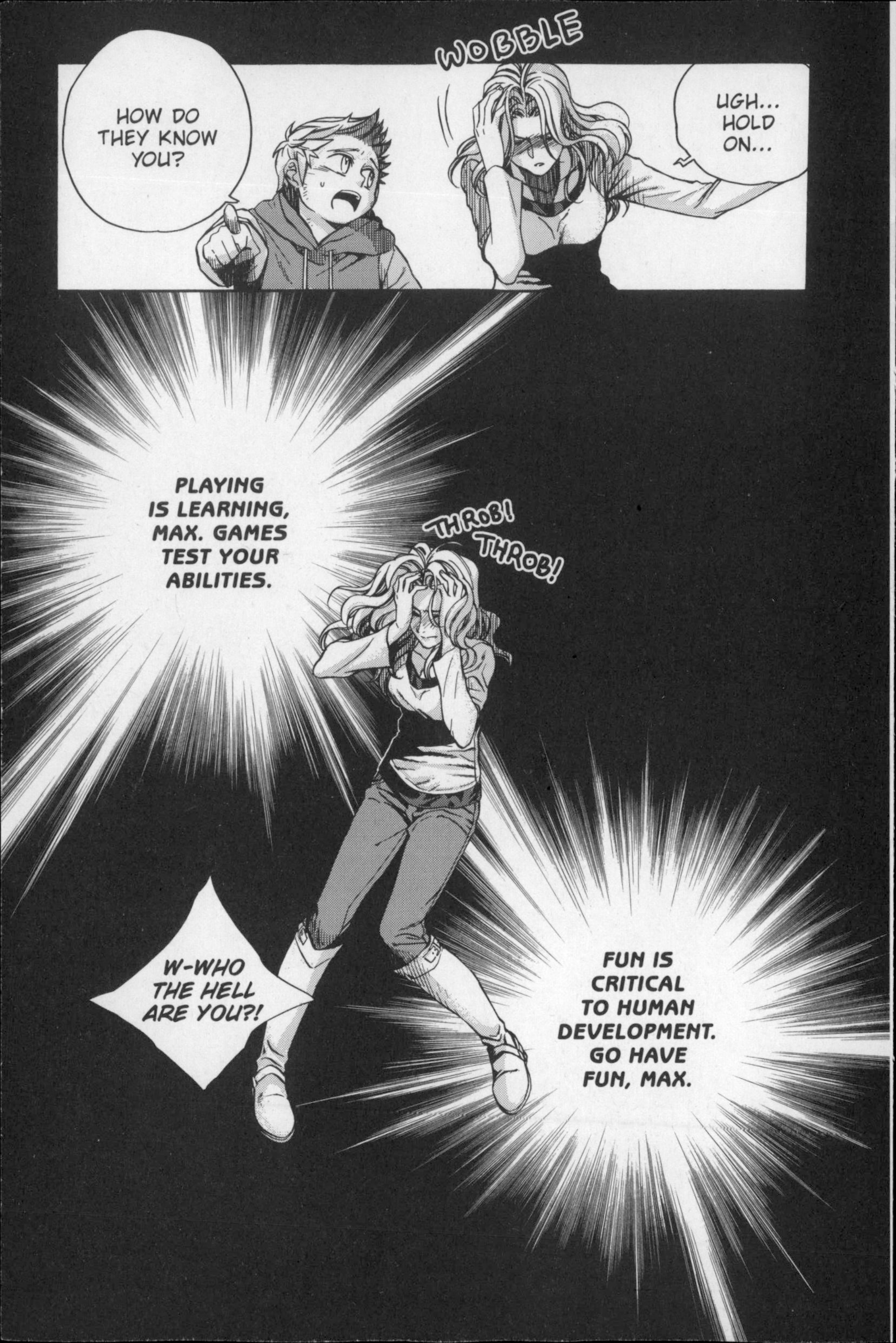
HOW DO THEY KNOW YOU?
WOBBLE
UGH... HOLD ON...
PLAYING IS LEARNING, MAX. GAMES TEST YOUR ABILITIES.
THROB! THROB!
W-WHO THE HELL ARE YOU?!
FUN IS CRITICAL TO HUMAN DEVELOPMENT. GO HAVE FUN, MAX.

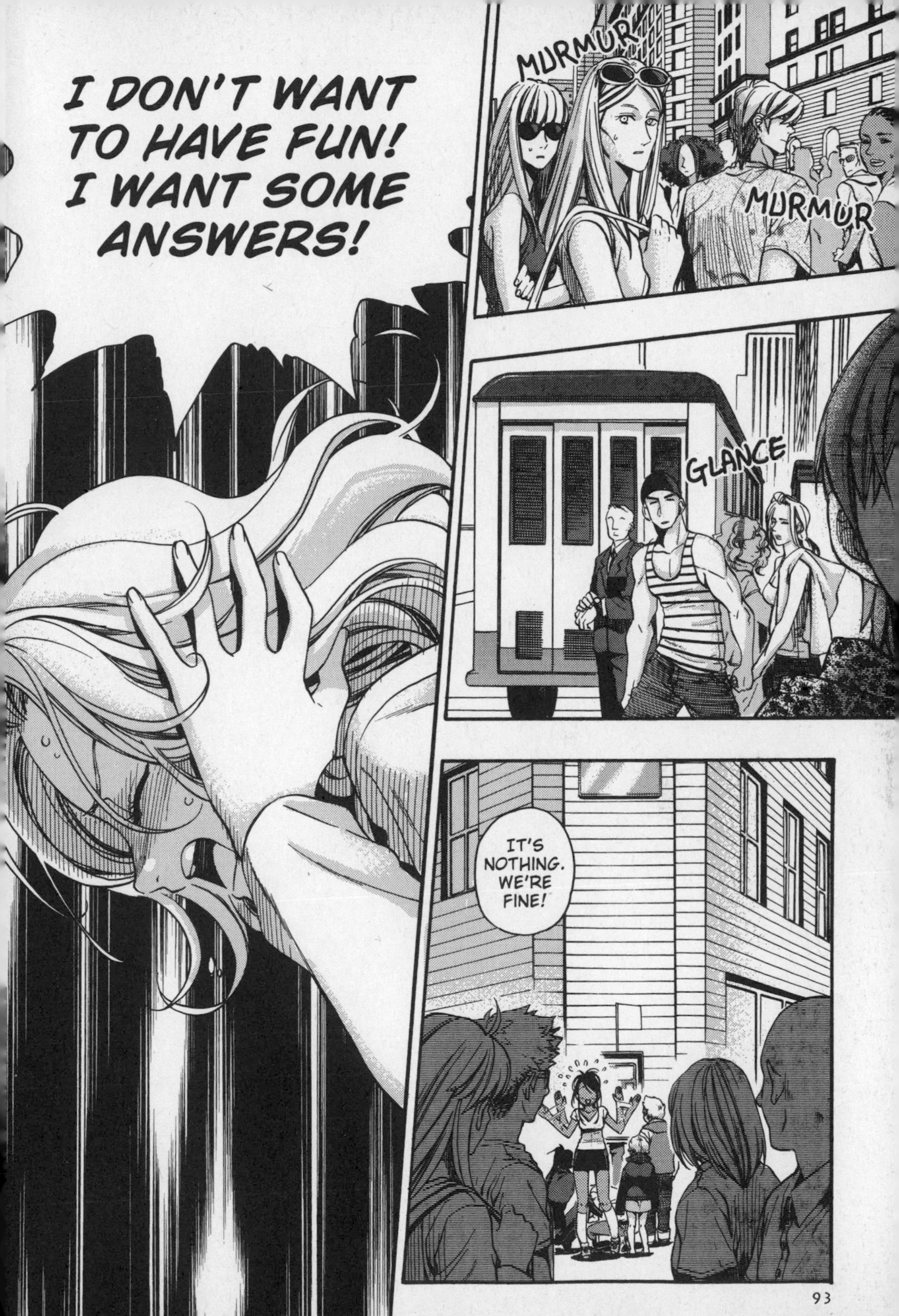
I DON'T WANT TO HAVE FUN! I WANT SOME ANSWERS!
MURMUR
MURMUR
GLANCE
IT'S NOTHING. WE'RE FINE!

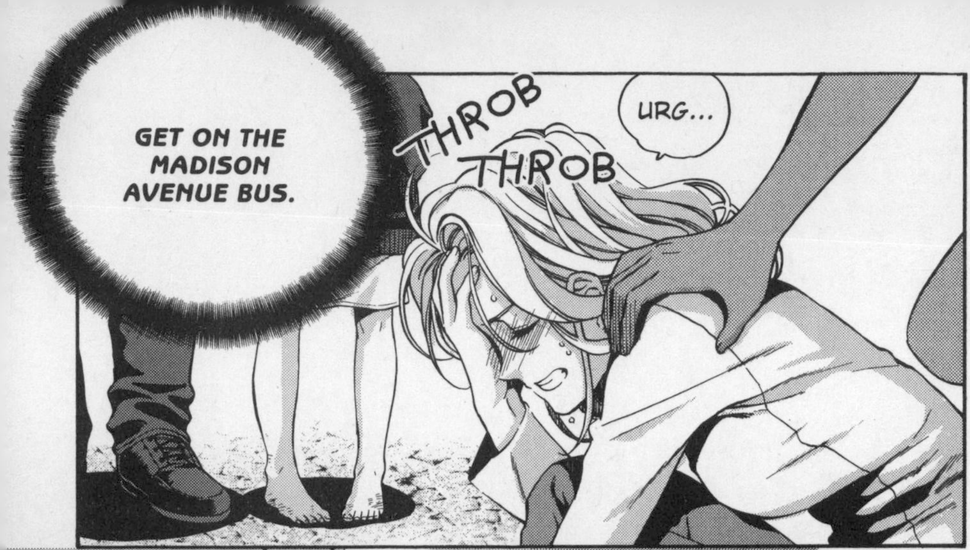
GET ON THE MADISON AVENUE BUS.
THROB
THROB
URG...
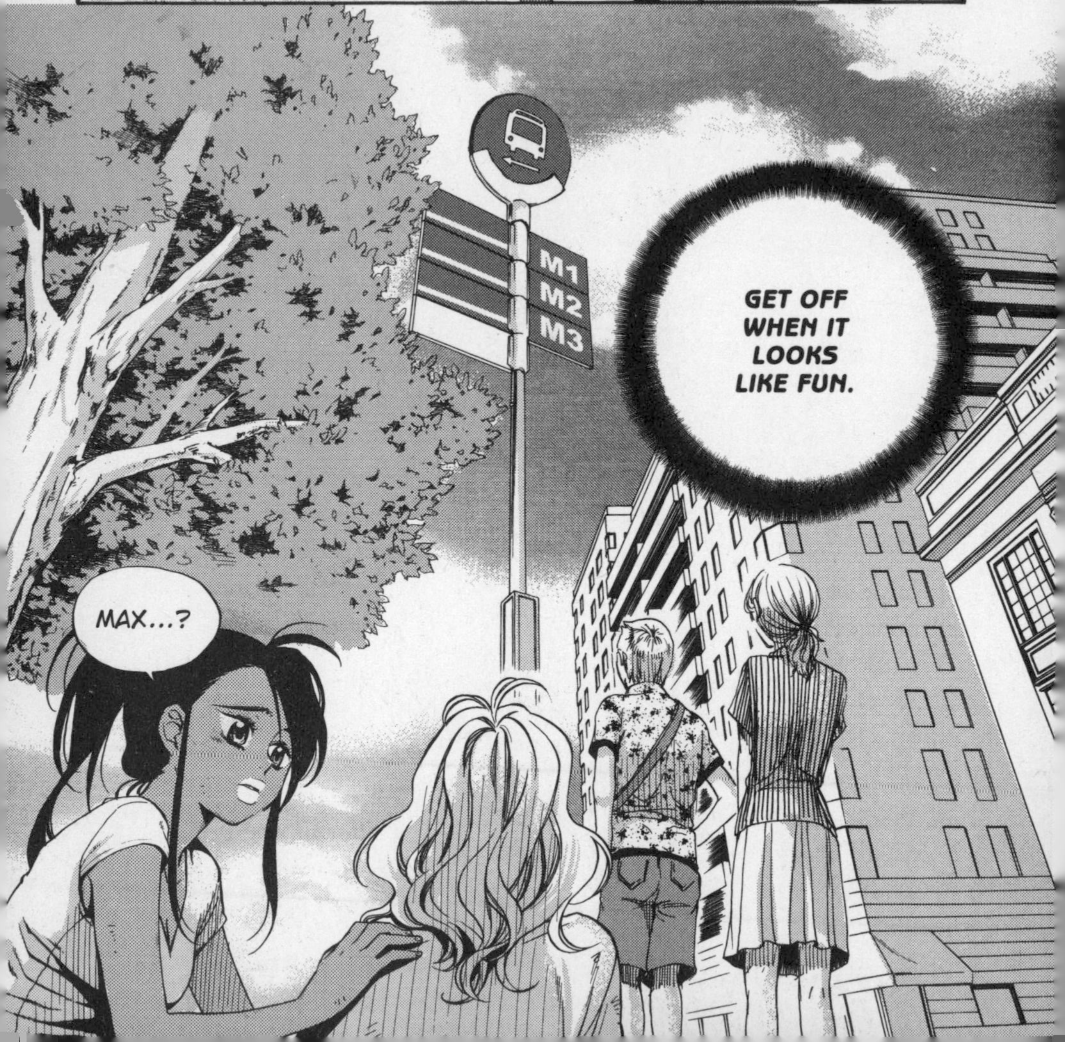
M1
M2
M3
GET OFF WHEN IT LOOKS LIKE FUN.
MAX...?

MAXIMUM RIDE
CHAPTER 11

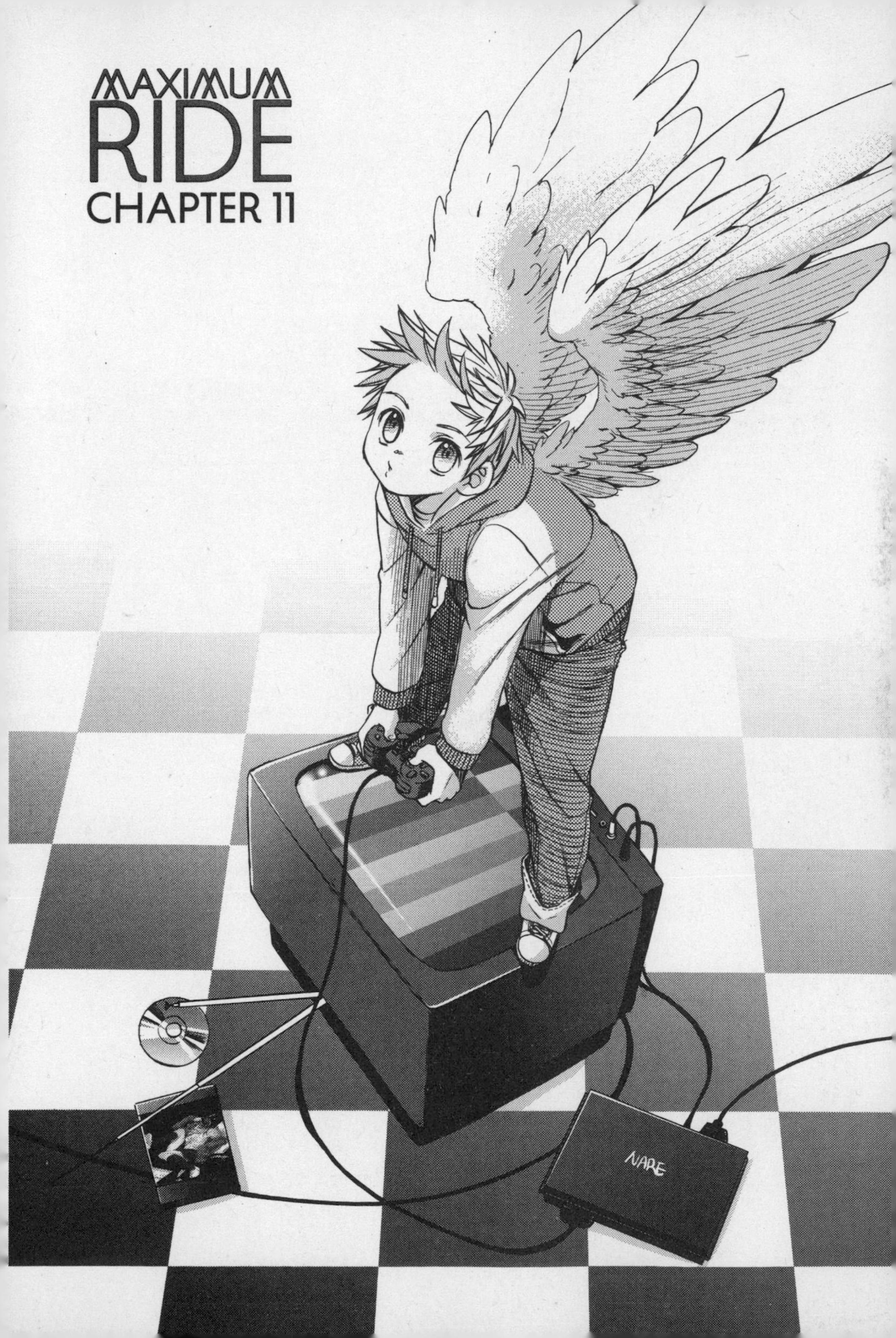
NARE

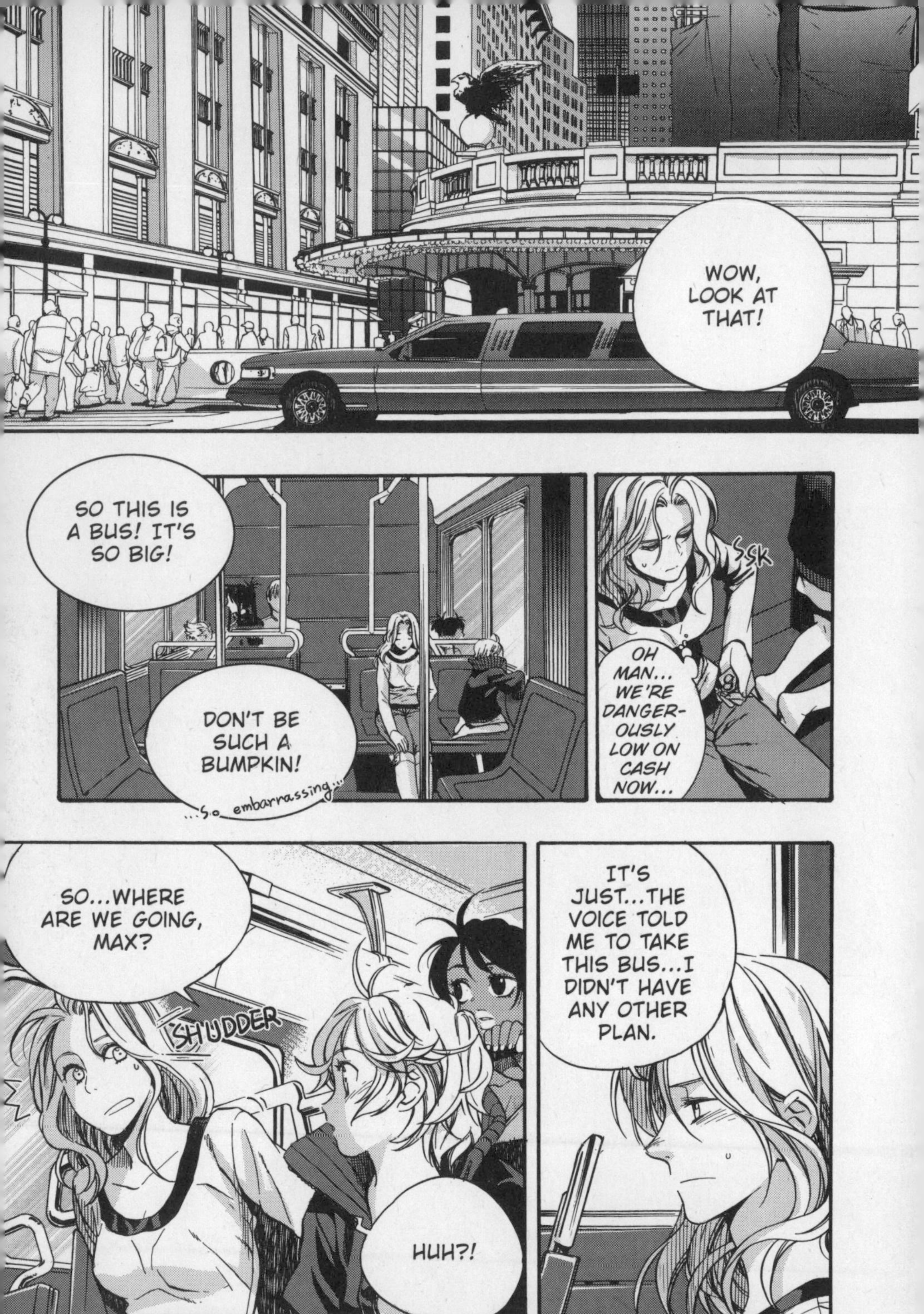
WOW, LOOK AT THAT!
SO THIS IS A BUS! IT'S SO BIG!
DON'T BE SUCH A BUMPKIN!
...So embarrassing...
SSK
OH MAN... WE'RE DANGEROUSLY LOW ON CASH NOW...
SO...WHERE ARE WE GOING, MAX?
SHUDDER
HUH?!
IT'S JUST...THE VOICE TOLD ME TO TAKE THIS BUS...I DIDN'T HAVE ANY OTHER PLAN.

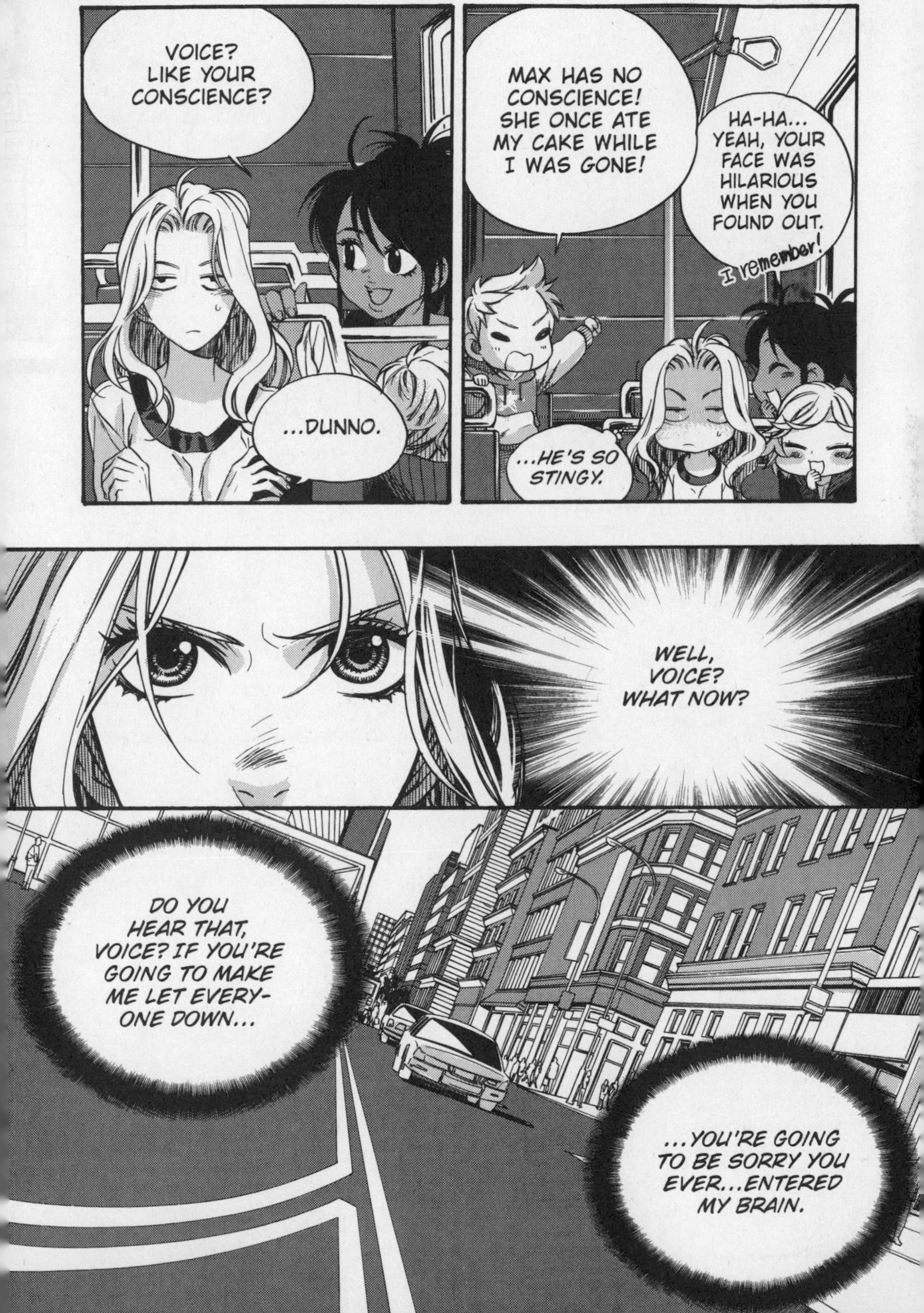
VOICE? LIKE YOUR CONSCIENCE?
...DUNNO.
MAX HAS NO CONSCIENCE! SHE ONCE ATE MY CAKE WHILE I WAS GONE!
HA-HA... YEAH, YOUR FACE WAS HILARIOUS WHEN YOU FOUND OUT.
I remember!
...HE'S SO STINGY.
WELL, VOICE? WHAT NOW?
DO YOU HEAR THAT, VOICE? IF YOU'RE GOING TO MAKE ME LET EVERY-ONE DOWN...
...YOU'RE GOING TO BE SORRY YOU EVER...ENTERED MY BRAIN.

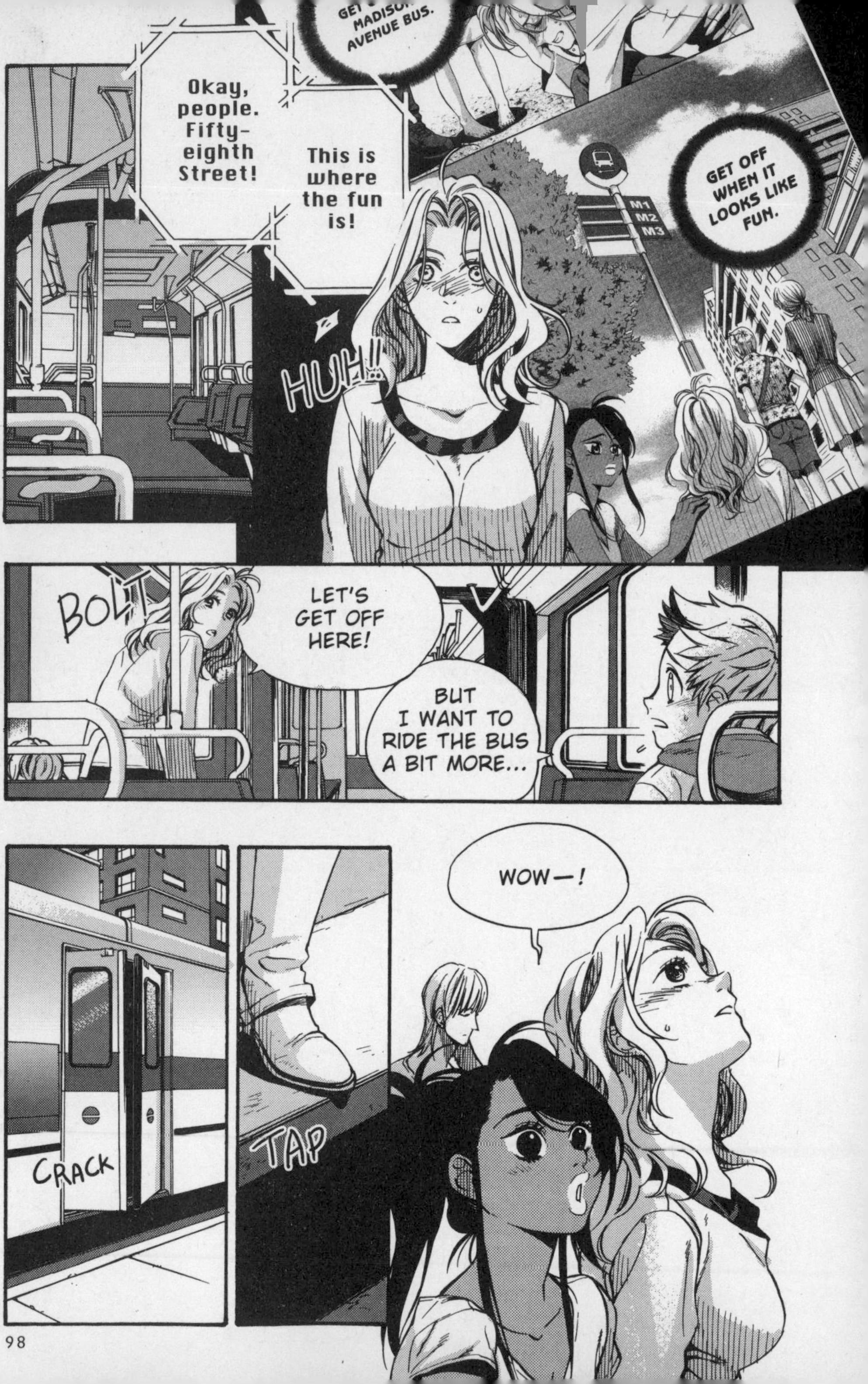
Okay, people. Fifty-eighth Street!
This is where the fun is!
MADISON AVENUE BUS.
HUH!!
GET OFF WHEN IT LOOKS LIKE FUN.
BOLT
LET'S GET OFF HERE!
BUT I WANT TO RIDE THE BUS A BIT MORE...
CRACK
TAP
WOW—!

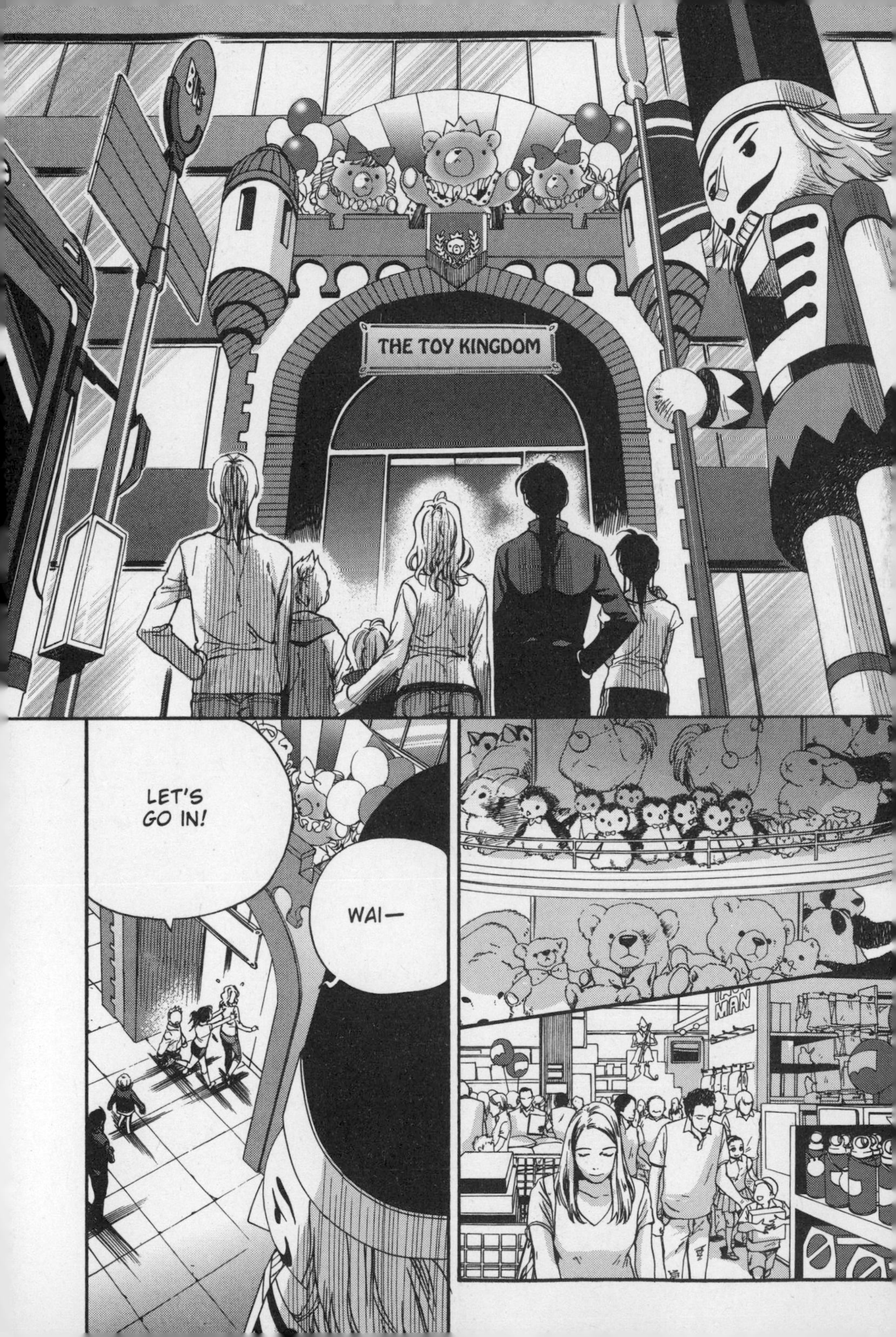
THE TOY KINGDOM
LET'S GO IN!
WAI—

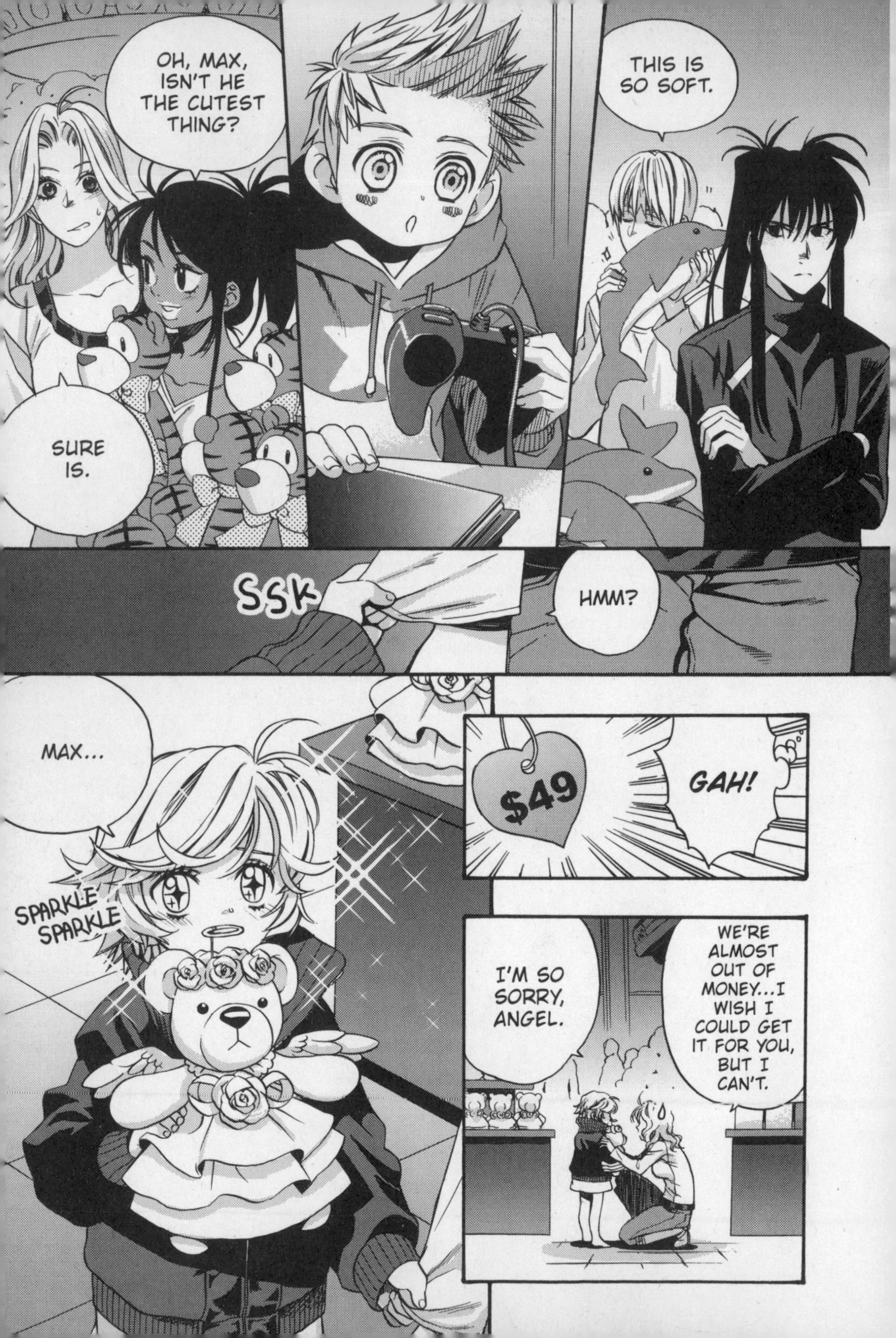
OH, MAX, ISN'T HE THE CUTEST THING?
SURE IS.
THIS IS SO SOFT.
SSK
HMM?
MAX...
SPARKLE SPARKLE
$49
GAH!
I'M SO SORRY, ANGEL.
WE'RE ALMOST OUT OF MONEY...I WISH I COULD GET IT FOR YOU, BUT I CAN'T.

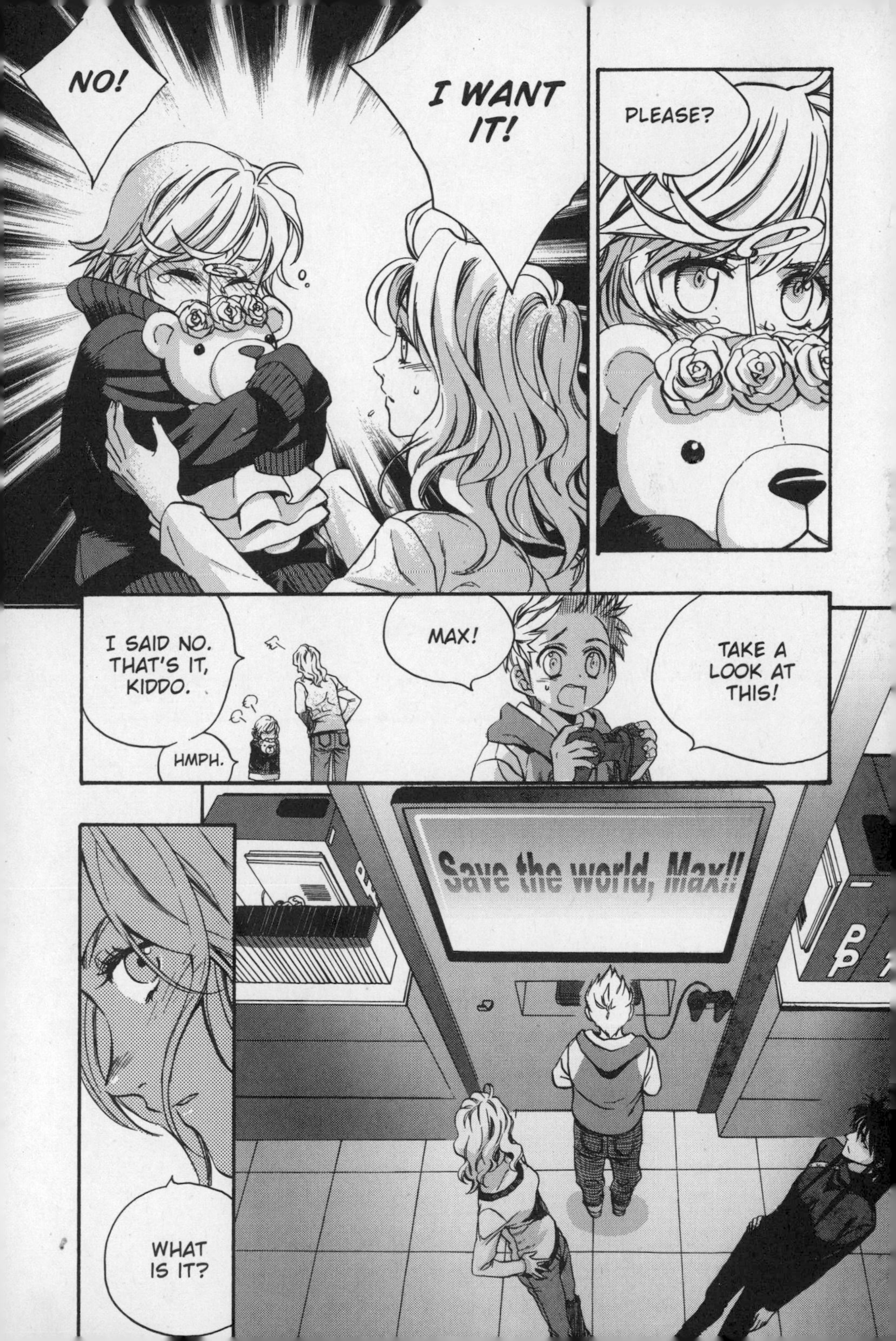
NO!
I WANT IT!
PLEASE?
I SAID NO. THAT'S IT, KIDDO.
HMPH.
MAX!
TAKE A LOOK AT THIS!
WHAT IS IT?
Save the world, Max!!

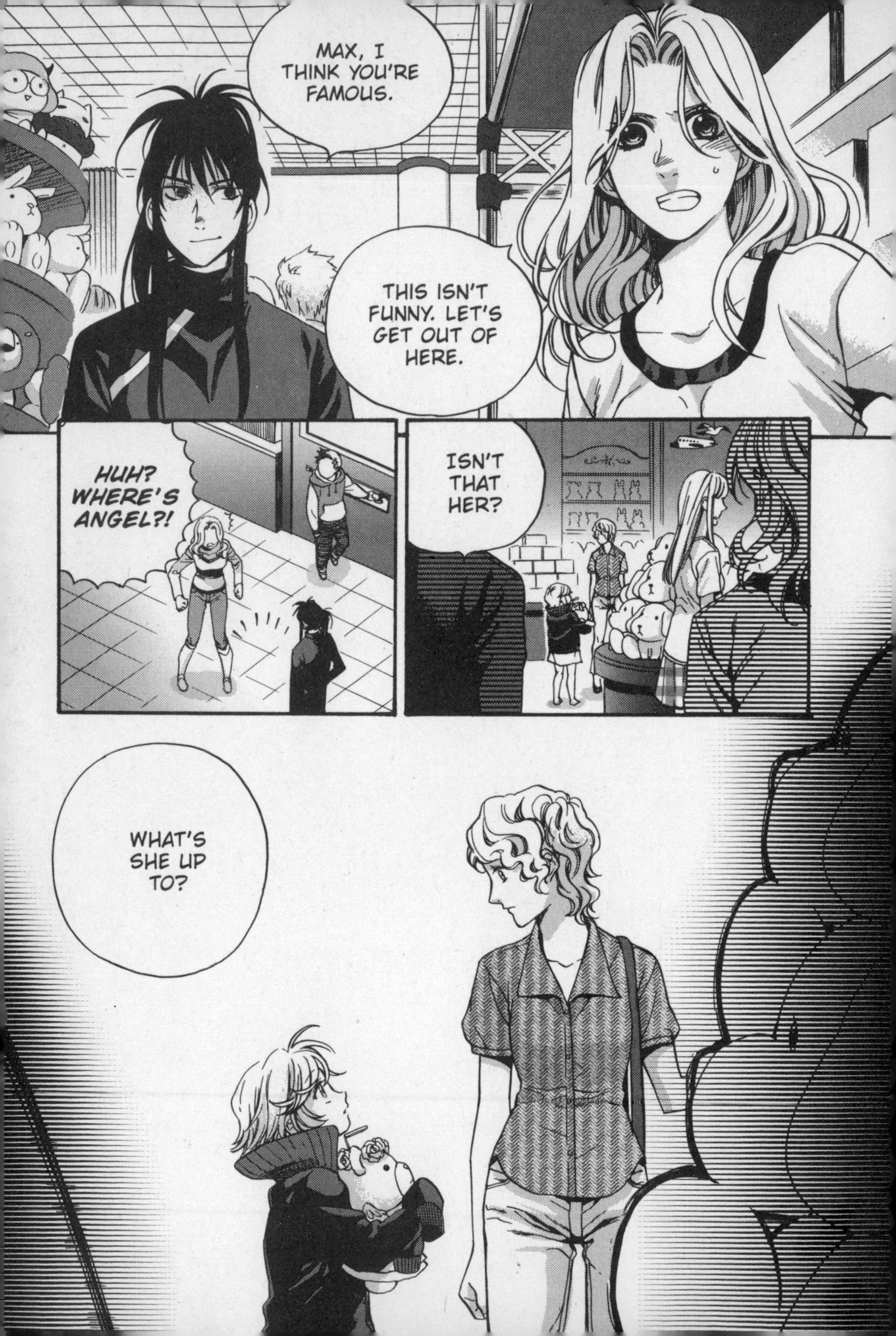
MAX, I THINK YOU'RE FAMOUS.
THIS ISN'T FUNNY. LET'S GET OUT OF HERE.
HUH? WHERE'S ANGEL?!
ISN'T THAT HER?
WHAT'S SHE UP TO?

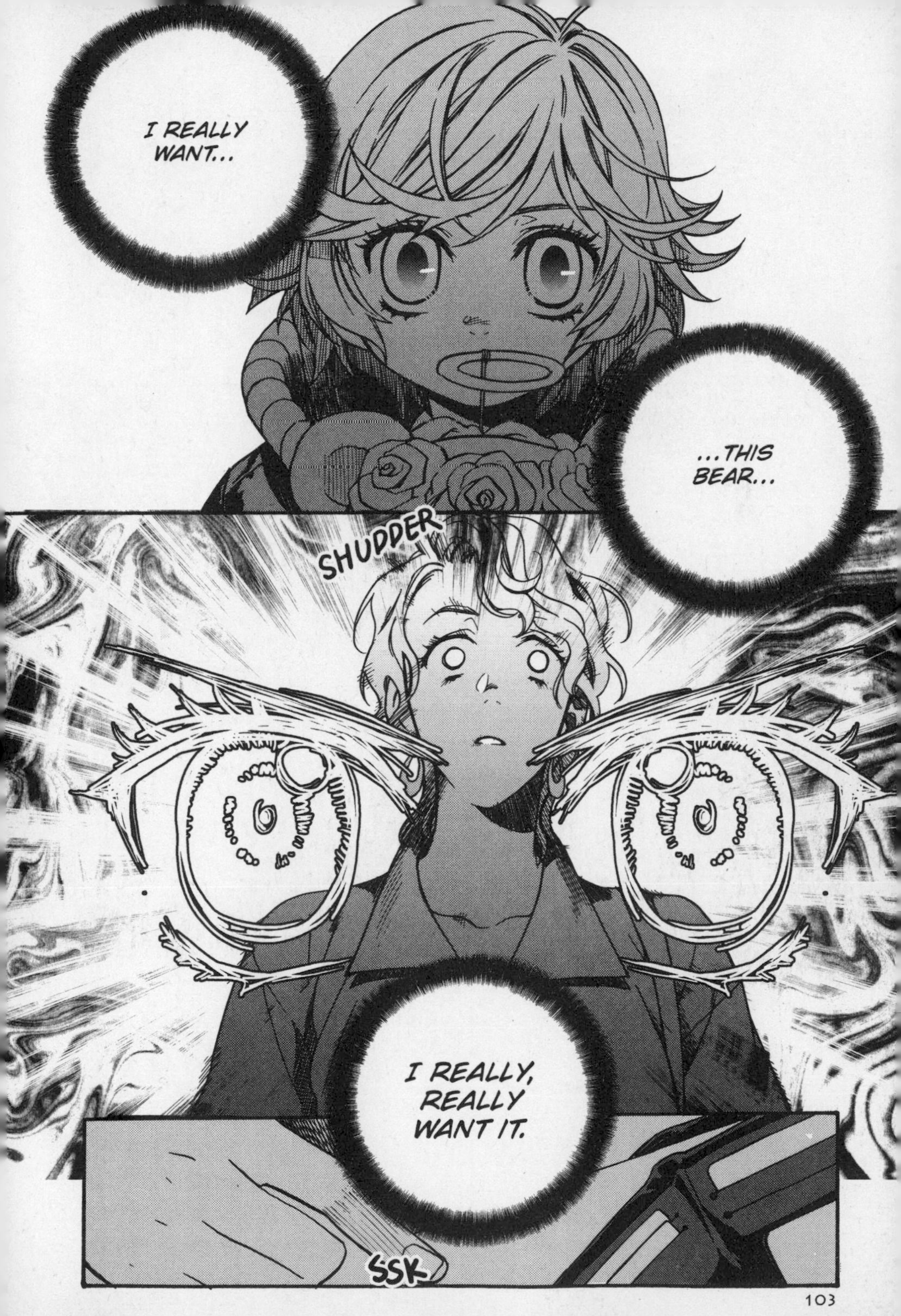
I REALLY WANT...
...THIS BEAR...
SHUDDER
I REALLY, REALLY WANT IT.
SSK

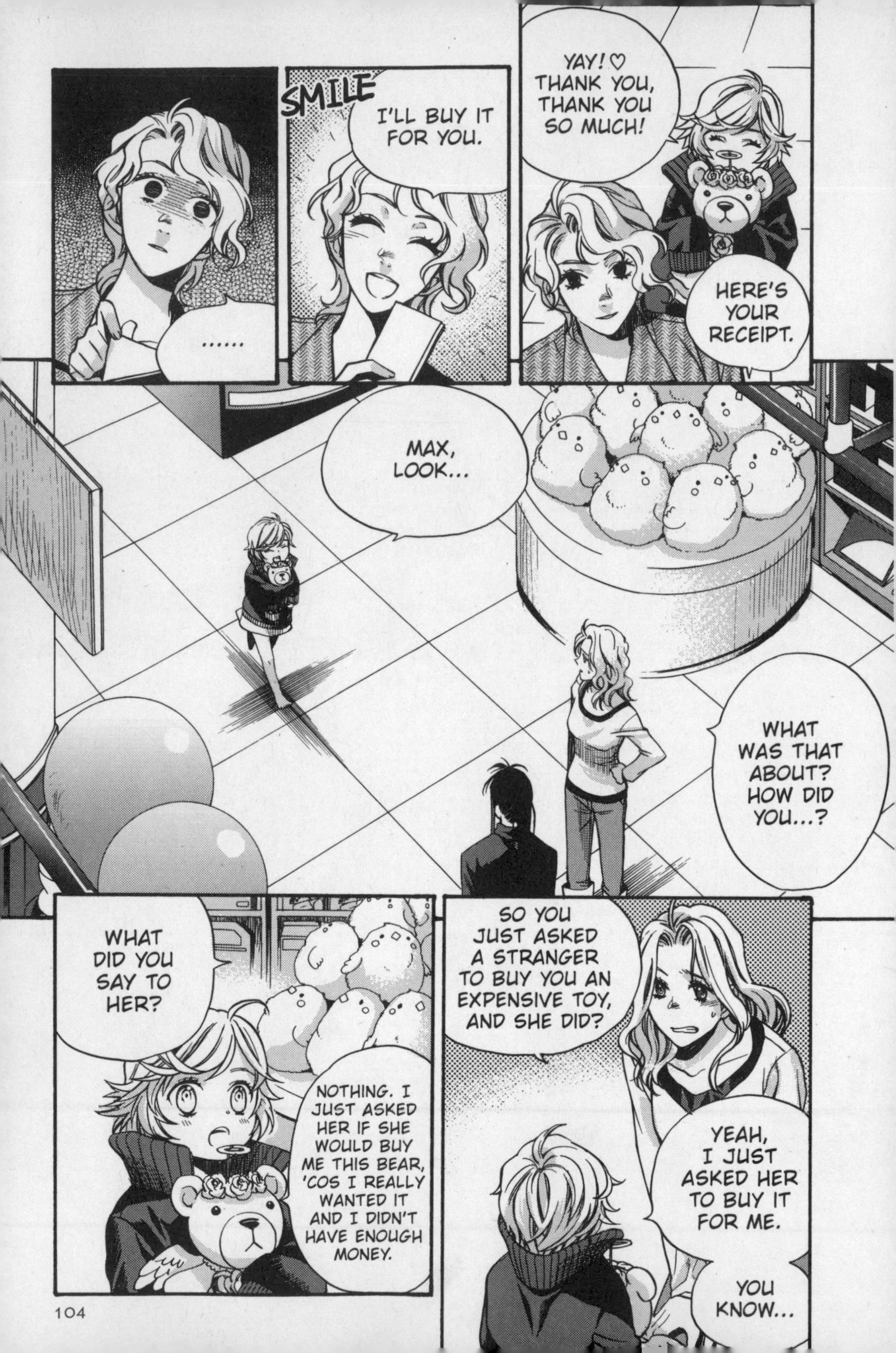
......
SMILE
I'LL BUY IT FOR YOU.
YAY! ♡ THANK YOU, THANK YOU SO MUCH!
HERE'S YOUR RECEIPT.
MAX, LOOK...
WHAT WAS THAT ABOUT? HOW DID YOU...?
WHAT DID YOU SAY TO HER?
NOTHING. I JUST ASKED HER IF SHE WOULD BUY ME THIS BEAR, 'COS I REALLY WANTED IT AND I DIDN'T HAVE ENOUGH MONEY.
SO YOU JUST ASKED A STRANGER TO BUY YOU AN EXPENSIVE TOY, AND SHE DID?
YEAH, I JUST ASKED HER TO BUY IT FOR ME.
YOU KNOW...

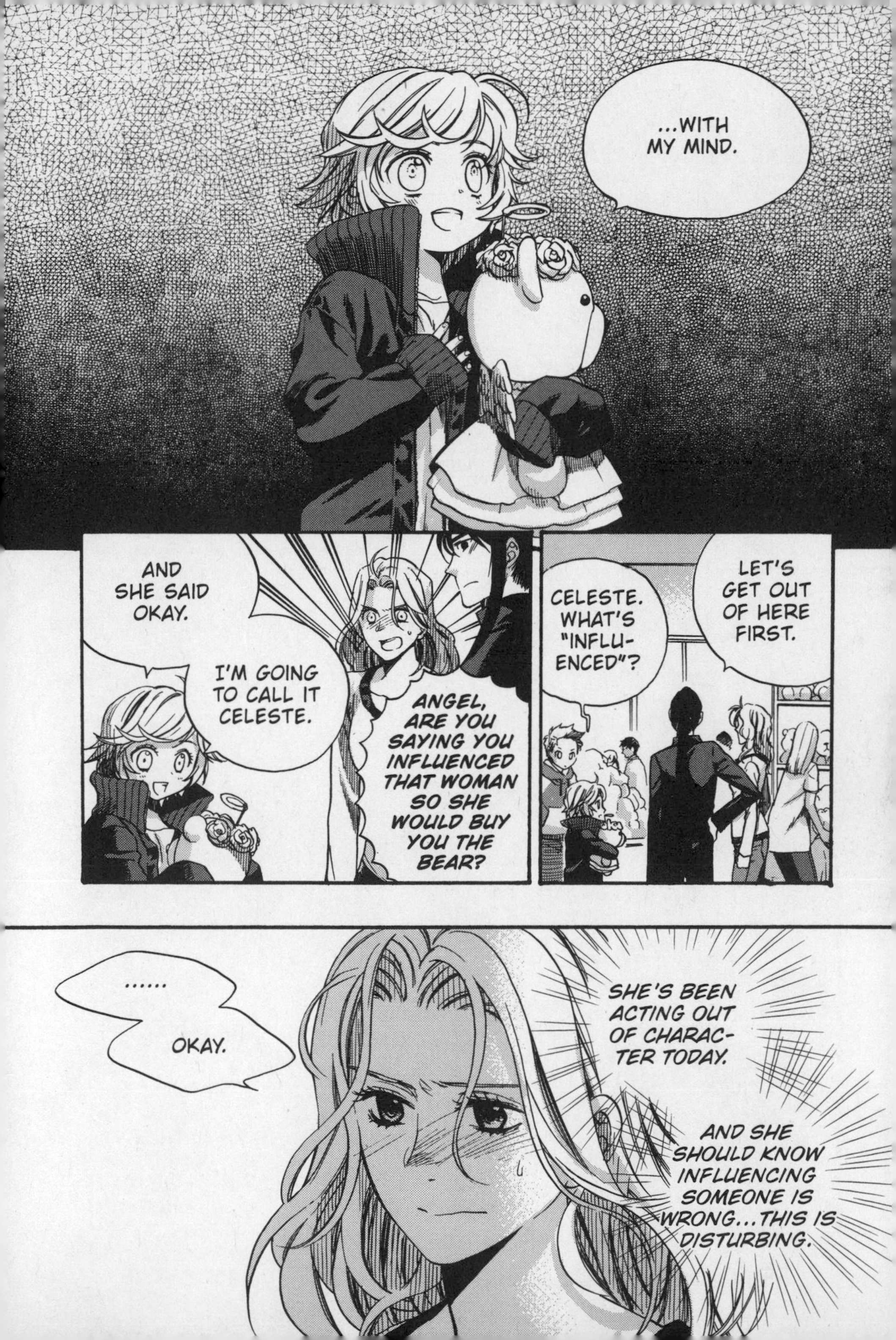
...WITH MY MIND.
AND SHE SAID OKAY.
I'M GOING TO CALL IT CELESTE.
ANGEL, ARE YOU SAYING YOU INFLUENCED THAT WOMAN SO SHE WOULD BUY YOU THE BEAR?
CELESTE. WHAT'S "INFLU-ENCED"?
LET'S GET OUT OF HERE FIRST.
......
OKAY.
SHE'S BEEN ACTING OUT OF CHARAC-TER TODAY.
AND SHE SHOULD KNOW INFLUENCING SOMEONE IS WRONG...THIS IS DISTURBING.

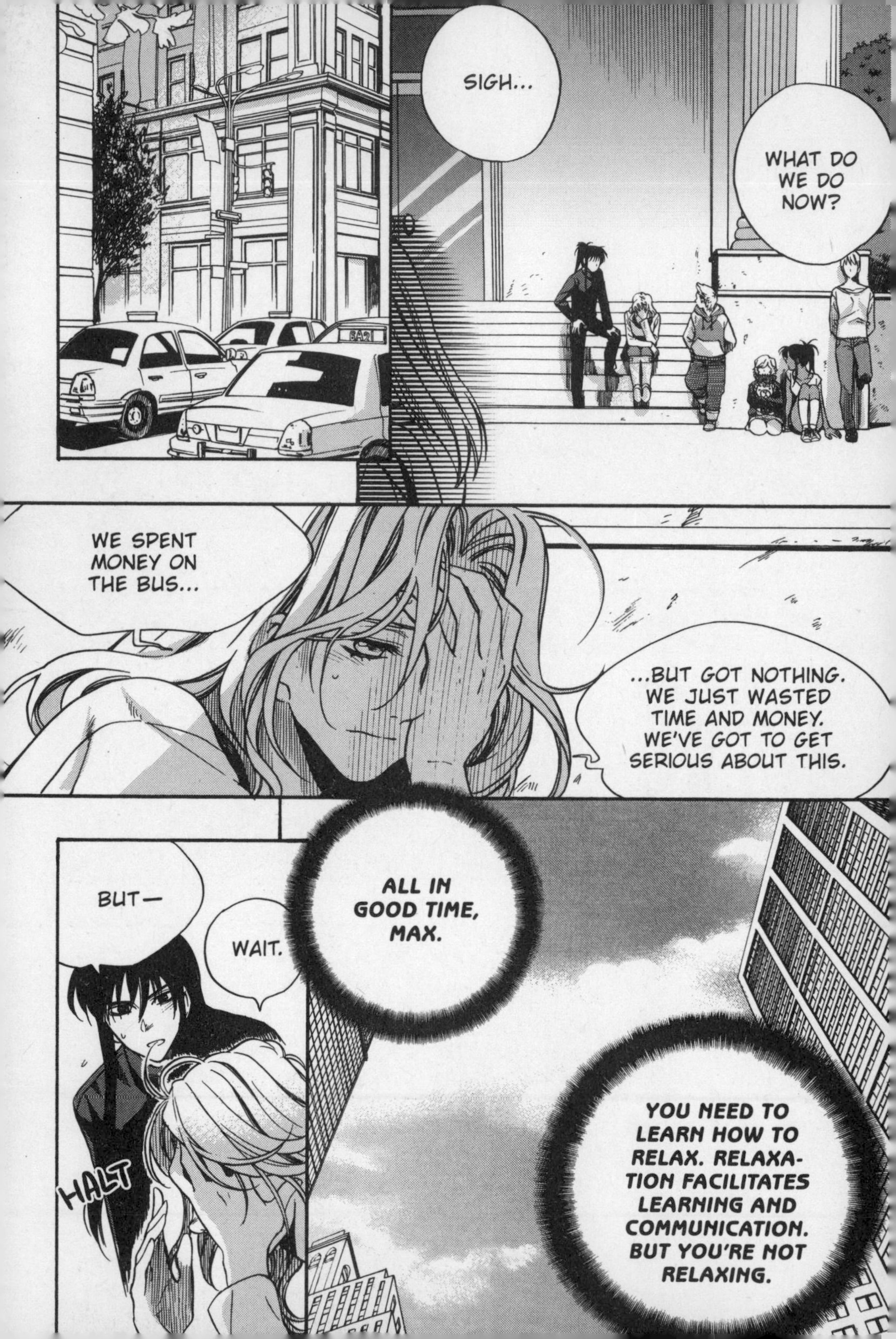
SIGH...
WHAT DO WE DO NOW?
WE SPENT MONEY ON THE BUS...
...BUT GOT NOTHING. WE JUST WASTED TIME AND MONEY. WE'VE GOT TO GET SERIOUS ABOUT THIS.
BUT—
WAIT.
HALT
ALL IN GOOD TIME, MAX.
YOU NEED TO LEARN HOW TO RELAX. RELAXA-TION FACILITATES LEARNING AND COMMUNICATION. BUT YOU'RE NOT RELAXING.

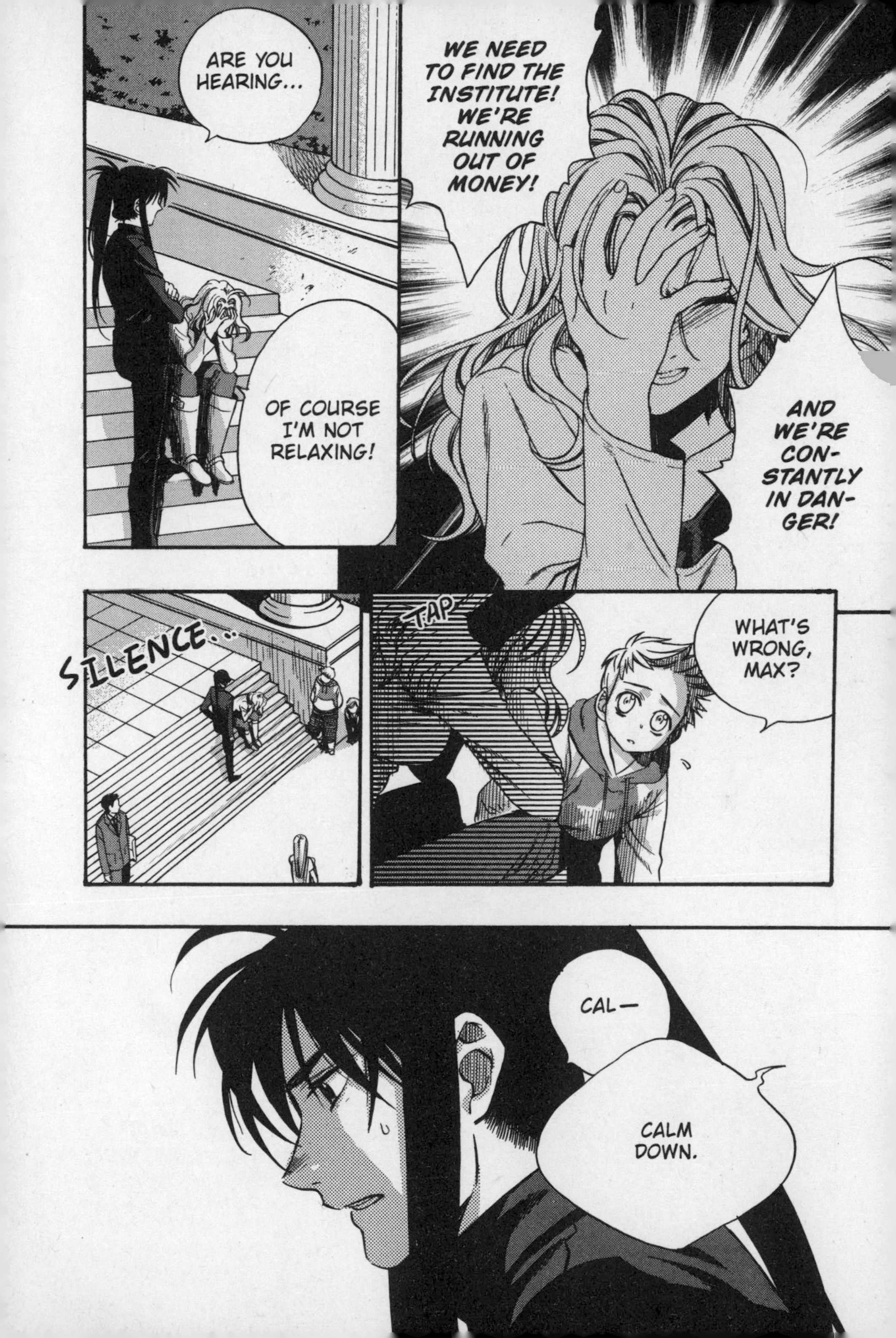
ARE YOU HEARING...
OF COURSE I'M NOT RELAXING!
WE NEED TO FIND THE INSTITUTE! WE'RE RUNNING OUT OF MONEY!
AND WE'RE CON-STANTLY IN DAN-GER!
SILENCE...
TAP
WHAT'S WRONG, MAX?
CAL—
CALM DOWN.

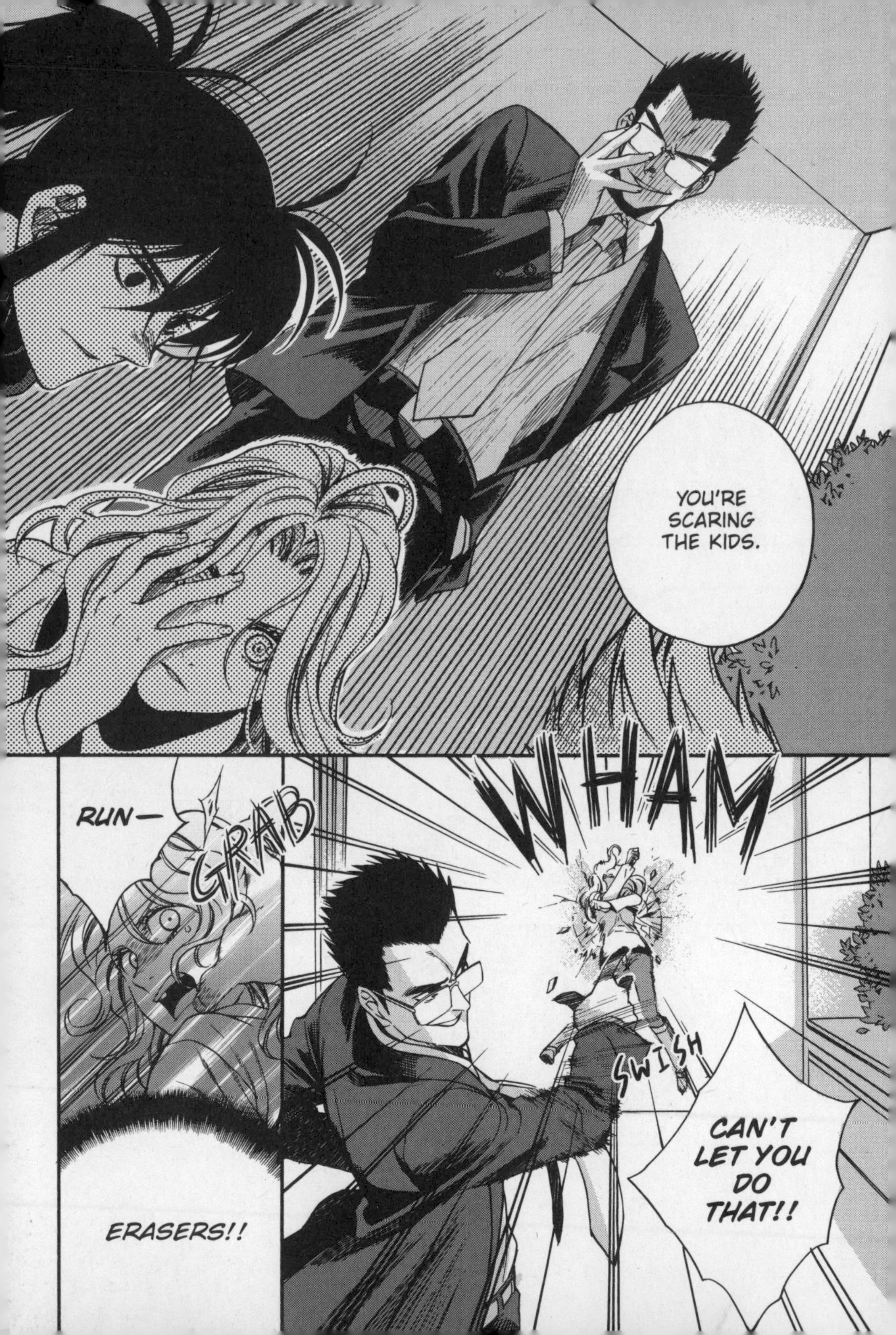
YOU'RE SCARING THE KIDS.
RUN—
GRAB
ERASERS!!
WHAM
SWISH
CAN'T LET YOU DO THAT!!

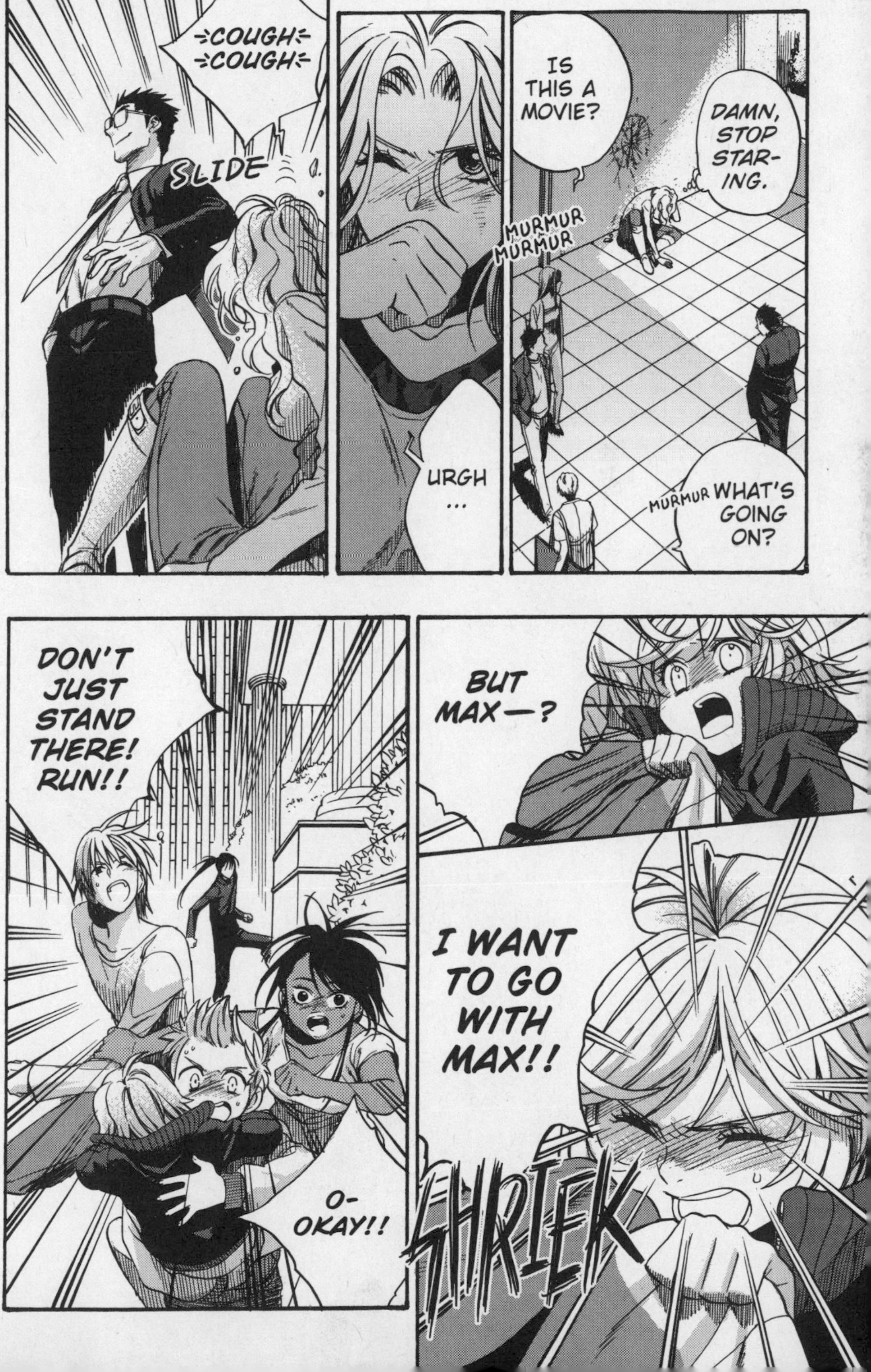

COUGH COUGH
SLIDE
URGH ...
IS THIS A MOVIE?
DAMN, STOP STARING.
MURMUR MURMUR
MURMUR
WHAT'S GOING ON?
DON'T JUST STAND THERE! RUN!!
O-OKAY!!
BUT MAX—?
I WANT TO GO WITH MAX!!
SHRIEK

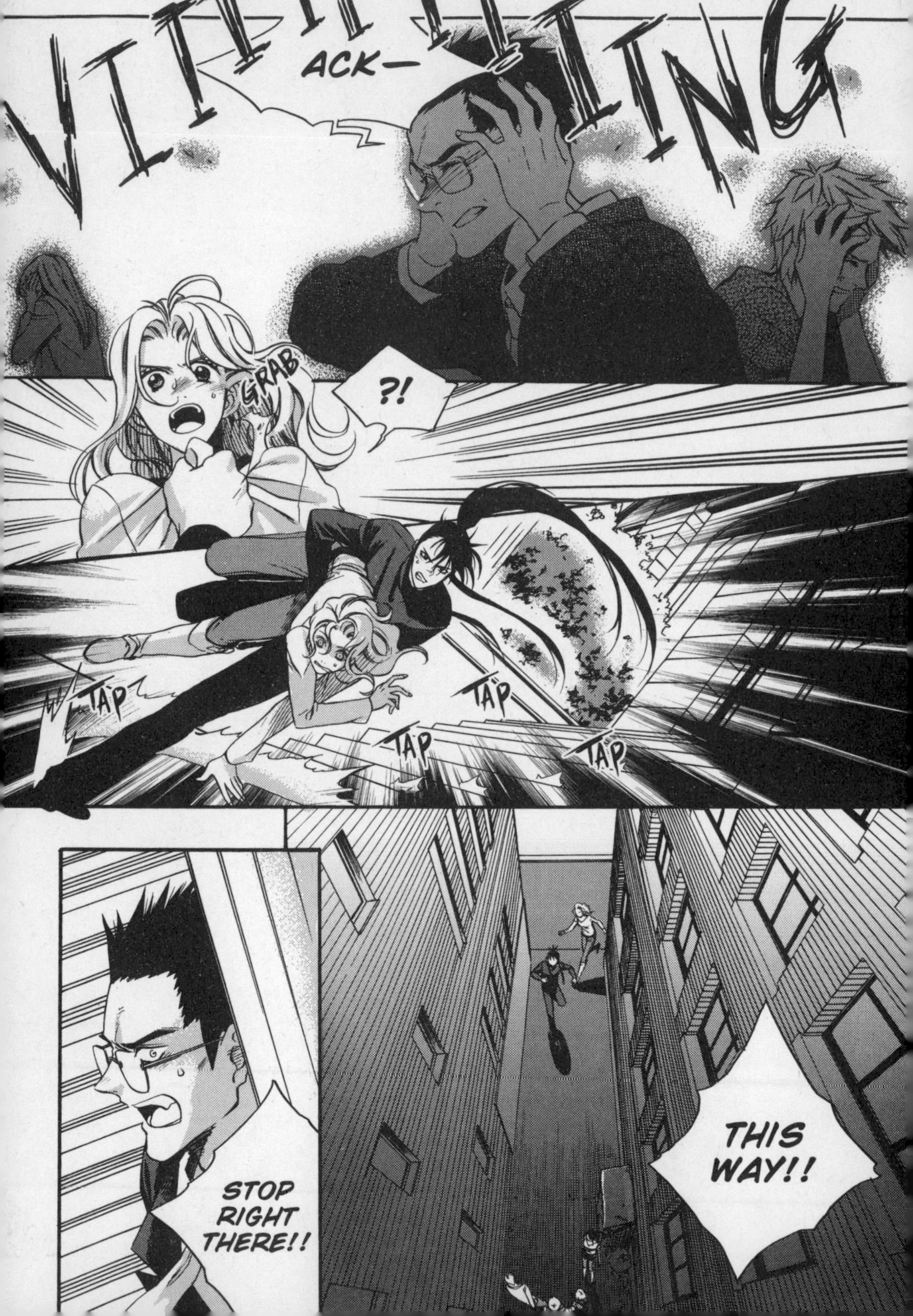
VIIIIIIIING
ACK—
GRAB
?!
TAP
TAP
TAP
TAP
STOP RIGHT THERE!!
THIS WAY!!

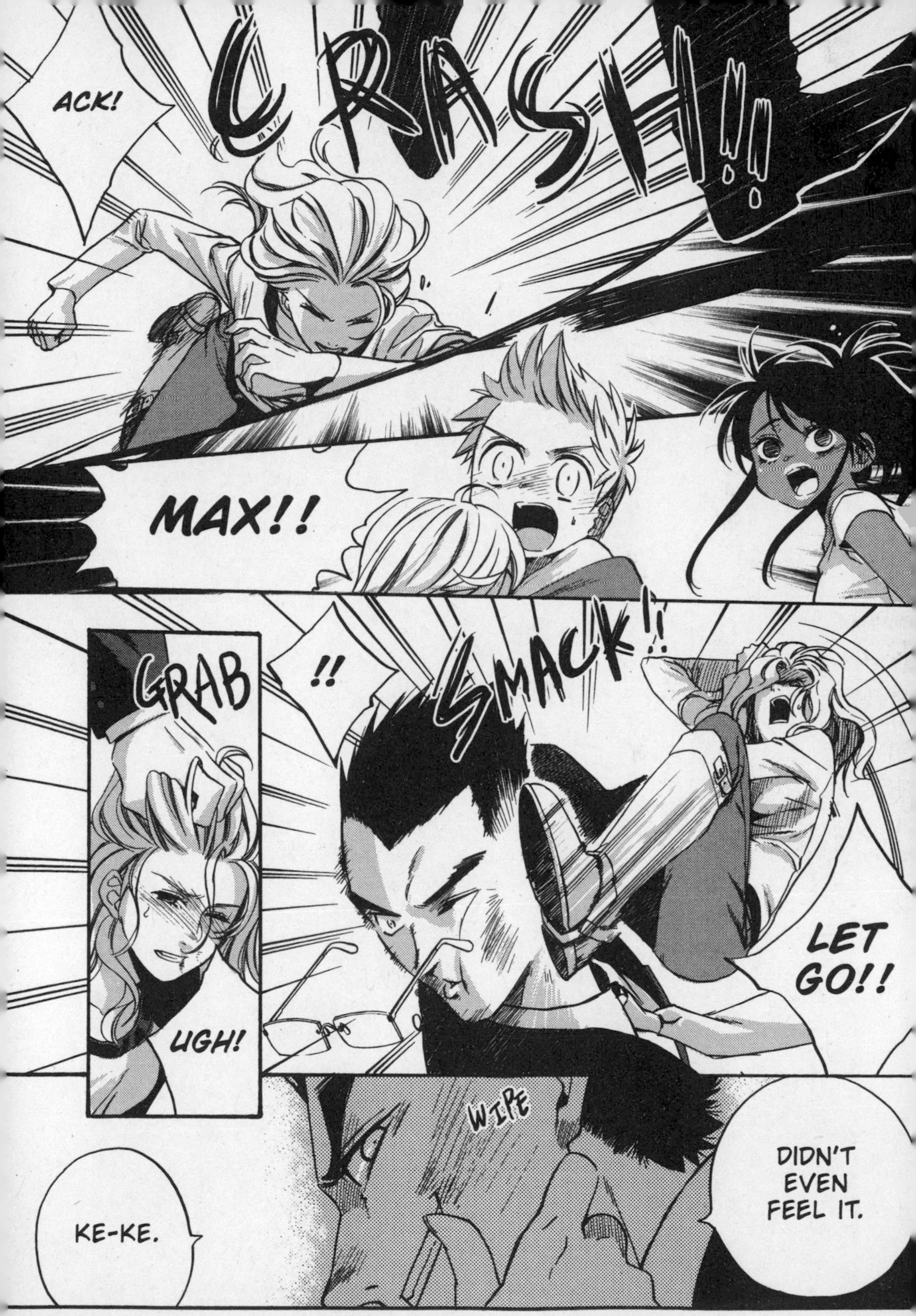
ACK!
CRASH!!
MAX!!
GRAB
!!
SMACK!!
UGH!
LET GO!!
WIPE
KE-KE.
DIDN'T EVEN FEEL IT.

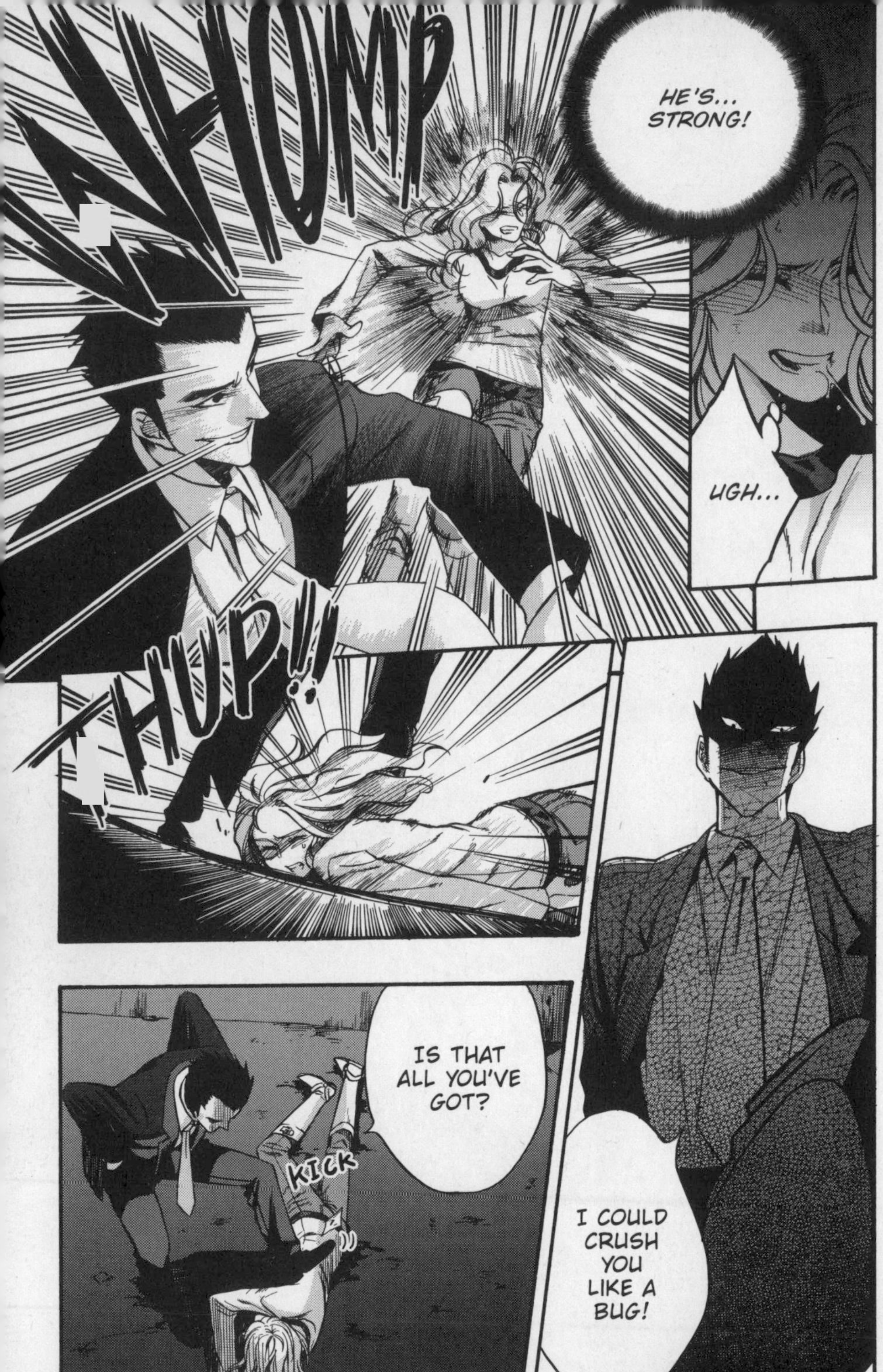
WHUMP
HE'S... STRONG!
UGH...
THUP!!
IS THAT ALL YOU'VE GOT?
KICK
I COULD CRUSH YOU LIKE A BUG!

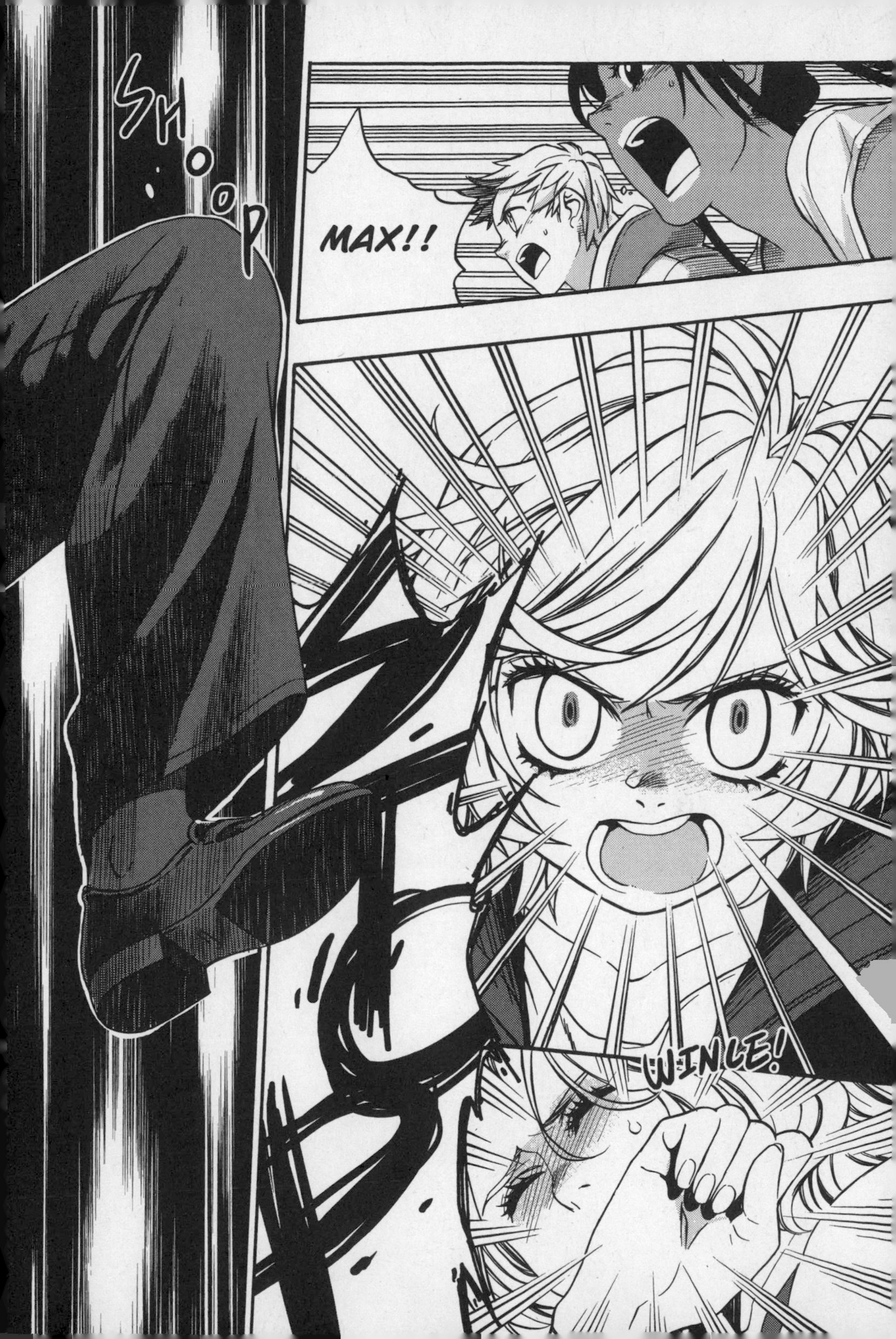
MAX!!
SHOOP
WINCE!

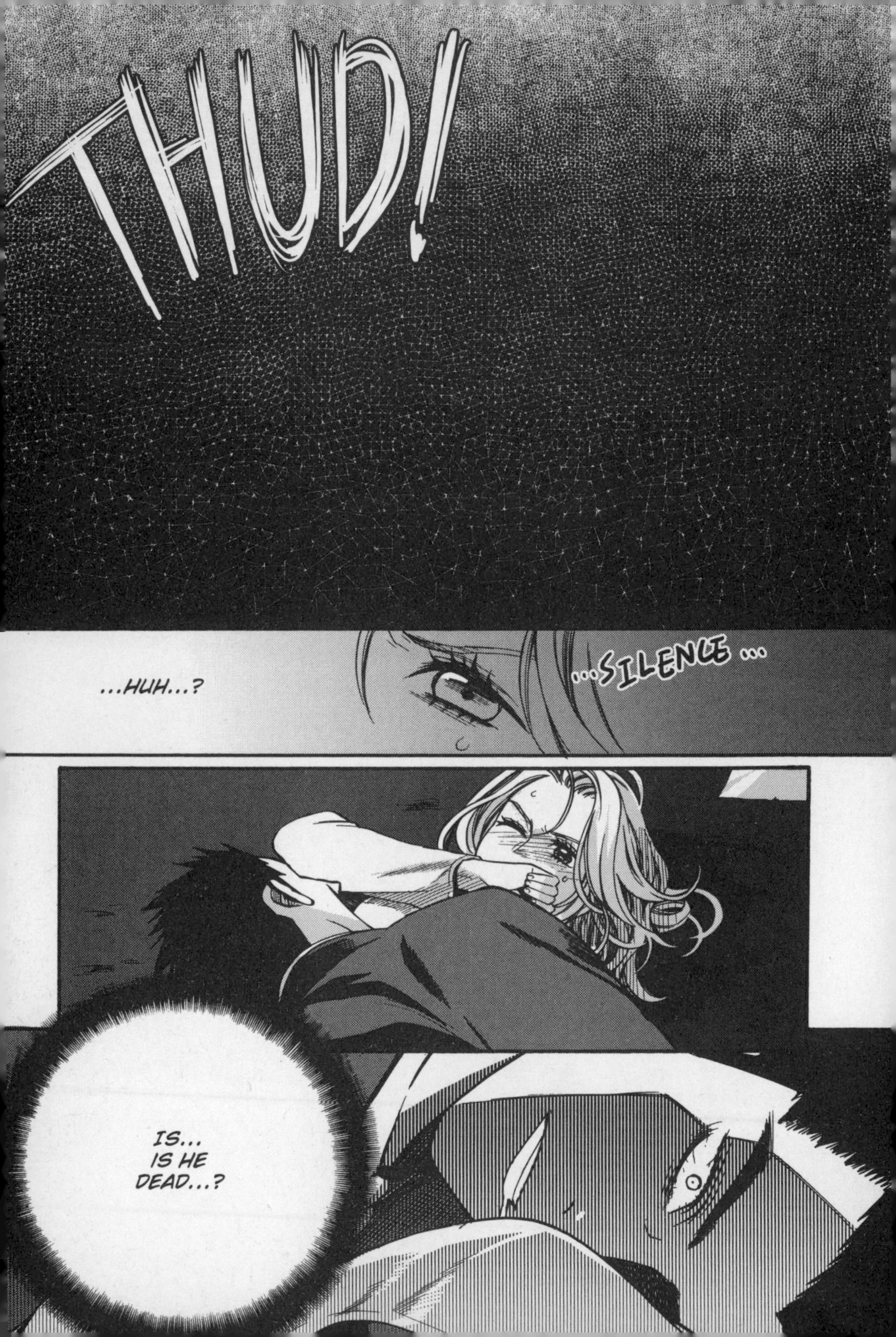
THUD!
...HUH...?
...SILENCE...
IS... IS HE DEAD...?

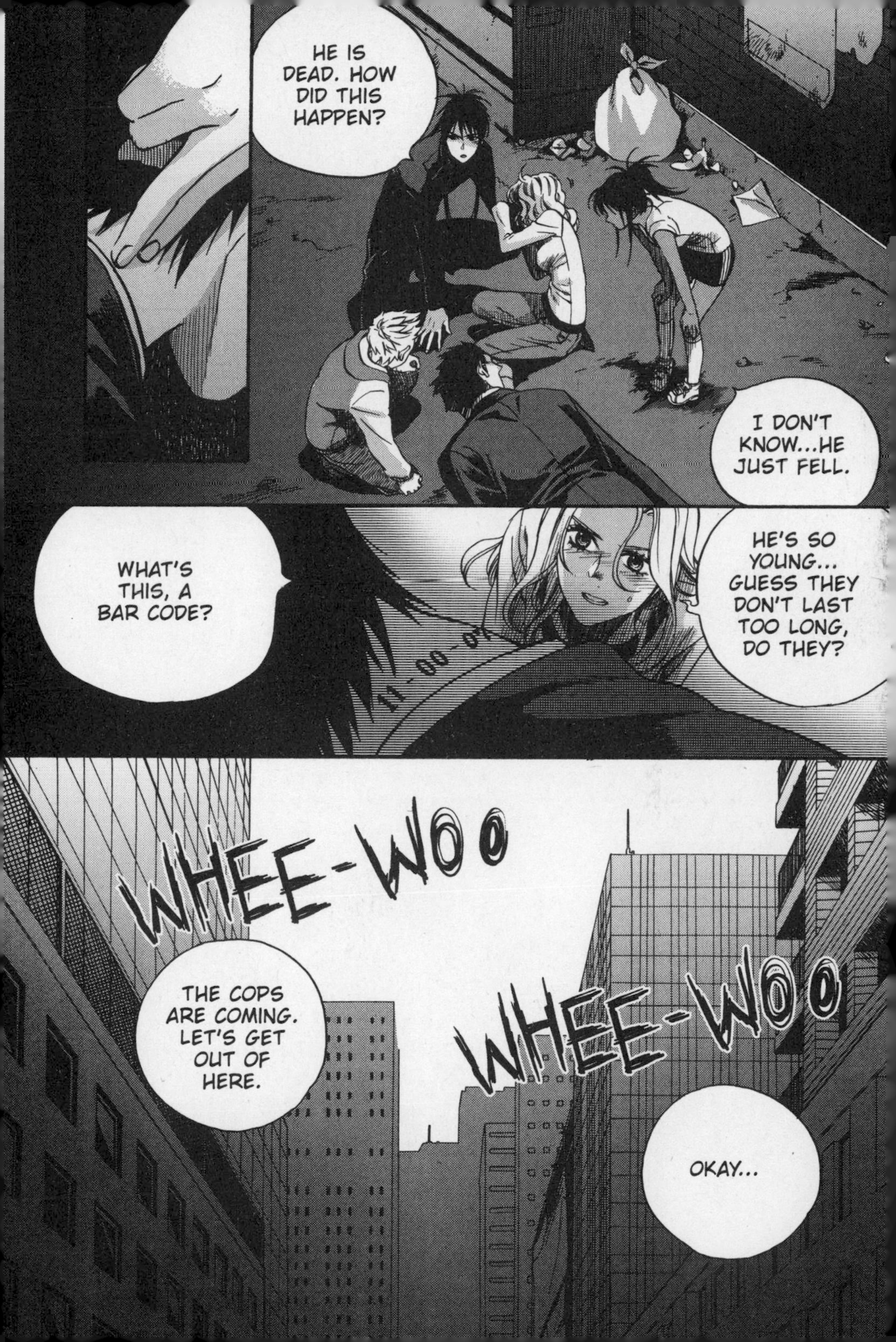
HE IS DEAD. HOW DID THIS HAPPEN?
I DON'T KNOW...HE JUST FELL.
WHAT'S THIS, A BAR CODE?
HE'S SO YOUNG... GUESS THEY DON'T LAST TOO LONG, DO THEY?
WHEE-WOO
THE COPS ARE COMING. LET'S GET OUT OF HERE.
WHEE-WOO
OKAY...

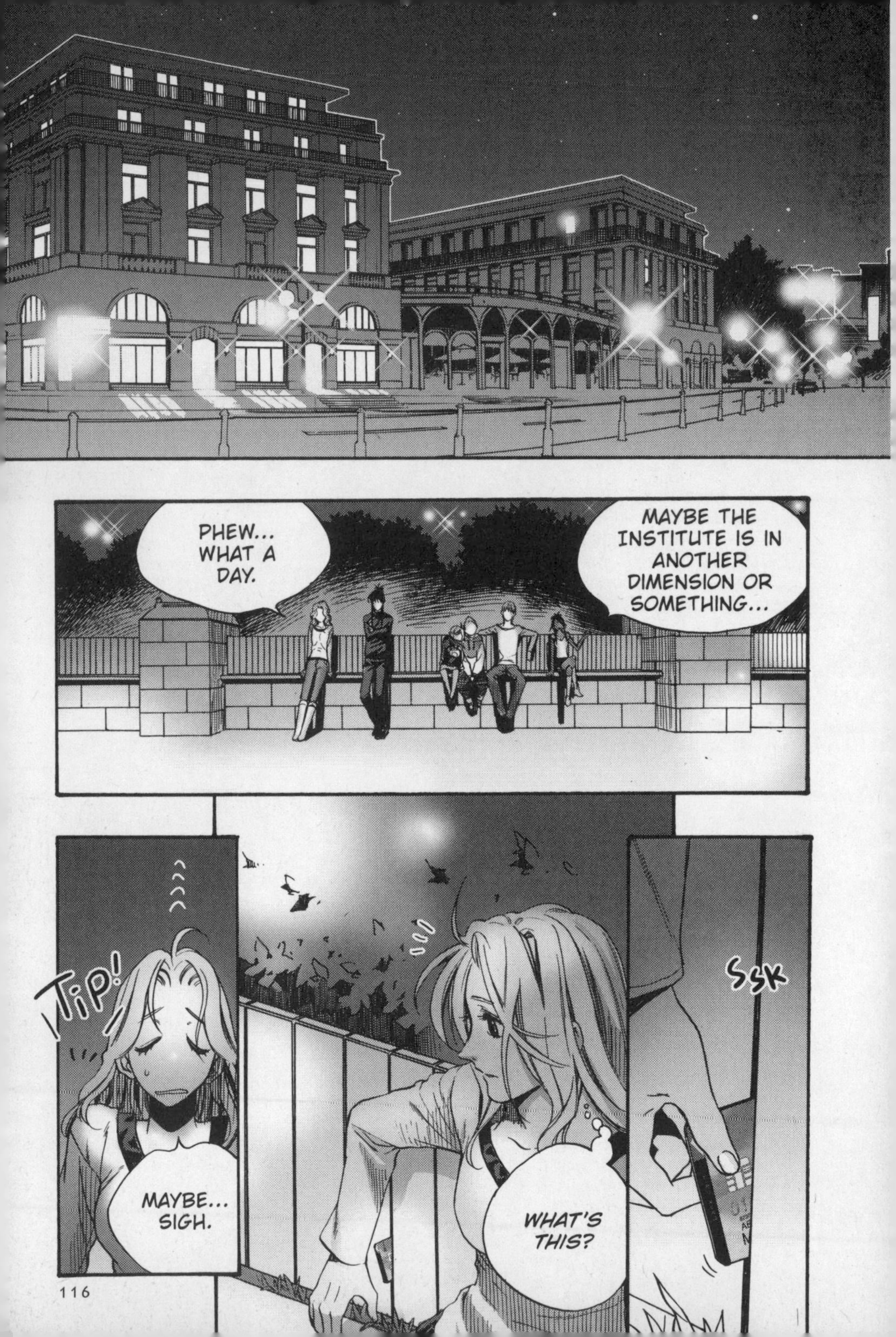
PHEW... WHAT A DAY.
MAYBE THE INSTITUTE IS IN ANOTHER DIMENSION OR SOMETHING...
TIP!
MAYBE... SIGH.
WHAT'S THIS?
SSK

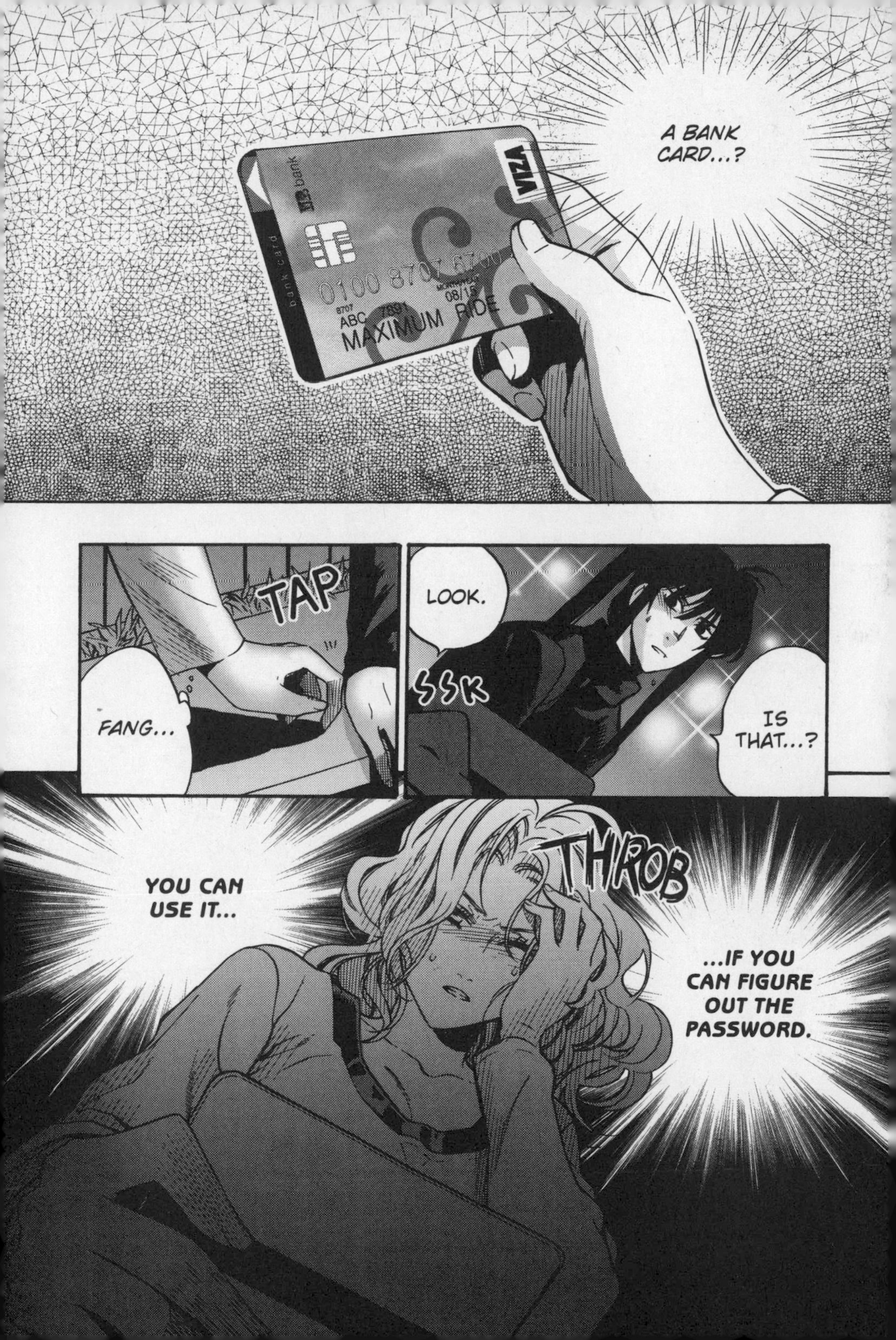
VISA
MAXIMUM RIDE
A BANK CARD...?
TAP
FANG...
LOOK.
SSK
IS THAT...?
YOU CAN USE IT...
THROB
...IF YOU CAN FIGURE OUT THE PASSWORD.

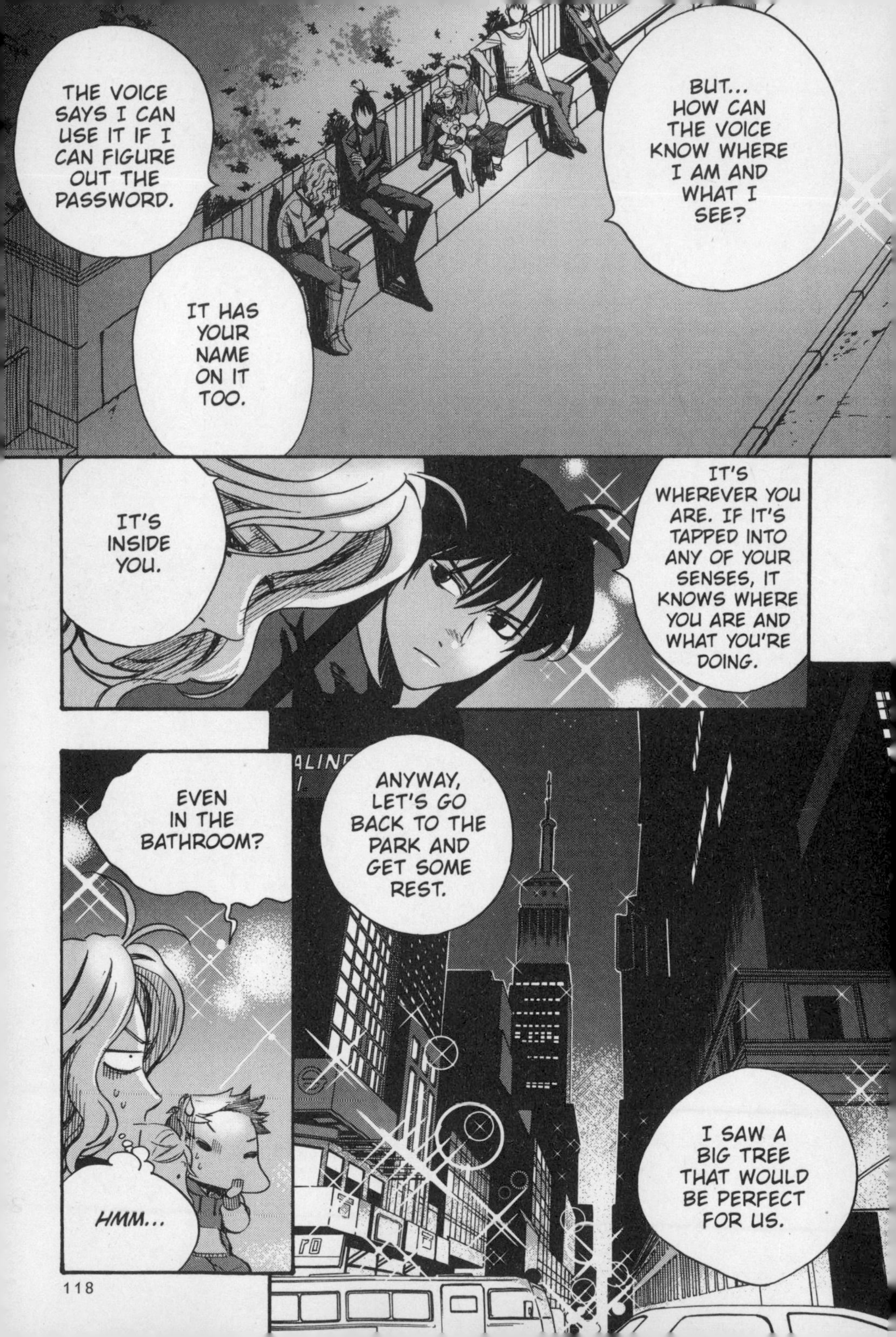
THE VOICE SAYS I CAN USE IT IF I CAN FIGURE OUT THE PASSWORD.
IT HAS YOUR NAME ON IT TOO.
BUT... HOW CAN THE VOICE KNOW WHERE I AM AND WHAT I SEE?
IT'S INSIDE YOU.
IT'S WHEREVER YOU ARE. IF IT'S TAPPED INTO ANY OF YOUR SENSES, IT KNOWS WHERE YOU ARE AND WHAT YOU'RE DOING.
EVEN IN THE BATHROOM?
HMM...
ANYWAY, LET'S GO BACK TO THE PARK AND GET SOME REST.
I SAW A BIG TREE THAT WOULD BE PERFECT FOR US.

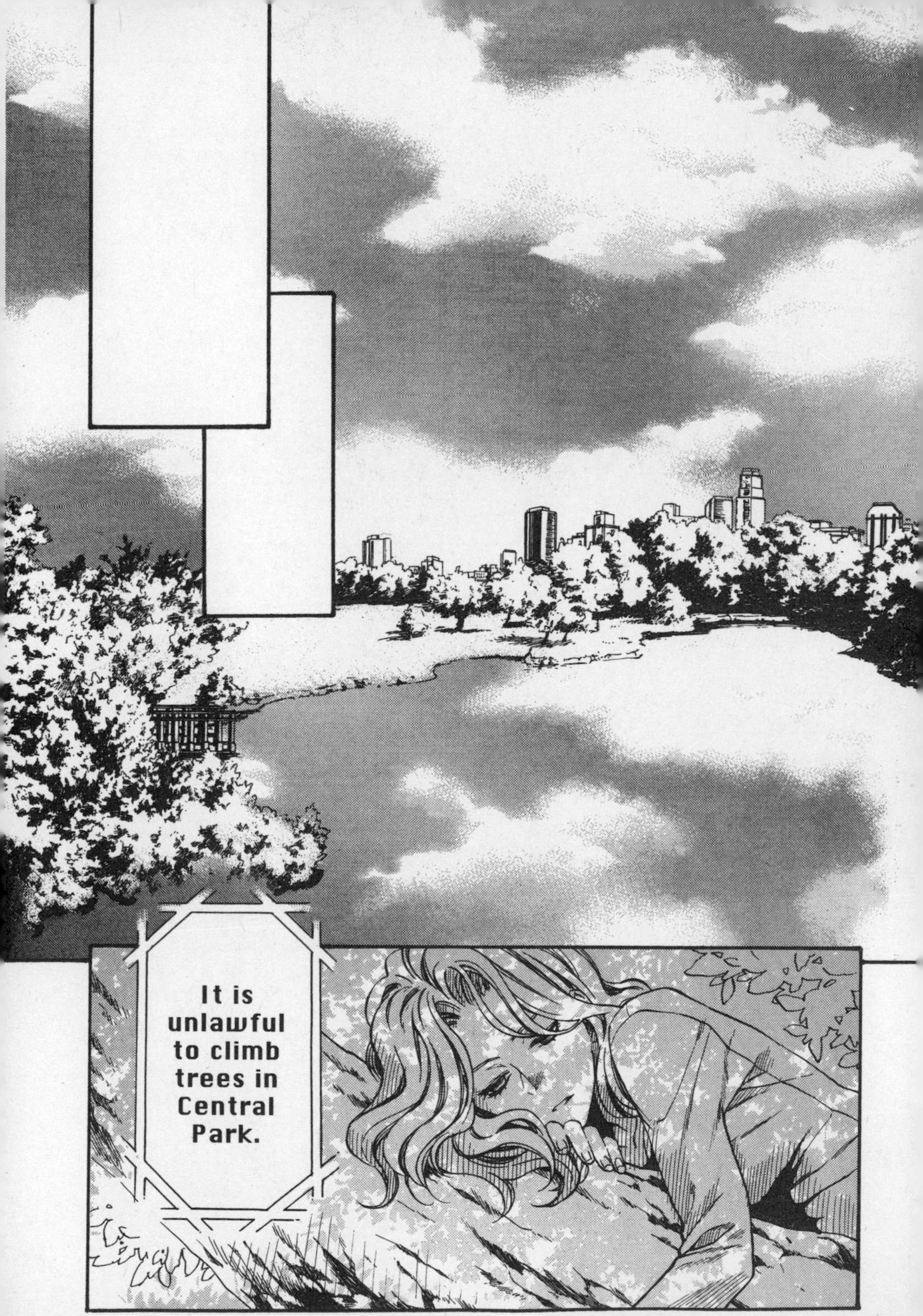
It is unlawful to climb trees in Central Park.

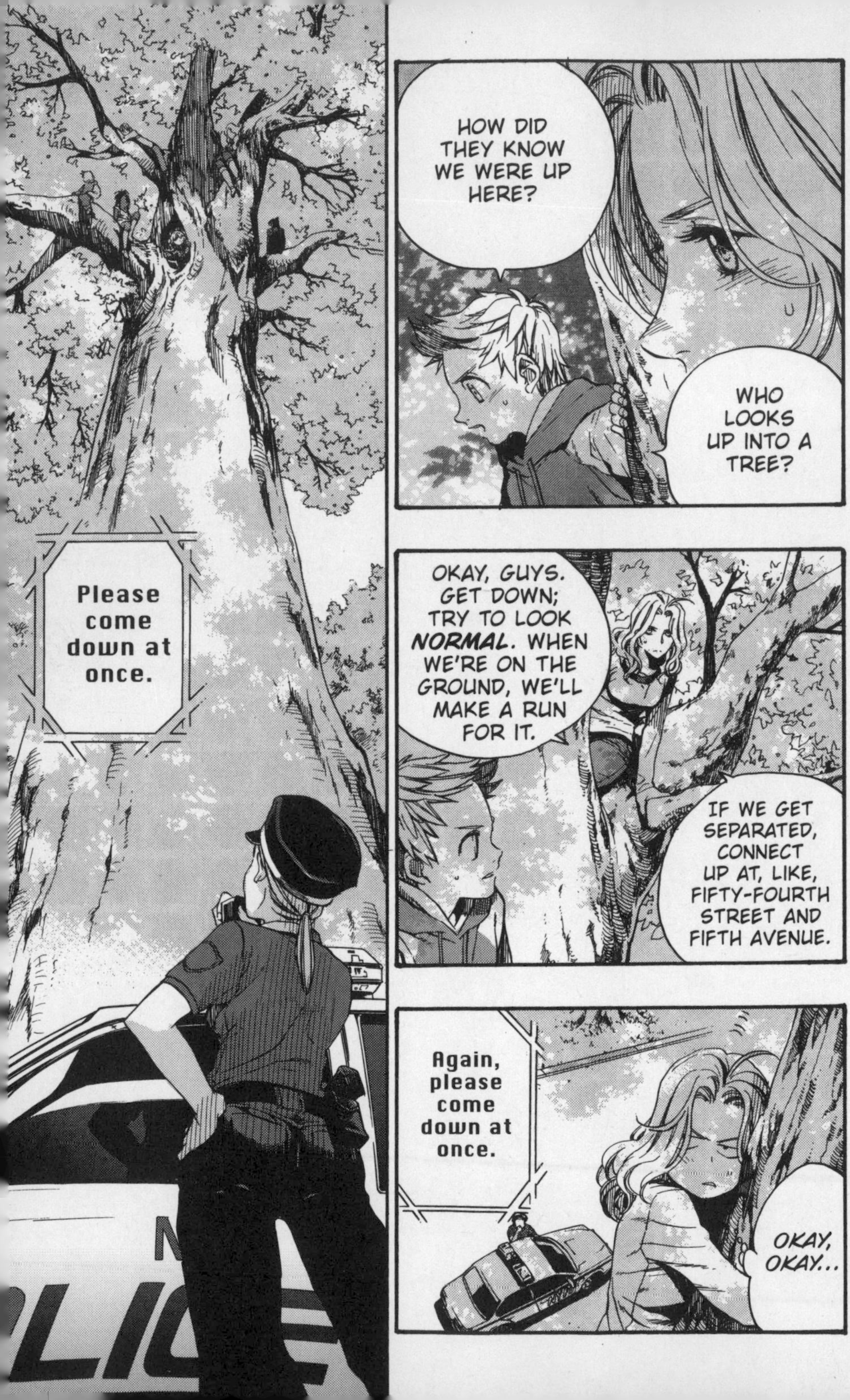
Please come down at once.
HOW DID THEY KNOW WE WERE UP HERE?
WHO LOOKS UP INTO A TREE?
OKAY, GUYS. GET DOWN; TRY TO LOOK *NORMAL*. WHEN WE'RE ON THE GROUND, WE'LL MAKE A RUN FOR IT.
IF WE GET SEPARATED, CONNECT UP AT, LIKE, FIFTY-FOURTH STREET AND FIFTH AVENUE.
Again, please come down at once.
OKAY, OKAY...

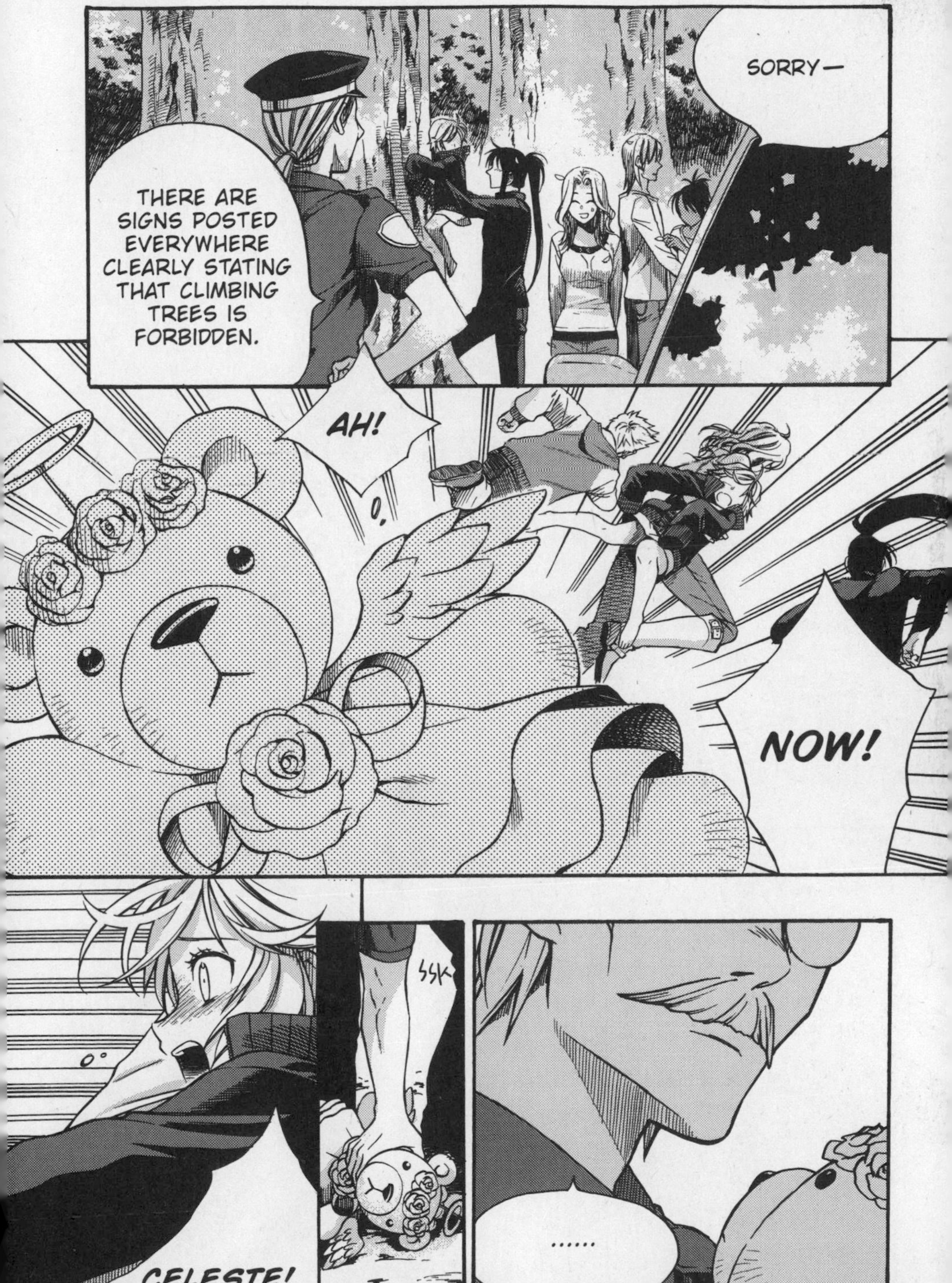
THERE ARE SIGNS POSTED EVERYWHERE CLEARLY STATING THAT CLIMBING TREES IS FORBIDDEN.
SORRY—
AH!
NOW!
CELESTE!
SSK
......

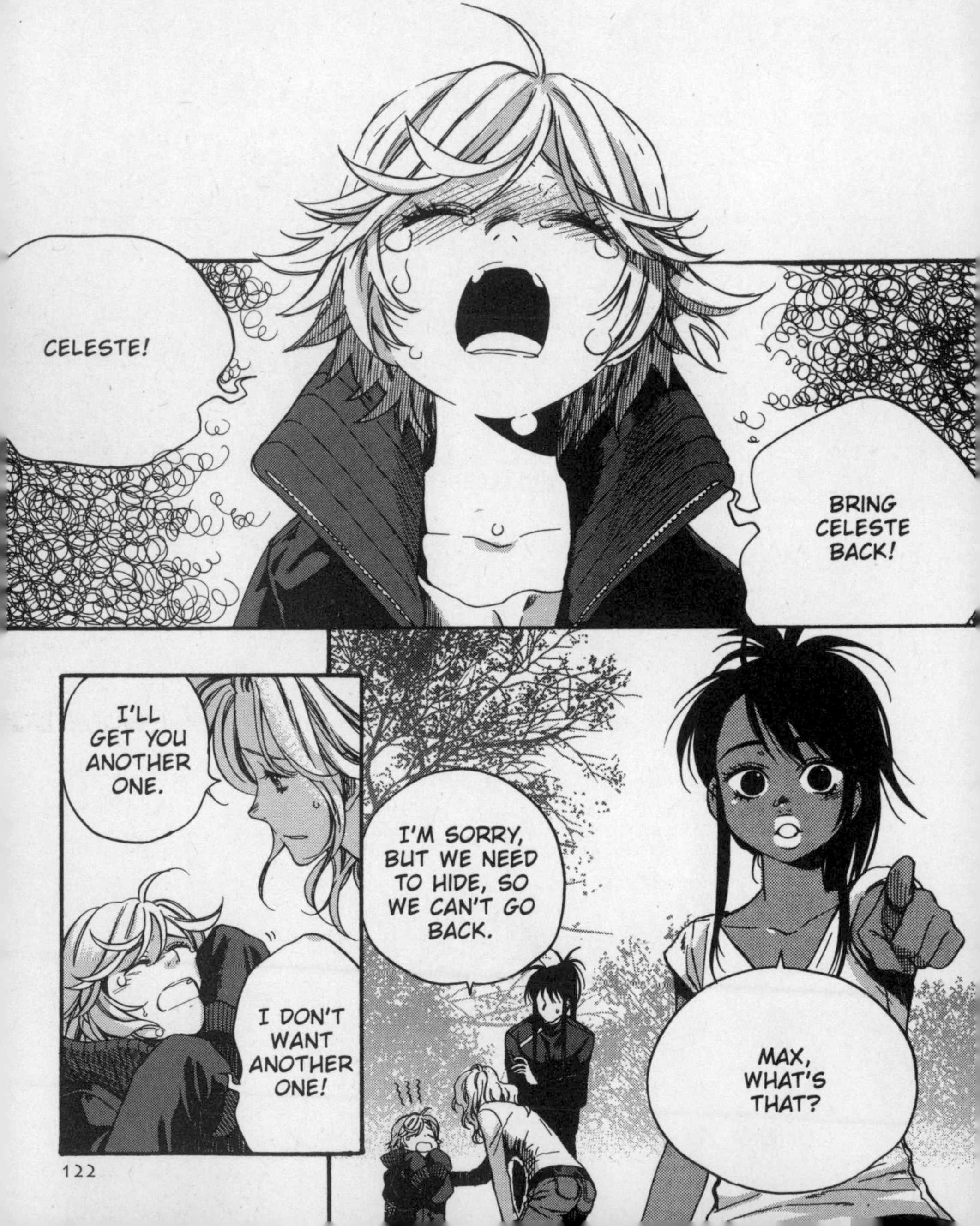
CELESTE!
BRING CELESTE BACK!
I'LL GET YOU ANOTHER ONE.
I DON'T WANT ANOTHER ONE!
I'M SORRY, BUT WE NEED TO HIDE, SO WE CAN'T GO BACK.
MAX, WHAT'S THAT?

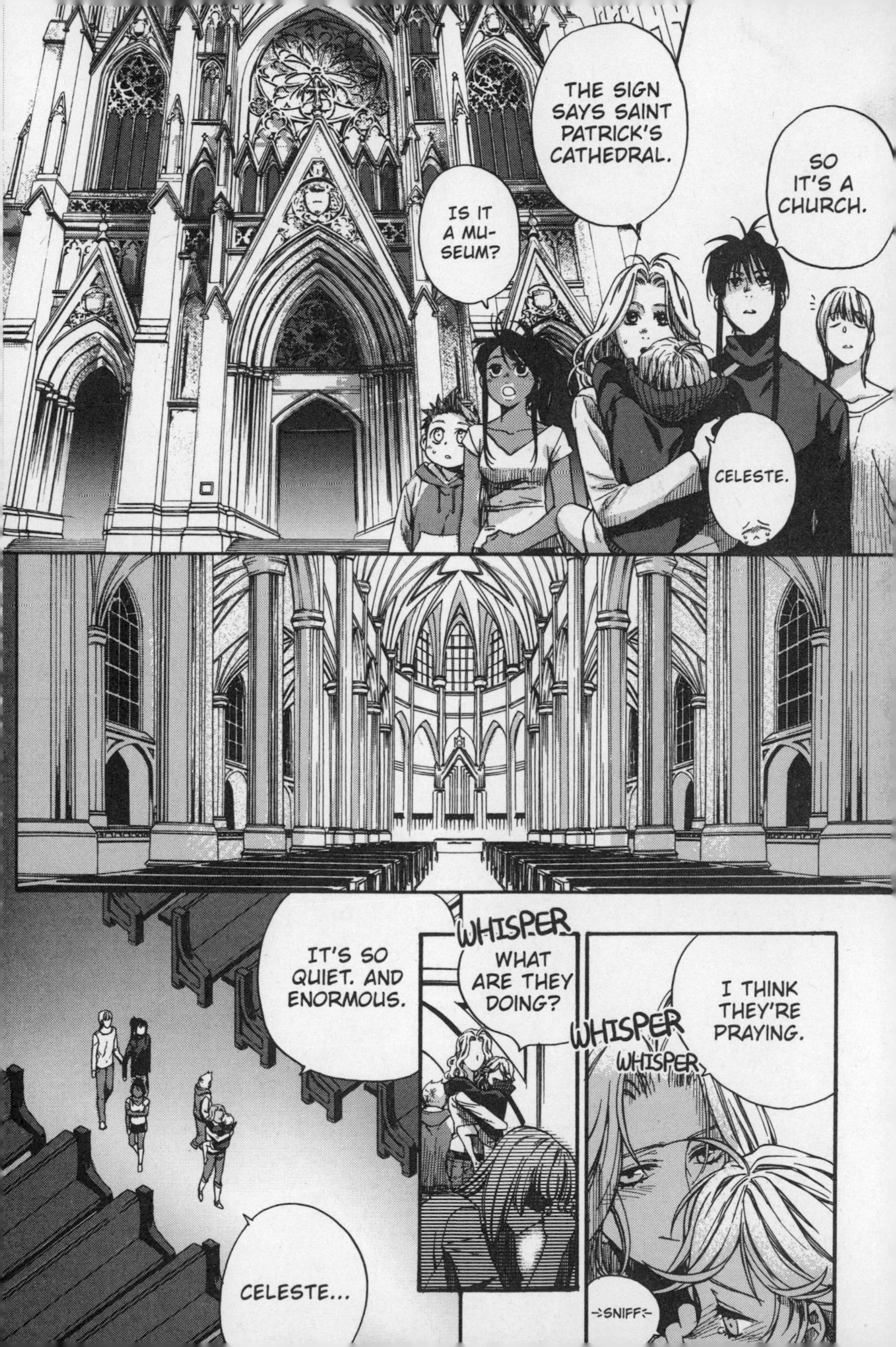
IS IT A MU-SEUM?
THE SIGN SAYS SAINT PATRICK'S CATHEDRAL.
SO IT'S A CHURCH.
CELESTE.
IT'S SO QUIET. AND ENORMOUS.
CELESTE...
WHISPER
WHAT ARE THEY DOING?
WHISPER
WHISPER
I THINK THEY'RE PRAYING.
SNIFF

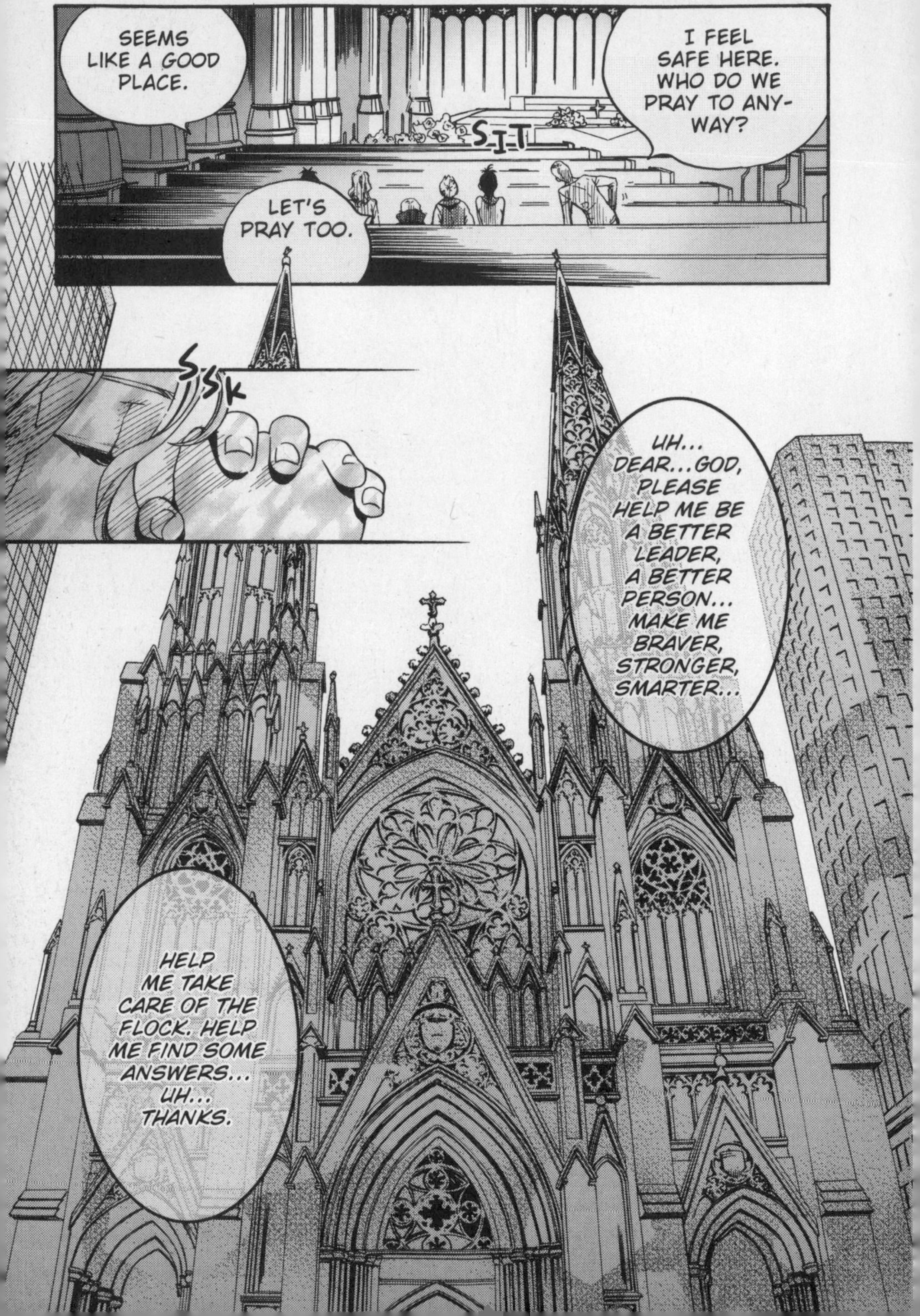
SEEMS LIKE A GOOD PLACE.
I FEEL SAFE HERE. WHO DO WE PRAY TO ANY-WAY?
SIT
LET'S PRAY TOO.
SSK
UH... DEAR...GOD, PLEASE HELP ME BE A BETTER LEADER, A BETTER PERSON... MAKE ME BRAVER, STRONGER, SMARTER...
HELP ME TAKE CARE OF THE FLOCK. HELP ME FIND SOME ANSWERS... UH... THANKS.

MAXIMUM
RIDE

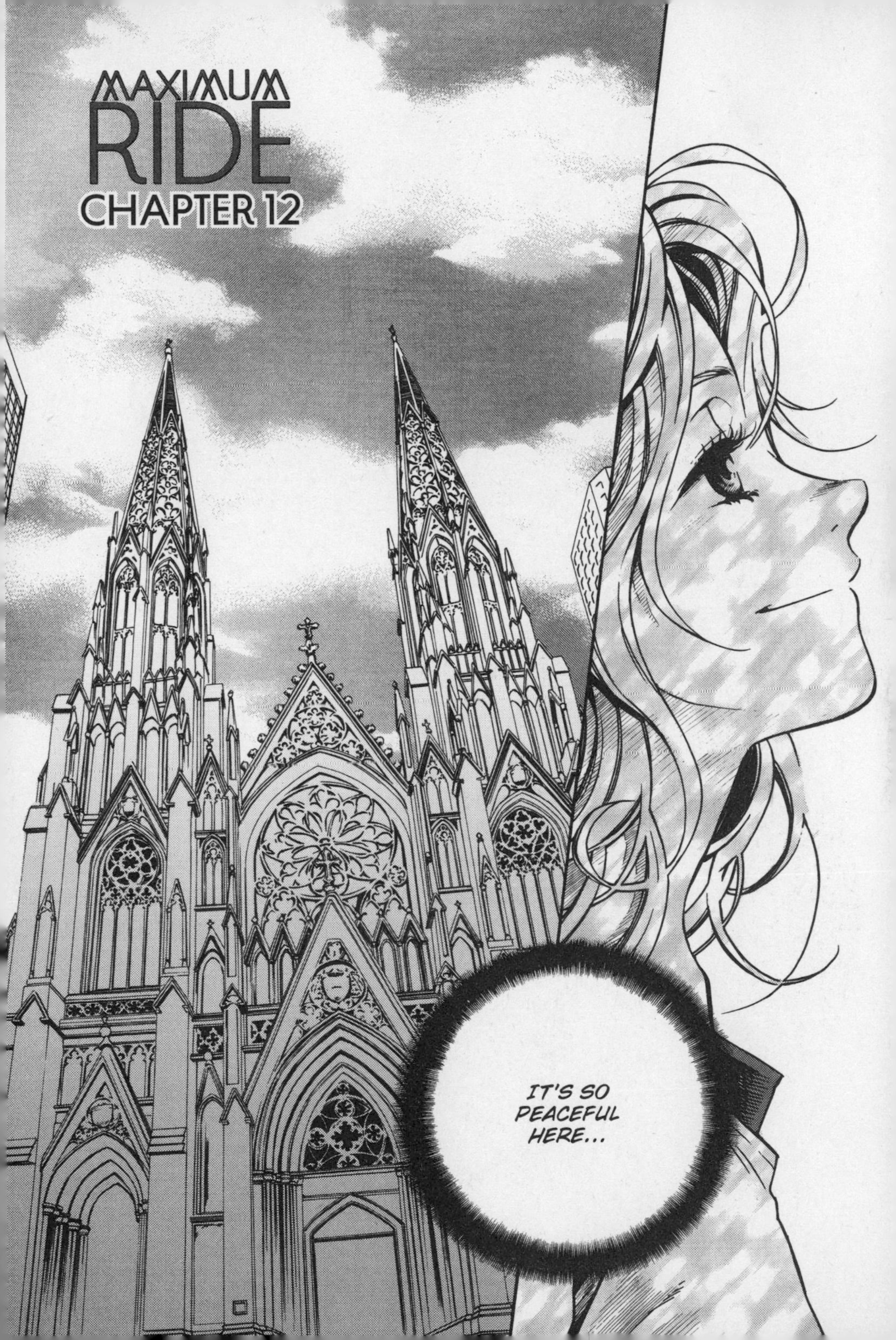
MAXIMUM RIDE
CHAPTER 12
IT'S SO PEACEFUL HERE...

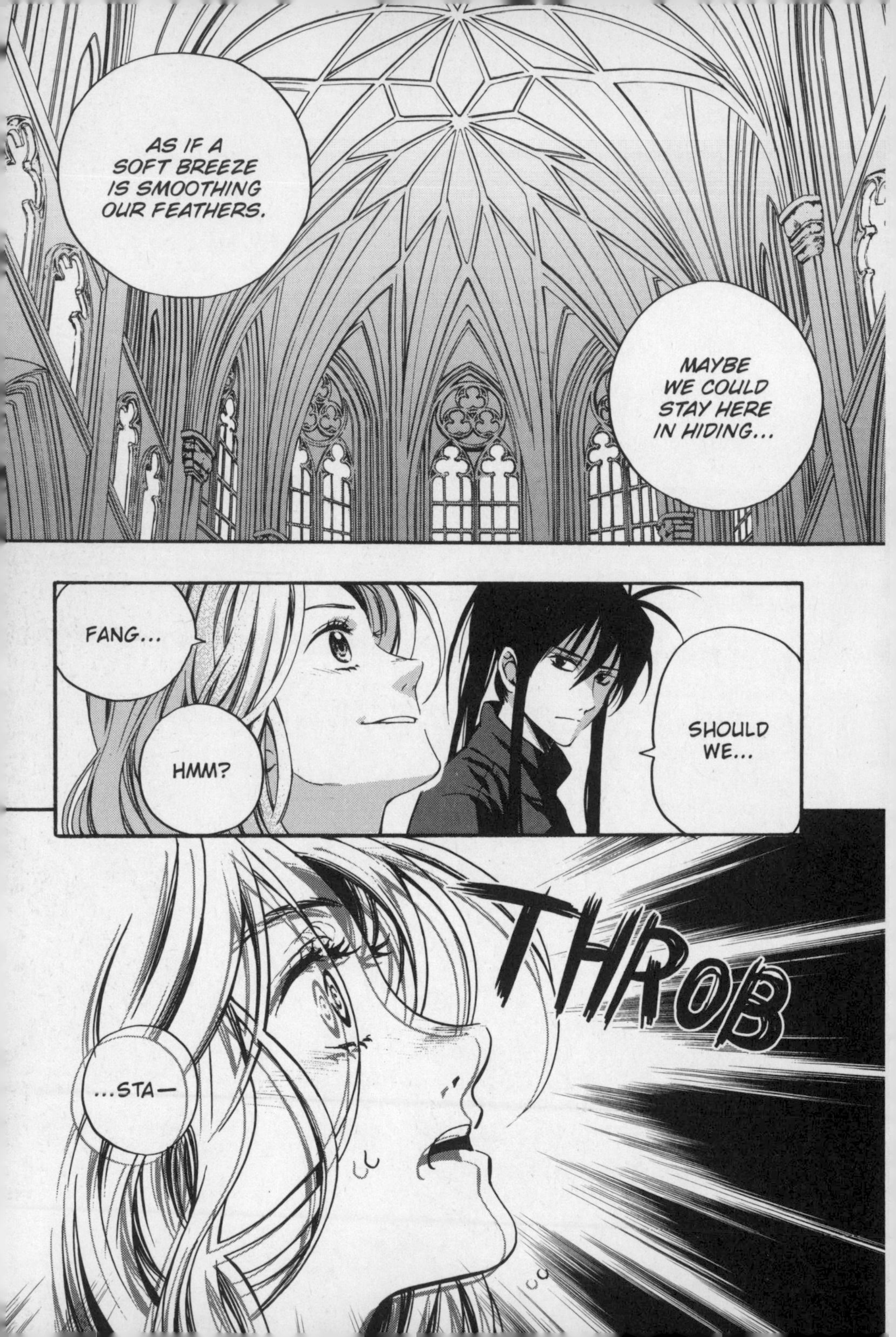
AS IF A SOFT BREEZE IS SMOOTHING OUR FEATHERS.
MAYBE WE COULD STAY HERE IN HIDING...
FANG...
HMM?
SHOULD WE...
THROB
...STA—

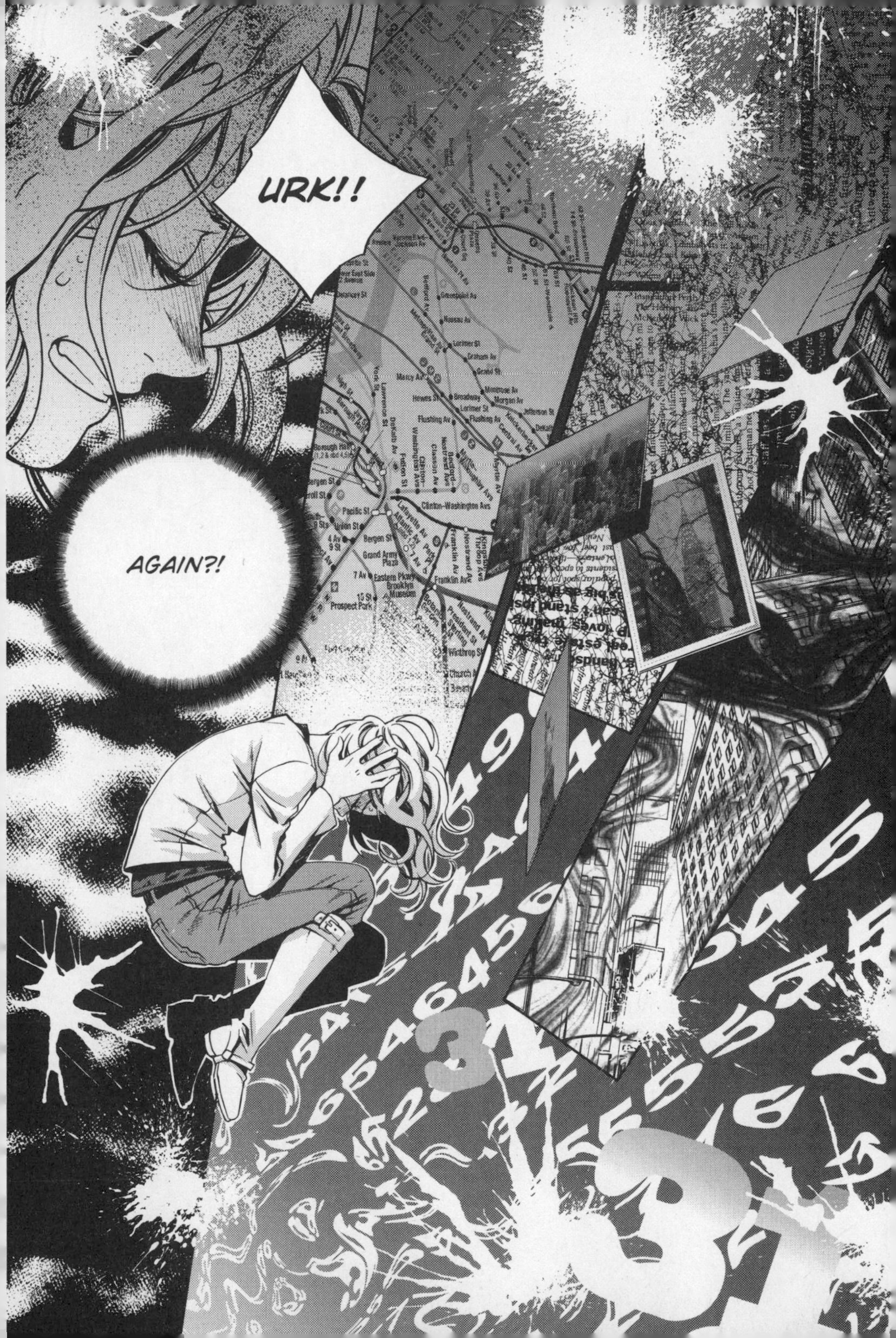
URK!!
AGAIN?!

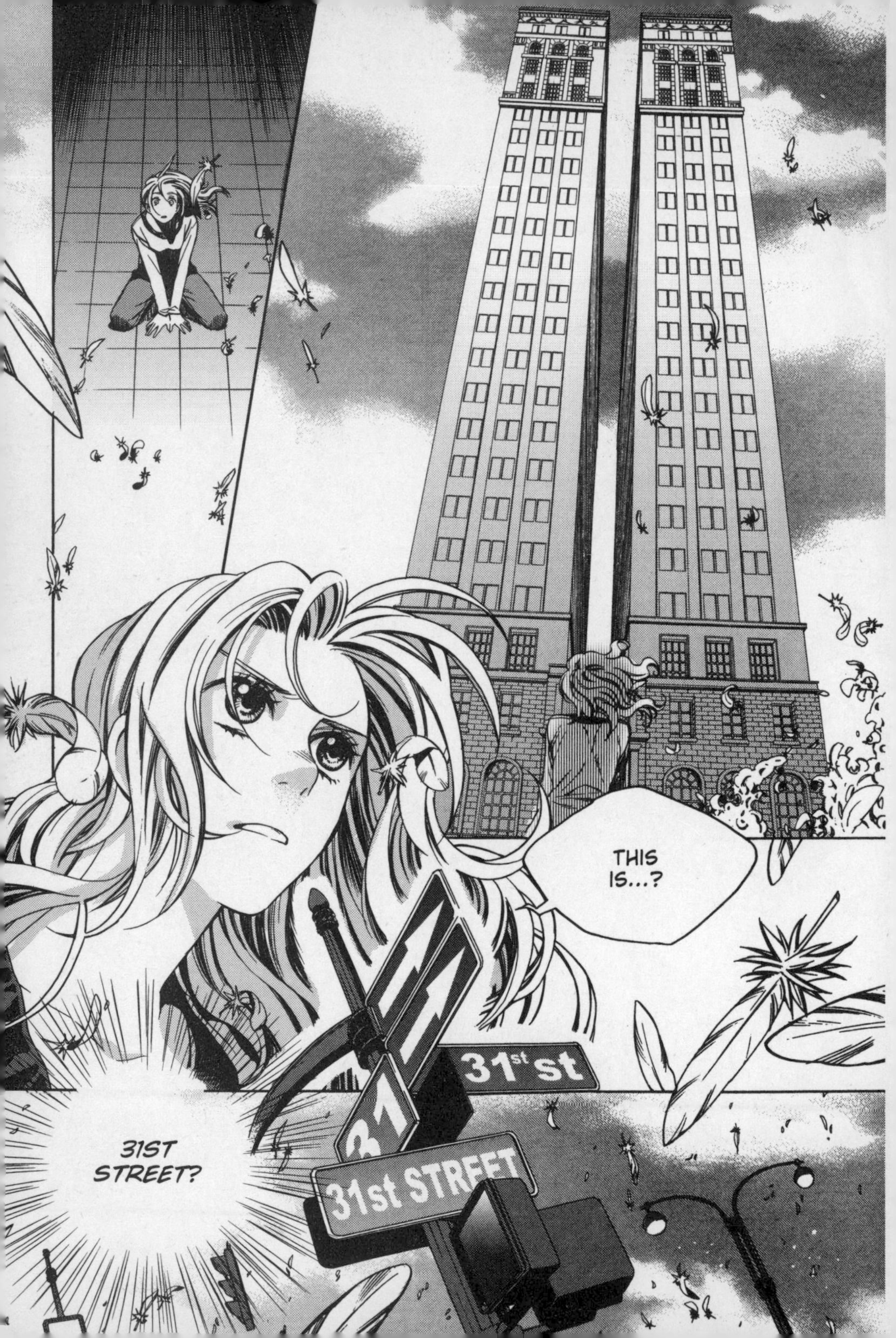
THIS IS...?
31ST STREET?
31st st
31st STREET

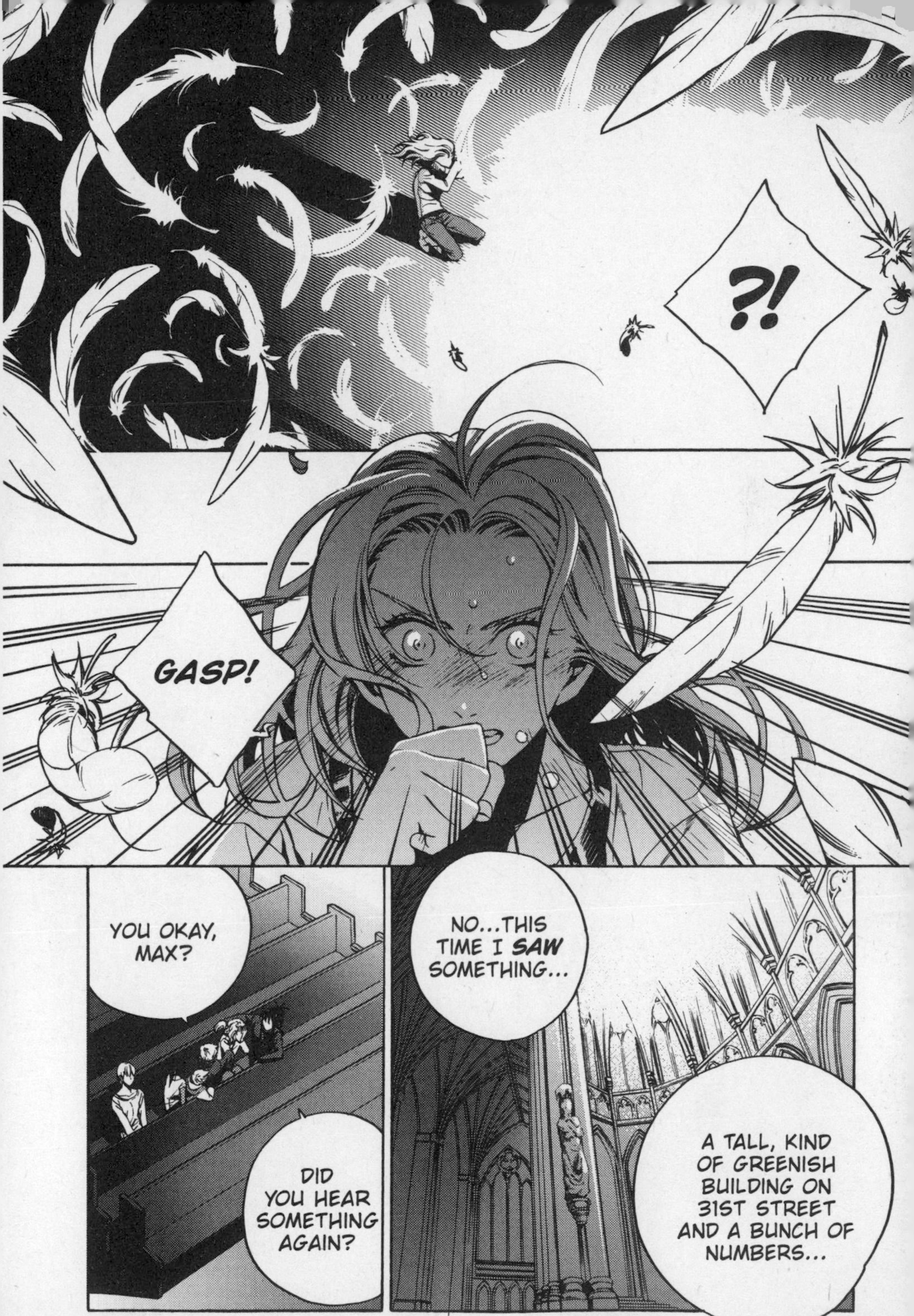
?!
GASP!
YOU OKAY, MAX?
DID YOU HEAR SOMETHING AGAIN?
NO...THIS TIME I SAW SOMETHING...
A TALL, KIND OF GREENISH BUILDING ON 31ST STREET AND A BUNCH OF NUMBERS...

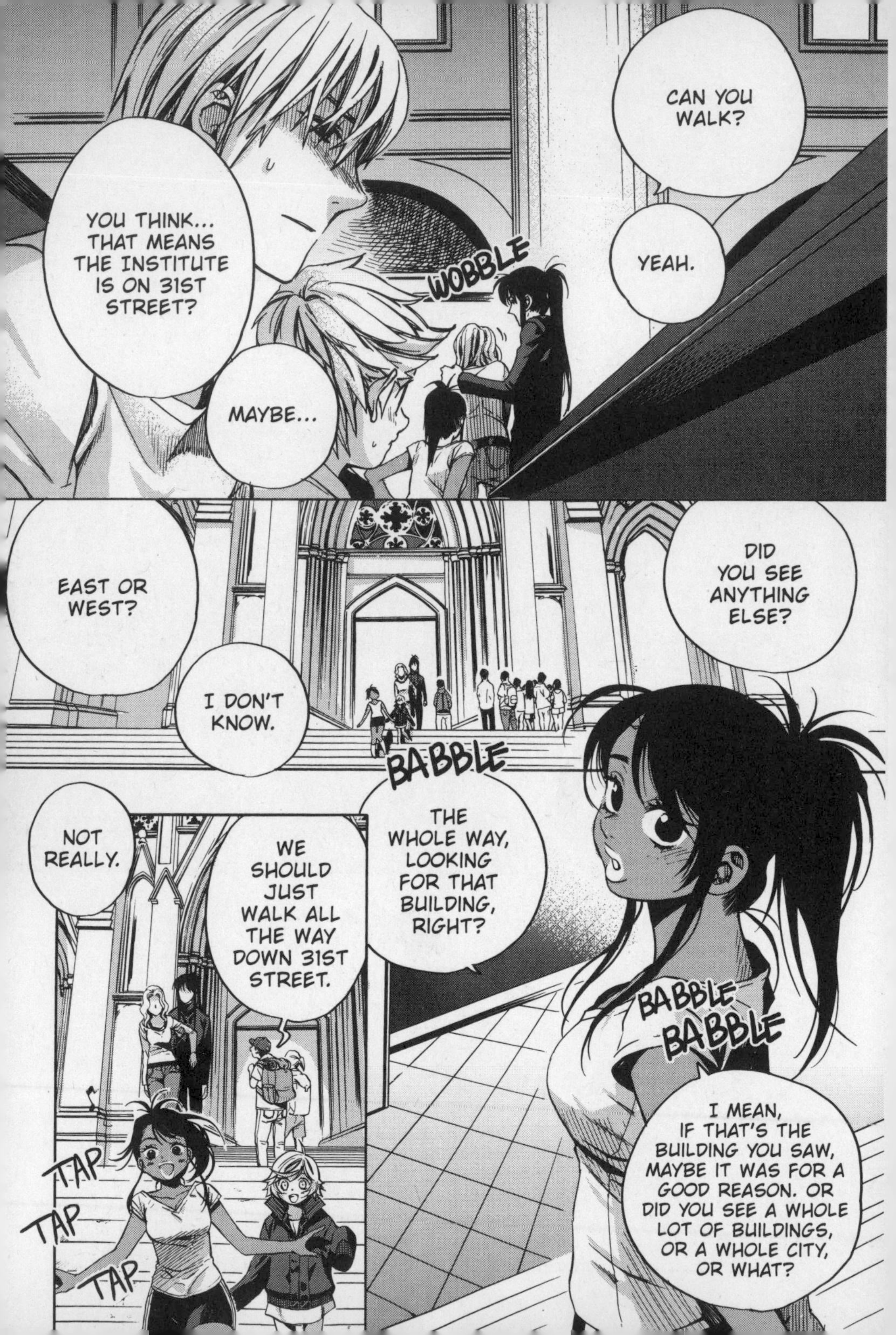
YOU THINK... THAT MEANS THE INSTITUTE IS ON 31ST STREET?
MAYBE...
CAN YOU WALK?
WOBBLE
YEAH.
EAST OR WEST?
I DON'T KNOW.
DID YOU SEE ANYTHING ELSE?
BABBLE
NOT REALLY.
WE SHOULD JUST WALK ALL THE WAY DOWN 31ST STREET.
TAP
TAP
TAP
THE WHOLE WAY, LOOKING FOR THAT BUILDING, RIGHT?
BABBLE BABBLE
I MEAN, IF THAT'S THE BUILDING YOU SAW, MAYBE IT WAS FOR A GOOD REASON. OR DID YOU SEE A WHOLE LOT OF BUILDINGS, OR A WHOLE CITY, OR WHAT?

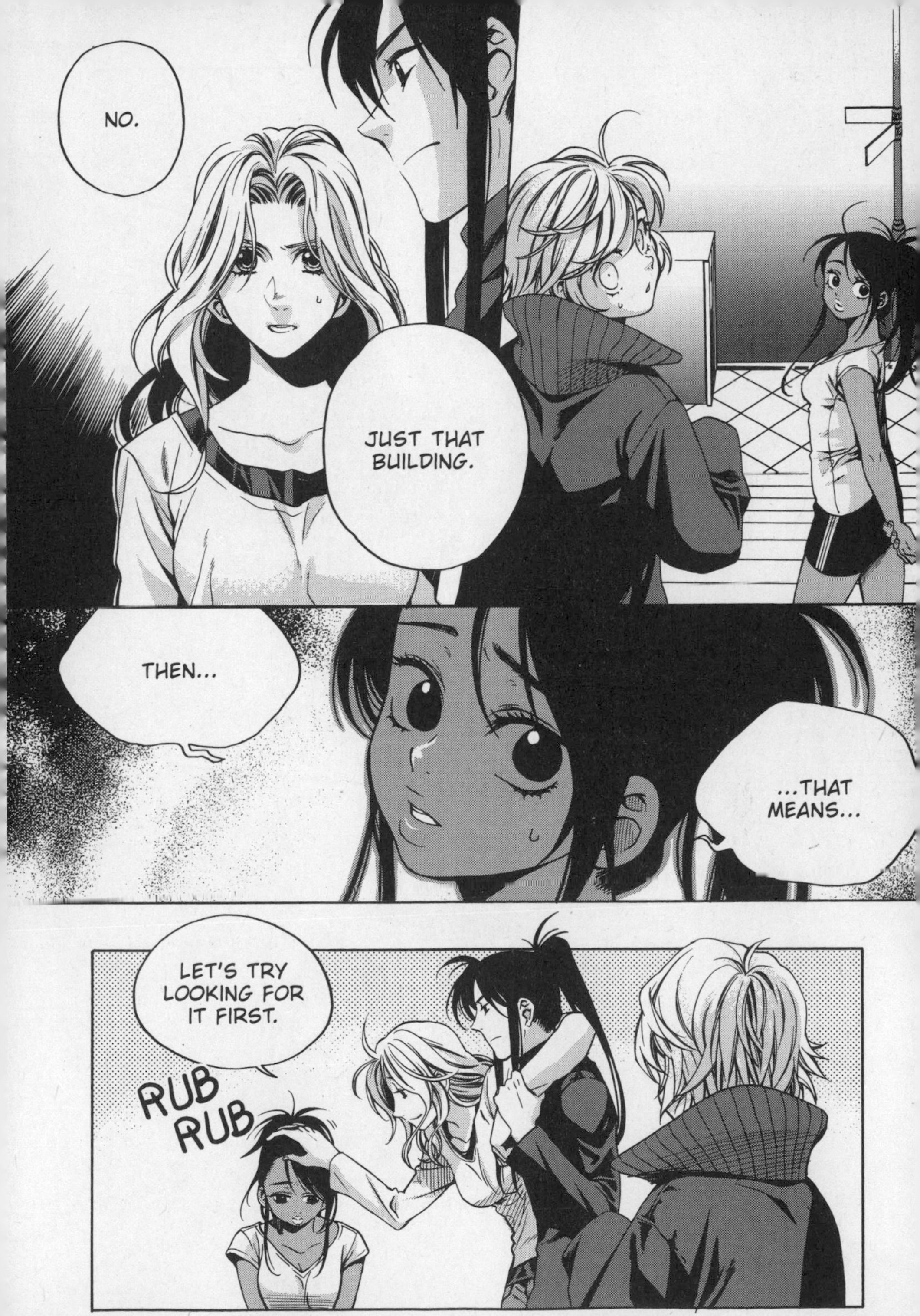
NO.
JUST THAT BUILDING.
THEN...
...THAT MEANS...
LET'S TRY LOOKING FOR IT FIRST.
RUB RUB

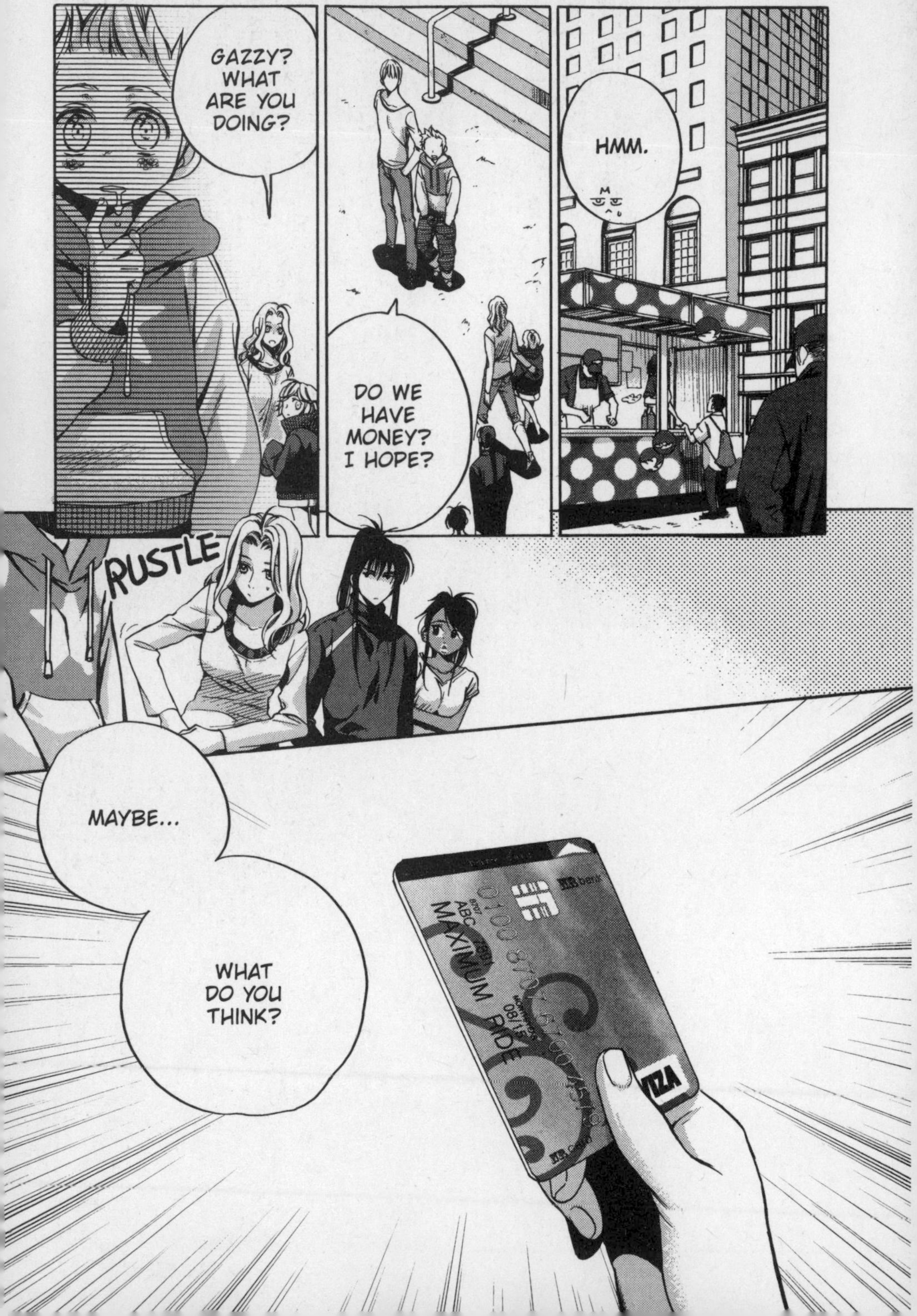
GAZZY? WHAT ARE YOU DOING?
DO WE HAVE MONEY? I HOPE?
HMM.
RUSTLE
MAYBE...
WHAT DO YOU THINK?
MAXIMUM RIDE
VIZA

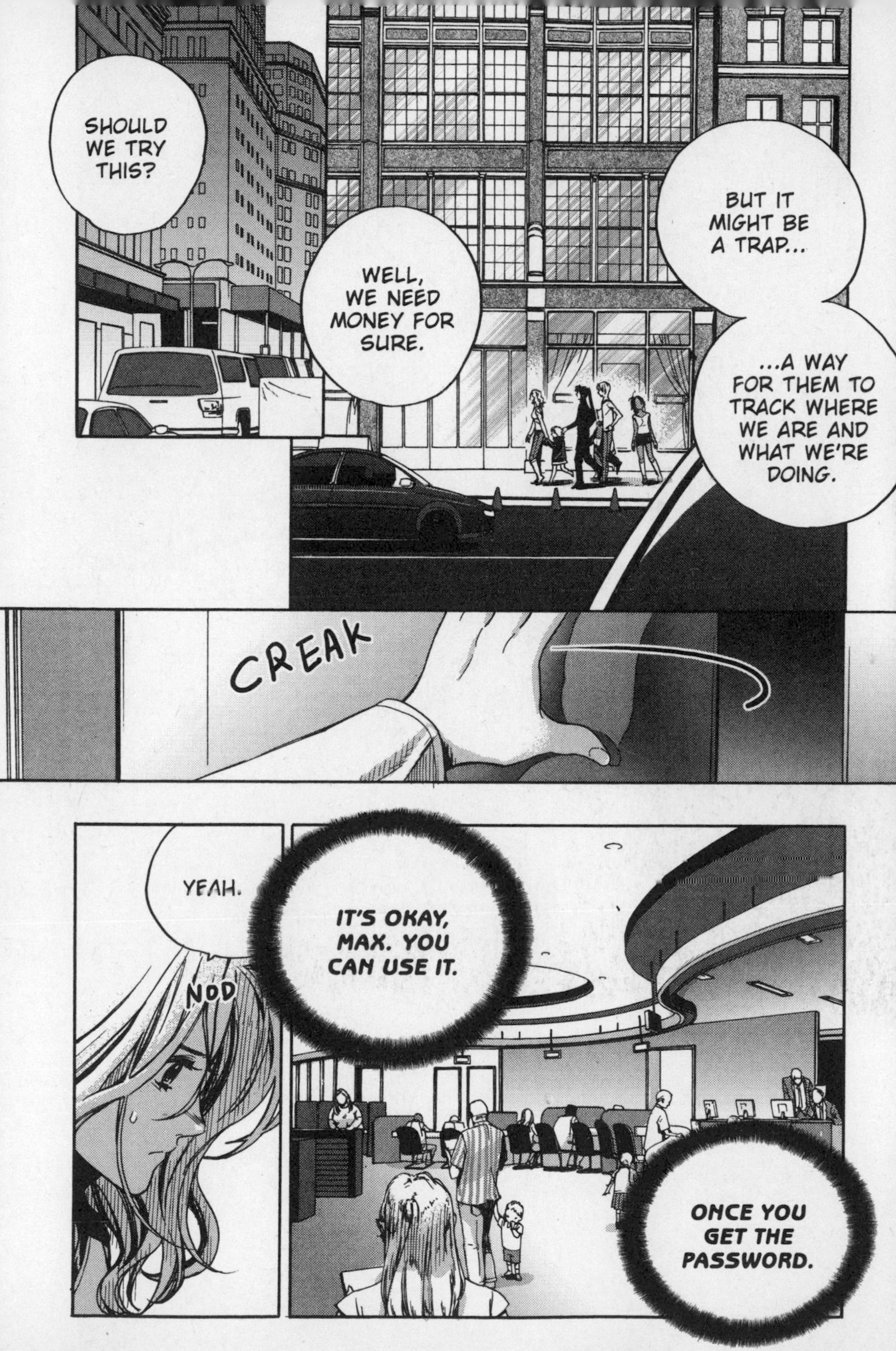
SHOULD WE TRY THIS?
WELL, WE NEED MONEY FOR SURE.
BUT IT MIGHT BE A TRAP...
...A WAY FOR THEM TO TRACK WHERE WE ARE AND WHAT WE'RE DOING.
CREAK
YEAH.
NOD
IT'S OKAY, MAX. YOU CAN USE IT.
ONCE YOU GET THE PASSWORD.

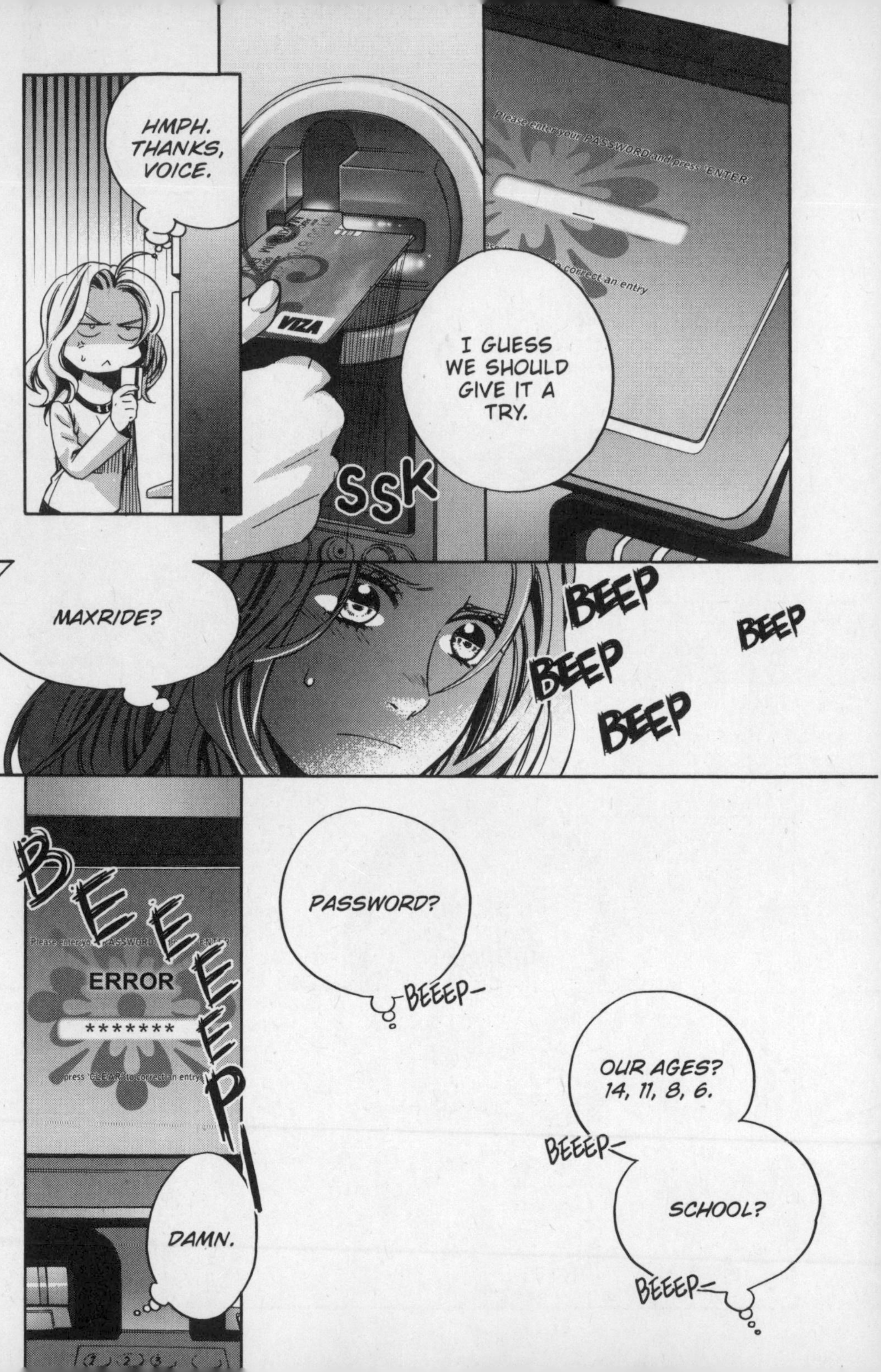
HMPH. THANKS, VOICE.
VIZA
SSK
Please enter your PASSWORD and press 'ENTER'
I GUESS WE SHOULD GIVE IT A TRY.
MAXRIDE?
BEEP
BEEP
BEEP
BEEP
BEEEEEP!
ERROR
****
DAMN.
PASSWORD?
-BEEEP-
OUR AGES? 14, 11, 8, 6.
BEEEP—
SCHOOL?
BEEEP—

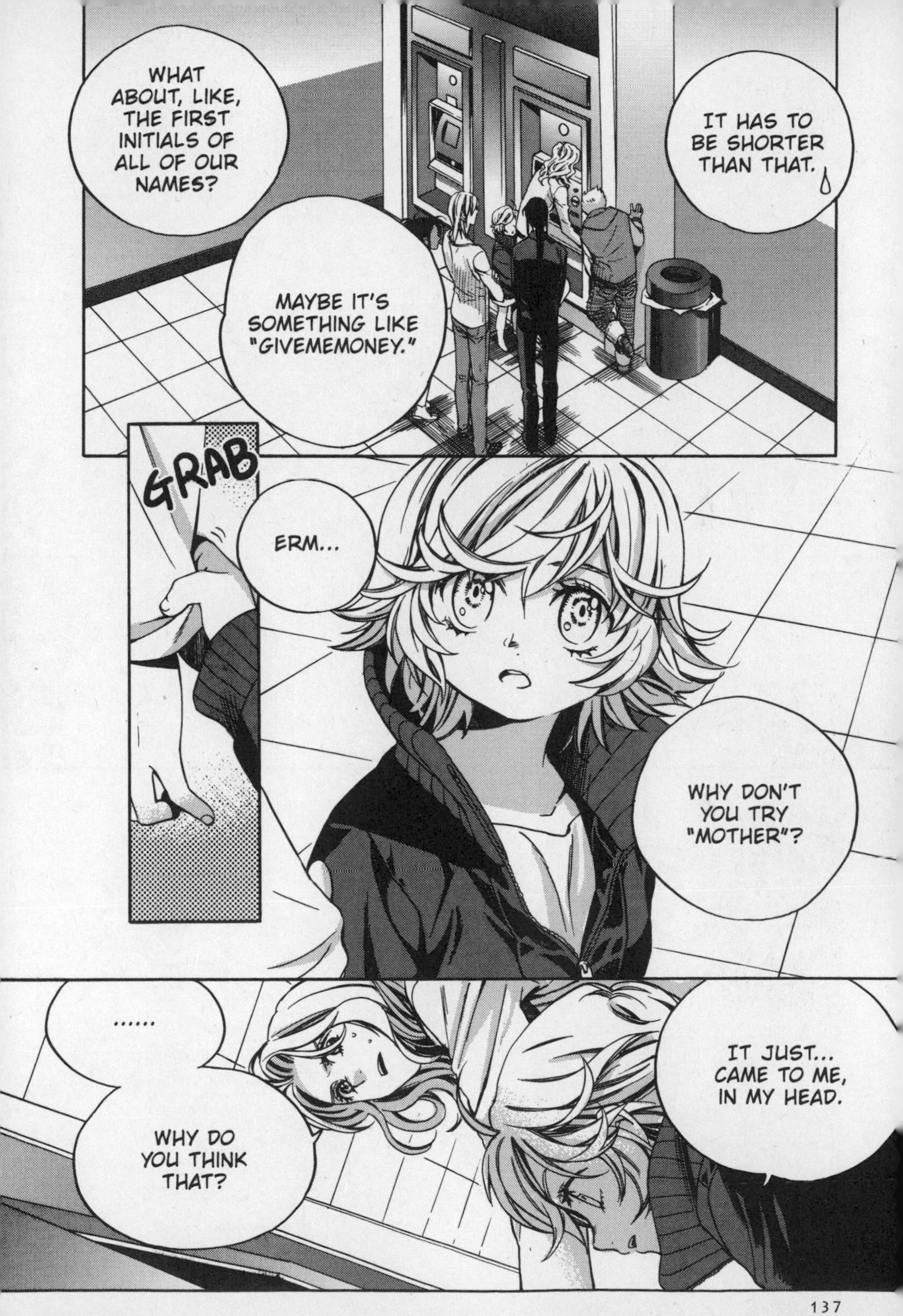
WHAT ABOUT, LIKE, THE FIRST INITIALS OF ALL OF OUR NAMES?
MAYBE IT'S SOMETHING LIKE "GIVEMEMONEY."
IT HAS TO BE SHORTER THAN THAT.
GRAB
ERM...
WHY DON'T YOU TRY "MOTHER"?
......
WHY DO YOU THINK THAT?
IT JUST... CAME TO ME, IN MY HEAD.

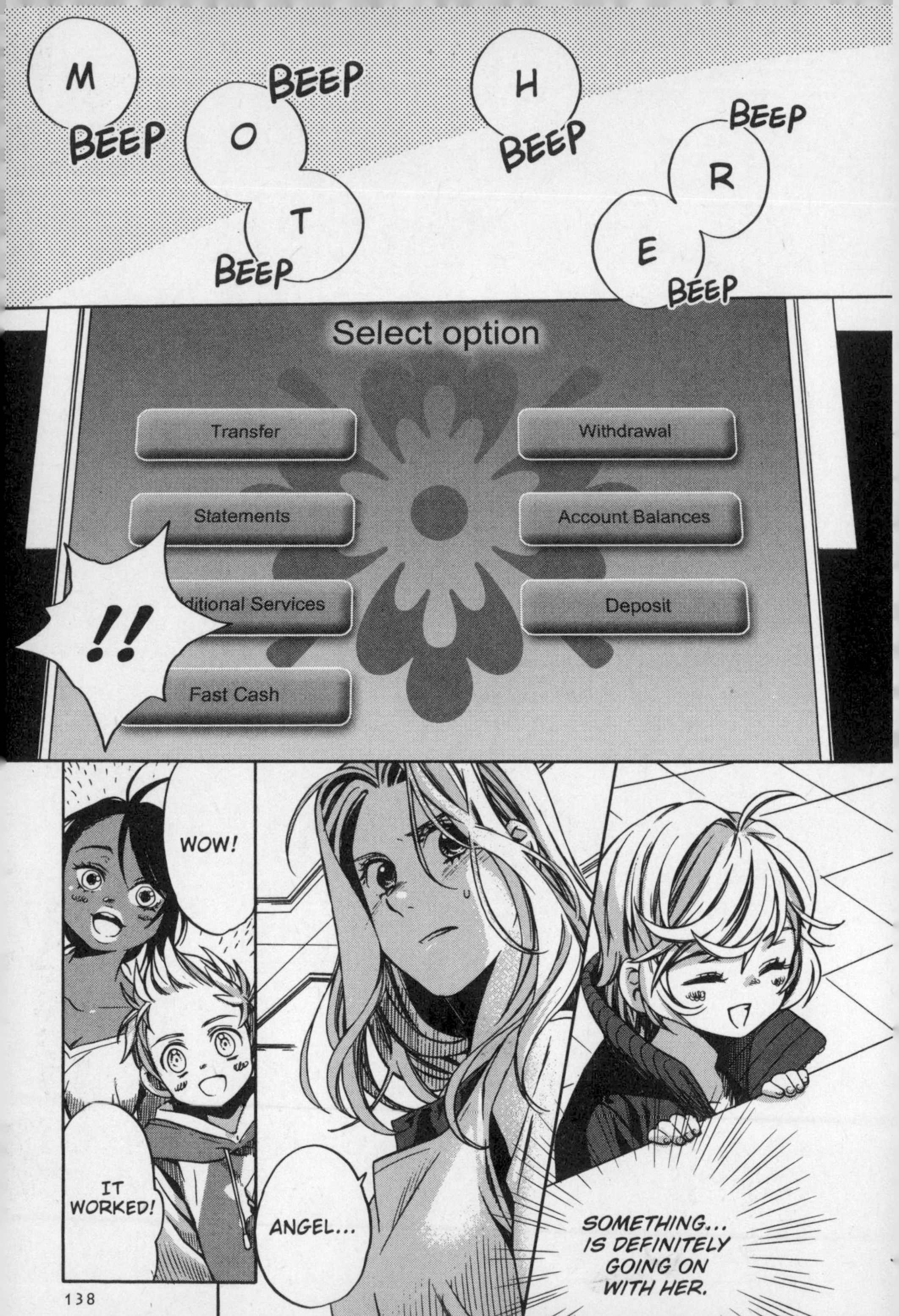
M
BEEP
O
BEEP
T
BEEP
H
BEEP
BEEP
R
E
BEEP
Select option
Transfer
Withdrawal
Statements
Account Balances
ditional Services
Deposit
Fast Cash
!!
WOW!
IT WORKED!
ANGEL...
SOMETHING... IS DEFINITELY GOING ON WITH HER.

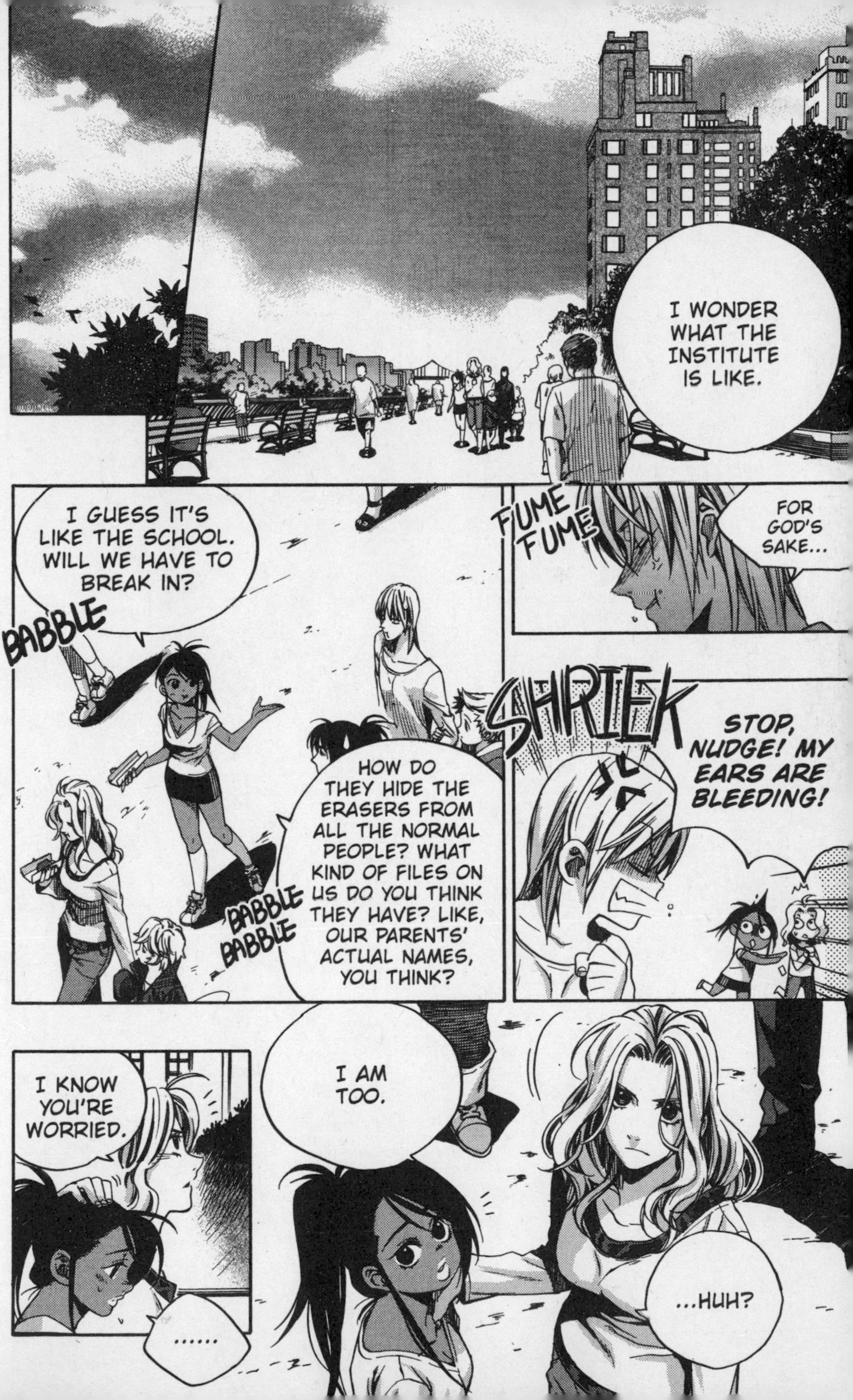
I WONDER WHAT THE INSTITUTE IS LIKE.
I GUESS IT'S LIKE THE SCHOOL. WILL WE HAVE TO BREAK IN?
BABBLE
FUME FUME
FOR GOD'S SAKE...
HOW DO THEY HIDE THE ERASERS FROM ALL THE NORMAL PEOPLE? WHAT KIND OF FILES ON US DO YOU THINK THEY HAVE? LIKE, OUR PARENTS' ACTUAL NAMES, YOU THINK?
BABBLE BABBLE
SHRIEK
STOP, NUDGE! MY EARS ARE BLEEDING!
I KNOW YOU'RE WORRIED.
I AM TOO.
....
...HUH?

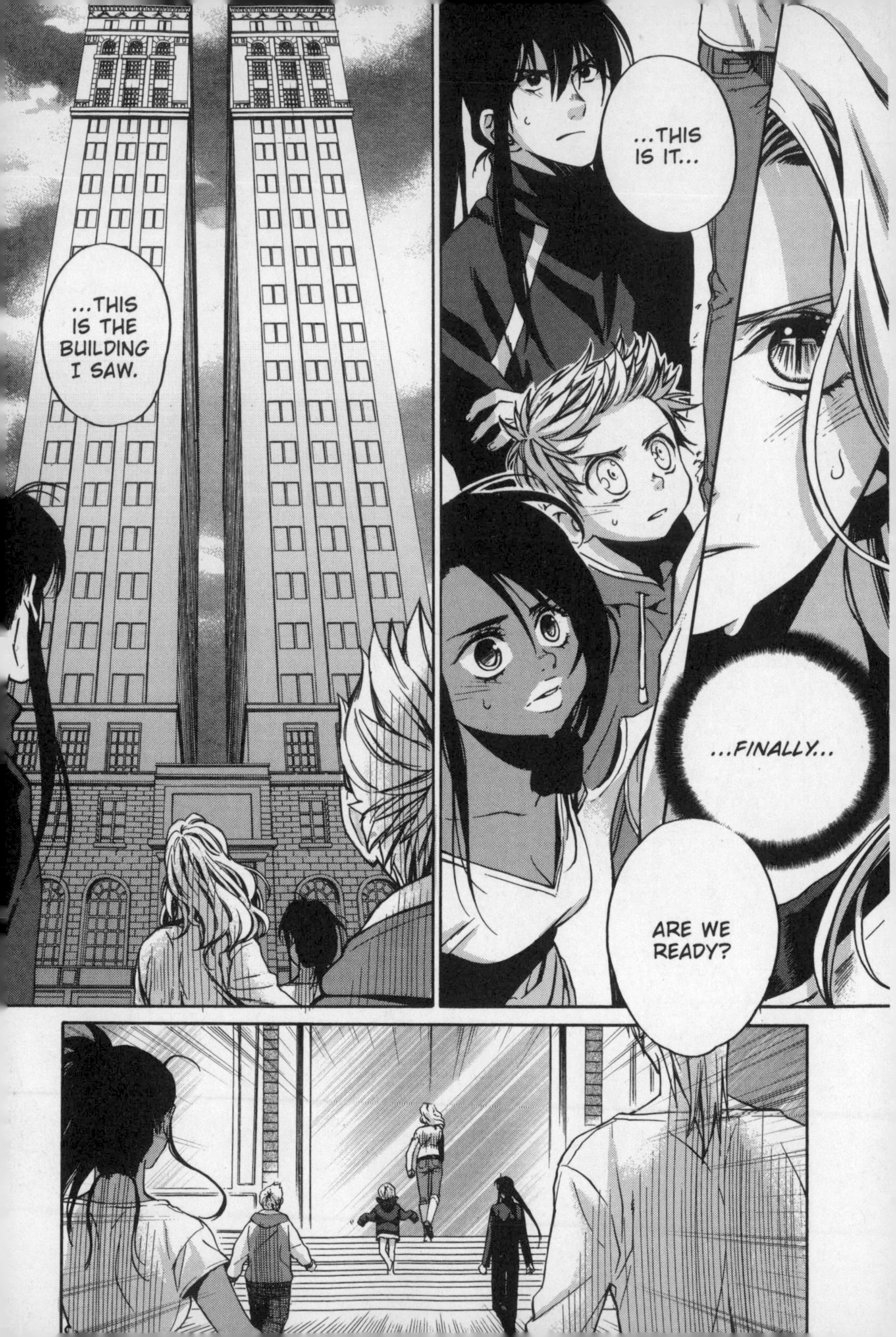
...THIS IS THE BUILDING I SAW.
...THIS IS IT...
...FINALLY...
ARE WE READY?

TAP

HERE.

2901
2902
2903
2904

1004 P
1005 C.C.C
1006 YEN PRESS
1007 HAKUSAN

INSTITUTE
...FOR...
HIGHER...
LIVING...

World
CNT insurance
FILL SYSTEM

2902
2903
2904

1003 NFN
1004 panasonic
1005 C.C.C

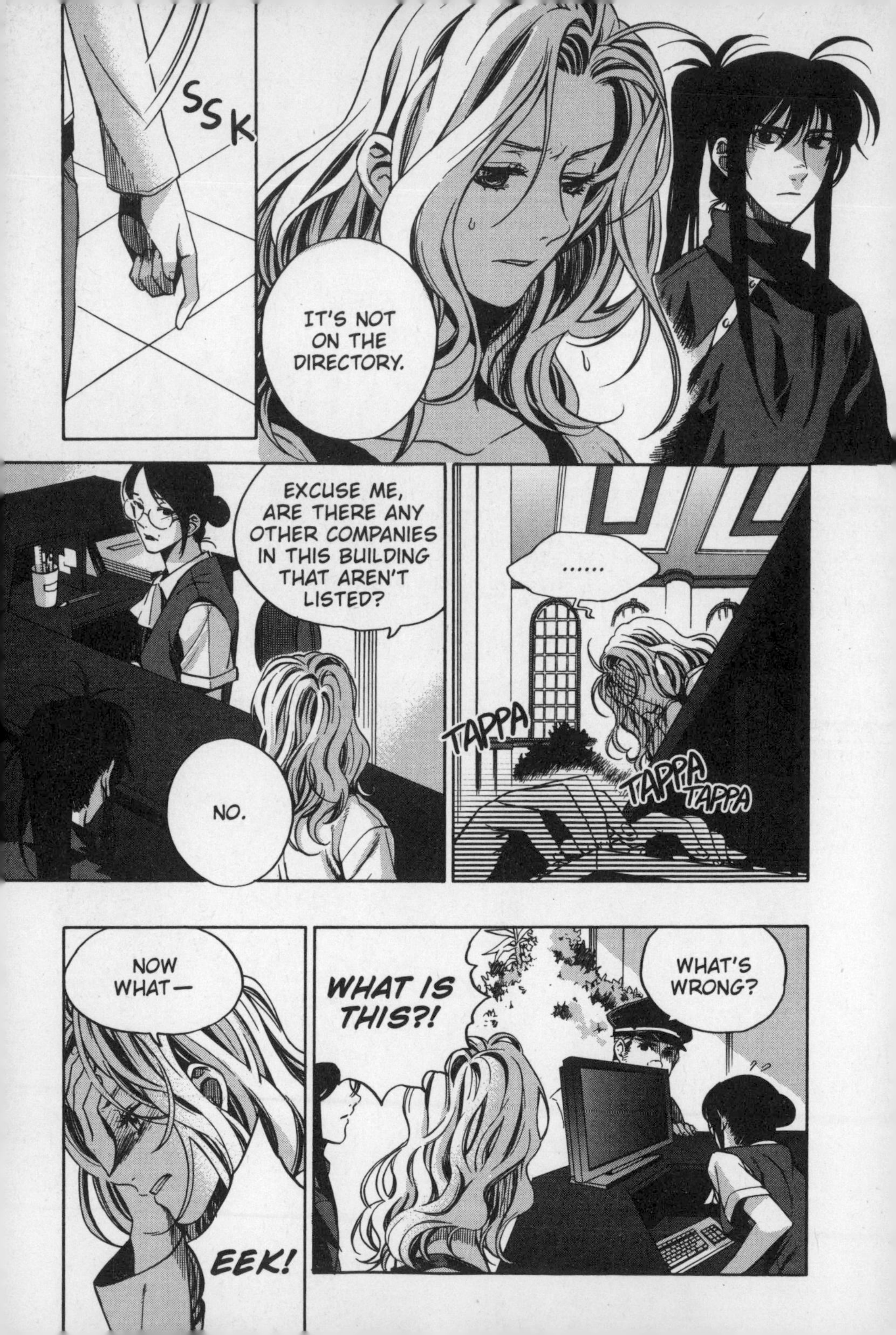
SSK
IT'S NOT ON THE DIRECTORY.
EXCUSE ME, ARE THERE ANY OTHER COMPANIES IN THIS BUILDING THAT AREN'T LISTED?
NO.
......
TAPPA
TAPPA TAPPA
NOW WHAT—
EEK!
WHAT IS THIS?!
WHAT'S WRONG?

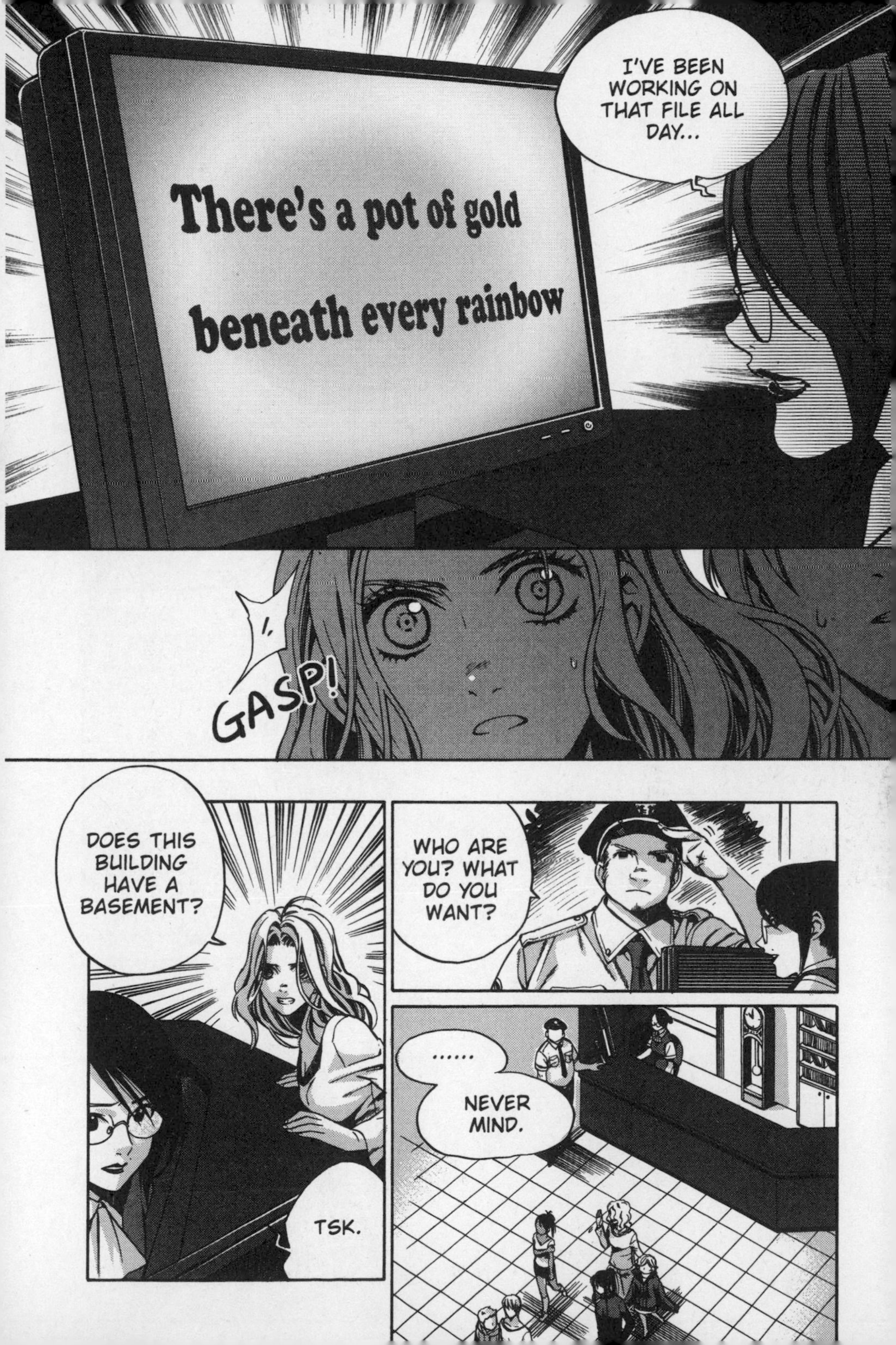
There's a pot of gold beneath every rainbow
I'VE BEEN WORKING ON THAT FILE ALL DAY...
GASP!
DOES THIS BUILDING HAVE A BASEMENT?
TSK.
WHO ARE YOU? WHAT DO YOU WANT?
......
NEVER MIND.

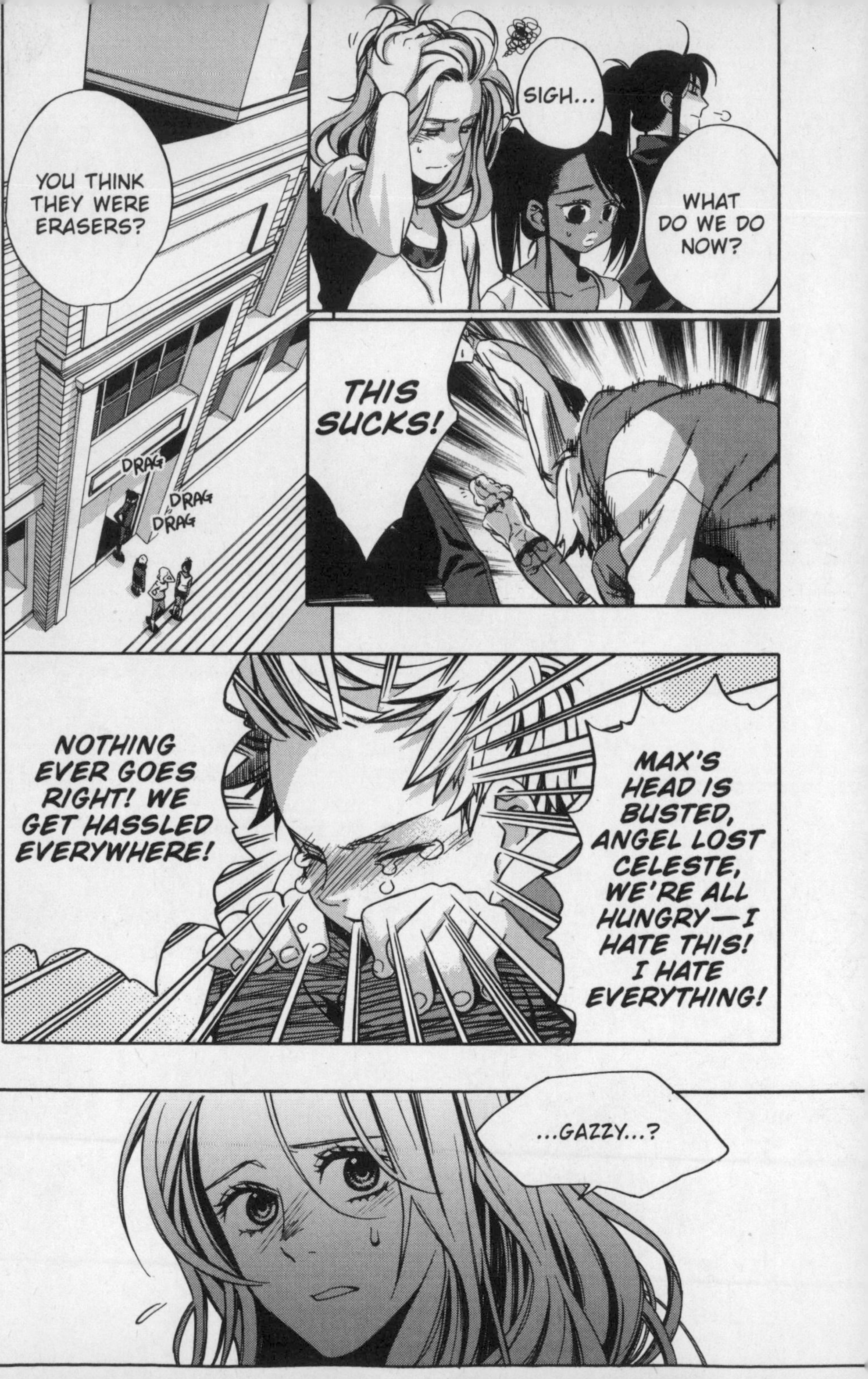
YOU THINK THEY WERE ERASERS?
DRAG
DRAG
DRAG
SIGH...
WHAT DO WE DO NOW?
THIS SUCKS!
NOTHING EVER GOES RIGHT! WE GET HASSLED EVERYWHERE!
MAX'S HEAD IS BUSTED, ANGEL LOST CELESTE, WE'RE ALL HUNGRY—I HATE THIS! I HATE EVERYTHING!
...GAZZY...?

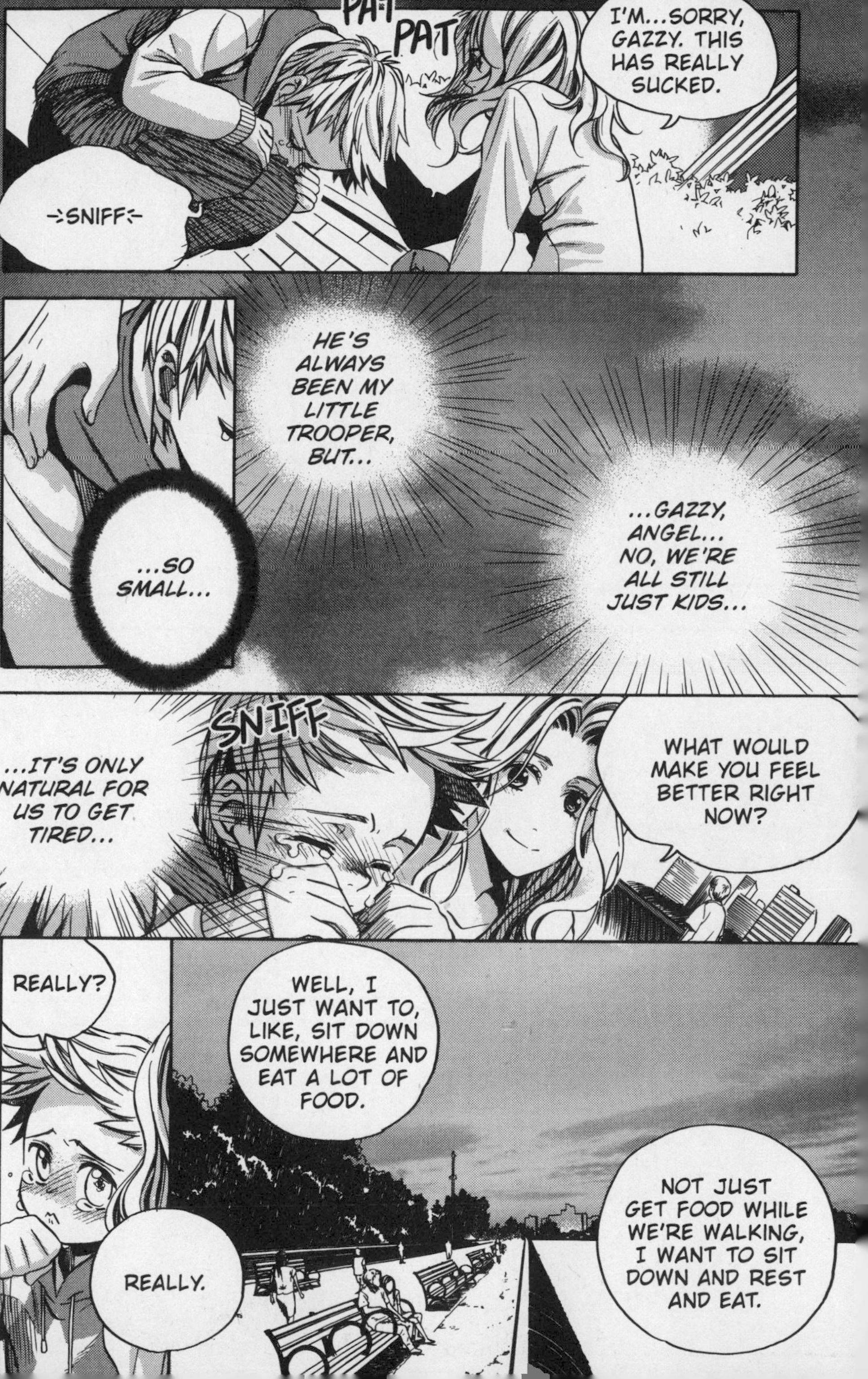
PAT PAT
I'M...SORRY, GAZZY. THIS HAS REALLY SUCKED.
-SNIFF-
HE'S ALWAYS BEEN MY LITTLE TROOPER, BUT...
...SO SMALL...
...GAZZY, ANGEL... NO, WE'RE ALL STILL JUST KIDS...
...IT'S ONLY NATURAL FOR US TO GET TIRED...
SNIFF
WHAT WOULD MAKE YOU FEEL BETTER RIGHT NOW?
REALLY?
REALLY.
WELL, I JUST WANT TO, LIKE, SIT DOWN SOMEWHERE AND EAT A LOT OF FOOD.
NOT JUST GET FOOD WHILE WE'RE WALKING, I WANT TO SIT DOWN AND REST AND EAT.

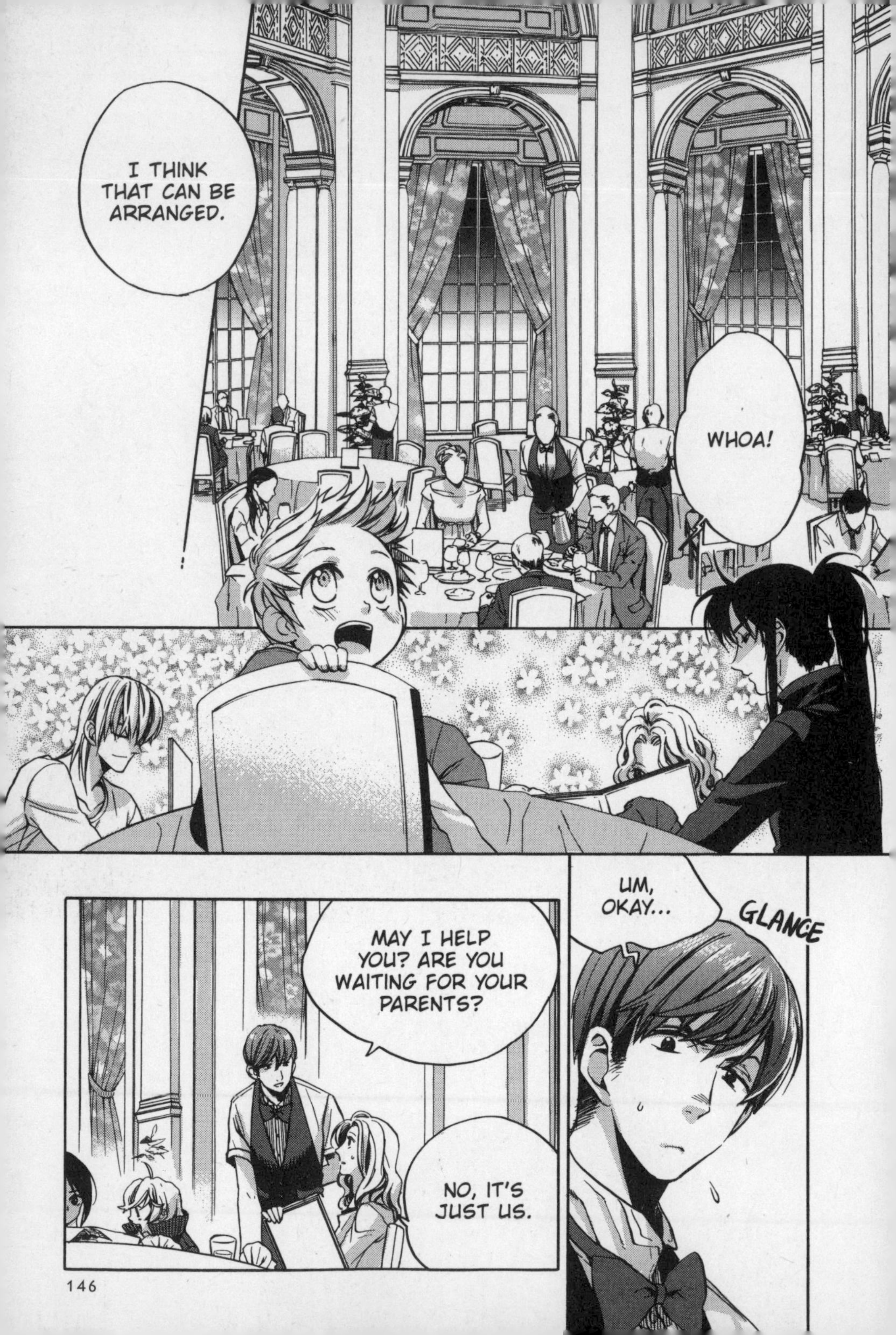
I THINK THAT CAN BE ARRANGED.
WHOA!
MAY I HELP YOU? ARE YOU WAITING FOR YOUR PARENTS?
NO, IT'S JUST US.
UM, OKAY...
GLANCE

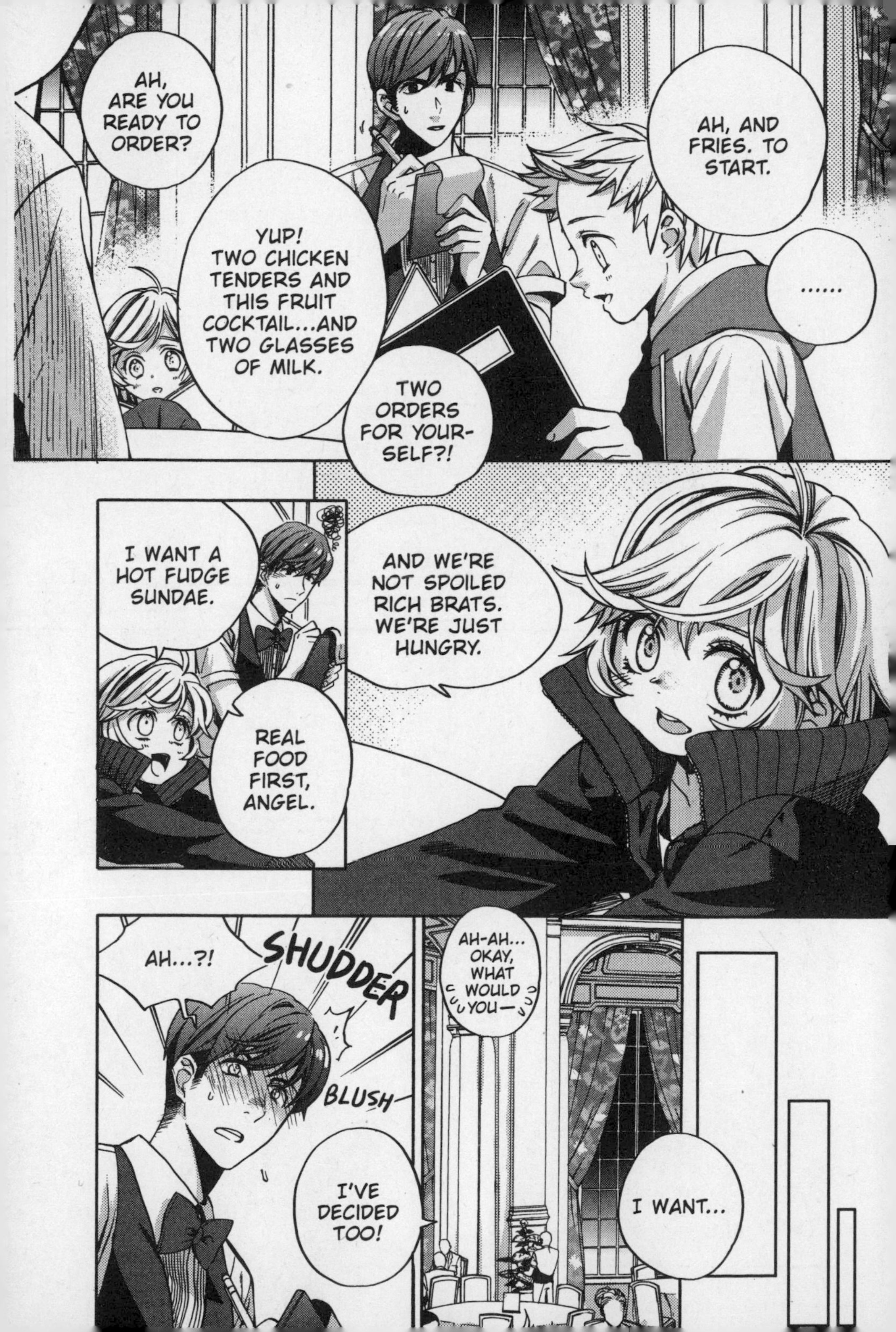
AH, ARE YOU READY TO ORDER?
YUP! TWO CHICKEN TENDERS AND THIS FRUIT COCKTAIL...AND TWO GLASSES OF MILK.
AH, AND FRIES. TO START.
......
TWO ORDERS FOR YOUR-SELF?!
I WANT A HOT FUDGE SUNDAE.
REAL FOOD FIRST, ANGEL.
AND WE'RE NOT SPOILED RICH BRATS. WE'RE JUST HUNGRY.
AH...?!
SHUDDER
BLUSH
I'VE DECIDED TOO!
AH-AH... OKAY, WHAT WOULD YOU—
I WANT...

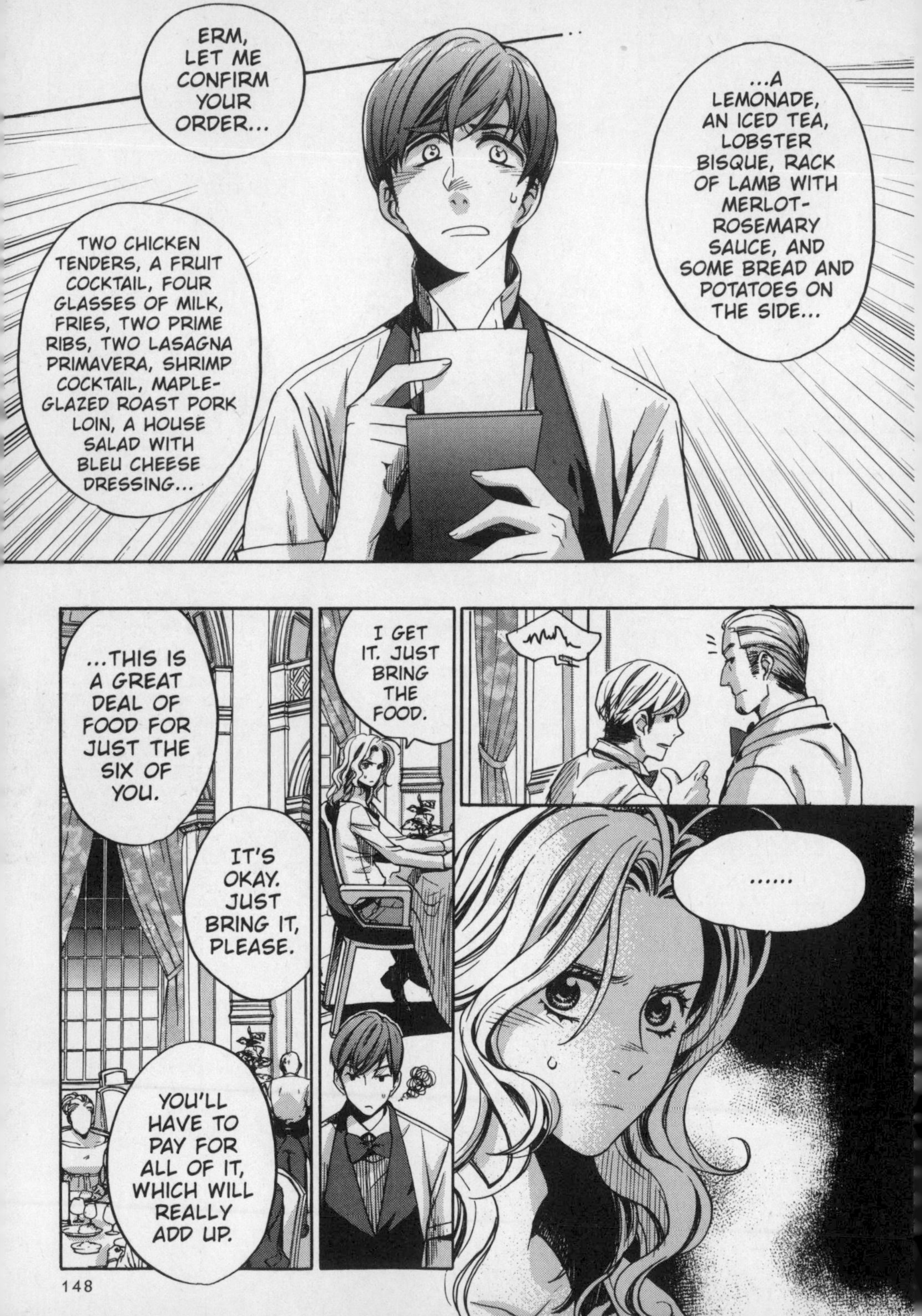
ERM, LET ME CONFIRM YOUR ORDER...
TWO CHICKEN TENDERS, A FRUIT COCKTAIL, FOUR GLASSES OF MILK, FRIES, TWO PRIME RIBS, TWO LASAGNA PRIMAVERA, SHRIMP COCKTAIL, MAPLE-GLAZED ROAST PORK LOIN, A HOUSE SALAD WITH BLEU CHEESE DRESSING...
...A LEMONADE, AN ICED TEA, LOBSTER BISQUE, RACK OF LAMB WITH MERLOT-ROSEMARY SAUCE, AND SOME BREAD AND POTATOES ON THE SIDE...
...THIS IS A GREAT DEAL OF FOOD FOR JUST THE SIX OF YOU.
IT'S OKAY. JUST BRING IT, PLEASE.
YOU'LL HAVE TO PAY FOR ALL OF IT, WHICH WILL REALLY ADD UP.
I GET IT. JUST BRING THE FOOD.
......

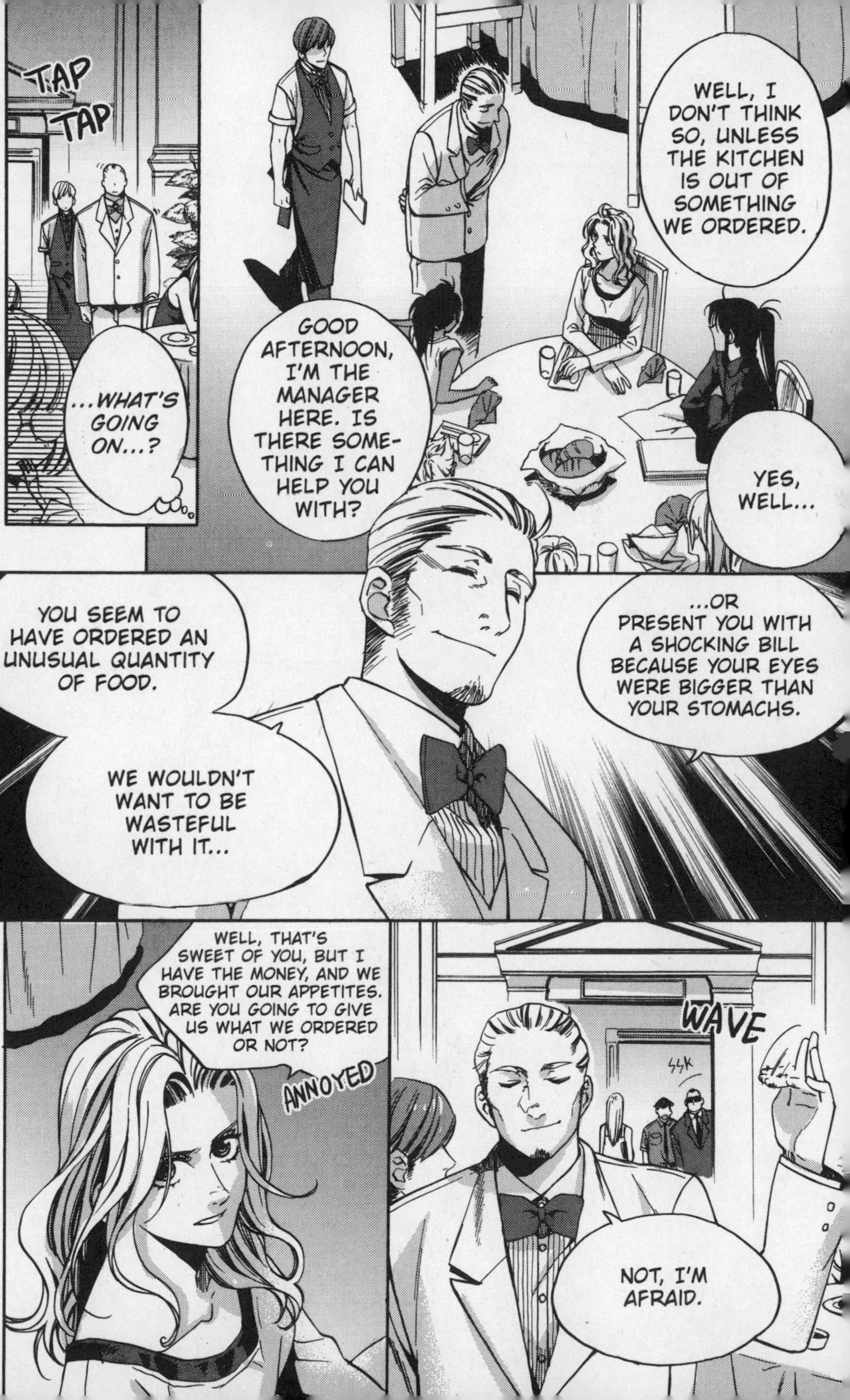
TAP
TAP
...WHAT'S GOING ON...?
GOOD AFTERNOON, I'M THE MANAGER HERE. IS THERE SOMETHING I CAN HELP YOU WITH?
WELL, I DON'T THINK SO, UNLESS THE KITCHEN IS OUT OF SOMETHING WE ORDERED.
YES, WELL...
YOU SEEM TO HAVE ORDERED AN UNUSUAL QUANTITY OF FOOD.
WE WOULDN'T WANT TO BE WASTEFUL WITH IT...
...OR PRESENT YOU WITH A SHOCKING BILL BECAUSE YOUR EYES WERE BIGGER THAN YOUR STOMACHS.
WELL, THAT'S SWEET OF YOU, BUT I HAVE THE MONEY, AND WE BROUGHT OUR APPETITES. ARE YOU GOING TO GIVE US WHAT WE ORDERED OR NOT?
ANNOYED
WAVE
SSK
NOT, I'M AFRAID.

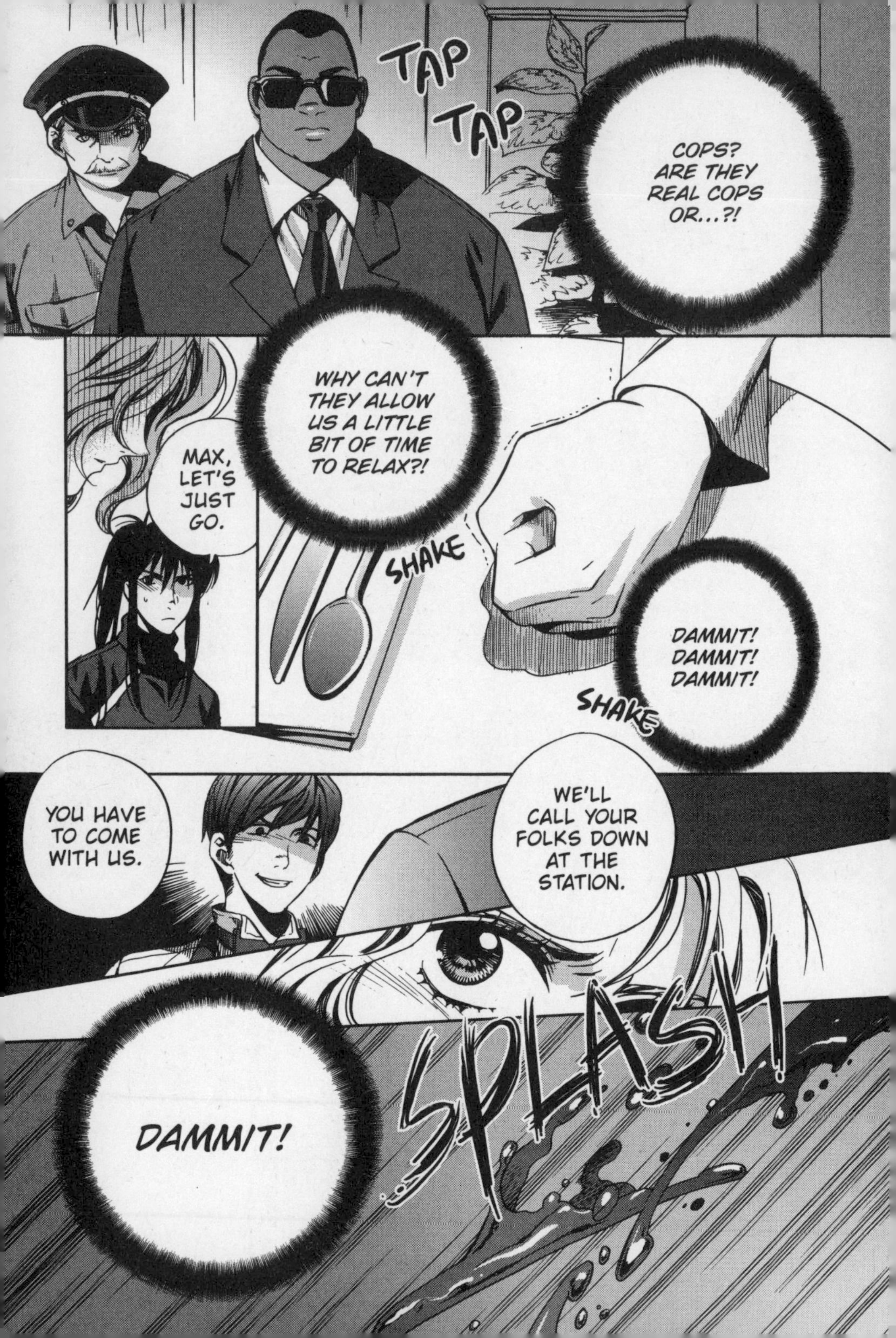
TAP
TAP
COPS? ARE THEY REAL COPS OR...?!
MAX, LET'S JUST GO.
WHY CAN'T THEY ALLOW US A LITTLE BIT OF TIME TO RELAX?!
SHAKE
DAMMIT! DAMMIT! DAMMIT!
SHAKE
YOU HAVE TO COME WITH US.
WE'LL CALL YOUR FOLKS DOWN AT THE STATION.
DAMMIT!
SPLASH!

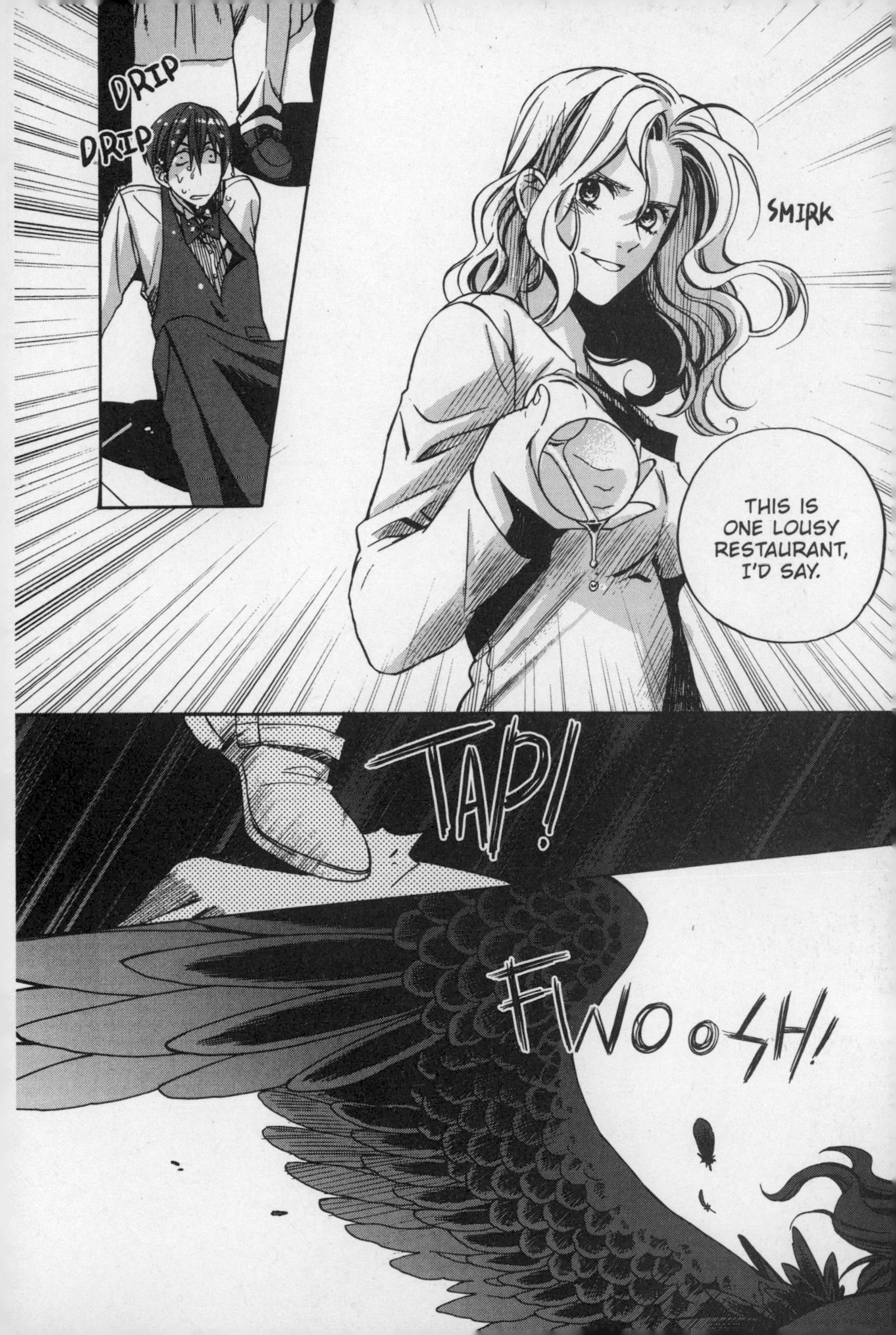
DRIP
DRIP
SMIRK
THIS IS ONE LOUSY RESTAURANT, I'D SAY.
TAP!
FWOOSH!

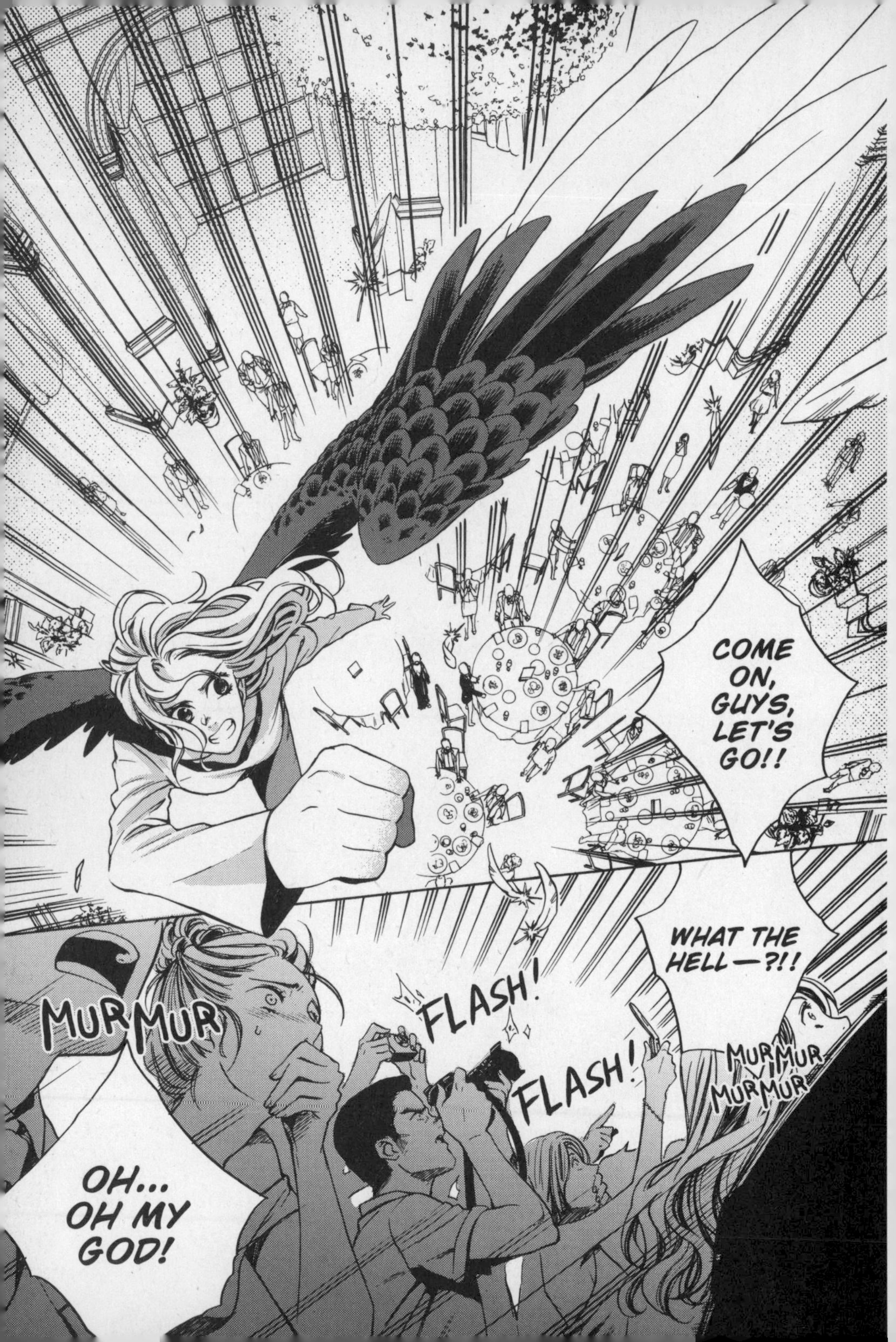
COME ON, GUYS, LET'S GO!!
MURMUR
FLASH!
WHAT THE HELL—?!!
FLASH!
MURMUR MURMUR
MURMUR MURMUR
OH... OH MY GOD!

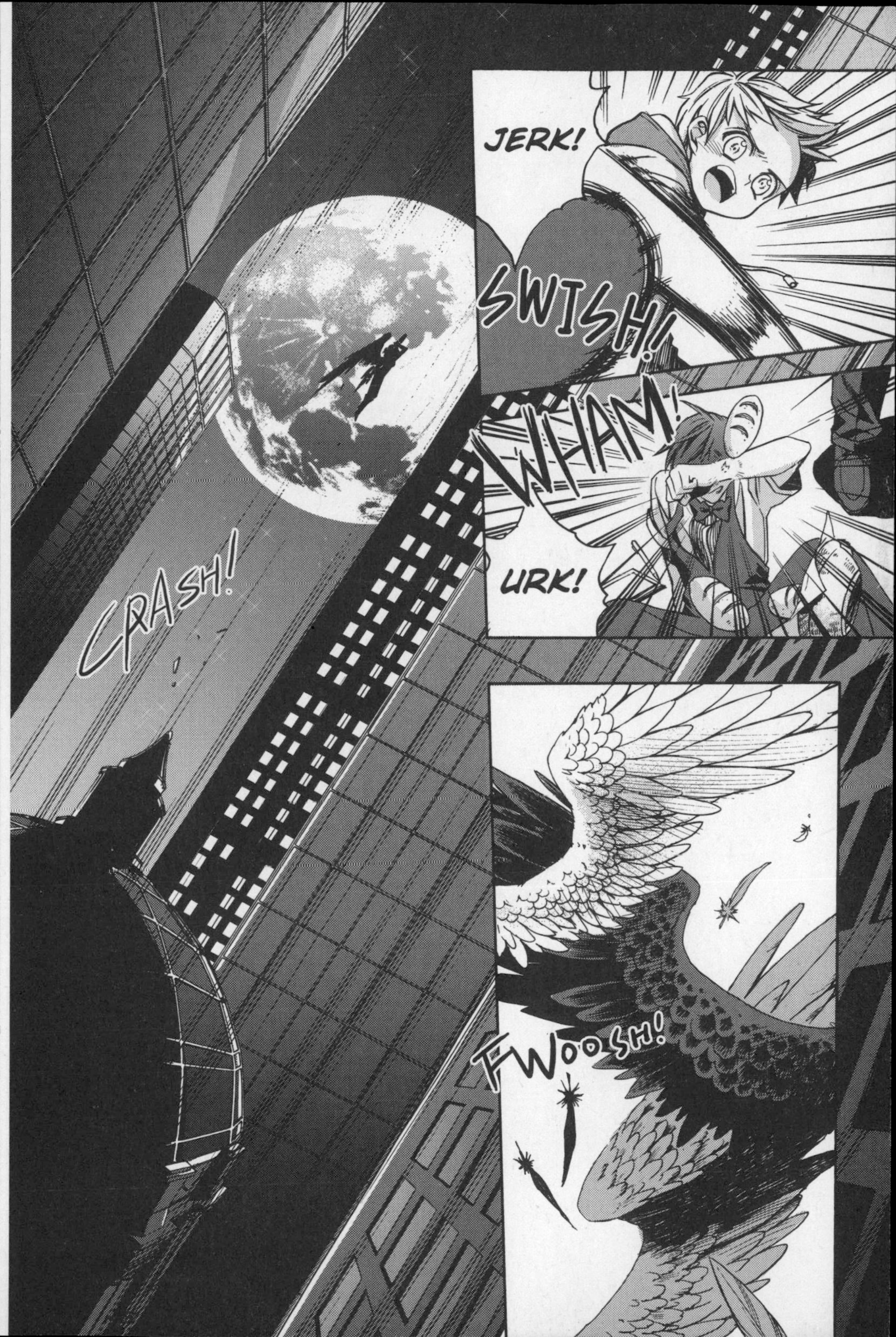
CRASH!
JERK!
SWISH!
WHAM!
URK!
FWOOSH!

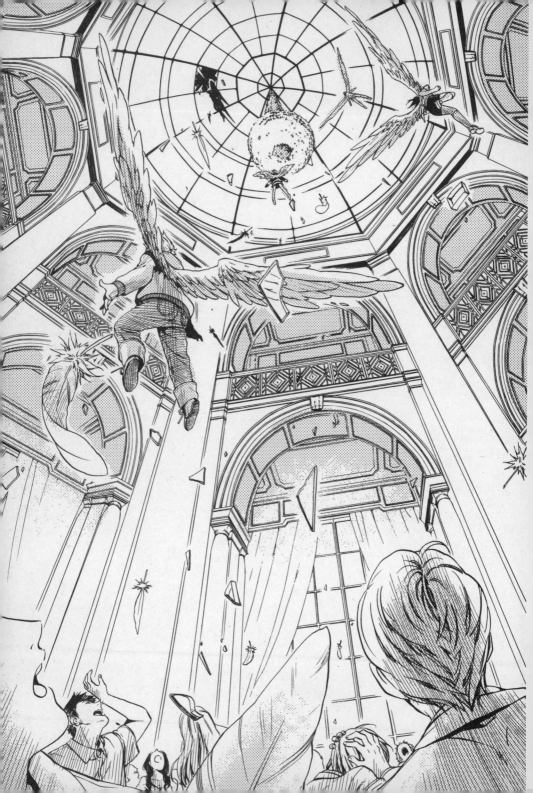

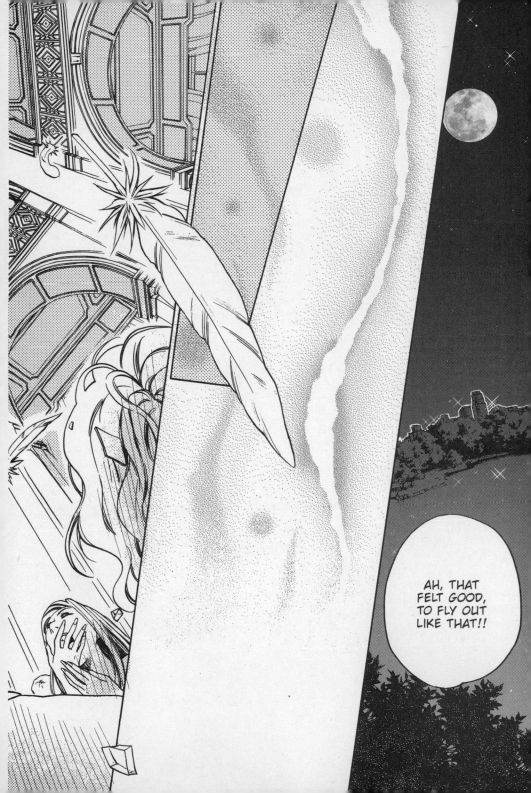

AH, THAT
FELT GOOD,
TO FLY OUT
LIKE THAT!!

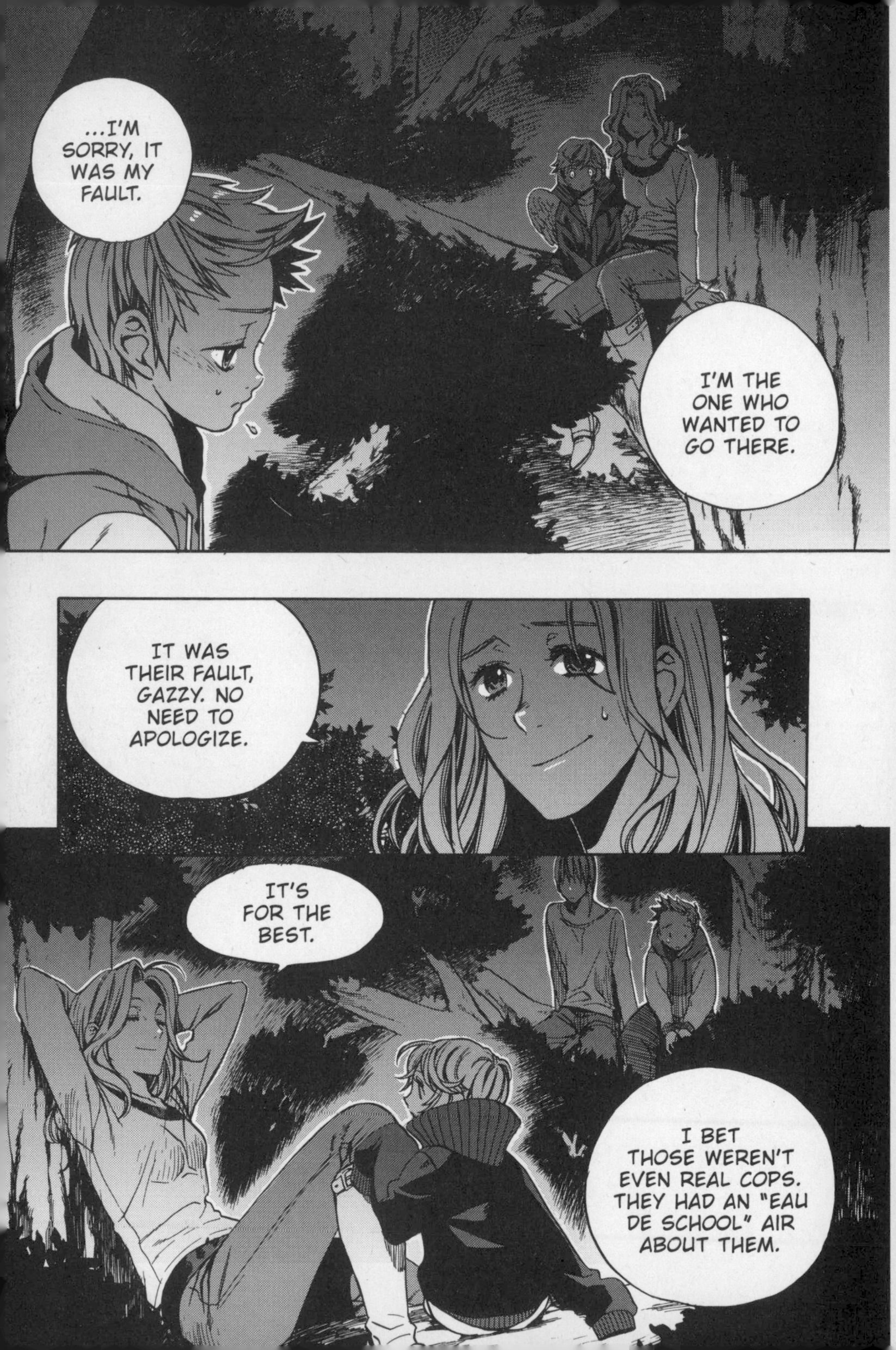
...I'M SORRY, IT WAS MY FAULT.
I'M THE ONE WHO WANTED TO GO THERE.
IT WAS THEIR FAULT, GAZZY. NO NEED TO APOLOGIZE.
IT'S FOR THE BEST.
I BET THOSE WEREN'T EVEN REAL COPS. THEY HAD AN "EAU DE SCHOOL" AIR ABOUT THEM.

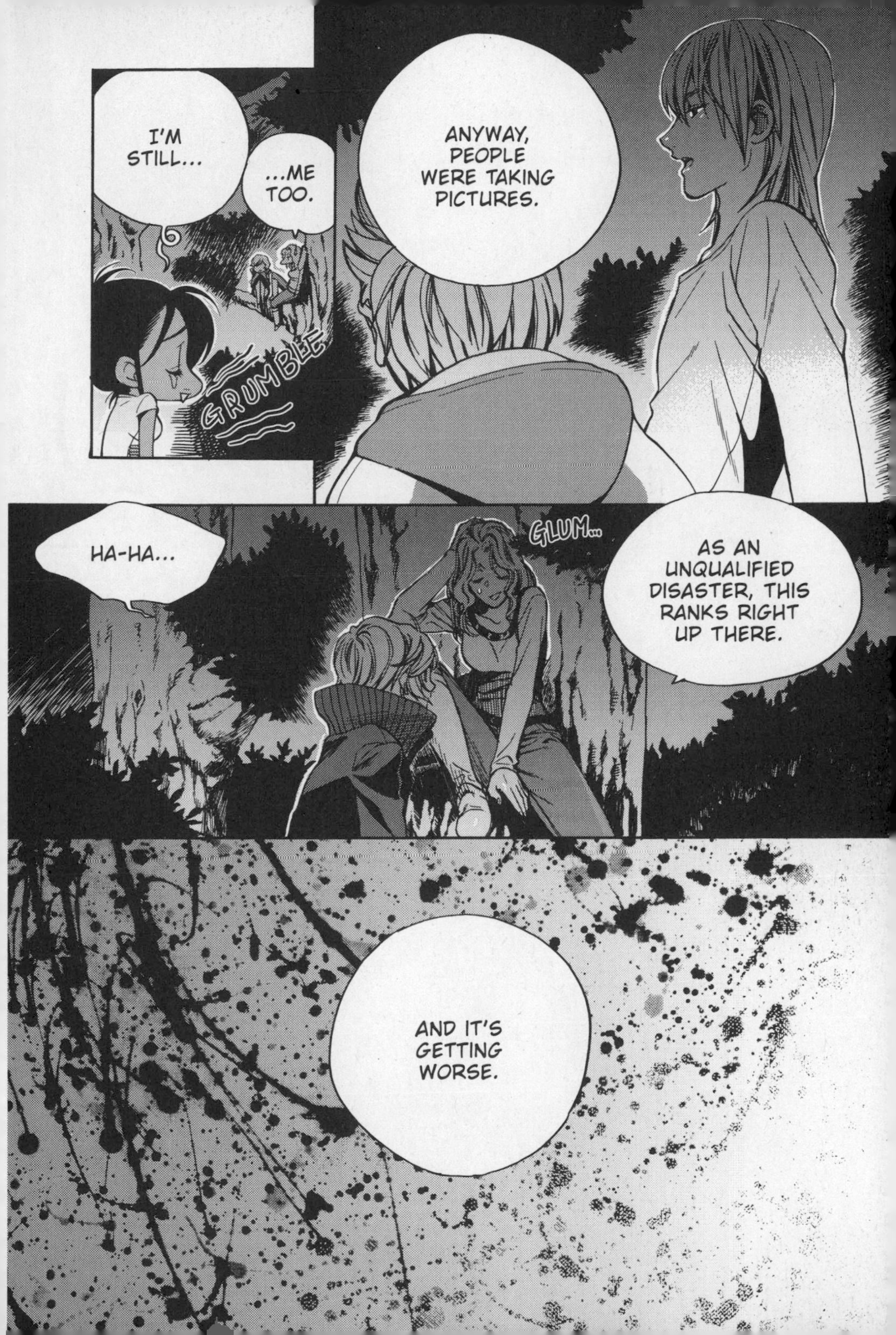
I'M STILL...
...ME TOO.
GRUMBLE
ANYWAY, PEOPLE WERE TAKING PICTURES.
HA-HA...
GLUM...
AS AN UNQUALIFIED DISASTER, THIS RANKS RIGHT UP THERE.
AND IT'S GETTING WORSE.

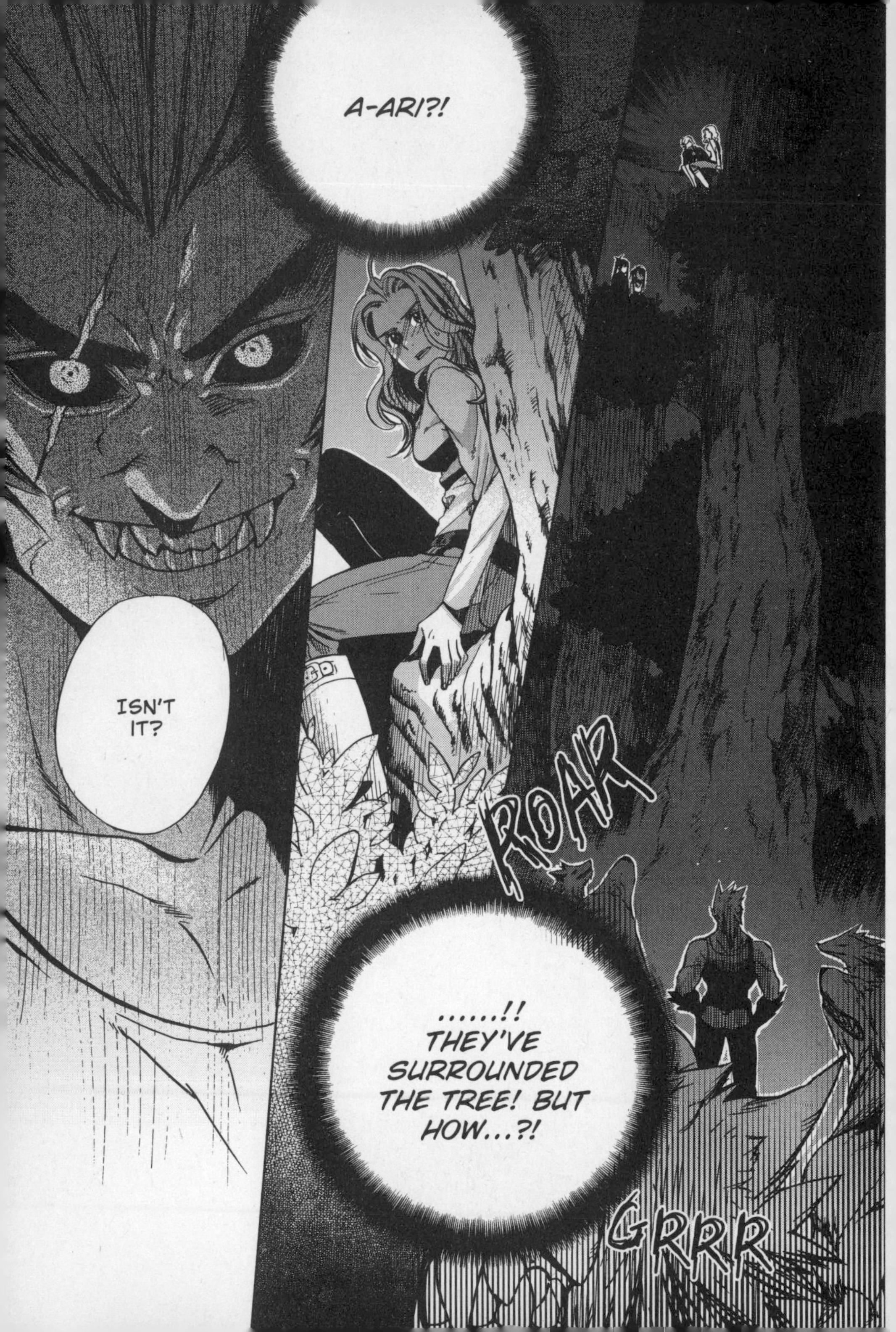
ISN'T IT?
A-ARI?!
ROAR
......!! THEY'VE SURROUNDED THE TREE! BUT HOW...?!
GRRR

MAXIMUM RIDE
CHAPTER 13

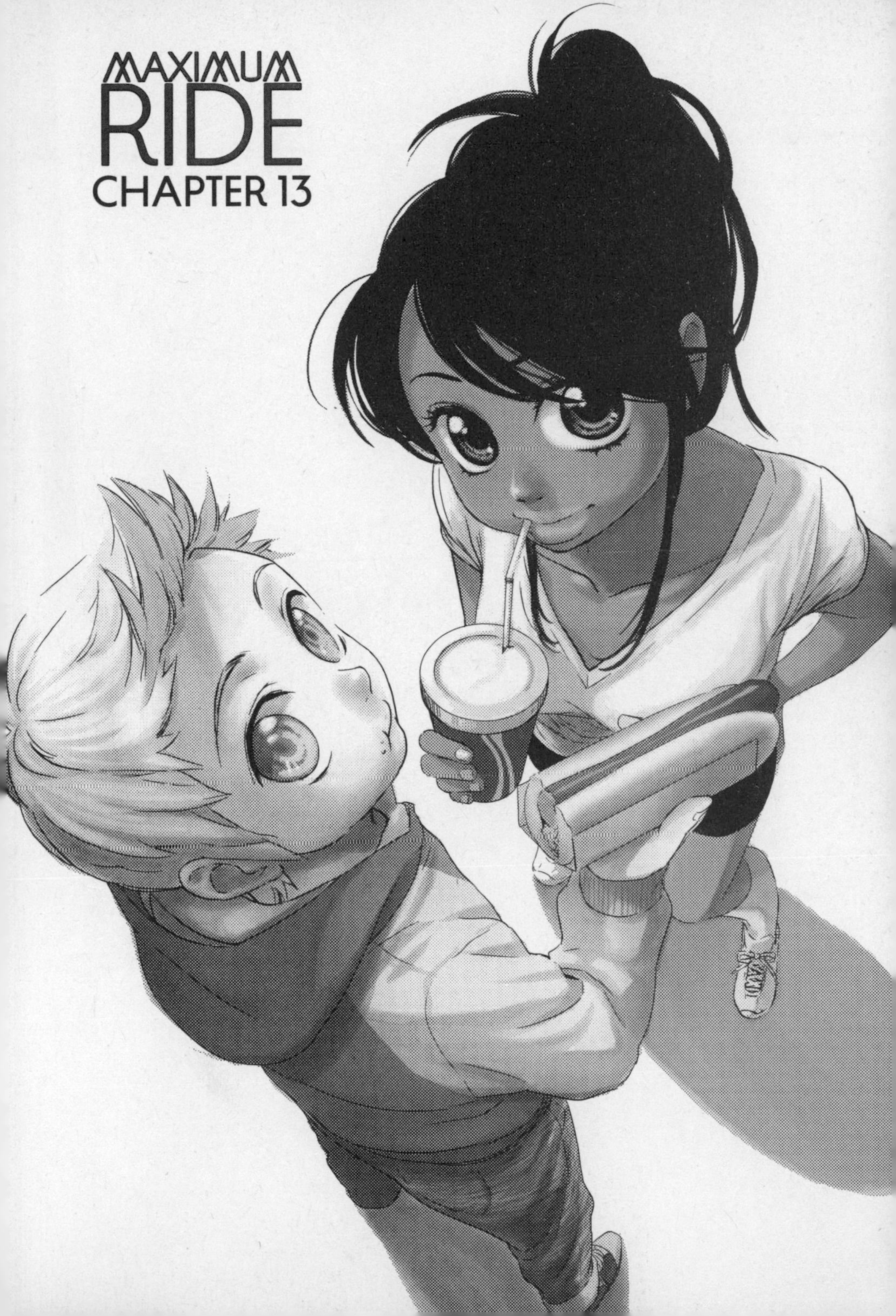

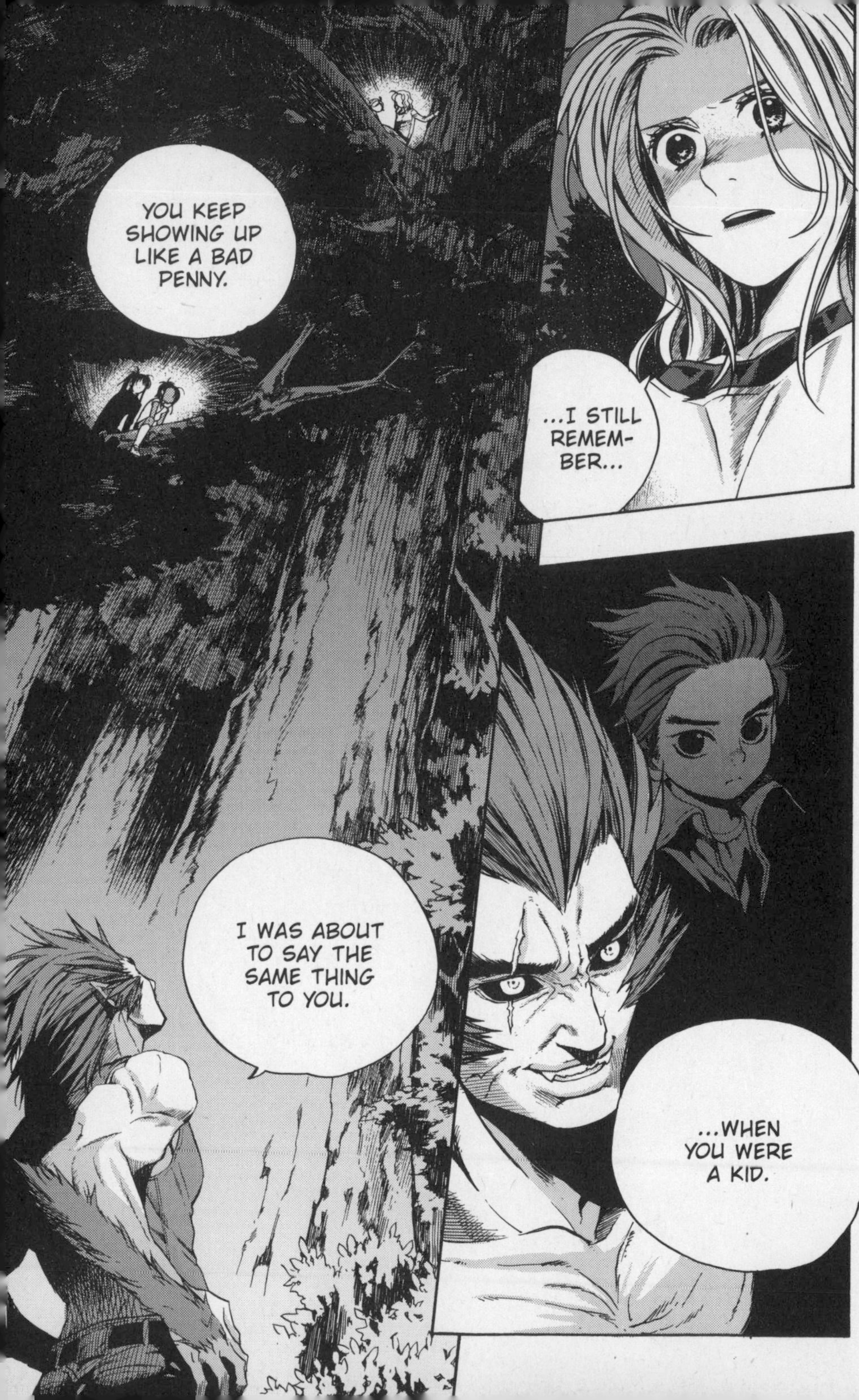
YOU KEEP SHOWING UP LIKE A BAD PENNY.
I WAS ABOUT TO SAY THE SAME THING TO YOU.
...I STILL REMEM-BER...
...WHEN YOU WERE A KID.

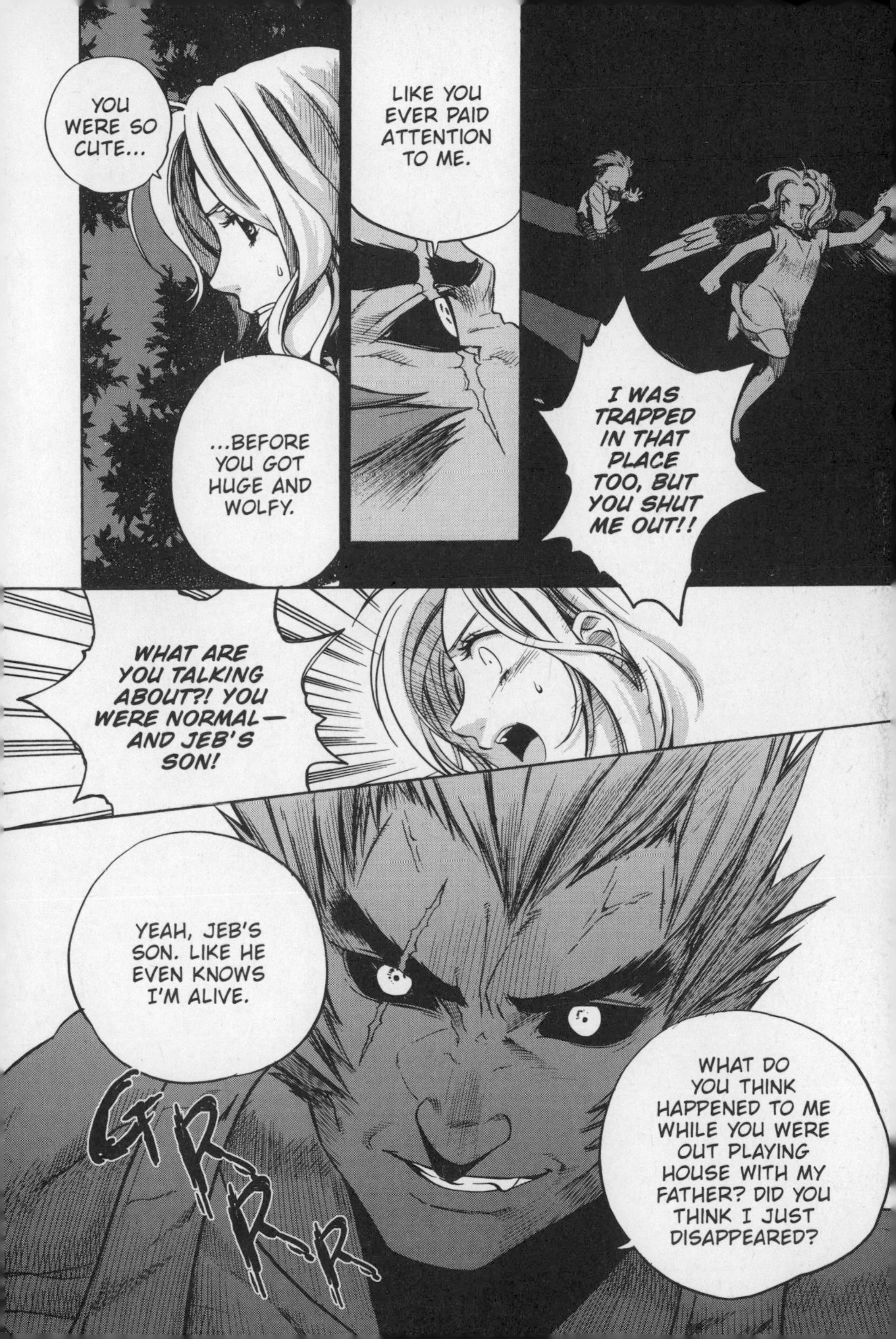
YOU WERE SO CUTE...
...BEFORE YOU GOT HUGE AND WOLFY.
LIKE YOU EVER PAID ATTENTION TO ME.
I WAS TRAPPED IN THAT PLACE TOO, BUT YOU SHUT ME OUT!!
WHAT ARE YOU TALKING ABOUT?! YOU WERE NORMAL—AND JEB'S SON!
YEAH, JEB'S SON. LIKE HE EVEN KNOWS I'M ALIVE.
GRR-R
WHAT DO YOU THINK HAPPENED TO ME WHILE YOU WERE OUT PLAYING HOUSE WITH MY FATHER? DID YOU THINK I JUST DISAPPEARED?

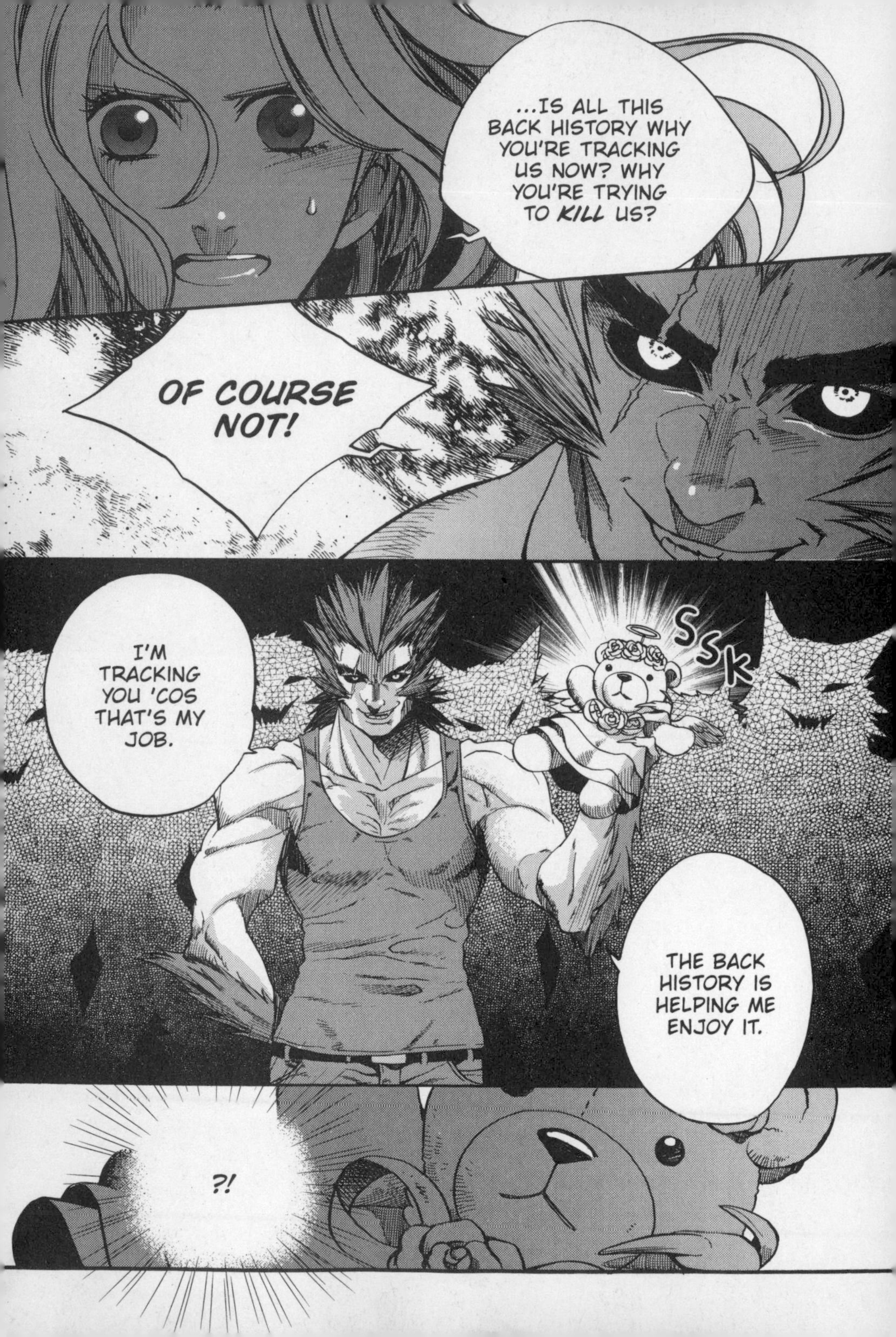
...IS ALL THIS BACK HISTORY WHY YOU'RE TRACKING US NOW? WHY YOU'RE TRYING TO KILL US?
OF COURSE NOT!
I'M TRACKING YOU 'COS THAT'S MY JOB.
SSK
THE BACK HISTORY IS HELPING ME ENJOY IT.
?!

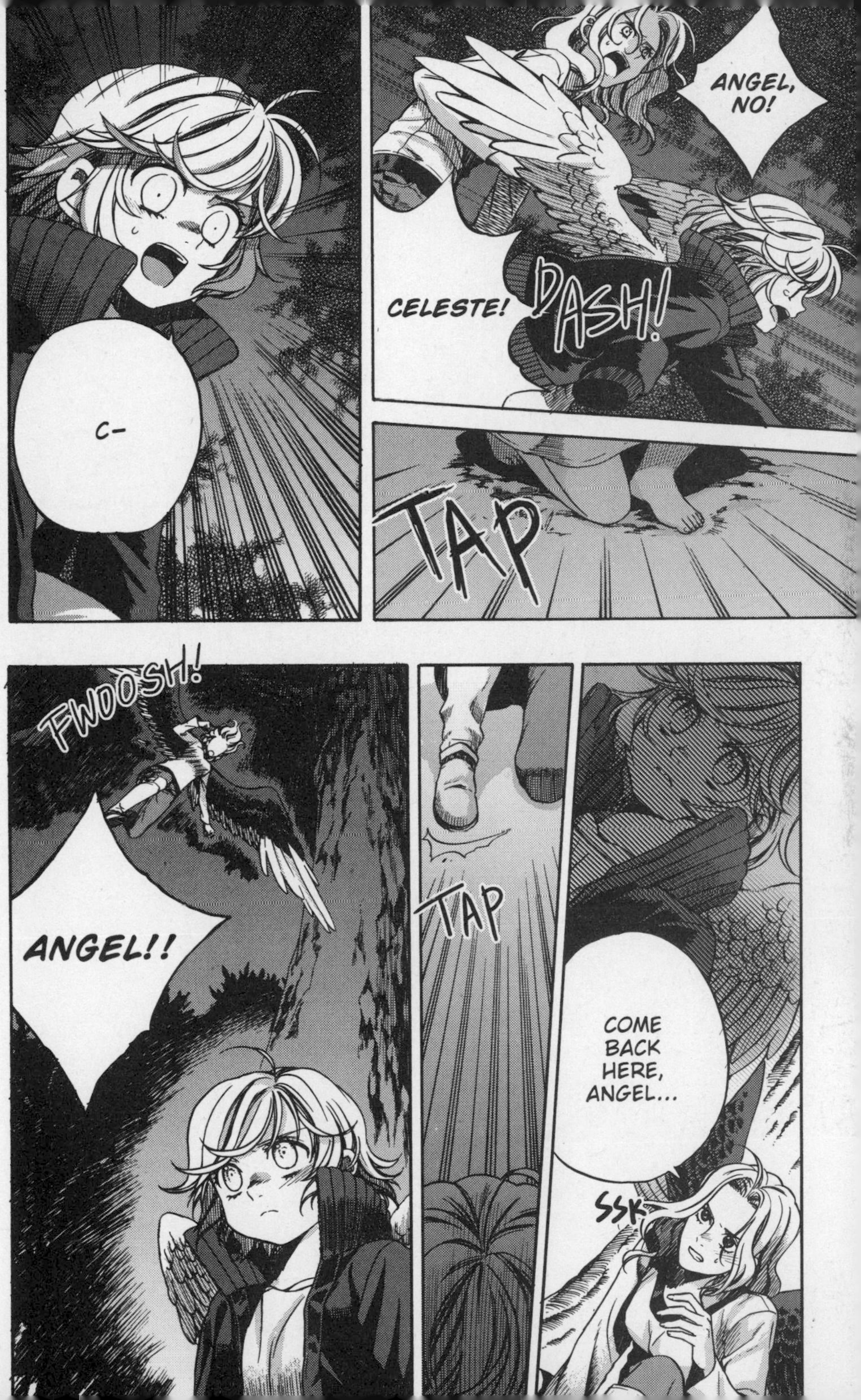
C–
ANGEL, NO!
CELESTE!
DASH!
TAP
FWOOSH!
ANGEL!!
TAP
COME BACK HERE, ANGEL...
SSK

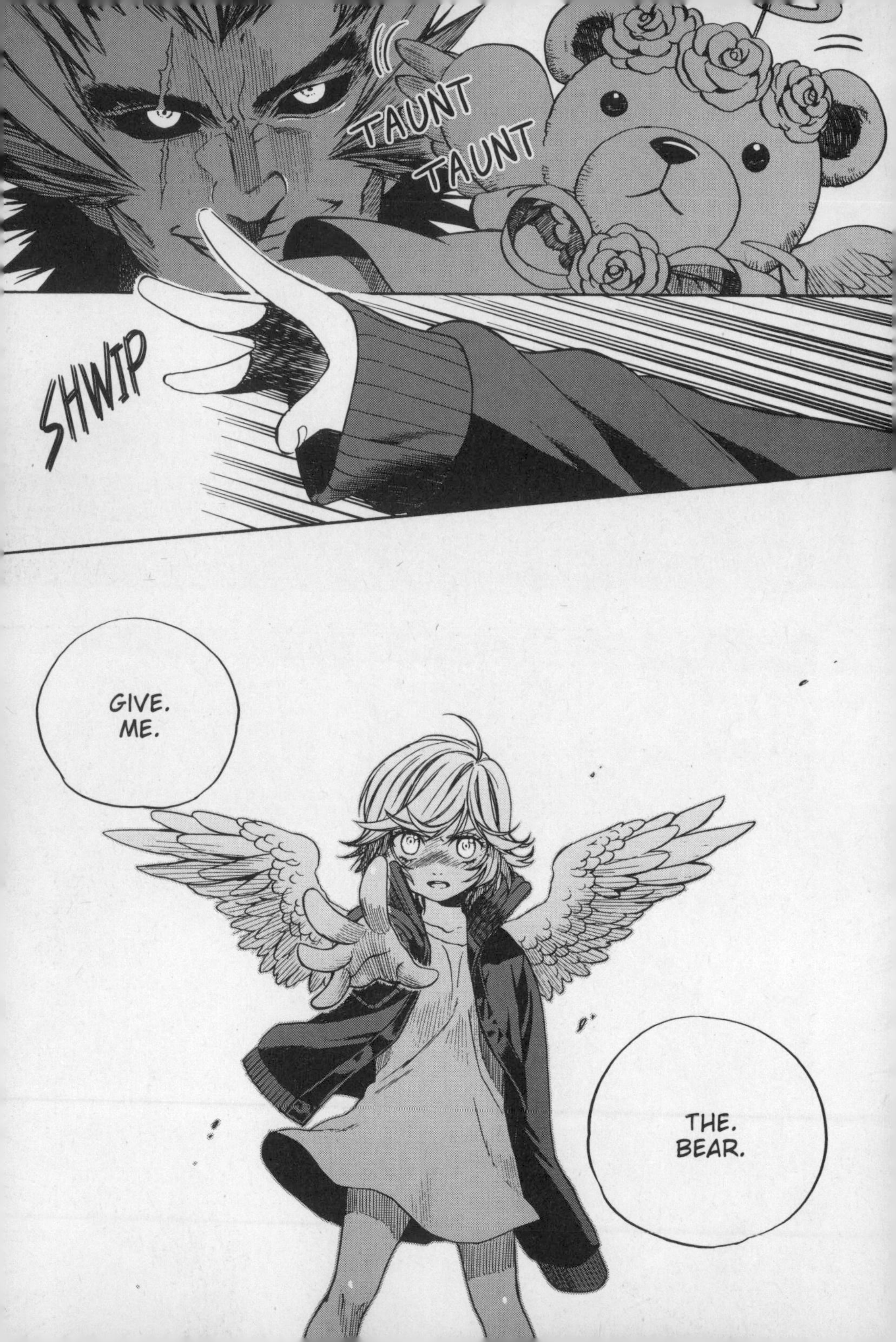
TAUNT
TAUNT
SHWIP
GIVE. ME.
THE. BEAR.

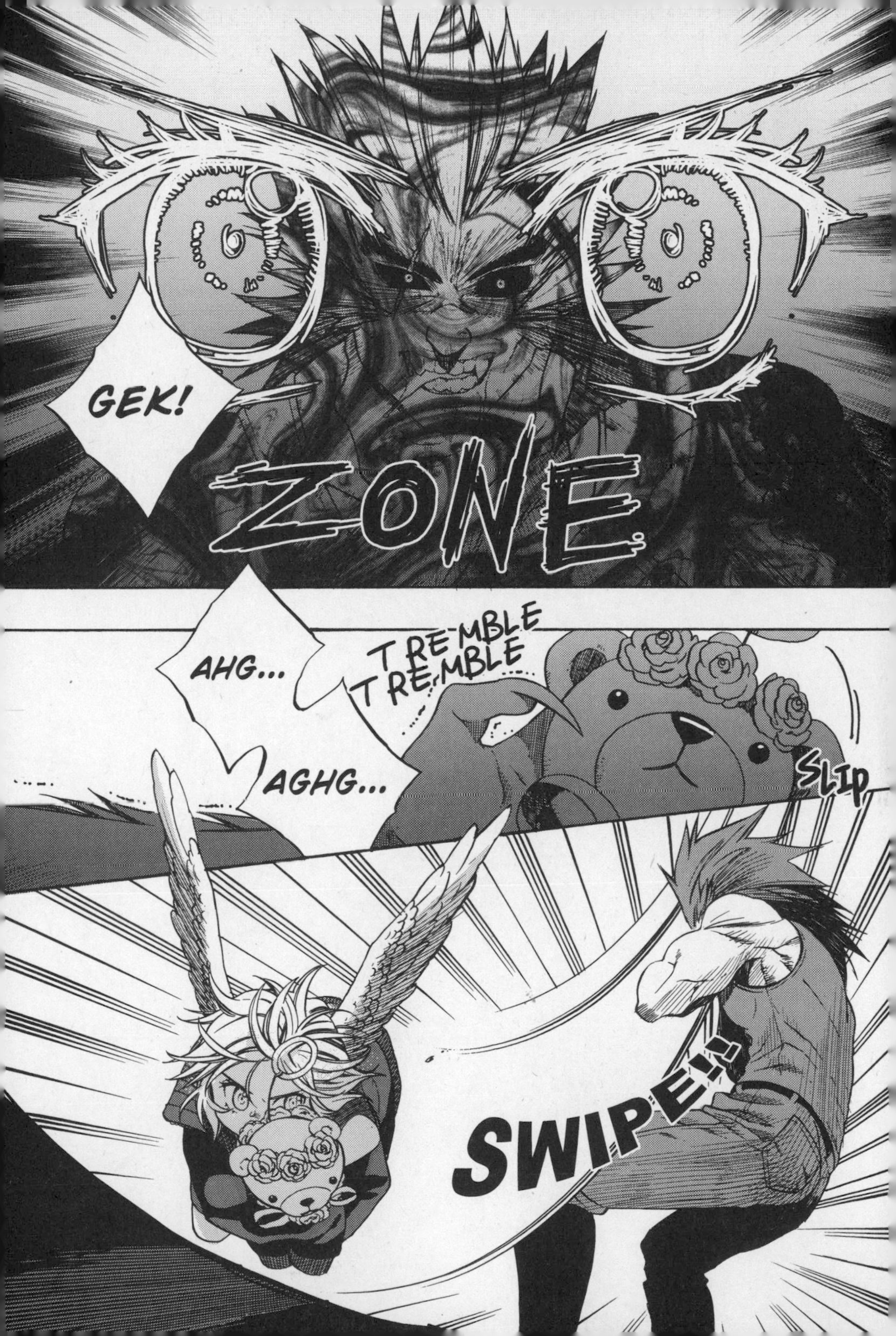
GEK!
ZONE
AHG...
TREMBLE TREMBLE
AGHG...
SLIP
SWIPE!!

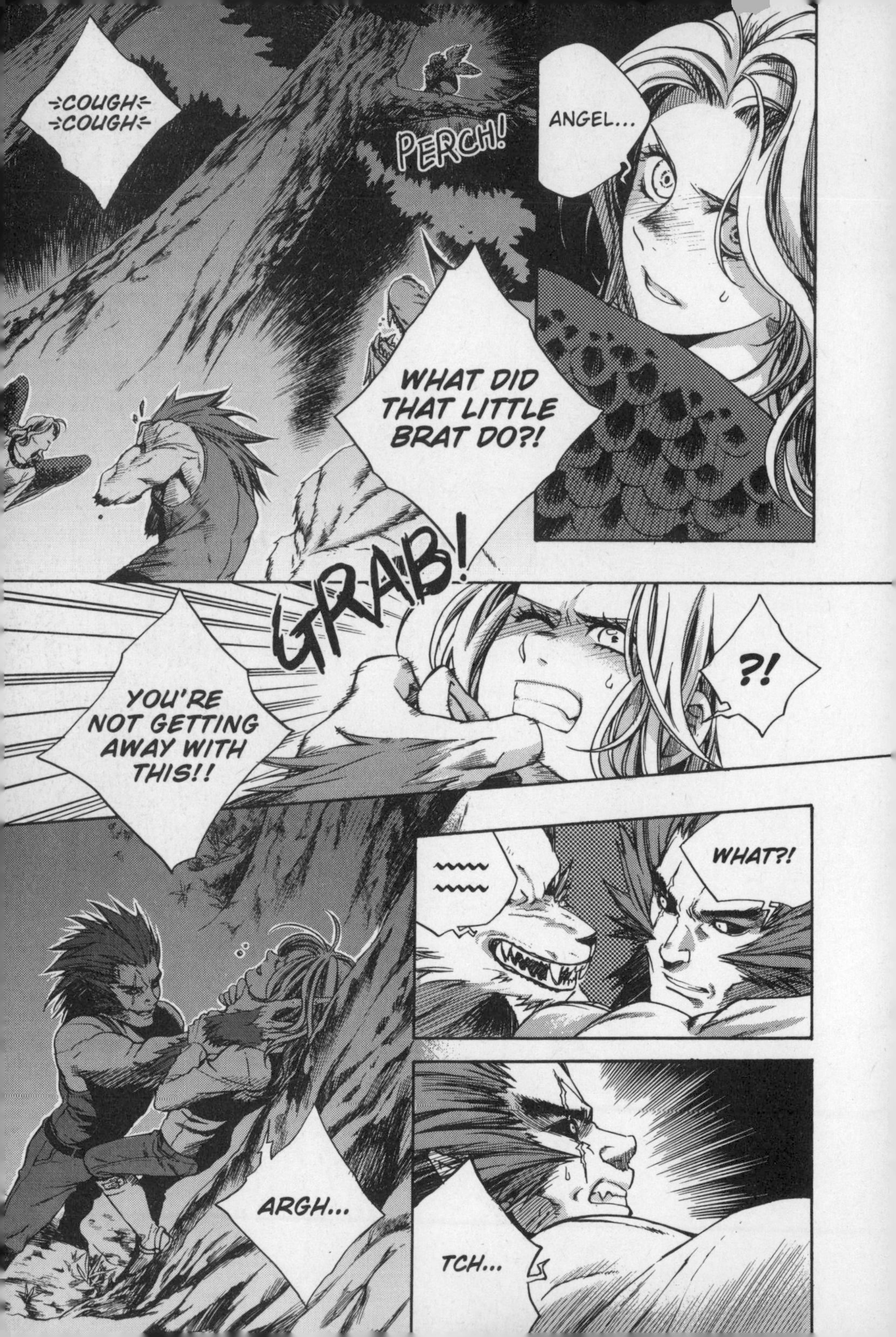

COUGH COUGH
PERCH!
ANGEL...
WHAT DID THAT LITTLE BRAT DO?!
GRAB!
YOU'RE NOT GETTING AWAY WITH THIS!!
?!
ARGH...
~~~ ~~~
WHAT?!
TCH...
~~~

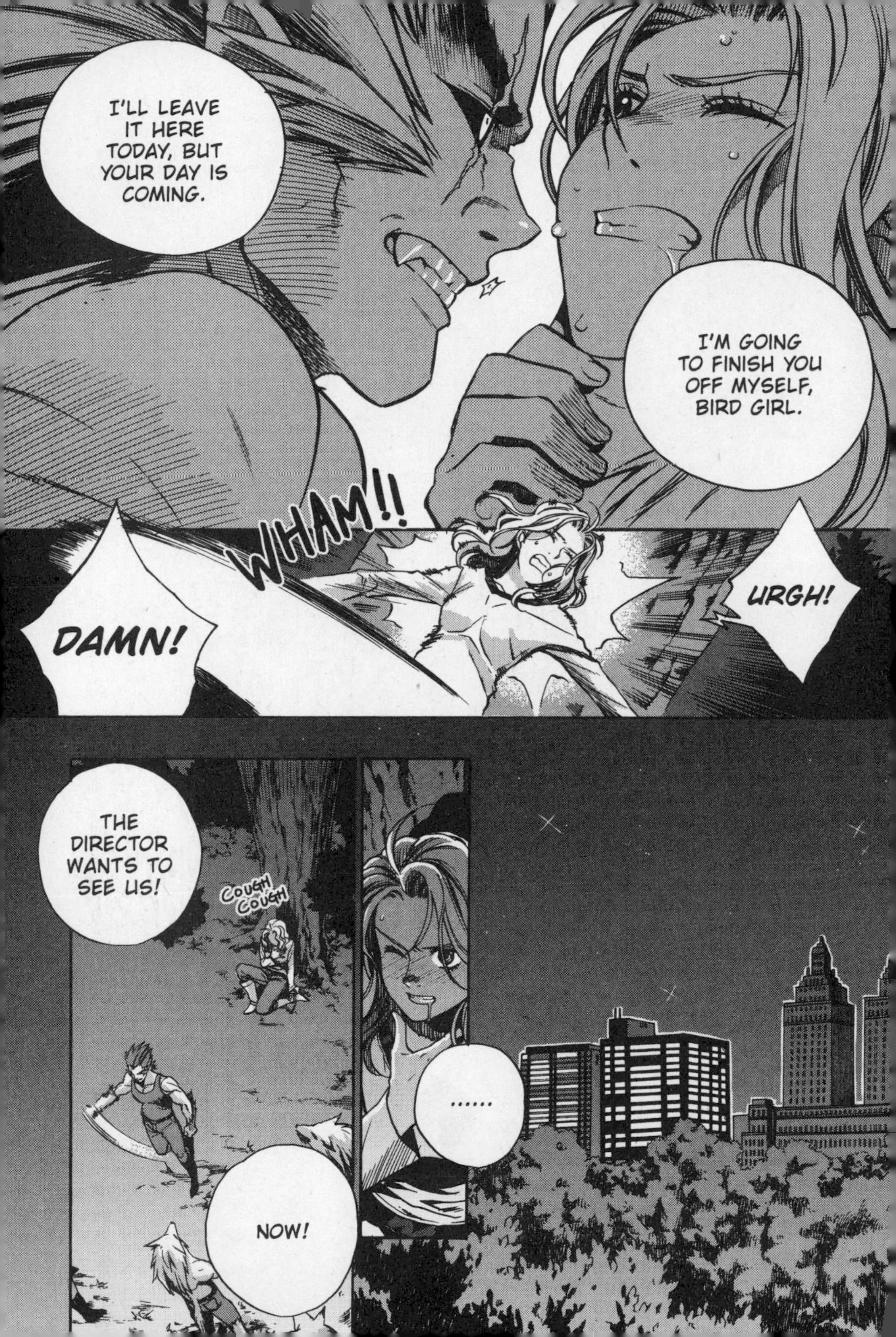
I'LL LEAVE IT HERE TODAY, BUT YOUR DAY IS COMING.
I'M GOING TO FINISH YOU OFF MYSELF, BIRD GIRL.
DAMN!
WHAM!!
URGH!
THE DIRECTOR WANTS TO SEE US!
COUGH COUGH
NOW!
......

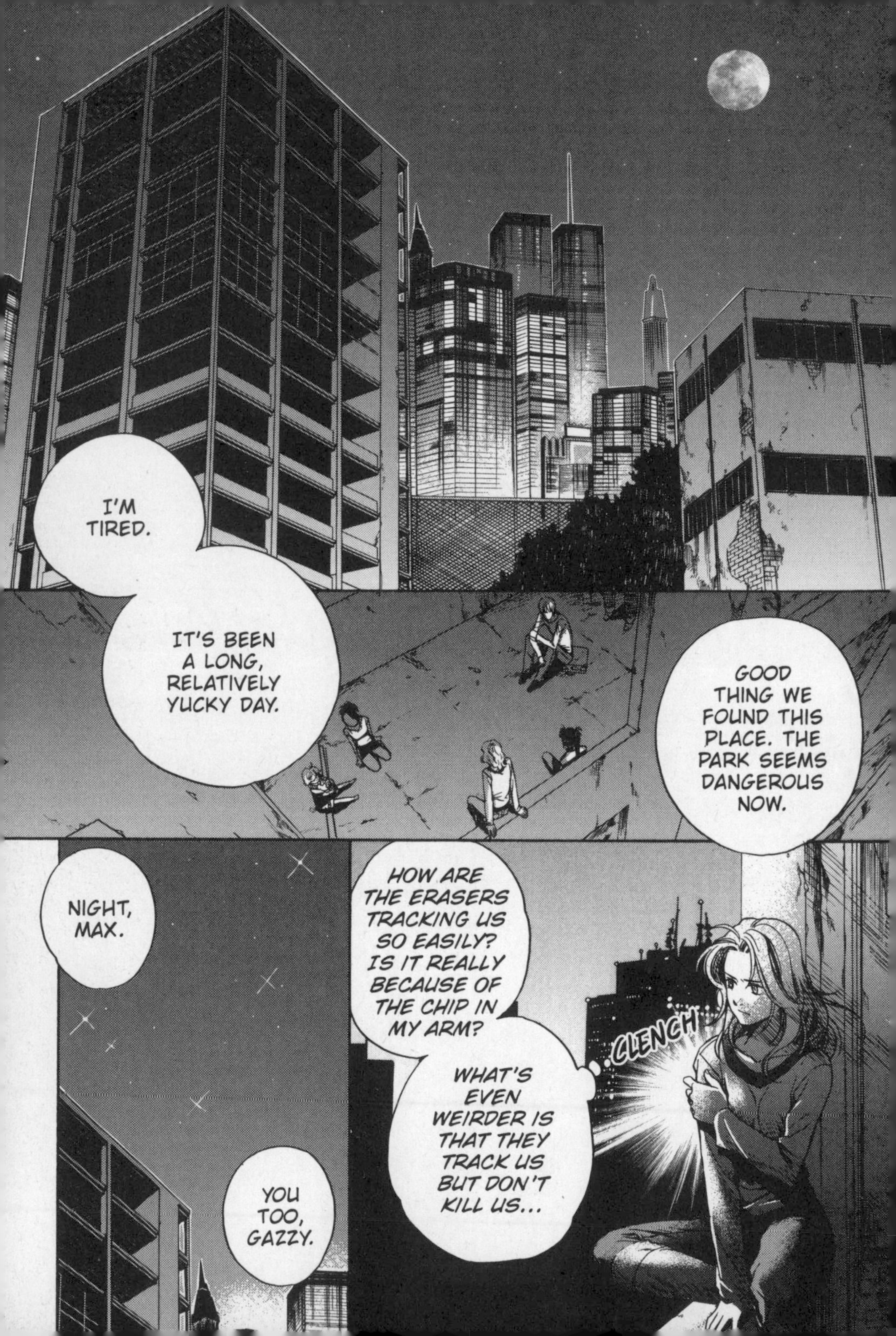
I'M TIRED.
IT'S BEEN A LONG, RELATIVELY YUCKY DAY.
GOOD THING WE FOUND THIS PLACE. THE PARK SEEMS DANGEROUS NOW.
NIGHT, MAX.
YOU TOO, GAZZY.
HOW ARE THE ERASERS TRACKING US SO EASILY? IS IT REALLY BECAUSE OF THE CHIP IN MY ARM?
CLENCH
WHAT'S EVEN WEIRDER IS THAT THEY TRACK US BUT DON'T KILL US...

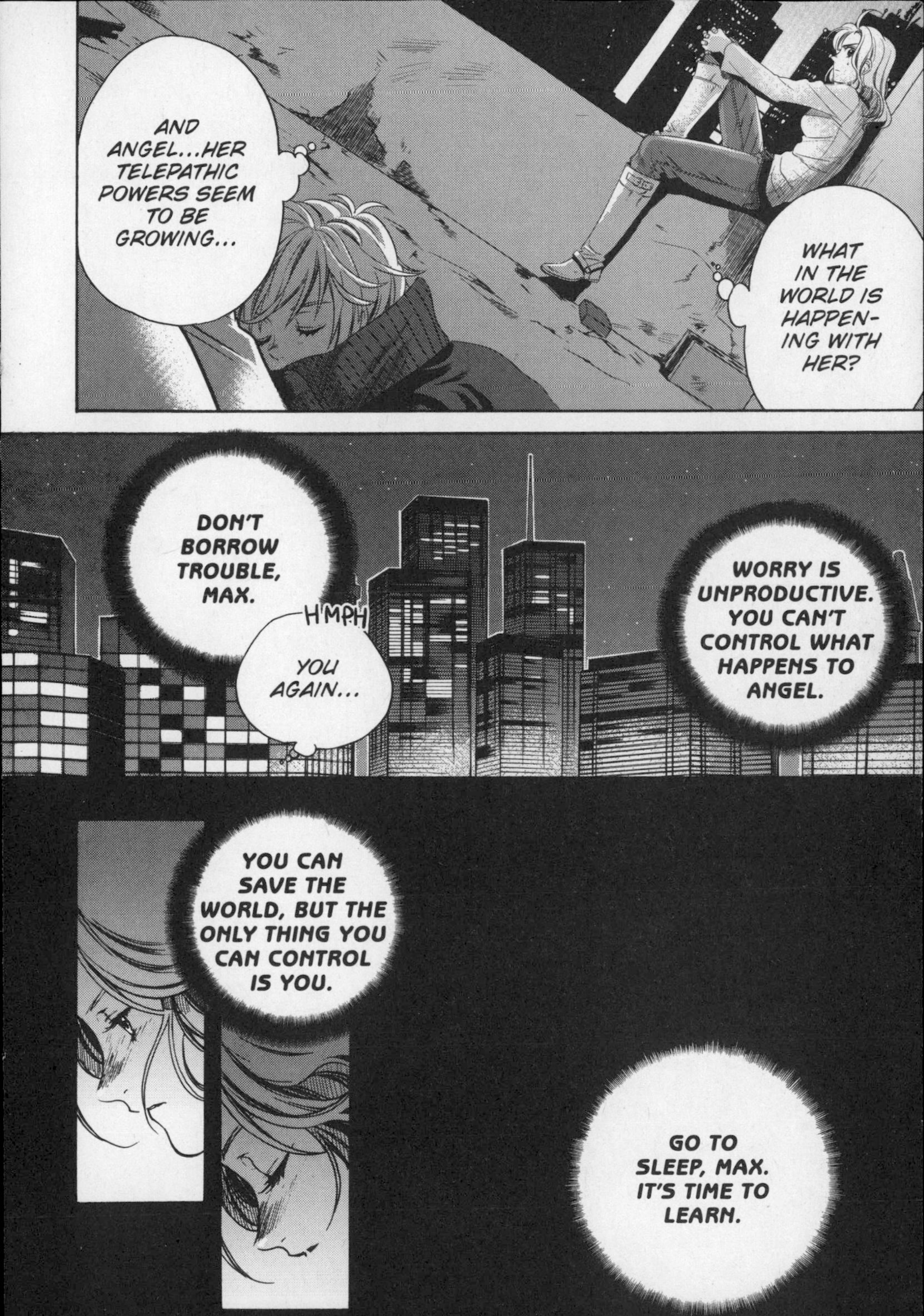

AND ANGEL...HER TELEPATHIC POWERS SEEM TO BE GROWING...
WHAT IN THE WORLD IS HAPPEN-ING WITH HER?
DON'T BORROW TROUBLE, MAX.
H'MPH
YOU AGAIN...
WORRY IS UNPRODUCTIVE. YOU CAN'T CONTROL WHAT HAPPENS TO ANGEL.
YOU CAN SAVE THE WORLD, BUT THE ONLY THING YOU CAN CONTROL IS YOU.
GO TO SLEEP, MAX. IT'S TIME TO LEARN.

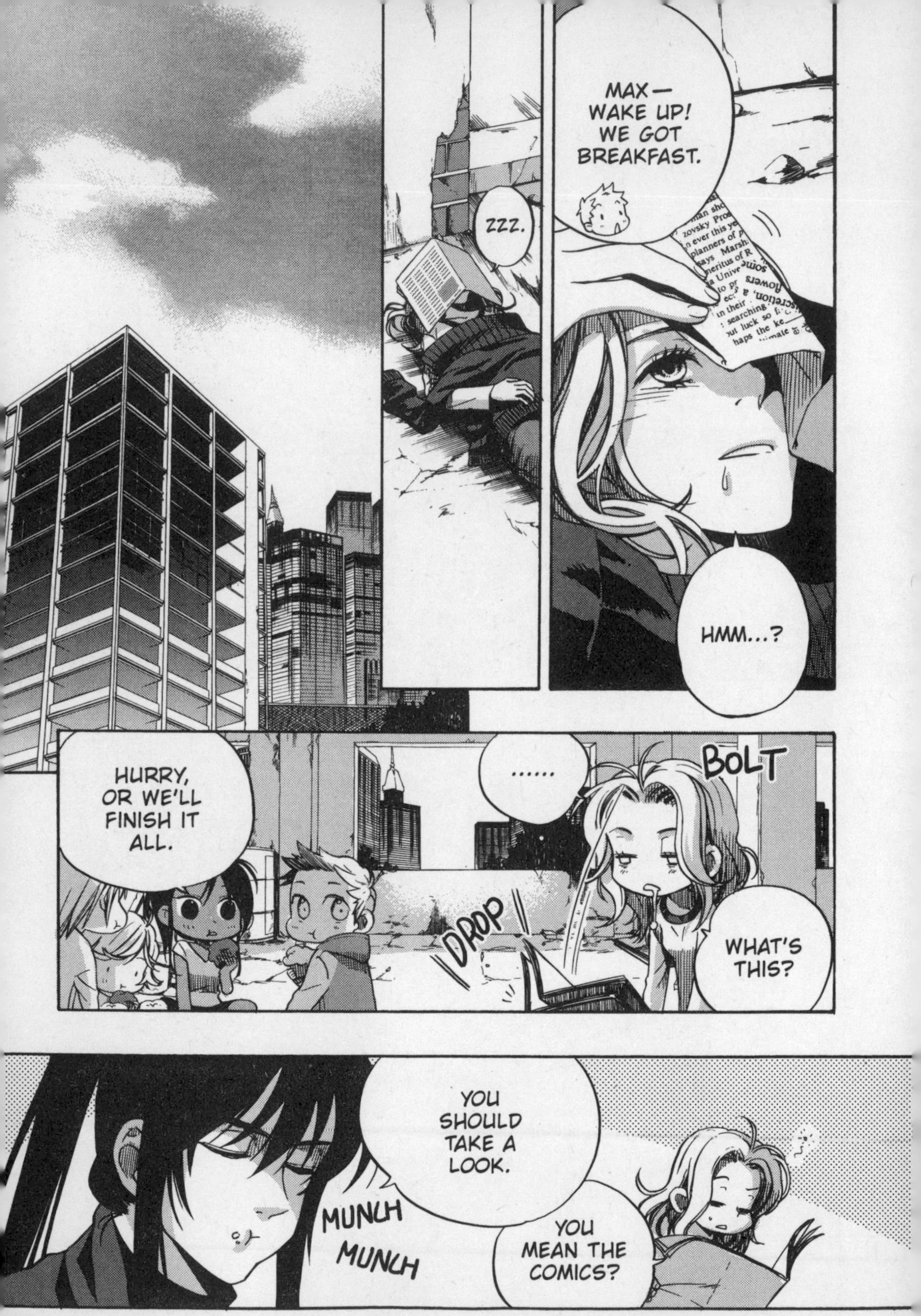
ZZZ.
MAX—WAKE UP! WE GOT BREAKFAST.
HMM...?
HURRY, OR WE'LL FINISH IT ALL.
......
BOLT
DROP
WHAT'S THIS?
YOU SHOULD TAKE A LOOK.
MUNCH MUNCH
YOU MEAN THE COMICS?

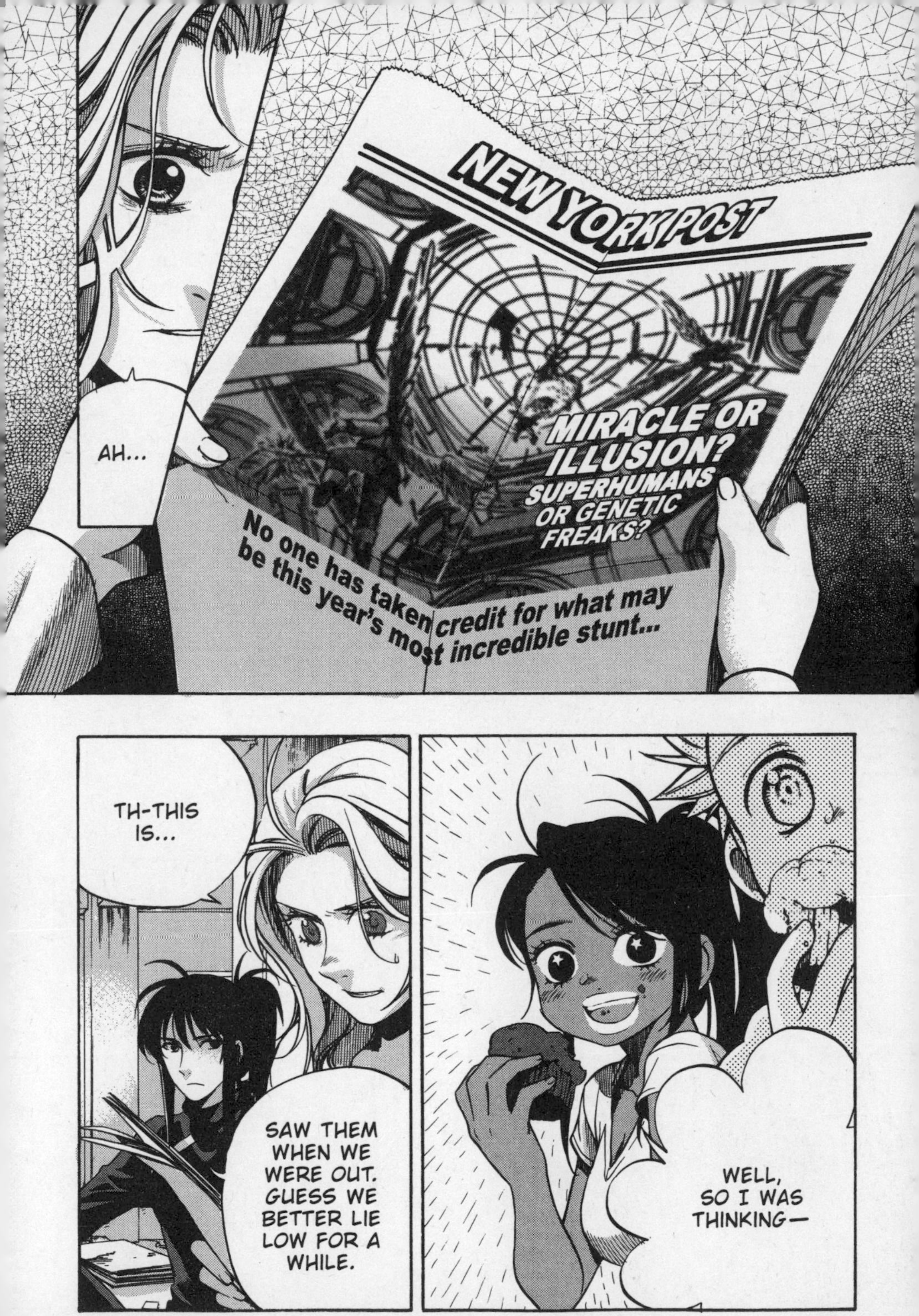
NEW YORK POST
MIRACLE OR ILLUSION? SUPERHUMANS OR GENETIC FREAKS?
No one has taken credit for what may be this year's most incredible stunt...
AH...
TH-THIS IS...
SAW THEM WHEN WE WERE OUT. GUESS WE BETTER LIE LOW FOR A WHILE.
WELL, SO I WAS THINKING—

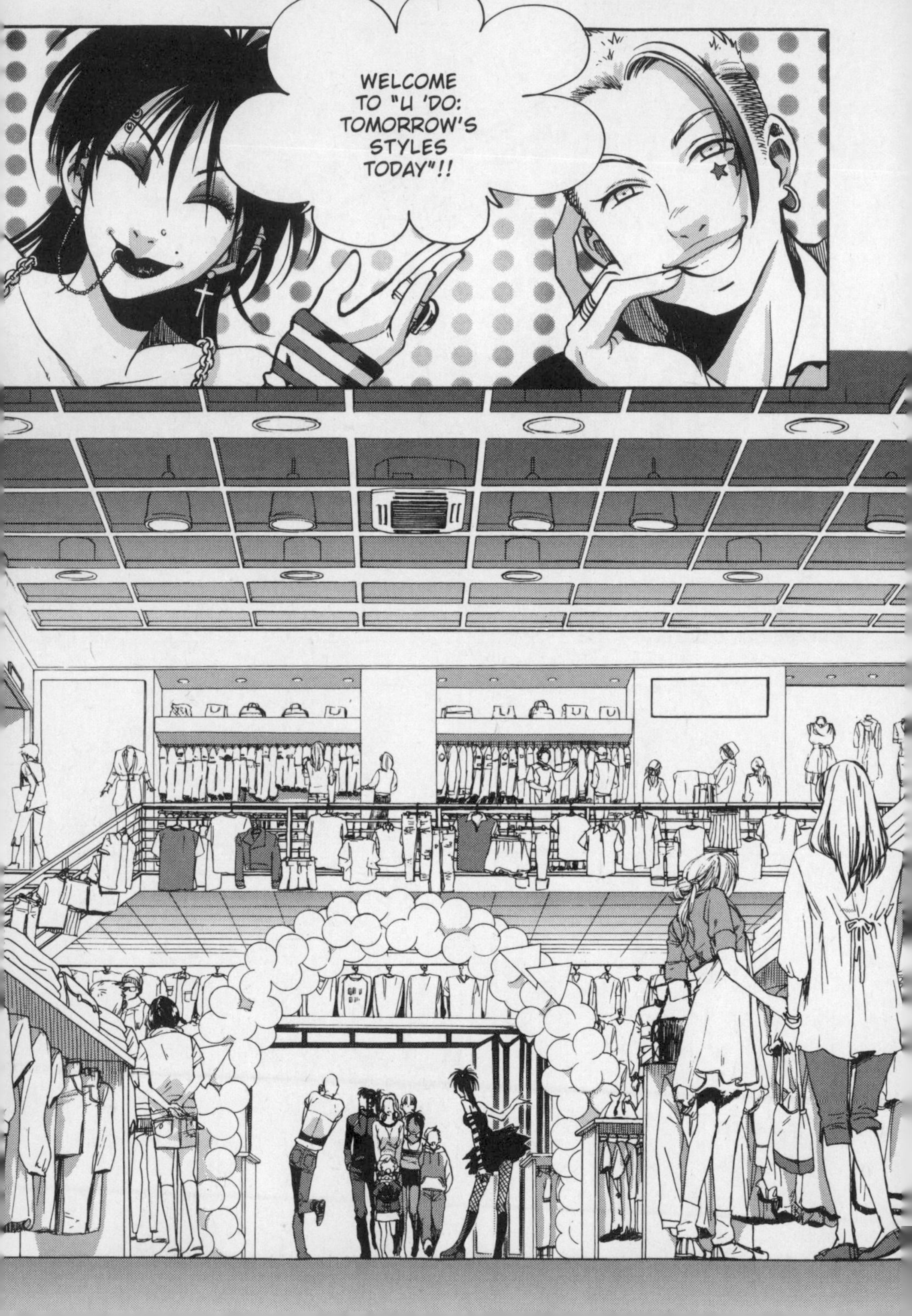
WELCOME TO "U 'DO: TOMORROW'S STYLES TODAY"!!

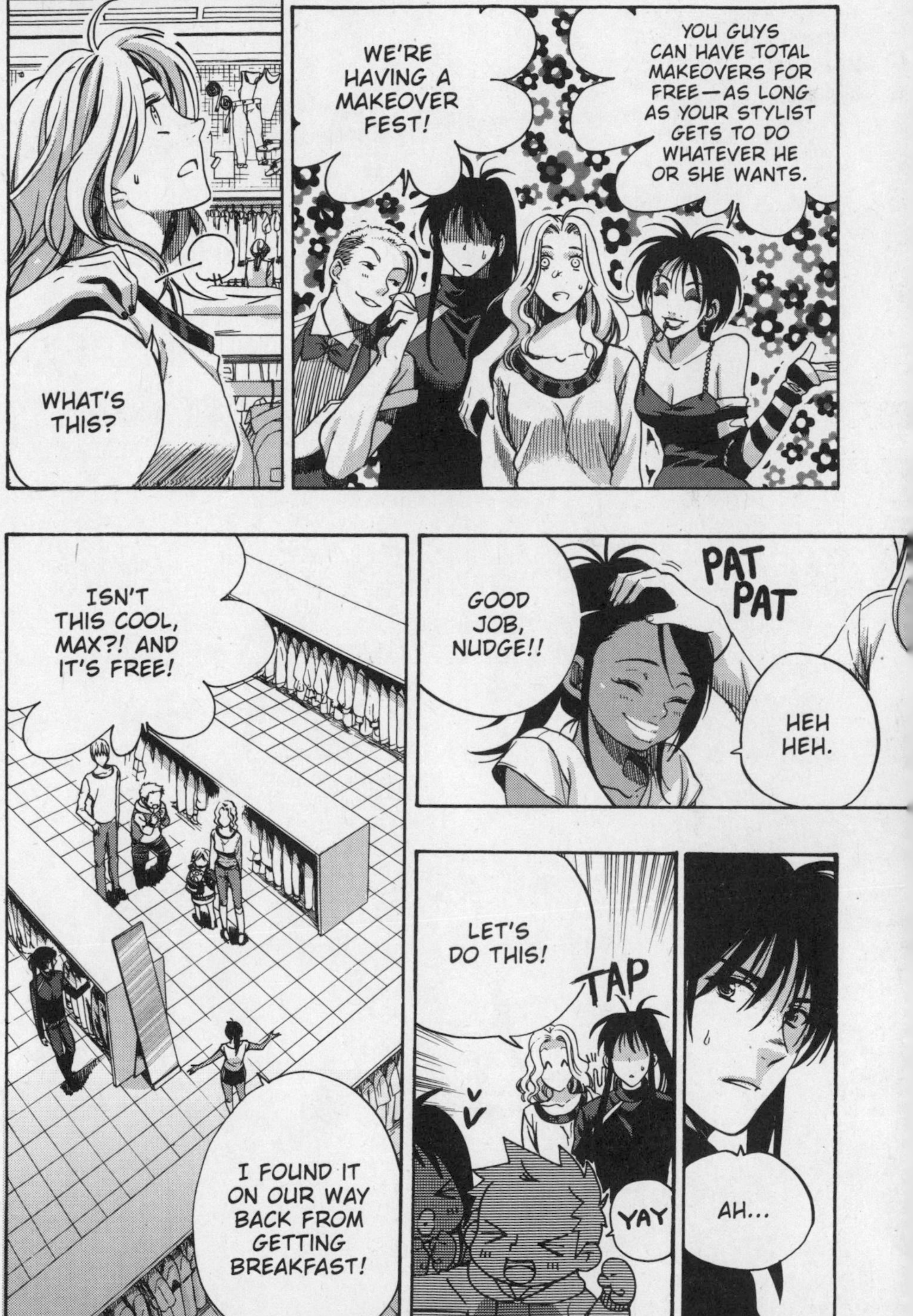
WHAT'S THIS?
WE'RE HAVING A MAKEOVER FEST!
YOU GUYS CAN HAVE TOTAL MAKEOVERS FOR FREE—AS LONG AS YOUR STYLIST GETS TO DO WHATEVER HE OR SHE WANTS.
ISN'T THIS COOL, MAX?! AND IT'S FREE!
I FOUND IT ON OUR WAY BACK FROM GETTING BREAKFAST!
GOOD JOB, NUDGE!!
PAT PAT
HEH HEH.
LET'S DO THIS!
TAP
YAY
AH...

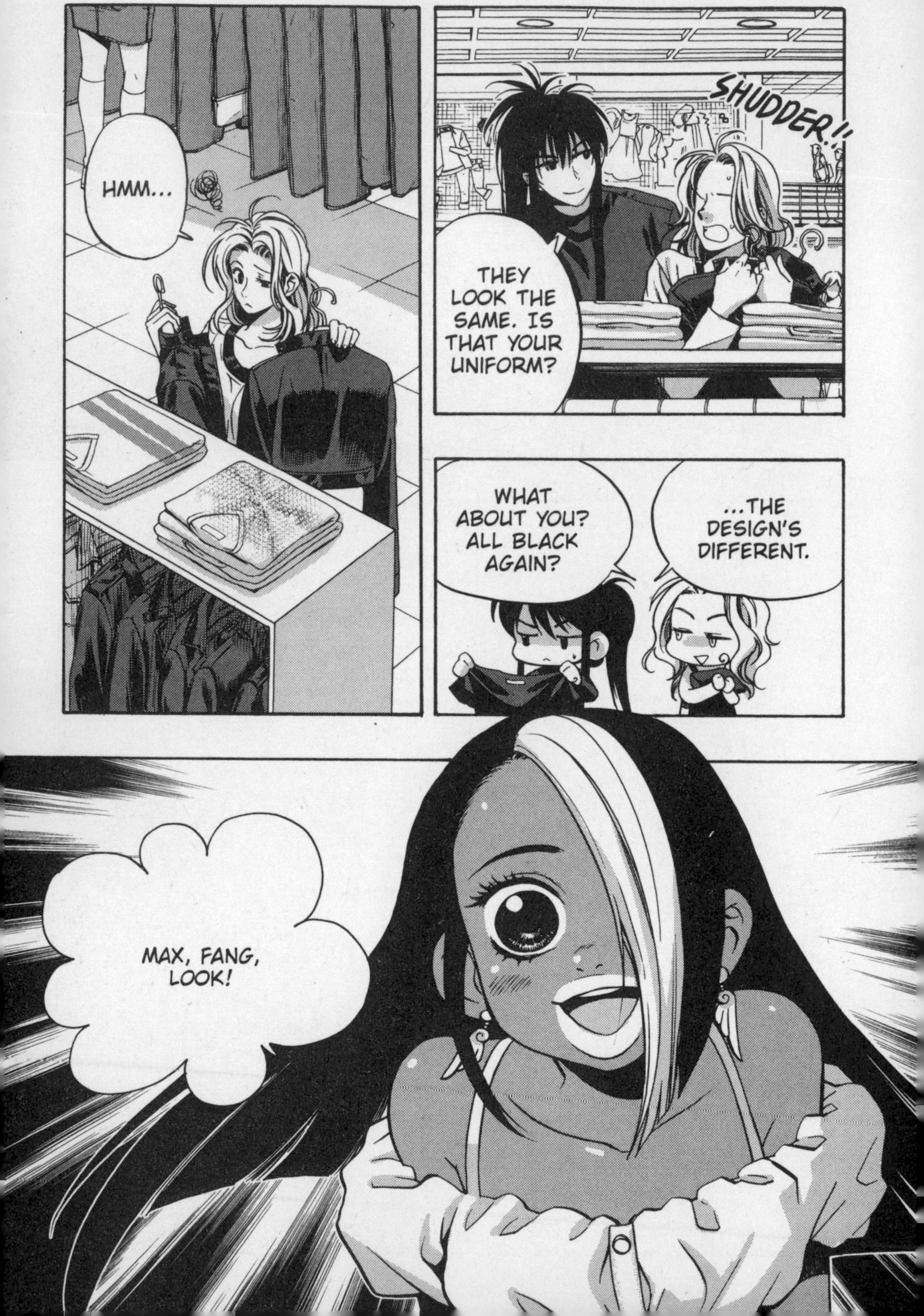
HMM...
SHUDDER!!
THEY LOOK THE SAME. IS THAT YOUR UNIFORM?
WHAT ABOUT YOU? ALL BLACK AGAIN?
...THE DESIGN'S DIFFERENT.
MAX, FANG, LOOK!

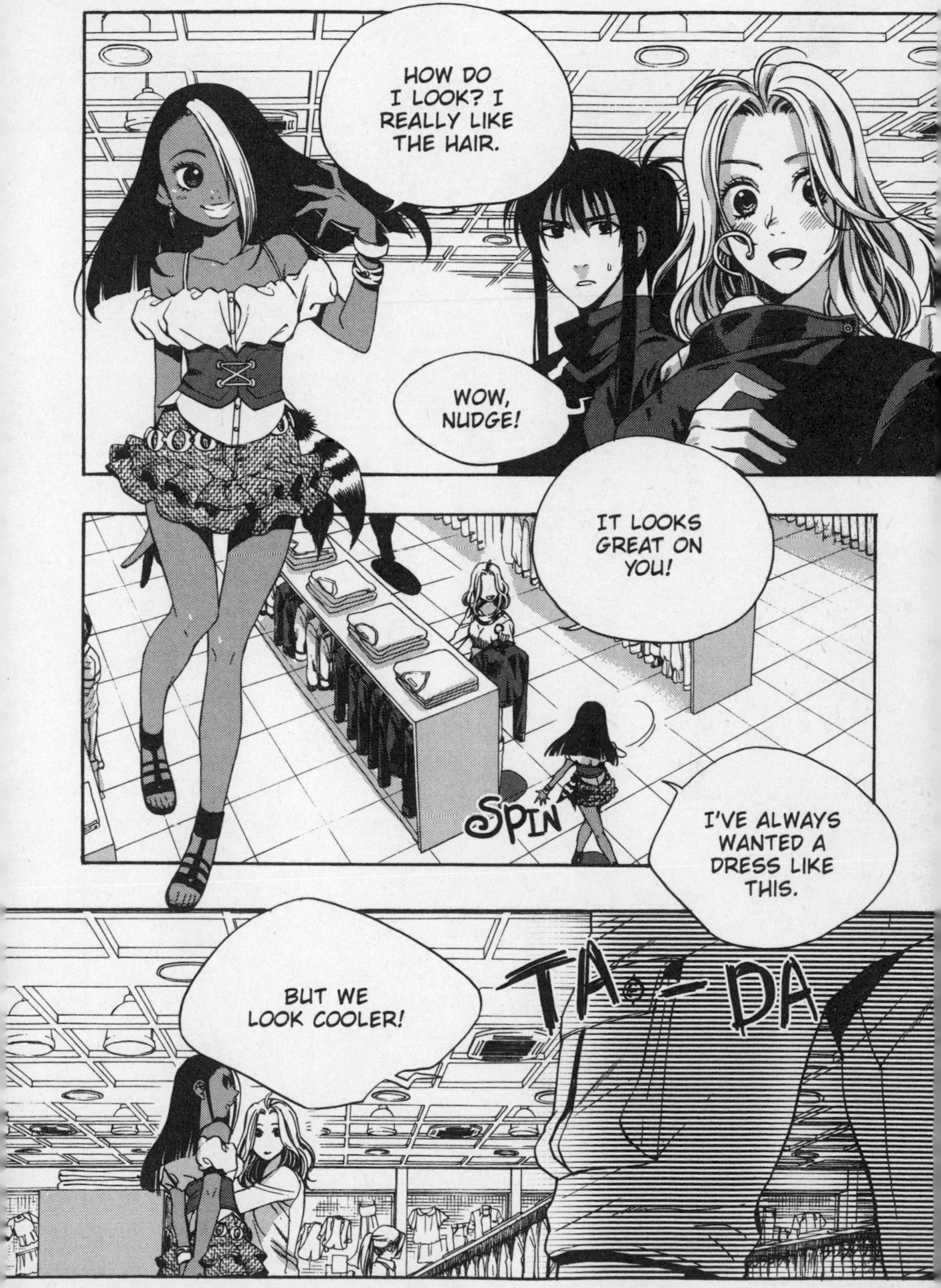
HOW DO I LOOK? I REALLY LIKE THE HAIR.
WOW, NUDGE!
IT LOOKS GREAT ON YOU!
SPIN
I'VE ALWAYS WANTED A DRESS LIKE THIS.
BUT WE LOOK COOLER!
TA-DA

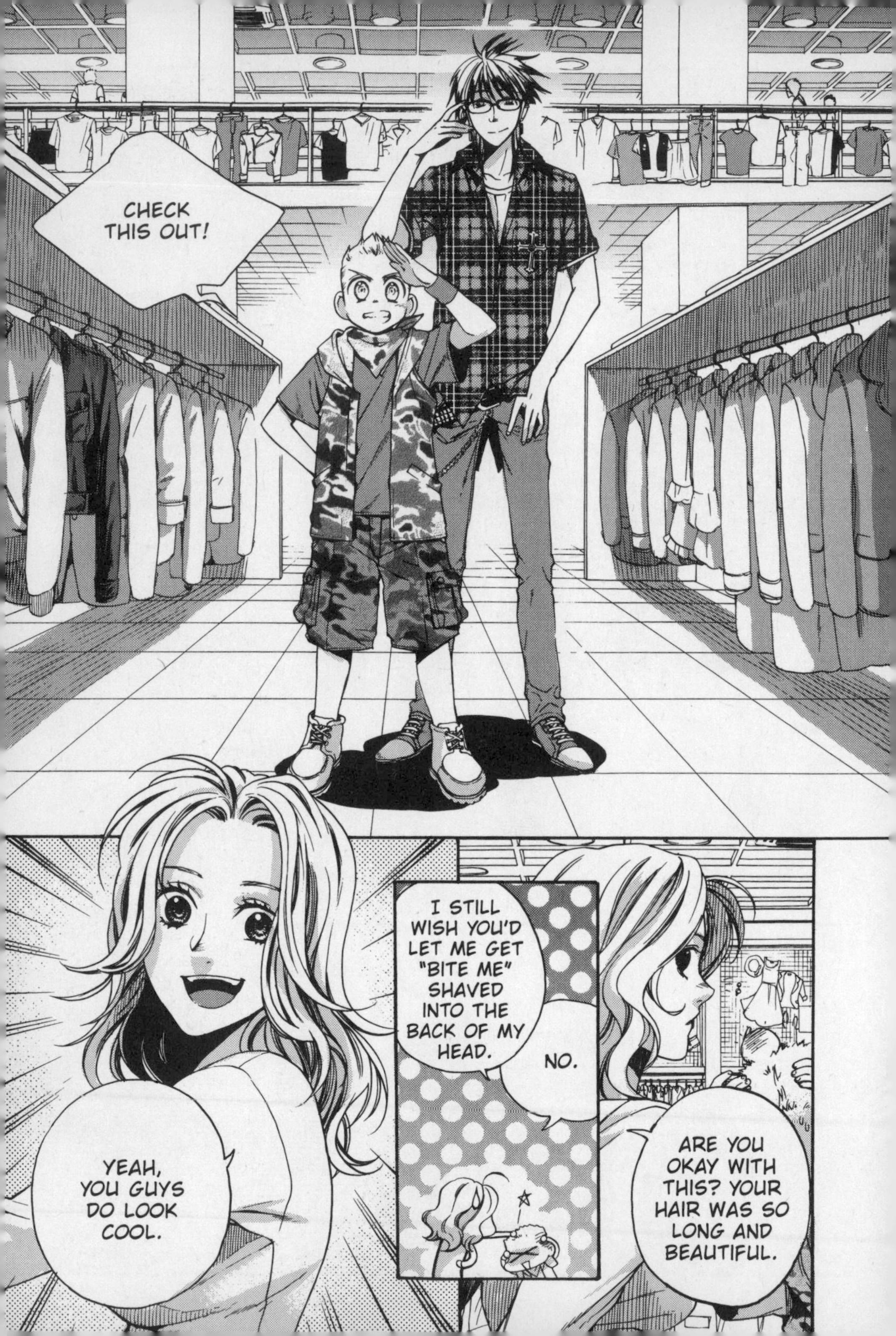
CHECK THIS OUT!
YEAH, YOU GUYS DO LOOK COOL.
I STILL WISH YOU'D LET ME GET "BITE ME" SHAVED INTO THE BACK OF MY HEAD.
NO.
ARE YOU OKAY WITH THIS? YOUR HAIR WAS SO LONG AND BEAUTIFUL.

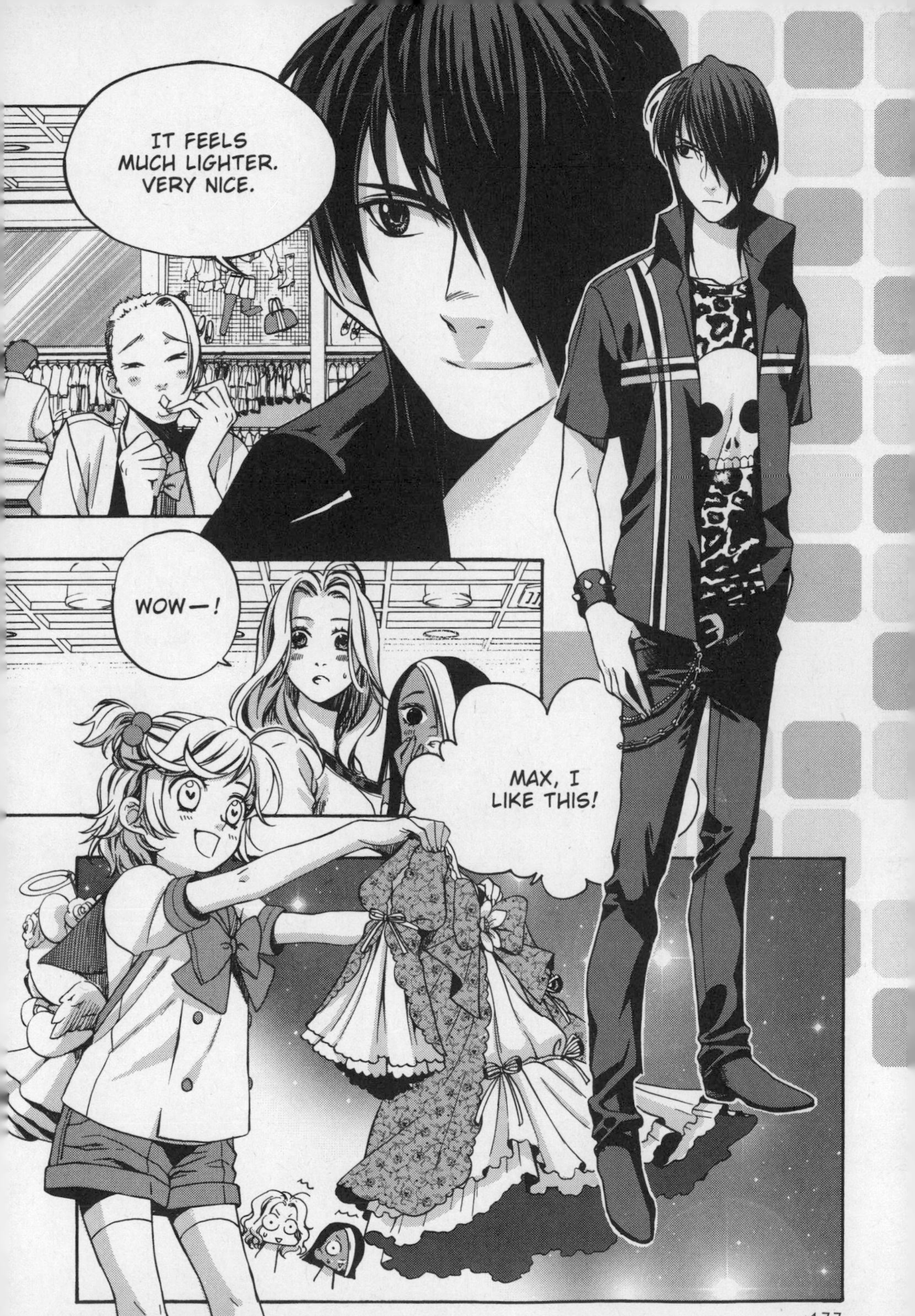
IT FEELS MUCH LIGHTER. VERY NICE.
WOW—!
MAX, I LIKE THIS!

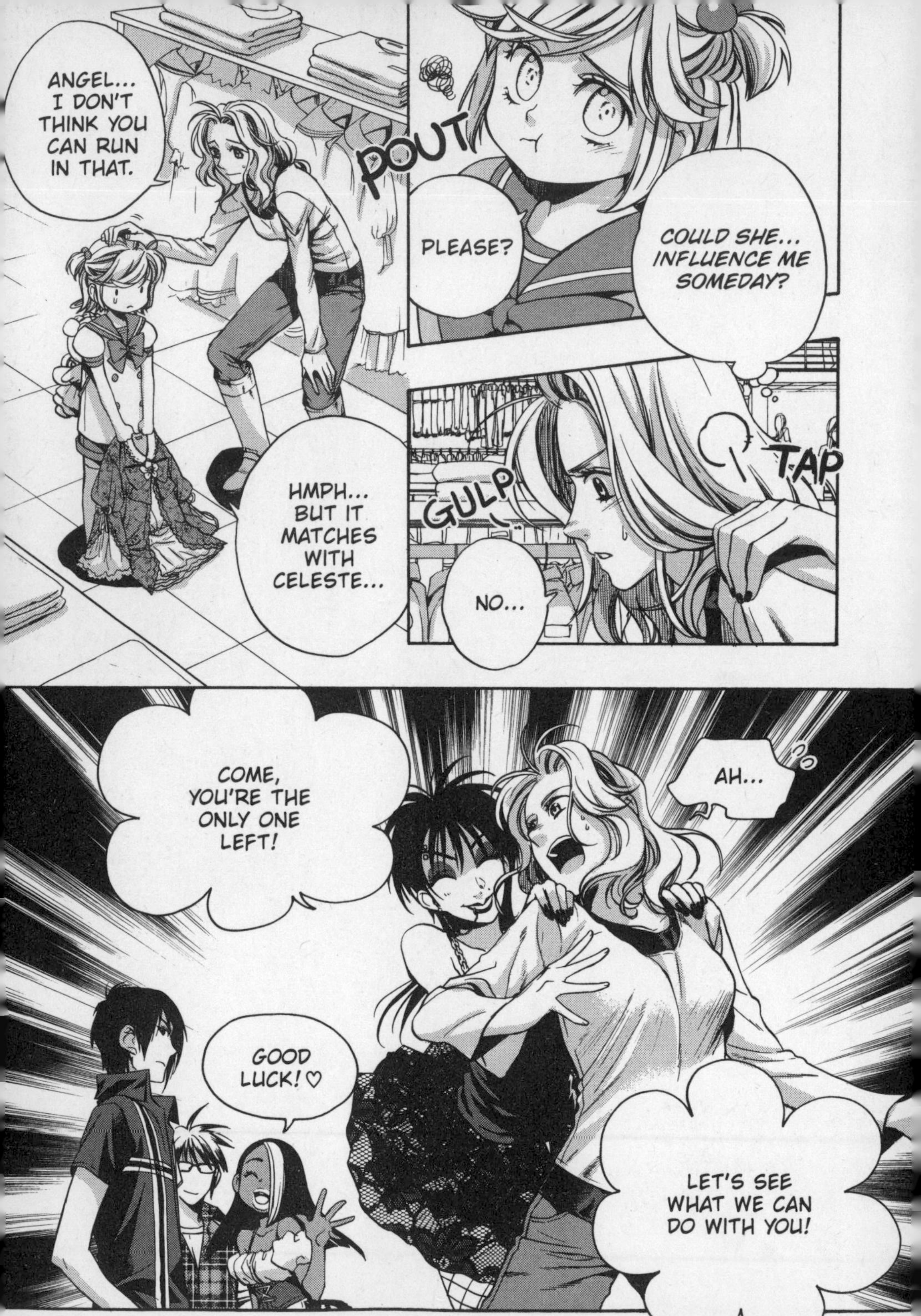
ANGEL... I DON'T THINK YOU CAN RUN IN THAT.
HMPH... BUT IT MATCHES WITH CELESTE...
POUT
PLEASE?
COULD SHE... INFLUENCE ME SOMEDAY?
GULP
TAP
NO...
COME, YOU'RE THE ONLY ONE LEFT!
AH...
GOOD LUCK! ♡
LET'S SEE WHAT WE CAN DO WITH YOU!

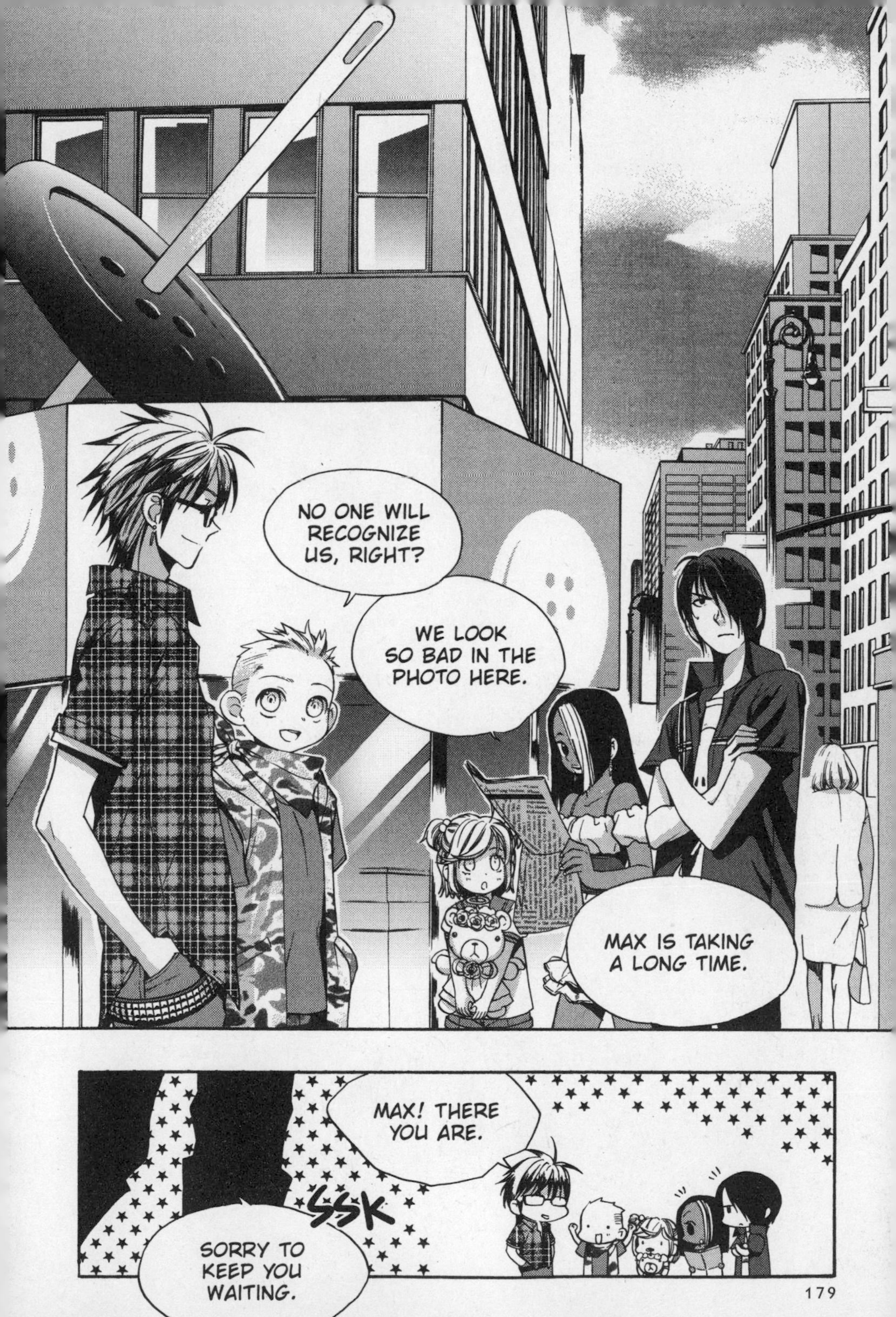
NO ONE WILL RECOGNIZE US, RIGHT?
WE LOOK SO BAD IN THE PHOTO HERE.
MAX IS TAKING A LONG TIME.
MAX! THERE YOU ARE.
SSK
SORRY TO KEEP YOU WAITING.

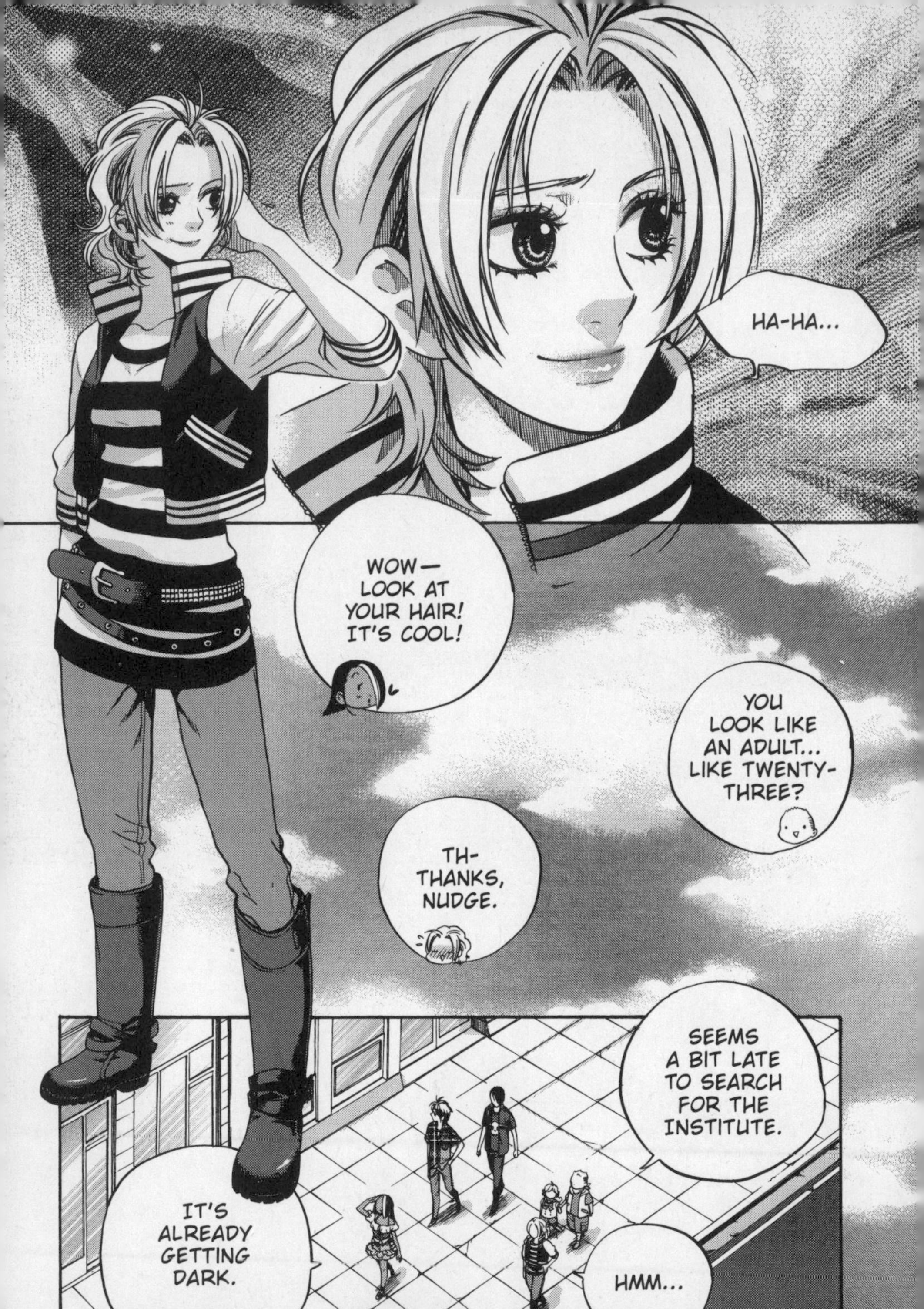
HA-HA...
WOW— LOOK AT YOUR HAIR! IT'S COOL!
YOU LOOK LIKE AN ADULT... LIKE TWENTY-THREE?
TH- THANKS, NUDGE.
SEEMS A BIT LATE TO SEARCH FOR THE INSTITUTE.
IT'S ALREADY GETTING DARK.
HMM...

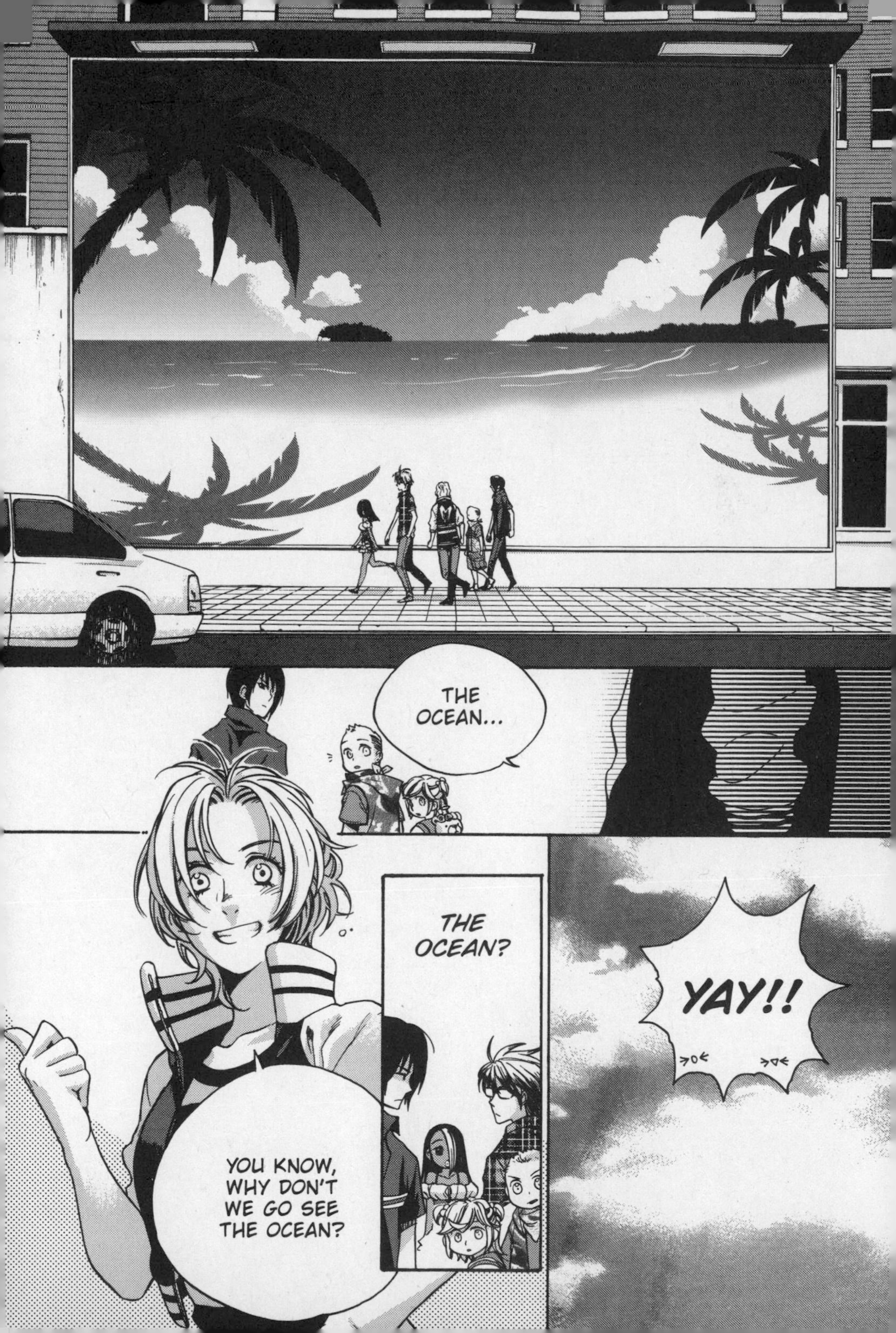
THE OCEAN...
YOU KNOW, WHY DON'T WE GO SEE THE OCEAN?
THE OCEAN?
YAY!!

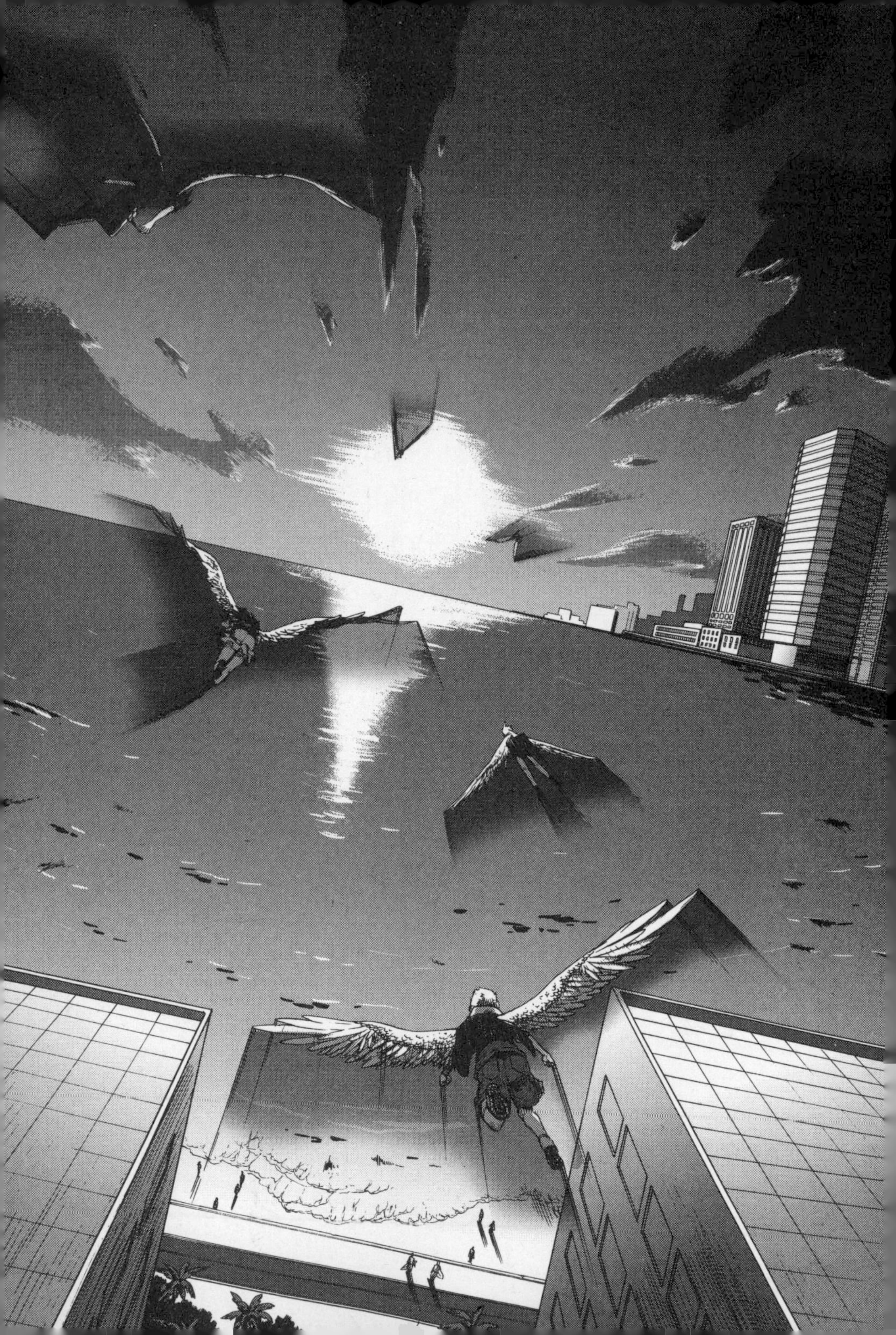

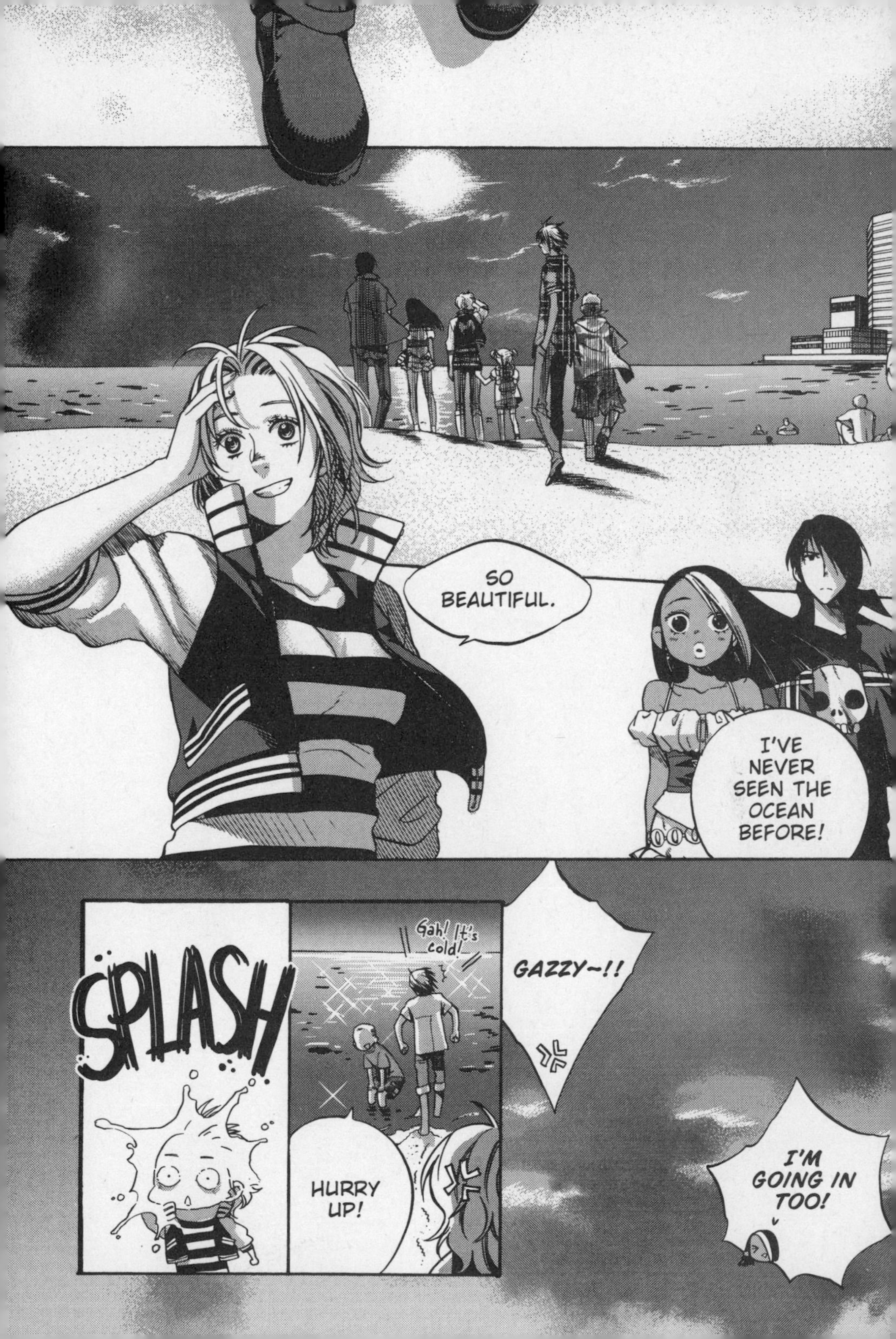

SO BEAUTIFUL.
I'VE NEVER SEEN THE OCEAN BEFORE!
SPLASH
Gah! It's cold!
HURRY UP!
GAZZY~!!
I'M GOING IN TOO!

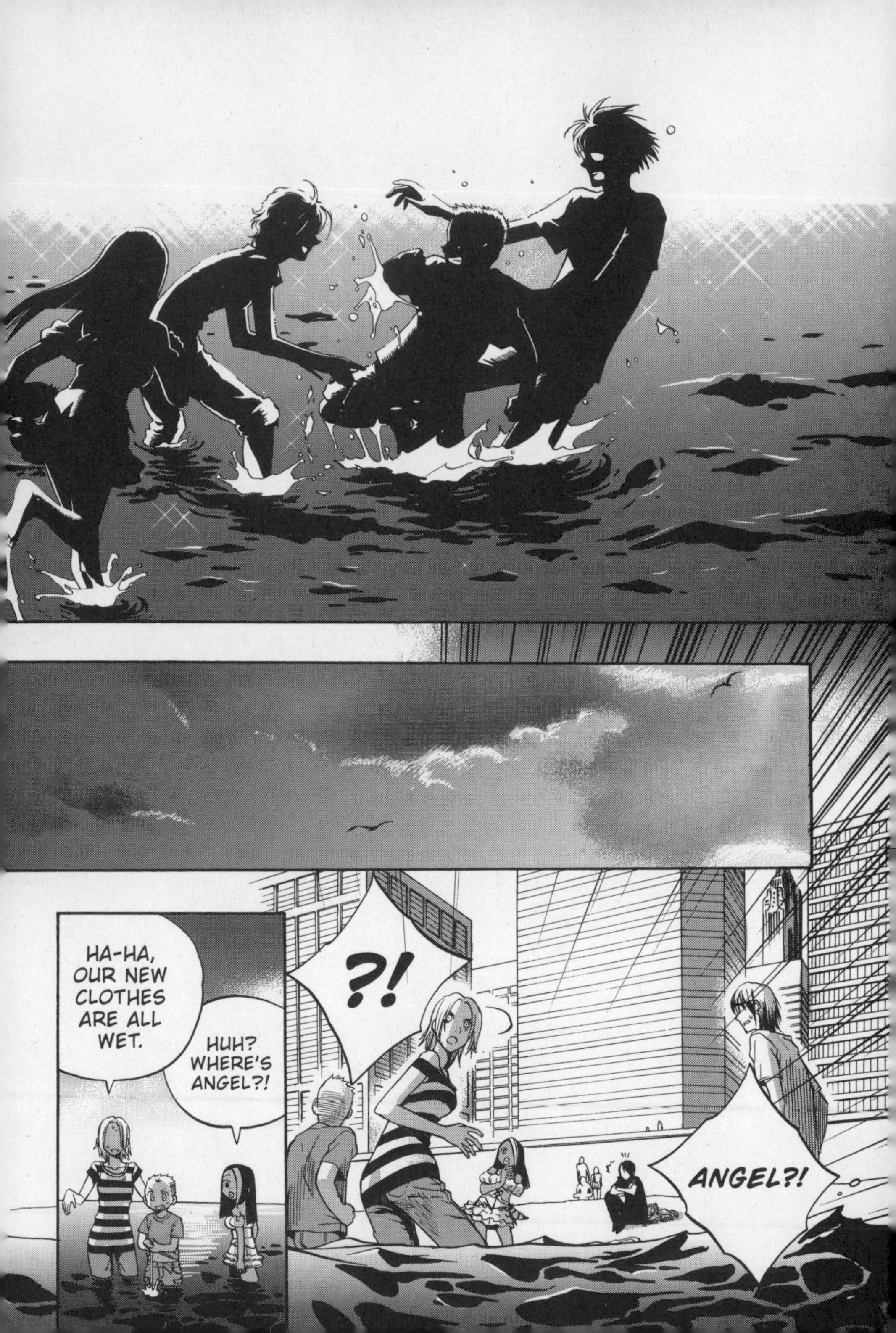
HA-HA, OUR NEW CLOTHES ARE ALL WET.
HUH? WHERE'S ANGEL?!
?!
ANGEL?!

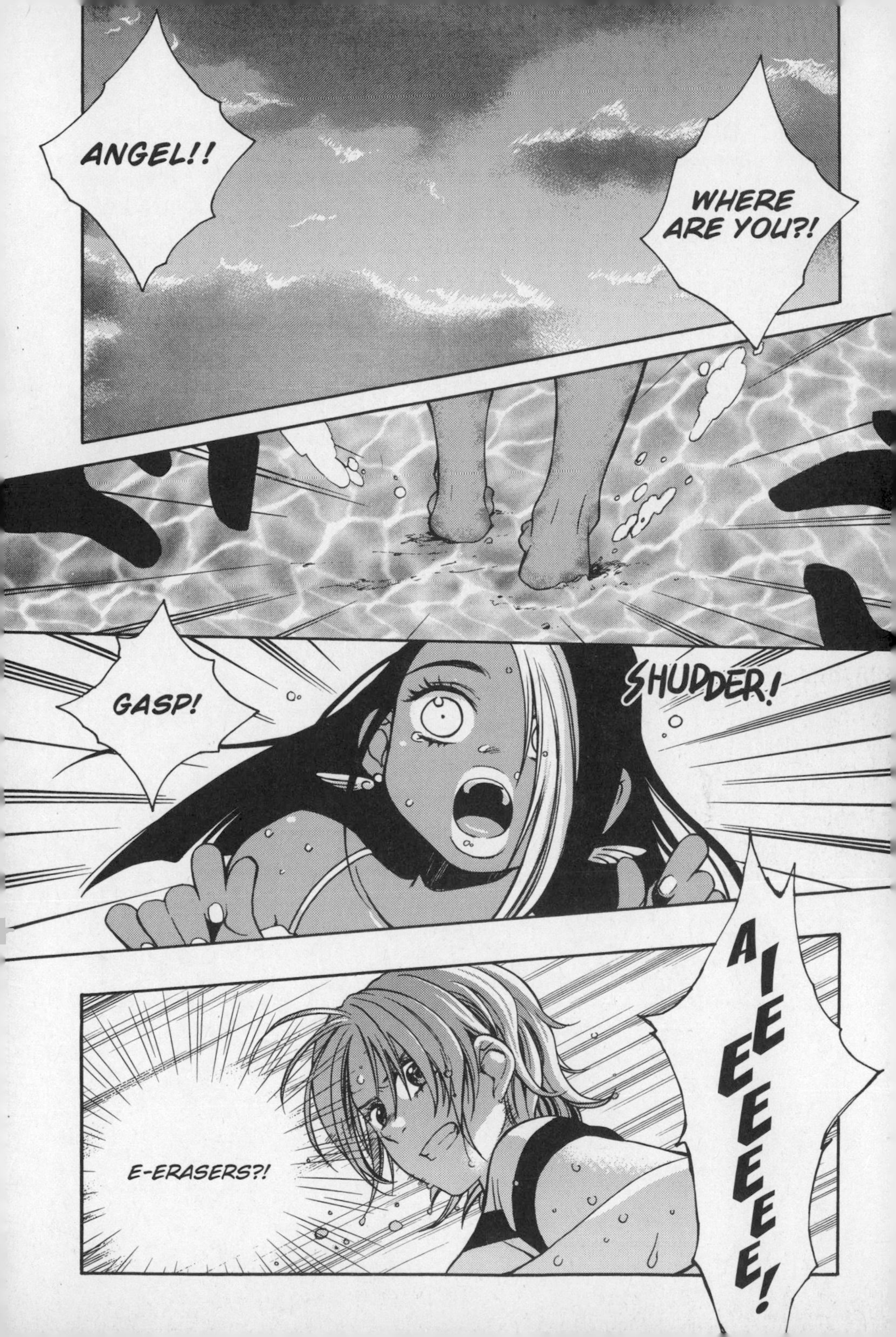
ANGEL!!
WHERE ARE YOU?!
GASP!
SHUDDER!
AIEEEEEEEE!
E-ERASERS?!

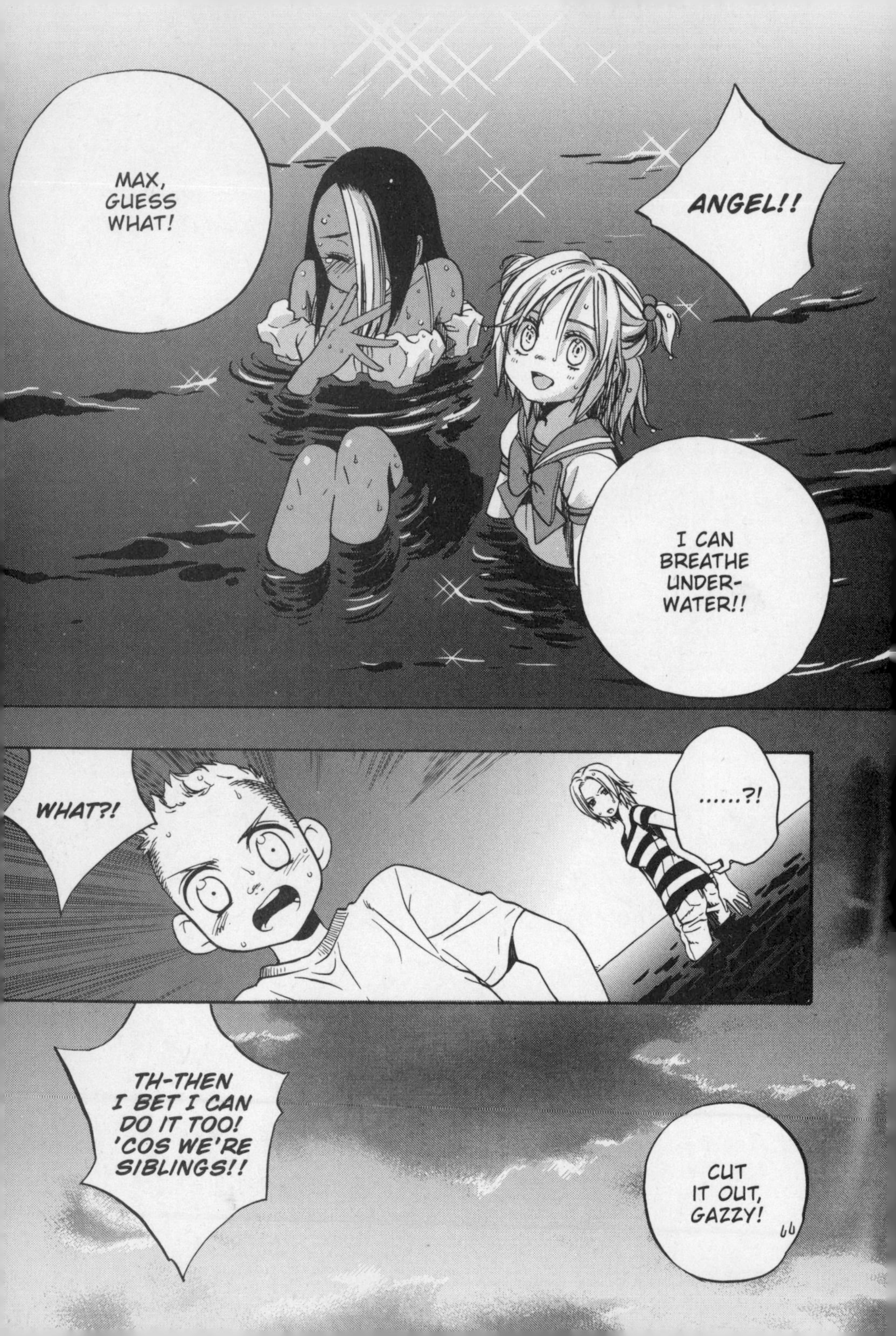
MAX, GUESS WHAT!
ANGEL!!
I CAN BREATHE UNDER-WATER!!
WHAT?!
......?!
TH-THEN I BET I CAN DO IT TOO! 'COS WE'RE SIBLINGS!!
CUT IT OUT, GAZZY!

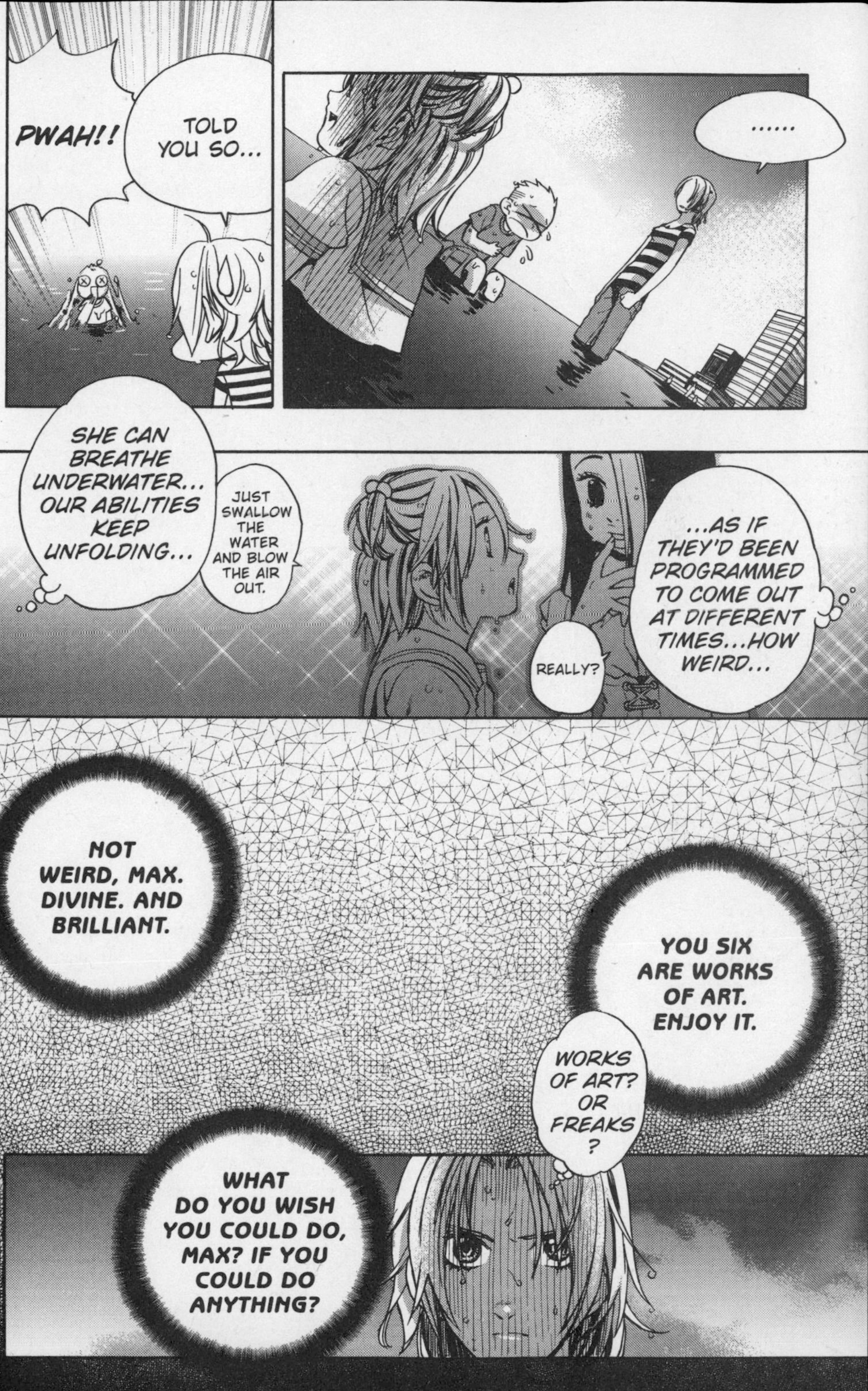
PWAH!!
TOLD YOU SO...
......
SHE CAN BREATHE UNDERWATER... OUR ABILITIES KEEP UNFOLDING...
JUST SWALLOW THE WATER AND BLOW THE AIR OUT.
REALLY?
...AS IF THEY'D BEEN PROGRAMMED TO COME OUT AT DIFFERENT TIMES...HOW WEIRD...
NOT WEIRD, MAX. DIVINE. AND BRILLIANT.
YOU SIX ARE WORKS OF ART. ENJOY IT.
WORKS OF ART? OR FREAKS?
WHAT DO YOU WISH YOU COULD DO, MAX? IF YOU COULD DO ANYTHING?

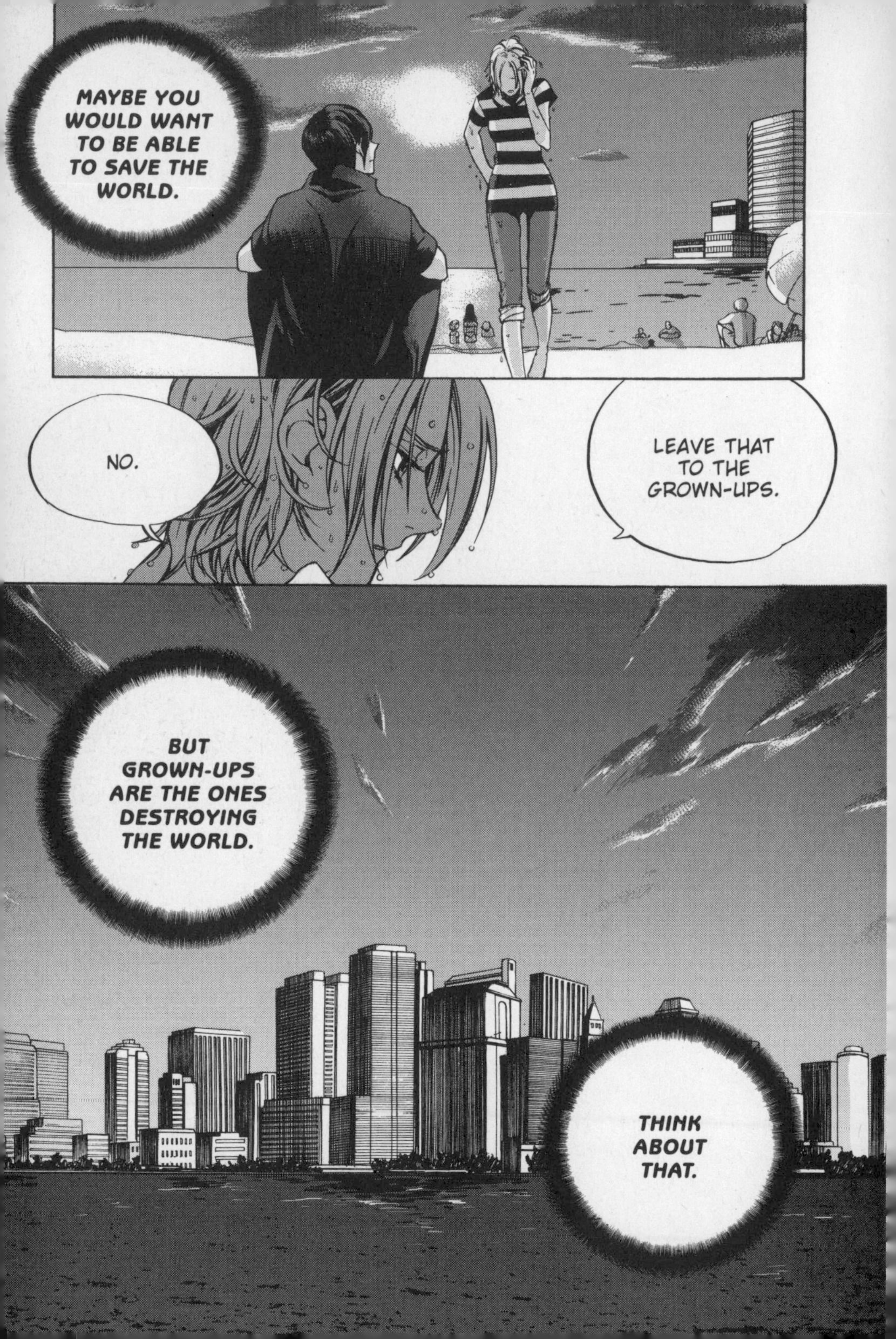
MAYBE YOU WOULD WANT TO BE ABLE TO SAVE THE WORLD.
NO.
LEAVE THAT TO THE GROWN-UPS.
BUT GROWN-UPS ARE THE ONES DESTROYING THE WORLD.
THINK ABOUT THAT.

MAXIMUM
RIDE

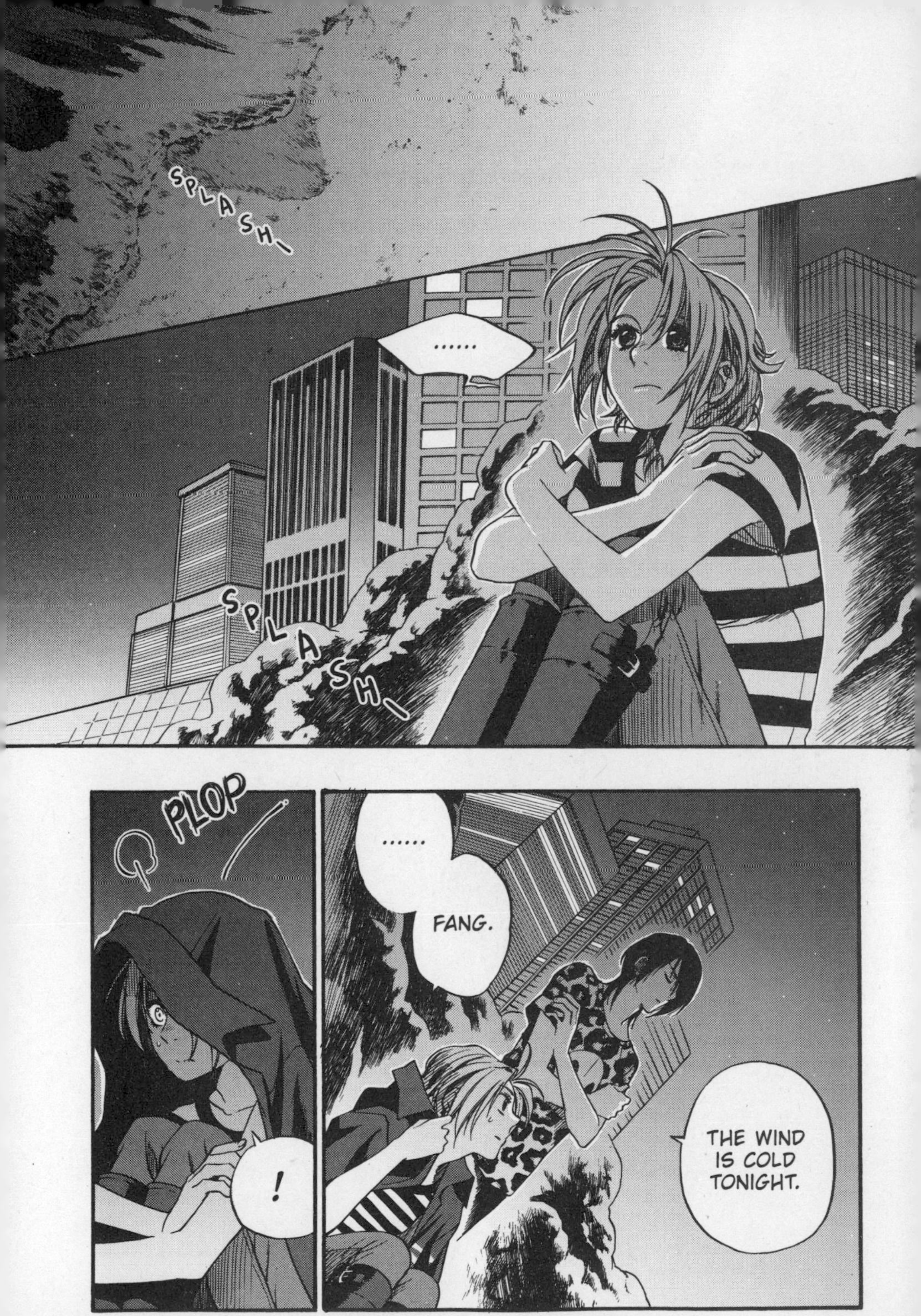
SPLASH
......
SPLASH
PLOP
!
......
FANG.
THE WIND IS COLD TONIGHT.

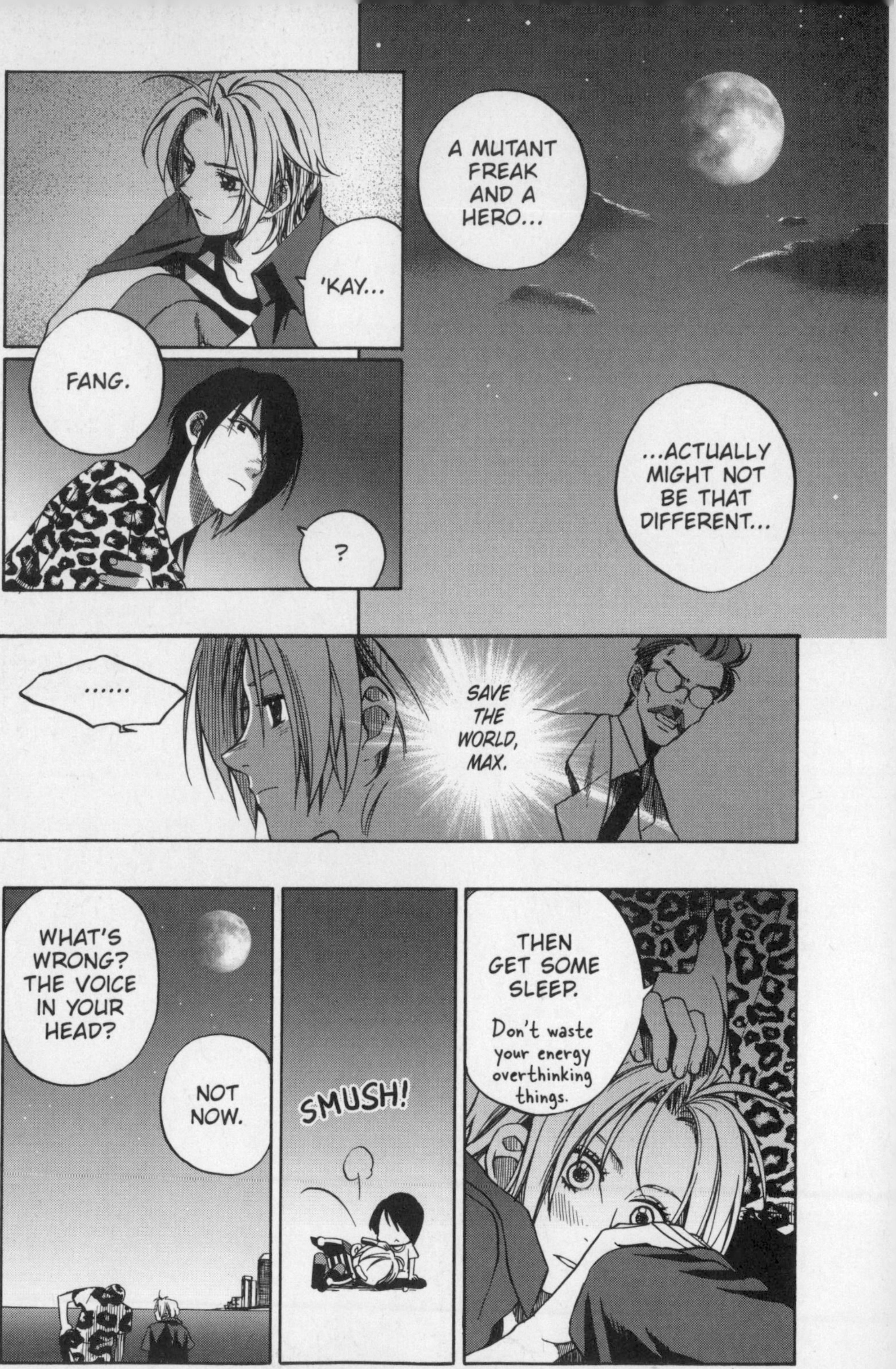
'KAY...
FANG.
?
A MUTANT FREAK AND A HERO...
...ACTUALLY MIGHT NOT BE THAT DIFFERENT...
......
SAVE THE WORLD, MAX.
WHAT'S WRONG? THE VOICE IN YOUR HEAD?
NOT NOW.
SMUSH!
THEN GET SOME SLEEP.
Don't waste your energy overthinking things.

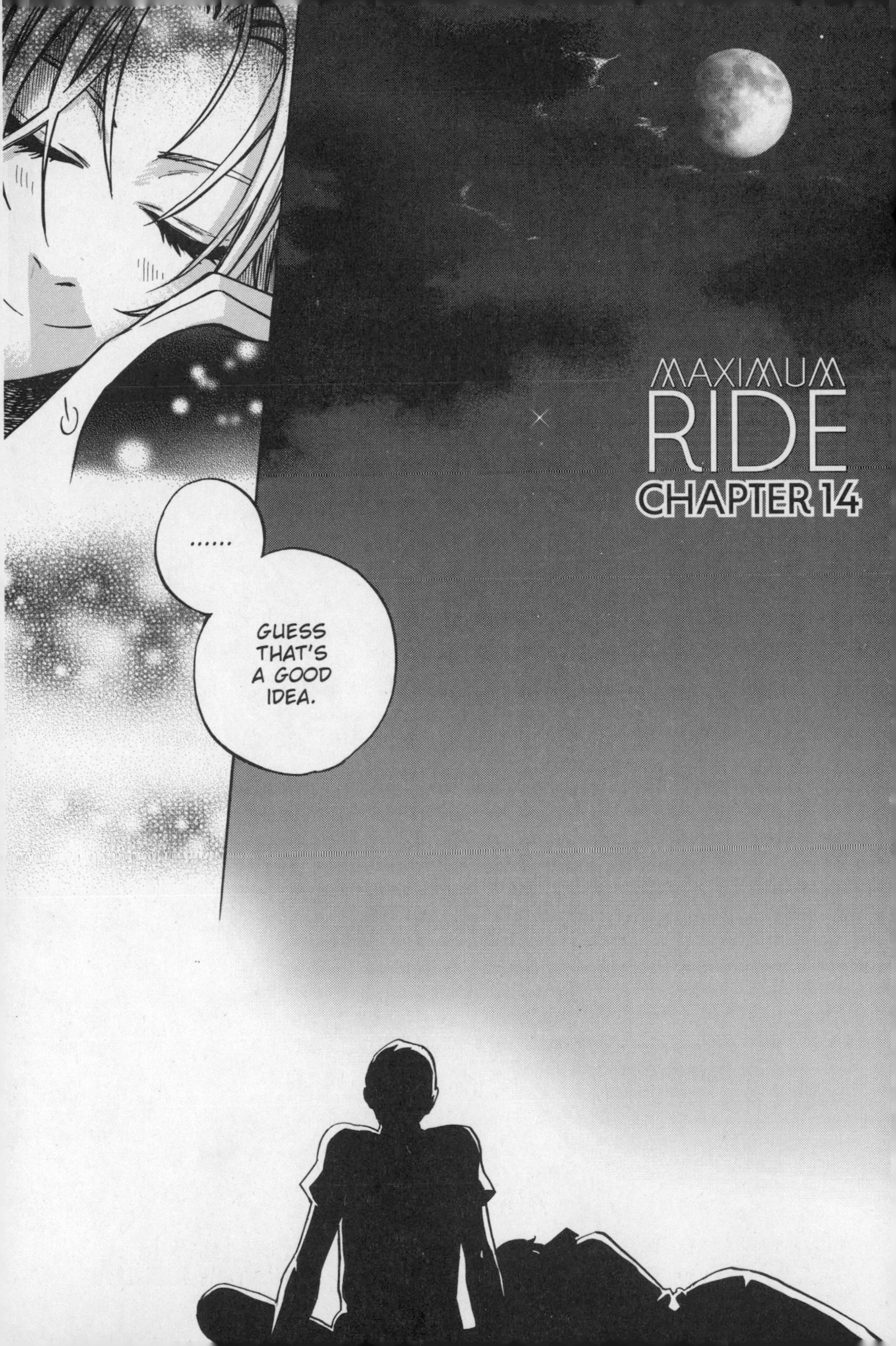

......
GUESS THAT'S A GOOD IDEA.
MAXIMUM RIDE
CHAPTER 14

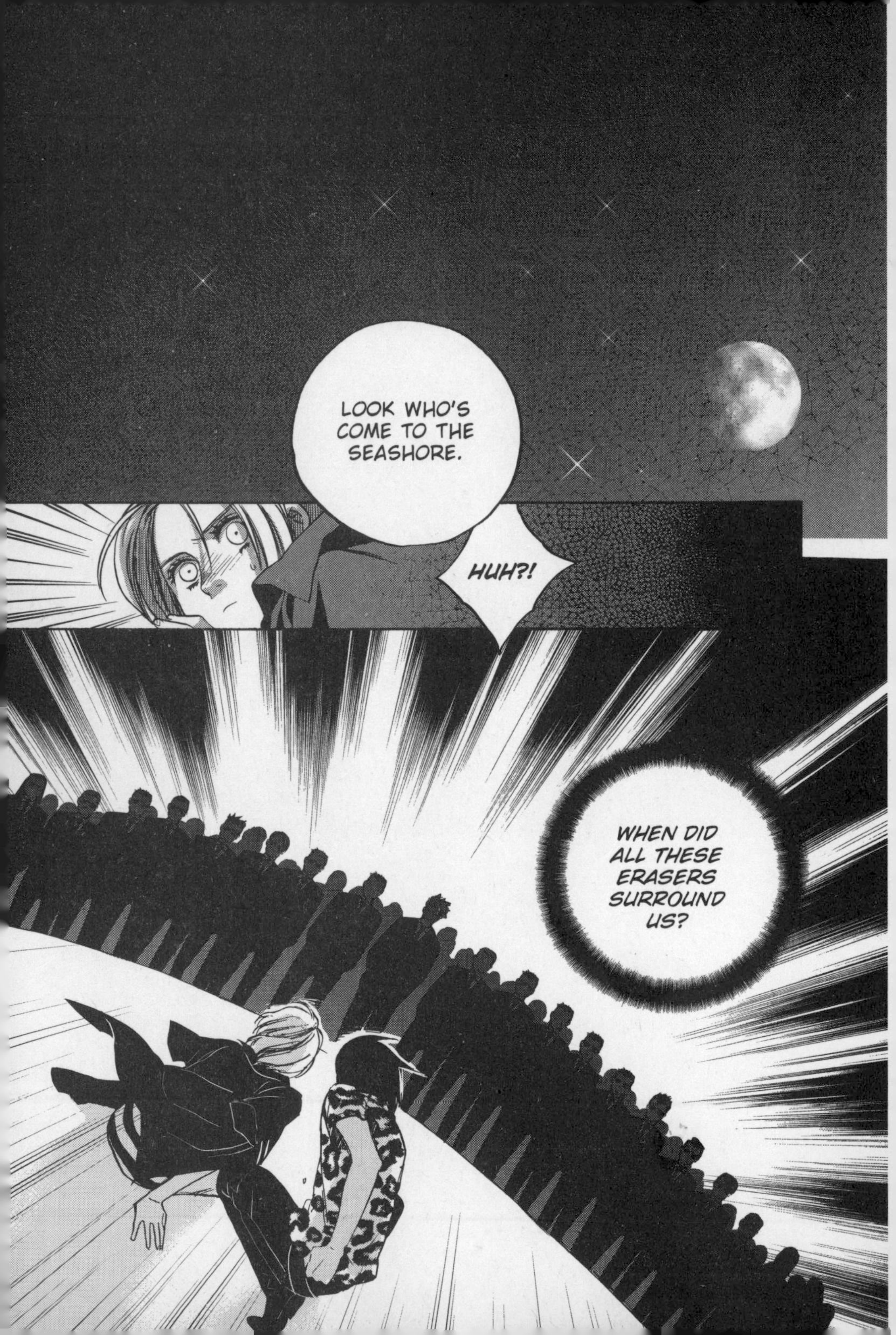
LOOK WHO'S COME TO THE SEASHORE.
HUH?!
WHEN DID ALL THESE ERASERS SURROUND US?

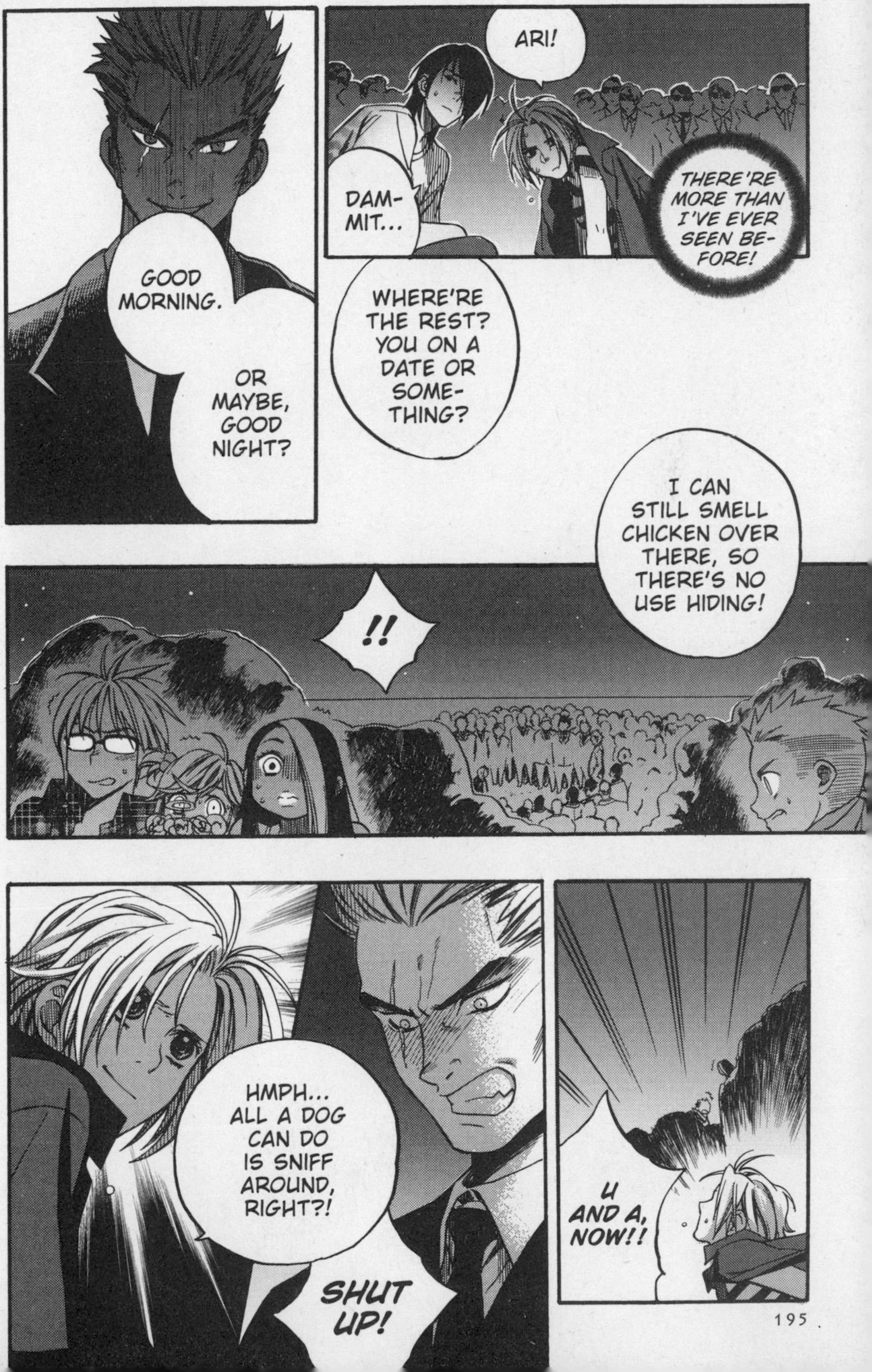
GOOD MORNING.
OR MAYBE, GOOD NIGHT?
ARI!
DAM-MIT...
THERE'RE MORE THAN I'VE EVER SEEN BE-FORE!
WHERE'RE THE REST? YOU ON A DATE OR SOME-THING?
I CAN STILL SMELL CHICKEN OVER THERE, SO THERE'S NO USE HIDING!
!!
HMPH... ALL A DOG CAN DO IS SNIFF AROUND, RIGHT?!
SHUT UP!
U AND A, NOW!!

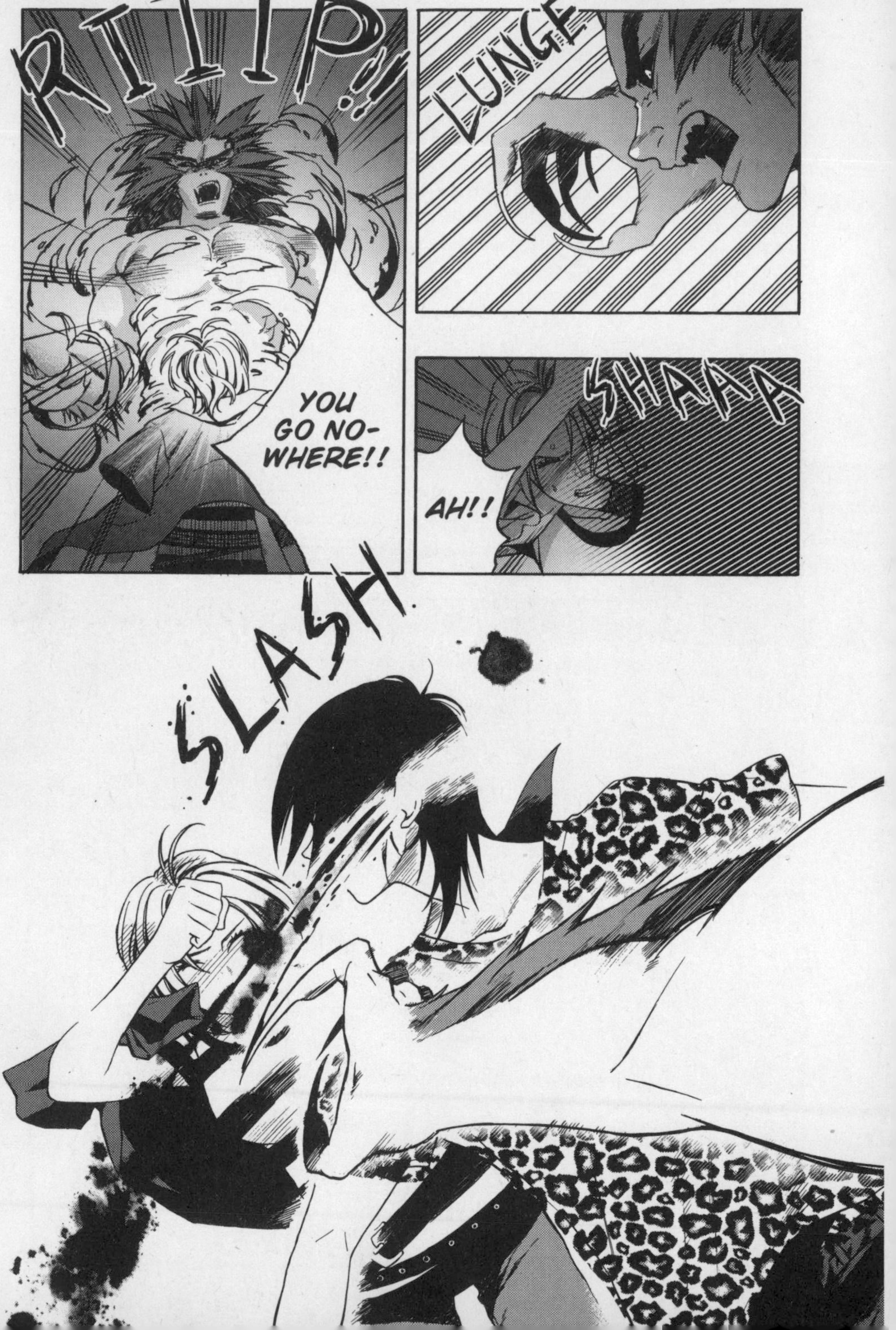
RIIIP!!!
YOU GO NO-WHERE!!
LUNGE
SHAAAA
AH!!
SLASH

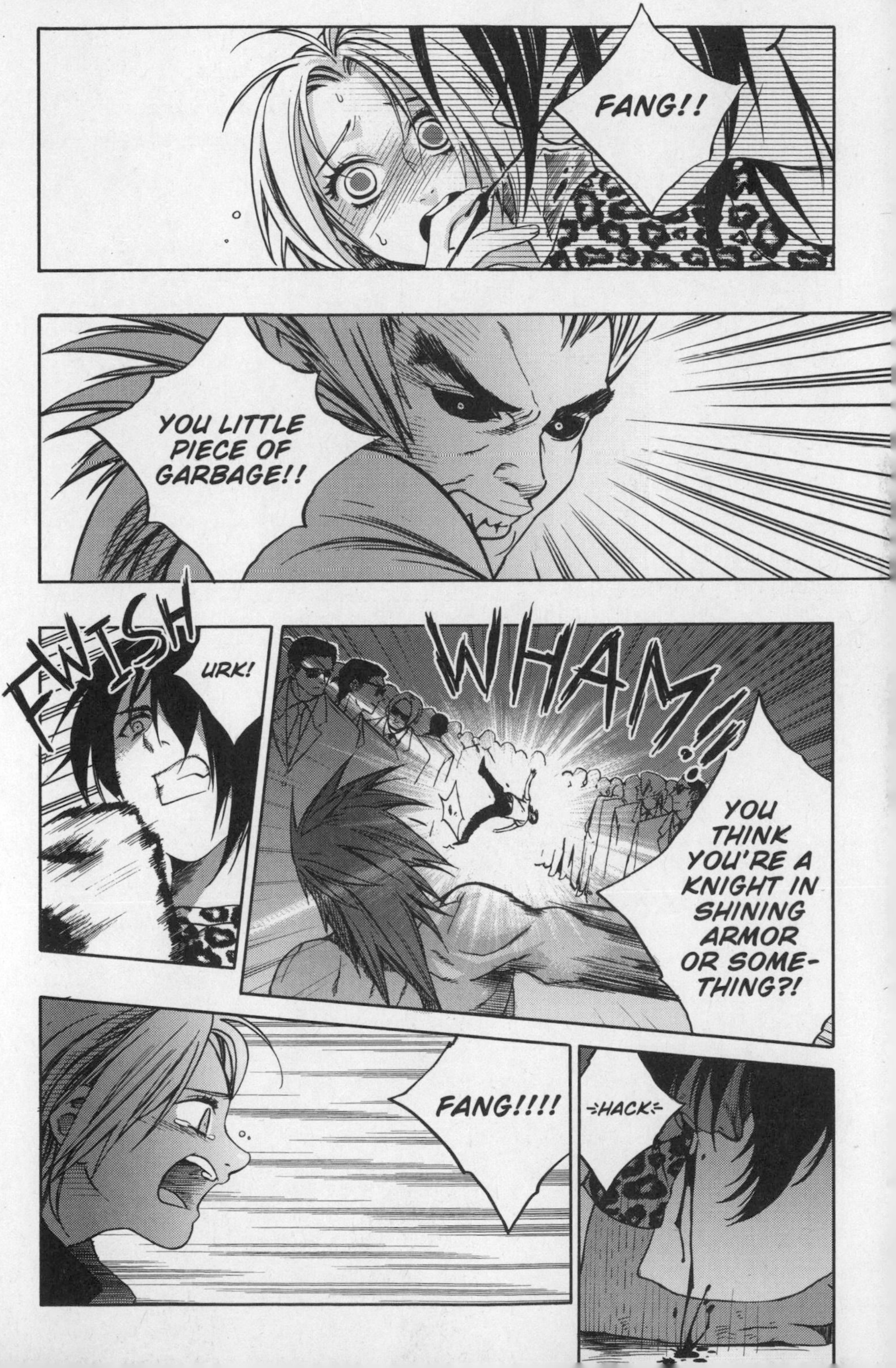
FANG!!
YOU LITTLE PIECE OF GARBAGE!!
FWISH
URK!
WHAM!!
YOU THINK YOU'RE A KNIGHT IN SHINING ARMOR OR SOME-THING?!
FANG!!!!
HACK

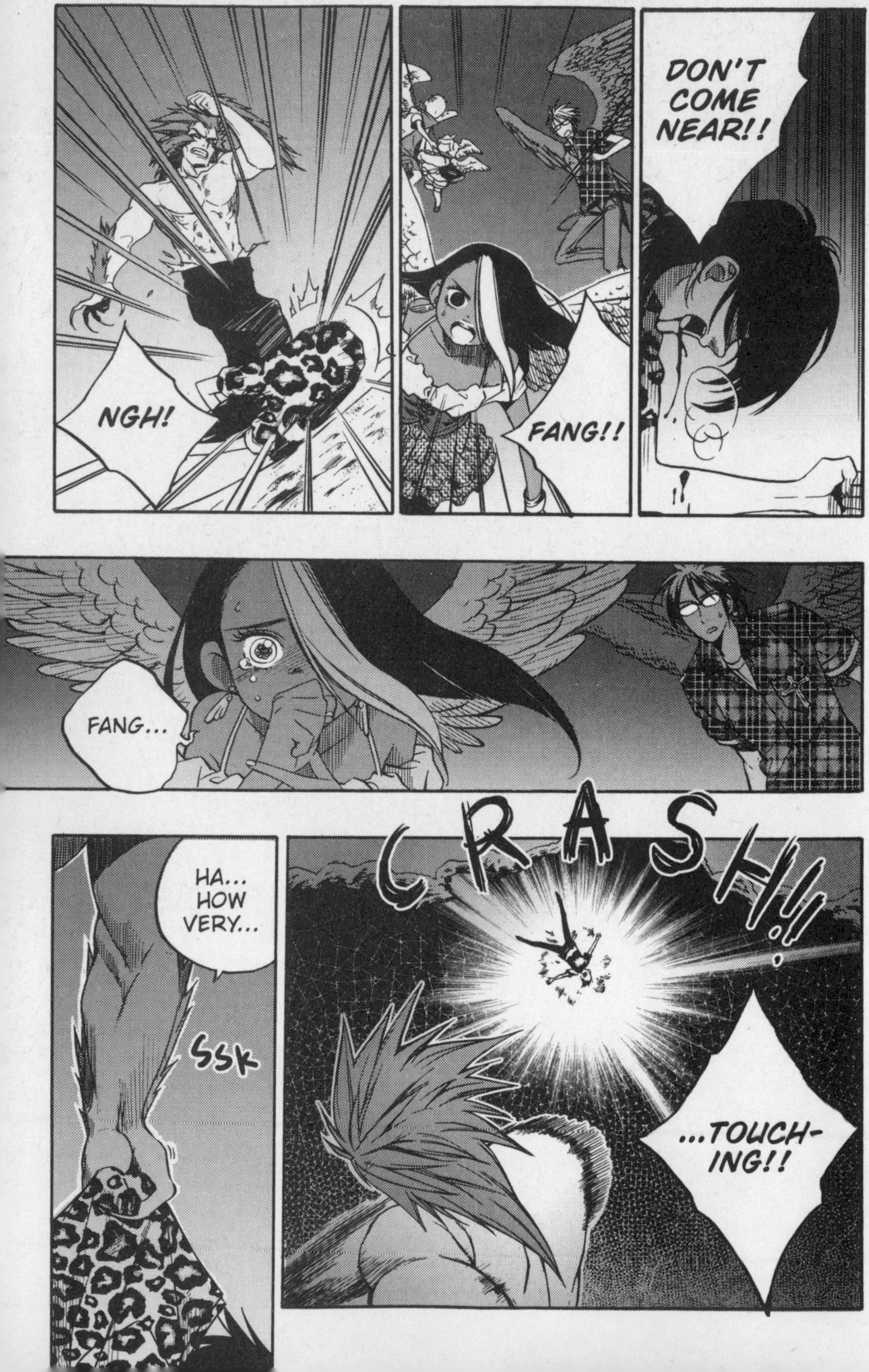
NGH!
FANG!!
DON'T COME NEAR!!
FANG...
HA... HOW VERY...
SSK
CRASH!!
...TOUCH-ING!!

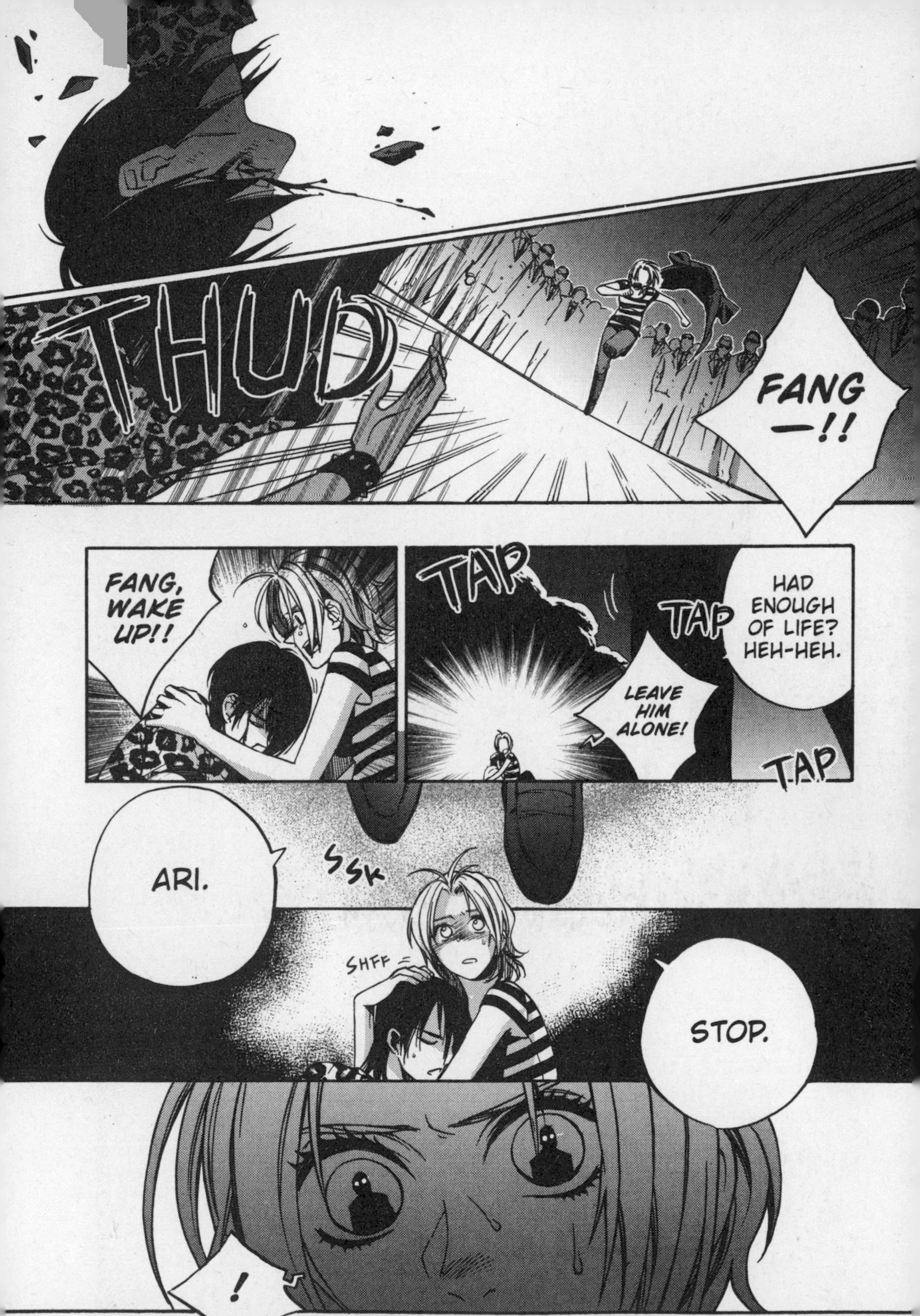
THUD
FANG—!!
FANG, WAKE UP!!
TAP
TAP
HAD ENOUGH OF LIFE? HEH-HEH.
LEAVE HIM ALONE!
TAP
ARI.
SSK
SHFF
STOP.
!

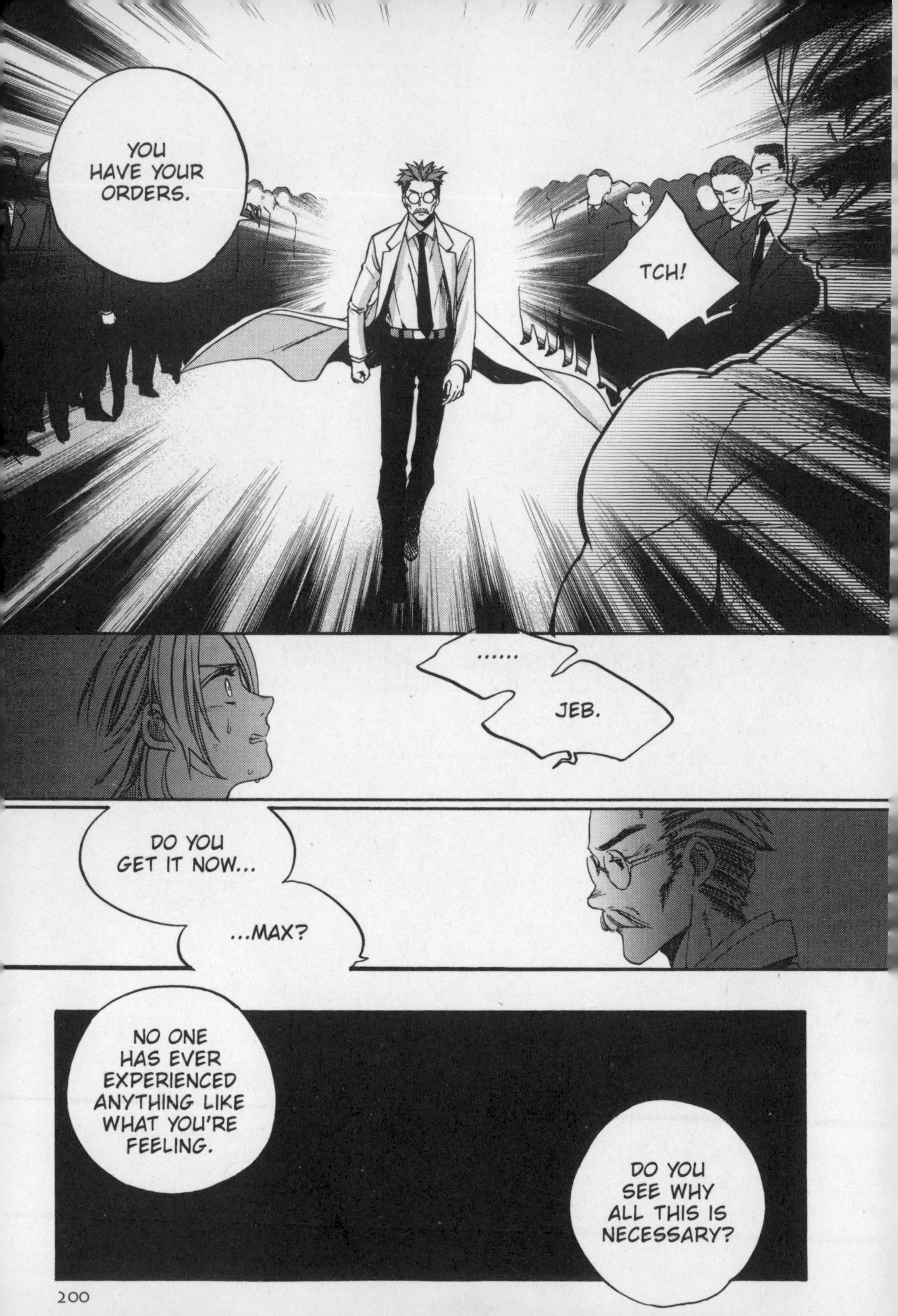
YOU HAVE YOUR ORDERS.
TCH!
......
JEB.
DO YOU GET IT NOW...
...MAX?
NO ONE HAS EVER EXPERIENCED ANYTHING LIKE WHAT YOU'RE FEELING.
DO YOU SEE WHY ALL THIS IS NECESSARY?

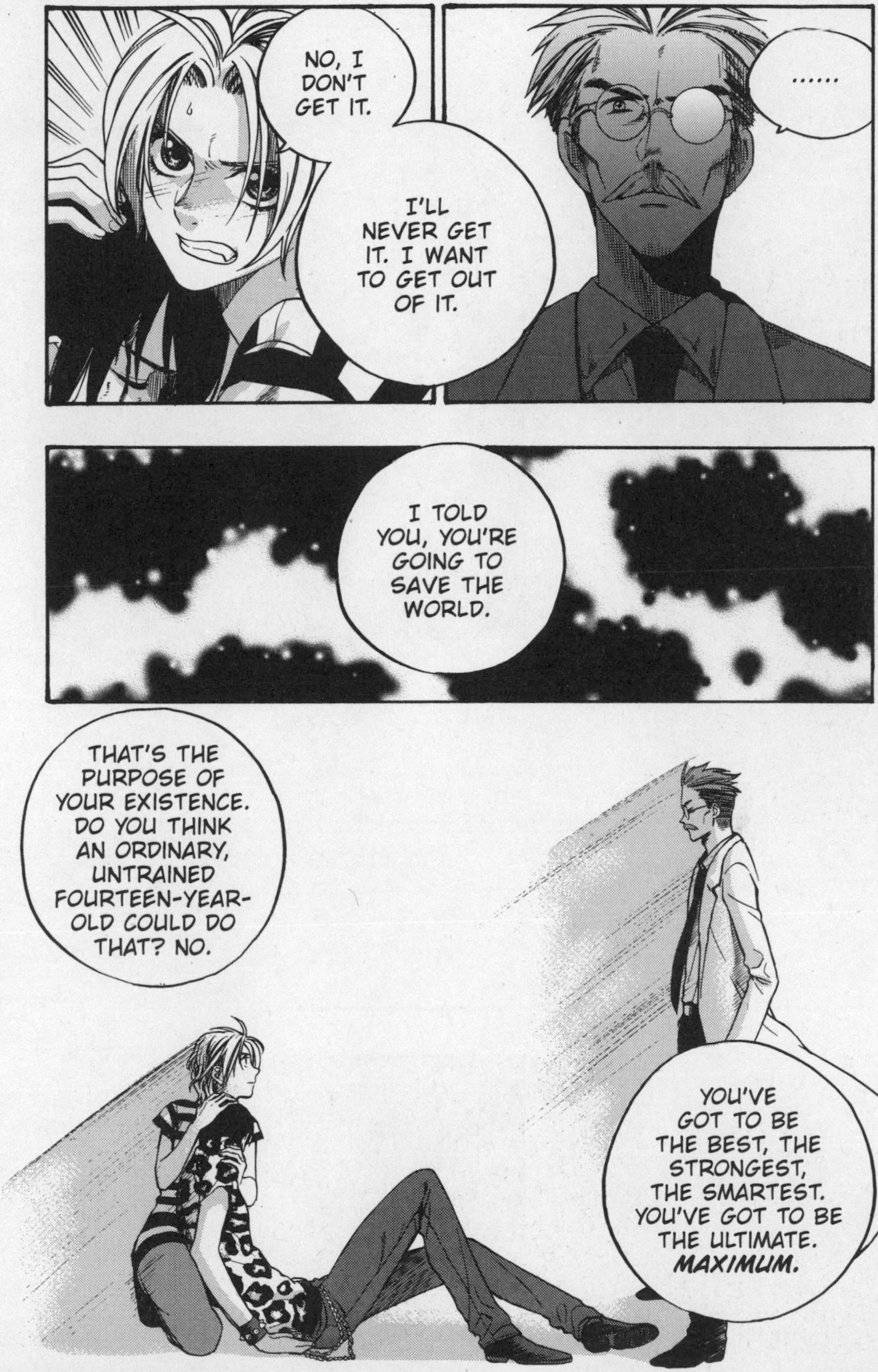
NO, I DON'T GET IT.
I'LL NEVER GET IT. I WANT TO GET OUT OF IT.
......
I TOLD YOU, YOU'RE GOING TO SAVE THE WORLD.
THAT'S THE PURPOSE OF YOUR EXISTENCE. DO YOU THINK AN ORDINARY, UNTRAINED FOURTEEN-YEAR-OLD COULD DO THAT? NO.
YOU'VE GOT TO BE THE BEST, THE STRONGEST, THE SMARTEST. YOU'VE GOT TO BE THE ULTIMATE. MAXIMUM.

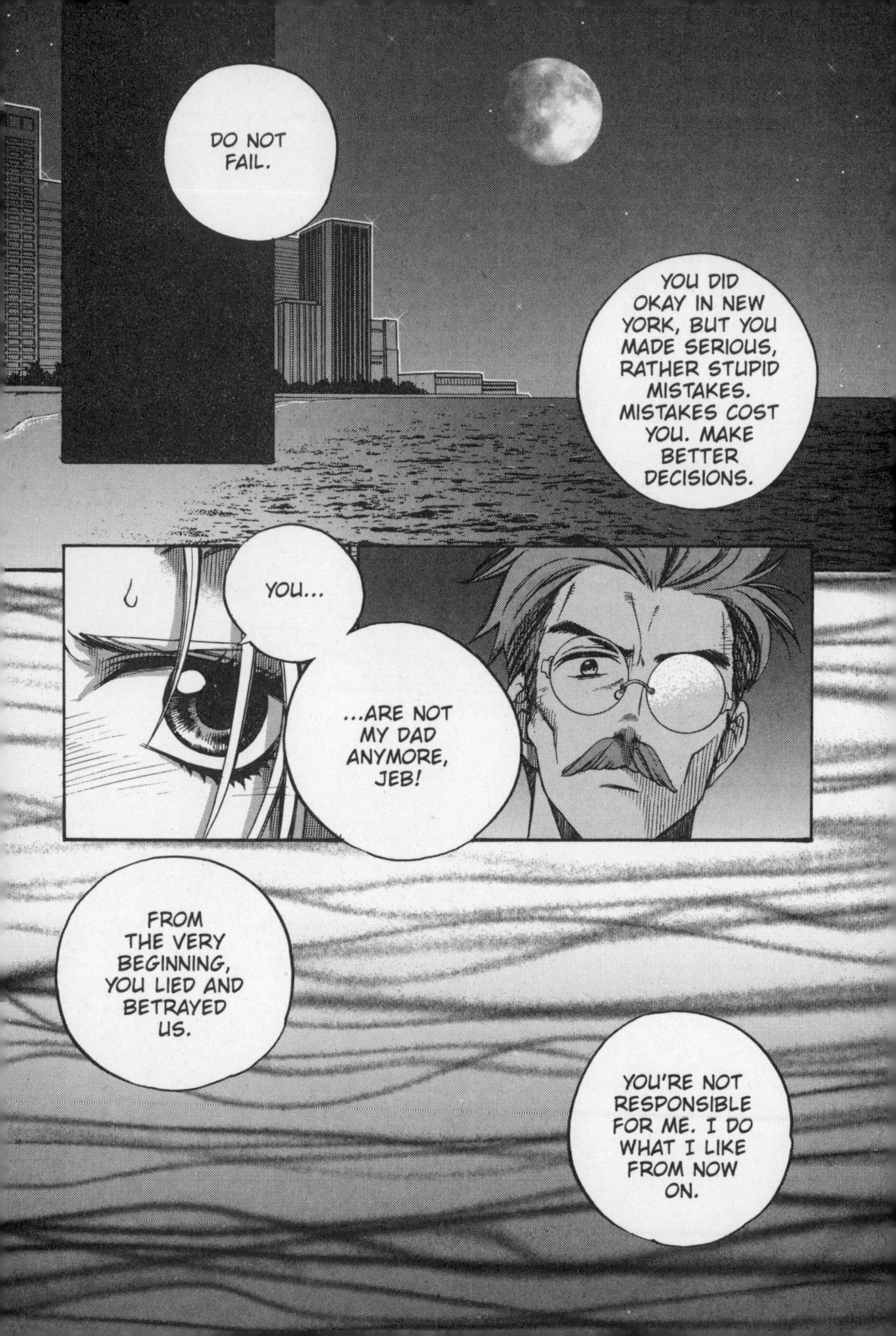
DO NOT FAIL.
YOU DID OKAY IN NEW YORK, BUT YOU MADE SERIOUS, RATHER STUPID MISTAKES. MISTAKES COST YOU. MAKE BETTER DECISIONS.
YOU...
...ARE NOT MY DAD ANYMORE, JEB!
FROM THE VERY BEGINNING, YOU LIED AND BETRAYED US.
YOU'RE NOT RESPONSIBLE FOR ME. I DO WHAT I LIKE FROM NOW ON.

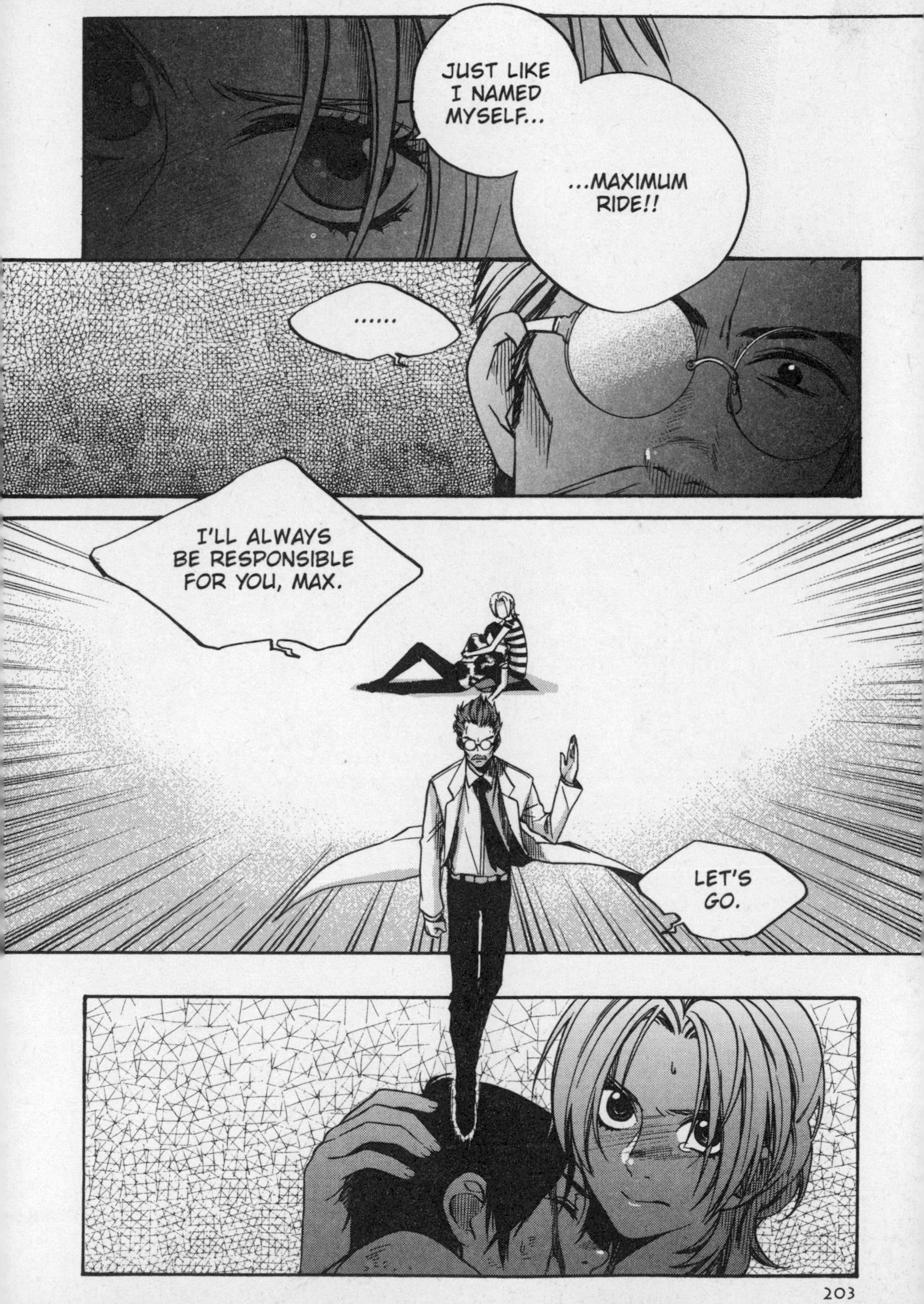
JUST LIKE I NAMED MYSELF...
...MAXIMUM RIDE!!
......
I'LL ALWAYS BE RESPONSIBLE FOR YOU, MAX.
LET'S GO.

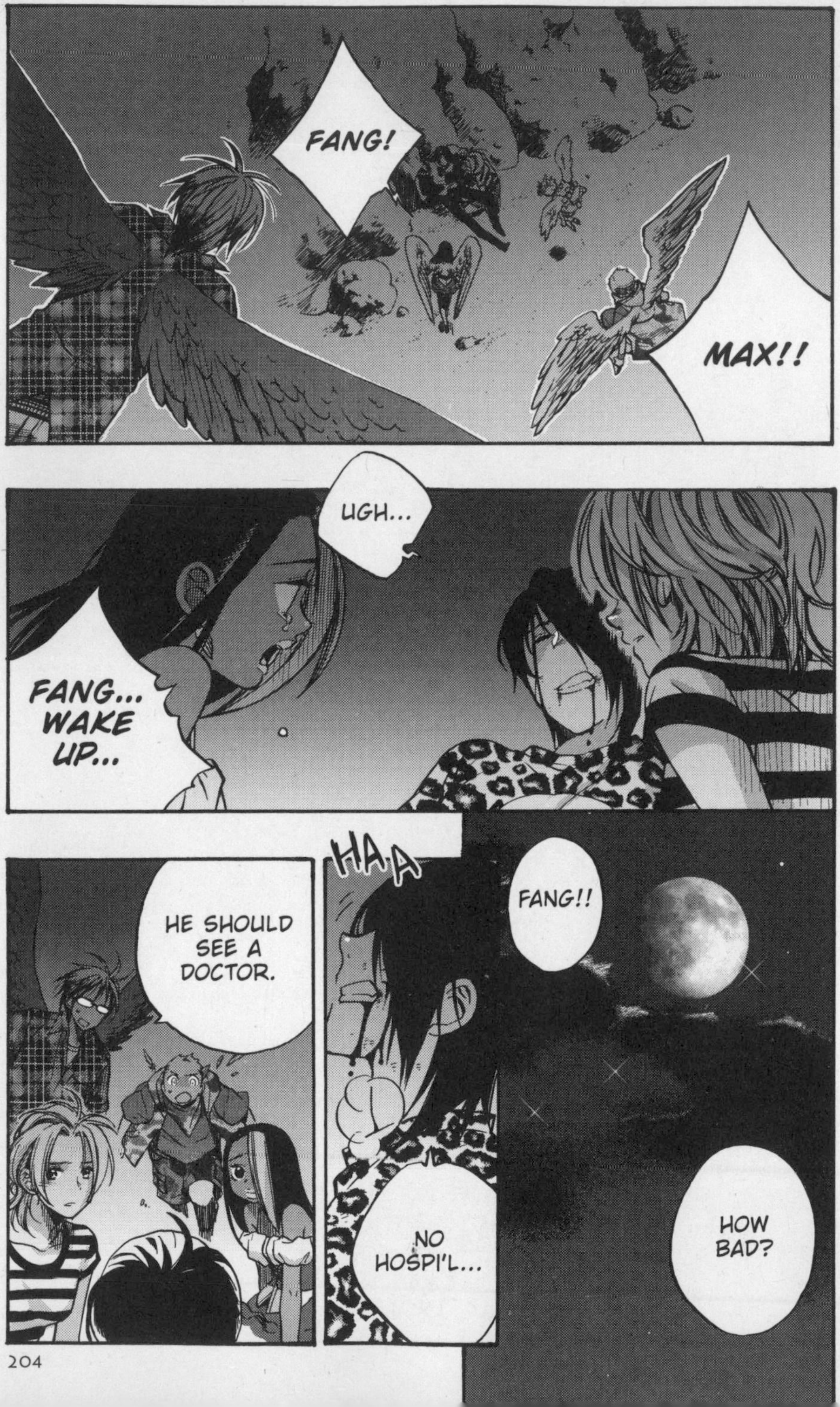

FANG!
MAX!!
FANG... WAKE UP...
UGH...
HE SHOULD SEE A DOCTOR.
HAA
NO HOSPI'L...
FANG!!
HOW BAD?

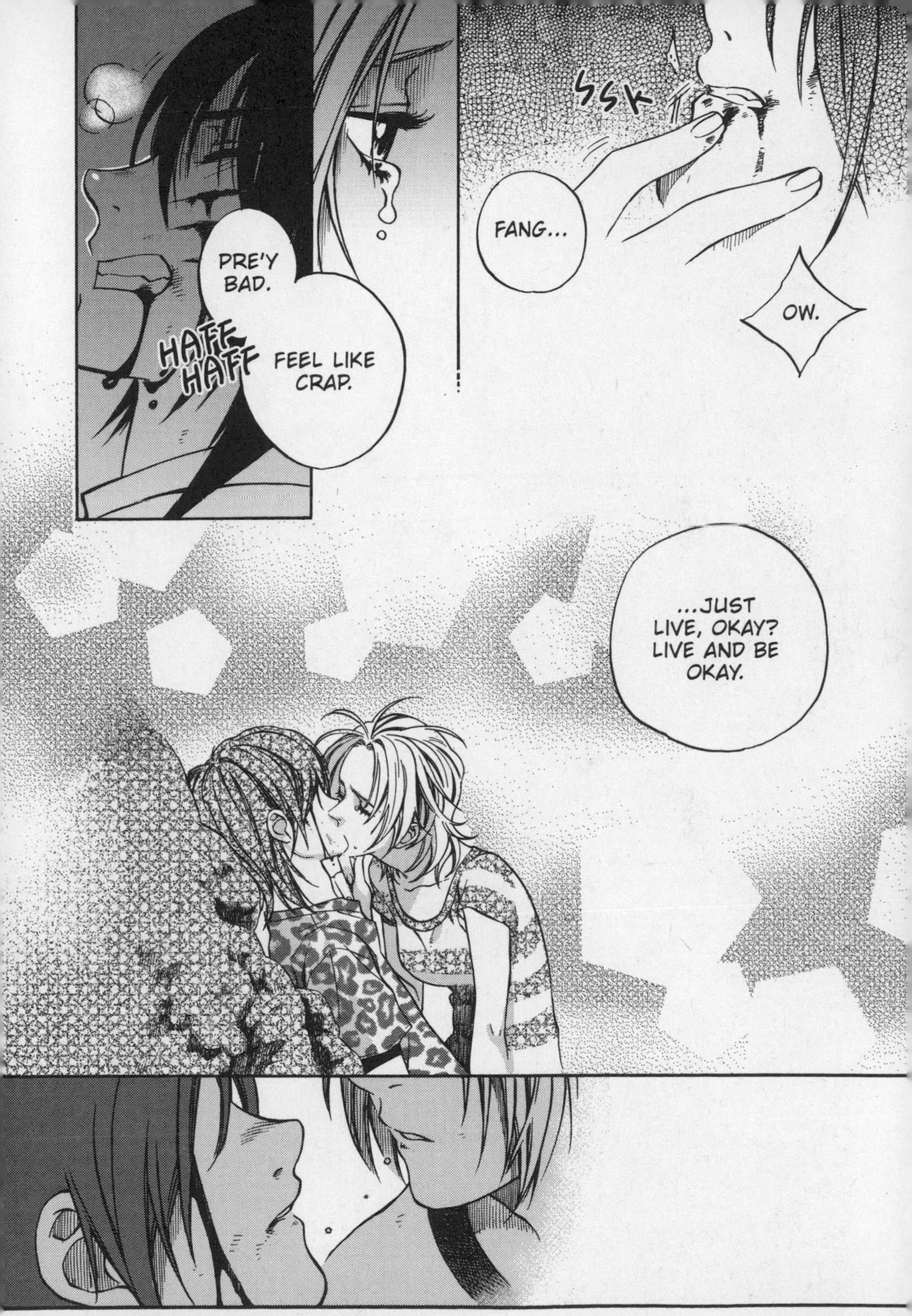
PRE'Y BAD.
HAFF HAFF
FEEL LIKE CRAP.
SSK
FANG...
OW.
...JUST LIVE, OKAY? LIVE AND BE OKAY.

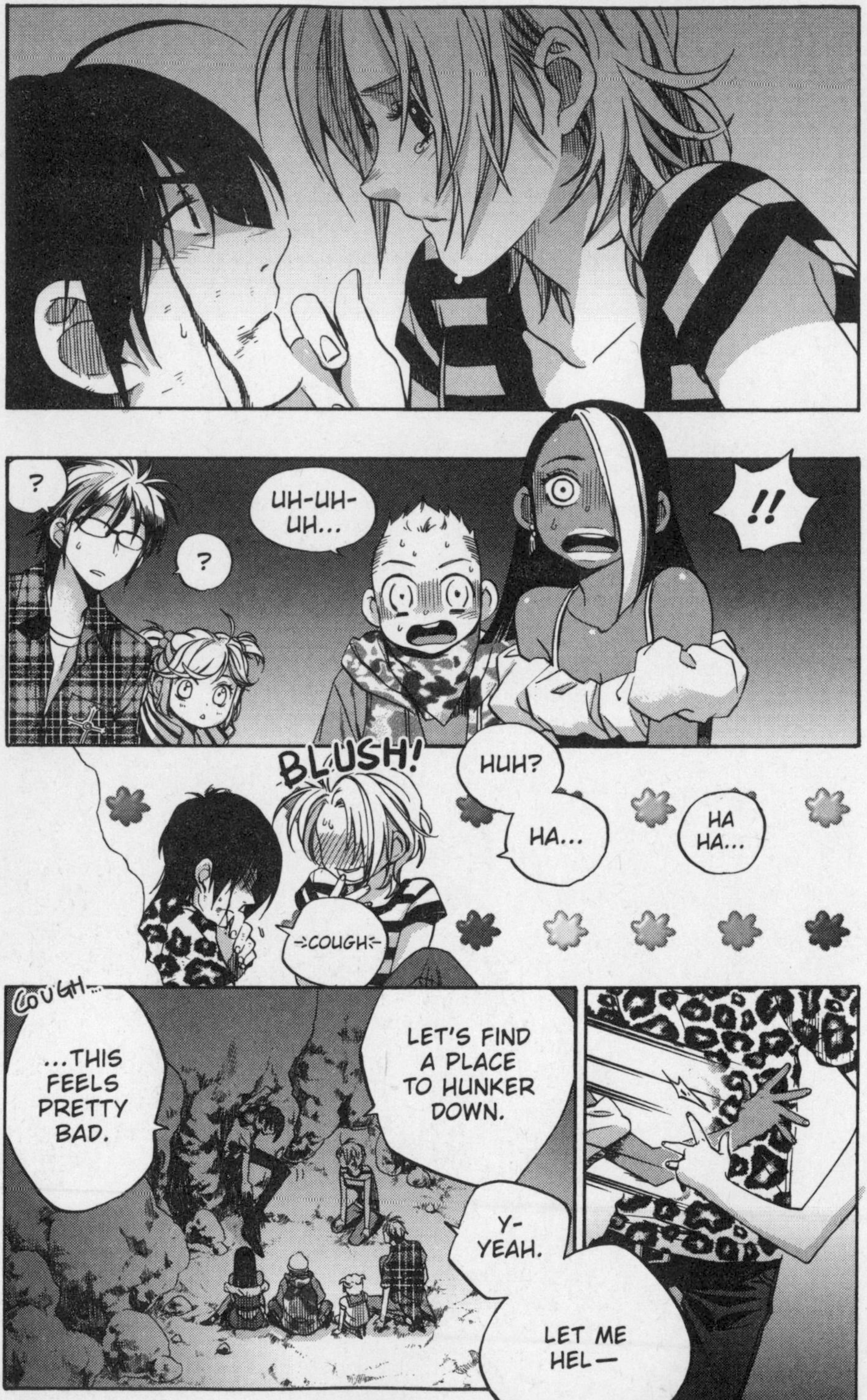
?
?
UH-UH-UH...
!!
BLUSH!
HUH?
HA...
HA HA...
-COUGH-
COUGH...
...THIS FEELS PRETTY BAD.
LET'S FIND A PLACE TO HUNKER DOWN.
Y-YEAH.
LET ME HEL—

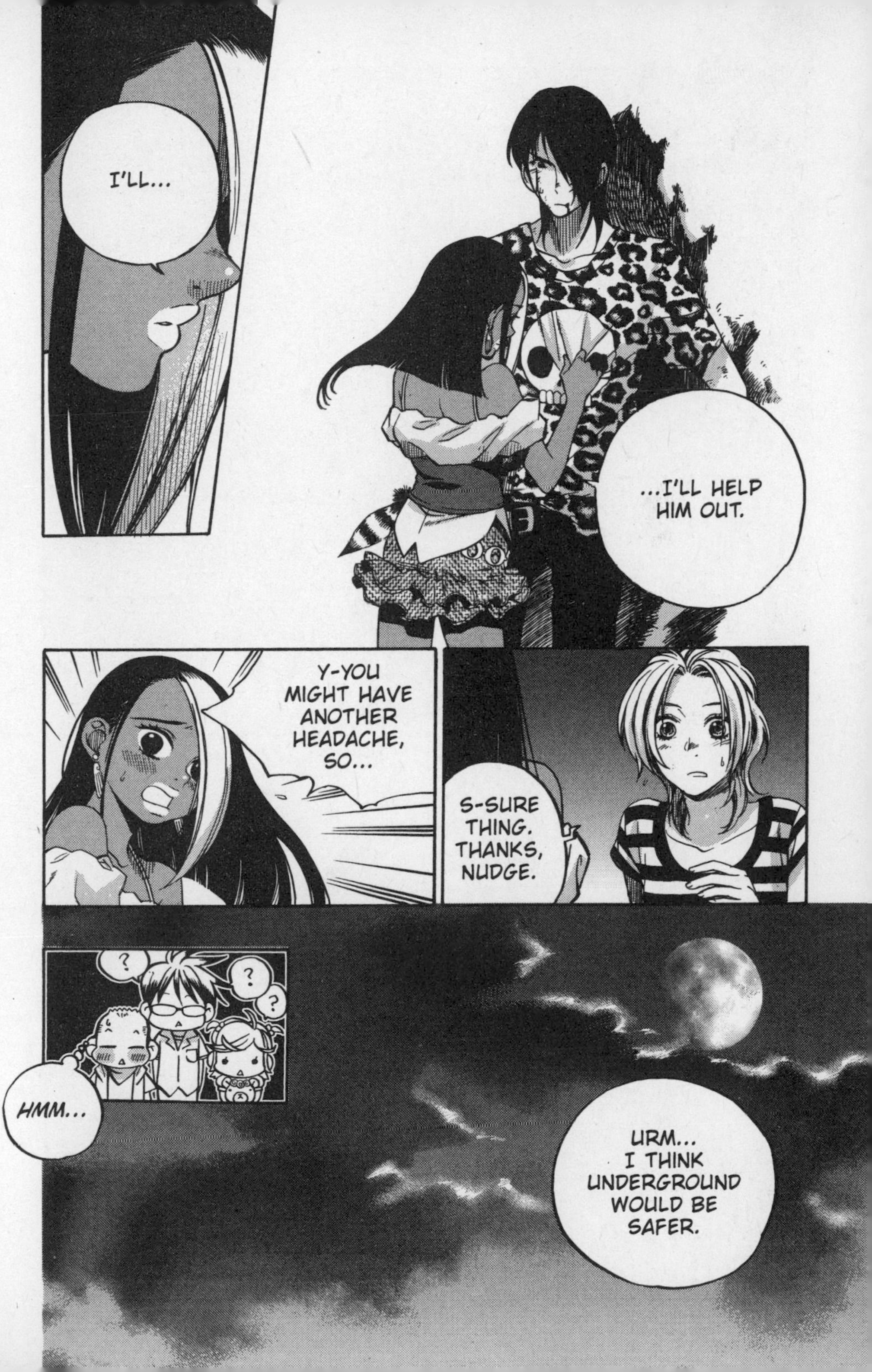
I'LL...
...I'LL HELP HIM OUT.
Y-YOU MIGHT HAVE ANOTHER HEADACHE, SO...
S-SURE THING. THANKS, NUDGE.
HMM...
URM... I THINK UNDERGROUND WOULD BE SAFER.

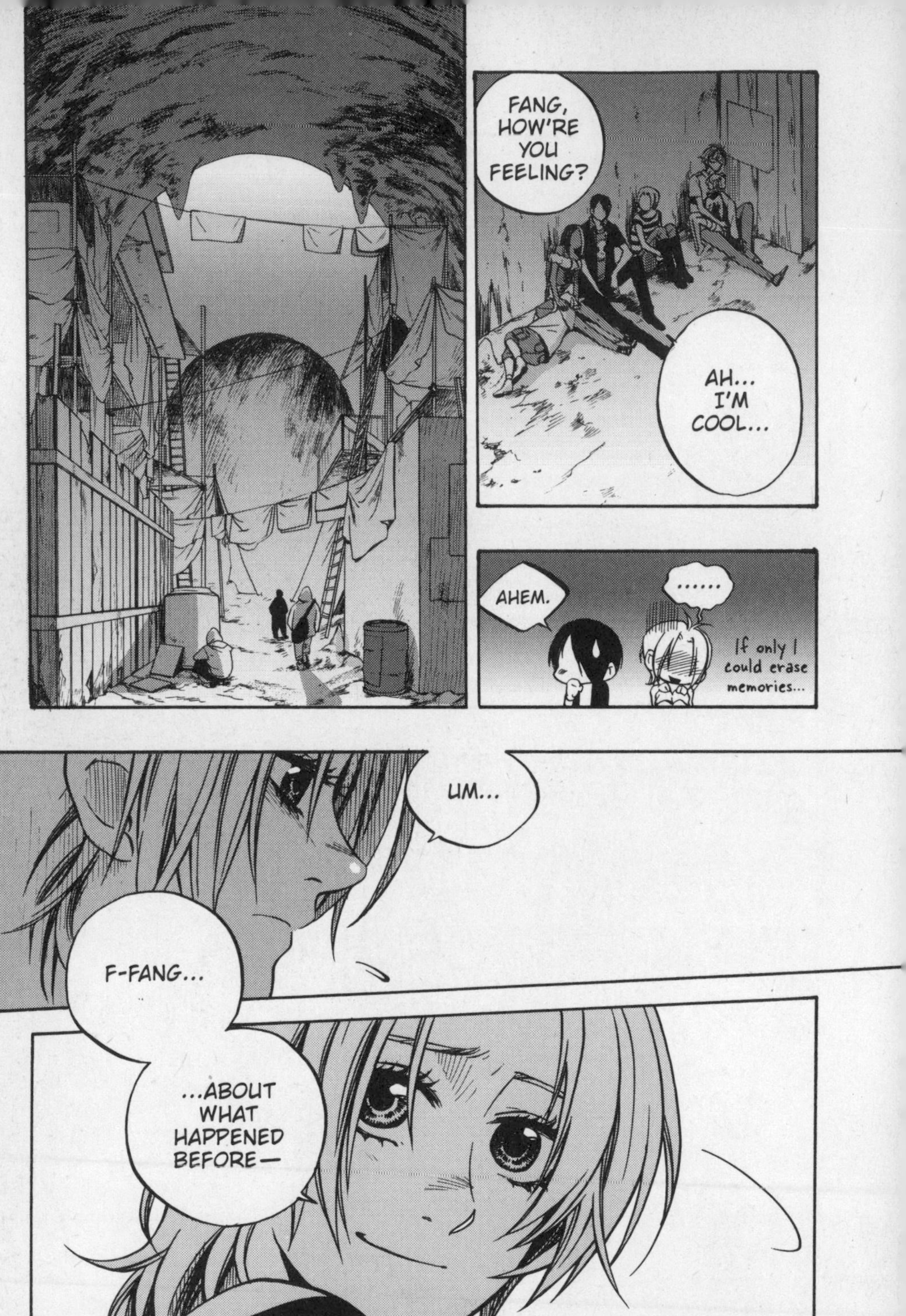

FANG, HOW'RE YOU FEELING?
AH... I'M COOL...
AHEM.
......
If only I could erase memories...
UM...
F-FANG...
...ABOUT WHAT HAPPENED BEFORE—

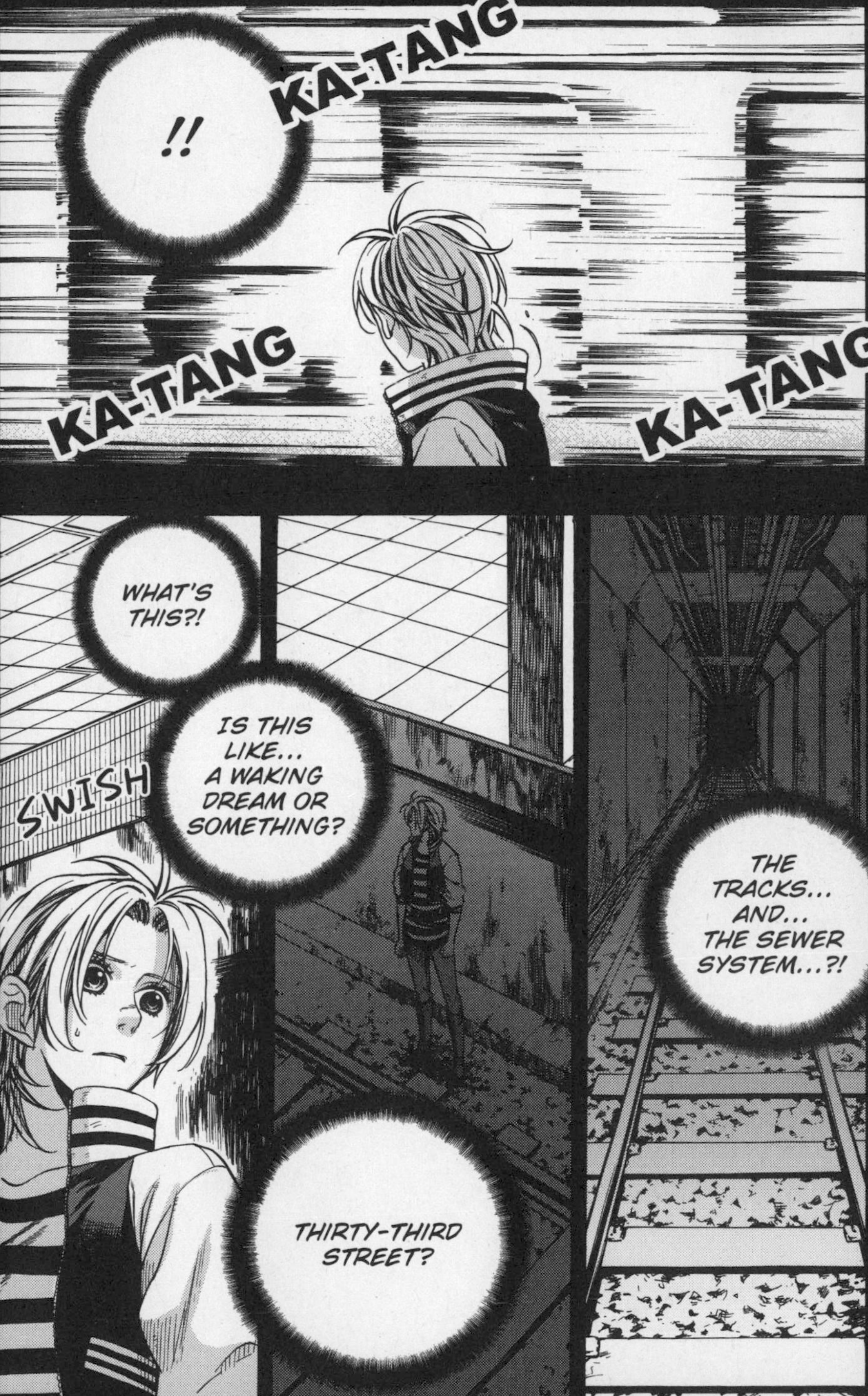
!!
KA-TANG
KA-TANG
KA-TANG
WHAT'S THIS?!
IS THIS LIKE... A WAKING DREAM OR SOMETHING?
SWISH
THIRTY-THIRD STREET?
THE TRACKS... AND... THE SEWER SYSTEM...?!

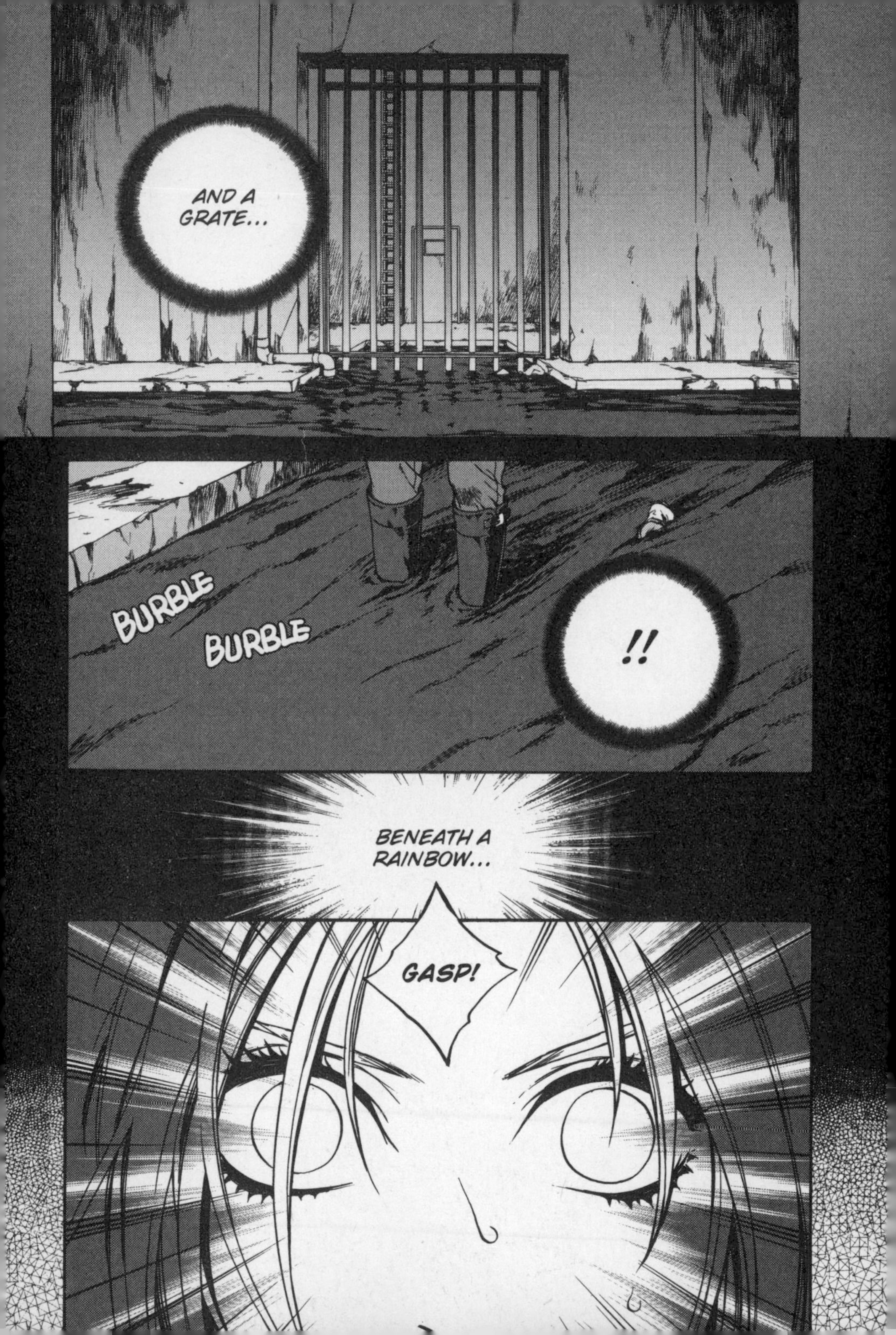
AND A GRATE...
!!
BURBLE
BURBLE
BENEATH A RAINBOW...
GASP!

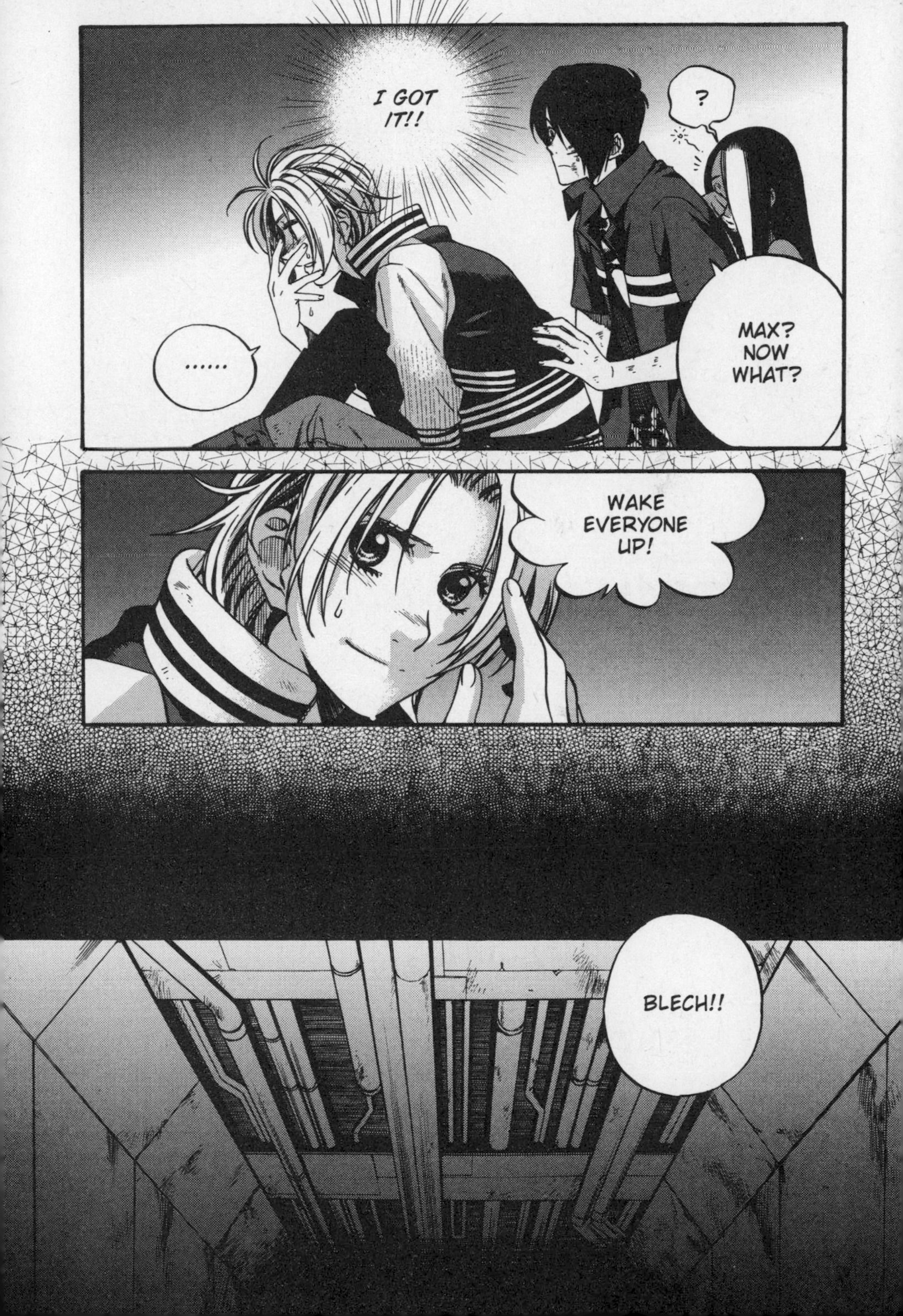
I GOT IT!!
?
......
MAX? NOW WHAT?
WAKE EVERYONE UP!
BLECH!!

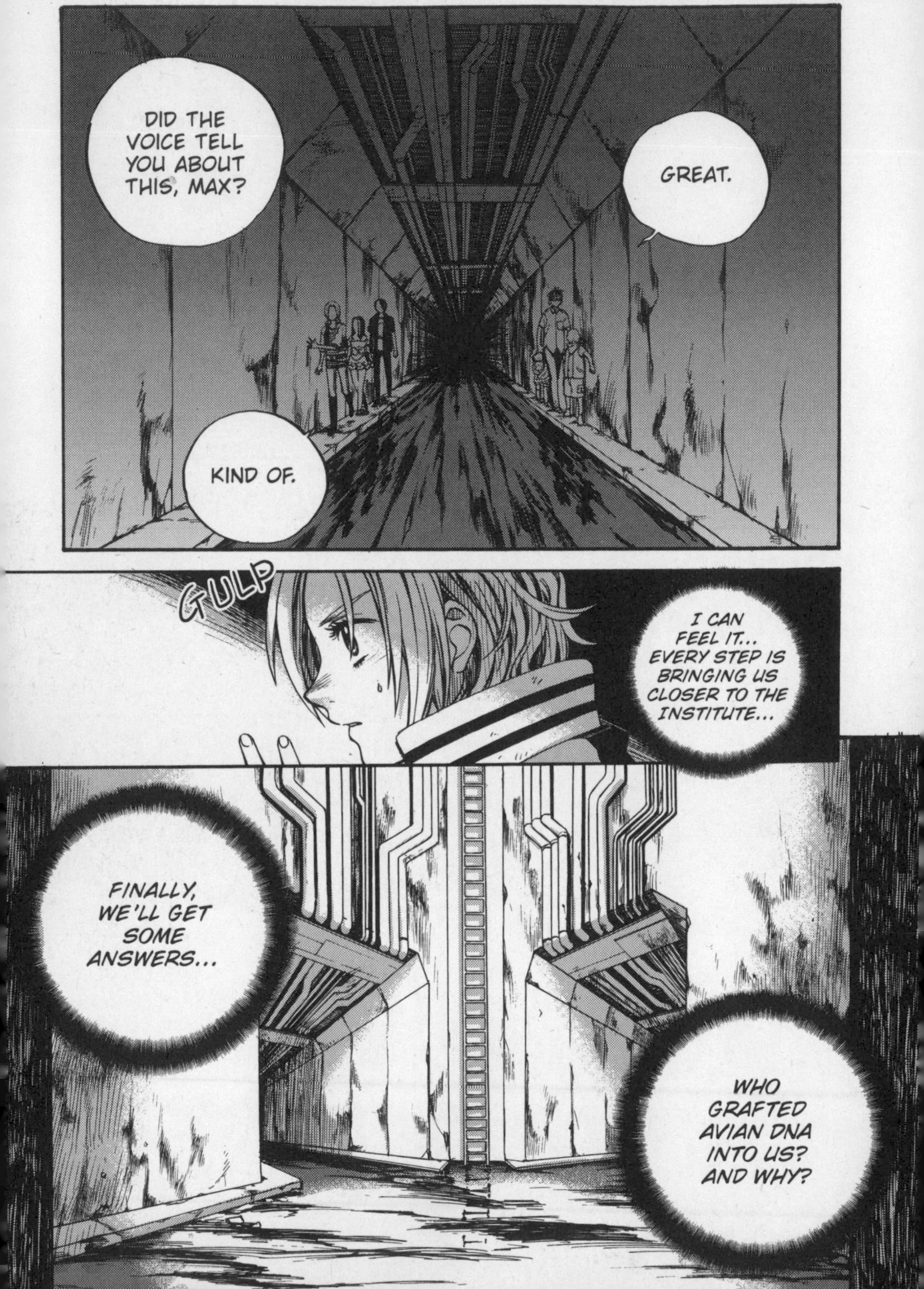
DID THE VOICE TELL YOU ABOUT THIS, MAX?
GREAT.
KIND OF.
GULP
I CAN FEEL IT... EVERY STEP IS BRINGING US CLOSER TO THE INSTITUTE...
FINALLY, WE'LL GET SOME ANSWERS...
WHO GRAFTED AVIAN DNA INTO US? AND WHY?

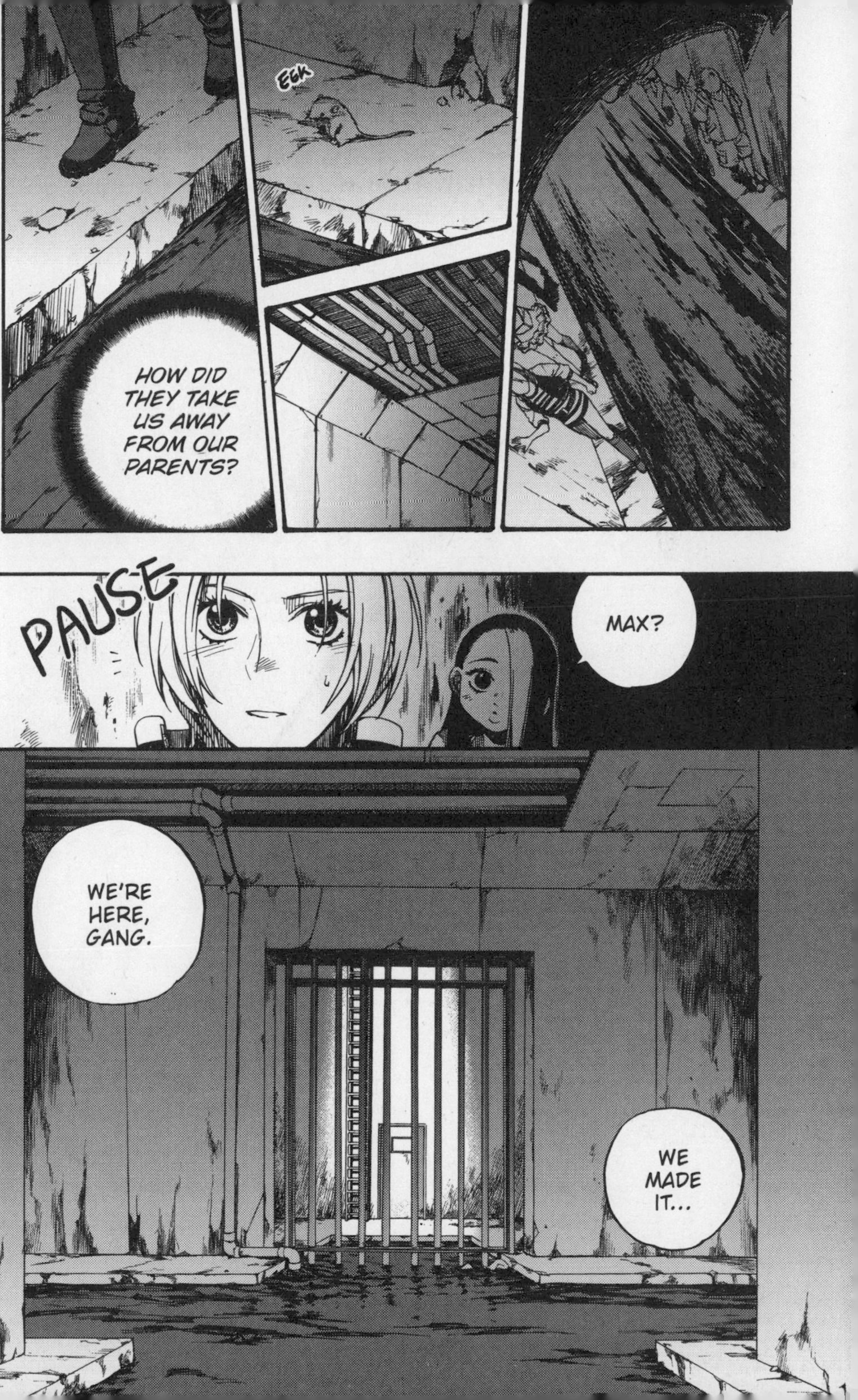
EEK
HOW DID THEY TAKE US AWAY FROM OUR PARENTS?
PAUSE
MAX?
WE'RE HERE, GANG.
WE MADE IT...

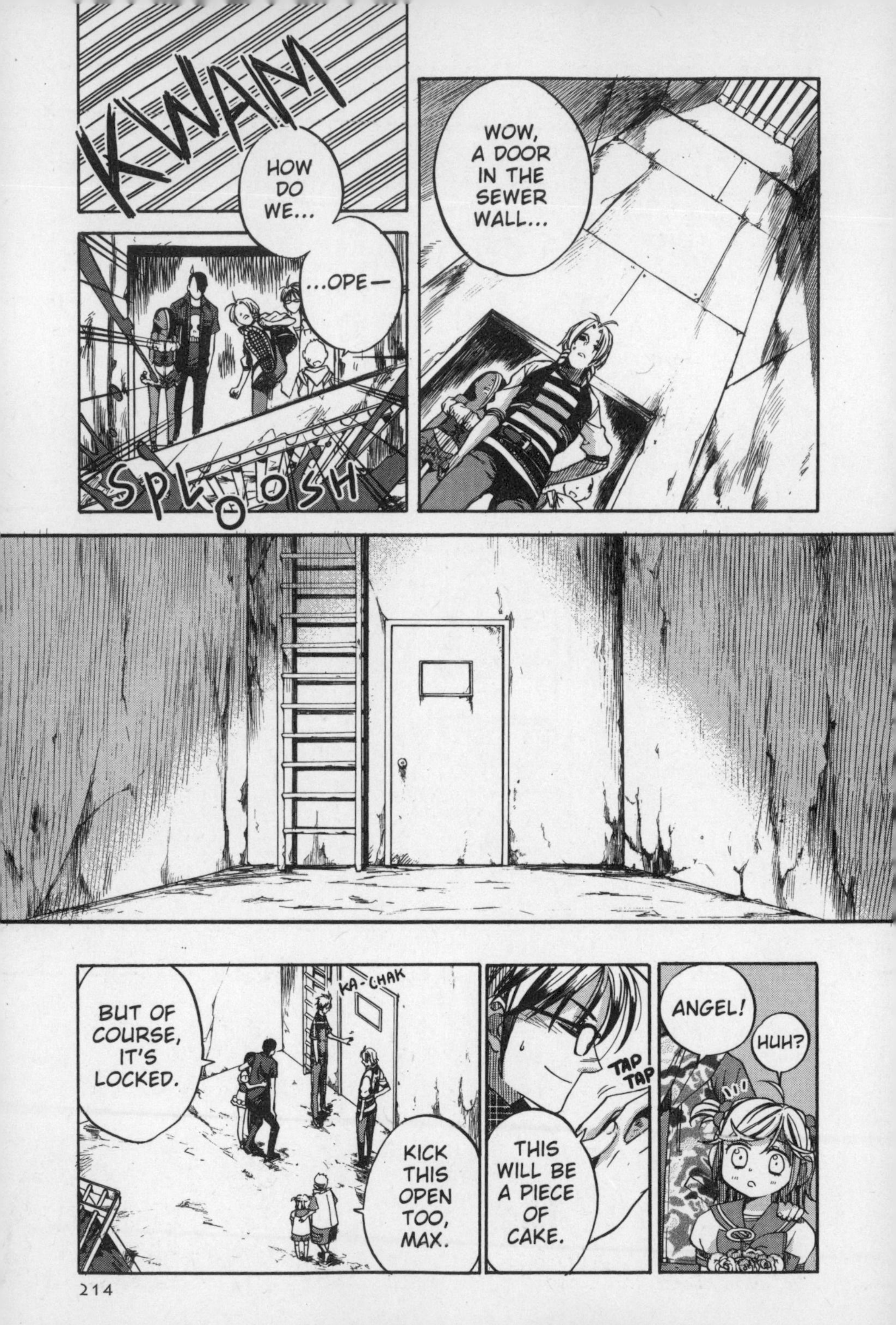
KWAM
HOW DO WE...
...OPE—
SPLOOSH
WOW, A DOOR IN THE SEWER WALL...
BUT OF COURSE, IT'S LOCKED.
KA-CHAK
KICK THIS OPEN TOO, MAX.
TAP TAP
THIS WILL BE A PIECE OF CAKE.
ANGEL!
HUH?

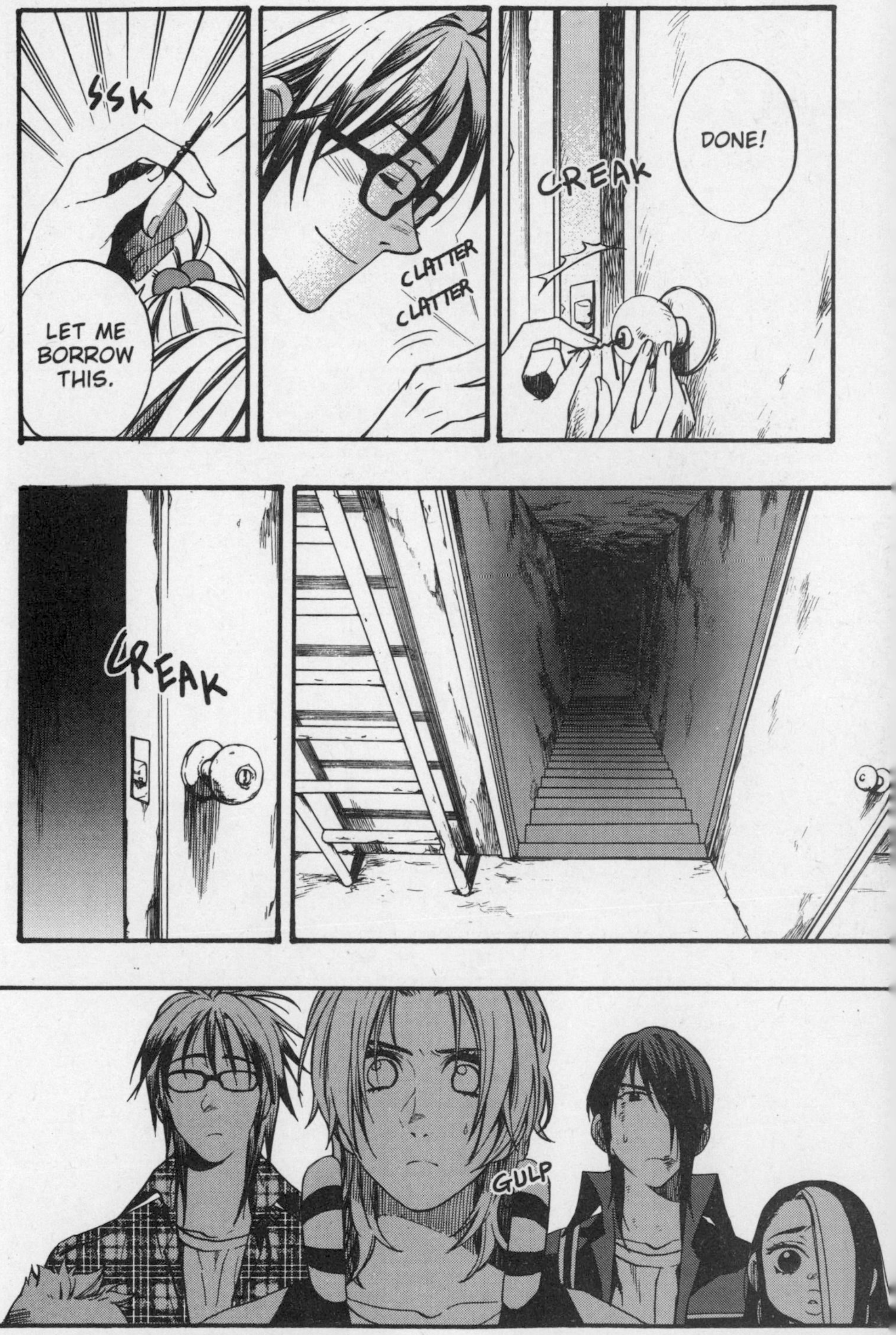
SSK
LET ME BORROW THIS.
CLATTER CLATTER
CREAK
DONE!
CREAK
GULP

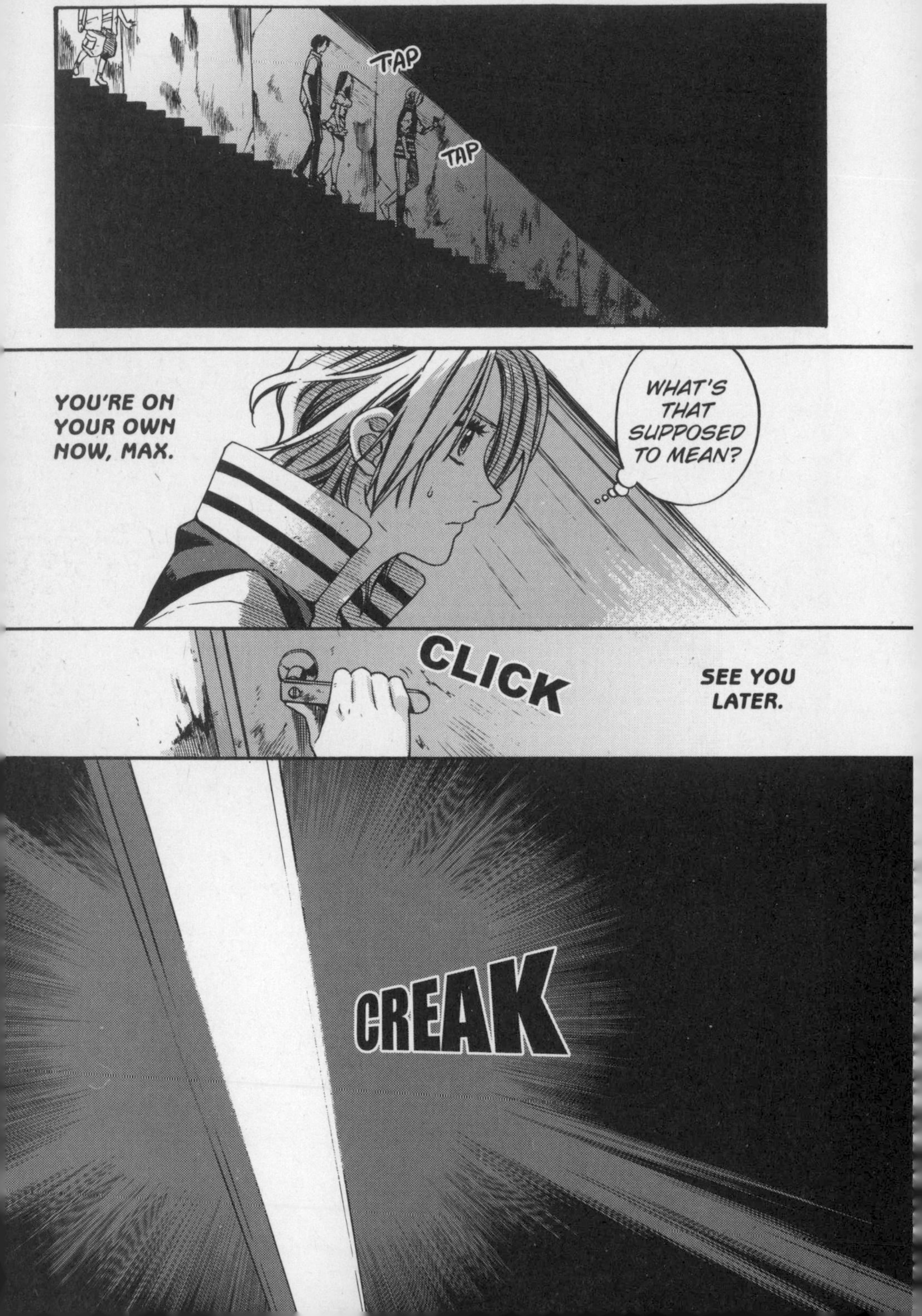
TAP
TAP
YOU'RE ON YOUR OWN NOW, MAX.
WHAT'S THAT SUPPOSED TO MEAN?
CLICK
SEE YOU LATER.
CREAK

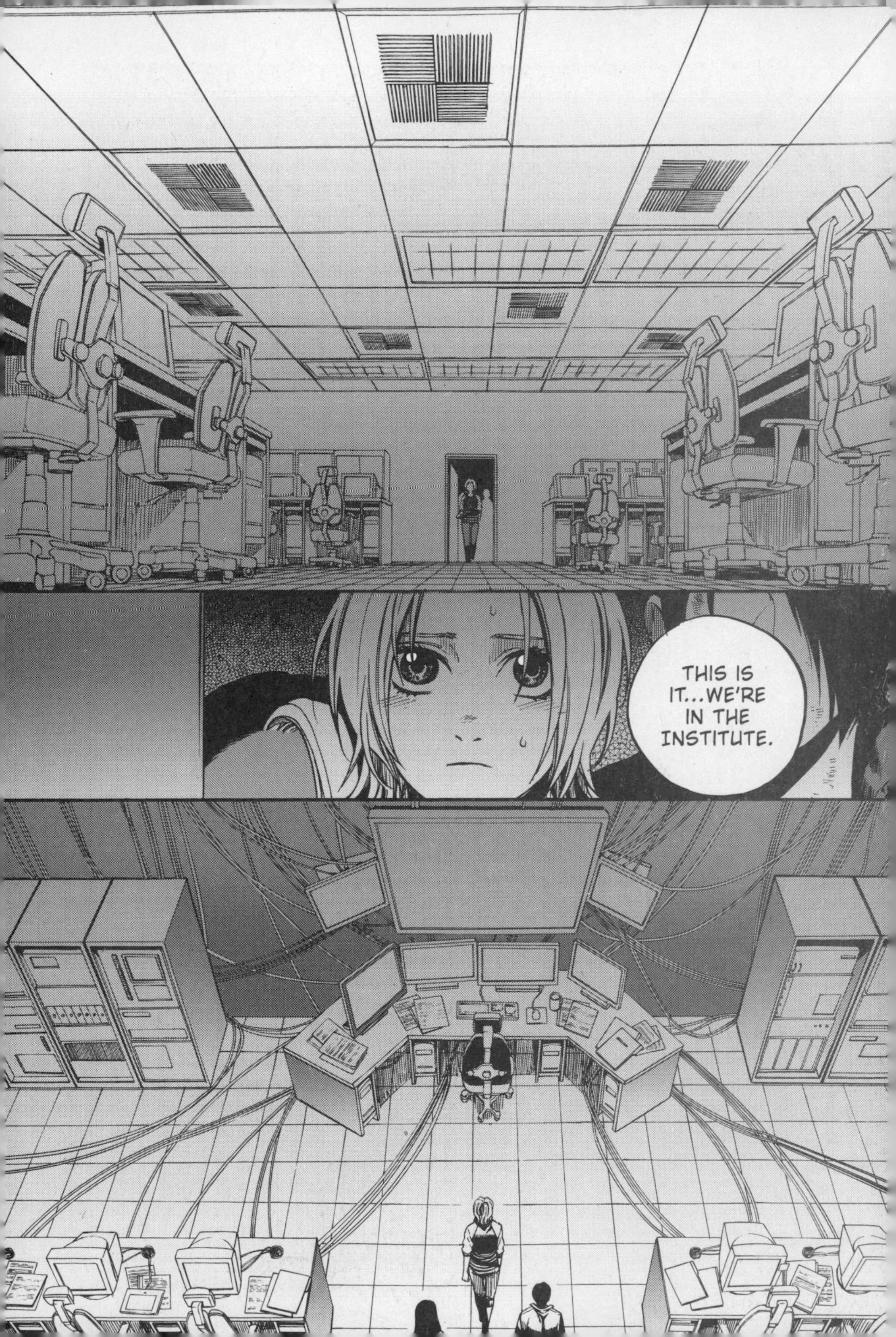
THIS IS IT...WE'RE IN THE INSTITUTE.

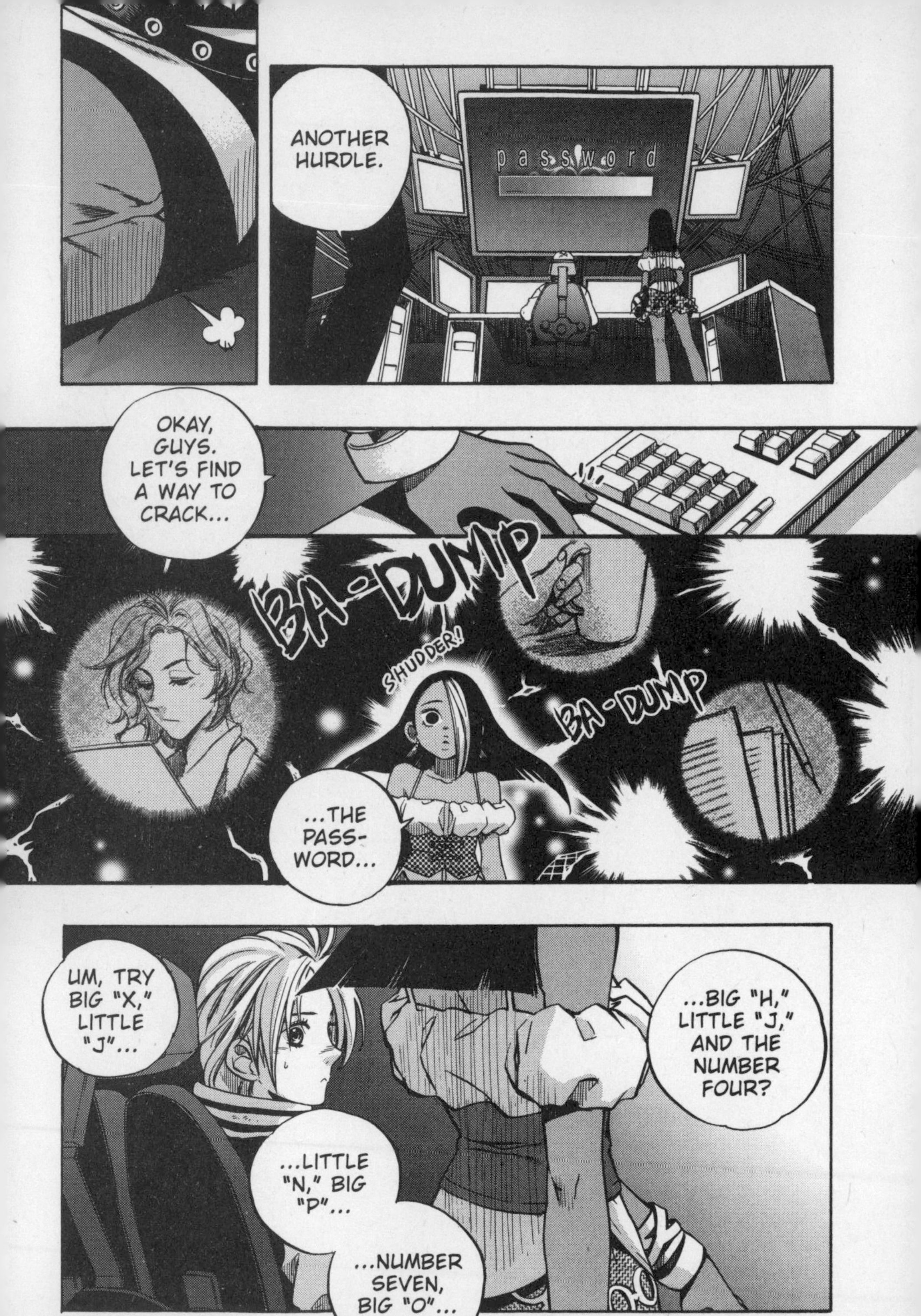

ANOTHER HURDLE.
password
OKAY, GUYS. LET'S FIND A WAY TO CRACK...
BA-DUMP
SHUDDER!
BA-DUMP
...THE PASS-WORD...
UM, TRY BIG "X," LITTLE "J"...
...LITTLE "N," BIG "P"...
...NUMBER SEVEN, BIG "O"...
...BIG "H," LITTLE "J," AND THE NUMBER FOUR?

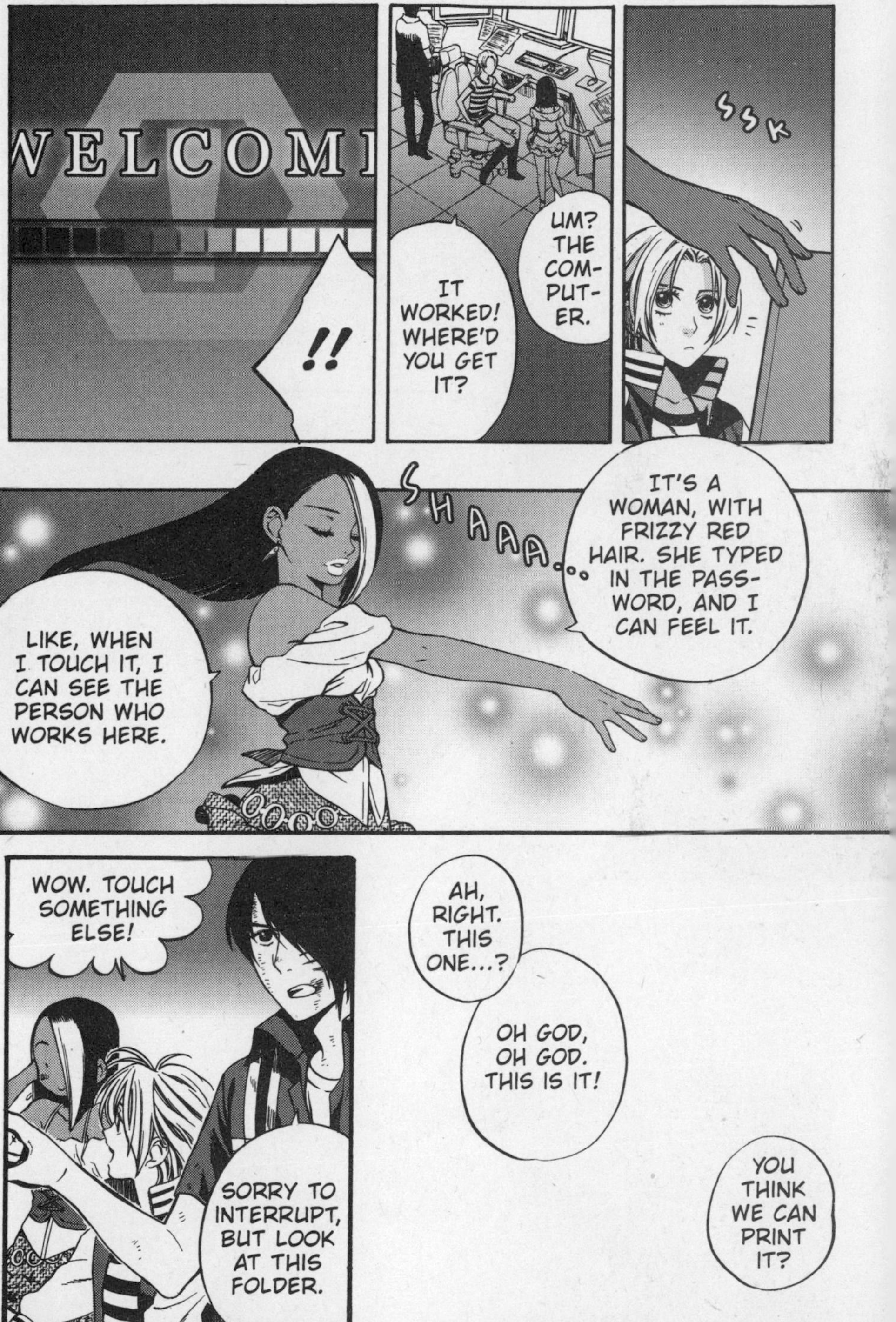
WELCOM
!!
IT WORKED! WHERE'D YOU GET IT?
UM? THE COMPUTER.
SSK
SHAAAA...
IT'S A WOMAN, WITH FRIZZY RED HAIR. SHE TYPED IN THE PASSWORD, AND I CAN FEEL IT.
LIKE, WHEN I TOUCH IT, I CAN SEE THE PERSON WHO WORKS HERE.
WOW. TOUCH SOMETHING ELSE!
SORRY TO INTERRUPT, BUT LOOK AT THIS FOLDER.
AH, RIGHT. THIS ONE...?
OH GOD, OH GOD. THIS IS IT!
YOU THINK WE CAN PRINT IT?

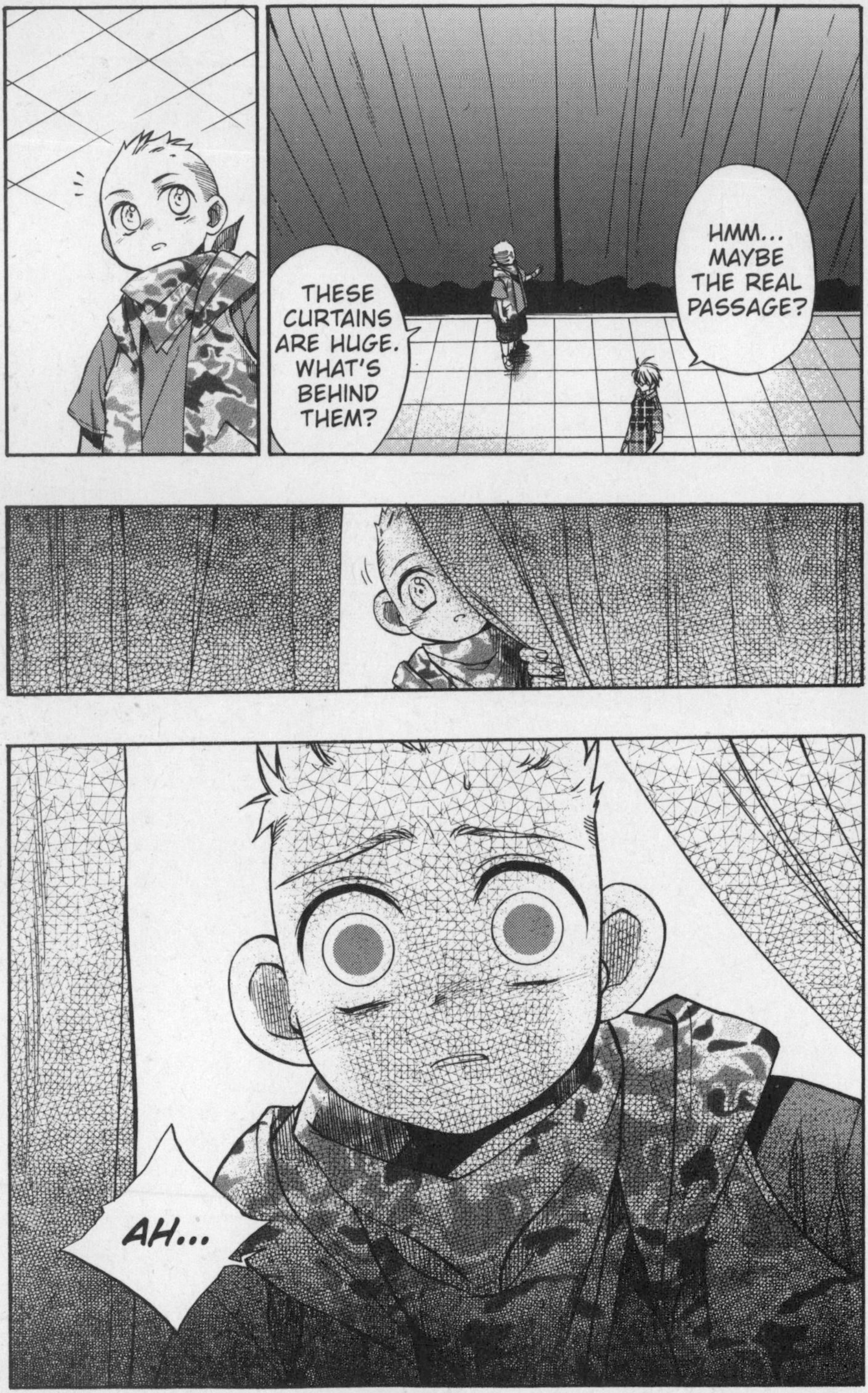
THESE CURTAINS ARE HUGE. WHAT'S BEHIND THEM?
HMM... MAYBE THE REAL PASSAGE?
AH...

MAXIMUM
RIDE

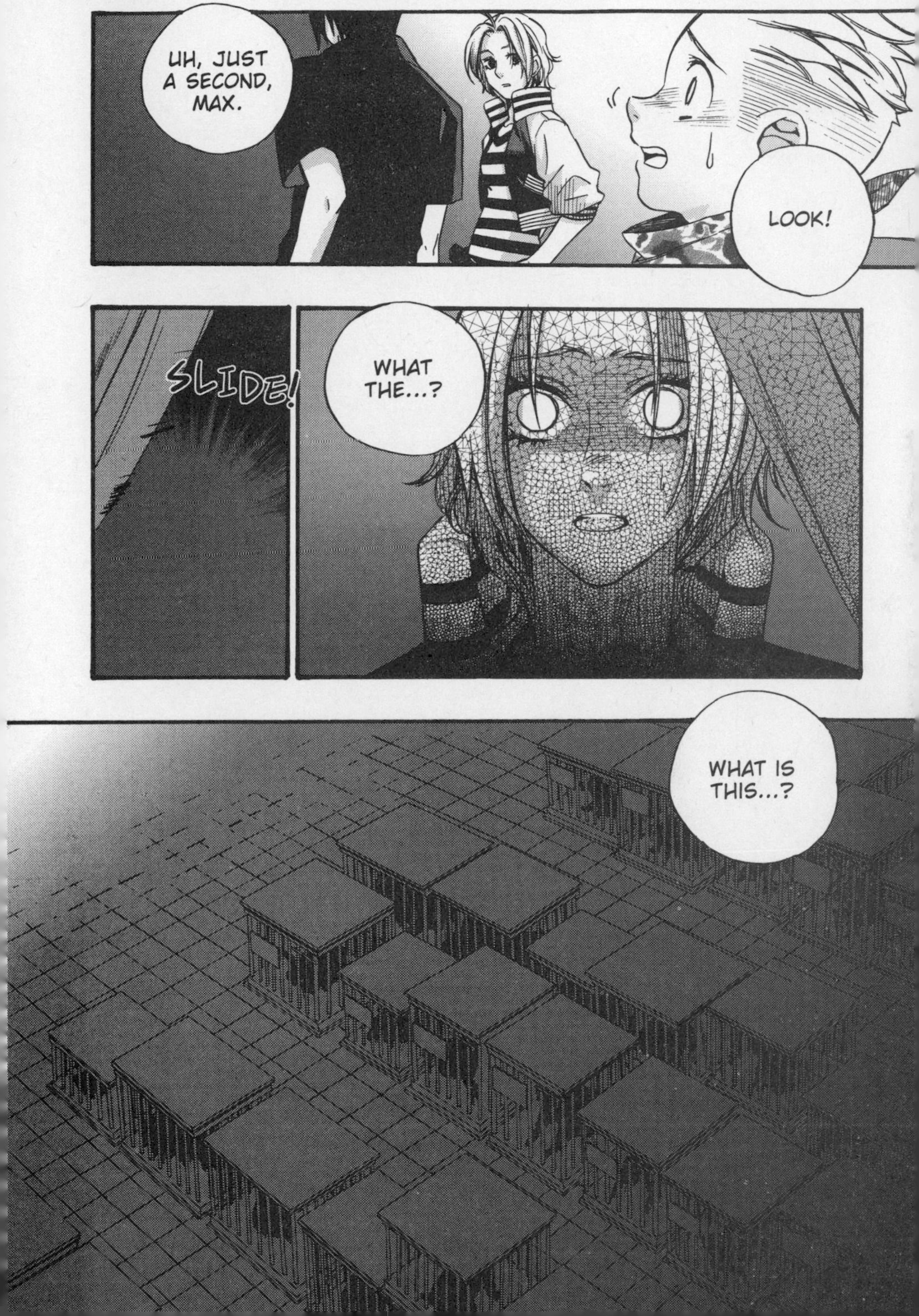
UH, JUST A SECOND, MAX.
LOOK!
SLIDE!
WHAT THE...?
WHAT IS THIS...?

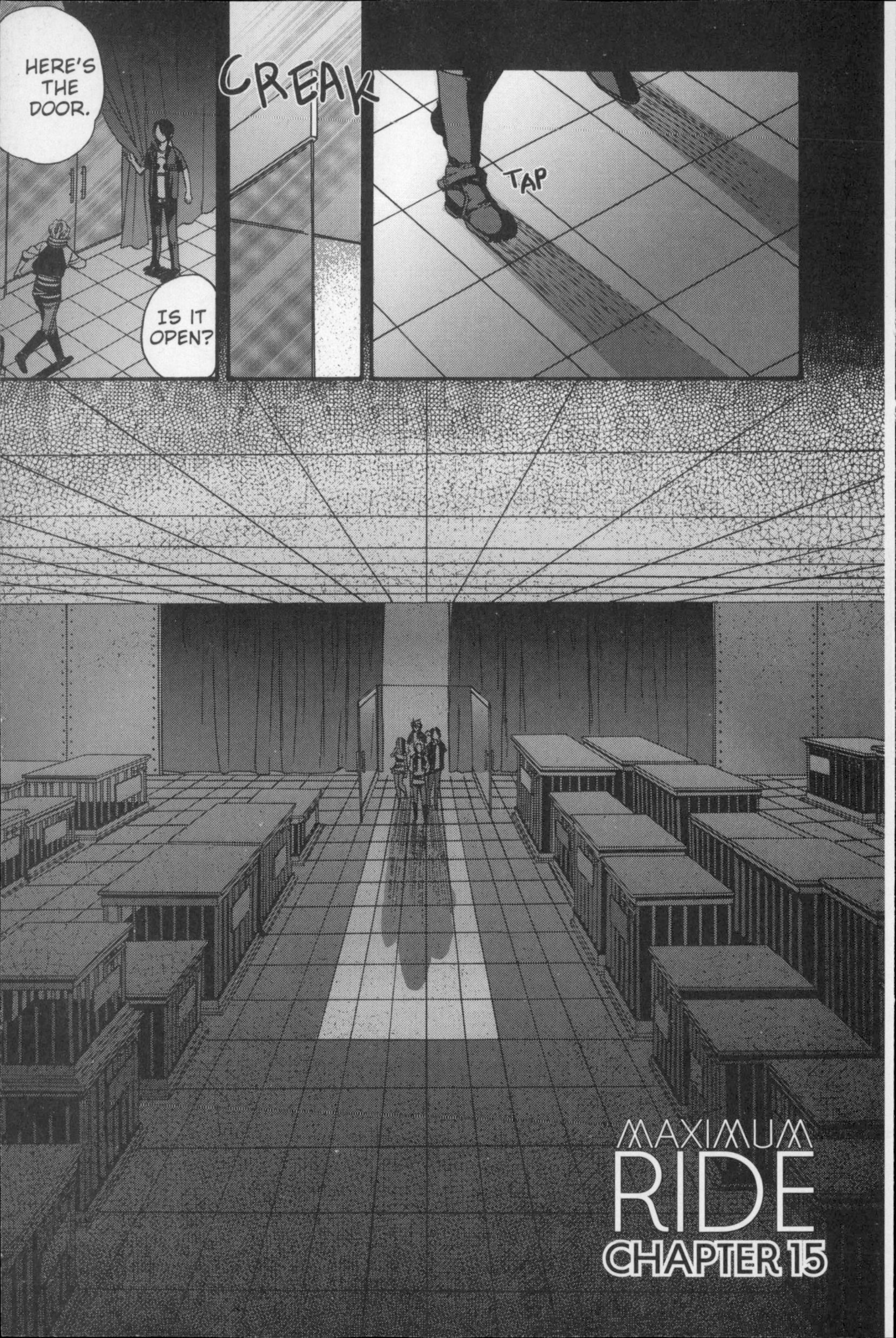
HERE'S THE DOOR.
IS IT OPEN?
CREAK
TAP
MAXIMUM RIDE
CHAPTER 15

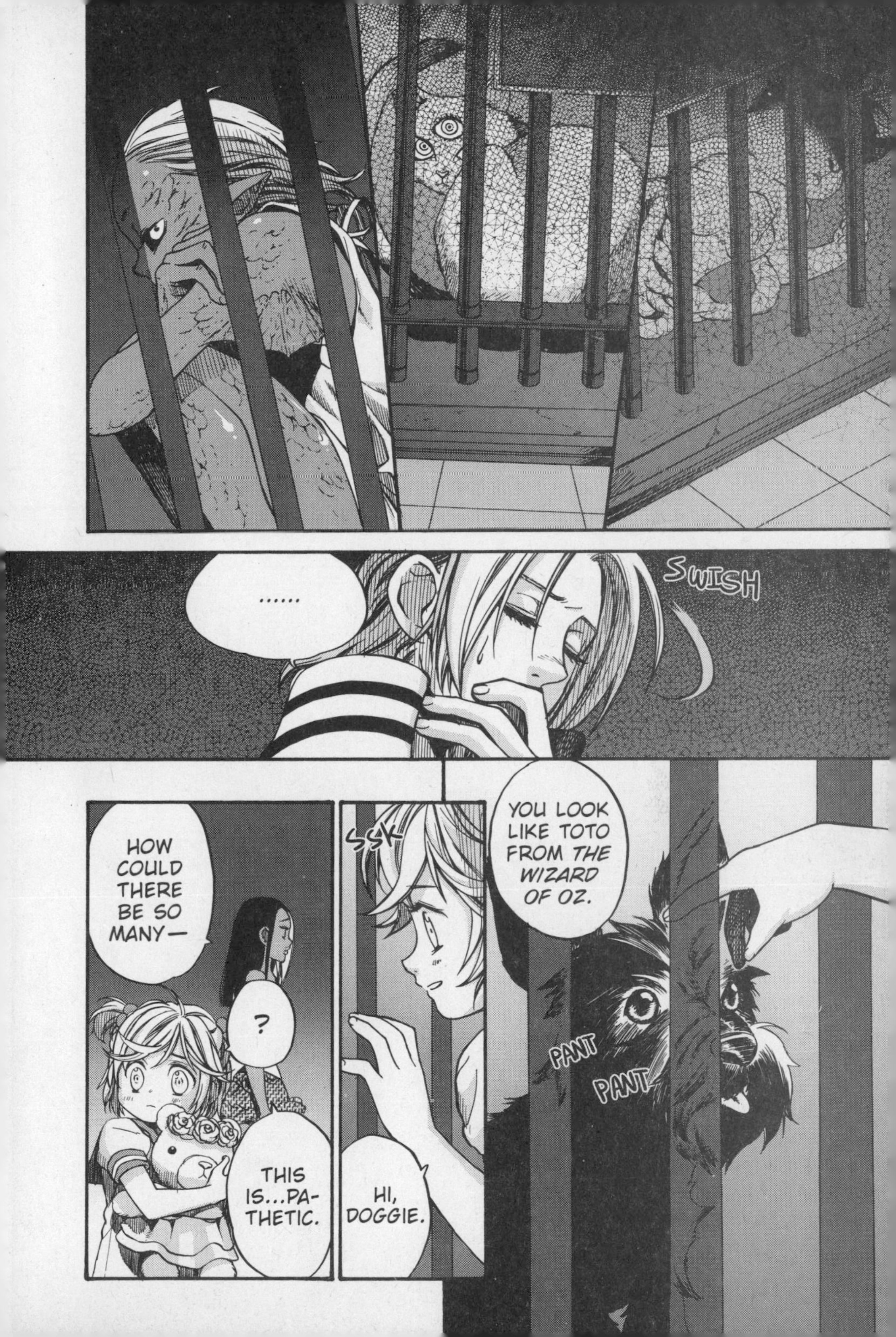
......
SWISH
HOW COULD THERE BE SO MANY—
?
THIS IS...PA-THETIC.
SSK
YOU LOOK LIKE TOTO FROM *THE WIZARD OF OZ*.
PANT
PANT
HI, DOGGIE.

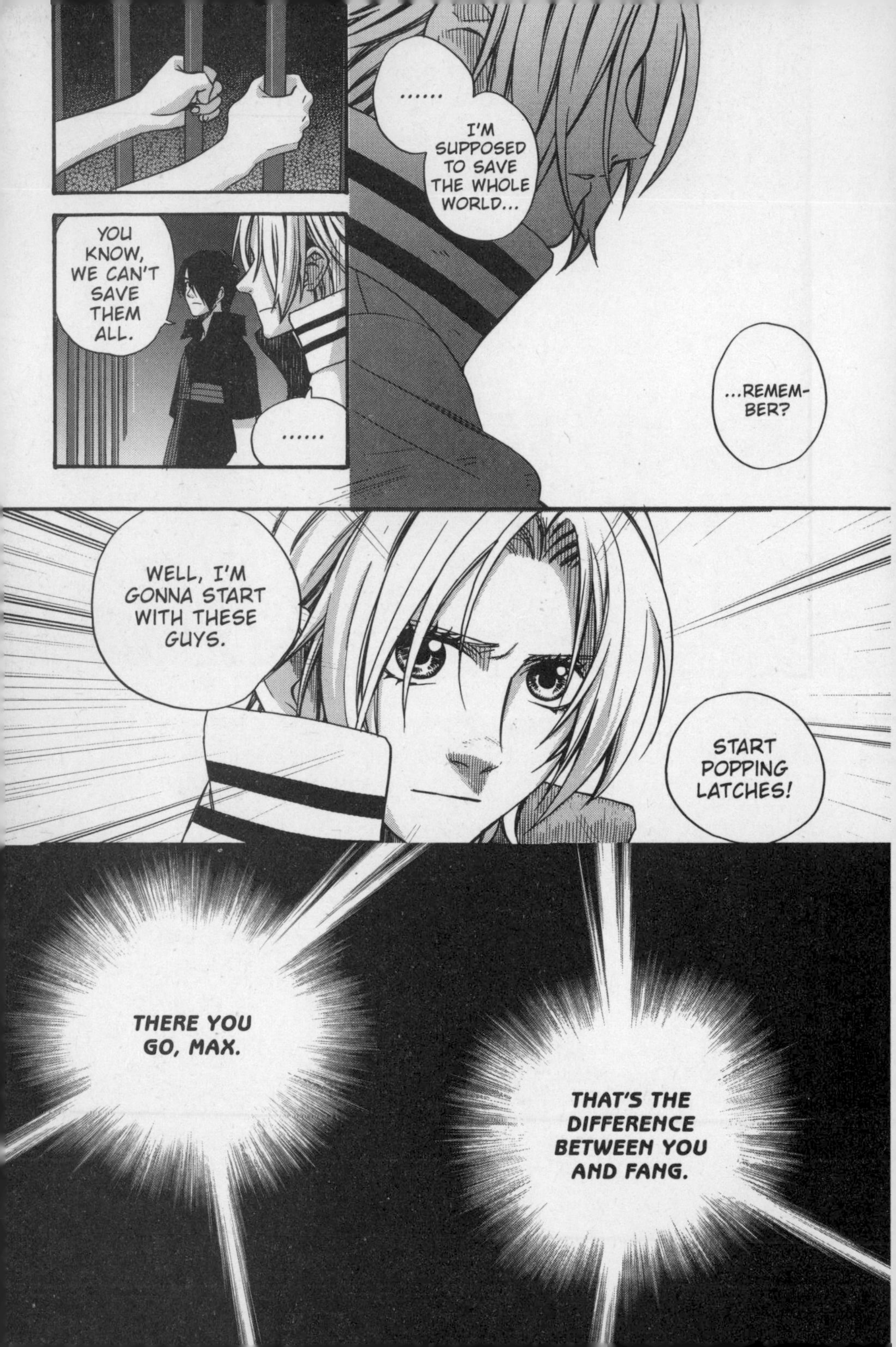
YOU KNOW, WE CAN'T SAVE THEM ALL.
......
......
I'M SUPPOSED TO SAVE THE WHOLE WORLD...
...REMEMBER?
WELL, I'M GONNA START WITH THESE GUYS.
START POPPING LATCHES!
THERE YOU GO, MAX.
THAT'S THE DIFFERENCE BETWEEN YOU AND FANG.

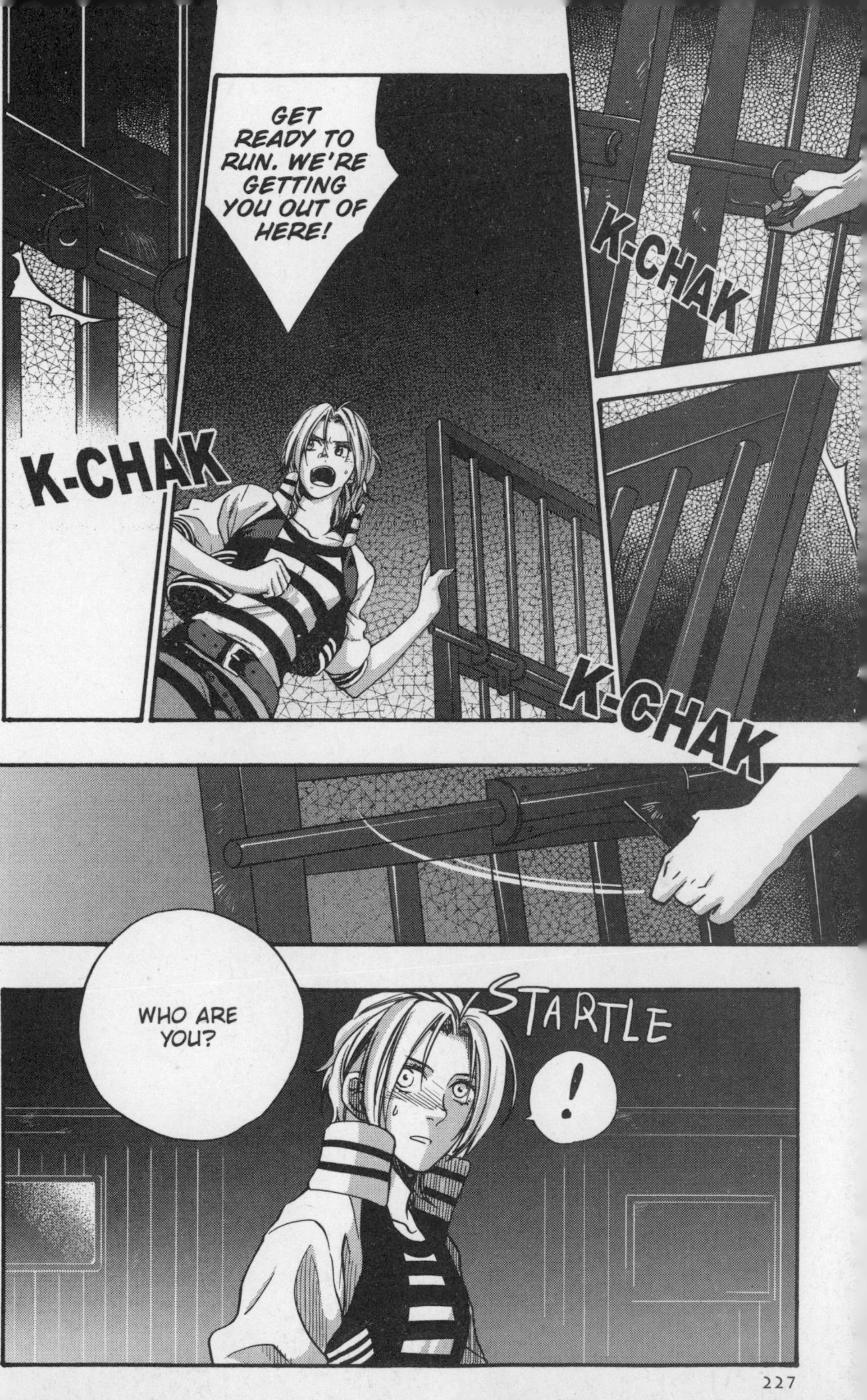
GET READY TO RUN. WE'RE GETTING YOU OUT OF HERE!
K-CHAK
K-CHAK
K-CHAK
WHO ARE YOU?
STARTLE
!

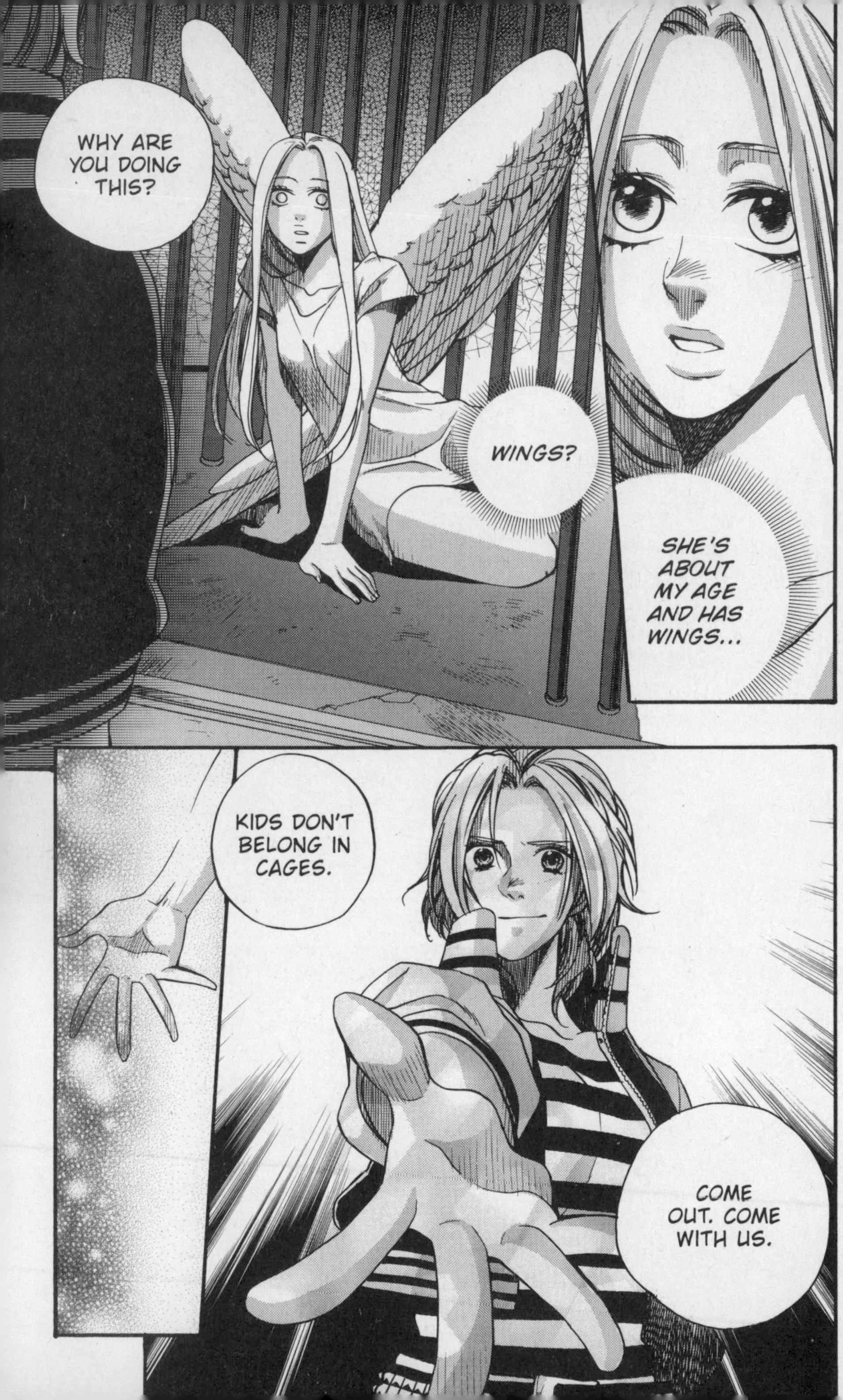
WHY ARE YOU DOING THIS?
WINGS?
SHE'S ABOUT MY AGE AND HAS WINGS...
KIDS DON'T BELONG IN CAGES.
COME OUT. COME WITH US.

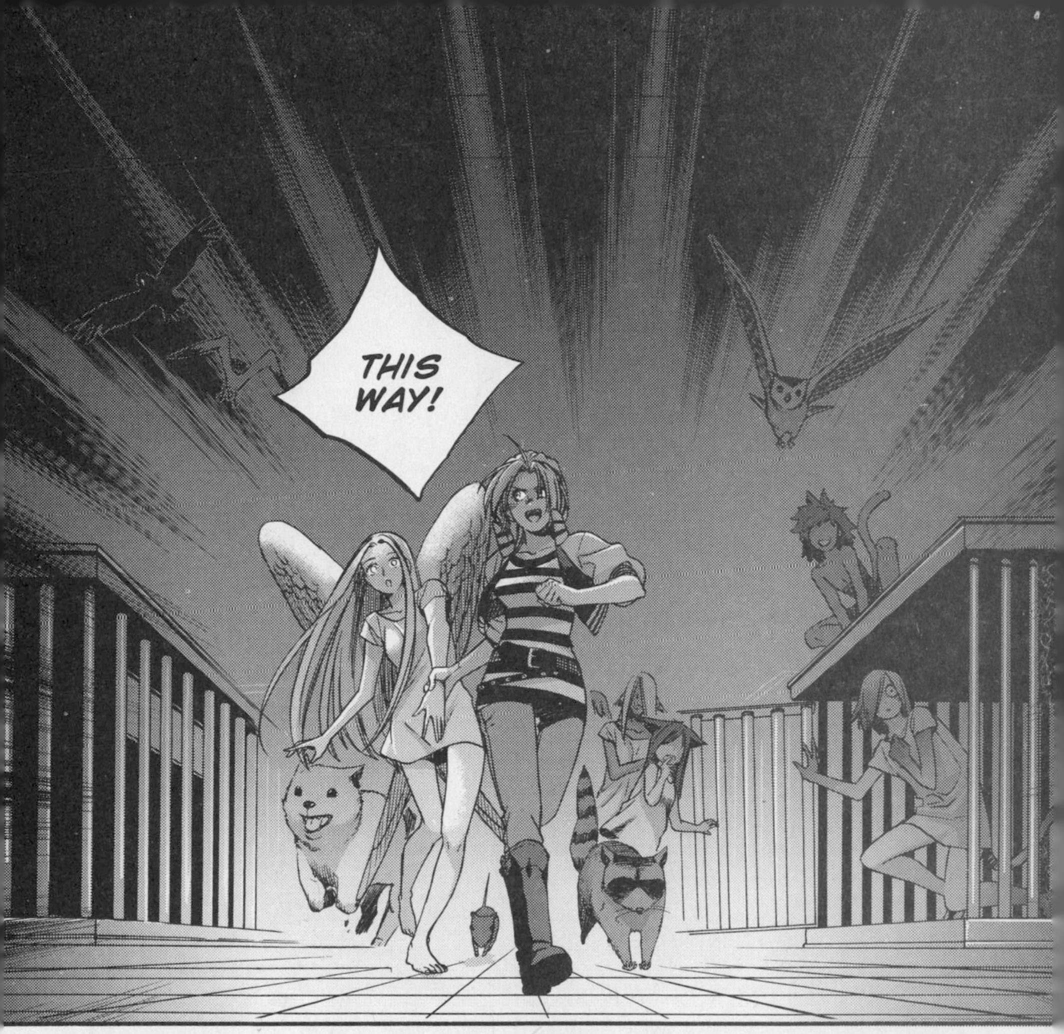
THIS WAY!

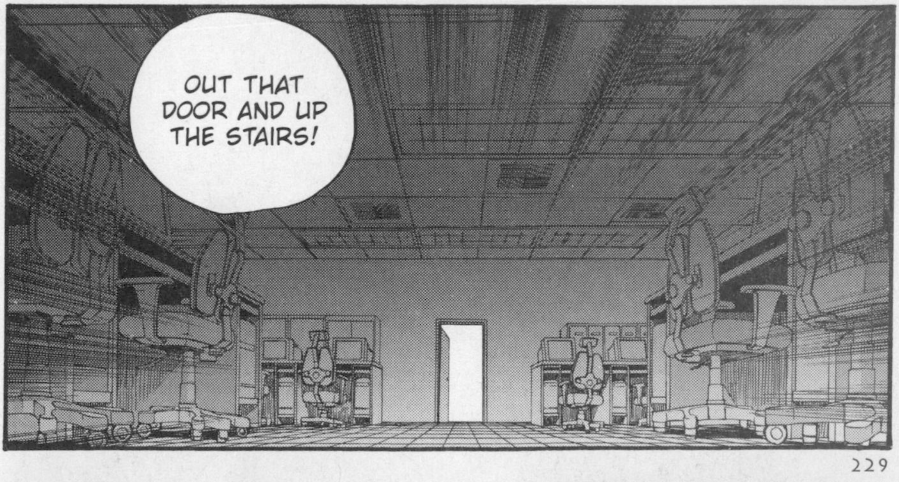
OUT THAT DOOR AND UP THE STAIRS!

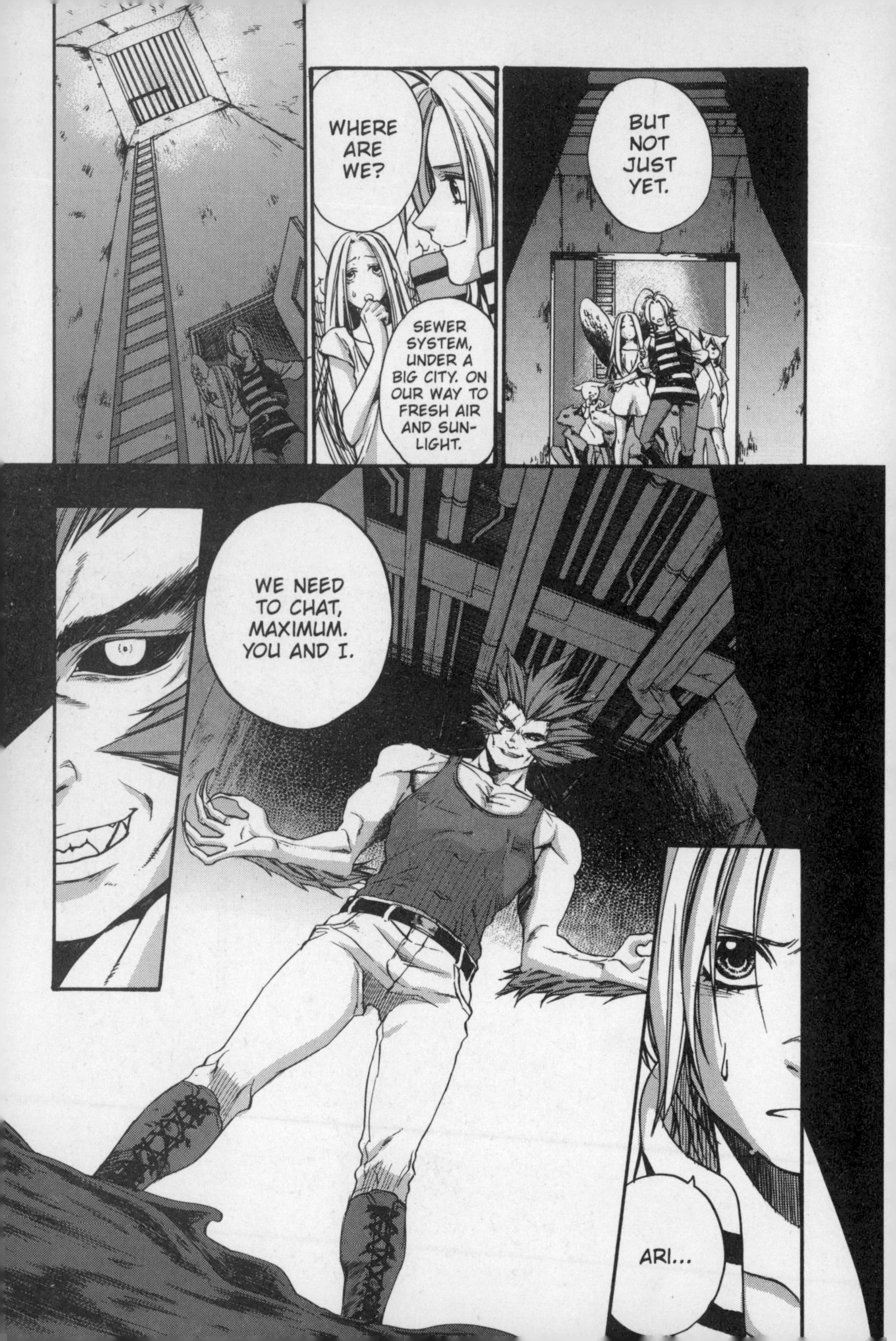
WHERE ARE WE?
SEWER SYSTEM, UNDER A BIG CITY. ON OUR WAY TO FRESH AIR AND SUN-LIGHT.
BUT NOT JUST YET.
WE NEED TO CHAT, MAXIMUM. YOU AND I.
ARI...

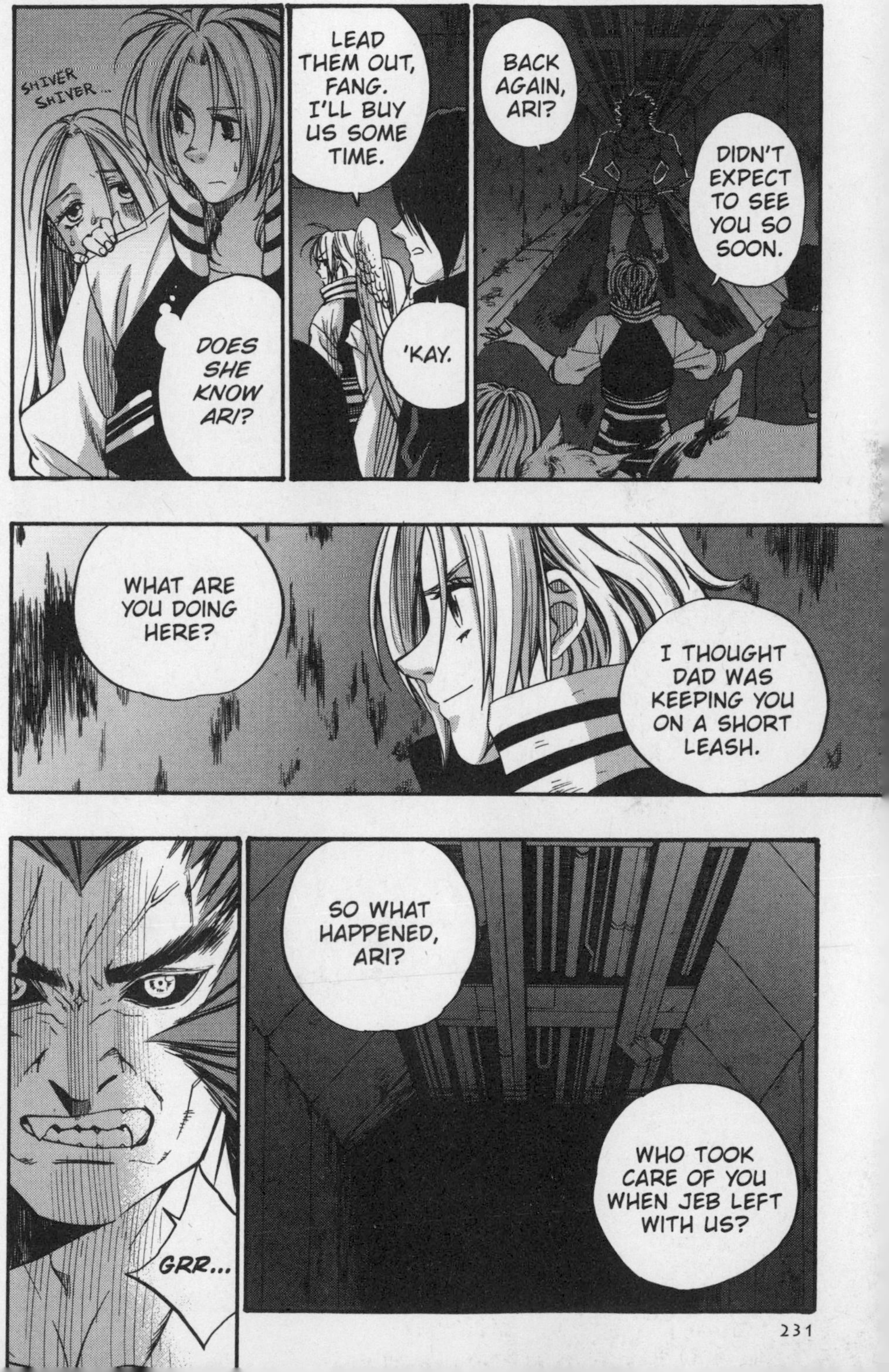
SHIVER SHIVER...
DOES SHE KNOW ARI?
LEAD THEM OUT, FANG. I'LL BUY US SOME TIME.
'KAY.
BACK AGAIN, ARI?
DIDN'T EXPECT TO SEE YOU SO SOON.
WHAT ARE YOU DOING HERE?
I THOUGHT DAD WAS KEEPING YOU ON A SHORT LEASH.
GRR...
SO WHAT HAPPENED, ARI?
WHO TOOK CARE OF YOU WHEN JEB LEFT WITH US?

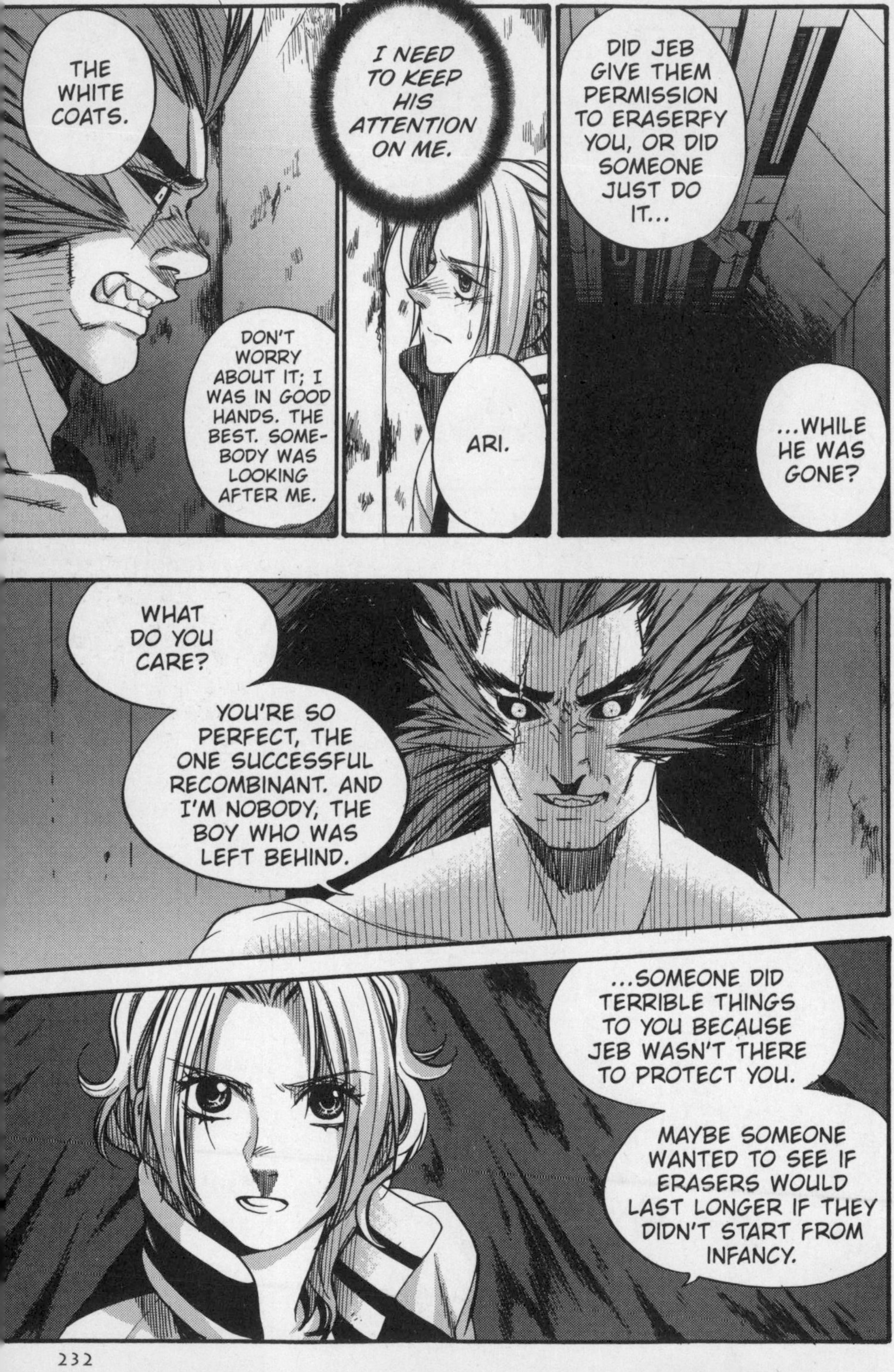
THE WHITE COATS.
DON'T WORRY ABOUT IT; I WAS IN GOOD HANDS. THE BEST. SOMEBODY WAS LOOKING AFTER ME.
I NEED TO KEEP HIS ATTENTION ON ME.
ARI.
DID JEB GIVE THEM PERMISSION TO ERASERFY YOU, OR DID SOMEONE JUST DO IT...
...WHILE HE WAS GONE?
WHAT DO YOU CARE?
YOU'RE SO PERFECT, THE ONE SUCCESSFUL RECOMBINANT. AND I'M NOBODY, THE BOY WHO WAS LEFT BEHIND.
...SOMEONE DID TERRIBLE THINGS TO YOU BECAUSE JEB WASN'T THERE TO PROTECT YOU.
MAYBE SOMEONE WANTED TO SEE IF ERASERS WOULD LAST LONGER IF THEY DIDN'T START FROM INFANCY.

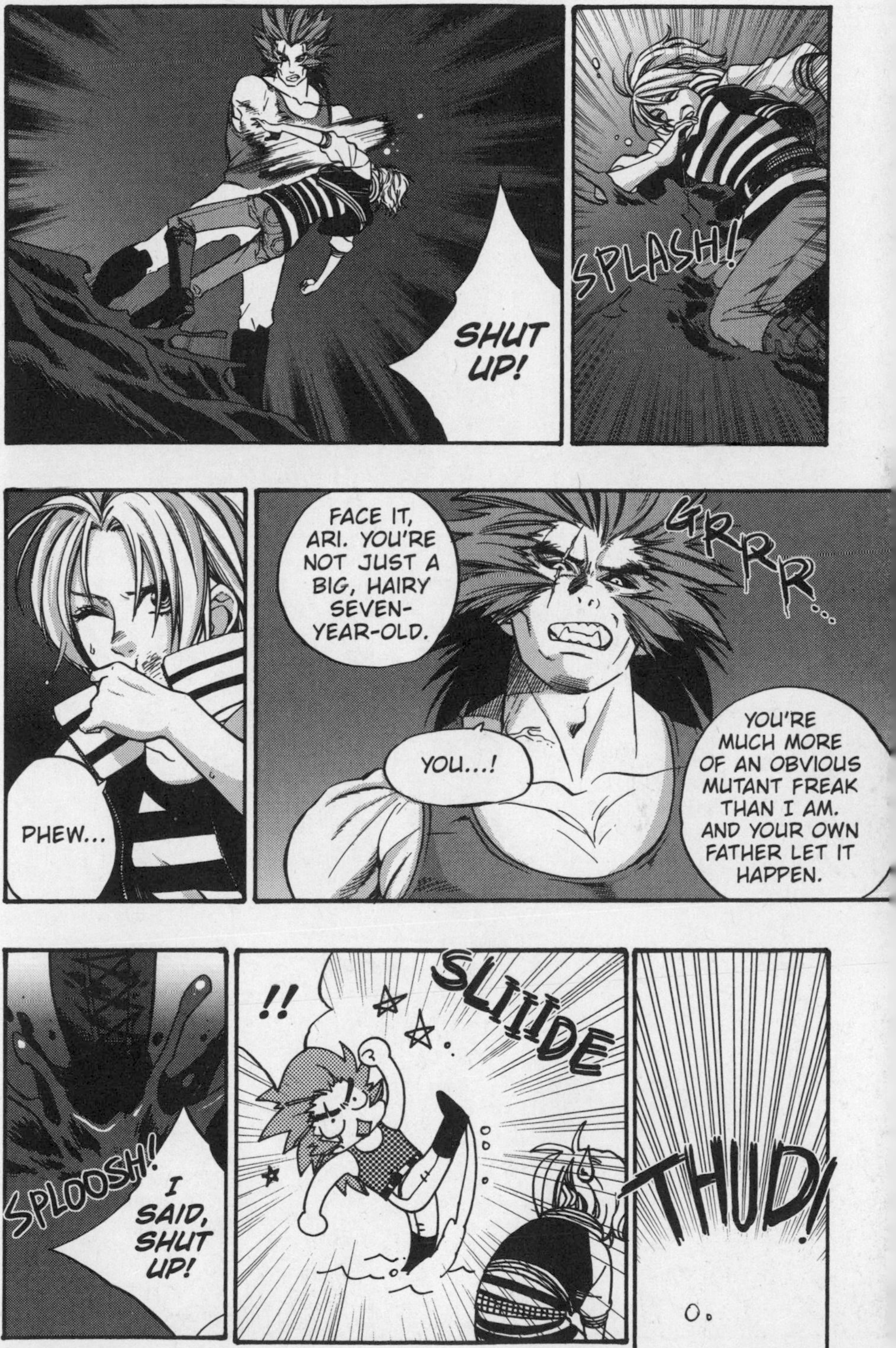
SHUT UP!
SPLASH!
PHEW...
FACE IT, ARI. YOU'RE NOT JUST A BIG, HAIRY SEVEN-YEAR-OLD.
GRRRR...
YOU...!
YOU'RE MUCH MORE OF AN OBVIOUS MUTANT FREAK THAN I AM. AND YOUR OWN FATHER LET IT HAPPEN.
SPLOOSH!
I SAID, SHUT UP!
!!
SLIIIDE
THUD!

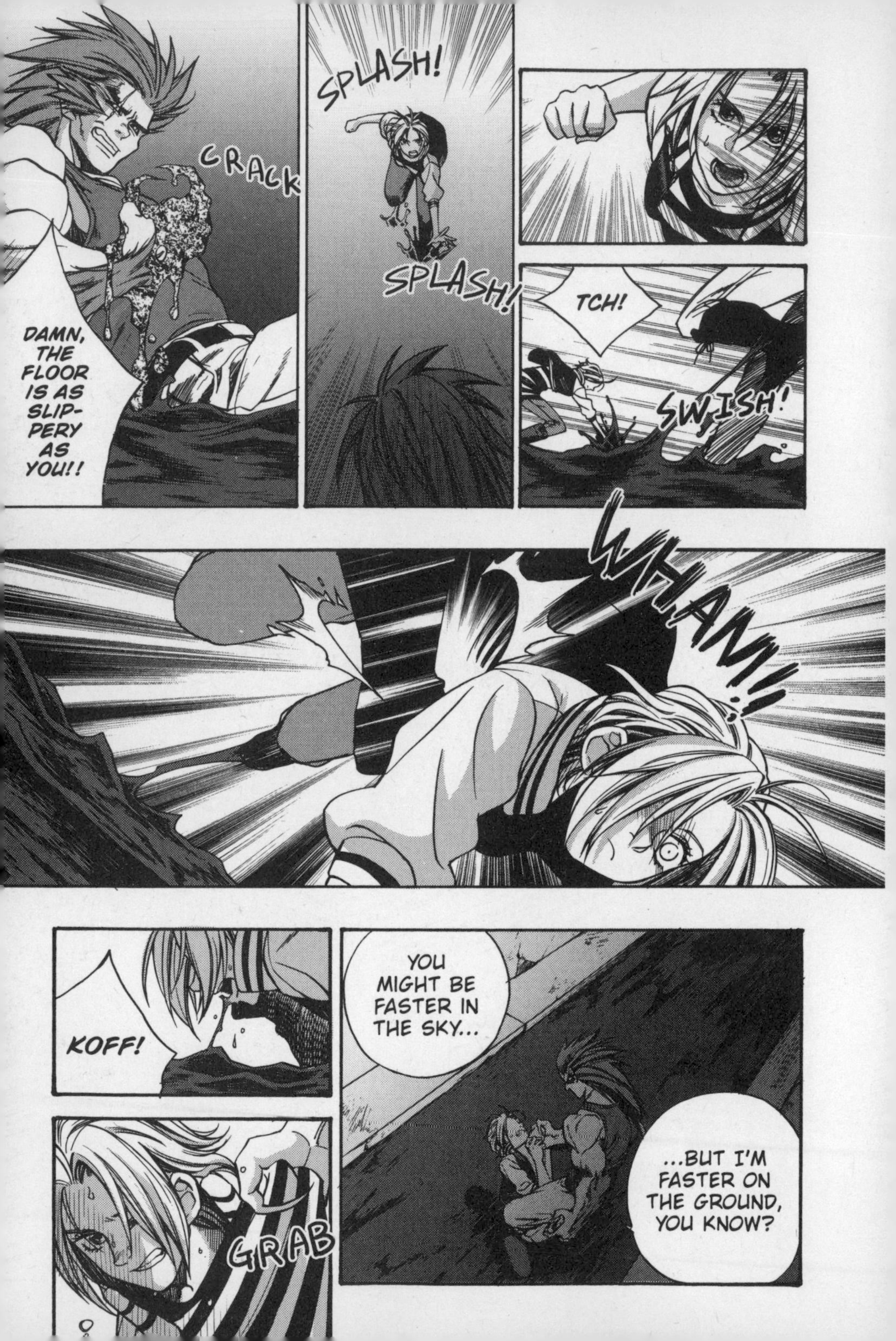
CRACK
DAMN, THE FLOOR IS AS SLIPPERY AS YOU!!
SPLASH!
SPLASH!
TCH!
SWISH!
WHAM!!
KOFF!
GRAB
YOU MIGHT BE FASTER IN THE SKY...
...BUT I'M FASTER ON THE GROUND, YOU KNOW?

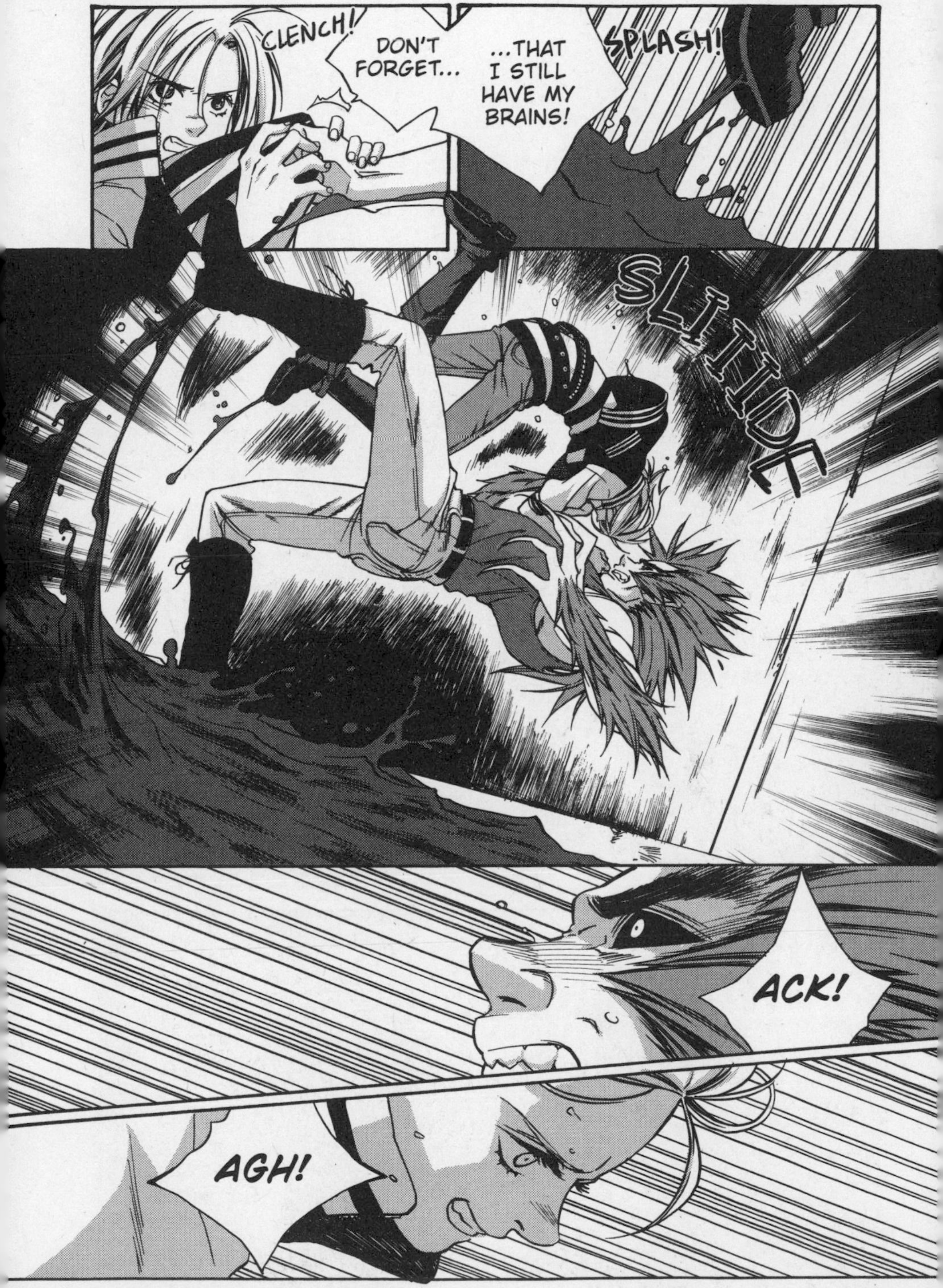
CLENCH!
DON'T FORGET...
...THAT I STILL HAVE MY BRAINS!
SPLASH!
SLIIIDE
ACK!
AGH!

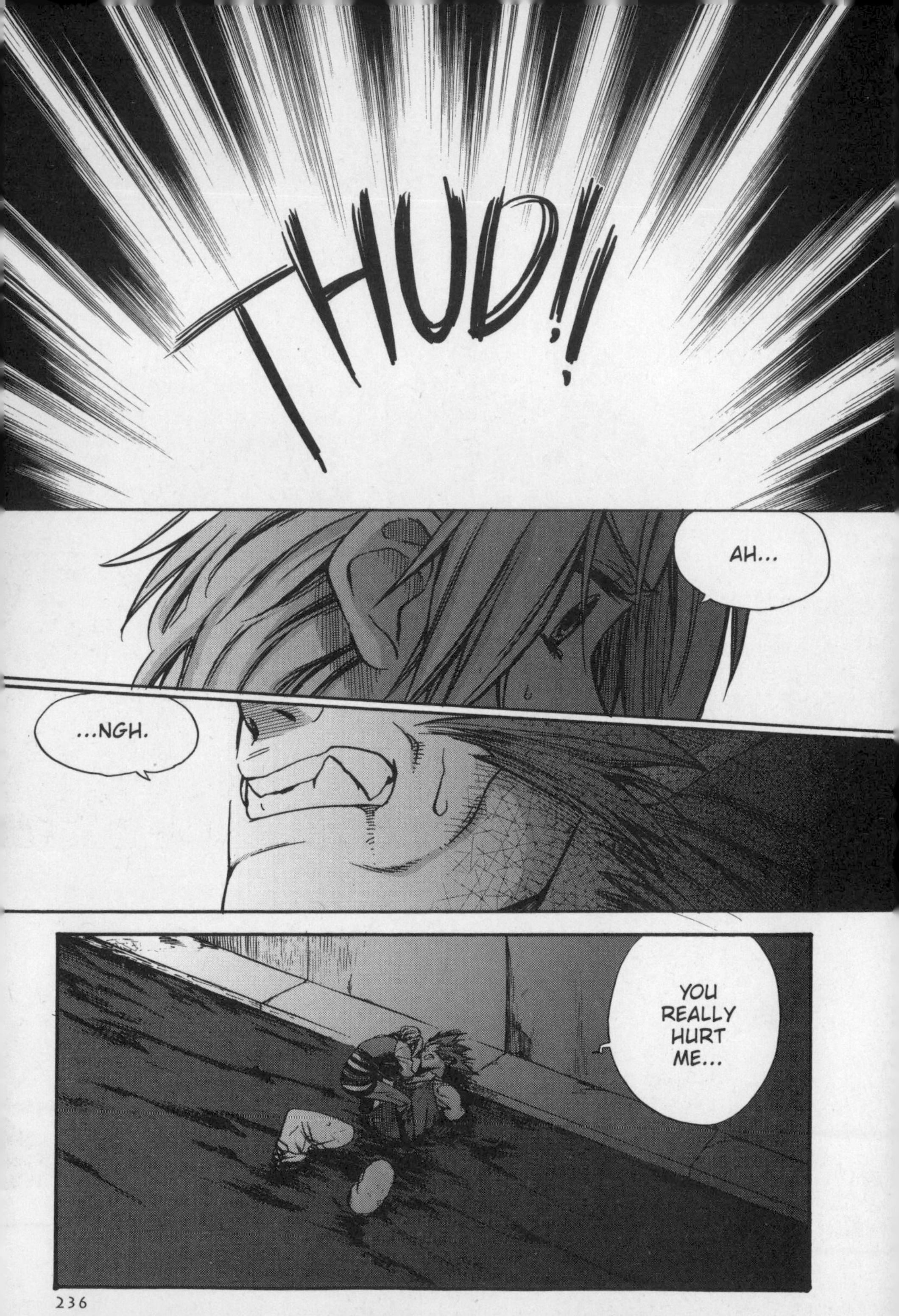
THUD!!
AH...
...NGH.
YOU REALLY HURT ME...

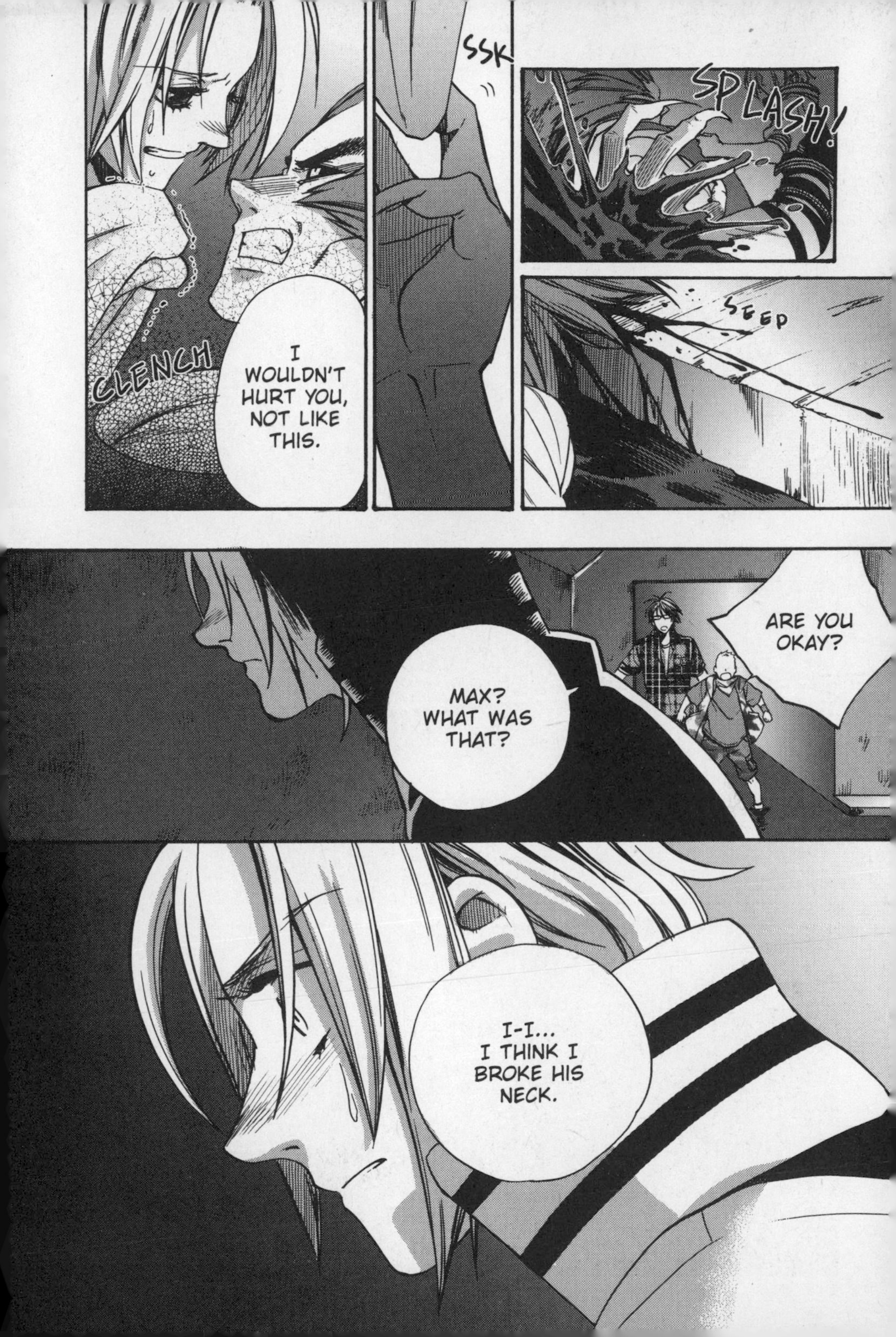
CLENCH
I WOULDN'T HURT YOU, NOT LIKE THIS.
SSK
SPLASH!
SEEP
MAX? WHAT WAS THAT?
ARE YOU OKAY?
I-I... I THINK I BROKE HIS NECK.

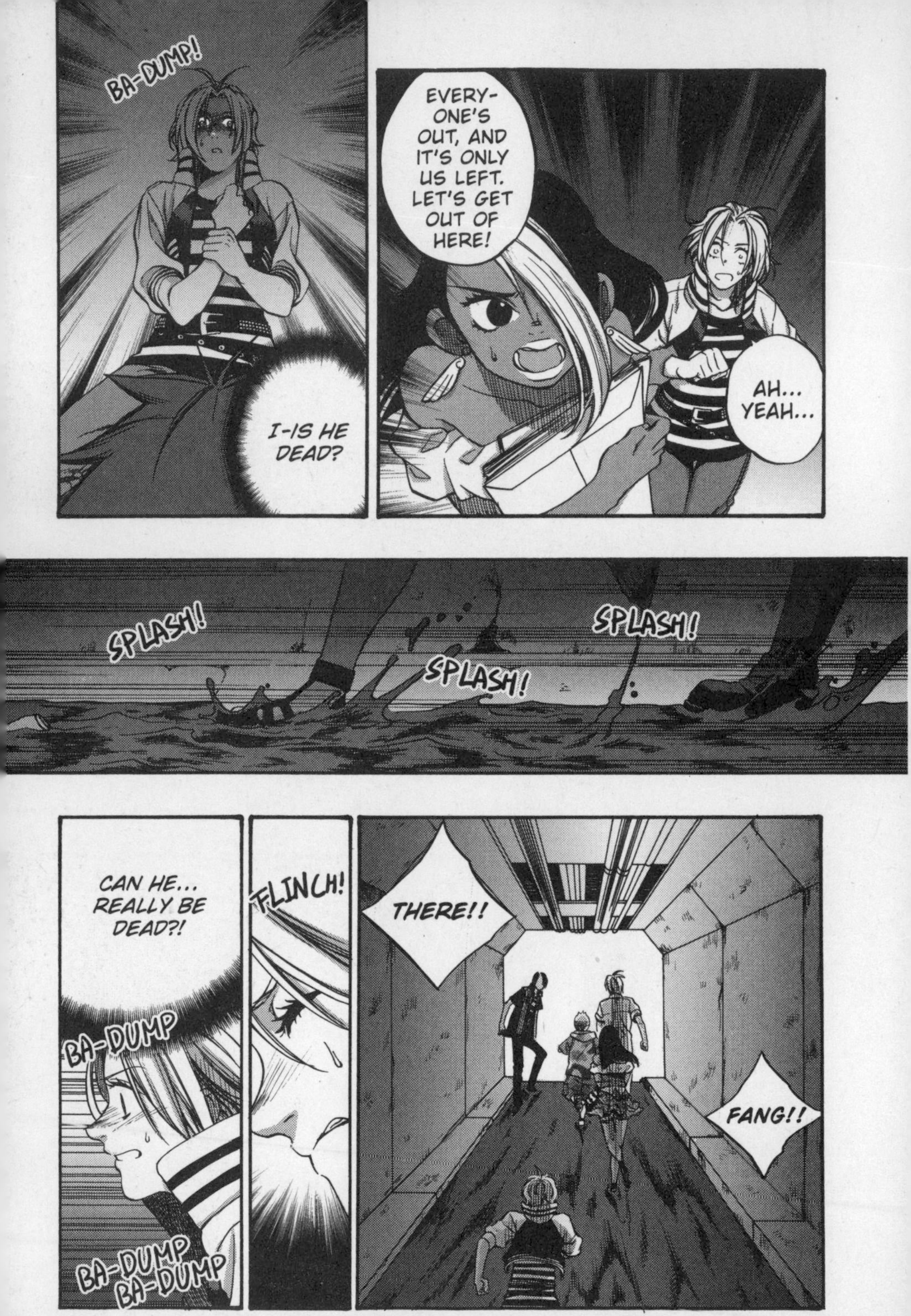
BA-DUMP!
I-IS HE DEAD?
EVERY-ONE'S OUT, AND IT'S ONLY US LEFT. LET'S GET OUT OF HERE!
AH... YEAH...
SPLASH!
SPLASH!
SPLASH!
CAN HE... REALLY BE DEAD?!
BA-DUMP
BA-DUMP BA-DUMP
FLINCH!
THERE!!
FANG!!

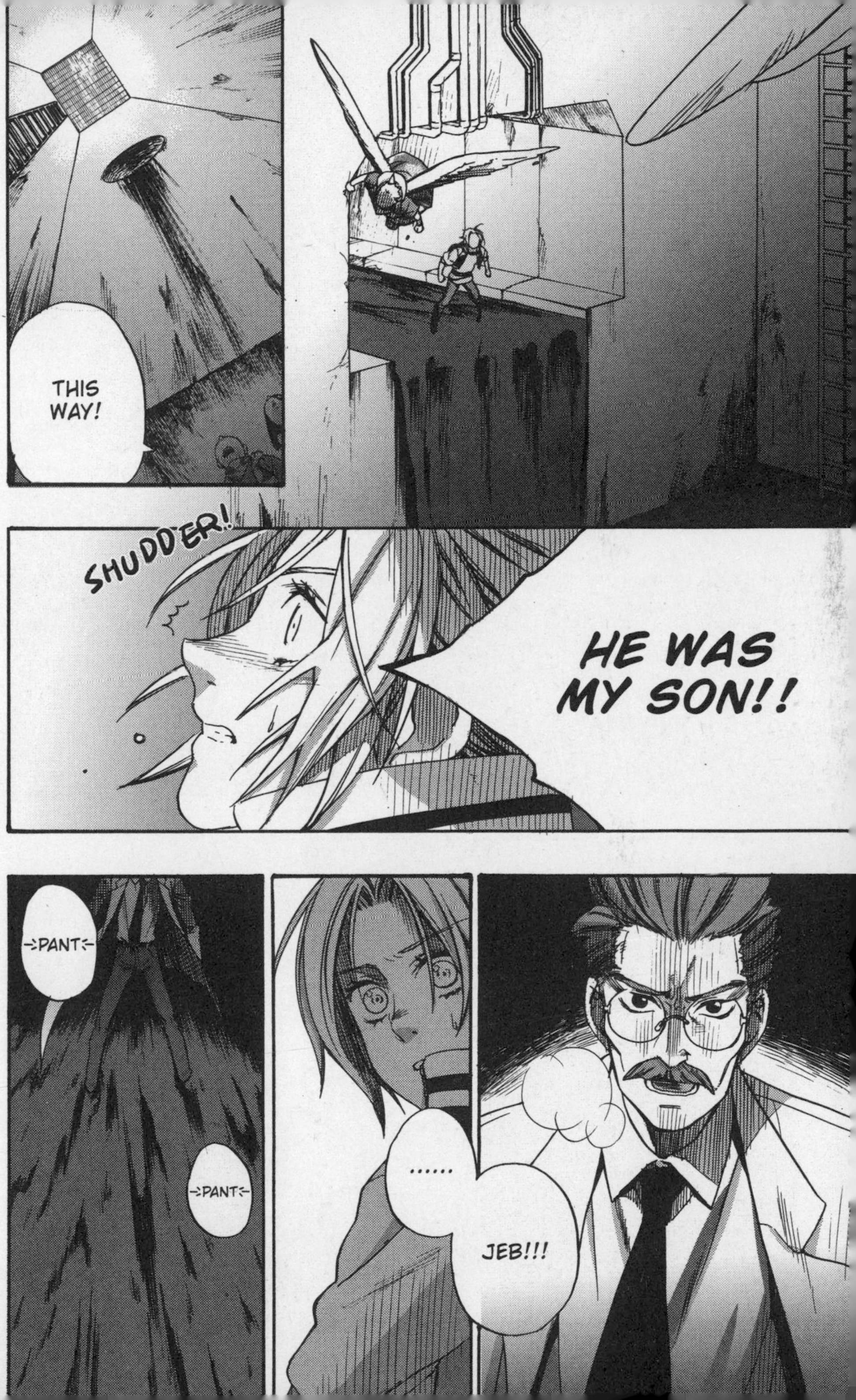
THIS WAY!
SHUDD'ER!
HE WAS MY SON!!
-PANT-
-PANT-
......
JEB!!!

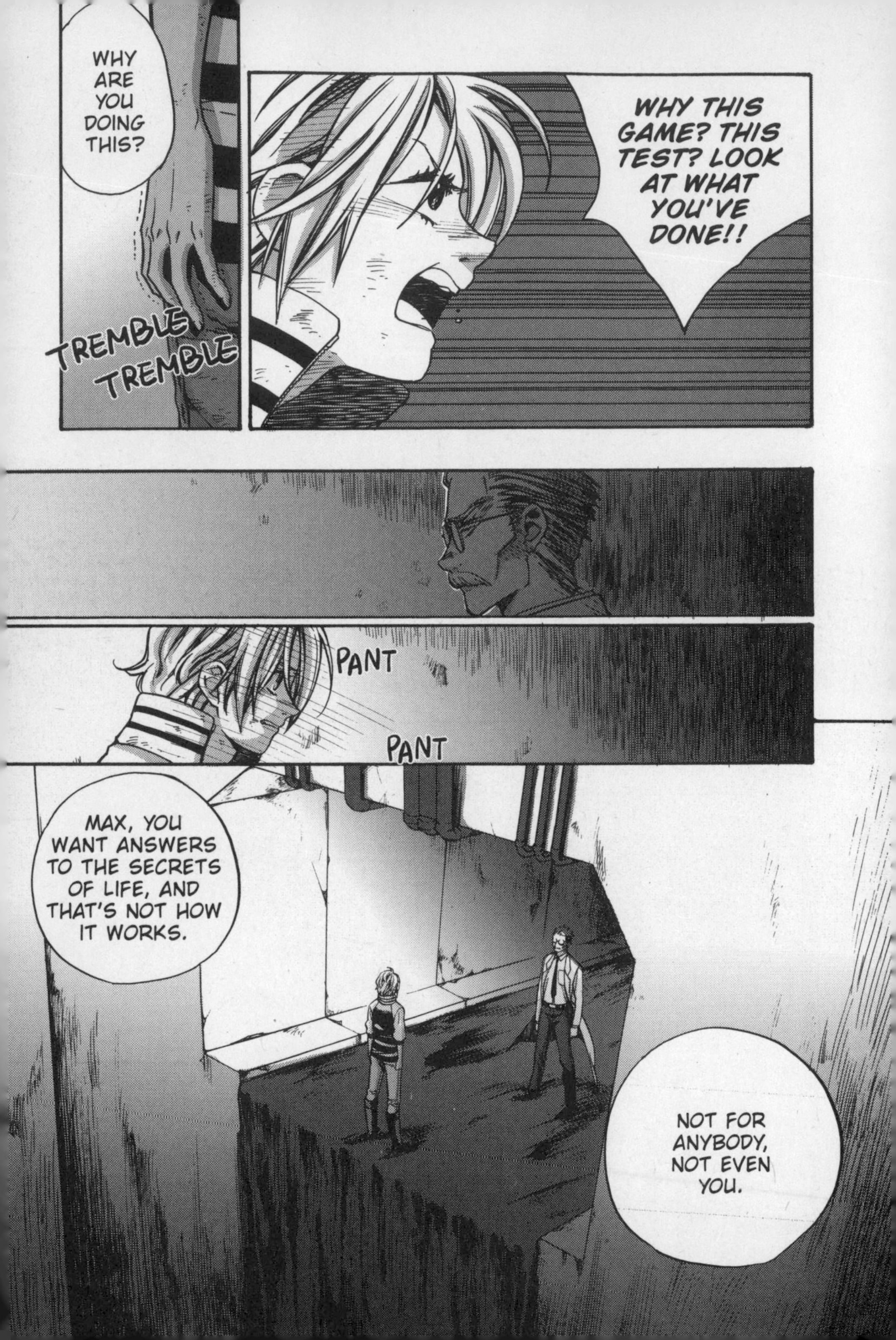
WHY ARE YOU DOING THIS?
TREMBLE TREMBLE
WHY THIS GAME? THIS TEST? LOOK AT WHAT YOU'VE DONE!!
PANT
PANT
MAX, YOU WANT ANSWERS TO THE SECRETS OF LIFE, AND THAT'S NOT HOW IT WORKS.
NOT FOR ANYBODY, NOT EVEN YOU.

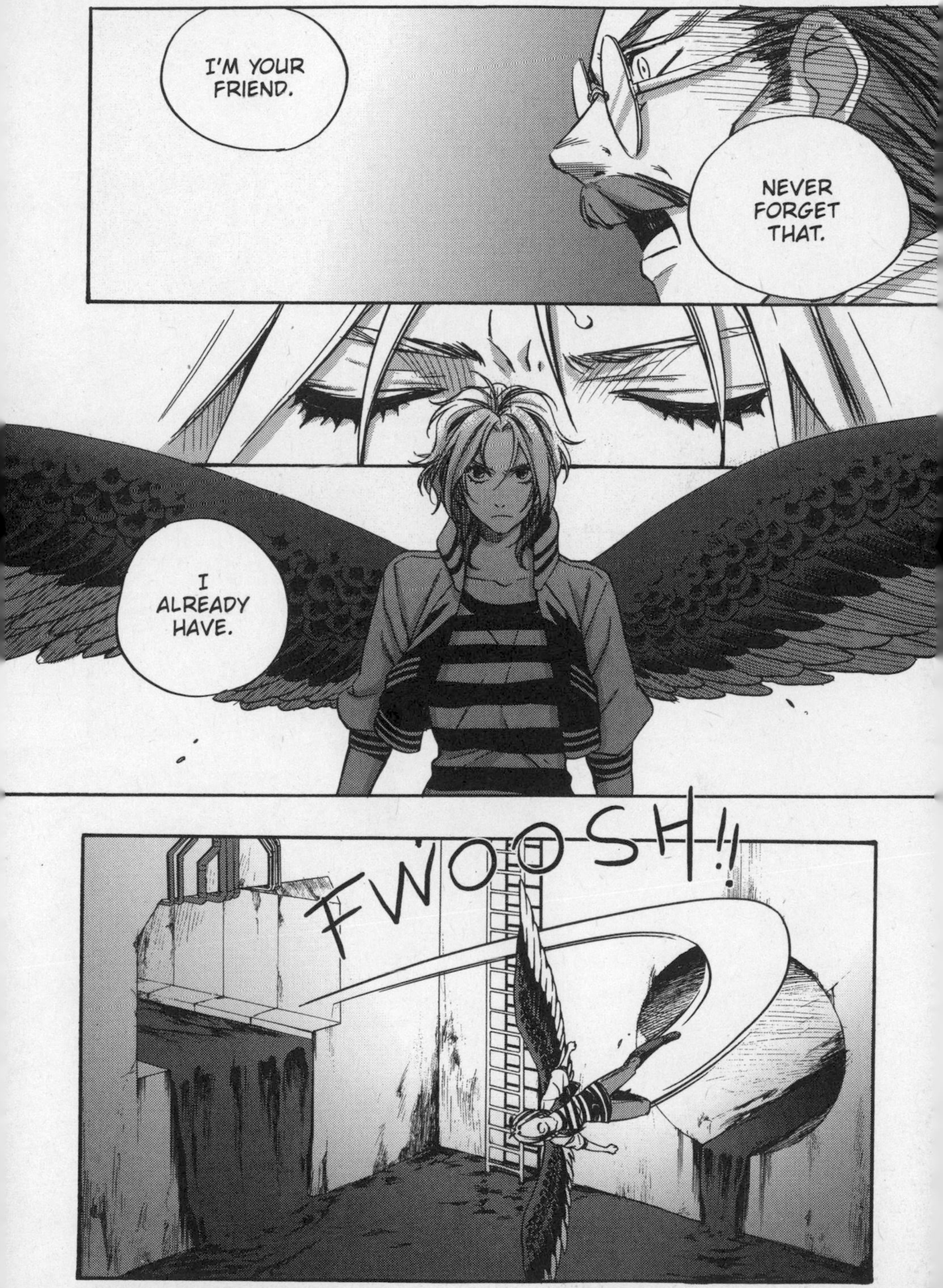
I'M YOUR FRIEND.
NEVER FORGET THAT.
I ALREADY HAVE.
FWOOSH!!

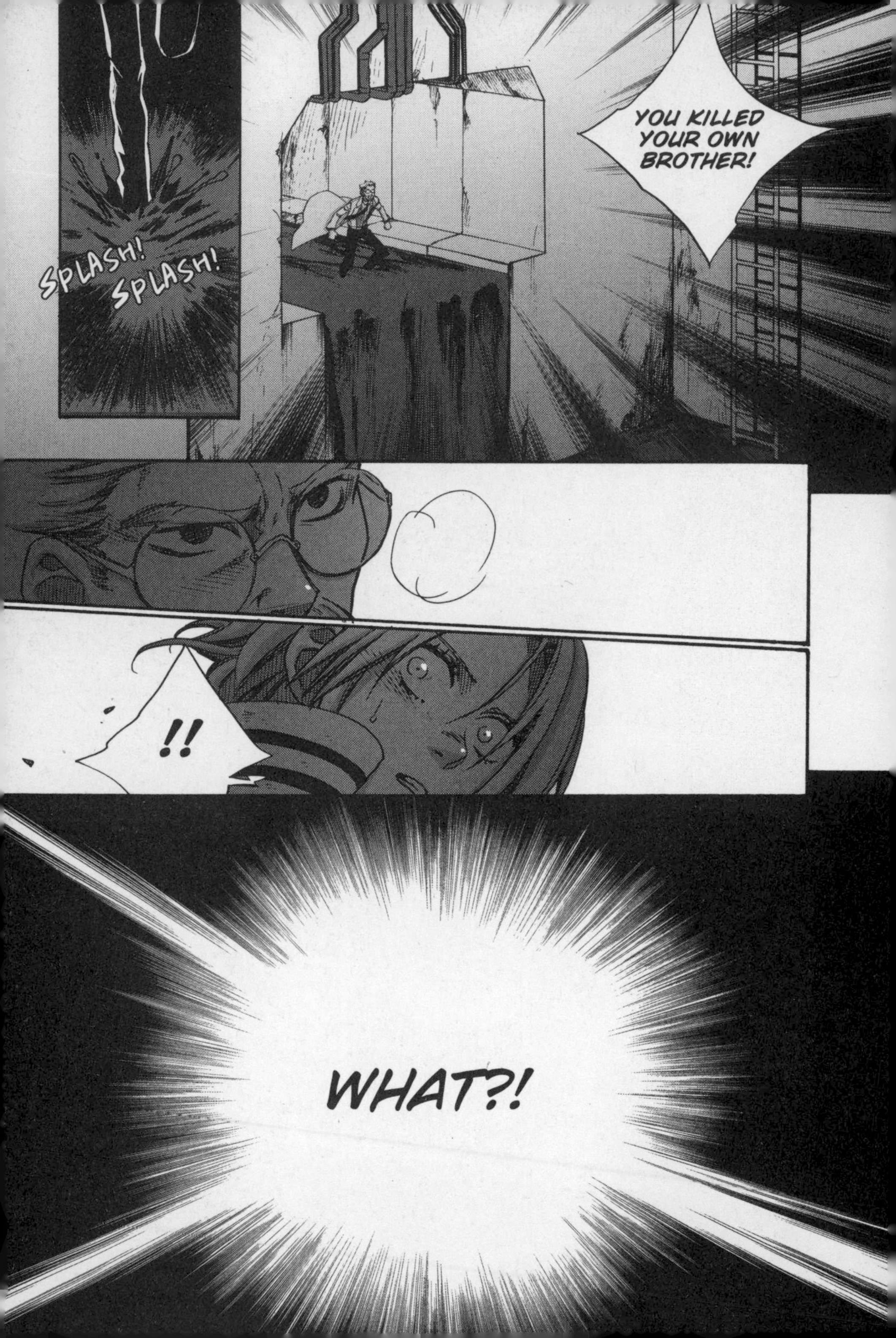
SPLASH! SPLASH!
YOU KILLED YOUR OWN BROTHER!
!!
WHAT?!

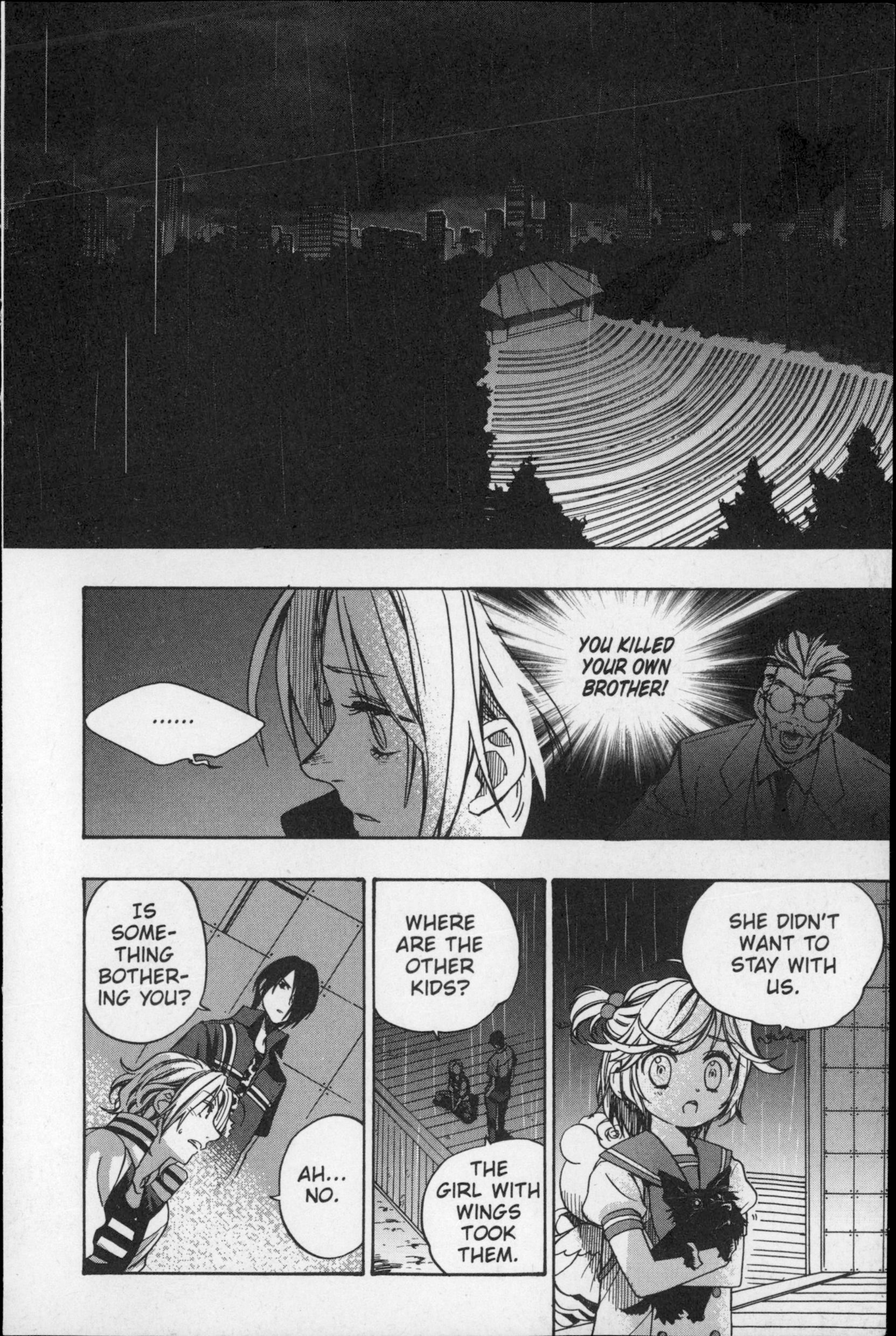
......
YOU KILLED YOUR OWN BROTHER!
IS SOME-THING BOTHER-ING YOU?
AH... NO.
WHERE ARE THE OTHER KIDS?
THE GIRL WITH WINGS TOOK THEM.
SHE DIDN'T WANT TO STAY WITH US.

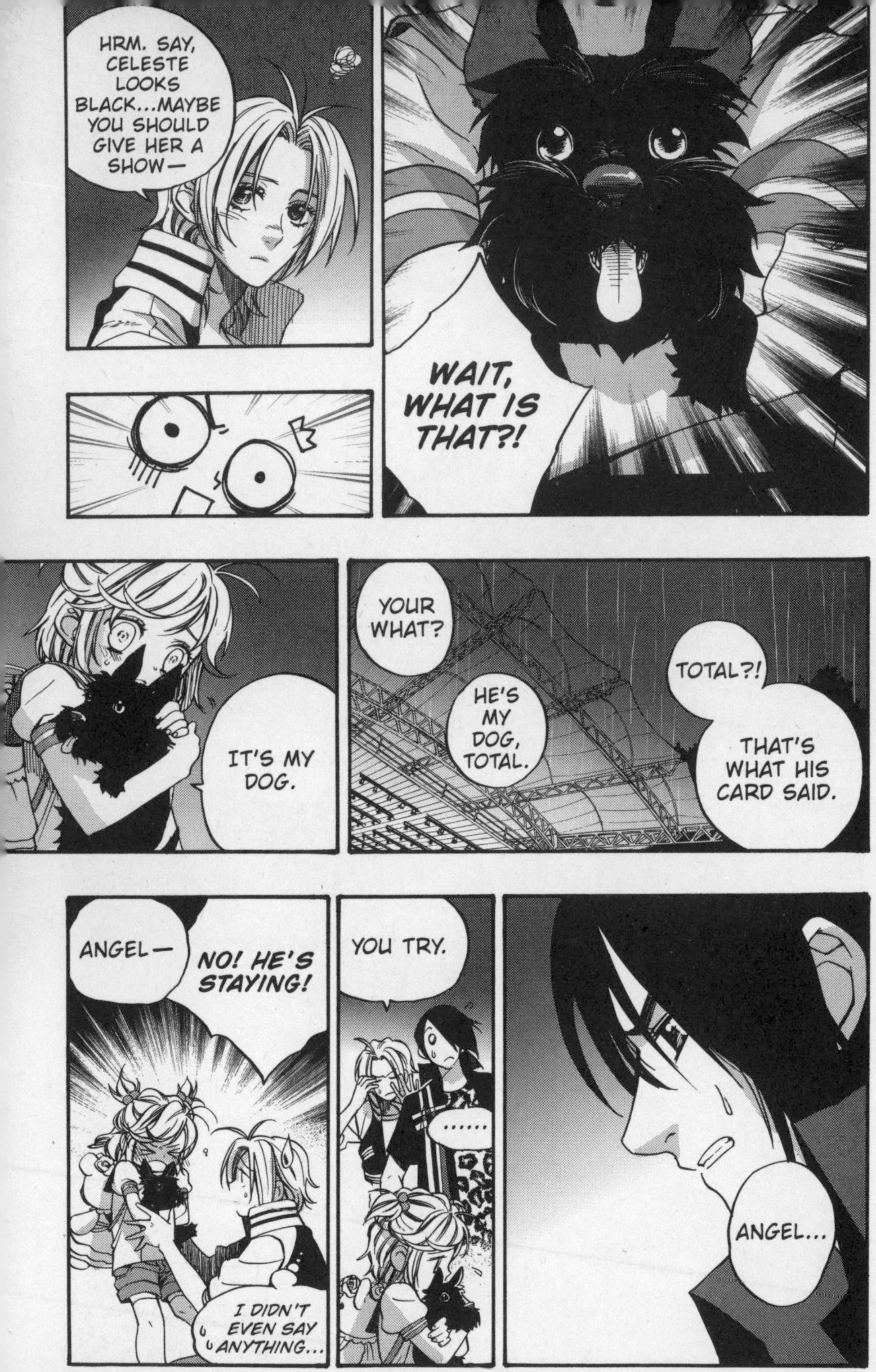

HRM. SAY, CELESTE LOOKS BLACK...MAYBE YOU SHOULD GIVE HER A SHOW—
WAIT, WHAT IS THAT?!
IT'S MY DOG.
YOUR WHAT?
HE'S MY DOG, TOTAL.
TOTAL?!
THAT'S WHAT HIS CARD SAID.
ANGEL—
NO! HE'S STAYING!
I DIDN'T EVEN SAY ANYTHING...
YOU TRY.
......
ANGEL...

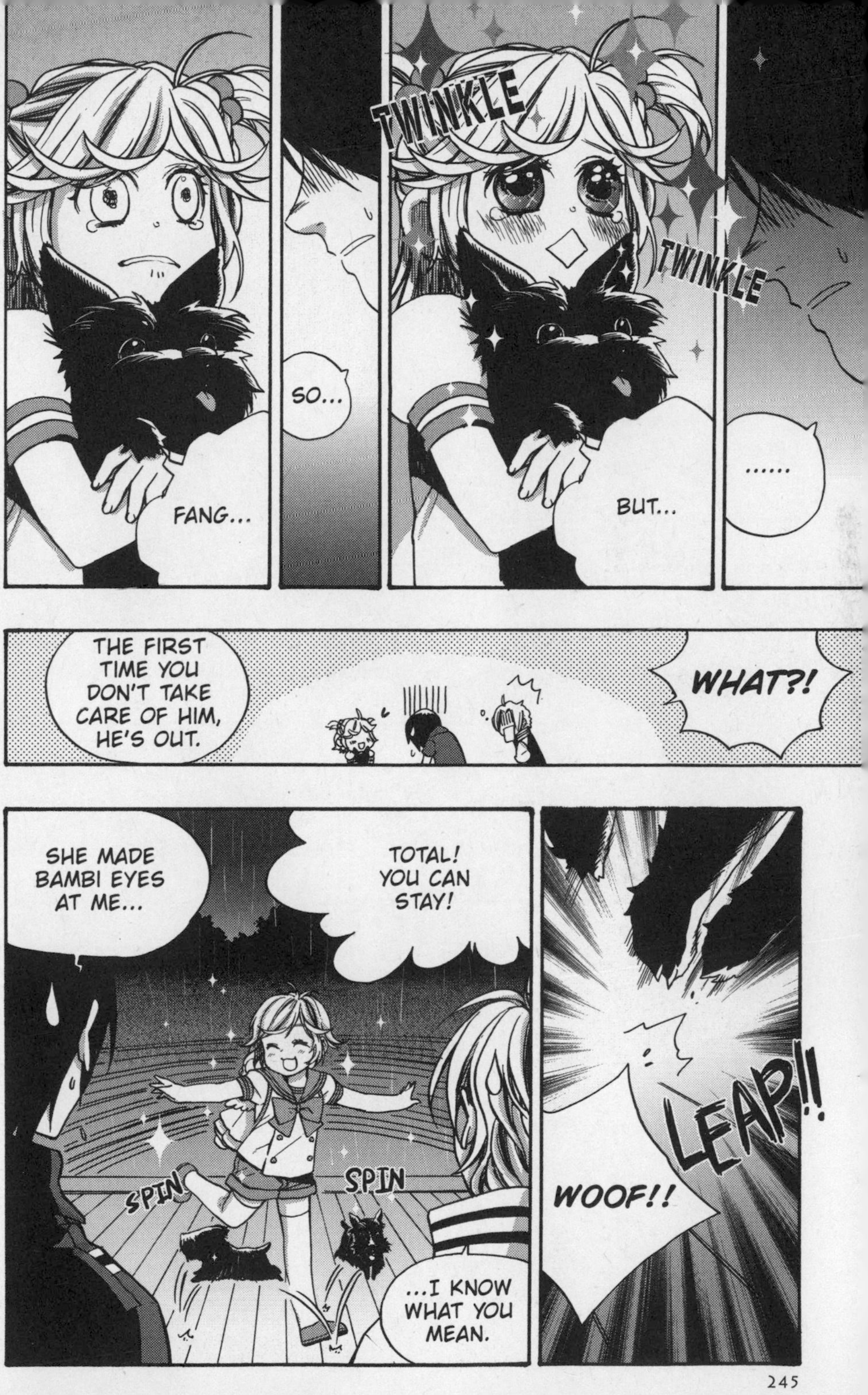
FANG...
SO...
TWINKLE
TWINKLE
BUT...
......
THE FIRST TIME YOU DON'T TAKE CARE OF HIM, HE'S OUT.
WHAT?!
SHE MADE BAMBI EYES AT ME...
TOTAL! YOU CAN STAY!
SPIN
SPIN
...I KNOW WHAT YOU MEAN.
LEAP!!
WOOF!!

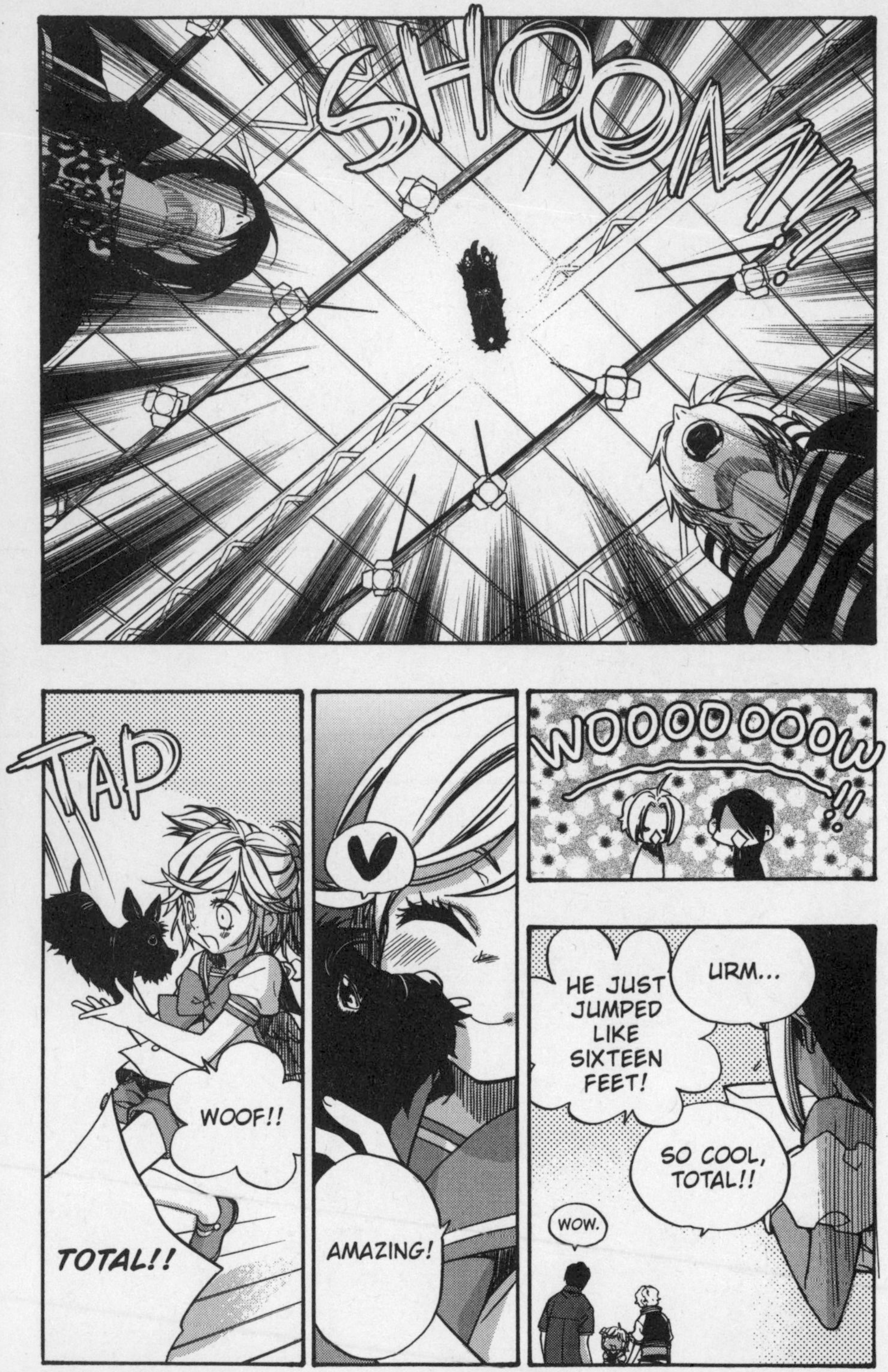
SHOOOM!!
TAP
WOOF!!
TOTAL!!
AMAZING!
WOOOOOOOW!!
HE JUST JUMPED LIKE SIXTEEN FEET!
URM...
SO COOL, TOTAL!!
WOW.

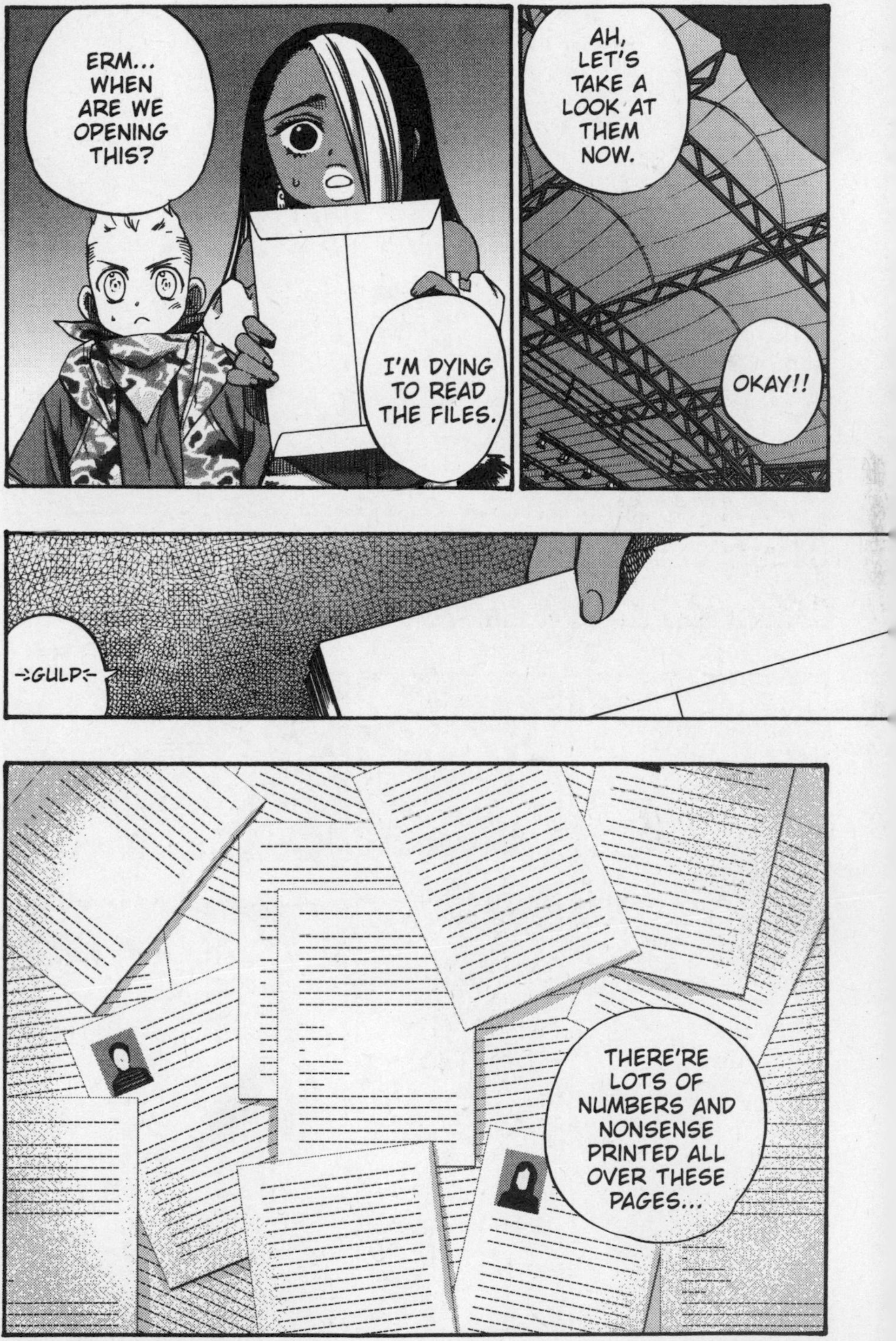
ERM... WHEN ARE WE OPENING THIS?
I'M DYING TO READ THE FILES.
AH, LET'S TAKE A LOOK AT THEM NOW.
OKAY!!
-GULP-
THERE'RE LOTS OF NUMBERS AND NONSENSE PRINTED ALL OVER THESE PAGES...

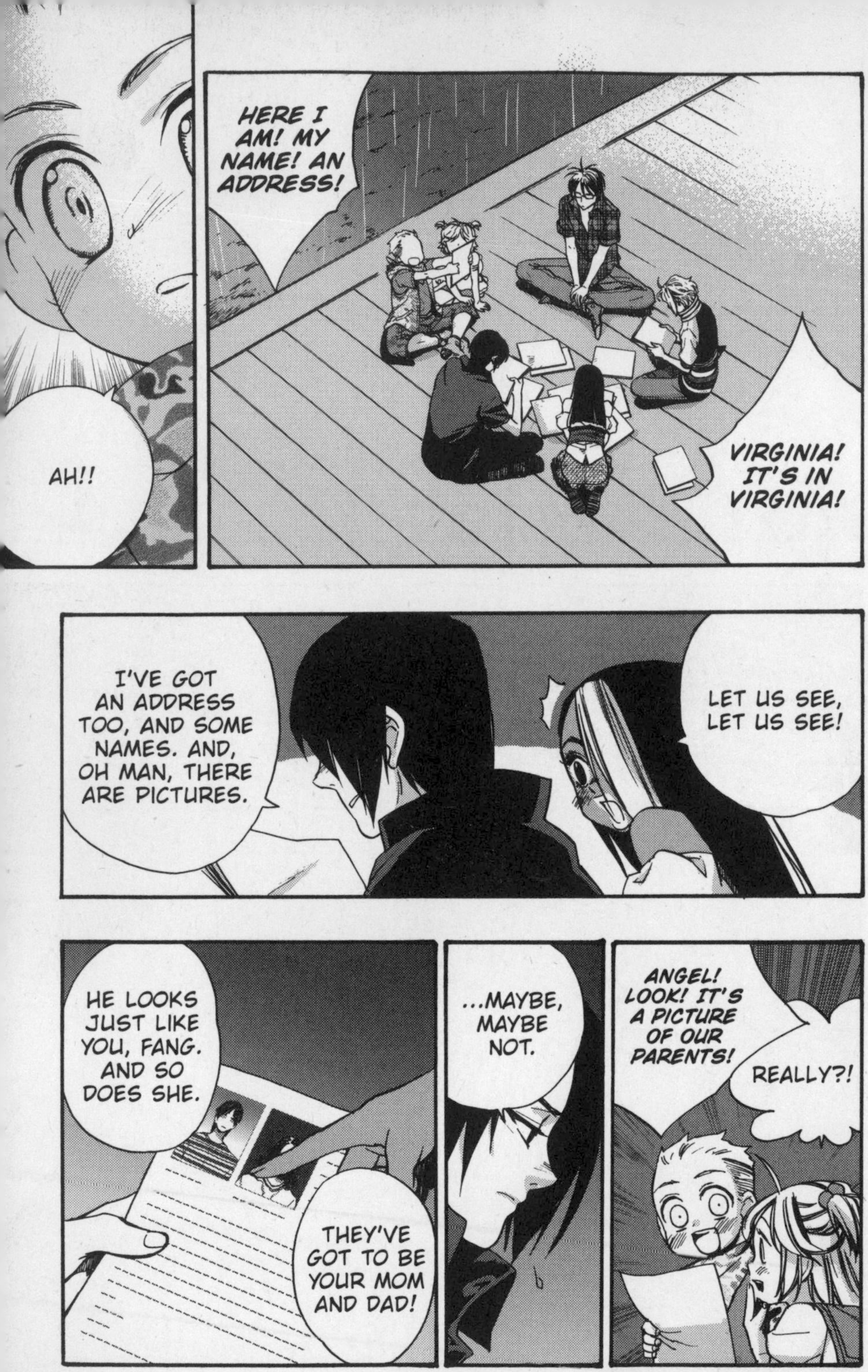
AH!!
HERE I AM! MY NAME! AN ADDRESS!
VIRGINIA! IT'S IN VIRGINIA!
I'VE GOT AN ADDRESS TOO, AND SOME NAMES. AND, OH MAN, THERE ARE PICTURES.
LET US SEE, LET US SEE!
HE LOOKS JUST LIKE YOU, FANG. AND SO DOES SHE.
THEY'VE GOT TO BE YOUR MOM AND DAD!
...MAYBE, MAYBE NOT.
ANGEL! LOOK! IT'S A PICTURE OF OUR PARENTS!
REALLY?!

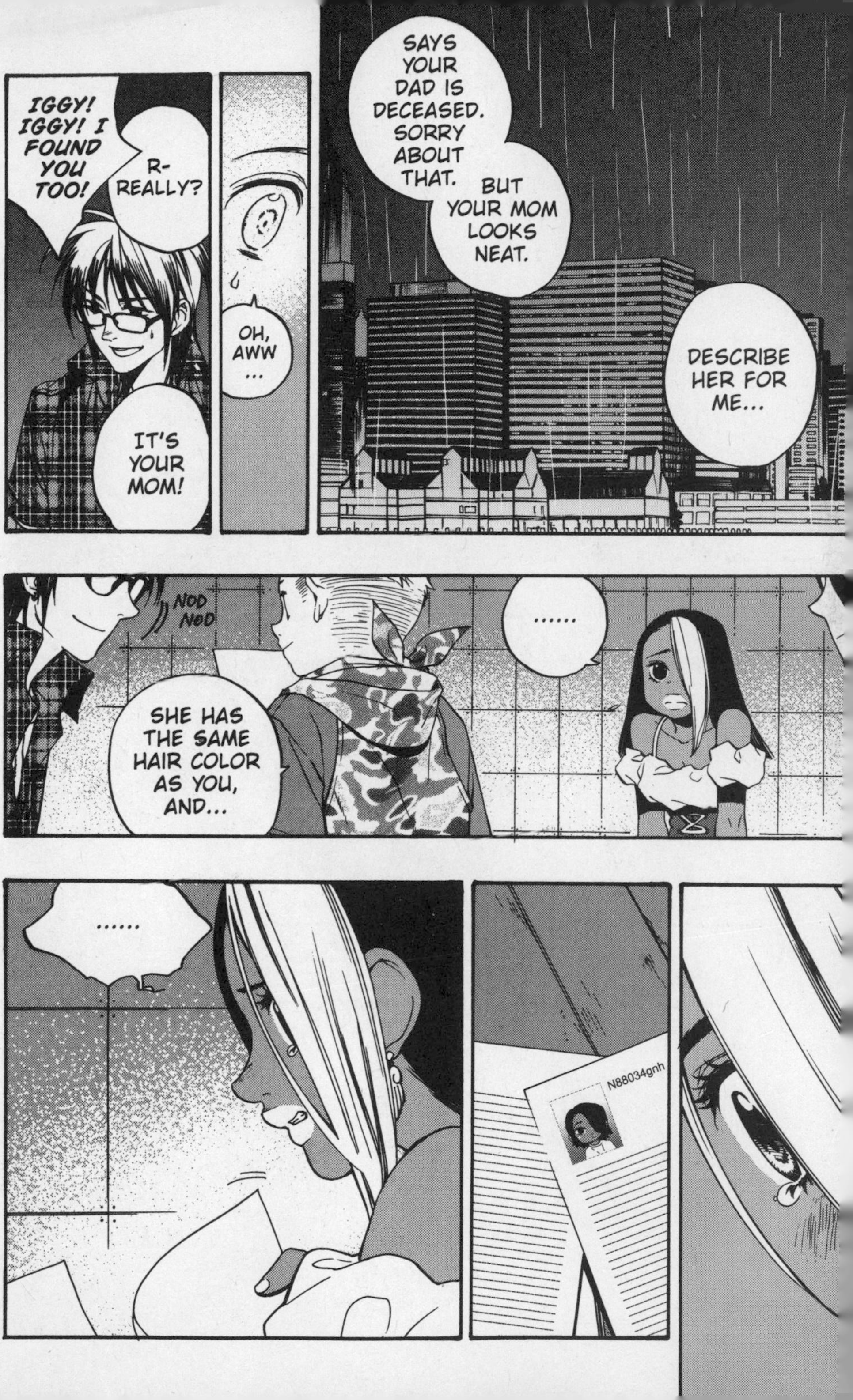
IGGY! IGGY! I FOUND YOU TOO!
R-REALLY?
IT'S YOUR MOM!
OH, AWW ...
SAYS YOUR DAD IS DECEASED. SORRY ABOUT THAT.
BUT YOUR MOM LOOKS NEAT.
DESCRIBE HER FOR ME...
NOD NOD
SHE HAS THE SAME HAIR COLOR AS YOU, AND...
......
......
N88034gnh

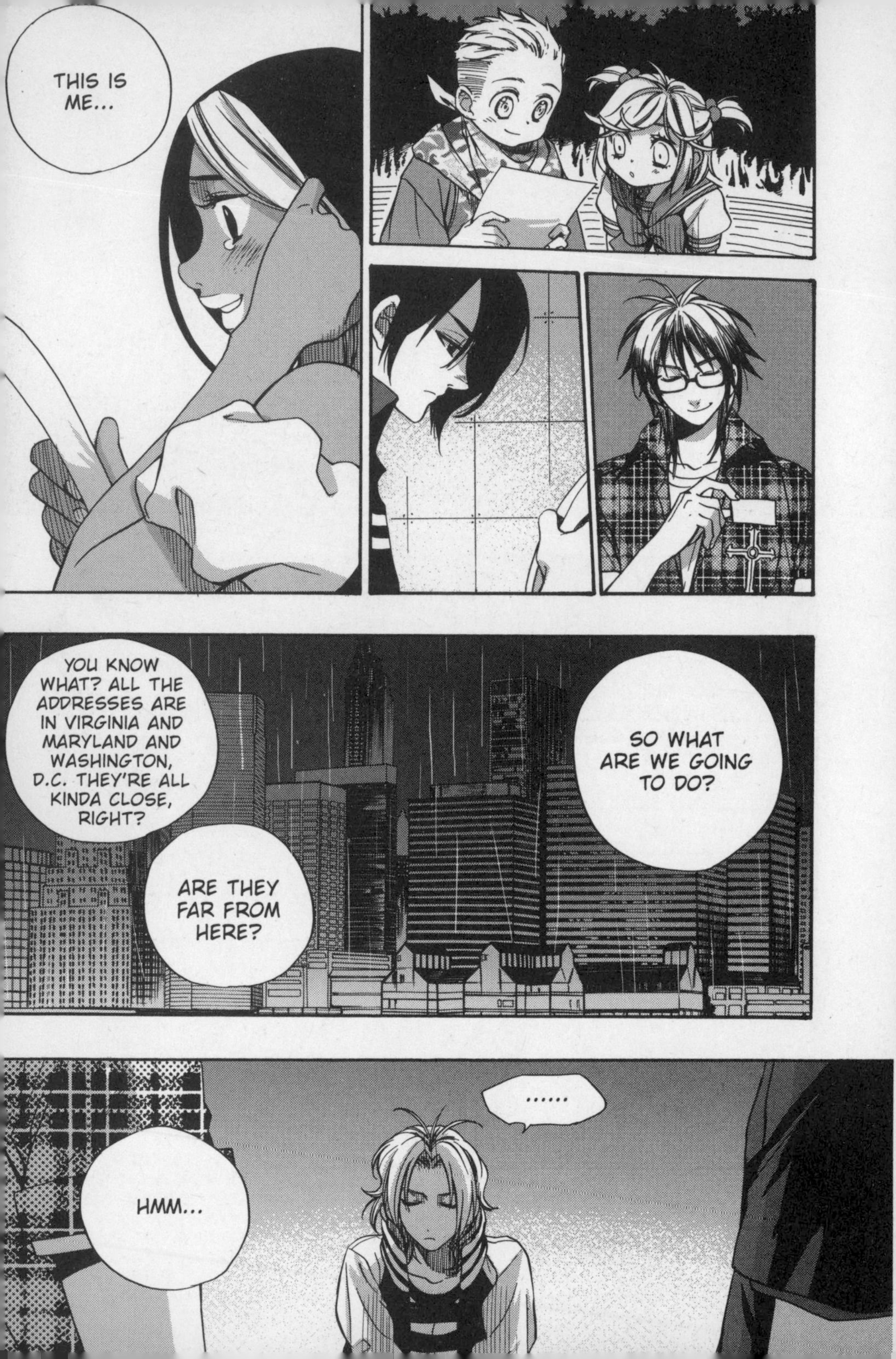
THIS IS ME...
YOU KNOW WHAT? ALL THE ADDRESSES ARE IN VIRGINIA AND MARYLAND AND WASHINGTON, D.C. THEY'RE ALL KINDA CLOSE, RIGHT?
ARE THEY FAR FROM HERE?
SO WHAT ARE WE GOING TO DO?
......
HMM...

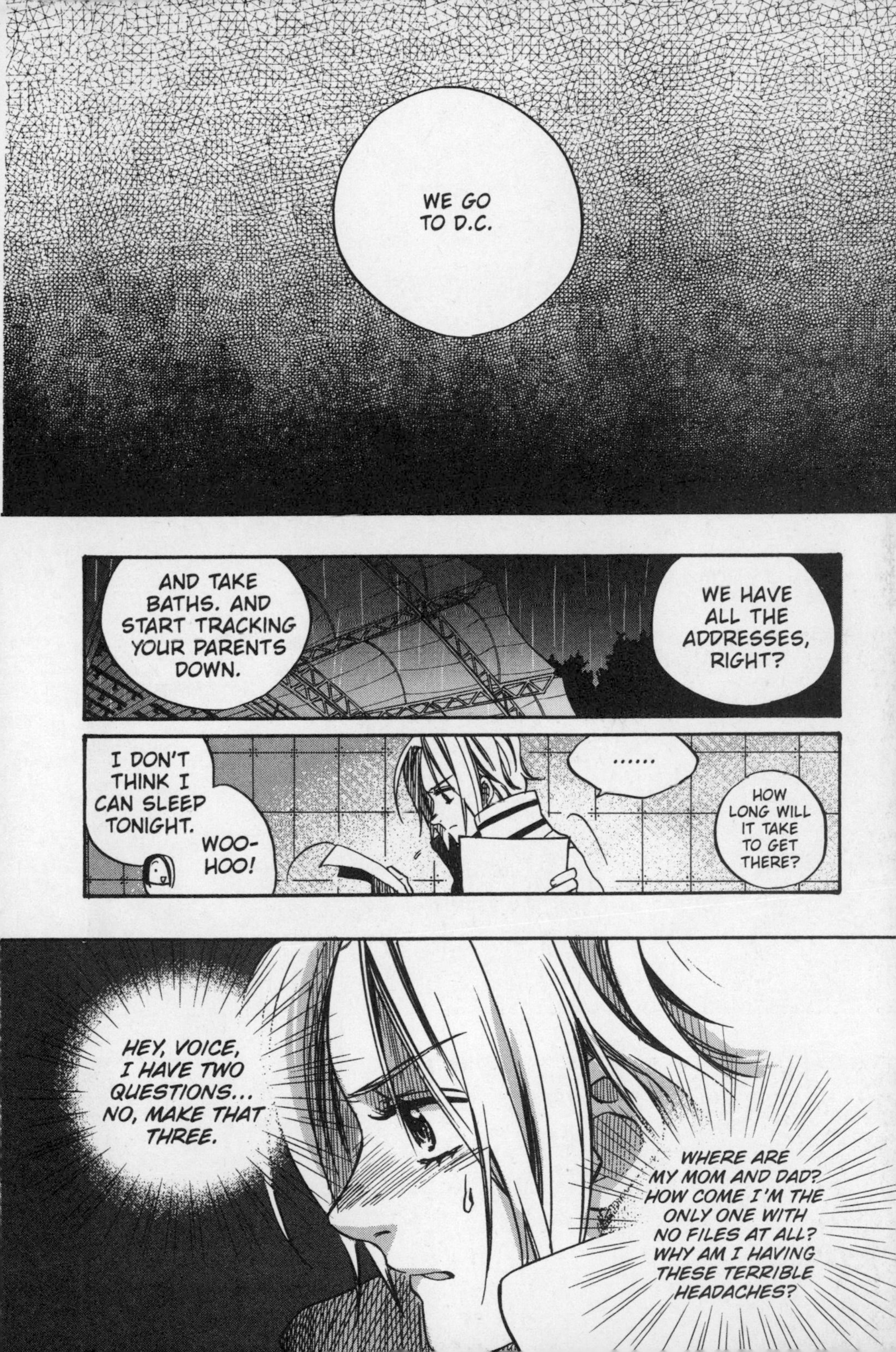
WE GO TO D.C.
AND TAKE BATHS. AND START TRACKING YOUR PARENTS DOWN.
WE HAVE ALL THE ADDRESSES, RIGHT?
I DON'T THINK I CAN SLEEP TONIGHT.
WOO-HOO!
......
HOW LONG WILL IT TAKE TO GET THERE?
HEY, VOICE, I HAVE TWO QUESTIONS... NO, MAKE THAT THREE.
WHERE ARE MY MOM AND DAD? HOW COME I'M THE ONLY ONE WITH NO FILES AT ALL? WHY AM I HAVING THESE TERRIBLE HEADACHES?

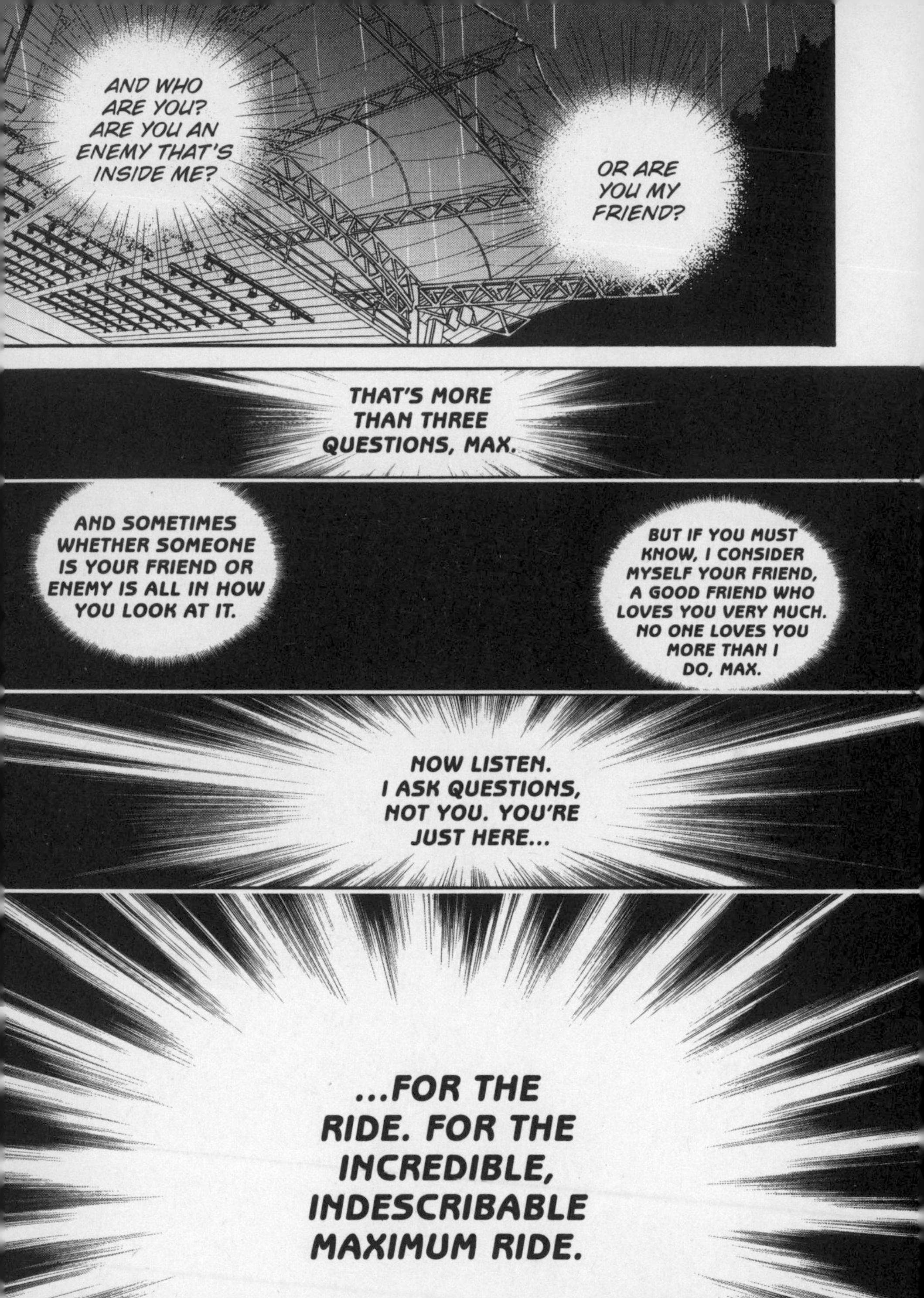

To be continued in MAXIMUM RIDE, Vol. 3!

STOP BY
AND SEE US
IN THE NEXT
VOLUME!

Read on to enjoy a
sneak preview of FANG,
Maximum Ride's
newest adventure
from bestselling author
James Patterson.

JAMES PATTERSON

FANG

ON SALE MARCH 15, 2010

PART 1

Meeting Doctor God

I'm a girl of extremes. When I love something, I'm like a puppy dog (without all the licking). When I'm cranky, I'm a wasp (like, a whole hive of 'em). And when I'm angry, I'm a mother bear with a predator after her cubs: dangerous.

I say this because lately my life seemed to be all about extremes. Like right now, for instance. I was soaring twenty thousand feet in the air with the five people I loved most in the world—and no, we weren't on a plane, hang-gliding, or hot air ballooning. We preferred to use good old-fashioned wings. The technology's been around for eons.

If you've ever dreamed you could fly, I can confirm that it's all that and better. Even if you're desperately flying through a subway tunnel to save your life, it's still off the charts. But today, flying over Africa ... it was as good as it ever gets. Maybe the best part was that for the first time in a dog's age, we weren't on the run from madmen. We were on a mission—to do good.

"Max!" Iggy called over to me. "Why did they name themselves Chad? I mean, Chad. It's like naming a whole country Biff or Trey. I don't get it."

"Ig, don't be ignorant," I scoffed. "It's not like all the people there named themselves."

"Why not? We named ourselves," Nudge noted, as if I needed to be reminded that we were raised in a lab under the supervision of science geeks.

"Only 'cause we're special." I gestured to her twelve-foot wingspan. "Hey, check that out!" I pointed to a Martian-like rock formation in the distance.

Fang turned his head and gave me one of his classic half smiles—you know, like the kind of smile Mona Lisa would have had if she were a guy. A teenage guy with longish scruffy hair, dark eyes, and a leather jacket. Mmmmm.

The whole trip had been as exhilarating as one of Fang's killer smiles. Even the hundreds of miles of shifting, mysterious desert dunes had been amazing. We're world travelers and all—we've lived in wilds as extreme as Death Valley and Antarctica—but there was something downright otherworldly about what I'd seen below as we crossed over—oh, crap, I'd forgotten the names of all of the different countries.

"Mauritania, Algeria, Mali, Niger, and Chad together are about sixty-eight percent desert," Angel recited, reading my mind. Literally. She's powerful like that.

"Whatever. It's too much freaking desert," Angel's brother, Gazzy, complained. "I wouldn't mind seeing a few cows chomping away on some grass right about now."

"A-plus-plus on the geography quiz, Angel. Gazzy, Iggy, extra credit when you check your attitudes at the door." Even without parents, somehow I'd picked up the language. Seems to work when you're the leader. "Listen, I know some of you are a little cranky from the long flight, but this is our chance to finally help people. Real people," I emphasized, as if we'd grown up in a plastic bubble or something. Well, we kind of had. Do dog crates in labs count?

"Real people," Fang clarified. "As in, not just a bunch of wack-job scientists."

"Yup. Did it ever occur to you guys," I continued grandly, "that when we were told we had to save the world, it might have actually meant saving people—like, one at a time? Sending a message around the world about people in need is great and all, but actually feeding people, giving people medical help and stuff? We've never done that before. I mean, this could be it, guys. Our destiny."

"Max is right," Angel agreed, in a very un-Angel-like manner. We didn't see eye-to-eye on much these days.

"Word on the street is that you have to save the world, Max," Iggy reminded me. "The rest of us? Not so much."

Twit. Always trying to take the easy way out.

Not Fang, though. "Hey, Max, wherever you go to save the world—I will follow ..." He did the killer half-smile thing. "Mother Teresa."

My stomach flip-flopped as if I'd folded my wings and plunged into freefall. Hello, Max the Puppy.

I had exactly five seconds to enjoy sainthood before I caught sight of three black dots in the distance—and they appeared to be moving straight toward us.

Looked like Mama Bear's cubs were in danger. And you know what that meant:

Bye-bye, Saint Max. Time to be a hellion again.

2

"Incoming!" I shouted to my flock. "Down, down, down!"

Fast-moving objects directed at the flock usually belong to one of three categories: bullets, mutant beings with a taste for bird kid, or vehicles hired by an evil megalomaniac wanting to kidnap us and use our powers. Which might explain why I was working on the assumption that the three black dots meant one thing and one thing only: imminent death.

"Max! Relax!" Fang managed to stop me before I could execute my dive. "I think those are the CSM cargo planes."

It was the Coalition to Stop the Madness (CSM), the activist group my non-winged mom was involved with, that had asked us to go on this humanitarian relief mission to Chad and to help publicize the work they were doing there. And what with our previous adventures helping them combat global warming and ocean pollution, we were slowly being turned from feral, scavenging outlaws on the lam into Robin Hoody do-gooders. Meanwhile, I was still supposed to save the world at some point. My calendar was full, full, full.

So full that I'd forgotten this was the part of the journey where we were supposed to meet up with the CSM planes so we could be guided into the refugee camp.

I gave Fang a thank-you-for-saving-me-from-myself look. When his eyes met mine, I shivered down to my sneakered toes.

Gazzy called over to me, "I can't see anything!"

"I can't see anything either!" Iggy complained.

"I'm rolling my eyes, Ig." I had to tell him that because he couldn't see me do it, what with his blindness and all.

"No, there's, like, dust clouds below," Gazzy clarified.

I glanced down, and sure enough—the blurry endlessness of sand was even more blurry.

"Not dust devils," Fang said. His dark feathers were covered with a layer of dust, and grit was caked around his eyes and mouth.

"No." I peered downward again.

Just then Angel said, "Uh-oh," which is always enough to make my blood run cold. In the next second, I focused sharply on a few dark specks at the front of the dust clouds. One of the dark specks raised a tiny dark toothpick.

This time I knew for sure that I wasn't overreacting.

"Guns!" I shouted. "They've got guns!"

3

"Quick! Up!" Fang shouted, just as the first bullets strafed the air around me with ominous hisses.

I angled myself upward, only to see the shiny silver underbelly of one of the CSM planes, now flying right above us. It was pressing downward—the rough landing strip was maybe a quarter mile away.

"Drop back!" I yelled. We all went vertical as the planes continued to come down practically on our heads. To escape from the bullets, we'd had to fly up right under them. The engines were way too close—the noise was deafening.

"Watch it!" I yelled, as one plane's landing gear almost hit Iggy. "Drop down! Drop down!" Bullets are bad, but getting smushed by landing gear, toasted by jet engine exhaust, or sucked into the front of an engine were all much less fixable.

I could now make out the sun-browned faces of the men on . . . oh, geez, were those camels? The men continued to aim their rifles at us, and I felt a bullet actually whiz by my hair. In about half a second, my brain processed the following thoughts lightning fast:

1) A bullet hitting the fuel tank on a plane:
   not a good situation.
2) Slowing down not good: slow + bird kids = drop like rocks.
3) Speeding up not good: fast bird kids + faster planes = getting flattened.
4) The only choice was to go on the offensive.

Fortunately, I'm very comfortable with being offensive—at least on the not-infrequent occasions when someone's trying to gun down my flock.

"Dive!" I shouted. "Knock 'em down!"

I tucked my wings flat against my back and began to race groundward like a rocket. At this speed, these shooters would need radar and a heat tracer to land a bullet on me. I could actually see the whites of their eyes now, which were widening in surprise.

"Hai-yah!" I screamed—just for fun, really—as I swung my feet down and came to a screeching halt by smashing my heels right into a rider's back. He flew off the camel, rifle pinwheeling through the air, and felt the joy of being airborne himself for about three seconds before he landed right in front of his pal's camel.

"Get the rest!" I ordered the flock. "Free the beasts!"

There were about ten of these armed riders—no match for six hot, angry bird kids. We were used to dodging bullets; these guys were not used to aiming at fast-moving flying mutants. And the bonuses of being aloft are infinite: Snatching a rifle from the grip of a maniacal shooter isn't as hard as you might think when you're coming from above and behind.

Iggy flew in sideways and smacked one guy right off his camel, and

Gazzy folded his wings around another's face, causing him to panic and fall. I grabbed a gun and used it like a baseball bat, neatly clipping one guy in the gut, knocking him right off his ride. Unfortunately, I didn't rise in time.

Which meant that for the first time in bird kid history, I got plowed into by a panicky galloping camel—with no sense of humor. Its head hit me in the stomach, and I flipped over its neck, landing hard on the saddle.

"Awesome move, Max!" I heard Nudge call from somewhere behind me. Wasn't she busy helping to take these guys out?

My Indiana Jones moment lasted about a second before I was lurched off the beast. Just as my feet hit the sand, I managed to grab a rein and hang on for dear life.

My wings were useless—there was no room to stretch them out—and my ankles were literally sanded raw before I was able to pull myself up hand over hand and eventually clamber back onto the saddle.

"Whoa, Nelly!" I croaked, gagging on dust. I gripped the saddle with my knees and pulled back on the reins.

This camel did not speak English, apparently. It stretched its neck and ran faster.

"Up and away, Max!" Fang yelled. I dropped the reins, popped to my feet on top of the saddle, and jumped hard, snapping out my wings. And just like that, I became lighter than air, stronger than steel . . . and faster than a speeding camel.

I watched it race off, terrified, toward the nearest village. Someone was about to inherit a traumatized camel.

This mission was off to a good start.

MAXIMUM RIDE: THE MANGA②

JAMES PATTERSON
& NARAE LEE

Adaptation and Illustration: NaRae Lee

Lettering: Abigail Blackman

Yen Press
1290 Avenue of the Americas
New York, NY 10104

Visit us at yenpress.com
facebook.com/yenpress
twitter.com/yenpress
yenpress.tumblr.com
instagram.com/yenpress

First Yen Press Edition: October 2009

Yen Press is an imprint of Yen Press, LLC.
The Yen Press name and logo are trademarks of Yen Press, LLC.

The publisher is not responsible for websites (or their content) that are not owned by the publisher.

ISBN: 978-0-7595-2968-7

20 19 18

WOR

Printed in the United States of America